Third Edition

Public & Private
Families

AN INTRODUCTION

ANDREW J. CHERLIN

Johns Hopkins University

Boston   Burr Ridge, IL   Dubuque, IA   Madison, WI   New York   San Francisco   St. Louis
Bangkok   Bogotá   Caracas   Kuala Lumpur   Lisbon   London   Madrid   Mexico City
Milan   Montreal   New Delhi   Santiago   Seoul   Singapore   Sydney   Taipei   Toronto

McGraw-Hill Higher Education

*A Division of The **McGraw-Hill** Companies*

PUBLIC AND PRIVATE FAMILIES: AN INTRODUCTION

Published by McGraw-Hill, an imprint of The McGraw-Hill Companies, Inc. 1221 Avenue of the Americas, New York, NY, 10020. Copyright © 2002, 1999, 1996, by The McGraw-Hill Companies, Inc. All rights reserved. No part of this publication may be reproduced or distributed in any form or by any means, or stored in a database or retrieval system, without the prior written consent of The McGraw-Hill Companies, Inc., including, but not limited to, in any network or other electronic storage or transmission, or broadcast for distance learning.

This book is printed on acid-free paper.

1 2 3 4 5 6 7 8 9 0 WCK/WCK 0 9 8 7 6 5 4 3 2 1

ISBN 0-07-240544-9

Editorial director: *Phillip A. Butcher*
Senior sponsoring editor: *Sally Constable*
Senior developmental editor: *Rhona Robbin*
Editorial coordinator: *Alyson DeMonte*
Senior marketing manager: *Daniel M. Loch*
Senior project manager: *Kimberly D. Hooker*
Manager, new book production: *Melonie Salvati*
Freelance design coordinator: *Laurie J. Entringer*
Cover design: *Heidi Jean Baughman*
Interior design: *Laurie Entringer*
Photo research coordinator: *Judy Kausal*
Photo researcher: *Barbara Salz*
Supplement producer: *Nate Perry*
Media Producer: *Jessica Bodie*
Compositor: *Shepherd Incorporated*
Typeface: *10.5/12 Garamond*
Printer: *Quebecor World Versailles Inc.*

Library of Congress Cataloging-in-Publication Data
Cherlin, Andrew J., 1948–
    Public and private families : an introduction / Andrew J. Cherlin
    —3rd ed.
        p.   cm.
    Includes bibliographical references and indexes.
    ISBN 0-07-240544-9 (alk. paper)
    1. Family—United States. 2. Family. 3. Family policy. I. Title.
HQ536.C44 2002
306.85—dc21   2001030952

www.mhhe.com

About the Author

Andrew J. Cherlin is Benjamin H. Griswold III Professor of Public Policy in the Department of Sociology at Johns Hopkins University. He received a B.S. from Yale University in 1970 and a Ph.D. in sociology from the University of California at Los Angeles in 1976. His books include *Marriage, Divorce, Remarriage* (revised and enlarged edition, 1992), *Divided Families: What Happens to Children when Parents Part* (with Frank F. Furstenberg, Jr., 1991), *The Changing American Family and Public Policy* (1988), and *The New American Grandparent: A Place in the Family, A Life Apart* (with Frank F. Furstenberg, Jr., 1986). In 1989–1990 he was chair of the Family Section of the American Sociological Association. In 1999 he was president of the Population Association of America, the scholarly organization for demographic research.

Professor Cherlin is a recipient of a MERIT (Method to Extend Research in Time) Award from the National Institutes of Health for his research on the effects of family structure on children. His recent articles include "Stepfamilies in the United States: A Reconsideration," in the *Annual Review of Sociology;* "Longitudinal Studies of the Effects of Divorce on Children," in *Science;* "Effects of Parental Divorce on Mental Health throughout the Life Course," in the *American Sociological Review;* "Going to Extremes: Family Structure, Children's Well-Being, and Social Science," in *Demography;* and "By the Numbers" and "I'm OK, You're Selfish," both in *The New York Time Magazine.* He also has written many short articles for the *New York Times,* the *Washington Post, Newsweek,* and other periodicals. He has been interviewed on *ABC News Nightline,* the *Today Show,* network evening news programs, National Public Radio's *All Things Considered,* and other news programs and documentaries.

For Claire and Reid

Contents in Brief

Contents

Part Two   Race, Ethnicity, Class, and the State 109

Chapter 4   *Social Class and Families 111*

Part Four	Links across the Generations 313

Chapter 10 *Children and Parents* 315

Chapter 13 *Divorce* 415

List of Boxes

How Do Sociologists Know What They Know?

Preface

The sociology of the family is deceptively hard to study. Unlike, say, physics, the topic is familiar (a word whose very root is Latin for "family") because virtually everyone grows up in families. Therefore, it can seem "easy" to study the family because students can bring to bear their personal knowledge of the subject. Some textbooks play to this familiarity by mainly providing students with an opportunity to better understand their private lives. The authors never stray too far from the individual experiences of their readers, focusing on personal choices such as whether to marry and whether to have children. To be sure, giving students insight into the social forces that shape their personal decisions about family life is a worthwhile objective. Nevertheless, the challenge of writing about the sociology of the family is to also help students understand that the significance of families extends beyond personal experience. Today, as in the past, the family is the site of not only private decisions but also activities that matter to our society as a whole.

These activities center on taking care of people who are unable to fully care for themselves, most notably children and the elderly. Anyone who follows social issues knows of the often-expressed concern about whether, given developments such as the increases in divorce and childbearing outside of marriage, we are raising the next generation adequately. Anyone anxious about the well-being of the rapidly growing elderly population (as well as the escalating cost of providing financial and medical assistance to the elderly) knows the concern about whether family members will continue to provide adequate assistance to them. Indeed, rarely does a month pass without these issues appearing on the covers of magazines and the front pages of newspapers.

In this textbook, consequently, I have written about the family in two senses: the *private family,* in which we live most of our personal lives, and the *public family,* in which adults perform tasks that are important to society. My goal is to give students a thorough grounding in both aspects. It is true that the two are related—taking care of children adequately, for instance, requires the love and affection that family members express privately toward each other. But the public side of the family deserves equal time with the private side.

Organization

This book is divided into six parts and 15 chapters. Part One ("Introduction") introduces the concepts of the public and private families and examines how sociologists and other social scientists study them. It provides an overview of the history of the family and then examines the central concept of gender. Part Two ("Race, Ethnicity, Class, and the State") deals with the larger social structures in which family relations are embedded: social class hierarchies, and racial and ethnic divisions. A chapter is then devoted to the influences of the nation-state on family life. In Part Three ("Sexuality, Partnership, and Marriage"), the focus shifts to the private family. The section first examines the emergence of the modern concept of sexuality and the formation of partnerships through dating, courtship, and cohabitation. It then focuses on persistence and change in the institution of marriage.

Part Four ("Links across the Generations") explores how well the public family is meeting its caretaking responsibilities for children and the elderly. Part Five ("Conflict and Disruption") deals with the consequences of conflict in family life. It first studies violence against wives, partners, and children. Then divorce, remarriage, and stepfamilies are discussed. Finally, in Part Six ("Family and Society"), I discuss where the great social changes of the twentieth century have left the institution of the family.

Special Features

This textbook differs from others in several ways, as described below.

It explores the public and the private family. This public/private distinction that underlies the book's structure is intended to provide a more balanced portrait of contemporary life. Furthermore, the focus on the public family leads to a much greater emphasis on government policy toward the family than in most other textbooks. In fact, every chapter except the first includes a short, boxed essay under the general title, "Families and Public Policy." This edition features new essays on parents' rights, work-family legislation since 1945, and fragile familes. Given the attention currently paid to issues such as these, the essays should stimulate student interest and make the book relevant to current political debates.

It highlights family life in other cultures. Although the emphasis in the book is on the contemporary United States and other Western nations, no text should ignore the important historical and cross-cultural diversity of families. Consequently, in addition to relevant material in the body of the text, I have also included in every chapter except the first a boxed essay under the title, "Families in Other Cultures." New to this edition are essays on transnational families and on public opinion toward government assistance for working parents. Adopters of the previous editions of the text have said that their students find these boxes intriguing and that they (and the policy boxes) provide good starting points for class discussions.

It includes distinctive chapters. The attention to the public family led me to write several chapters that are not included in some sociology of the family textbooks. These include Chapter 6, "The Family, the State, and Social Policy", Chapter 10, "Children and Parents"; and Chapter 11, "The Elderly and Their Families." These chapters examine issues of great current interest, such as income assistance to poor families, the effects of out-of-home childcare, and the costs of the Social Security and Medicare programs. Throughout these and other chapters, variations by race, ethnicity, and gender are explored.

It gives special attention to the research methods used by family sociologists. To give students an understanding of how sociologists study the family, I include a section in Chapter 1 titled, "How Do Family Sociologists

Know What They Know?" This material explains the ways that family sociologists go about their research. Then in seven chapters, I include boxed essays under a similar title on subjects ranging from national surveys to feminist research methods to archival research. Instructors who used the previous edition of this text said that this material gives their students a better understanding of how sociological research is carried out and of the strengths and limitations of various methodological approaches.

It features "Families on the Internet" sections. Since I wrote the first edition of this textbook, the World Wide Web has changed from a pleasant diversion to an essential information-gathering tool. Almost every chapter contains information that I gathered from the Web, including the most up-to-date demographic statistics from government statistical sites such as the Bureau of the Census web page. While using the Internet, I realized that it can be not only an indispensable research tool but also a powerful instructional tool. Consequently, at the end of each chapter is a section titled "Families on the Internet," in which I list web sites that students may find useful. In this edition, students are also asked to answer questions when they visit the sites suggested in these sections. Instructors should also find many of these sites to be excellent sources of information for student papers and presentations.

Pedagogy

Each chapter begins in a way that engages the reader: the neither-men-nor-women *berdaches* of many Native American tribes; the nineteenth-century diary in which Maud Rittenhouse described her suitors; the story of American men who fly to Russia in search of brides; the case of Danny Henrikson, taken from a stepfather who raised him and awarded by a judge to a father he did not know; and so forth. And each of the six parts of the book is preceded by a brief introduction that sets the stage.

In addition, several new features make this edition easier to use and should stimulate students' critical thinking.

- Each chapter includes the following types of questions:
    1. Looking Forward—questions that preview the chapter themes and topics.
    2. Ask Yourself—Two questions, which appear at the end of each of the three types of boxes.
    3. Looking Back—Looking Forward questions reiterated at the end of each chapter, around which the chapter summaries are organized.
    4. Thinking About Families—five questions, which appear at the end of each chapter and are designed to encourage critical thinking. Two of the five questions focus on the "public" and the "private" family.
- "Families on the Internet" sections now ask students to answer questions when they visit the sites suggested in these sections.
- Cross-reference icon: These icons, embedded in the text, point readers to the exact page where an important concept was introduced in an earlier chapter.
- More headings and summary tables.

- Boxes and "Families on the Internet" sections include the Online Learning Center web site URL to signal that content updates are available on the web site.
- This edition features a new, full-color design that enabled me to select contemporary photos and to use color effectively in graphs and tables.

What's New in Each Chapter?

First, users of past editions will find a slightly different chapter order. Chapters 7, 8, and 9 in the second edition have been combined into new Chapter 7, "Sexuality" and new Chapter 8, "Cohabitation and Marriage." Moreover, I now present the chapters on children and the elderly (which constitute Part Four) before the chapters on domestic violence, divorce, and remarriage and stepfamilies (which constitute Part Five). Every chapter has new material.

Chapter 1   Public and Private Families

- Update on the opening vignette—Vermont's domestic partner law
- Table 1.1, The Public Family and the Private Family

Chapter 2   The History of the Family

- Expanded coverage of Native American families: discussion of kinship among the Apache of Arizona
- Expanded discussion of affection and individualism in the medieval European family
- Updated statistics on immigration, marriage, and women in the workforce
- Section on the African cultural heritage, including an expanded discussion of marriage as a process
- Section on the Asian cultural heritage
- Section on generational changes in the life course, with graph

Chapter 3   Gender and Families

- Section on the gestational construction of gender, including hormonal, biosocial, and evolutionary influences
- Section on masculinity and the recent men's movement
- Updated statistics on the earnings gap and the sex ratio in China

Chapter 4   Social Class and Families

- Updated and expanded opening vignette
- Updated statistics on social class structure, homelessness, the labor market, poverty trends, and dual-earner couples

Chapter 5   Race, Ethnicity, and Families

- Opening vignette on the "new second generation" of immigrants
- Updated statistics on racial and ethnic populations in the United States, marriage rates, out-of-wedlock birth rates, income levels, and interracial marriage rates
- Updated Families and Public Policy box on the counting of multiracial families in Census 2000
- Updated table showing the decline of marriage by race
- Updated figure showing married-couple households by race and income group
- Discussion of residential patterns of middle-class African-American families
- Updated figure showing total fertility rates of racial and ethnic groups

- Families in Other Cultures box on transnational families
- Updated figure showing out-of-wedlock births by racial and ethnic groups
- Section on social capital and immigrant families

Chapter 6   The Family, the State, and Social Policy

- Families in Other Cultures box on public opinion toward government assistance for working parents
- Updated statistics on U.S. government assistance to poor and nonpoor families and the proportion of American children born outside marriage by race
- Section on abortion policy moved from previous Chapter 10 and updated
- Updated graph showing race and ethnicity of parents receiving TANF
- Updated coverage of the "marriage penalty," the earned income tax credit, and the number of families receiving TANF

Chapter 7   Sexuality

- Section on adolescent sexuality, pregnancy, and childbearing outside of marriage moved from previous Chapter 8.
- Graph showing percentages of first births in the United States, conceived and born before or after marriage, 1930–1994
- Families and Public Policy box on the U.S. policy response to AIDS formerly in the text
- Expanded discussion of selection effects combined with material from previous Chapter 8
- Updated statistics on sexual attitudes, AIDS, and teenage childbearing
- Updated graph showing AIDS deaths in the United States by race and ethnicity

Chapter 8   Cohabitation and Marriage

- Single new chapter on cohabitation and marriage which replaces previous Chapters 8 and 9
- Opening vignette on a brokered marriage between an American man and a Ukrainian woman
- Updated statistics on age at first marriage, expected marriage rates, cohabitation, and gay and lesbian partnerships
- Discussion of the characteristics of cohabiting couples, including educational level, marital status (divorced or never married), and the presence of children in the household
- Discussion of births to cohabiting couples
- Discussion of the duration and outcome of cohabiting relationships
- Updated Families and Public Policy box on domestic partnerships
- Discussion of domestic partnerships among gay and lesbian couples
- Expanded discussion of the benefits of marriage for women

Chapter 9   Work and Families (previously Chapter 10)

- Updated vignette showing shift in marital power after a wife's earnings increased
- Updated graph showing labor force participation rates of married women with children
- Updated statistics on labor force participation rates of married women by race and children's age; women's earnings relative to men's by race; share of professional degrees earned; family responsibilities of employed workers; percentage of workers with flexible schedules and work-at-home arrangements; and international parental leave policies

- Updated section on division of housework among husbands and wives, including updated graph
- Updated discussion of men's attitudes toward housework
- New section on overwork among salaried professionals and underwork among wage-earning sales and service workers
- New statistics on the effect of work responsibilities on home life; the percentage of parents working night or weekend shifts; divorce among parents working the night shift; and gender of projected new entrants to the labor force
- New Families and Public Policy box on trends in work-family legislation since 1945, with graph

Chapter 10   Children and Parents (previously Chapter 14)

- New Families and Public Policy box on parents' rights (the Elián González case and *Troxel* v. *Granville*)
- New discussion of parenting styles among ethnic and racial minorities
- Updated discussion of the effect of fathers on children's lives, including a new section on the effect of nonresident fathers
- Updated discussions of the effect of poverty and divorce on children
- Updated statistics on childcare, including a new graph showing relative reliance on different types of childcare
- Updated discussion of the effect of childcare on children, including infants
- Updated discussion of gay and lesbian families, including those formed by artificial insemination, and their effect on children
- Updated discussion of historical trends in the well-being of children, including an updated graph showing child poverty rates
- Updated How Do Sociologists Know What They Know? box on measuring the well-being of children
- Updated discussion of historical trends in the well-being of children from different social classes
- Updated Families in Other Cultures box, including an updated graph showing child poverty rates in 25 countries

Chapter 11   The Elderly and Their Families (previously Chapter 15)

- A new section on changing patterns of dying and their effects on the widowed and on children and grandchildren
- Updated statistics on life expectancy, the aged population, poverty among the aged, grandparents as childcare providers, residency in nursing homes, government expenditures for Social Security and Medicare, government and private expenditures for nursing home care, and nursing home costs

Chapter 12   Domestic Violence (previously Chapter 11)

- Expanded definition of domestic violence (includes intimate partners and stalking)
- Two new graphs showing percentage of physical assaults by type of assault and gender of victim
- Updated statistics on domestic violence, partner rape, and child abuse
- New section on marital status of couples reporting domestic violence
- Expanded discussion of the Puritan attitude toward the use of physical force in childrearing
- Updated graph showing percentage of child abuse cases by type of abuse

- Updated Families and Public Policy box on foster care
- Updated Families in Other Cultures box on wife beating in the developing world

Chapter 13   Divorce (previously Chapter 12)

- Updated vignette on covenant marriage
- Updated statistics on divorce rates, child support, and single-parent families headed by fathers
- Updated graph showing the divorce rate over time
- Updated discussion of the effect of personal and family background on the likelihood of divorce
- Updated figure showing the award and receipt of child support
- Updated box on the enforcement of child support obligations
- Updated discussion of the effect of multiple transitions on children
- Updated discussion of children's long-term adjustment to divorce

Chapter 14   Remarriage and Stepfamilies (previously Chapter 13)

- Expanded section on building stepfamilies, including summary table
- Updated discussion of stepchildren's relations with stepparents
- Updated discussion of the effects of remarriage on children

Chapter 15   Social Change and Families (previously Chapter 16)

- New opening vignette on Americans' attitudes toward family life and recent changes in the family
- New Families and Public Policy box on fragile families
- Updated statistics on foreign birth rates and children without health insurance
- Revised sections on encouraging two-parent families and assisting single-parent families

Supplements

This text is accompanied by a variety of instructional resources designed to enhance classroom instruction and to support instructors with long experience as well as those teaching the family course for the first time.

PUBLIC AND PRIVATE FAMILIES: A READER, 2/E

Edited by the text's author and keyed to text chapters, this reader includes articles and book excerpts by family sociologists and other writers on a variety of issues facing families today. A special discount is available when the text and reader are ordered as a package.

INSTRUCTOR'S MANUAL AND TEST BANK

This manual, prepared by Bahira Sherif of the University of Delaware, and Anne Smith Hastings of the University of North Carolina, Chapel Hill, includes the following elements: detailed chapter outlines; lecture ideas; student projects and review questions; suggested readings and films; and a test bank with multiple choice, matching, true-false, short-answer, and essay questions for each chapter. In addition to the printed format, the test items are available on CD-ROM for test construction.

ONLINE LEARNING CENTER WEB SITE

Students and instructors are invited to visit the book's Online Learning Center, the text-specific web site, at www.mhhe.com/cherlin. The content for the Online Learning Center was developed by Diane Levy of the University of North Carolina, Wilmington, and Lynn Newhart of Rockford College in Illinois. This web site offers an extensive variety of resources and activities, including chapter quizzes, key terms, learning objectives, author audio clips, Internet exercises, interactive activities, PowerPoint slides, relevant URLs for Census updates, and more. It's also possible to link directly to Internet sites from the Online Learning Center. The URL for the Online Learning Center appears in the boxes and *Families on the Internet* sections throughout the text, reminding readers to visit the Online Learning Center homepage for content updates.

PAGEOUT

All online content for *Public and Private Families, 3/e* is supported by WebCT, eCollege.com, and Blackboard. Additionally, McGraw-Hill's PageOut service is available to get you and your course up and running online in a matter of hours— at no cost! PageOut was designed for instructors just beginning to explore web options. Even the novice computer user can create a course web site with a template provided by McGraw-Hill (no programming knowledge required). PageOut lets you offer your students instant access to your syllabus, lecture notes, and original material. And, using PageOut, you can pull any of the McGraw-Hill content from the Cherlin Online Learning Center web site into your web site. To find out more about PageOut, ask your McGraw-Hill representative for details, or fill out the form at www.mhhe.com/pageout.

POWERWEB

Offered free with the text, and accessible from a link on the Cherlin Online Learning Center, PowerWeb is a turnkey solution for adding the Internet to a course. PowerWeb is a password-protected web site developed by McGraw-Hill/Dushkin that offers instructors and students the following materials: refereed, course-specific web links and articles, student study tools, interactive exercises, weekly updates with assessment, material on how to conduct research on the Internet, daily news feed of topic-specific news, message board for instructors, and access to Northern Light Research Engine.

POWERPOINT SLIDES

PowerPoint slides, prepared by Catherine Robertson of Grossmont College in California, feature the 480 charts, graphs and detailed chapter outlines.

VIDEOS

McGraw-Hill offers adopters a variety of videotapes that are suitable for classroom use in conjunction with the textbook.

Acknowledgments

To write a book this comprehensive requires the help of many people. At McGraw-Hill, senior sponsoring editor Sally Constable provided me with editorial guidance, senior developmental editor Rhona Robbin provided invaluable help in reorganizing and revising the chapters, and freelance editor Elizabeth Morgan provided expert editing of the manuscript. At Johns Hopkins, Jean Davis provided able research assistance. In addition, the following people read drafts of chapters and provided suggestions for improvements:

Igolima T. D. Amachree, Western Illinois University

Loretta E. Bass, University of Oklahoma

Brian E. Copp, University of Wisconsin—River Falls

Lynda Dickson, University of Colorado—Colorado Springs

Barbara Dobling, Kirkwood Community College

Thomas P. Egan, Eastern Kentucky University

Lee K. Frank, Community College of Allegheny County

Michael Goslin, Tallahassee Community College

Pamela Guzman, California State University at Fullerton

Jennifer Hamer, Southern Illinois University—Edwardsville

Shirley J. Harkess, University of Kansas

Linda Sam Lenox, Northeastern University

Diane Levy, University of North Carolina—Wilmington

Bahira Sherif, University of Delaware

Curt Sobolewski, Penn State University

Teresa Swartz, Hamline University

Elaine Wethington, Cornell University

Anna Zajicek, University of Arkansas

Andrew J. Cherlin

Viewing the Family Through Two Lenses

The Private Family

This text considers aspects of intimate relationships in its examination of the private family in which people live most of their personal lives.

The Public Family

This text also describes how families do socially important work such as raising children and caring for the elderly.

"Families and Public Policy" Boxes

In its focus on the public family, this text explores the impact of government policies on families.

Reflecting the Rich Diversity of Today's Families

Families in Other Cultures
Love and Marriage in Japan

Is love necessary for a lasting marriage? Most Americans would say yes, of course. But marriage in other cultures suggests a different answer. Consider Japan: Marriages among the older generation, especially in rural areas, were stable but often loveless. In 1996, Yuri Uemura, an elderly woman in the town of Omiya told a *New York Times* reporter, "There was never any love between me and my husband. But, well, we survived" (Kristof, 1996). In 40 years, she said, her husband had never told her he liked her, never held her hand, never given her a present, never said "thank you," and never shown affection in any way.

Yet their marriage endured, as did most others. Until the 1980s, Japan had one of the lowest rates of divorce in the developed world. Love, however, was not the main ingredient keeping couples together. In part, strong social pressure kept couples together. Becoming divorced was shameful, a sign of individual weakness or moral failing. Marriages were also held together by a strict division of labor. Women were responsible for nearly all of the housework and childrearing. Japanese men did, and still do, much less housework and childcare than men in Western countries such as the United States. National studies of time use in Japan from 1965 to 1990 show that husbands do only 10 percent of the housework and childcare (Tsuye, 1992; see Chapter 9 for figures for U.S. husbands).

Marriages in Japan were also held together by low expectations for love and companionship. Japanese adults viewed marriage more in terms of social roles, such as mother or wage earner, than in terms of pleasurable relationships between the wife and husband. A woman's primary family role was as mother to her children rather than as companion to her husband (Hsia & Scanzoni, 1996). With expectations low, married couples did not experience the kinds of crises Americans do if one spouse's affection for the other falters.

But marriage in Japan is changing. Women's roles are becoming more varied. Between 1965 and 1990, the proportion of married women aged 20 to 54 who were paid employees in nonagricultural industries rose from 15 to 41 percent (Tsuye, 1992). Attitudes about women's roles are also changing. A series of national opinion surveys in Japan from 1972 to 1990 have asked women and men whether they agree with the statement that "the external world is for men and the domestic world is for women." In 1972, 83 percent of women and 84 percent of men agreed; but by 1990 just 25 percent of women and 35 percent of men agreed (Tsuye, 1992). Moreover, young adults, particularly in cities, expect more companionship from their spouses.

In these ways, Japanese marriages have become more like Western marriages, which are based on a less-strict division of labor, a larger role for married women outside the household, and more love and companionship. But these changes have also helped to produce a sharp increase in divorce. Between 1980 and 1994, the percentage of Japanese marriages that were projected to end in divorce increased from 20 percent to 29 percent (Yamamoto & Kojima, 1996). While still lower than the projection of about 50 percent in the United States, the rising divorce rate has prompted concern in Japan.

Attitudes have changed among the older generation as well. "The other day, he tried to pour me a cup of tea," Mrs. Uemura said of her husband (Kristof, 1996, p. 12). "It was a big change. I told all my friends." Yet as divorce has become more acceptable, there has also been a surge of divorces among older, traditional married couples, according to reports from demographers (Tsuye, personal communication). In support of this observation, national data show that the average age of people at the time of divorce has been increasing (Yamamoto & Kojima, 1996). Apparently, the

Japanese marriages, long rooted in a strict division of labor, are increasingly based on love and companionship.

reduced stigma of divorce has led some couples in long-term, relatively loveless marriages to break up.

The changes in Japanese marriage over the last few decades suggest that love and companionship do not keep couples together. In fact, the divorce rates in societies in which marriage is primarily a working partnership are generally lower than in societies in which marriage is defined in terms of love and companionship. Once marriage becomes a companionship rather than a working partnership, people who are dissatisfied with the level of love and closeness in their marriages feel justified in obtaining a divorce. As a result, Western-style marriages, while emotionally satisfying to each spouse, also lead to a higher rate of divorce.

Ask Yourself

1. Have there been any divorces in your family? If so, in which generation did they occur? Was the lack of love and companionship a major complaint?

2. Besides the increase in the number of married women in the Japanese workforce, what other factors might account for the change in Japanese attitudes toward love and marriage?

www.mhhe.com/cherlin

In general, parents take control of the matchmaking process when the choice of whom to marry is too important to them to be left to their children alone. In the past, a good marriage and many children were crucial to the survival of the household. A son who would inherit the farm needed a wife to help him and to have children who would provide more help. A woman needed to marry a man whose parents owned land, or whose relatives owned cattle, or who would inherit a trade. It is probable that throughout human history practical considerations have dominated the search for a spouse. I think it likely that only within the past 100 years in the Western nations—and within the past few decades in newly developed nations—has the standard of living improved so much that young adults have had the luxury of paying more attention to a partner's personality than to his or her industriousness or family worth.

Parental influence also erodes when children can find ways of making a living that don't depend on their parents' resources. In eighteenth-century Austria, the heir to the farm had no other good sources of income and couldn't marry without his father's permission. Often permission wasn't granted until the father retired. A folk song of the time expressed the frustration of the unmarried son:

Father when ya gonna gimme the farm,
Father when ya gonna sign it away?
My girl's been growin' every day,
And single no longer wants to stay (Berkner, 1972).

Grandmothers typically play a larger role in childrearing in African-American families than they do in other families.

mothers are divorced. The divorced mothers are more likely to have avoided economic problems prior to the breakup of their marriages; the never-married mothers are more likely to have lived persistently in poverty.

In addition, it is more common among poor black children than among poor white children to be raised by a grandmother—particularly among children whose mothers (and often grandmothers) were teenagers when they gave birth. In these families, teenage childbearing compresses the generations, producing grandmothers who are in their thirties and forties rather than their fifties and sixties (Burton, 1990). To be sure, many young grandmothers provide crucial support and excellent childcare. Moreover, the role of the grandmother in African-American families is stronger, in general, than in European-American families. [➤ p. 152] Nevertheless, some grandmothers may not be at a life stage at which they expect to be caring for grandchildren, and they may be holding jobs themselves. Psychologist P. Lindsay Chase-Lansdale and her colleagues videotaped interactions between young African-American mothers and their children, and between grandmothers and the same children, in two kinds of families: those in which the three generations lived in the same household and those in which the grandmother lived in a separate household (Chase-Lansdale, Brooks-Gunn, & Zamsky, 1994). To the research group's surprise, the quality of parenting—by both the mother and the grandmother—was *lower* when the three generations lived in the same household. The only exception occurred when the mother had given birth in her early teens. It seems likely that a selection effect [➤ p. 223] is at work: Young mothers who have the financial and psychological resources to live on their own probably are more competent, on average, at raising a child. Mothers who have fewer resources are more likely to live with grandmothers. Joint residence is an arrangement often born of necessity. It has mixed effects on children in poor families (McLoyd et al. 2000).

Thought-Provoking "Families in Other Cultures" Boxes

These essays broaden students' understanding of family life in other cultures. Topics include missing girls in China, transnational families, and public opinion toward government assistance for working families.

Strong Coverage of Family Diversity in the United States

This edition provides expanded coverage of the impact of race, ethnicity, class, and gender on families in the United States.

Explaining How Sociologists Study Families

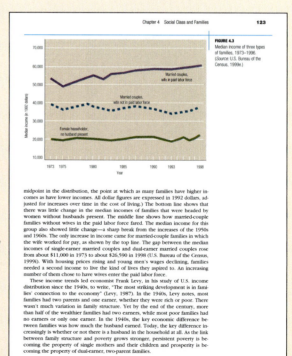

Studying Families

"How Do Sociologists Know What They Know?" boxes show students how sociologists study families, exploring approaches such as national surveys, archival research, and feminist research methods.

Presenting Current Findings

This text highlights important research findings in graphs and tables and explains the significance of these findings in the text narrative.

Exploring Public Policy Issues Affecting Families

438 Part V Conflict, Disruption, and Reconstitution

Families and Public Policy *Enforcing Child Support Obligations*

Children in single-parent families would benefit if every absent parent knew he or she would have to pay child support. This has been the goal of several new laws that were enacted in the 1980s and 1990s. Since 1994, for example, all parents who have been ordered by the courts to pay child support have had their payments deducted automatically from their paychecks. Moreover, states are now required to adopt guidelines for the amount of child support a parent should pay, according to income and number of children; judges must follow these guidelines or state in writing why they didn't (Cherlin, 1993).

The 1996 welfare reform act [➡ p. 191] contained a number of additional measures to strengthen the system. For instance, it provided more support for programs to establish paternity in hospitals at the birth of the children, and it penalized welfare recipients who failed to cooperate. It required employers to send the names of newly hired employees to state and federal agencies that will match the names against lists of parents who have not paid child support obligations. It allowed states to deny occupational and driver's license renewals to parents who fail to pay (U.S. Administration for Children and Families, 1996). In fact, toughening child support enforcement has been one of the most popular family policies among both conservatives and liberals. Conservatives favor tougher enforcement because making fathers pay is consistent with their belief that parents should take responsibility for the well-being of their children. (Although the law applies equally to absent mothers who owe child support payments, in practice the vast majority of payments are collected from fathers and distributed to mothers.) The new measures send a message to fathers that they can leave their marriages, but they can't leave their children. Conservatives hope that the measures will deter men from fathering children they can't, or don't intend to, support. Liberals favor tougher measures because increased collection of child support payments will provide more economic support to children in low-income single-parent families.

There is evidence that these measures are producing results. Between 1993 and 1997, the proportion of custodial mothers who reported receiving the full amount of child support they had been awarded increased by 30 percent (U.S. Bureau of the Census, 2000a). However, most of the measures help middle-class single parents more than poor single parents and their children. Most middle-class single mothers are divorced, and can obviously identify the fathers of their children. Moreover, most middle-class fathers are employed and can make some child support payments. Many poor single mothers, in contrast, were never married to the fathers of their children. Even when the fathers can be identified and located, they may not be employed, and thus may not be able to pay much in child support. Consequently, some experts warn that child support programs that stress enforcement of divorce decrees will not work for poor families. Rather, these experts advocate programs to increase the earnings capacity of single fathers, so that they can afford to pay child support (Meyer, 1999).

Ask Yourself

1. Do you know anyone who has had difficulty collecting court-ordered child support payments? If so, was the problem caused by the absent parent's inability to pay or simply an unwillingness to pay?
2. Besides the measures described here, what other steps could government take to improve the economic well-being of children in single-parent families?

www.mhhe.com/cherlin

another 21 percent had incomes less than twice the poverty line. Yet few single fathers are granted child support awards, since most have higher incomes than their ex-wives. Nevertheless, some single fathers with low incomes may need assistance from their former wives.

About 4 percent of all children in 1998 lived in single-father families (U.S. Bureau of the Census 1998b). Our mental image of the single-father family is the divorced dad living alone with his children. However, only one-fourth of single-father families consist of divorced men living alone with their children. Of the rest, most are sharing their households with mothers, sisters, or new girlfriends, who may be doing much of the childcare (Eggebeen, Snyder, & Manning, 1996). Yet the census counts them as "single-father families" as long as the mother of the child is not in the household.

146 Part II Race, Ethnicity, Class, and the State

Families and Public Policy *How Should Multiracial Families Be Counted?*

How can a child whose parents have different races have only one? Logically impossible, you might think; but until 1997, federal government statistical policy required that individuals check just one race for themselves or their children on official forms such as the Census of Population. And before 1997, the government recognized four races: (1) white, (2) black, (3) Asian and Pacific Islander, and (4) American Indian and Alaska Native. It also required its agencies, in a separate question, to ask about membership in one ethnic group: Spanish or Hispanic origin.

Interracial couples represent a small but growing share of all families. About 2.5 percent of married couples were interracial in 1998 (U.S. Bureau of the Census, 1999g). Their numbers are large enough, however, that they have become a visible presence and a reminder that the old categories may not fit much longer. In 1993, Representative Thomas Sawyer of Ohio, chair of the subcommittee of the House of Representatives that oversees the census and statistical policy, listened to the testimony of Susan Graham, an advocate for multiracial children and a mother of two of them. She told Representative Sawyer:

> *When I received my 1990 census form, I realized there was no race category for my children. I called the Census Bureau. After checking with supervisors, the Bureau finally gave me their answer, the children should take the race of the mother. When I objected and asked why my children should be classified as their mother's race only, the Census Bureau representative said to me, in a very hushed voice, "Because in cases like these, we always know who the mother is and not the father" (U.S. House of Representatives, Committee on Post Office and Civil Service, Hearings, 1994).*

Ms. Graham said her son had been classified as white by the census but black by the school he attended. Her solution: Add a new category, "Multiracial," to the official government list and to the 2000 Census. Yet this seemingly logical step was opposed by many of the political leaders of the minority groups that would be most affected. They opposed a multiracial category because the statistics that agencies collect are used not just to describe the population but also to determine whether federal laws have been carried out. Congress and the courts use the information on race and ethnicity from the census to determine whether congressional districts are providing fair representation to blacks and Hispanics. Agencies that oversee banks use the information to determine whether banks are willing to loan money to members of racial-ethnic groups. Other agencies use the information from employers to determine whether employers are discriminating on the basis of race or ethnicity. Consequently, the political leaders opposed a multiracial category because they feared it would lower the number of blacks, Hispanics, or Asians counted in the census and would therefore dilute the political power that comes with greater numbers (Wright, 1994).

Faced with this dilemma, the government considered what, if anything, to do about Susan Graham's children and the many others like them when it fielded the 2000 Census of Population. In 1997, a government statistical committee decided that the 2000 Census (and all other government surveys) would allow individuals to choose more than one race; but it rejected a separate "multiracial" category. It also decided to place the question about Hispanic ethnicity before the question on race (rather than after it, which was the old policy), a change that probably increased the number of people who said they were "Hispanic." So when Americans filled out the 2000 Census, they saw the ethnic and racial questions shown in the figure. First they were asked whether they were "Spanish/Hispanic/Latino," and

the blue columns show, more than 80 percent of Asian-American family households were headed by a married couple, the highest percentage of any of the five groups. In contrast, just 44 percent of African-American family households were headed by married couples—the lowest percentage of any of the groups. Non-Hispanic whites, Hispanics, and Native Americans were in between. Correspondingly, African Americans had the highest percentage of family households headed by an unmarried woman and Asian Americans had the lowest. Few households in any group were headed by an unmarried male, as the middle columns show.[2]

[2](O'Hare, 1992). The data were taken from 1990 Census Summary Tape File 1C. By "unmarried," I mean never married, divorced, separated, or widowed.

496 Part VI Family and Society

Families and Public Policy *Fragile Families*

Once nearly all two-parent families were started by married couples. Today, about 1.5 million unmarried cohabiting couples have children (U.S. Bureau of the Census, 1998b). Yet cohabiting parents often are ignored in official statistics. For example, the increasing trend toward childbearing outside of marriage is common knowledge, but most people are unaware that these births occur mainly to women who are cohabiting—usually with the child's father. In fact, the percentage of the supposedly "single" mothers who are cohabiting is growing (Bumpass & Lu, 2000).

In a recent study, researchers interviewed random samples of unmarried mothers in hospitals in Austin, Texas, and Oakland, California, just after they had given birth. They also interviewed the fathers when possible. They were surprised to find that over half the mothers were living with the fathers when the children were born. Moreover, at the time of the births, 80 percent of the mothers said that their chances of marrying the father were 50-50 or better (Garfinkel & McLanahan, 2000). Clearly, cohabitation is common among unmarried mothers in these two cities, and most are cohabiting with the father of their children.

Yet many of these relationships end quickly. The 1995 national survey found that among unmarried mothers, only about half of whites and one-fifth of African Americans married within five years of giving birth (Bumpass & Lu, 2000). Among those who married, not all of them married the father of their child. Little is known about why some woman marry, some continue to cohabit, and others break up with the father. The leaders of the Austin and Oakland research project, Irwin Garfinkel and Sara McLanahan, call the couples they studied "fragile families." They plan to reinterview the parents periodically, to learn more about their relationships.

Meanwhile, policymakers who wish to encourage the surprisingly large number of fragile families to stay together, whether through marriage or continued cohabitation, are considering whether to increase public support. While many of the mothers have access to job training and employment counseling through the welfare system, the fathers typically do not. Furthermore, some of the fathers owe child support payments to the mothers of other children. Providing fathers with job training, counseling, and assistance with child support obligations may well increase their chances of remaining with the mothers of their children.

Ask Yourself

1. Do you know a cohabiting couple that has children? If so, do you think these parents see themselves as a fragile family? Do you expect them to be together five years from now?
2. If you were a sociologist, what questions would you ask about the trend toward childbearing among cohabiting couples? How would you go about answering them?

www.mhhe.com/cherlin

coverage they are very expensive. Programs targeted on the poor are cheaper but command less political support.

One universal program that was nearly established in 1994 was a national health insurance system. The failure of Congress to enact it was particularly unfortunate from the standpoint of family policy because universal health insurance would be a major antipoverty measure for children. The most obvious reason is that so many children, an estimated 11 million in 1997, are not covered (U.S. Bureau of the Census, 1999d). In addition, the lack of health insurance benefits in many part-time and low-wage jobs creates a perverse incentive for parents to apply for, or remain on, the public assistance rolls. This is because parents and children receiving public assistance also receive health insurance through the Medicaid program for the poor. When a parent gives up public assistance to take a job, she may find that she loses all her medical coverage, and she may decide that having protection from large medical bills dictates that she quit her job. The problem has been eased by recent expansions of Medicaid to some children in nonwelfare, low-income families, but the parents of these children are still at high risk of not having health insurance.

Focus on Public Policy Issues

Boxed essays in all but the first chapter examine the impact of government policies on families. New to this edition are essays on trends in work-family legislation, parents' rights, and strategies to assist fragile families.

The teenage birthrate has been declining, but the proportion of teenage mothers who are unmarried has been increasing.

- A modest decline in adolescent sexual activity occurred in the 1990s, particularly for boys. At that time, condom use increased.
- The historical difference in the sexual activity of adolescent boys and girls has nearly disappeared.
- The increases in adolescent sexual activity have been greater for the middle class and whites than for other groups, although sexual activity is still more common among the poor and African Americans.

Yet even with the declines that occurred in the 1990s, adolescent sexual activity still was much more widespread than it had been at mid-century, especially for girls. Coupled with a rising age at marriage, this increase in sexual activity among adolescents led to a greater proportion of teenage pregnancies and births outside marriage.

THE TEENAGE PREGNANCY "PROBLEM"

Most people have read or heard something about the teenage pregnancy "problem," but few people have a good understanding of exactly what the problem is.

A Close Look at Teen Pregnancy

Chapter 7, "Sexuality," includes a discussion of adolescent sexuality and explores the causes and consequences of teenage pregnancy and childbearing.

Strong Treatment of Work-Family Issues

Special attention is given to work/family issues in this edition. New data on the effect of work responsibilities on home life, an updated section on the effects of childcare on children, and new material on overworked professionals and underworked blue-collar workers are some examples of this coverage.

Expanded Coverage of Cohabitation

Chapter 8, "Cohabitation and Marriage," provides expanded coverage of cohabitation that includes information on the characteristics of cohabiting couples and on the duration and outcome of cohabiting relationships.

Families and Public Policy

Putting Work-Family Issues on the Agenda

Half a century ago, the breadwinner-homemaker family was at its peak. Few married women with young children worked outside the home, and few members of Congress favored assistance for employed mothers. But today several laws provide benefits for working parents, and Congress seems poised to pass more legislation. When and how did this change?

Sociologist Paul Burstein and his colleagues examined this question by counting the number of members of Congress who sponsored (officially supported) various kinds of work-family bills between 1945 and 1990 (Burstein & Bricher, 1997; Burstein, Bricher, & Einwohner, 1995; and Burstein & Wierzbicki, 2000).

The results are presented in Figure 9.4, which shows the number of sponsors for three different types of legislation over the 45-year period. Though most of the bills did not become law, their content is informative. The first type, "separate spheres" bills,

contained proposals that would support families in which the husband worked outside the home and the wife did not. An example was legislation that would have limited the number of hours women could work, to protect their ability to be good mothers. Unthinkable today, such bills were commonplace in the first half of the twentieth century. The black line in the chart shows a modest but steady number of sponsors for these bills throughout the 1945–1990 period.

The second type of legislation, "Equal opportunity" bills, was based on the premise that working women were entitled to the same opportunities as working men. For instance, they might require employers to pay equal wages to women and men doing the same job. Such an idea might seem obvious, but before the 1960s many employers paid women less than men, on the theory that men were the main earners for their families and so deserved more than

women. The green line in Figure 9.4 shows a modest number of sponsors for equal-opportunity bills until the mid-1960s, after which sponsorships rose sharply. Not coincidentally, the mid-1960s were the era of the civil rights movement and the birth of the modern feminist movement.

Most recently, legislators have supported "work-family accommodation," including an income tax credit for child care expenses. These bills attempt to help parents combine paid work with childrearing. The white line in Figure 9.4 shows that sponsorship of this type of bill was rare through most of the period, but rose dramatically over the last 10 years. Had the study continued into the 1990s, it undoubtedly would have shown further growth. In 1993, for example, Congress passed the Family and Medical Leave Act, which allows workers to take time off to care for newborns and seriously ill children or to handle other family medical emergencies.

During the 1980s and 1990s, corporations began to address these concerns. They did so largely out of self-interest. The Census Bureau estimates that 62 percent of the new entrants to the labor force between 1998 and 2006 will be women, many of whom will have family responsibilities (U.S. Bureau of the Census, 1999d). Employers who wish to recruit and retain good workers realize that they must make their jobs attractive to people who are caring for children—and to the growing number who are caring for elderly parents. Most large firms now have some personnel policies to help employees with family responsibilities (Glass & Estes, 1997). Small firms are much less likely to offer family-friendly policies for several reasons:

- They typically do not invest as much time and money training new workers, so they don't have as much to lose if employees quit because of family-related problems.
- They don't have the volume of workers necessary to make services such as on-site childcare cost-effective.
- Because of their lower sales revenues, they cannot pass along the costs of the policies to consumers as easily as large firms can.

A majority of first marriages are preceded by cohabitation.

national survey of women ages 19 to 44, 59 percent of those without a high-school degree had cohabited, compared to 37 percent of those with a college degree (Bumpass & Lu, 2000). To be sure, cohabitation has increased greatly among the well-educated, but it has also increased among the less well-educated.

- Although we read more about young people living together before a first marriage, cohabitation is more common before a remarriage than before a first marriage. Indeed, the great majority of remarriages are preceded by a period of cohabitation (Smock, 2000).
- Although the common image is one of a childless couple, a surprising number of cohabiting couples have children: In the 1995 survey, 15 percent had children from the current relationship, and 35 percent had children from a previous relationship (Bumpass & Lu, 2000).

The last fact may be the most startling. About 40 percent of the births listed in official statistics as occurring outside of marriage are in reality births to cohabiting couples (Bumpass & Lu, 2000). One recent study of unmarried mothers who had just given birth found that 44 percent of them were living with the fathers of their children (Center for Research on Child Well-Being, 2000). In fact, over the past decade or so,

Providing a Variety of Learning Aids

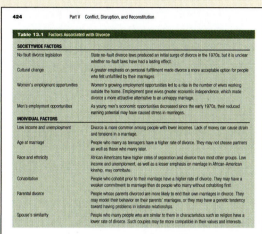

Helpful Summary Tables

Tables summarize important concepts and provide comparisons of key topics. Several new tables are included in this edition.

Other Learning Aids

* "Looking Forward" preview questions
* "Ask Yourself" questions in boxed essays
* Marginal Glossary
* Cross-reference icons

Effective End-of-Chapter Resources

Each chapter concludes with a chapter summary organized around key questions raised at the beginning of the chapter, critical thinking questions ("Thinking About Families"), Key Terms with page references, and Internet activities ("Families on the Internet.").

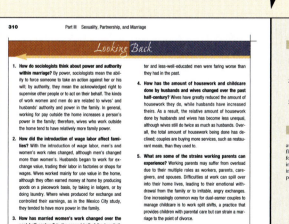

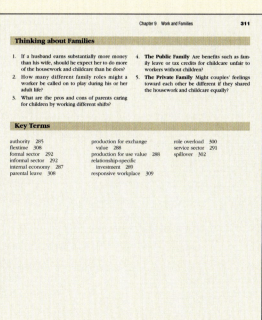

Part One

Introduction

The family has two aspects. It is, first, the place where we experience much of our private lives. It is where we give and receive love, share our hopes and fears, work through our troubles, and relax and enjoy ourselves. Second, it is a setting in which adults perform tasks that are of importance to society, particularly raising children and assisting elderly parents. To be sure, people undertake these tasks not to perform a public service but rather to express love, affection, and gratitude. Nevertheless, family caretaking benefits us all by raising the next generation and by reducing our collective responsibility for the elderly. Indeed, one frequently expressed source of concern these days is whether changes in family life have reduced parents' abilities to raise their children well. • This book is about both the private and public aspects of families. It examines the contributions of family life not only to personal satisfaction but also to public welfare. The first three chapters provide an introduction to this perspective. • Chapter 1 explores the most useful ways to think about families. It reviews the debates about family life today; and it examines the approaches that sociologists and other social scientists use to study families. • Chapter 2 provides an overview of the history of the family. A knowledge of family life in the past can help us to understand families today. Over the past few decades, family historians have produced many studies that provide useful insights. • The experiences of women and men in families differ greatly. Consequently, gender—the social and cultural characteristics that distinguish women and men—will be discussed throughout the book. Chapter 3 begins this discussion by examining the construction and maintenance of gender differences.

Public and Private Families

Looking Forward

1. How do Americans feel about marriage and the family?

2. What do families do that is important for society? What do families do that is important for the individuals in them?

3. What are the grounds for being optimistic or pessimistic about the state of the family?

4. How do sociologists go about studying the family?

5. What are the leading theoretical approaches to studying the family?

On December 17, 1990, three couples walked into the State of Hawaii marriage license bureau in Honolulu and requested licenses. In love and ready to commit to their partners, these women and men weren't much different from typical applicants, except in one crucial respect: All were in same-sex partnerships. The bureau refused to issue them marriage licenses. This did not come as a surprise to the two lesbian couples and the gay male couple; indeed, they had intentionally entered as a group in order to create the grounds for a lawsuit. Following the denial of their requests, they sued the State of Hawaii, charging that it is an unconstitutional violation of their rights to restrict marriage to heterosexual couples.

A lower court judge ruled against the couples and in favor of the State's interpretation of the marriage laws. But after the couples appealed, the Hawaii Supreme Court disagreed with the lower court ruling (*Baehr* v. *Lewin,* 1993). It sent the case back to the lower court with orders to retry the case and to grant the marriage licenses unless the State could show that it "furthers a compelling state interest" to exclude same-sex couples. Three years later, testimony in the case, *Baehr* v. *Miike,* began before Judge Kevin S. C. Chang. News of the impending case had attracted great interest around the country. Opponents of same-sex marriage had even persuaded the U.S. Congress to pass the Defense of Marriage Act (Public Law 104-199), which decreed that other states need not recognize a marriage license granted to a same-sex couple in Hawaii or elsewhere. Many states also enacted measures stating that they would not recognize such marriages.

Attorneys for the two sides—the couples and the State of Hawaii—presented a total of eight witnesses. Two were sociologists who study the family, one for each side: David Eggebeen of Pennsylvania State University testified in opposition to allowing same-sex marriages, and Pepper Schwartz of the University of Washington testified in favor of allowing them. Both testified as expert witnesses whose knowledge and experience qualified them to advise the court on the matter.[1]

The prominent role of sociologists in this landmark case demonstrates how much the field of the sociology of the family has become entwined with public debates about important social issues such as (alphabetically) abortion, caring for the frail elderly, children's well-being, the decline of marriage, divorce, gay and

---

[1]In the spirit of full disclosure, let me state that I signed a friend-of-the-court brief in favor of extending marriage to same-sex couples.

lesbian families, teenage childbearing, welfare, and women's equality. To be sure, the private relations between husbands and wives, intimate partners, and parents and children make up a large part of the field. In fact, the roots of twentieth-century sociology of the family lie in the study of marital interaction. But the field has also acquired a public dimension based on sociologists' studies of issues of concern.

Eggebeen and Schwartz's testimony reflects the way sociologists think about the family and the kinds of social scientific arguments they make. That they disagreed demonstrates that the evidence sociologists cite often lends itself to more than one interpretation. Often, the final interpretation—in this case the law about who may marry whom—must reflect moral or political beliefs that sociologists cannot prescribe.

David Eggebeen, testifying first, defined marriage in terms of **procreation:** having and raising children.

> EGGEBEEN: *Well, to me it's the . . . the conclusion is clear that marriage represents a gateway to becoming a parent. When people get married, by an extraordinary margin they intend to become parents.*
>
> ATTORNEY FOR THE STATE: *So in the minds of people, marriage would be synonymous with having children?*
>
> EGGEBEEN: *When 98 percent of the married individuals intend to become parents, I would say that's a very valid conclusion.[2]* (trial transcript, September 11, 1996, p. 42)

procreation the process of having and raising children

Eggebeen then suggested reasons why gay marriages may not provide optimal settings for raising children. He cited research showing that children's well-being is, on average, lower in some respects in single-parent families and stepfamilies than in two-parent families. And gay couples with children are like stepfamilies, he argued, because often the children were conceived in heterosexual unions that the gay parent later left to live with a gay partner. In other words, he argued that gay marriages should be discouraged because they might not be as good for children as heterosexual marriages. Although some gay parents may do excellent jobs of raising their children, he acknowledged, on average they aren't as good.

Eggebeen's criteria emphasize one of the most public aspects of family life: the raising of the next generation, on which society depends. The belief that raising children is the central task of marriage is an old one, going back to the days when the survival of a family line couldn't be taken for granted. Procreation was seen as socially important work—not the sort of thing to risk by undertaking radical changes in marriage. Eggebeen admitted that there wasn't much research on whether or not same-sex couples are fit parents; but he drew the conservative conclusion that, in the absence of data, society should not take what he sees as a risk to children's development:

> EGGEBEEN: *. . . my professional opinion is that if we do not have the studies done . . . that allow us to make generalizations, then my opinion is that we should not make any changes in how we view marriage or legal changes in marriages that would lead to [legalized gay marriage]* (tr., September 11, p. 88).

---

[2]Eggebeen was referring to Jacobson and Heaton (1991), who reported that in a national survey 2.8 percent of men and 3.5 percent of women 39 or younger said that they did not have children already and did not intend to have any.

In contrast, Pepper Schwartz, testifying on behalf of the couples, defined marriage more in terms of the private rewards it provides to adults than in terms of childrearing.

> *ATTORNEY FOR THE COUPLES: Well, on the topic of what marriage means to people, Doctor Schwartz, why do people get married?*
>
> *SCHWARTZ: . . . What people think of when they want marriage is they want companionship, they want love, they want trust, they want someone who will be with them through thick and thin. Now, I wouldn't say this is what marriage means in all cultures but in our own it's an aspiration for—for intimacy and security. And that is the definition of marriage as people first and primarily think of it* (tr., September 16, 1996, p. 59).

Children are an important part of marriage, she suggested, but they aren't as central as Eggebeen claimed:

> *Yes, having children is a deep desire of the majority of young Americans . . . most of whom want kids when they get married. But it isn't, I think the reason that everyone gets married. They get married to have this partnership. It [having children] is a reason among many that people want to be married* (tr., September 16, pp. 61–62).

As we will learn in Chapter 2, the view that private rewards such as intimacy and companionship are central to marriage wasn't widespread until the nineteenth and twentieth centuries. In a historical sense, it is a relatively new way to think about families. Schwartz's research, which has identified similarities and differences among married couples, heterosexual cohabiting couples, gay male couples, and lesbian couples, is focused mainly on the relationships among couples rather than on their childrearing (Blumstein & Schwartz, 1983; Schwartz, 1994).

But Schwartz and the attorneys for the couples realized that in order to win a favorable ruling from the judge, they had to address the question of whether allowing gay marriage is in the best interests of children. The attorneys for the couples knew that the other side would try to show that gay marriage was not in the best interests of children and that, therefore, prohibiting gay marriage furthered a "compelling state interest." So, under friendly questioning from the couples' attorneys, Schwartz was asked how effectively biological gay parents in same-sex partnerships serve the needs of their children. She replied that they were comparable to heterosexual parents. Asked what she based that conclusion on, she replied:

> *Well, I base it primarily on, I don't know, what must there be near twenty studies comparing lesbian mothers with their own biological children compared to heterosexual mothers with their own biological children* (tr., September 16, p. 87).

Eggebeen, as we have seen, had a different reading of the evidence: On average, he believed children would not fare as well in same-sex partnerships as in marriages. (We will review the evidence in Chapter 10.) But under cross-examination, he acknowledged that gay and lesbian couples are capable of raising a healthy child and that there are some who do an excellent job. He also acknowledged that children who are being raised by gay couples would be helped if the couples could marry because many legal benefits (e.g., social security survivor's benefits for widows and widowers) are reserved for married couples.

Still, Eggebeen's (and the State's) position was that although children now being raised in same-sex partnerships would benefit if the partners could marry, same-sex marriages should be discouraged because, on average, children do bet-

ter when raised by two biological parents. Therefore, they argued, the State has a compelling interest in prohibiting same-sex marriage. Schwartz (and the couples' attorneys) argued that the research base doesn't clearly show negative effects on children of being raised in gay partnerships and that making marriage available to them would increase the stability of their unions, give them important legal rights, and raise their status in the eyes of society. Thus, they concluded, the well-being of children might benefit, and is unlikely to suffer, if same-sex partners could marry.

Judge Chang listened to these arguments, studied the trial record and other materials, and on December 3, 1996, issued his ruling: The State of Hawaii had failed to prove that prohibiting same-sex marriage furthered a compelling interest.[3] He was not persuaded that enough negative evidence existed to plainly show that being raised by same-sex partners harms children, and he concluded that children being raised in same-sex partnerships would be helped if the partners were

[3]Findings of Fact and Conclusions of Law of Judge Kevin S. C. Chang, filed December 3, 1996. First Circuit Court, State of Hawaii.

allowed to marry. He therefore declared the law unconstitutional and prohibited the State of Hawaii from denying a marriage license solely because the applicants are of the same sex. Public opposition to the decision was so strong, however, that Hawaii voters approved an amendment to the state constitution that prohibited same-sex marriage, which meant that Judge Chang's ruling no longer applied. Yet the issue is still very much alive in other states. In Vermont in 2000, for example, the legislature, under pressure from the state's highest court, created a form of domestic partnership called a "civil union," which has many of the legal and economic benefits of marriage (Goldberg, 2000) (See Chapter 8.)

The same-sex marriage case shows that the sociology of the family deals with important social issues. Far from dealing with topics of limited academic interest, sociological studies of the family engage some of the most hotly debated and difficult social issues of our time. Nevertheless, the case also shows that sociological research can't, by itself, resolve moral and political issues. Sociological research can provide helpful information about social issues such as same-sex marriages. But in order to resolve these issues, citizens, legislators, and judges must also rely on values and principles that, strictly speaking, are outside the domain of sociological research.

The debate over same-sex marriages also shows the ambivalence Americans have toward the great changes in family life over the past half-century. This chapter will begin by examining the sources of that ambivalence. It will then consider fundamental questions raised by same-sex marriages: What is a family? What do families do that is important to society? What do families do that is meaningful to individuals? The chapter will then present the sharply contrasting views that sociologists have expressed about changes in family life. It will present the main research methods sociologists use to study the family. And it will conclude with a brief survey of the main theoretical perspectives that sociologists and others use to help explain why families do what they do.

American Ambivalence toward Marriage and the Family

The national uproar over the gay marriage case provided a puzzle: It was surprising to find, in a society in which sexual relations among unmarried adults are accepted, cohabiting unions are becoming the norm, and births outside of marriage are increasingly common, that so many people cared about the definition of marriage. Given the decreasing importance of marriage for sexual behavior and childbearing, why were so many people concerned? One obvious reason is widespread disapproval of homosexual activity. In a 1998 national survey, 64 percent of those questioned said that they thought sexual relations between two adults of the same sex was "always wrong" or "almost always wrong" (Davis, Smith, & Marsden, 1999).[4] But I think a more general reason is the profound ambivalence among many Americans toward marriage and the family. On the one hand, a family life centered on marriage remains the preference of most Americans. When young adults are asked their plans for the future, the overwhelming majority respond that they plan to marry and then have children. On the other hand, Americans are much more tolerant than they used to be of those who aren't married. In the 1950s, at the height of

[4]See Chapter 7.

the post–World War II baby boom, and again in 1976, national samples of Americans were asked what they would think about a person if all they knew was that he or she did not want to get married. In 1957, half responded that the person must be sick, selfish, immoral, or otherwise deficient. But in 1976, only a third responded negatively; most were neutral (Veroff, Douvan, & Kulka, 1981). To be unmarried in the 1950s was to be an outcast; in the 1970s—and even more so, I believe, in the 2000s—it is acceptable.

In fact, many of those who were so concerned about the outcome of the same-sex marriage case belong to a generation of women and men that has postponed marriage to an extent not seen since the beginning of the twentieth century. The postponement can be attributed to several factors, which are described more fully in subsequent chapters: the greater investment by young women in labor market skills and work experience, the decline in young men's earning power, the greater acceptance of premarital sex, the increase in cohabitation (unmarried couples living together), and the ability to avoid unwanted pregnancies and births through contraception and abortion. These developments have made women and men more independent of each other. Earlier in the twentieth century, in contrast to circumstances today, marriage was an economic necessity. Women and men needed to pool their resources in order to meet a minimum standard of living. Moreover, it was an expected, almost obligatory part of life.

Among the middle class today, marriage must compete with alternatives such as staying in school longer to obtain a higher degree, taking more time to develop a career, living with a partner without marrying, or childbearing outside marriage. Among middle-class young adults, this competition is increasingly judged by a single criterion: self-fulfillment. And by this criterion, marriage does not always come out the winner. Most Americans still want to marry but have less of a need to do so. Most want to have children, but they also value other uses of their time and money—such as investing in a career or building a vacation home. Many are ambivalent about marriage, at once drawn by its promise of intimacy and wary of its commitments and constraints.

The poor and near poor have not been immune to these cultural trends; but economics, of necessity, has played a greater role in their behavior. Since the early 1970s, the job prospects of men without a college education have deteriorated. Their earnings have declined so much that the average 50-year-old high school graduate was earning less in 1996 than the average 30-year-old high school graduate had earned 20 years earlier (Levy, 1998). Moreover, the income gap between the poorest and wealthiest families has widened.[5]

These cultural and economic changes have influenced what Americans think of marriage and parenthood. In 1999, the editors of the *New York Times Magazine* asked me to help design a national telephone survey about Americans' most important values (Cherlin, 1999). We presented randomly selected adults with a list of value statements and asked how important each one was to them. The list is displayed in Figure 1.1 in order of the percentage replying "very important." What is most interesting is the relative ranking of these value statements. The first four mostly reflect individualism ("being responsible for your own actions") and self-expression ("being able to communicate your feelings"). Note that "having children" only ranked sixth and "being married" ranked tenth. In fact, the

[5]See Chapter 4.

FIGURE 1.1

Percentage of adults replying "very important" when asked how important each of these values is to them. (*Source:* Cherlin, 1999.)

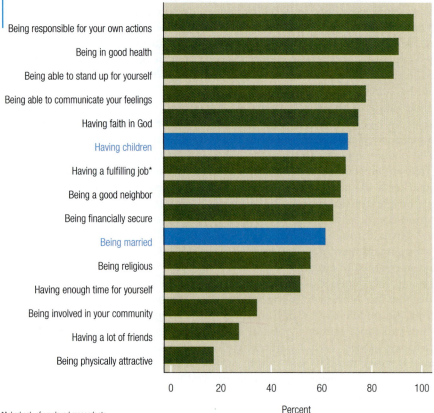

*Asked only of employed respondents

proportion of people who replied that "being married" was very important was less than the proportion who replied that "being a good neighbor" was very important. Overall, the rankings suggest that Americans value independence and self-expression more highly than playing the roles of parent or spouse.

What Is a Family?

The controversy about same-sex marriage and the widespread ambivalence about marriage raise the fundamental question of how to define a family. How it is defined has important social and economic consequences. On the level of morality, it is a statement of the kinds of personal relationships that we value highly. When President Jimmy Carter proposed a White House Conference on Families in the late 1970s, a bitter battle ensued between social conservatives who wanted the plural "families" replaced with "the family" in the title and liberals who wanted to preserve the original title. The social conservatives pressed the Carter administration to use the singular form because it symbolized their belief that there is only one proper kind of family: the "traditional" two-parent family in which the husband is employed outside the home and the wife cares for the children. Liberals fought off the conservative challenge, but the conference was seriously weakened by the controversy.

U.S. families are more diverse today than in earlier times because of the great changes that have occurred since the middle of the twentieth century. Single-parent families, extended families, and complex families formed by remarriages are among the kinds of families with which the two-parent, first-marriage family must share its spotlight.

The definition of the family is also important economically. Rules specifying who is a "family member" determine billions of dollars of government and corporate benefits. For example, I am eligible for health insurance coverage through my employer for my "family," which is defined as a spouse and children under 18. If I were unmarried but living with a woman who was the mother of my children, I could insure the children but not the mother. If I had been living for years with a man whom I considered my lifelong partner, I probably could not insure him. Moreover, how one defines a family plays an important role in the debate over whether the family has declined.

The definition of the family also varies from culture to culture. This book is primarily about families in the **Western nations,** the countries of Western Europe and the overseas English-speaking countries of the United States, Canada, Australia, and New Zealand. The main focus is on the family in the United States; but there are strong similarities between the American family and the family in other Western nations (Cherlin & Furstenberg, 1988). The primary unit in all these countries is the small, household-based family of parents and children. Young adults choose their spouses with modest input from their parents, and marriage is monogamous. (**Monogamy** is a marriage system in which persons cannot have more than one spouse.) Substantial proportions of married women

Western nations the countries of Western Europe and the overseas English-speaking countries of the United States, Canada, Australia, and New Zealand

monogamy a marriage system in which people are allowed only one spouse

work for pay outside the home (although that was not the case earlier in the twentieth century). Over the past few decades, nearly all the Western nations have undergone similar increases in cohabitation, childbearing outside of marriage, and divorce.

Nevertheless, we can draw important lessons by studying families elsewhere in the world. Therefore, this book will include numerous examples of family patterns in non-Western countries, including the developed nations of East Asia such as Japan and Taiwan, and developing countries through the world. In many of these countries, ties to parents and other kin play a larger part in the structure of the family. Often, parents provide substantial guidance to children in choosing spouses. In some countries, women rarely work outside the family home or compound. In many countries in Africa, Arabic Asia, and other areas, polygamous marriage is allowed. (**Polygamy** is a marriage system in which men or women [or both] are allowed to have more than one spouse at a time.) At the same time, significant changes have occurred in family patterns in much of the developing world over the past several decades; examining these changes can help us better understand the changes that have occurred closer to home. Similar insights can be drawn from studying the changes in family life in Western history. Each of the subsequent chapters of this book will include a separate, short essay on families in other cultures, with "other cultures" occasionally defined to include Western history.

For the United States and other Western nations, I would argue that there is no single definition of a family that is adequate for all purposes. Rather, how you define a family depends on what questions you want to answer. Two key questions are:

1. How well are family members taking care of children, the chronically ill, and the frail elderly?
2. How well are families providing the emotional satisfaction people value so highly—intimacy, love, personal fulfillment?

These questions address, respectively, the public responsibilities and the private pleasures the family is called upon to meet. For each of these questions, I submit, one of two definitions of the family will be helpful; I will call them the public family and the private family. These definitions provide two useful ways of looking at the same reality—and often the very same group of adults and children. Some observers may impose their own theological definitions of what constitutes a family from religious works such as the Bible or the Koran. But social science cannot determine the moral essence of the family, nor need it do so.

THE PUBLIC FAMILY

In examining the concept of the public family, it's useful to borrow a few terms from the field of economics. Economists who specialize in public welfare have introduced the notion of **externalities,** of which there are two types.[6] First, **negative externalities** occur when an individual or a business produces something that is beneficial to itself but imposes costs on other individuals or businesses. For example, factories that release sulfur dioxide through smokestacks impose a cost on everyone else by polluting the air. The factory gains by producing goods without having to install expensive smokestack scrubbers, but everyone else loses. Second, **positive externalities** occur when an individual or business produces something that benefits others but for which the producers are

---

polygamy a marriage system in which men or women (or both) are allowed to have more than one spouse

externalities benefits or costs that accrue to others when an individual or business produces something

negative externalities the costs imposed on other individuals or businesses when an individual or business produces something of value to itself

positive externalities benefits received by others when an individual or business produces something, but for which the producer is not fully compensated not fully compensated. For example, a corporation may start an expensive job training program in order to obtain qualified workers; but some of the workers may take jobs with rival firms after completing the training. The other firms obtain skilled workers without paying the cost of their training.

Some positive externalities involve the production of what are called **public goods.** These goods have a peculiar property: It is almost impossible to stop people who don't produce them from enjoying them. As a result, public goods are often produced in smaller quantities than is socially desirable. Suppose a town raises taxes to build a water filtration plant that cleans a polluted river. It cannot stop residents of other towns downstream from enjoying the cleaner water; yet these fortunate residents have paid nothing for the cleanup. In a situation like this, it is clearly in each town's interest to have some other town farther up the river produce the public good—the treatment plant. Yet if no town builds the plant, no one will enjoy cleaner water. One solution to this dilemma is for the county or state government to raise taxes in all the towns and then build the plant. Another is for the towns to reach an agreement whereby one will build the plant but all will contribute to the costs. Either solution compensates the producer of the public good for the benefits that others obtain.

public goods things that may be enjoyed by people who do not themselves produce them

Although it may seem like a long leap from factories to families, the concepts of externalities and public goods still apply. Families do produce valuable public goods—most notably, children (England & Folbre, 1999). For example, when I retire, I hope to receive a social security check from the government each month, just as retired people do today. The funds for those checks will come from payroll taxes paid by workers. After 2010, the many men and women born during the post–World War II baby boom will begin to reach retirement age; I hope to be one of them. Currently, there are about five persons of working age for each retired person; but by 2025 there may be only three persons of working age for every retired person.[7] This means that the burden of supporting the elderly will increase greatly. It's in my interest, then, for families to have and rear children today who will pay taxes when they grow up.

More, generally, it's in society's interest that today's children become good citizens with traits such as obeying the law, showing concern about others, and being informed voters. It's also in society's interest that they be productive workers who are willing and able to fill the needs of the economy. To be sure, critics charge that families often raise children in ways that reproduce existing inequalities between women and men (see Chapter 3), or between the working class and middle class (see Chapter 4). Nevertheless, what they do is of great public value. They are greenhouses growing the workers and citizens of tomorrow.

But children are costly to raise, and I will receive the same social security check whether or not the workers were raised by me. Therefore, it's in my economic interest to remain childless and to have every other family except mine raise children. Yet if everyone followed this strategy there would be no next generation. This dilemma is sometimes known as the **free-rider problem:** the tendency for people to obtain public goods by letting others do the work of

free-rider problem the tendency for people to obtain public goods by letting others do the work of producing them—metaphorically, the temptation to ride free on the backs of others

---

[6]A standard treatment of these topics can be found in Stiglitz (1988).

[7]Considering 20 to 64 as working age and 65 or older as retirement age. See Palmer and Gould (1986).

The public family: In another 10 years, will there be enough young workers paying taxes to support programs for the elderly such as Social Security and Medicare?

producing them—metaphorically, the temptation to ride free on the backs of others. Luckily, people have children for reasons other than economic self-interest. At the moment, however, they are barely having enough to replace the current generation of parents. Everyone benefits from the child rearing that parents do.[8] A National Academy of Sciences panel estimated that if the government had to purchase all the childcare services parents and relatives now provide for free, the cost would be $126 billion per year (Hayes, Palmer, & Zaslow, 1990).

In addition, families provide other services that have the character of public goods. As will be noted in Chapter 11, adult children still provide the bulk of the care for the frail elderly. If I am old and ill, I will benefit if I have adult children who will care for me. But others will also benefit from the care that my family provides. Without them, I would need more assistance from the government-funded medical insurance programs for the elderly (Medicare) and for the poor (Medicaid). Consequently, the care my family provides will keep government spending, and hence taxes, lower for everyone. The same logic applies to care that family members provide for the chronically ill.

The first definition, then, concerns the view of the family you take when you are concerned about the family's contribution to the public welfare—the useful services family members provide by taking care of one another. It is a definition of what I will call the **public family:** *One adult, or two adults who are related by marriage, partnership, or shared parenthood, who is/are taking care of dependents, and the dependents themselves.* Dependents are defined as children, the frail elderly, and the chronically ill. The family members usually reside in the same household, but that is not essential. For example, an elderly person may live in her own apartment but still receive daily assistance from her daughter or son. Nor is it essential that the family members be married or of the opposite sex. The important fact is that they are taking care of dependents and, in doing so,

public family one adult, or two adults who are related by marriage, partnership, or shared parenthood, who is/are taking care of dependents, and the dependents themselves

[8]This example holds only, however, for developed countries such as the United States, where the birthrate is at or below the level needed to replace the population. In developing countries with very high birthrates, children can impose negative externalities. Given the high death rates in the poorest developing countries, it is in the interest of a peasant farmer to have many children to ensure that at least one or two will still be alive when the farmer is too old to work. But if every family follows that logic, the land may become overpopulated and the country's development may slow. See Cain (1983).

producing public goods. This definition would include, of course, a married couple and their children or their elderly parents. But it would also include a divorced (or never-married) mother and her children, a cohabiting couple with children, a lesbian couple who are jointly raising a child that was born to one of them, or a gay man caring for a partner with AIDS. Note also who would be excluded by this definition: a childless married couple with no dependent or elderly relatives, or opposite-sex or same-sex cohabitors without children, the elderly, or ill dependents.

The boundaries of the public family are sometimes unclear. Suppose that after a divorce a father makes regular child support payments to his ex-wife and sees his children often. You might argue that he is still sharing parenthood and therefore part of the family under this definition. If the mother remarries, her new husband could also be considered part of the family. As will be discussed in later chapters, divorce, remarriage, and childbearing outside of marriage have made older notions of family boundaries unsatisfactory. Yet no social or legal consensus exists on what new boundaries should be accepted.

There is another kind of caretaking that goes on in many households with married or cohabiting couples, a kind that I have not included in the public family perspective. In most such households the wives (or women partners) do the majority of the housework: cooking, cleaning, shopping, washing, ironing. In doing so, they care for their husbands (or male partners), who do less than their share of the housework. Women's housework is socially valuable labor. Yet there is a difference between caring for husbands and caring for dependents such as children and the frail elderly: The latter are not capable of caring for themselves, whereas husbands are. When parents stop taking care of their children, the government is often obliged to step in and pay for the care. If wives stopped doing housework for their husbands, the government could tell husbands to care for themselves. That is why I have not listed childless couples under this definition.

The production of public goods invites public scrutiny, and public families are easily identifiable to outsiders by the presence of dependents. Because society has an interest in how well families manage the care of dependents, the law allows for some regulation of these families—despite strong sentiment in the United States against intervening in family matters. For example, we require families to send their children to school until age 16. And state social welfare agencies have the power to remove children from homes judged to be harmful. More recently, several states have required medical personnel to report suspected cases of physical abuse of children. The public family, then, is about caretaking and dependency. It points us toward the kinds of kinship ties that are important for nurturing the young and caring for the elderly and the ill. It is a useful perspective for answering questions such as: How adequately will our society raise the next generation? How will we care for the growing number of elderly persons?

THE PRIVATE FAMILY

At the same time, the family is much more than a public service institution. It also provides individuals with intimacy, emotional support, and love. Indeed, most people today think of the family and experience it in these private terms. Although some of the intimacy is expressed sexually, the family is also where we get hugs as children and back rubs as adults. It is where children form first attachments, teenagers take steps toward autonomy, and adults share their inner selves with someone else. The public family is not the most useful perspective in this regard because the central question is not how we will care for dependents or reproduce the workforce but, rather, how we will obtain the intimacy and emotional support we desire.

An appropriate definition of the private family must, therefore, encompass intimate relationships whether or not they include dependents. Yet if we are to maintain our focus on the family as a social institution, the definition still must encompass some rules for defining what kinds of intimate relationships constitute a family. The rules were relatively easy to formulate in the case of the public family: A dependent and a caregiver had to be present. Twenty or 30 years ago, it would also have been easy to find rules for the private family, but now it is much more difficult. At the earlier time, one could simply have adopted the definition of a family that was then, and is still now, used by the U.S. Bureau of the Census: A family is two or more persons, living in the same household, and related by blood, marriage, or adoption. The term **relationship by blood** means sharing a common ancestor, including cross-generational kinship ties such as parent and child (whose common ancestors are the parents' parents) or same-generation ties such as brother and sister (whose common ancestors are their parents). The Census Bureau definition would include a married couple with or without children as well as an unmarried mother and her child (who are related by "blood" or adoption). It is no longer satisfactory for several reasons. For example, consider the great rise in cohabitation since about 1970. Nearly half of all adults live with a partner before they marry, as mentioned earlier. According to the Census Bureau definition, a couple who live together for three years and then marry would not become a family until their wedding day. Some people might still support this definition on moral grounds, but it is increasingly out of step with the way young adults are leading their personal lives. Excluding cohabitation may still be valid as a statement of what family life should be, but it is deficient as a statement of what it is.

Moreover, Americans' increased tolerance of nonmarital relationships has led to a debate about whether to consider homosexual couples as families. The same-sex marriage trial in Hawaii was one manifestation of that debate. Advocates argue that most gay or lesbian couples who do not qualify as families under the Census Bureau definition because they are neither married nor related by blood have long-term intimate relationships that differ little in emotional content from heterosexual unions. Others, including some religious leaders, believe that heterosexual, marital unions are the only morally acceptable basis for family life. If one includes the care of dependents as part of the definition, as I have done above in defining the public family, the majority of gay and lesbian couples would be excluded. But if one's concern is with intimate relations, as mine is here in defining the private family, then gay and lesbian couples fit the definition descriptively.

Thus, it is difficult to define the family in terms of sentiment and intimacy because of the decline of marriage and of kinship by blood as the sole markers of family-like relationships among adults. It is difficult to know where to draw the line between private families and other kinds of intimate relationships, such as two people who live in separate apartments and see each other a few times a week. Where exactly is the boundary between family life and less intensive forms of intimacy? Here uncertainty is the challenge we must confront. Rapid change has undermined the consensus among Americans about the norms of family life—the social rules about what constitutes a family and how people should be-

relationship by blood
the sharing of a common ancestor, including cross-generation ties (such as parent and child) and same-generation ties (such as brother and sister)

have when they are in one. Let me offer, then, a definition of the **private family** not as an authoritative statement but rather as a starting point for analyzing this uncertainty: *two or more individuals who maintain an intimate relationship that they expect will last indefinitely—or, in the case of a parent and child, until the child reaches adulthood—and who live in the same household and pool their income and household labor.* This definition allows for children to be part of the private family, although the character of the intimacy between parents and children is clearly different from that between adult partners. It does not require that the individuals be of opposite sexes. The relationship must be one in which the commitment is long-term, in which the expectation is that the adult partners will stay together indefinitely. I do not require that they expect to stay together for life because it's not clear how many married couples even expect as much, given that about half of all marriages now end in divorce. The definition also includes the notion that the partnership usually is household-based and economic as well as intimate—shared residence, common budgets. This reflects my sense that intimate relationships in families are not merely erotic and emotionally supportive but also involve sharing the day-to-day details of managing one's life.

To be sure, individuals also receive emotional support and material assistance from kin with whom they are not in an intimate relationship. The word "family" is sometimes used in the larger sense of relationships with sisters, uncles, grandmothers, and so forth. These broader kinship ties are still an important part of the setting in which people embed their intimate relations to spouses, partners, and children. The usual definition of "kin" is the people who are related to you by descent (through your mother's or father's line) or marriage. Yet the concept of kinship is also becoming broader and harder to define, as this book will show. In settings as varied as sharing networks among low-income African Americans, friend-based support networks among lesbians and gay men, and middle-class networks of adults who are related only through the ties of broken marriages and remarriages, people are expanding the definition of kinship, creating kin, as it

private family two or more individuals who maintain an intimate relationship that they expect will last indefinitely—or in the case of a parent and child, until the child reaches adulthood—and who live in the same household and pool their income and household labor

Table 1.1 Two Ways of Looking at the American Family

	THE PUBLIC FAMILY	THE PRIVATE FAMILY
Examples	Married couple, cohabiting couple, or single parent with children Single person caring for ailing parent Gay person caring for partner with AIDS	Married or cohabiting couples without children Gay or lesbian couples without children
Main Functions	Raising the next generation Caring for the elderly Caring for the ill and disabled	Providing love and intimacy Providing emotional support
Key Challenge	Free-rider problem	Boundary problem

created kinship kinship ties that people have to construct actively

assigned kinship kinship ties that people more or less automatically acquire when they are born or when they marry

were, out of relationships that don't fit the old mold. In fact, throughout the book I will distinguish between what I will call **created kinship**—kinship ties that people have to construct actively—and **assigned kinship**—kinship ties that people more or less automatically acquire when they are born or when they marry. And I will return in the final chapter to the changing nature of kinship and its implications for family life.

TWO VIEWS, SAME FAMILY

No matter which perspective—public or private—you choose, many, perhaps most, family units will fit that perspective. That is to say, both perspectives may apply to the same family unit. A married couple may be providing each other with love and intimacy and also raising children. Indeed, the public and private dimensions of the family often overlap. For example, it's difficult for families to provide good childcare without love and emotional support. Moreover, even the private family is influenced by the larger society. As will be discussed in Chapter 2, the development of the private family depended upon, among other things, the availability of wages high enough so that family members no longer needed to focus their attention on day-to-day subsistence. The two perspectives, then, can be thought of as complementary and sometimes overlapping ways of looking at the same reality: the institution of the family.

Table 1.1 reviews the basic distinction between these two perspectives. The first row shows examples of families as seen through the public and private family perspectives. The second row shows the main functions of the family in the public and private domains. In raising the next generation of children—the workers, citizens, and parents of the future—parents and other caregivers are best viewed as carrying out the functions of the public family. The same can be said for caregivers of the frail elderly or for disabled individuals. In contrast, when providing love, intimacy, and emotional support, family members are carrying out the functions of the private family. The third row shows the key challenges families face in these two guises. It's in people's narrow self-interest to let others do the hard work of raising children or caring for the elderly—activities that benefit society as a whole. (And much of this care is provided by women outside of the paid workforce. See Chapter 9.) But if too many people try to ride free, our society may not invest enough time and effort in producing the next generation or in caring for the elderly. In fact, some social critics believe American society has already reached this point. As for the private family, its key challenge is maintaining its dominant position as the setting where people experience emotional gratification. With the decline of marriage, there are many kinds of relationships that provide intimacy, love, and sex. Will the private family continue to cohere as a social institution, or will its boundaries collapse into a sea of diverse, limited personal relationships?

In sum, to examine the contributions of families to the public welfare is to look at relationships through the lens of the public family. To examine the family's provisions of intimacy, love, and fulfillment is to look through the lens of the private family. Both perspectives are embedded in each of the chapters that follow. Which is better? Neither. They are two takes on the same reality. Many textbooks emphasize the private family by focusing primarily on interpersonal relationships in courtship, cohabitation, and marriage. In doing so, they pay less attention to the socially valuable work that families do. Although this book, too, will have much to say about the private family, it will also emphasize the public family. In addition to the essays on families in other cultures, each subsequent chapter will include a short essay on families and public policy; and chapters such as "The Family, the State, and Social Policy," "Children and Parents," and "The Elderly and Their Families" will be directed primarily toward public issues.

A SOCIOLOGICAL PERSPECTIVE ON THE FAMILY

In this book, the singular form "the family" rather than the plural form "families" will be used when discussing the family as a **social institution.** This term refers to a set of roles and rules that define a social unit of importance to society. The roles give us positions such as parent, child, spouse, ex-spouse, stepfather, partner, and so forth. The rules offer us guidance about how to act in these roles. But the use of the singular is not meant to imply that there is only one kind of family. On the contrary, there are many forms. Similarly, one might write about "the corporation" in a textbook on social organizations without implying that there is no difference between IBM and a chain of grocery stores. Or an author might discuss "the hospital" in a text on medical sociology while recognizing the difference between a giant teaching hospital in a central city and a community hospital out in the suburbs. In addition, referring to "the family" is not meant to imply that the interests of wives, husbands, and children are always identical—any more than that the interests of workers and managers in corporations are identical.

In all of these cases, the use of the singular would signal the study of the family as a social institution rather than just a set of interpersonal relationships. An institution can grow stronger or weaker over time; it can take on somewhat different forms at different times and places; and it can be difficult to define at its margins. But it is a visible structure that people can recognize and understand. It also does something important for society. The "family" fits this description. Its important functions include rearing children, caring for the elderly, and providing comfort and emotional support to its members.

If the family can be viewed as a social institution, then sociology can help us understand it better. Sociologists specialize in, among other topics, the study of institutions. They analyze the consequences for individuals of the roles that exist and the rules about how these roles should be played. For example, in my work analyzing remarriage after divorce, I have argued that some

social institution a set of roles and rules that define a social unit of importance to society

of the common problems occur because the rules of the institution of the family assume that individuals are in first marriages. There are no widely accepted norms for how harshly a stepparent can discipline his or her stepchild, nor for how much emotional and financial support a stepparent owes to a stepchild. This lack of norms can lead to confusion and conflict as remarried persons and their children attempt to build a successful stepfamily (Cherlin, 1978). (See Chapter 14.)

When sociologists study institutions, they also look outward. They search the social world for important external forces, such as the degree of opportunity provided by the labor market, the restrictions imposed by racial prejudice and discrimination, the domination of women by men, and the impact of new ideas and values. This book will discuss how forces such as these influence the family. In other words, sociologists argue that the family cannot be studied in a vacuum; rather, it must be studied in its social context. The sociological perspective on the family emphasizes the rules, roles, and relationships that are created and maintained by the larger society.

Marriage and the Family: Contrasting Sociological Viewpoints

Nevertheless, sociologists also have been uncertain about the current and future role of marriage and the family in American society. From the end of World War II to the late 1970s, rates of marriage, divorce, and childbearing went up and down in a roller-coaster pattern that left experts scurrying to keep up. The pace of change slowed in the 1980s and 1990s, allowing commentators to catch their breath and take stock of what had happened. Their assessments ranged from glee to gloom.

AN OPTIMISTIC VIEW

The optimists, most of whom are political liberals, claim that the family isn't in any great difficulty, it's just changing. Families, these observers remind us, have always been changing. What's more, so this argument goes, the family is good at adapting to change—it's a flexible, resilient institution. In this vein, the editors of a collection of essays write:

> *The American family is changing, but then it always seems to be changing. It is stable in its flexibility, its adaptation to changing social conditions. Instead of viewing with alarm the rapidity of change in family structures, we should step back a bit and be aware of the continuity of familial change* (Dornbusch & Strober, 1988).

No cause for alarm? What about the likelihood that about 40 percent of all children will witness the breakup of their parents' marriages and perhaps 10 percent will witness two divorces? Or that about 500,000 teenagers, many of them poor and unmarried, bear children every year? Or that one out of five children is living in a family with an income below the poverty line? The more forthright of the optimists face up to these facts but nevertheless argue that, as in the past, the family will adjust. They urge greater governmental effort in providing childcare for employed parents, helping teenage mothers finish school, ensuring that divorced fathers pay the child support they owe, and so forth. They note that wives in dual-earner marriages still bear most of the burden of cooking, cleaning, and childcare and urge fathers to do more.

The less forthright of the optimists merely step gingerly around divorce, child-bearing outside of marriage, and childhood poverty and instead accentuate the positive. And there are positives. Americans value the increased independence that they have achieved in their private lives; although this achievement is easy to criticize, few critics would volunteer to be the first to give up their own auton-omy. Moreover, the changes in women's work and family roles over the past few decades have given American women broader opportunities, the ability to leave abusive relationships, and much greater control of their own lives.

A PESSIMISTIC VIEW

The pessimists, who tend to be political conservatives, see the family in a very different light. Near the end of the introductory essay in his edited volume on marriage, Kingsley Davis, who was a leading sociological theorist, wrote:

> *The general direction of the changes in marriage that the present book documents during the last forty years is toward a weakening of marriage as an institution. If this goes far enough, and if no satisfactory substitute for marriage emerges, industrial societies will not survive. In fact they are not replacing themselves now, in either number or quality of the next generation. The nonindustrial two-thirds of the world, ill equipped to provide adequate education, is producing 92 percent of the world's next generation. There is thus no assurance that industrial societies, as we have known them, will survive* (Davis, 1985).

Whereas liberal defenders of family change focus on the emotionally enhanced relationships between adults and on the increased autonomy of women, conser-vatives such as Davis focus on instability and on children—and in Davis's case, on the lack of children in sufficient "number or quality." Without doubt, there are some valid issues about low birthrates that will be discussed in later chapters: How will a relatively smaller workforce pay for social security and health care benefits for a large elderly population? With fewer children and more women at work, will the elderly be able to rely on assistance from their families, as many do today? If low population growth means fewer new firms, will job opportunities be limited? Will the pace of technological innovation slow? Despite such ques-tions and concerns, the end of industrial societies, as we have known them, is not in sight. Moreover, as will be noted later, birthrates of women over age 30 in-creased in the 1980s as many later-marriers sought to make up for lost time.

Conservative critics, I think, tend to minimize the family's ability to adapt to new developments, such as the increased employment of married women or the introduction of the birth control pill. Dire warnings of the family's failing health have been put forth for decades. Consider this false alarm, written by an expert on the family during the low-birthrate years of the Great Depression:

> *The family is not indefinitely adaptable to modern society. . . . Only two logical alternatives appear feasible for governments wishing to induce births. They can go back to a rural-stable regime, or they can invent a new system of reproductive institutions* (Davis, 1937; Modell, 1985).

This fear of a shrinking population proved groundless. It turned out later that the family had not yet reached the limit of its ability to adapt and that governments did not have to invent a new system for encouraging births. What the expert did not and could not foresee was the great increase in births that occurred after World War II. Who was this expert? None other than Kingsley Davis, writing in 1937 at the beginning of his career. This is not to say that we should expect another baby boom, nor that the family is as malleable as its liberal champions proclaim. The point is rather that the family has shown an ability to adjust to changing circumstances that is often underestimated by conservatives, albeit overestimated by liberals. The problems of the contemporary family are real and should not be minimized, but they do not suggest that the institution of the family is fatally wounded.

STEERING A MIDDLE COURSE

Consequently, the challenge for a social scientist writing about the family—and for a reader—is to avoid the two extremes of boundless optimism and prophesies of doom. Too many observers stake out a position at one pole and try to defend it against all challengers. We must accept, rather, that the changes in the family have had both benefits and costs. Take divorce, for instance: Adults are freer to end unhappy marriages, which is an advance; but they do so through a process that is often gut-wrenching and economically draining for parents and traumatic for children. Moreover, we must realize that family change is continuing and that the end point if there will be one is not clear. It is too soon to know, for example, to what extent living together will supplant marriage. Except among the poor, cohabitation outside marriage has been noticeable only since about 1970, and it is still increasing. Although one can argue that cohabitation has not yet challenged the primacy of marriage in the United States, it is unclear what its impact will be 10 or 20 years from now. The changes in the family since midcentury have been so sharp and so recent that an eminent French demographer titled his book *La Famille Incertaine*—the uncertain family. He concluded that for observers of the family:

> *the attitude which makes the most sense is to accept that uncertainty is, for a time, our destiny, or rather the challenge we must confront. This should stimulate, not discourage, research. Without doubt, what research will reveal to us over the course of the coming years will not correspond to today's received wisdom*[9] (Roussel, 1989, p. 279).

In writing this book, I have tried to steer a middle course that respects the complexity and uncertainty of social changes in the family. First, I have attempted to confront both the costs and the benefits of the kinds of family lives Americans now live. It is more difficult to hold the pluses and minuses in one's head than to argue the case that changes have been unequivocally for the better—or for the worse; but I think it is necessary to do so. Second, I have tried not to envision an end point for a process that is still playing out. The implications of the great changes we will examine in this book defy a simple, assured summary.

Still, there is plenty of room in the middle ground for reasoned disagreements about the state of the American family. A number of observers concede that the family is in no danger of fading away but nevertheless insist that it is in decline.

---

[9]Louis Roussel, *La Famille Incertaine* (Paris: Editions Odile Jacob, 1989), quoted at 279. The translation is mine.

David Popenoe notes that marriage has become much more unstable and that there are acceptable alternatives—lifelong singlehood, cohabitation—to getting married at all. He argues that people value the survival and strength of the family unit less and self-fulfillment more. And he charges that parents are doing a poorer job of bringing up children due to the increase in single-parent families (a theme in David Eggebeen's testimony), the higher percentage of mothers working outside the home, and what he claims is a thinner family culture in the home (e.g., fewer joint activities, fewer family-centered traditions) (Popenoe, 1988, 1991).

Others admit that change has brought some problems but argue that, on balance, the family is not in decline—just becoming different and more diverse. They argue that American society can adjust to the new family forms, such as two-earner couples and single-parent households, by changing the ways in which the workplace and the school are organized. They assert that there is little evidence to back up the claim that having a working mother hurts children. Moreover, they ask, "decline for whom?" and note that the authority and stability of the 1950s family was achieved, in part, by severely limiting the opportunities of women. It is an important debate—one that I will touch upon throughout the book and then evaluate in the final chapter.

DIVERSITY

Both sides can agree on the growing diversity of American families. At midcentury, most families consisted of a married couple, neither of whom had been married to someone else previously, and their children. Beginning in the 1960s, however, family patterns were altered by great rises in divorce, childbearing outside of marriage, and, since about 1970, cohabitation. As a result, the first-marriage, two-parent family must now share its prominence with single-parent families and families formed by remarriages. The large numbers of immigrants from Latin America and Asia have brought their own cultural traditions, which often include a greater emphasis on ties to other kin beyond the parents-and-children household, such as grandparents, uncles, and aunts. Among African Americans, the percentage of two-parent households has declined greatly, while the importance of ties to other kin has increased. Across all racial and ethnic groups, married women have become much more likely to work outside the home. The causes of this growing diversity and its consequences for adults and children will be examined throughout this book.

How Do Family Sociologists Know What They Know?

Sociologists collect and analyze data consisting of observations of real families and the people in them. For the most part, they strive to analyze their data using objective, scientific methods. **Objectivity** means the ability to draw conclusions about a social situation that are unaffected by one's own beliefs. But it is much more difficult for a sociologist to be objective than it is for a natural or physical scientist. Sociologists not only study families, they live in them. They often have strong moral and political views of their own (indeed, strong views about social issues are what lead many people to become sociologists), and it is difficult to prevent those views from influencing one's research. In fact, there are some sociologists who argue that objectivity is so difficult to achieve that sociologists

objectivity the ability to draw conclusions about a social situation that are unaffected by one's own beliefs

shouldn't try. Rather, they argue, sociologists should try to do research that advances the social causes they believe in (Reinharz, 1992; see *How Do Sociologists Know What They Know?* Feminist Research Methods, in Chapter 3).

scientific method a systematic, organized series of steps that ensures maximum objectivity and consistency in researching a problem

hypothesis a speculative statement about the relationship between two or more factors

But most sociologists, although aware that their views can influence the way they interpret their data, model their research on the scientific method. For a detailed examination of the scientific method in sociology, consult any good introductory sociology textbook. For example, Schaefer (2001, p. 35) defines the **scientific method** as "a systematic, organized series of steps that ensures maximum objectivity and consistency in researching a problem." The essence of the scientific method is to formulate a hypothesis that can be tested by collecting and analyzing data. (A **hypothesis,** Schaefer and Lamm [1998] write, is "a speculative statement about the relationship between two or more factors" [p. 39].) It's easy to come up with a hypothesis (God is a woman), but the trick is to find one that can be shown to be true or false by examining data. Sociologists therefore tend to formulate very specific hypotheses about family life that can be confirmed or disconfirmed by observation. For example, sociologists have hypothesized that having a first child as a teenager lowers, on average, the amount of education a woman attains; and statistical data are consistent with this claim.

Even so, there are inherent limitations in how well social scientists can use the scientific method. The best way to confirm or disconfirm a relationship between two factors is to conduct an experiment in which all other factors are held constant. Scientists do this by randomly assigning subjects to one of two groups: an experimental group and a control group. For example, doctors will study whether a new drug speeds recovery from an illness by assembling a group of volunteers, all of whom have the illness, and then randomly giving half of them (the experimental group) the new drug. By randomizing, the doctors hope that all other confounding factors (such as past medical history) will be equalized between the two groups. Then they compare the average recovery times of the experimental group and the control group (those who did not receive the drug).

But it is rarely possible for sociologists to conduct randomized experiments on families. Without randomization, there is always the possibility that another, unobserved factor, lurking just beneath the surface, is causing the relationship we see. Consider again teenage childbearing. Women who have a first child as a teenager tend to come from families that have less education and less money, on average, than do other women. So the reason that teenage mothers attain less education may reflect their disadvantaged family backgrounds rather than having a child; in others words, they might have had less education even if they hadn't had children as teenagers. To truly settle this issue, a truth-seeking but cold-blooded sociologist would want to obtain a list of all families with teenage girls in the United States and then to assign *at random* some of the girls to have children and others to remain childless until their twenties. Because of the random assignment, teenage childbearing would be about as likely to occur in middle-class families as in poor families. In this way, the social scientist could eliminate family background as a cause of any differences that emerge between teenage mothers and nonmothers.

For very good ethical and legal reasons, of course, sociologists simply cannot conduct this type of study. Without random assignment, we can't be sure that having a child as a teenager *causes* a woman to have less education. Still, the lack of randomized experiments does not mean that sociologists should abandon the scientific method. Astronomers, after all, can't do experiments either. But this limitation makes the task of deciding whether a sociological study confirms or disconfirms a hypothesis more difficult.

If not from experiments, where does the data that family sociologists use come from? Generally, from one of two research methods. The first is the **survey,** a study in which individuals or households are randomly selected from a larger population and asked a fixed set of questions. Sociologists prepare a questionnaire and give it to a professional survey research organization. The organization then selects a sample of households randomly from an area (a city, a state, or the entire nation) and sends interviewers to ask the questions of one or more family members in the households. The responses are coded numerically (e.g., a "yes" answer is coded 1 and a "no" is coded 0), and the coded responses for all individuals are made available to the sociologists as a computer file.

The random selection of households is done to ensure that the people who are asked the questions are representative of the population in the area. This kind of random selection of households shouldn't be confused with conducting a randomized experiment. A random-sample survey is not an experiment because the households that are selected are *not* divided into an experimental group and a control group. Nevertheless, data from surveys provides sociologists with the opportunity to examine associations among characteristics of a large number of individuals and families. (See *How Do Sociologists Know What They Know?* The National Surveys, in this chapter.)

The advantage of the survey method (assuming that the households are randomly selected) is that its results are representative not only of the sample that was interviewed but also of the larger population in the area. The main disadvantage is the limited amount of information that can be gathered on each person or family. Most people won't participate in an interview that takes more than an hour or two. Moreover, the same set of questions is asked of everyone, with little opportunity to tailor the interview to each participant. Another disadvantage is that it's difficult to determine whether the people in the sample are responding honestly, especially if the questions touch upon sensitive issues. (See *How Do Sociologists Know What They Know?* Asking about Sensitive Behavior, in Chapter 7.)

The second widely used research method is the **observational study,** also known as *field research,* in which the researcher spends time directly observing each participant in the study—often much more time than an interviewer from a survey organization spends. The researcher may even join the group she or he is studying for a period of time. The individuals and families to be studied are not usually selected randomly; rather, the researcher tries to find families that have a particular set of characteristics he or she is interested in. For example, in a classic observational study of a low-income area of Boston, Herbert Gans (1982) moved into an Italian neighborhood for eight months and got to know many families well. He was able to argue that the stereotype of slum families as "disorganized" was not true. The strength of the observational method is that it can provide a much more detailed and nuanced picture of the individuals and families being studied than can the survey method. Sociologist-observers can view the full complexity of family behavior and can learn more about it.

The disadvantage of observational studies is that it is hard to know how representative the families being studied are of similar families. Because it takes a great deal of time to study a family in depth, observational studies typically are carried out with far fewer families than are surveys. Moreover, sociologists who do observational studies usually can't choose their families randomly by knocking on

survey a study in which individuals from a geographic area are selected, usually at random, and asked a fixed set of questions

observational study (also known as field research) a study in which the researcher spends time directly observing each participant

$\mathcal{S}$ociologists who study the family in the United States draw many of their findings from a series of national surveys that have been conducted over the past few decades. These surveys interview randomly selected samples of the U.S. population. They are similar to the opinion-poll surveys you see in the newspapers (e.g., what percent of the public thinks the president is doing a good job?), but they differ in several important ways:

- *They are larger* The surveys in the newspapers typically interview 500 to 1,500 individuals. The social scientific surveys typically interview 5,000 to 10,000 individuals or more. Because of this larger size, the social scientific surveys can provide reliable information on subgroups of the population, such as couples who are living together outside of marriage, currently divorced individuals, and never-married adults.
- *They are carried out using in-person interviews* In contrast, most of the newspaper polls are conducted by randomly dialing telephone numbers and speaking to people over the telephone. In-person interviews can be longer and more detailed (because people tire of telephone conversations more quickly than in-person conversations) and can be more flexible (e.g., the interviewer can give the subject a self-administered questionnaire for her husband or partner to fill out). But in-person interviews are also much more expensive to carry out.
- *They are longitudinal* Whereas the typical newspaper poll is a one-time activity, social scientists prefer a **longitudinal survey,** meaning a survey in which interviews are conducted several times at regular intervals. This design allows social scientists to study social change. The surveys typically select families or individuals at random and then reinterview them annually or biennially about how their lives are changing.
- *They are intended to be public resources* Most newspaper polls are meant for **primary analysis,** meaning they are analyzed by the people who collected the information. The data from these polls are then forgotten. The social scientific studies are designed for **secondary analysis,** meaning analysis of the data by people other than the group that collected it. The questionnaires are intentionally broad so that the interviewers can collect a wide range of information that will be of interest to many researchers. The results are coded numerically onto computer tapes or CD-ROMs and made available to anyone who wants to analyze them.
- *They are conducted by academic research centers rather than by commercial polling firms* The academic centers, such as the National Opinion Research Center at the University of Chicago and the Survey Research Center at the University of Michigan, typically take extra steps in designing and carrying out a survey so that the results are of better quality (e.g., the data conforms

---

longitudinal survey a survey in which interviews are conducted several times at regular intervals

primary analysis analysis of survey data by the people who collected the information

secondary analysis analysis of survey data by people other than those who collected it

doors or calling on the telephone because they must win a family's cooperation and trust before the family will agree to be studied in such detail. So although observational studies may yield a great deal of information about a small number of families, we may be unsure that we can generalize this knowledge to other similar families that weren't in the observational study.

Surveys and observational studies, consequently, have complementary strengths and limitations. They are summarized in Table 1.2. If the knowledge from sociological studies could be stored in a lake, a survey-based lake would be wide (because of the large number of people reached) but shallow (because of the limited time spent with each family), whereas an observationally based lake would be narrow but deep. Ideally, it would be best to employ both methods to study a problem, and some research projects attempt to do so. But to choose a large number of families randomly and then to send in sociologists to observe each family intensively over weeks and months is too expensive to be feasible. Moreover, the set of skills necessary to do survey research versus observational research is so distinct that sociologists tend to specialize in one or the other.

Sociologists sometimes use other research methods as well. For some topics, it is useful to examine historical sources. Chapter 8 describes a study in which

better to the statistical theory underlying random-sample surveys; a greater percentage of the selected subjects are reached and interviewed).

Because of the large sample size, longitudinal design, use of in-person rather than telephone interviews, and extra care in the fieldwork, the social scientific surveys are very expensive. Most are sponsored by U.S. government agencies such as the National Institutes of Health, the National Science Foundation, or the Bureau of Labor Statistics. The agencies support those large surveys to provide information on many research questions so that hundreds of researchers can analyze the data.

One such study is the National Survey of Families and Households. Interviews were first conducted during 1987 and 1988 with a randomly selected sample of 13,007 individuals, including oversamples of African Americans, Puerto Ricans, Mexican Americans, single-parent families, families with stepchildren,

cohabiting couples, and recently married persons. A broad range of questions about personal background and family life were asked. From 1992 to 1994, reinterviews were conducted with 10,007 of these individuals.

Another study is the Panel Study of Income Dynamics. In 1968, researchers at the University of Michigan interviewed 5,000 American households selected at random. They have reinterviewed the members of these households every year since then. When children grew up and left home, or adults divorced and moved out, the study followed them and interviewed them in their new households. The Panel Study of Income Dynamics greatly increased our knowledge of the economic fortunes of families over time. For example, the results indicate that few families are poor every year, but over the course of a decade many families, perhaps one-fourth, experience at least a year in which they are poor (Duncan, 1984).

Throughout the book, findings from these and other national surveys will be presented. Although not without limitations (See Chapter 7, *How Do Families Know What They Know?* Asking about Sensitive Behavior), they constitute a valuable resource to everyone interested in families, households, parents, and children. The "Families on the Internet" feature at the end of this chapter lists the World Wide Web addresses at which information about these surveys can be obtained.

Ask Yourself

1. Besides researchers, who else might be interested in the results of social scientific surveys? Can you think of any practical use for this information?

2. Why do you think researchers would want to see survey results for particular racial and ethnic groups or specific types of families?

www.mhhe.com/cherlin

Table 1.2 Comparing Survey Studies and Observational Studies			
WHO IS STUDIED	**HOW ARE THEY STUDIED**	**STRENGTHS**	**LIMITATIONS**
Survey Study			
Large, random sample of individuals or families	An interviewer asks questions from a predesigned questionnaire and records the answers	Results can be generalized to the population of interest	Only limited knowledge can be obtained; hard to judge honesty of responses
Observational Study			
Small, purposefully chosen sample of individuals or families	A researcher observes them in depth over a long period of time, sometimes participating in their daily activities	Detailed knowledge is obtained	Findings may not be representative of other, similar individuals or families

magazine articles from 1900 to 1979 were used to study changing conceptions of marriage. Occasionally, it is even possible to do an experiment. In the 1960s and 1970s, the Federal government sponsored experiments to learn about the consequences of providing families with a guaranteed minimum income. In several communities, families were selected and randomly divided into experimental and control groups. Families in the experimental group received checks from the experimenters if their incomes fell below a threshold. The results indicated that a guaranteed income produced some reduction in work effort and possibly an increase in marital disruption (Robins, Spiegelman, Weiner, & Bell, 1980).

These are the major methods that sociologists use to study families. In several of the chapters of this book, we will examine the methodology of key studies so that you may better understand how family sociologists develop their research findings.

Sociological Theory and the Family

The methods sociologists use and the questions they ask are influenced by sociological theory. Let me present a brief introduction to the theoretical perspectives that sociologists have developed for studying social institutions such as the family. These perspectives are best thought of as conceptual frameworks—road maps that show the important people and places, their characteristics, and how they relate to one another. I will draw upon these perspectives often in this book.

THE FUNCTIONALIST PERSPECTIVE

functionalist theory a sociological theory that attempts to determine the functions, or uses, of the main ways in which a society is organized

The dominant sociological perspective in the 1950s was **functionalist theory.** The functionalist theorists tried to determine the functions, or uses, of the main ways in which a society is organized. Functionalism had been developed earlier in the century by anthropologists who undertook field research among tribes and small societies in Africa, Asia, and Latin America. The anthropologists wanted to show that seemingly strange customs in other cultures had important uses and were valid, alternative ways of organizing a society—in other words, they wished to demonstrate that our culture was not superior to others. Their books documented the roles, relations, and practices of particular societies and then explained how these systems were able to maintain their societies' existences.

Beginning in the 1940s and continuing through the 1950s, numerous sociologists employed the functionalist approach to explain aspects of the ways social institutions were organized, including the institution of the family. The foremost practitioner of functionalism in sociology was Talcott Parsons, whose theoretical writings profoundly influenced other sociologists. Ironically, the effect of Parsons's writings about the American family was the opposite of the anthropologists' writings about exotic cultures. Whereas the anthropologists' message seemed to be that there were many valid ways of organizing family life, Parsons's message—whether intentional or not—seemed to be that the American family in the 1950s was the natural, superior form.

As will be described in Chapter 2, the middle-class ideal in the 1950s was the two-parent family in which the husband worked outside the home and the wife stayed home and did the housework and childcare. Robert Bales, a psychologist and colleague of Parsons on the Harvard faculty, had conducted a series of experiments with small groups, in which they were observed discussing how to go about some task. Bales claimed that in each group, one person emerged as the "instrumental" leader who led the group discussion about how to accomplish the task they had been assigned. A different person emerged as the "expressive" or "socioemotional" leader who kept up the group's spirit with warm, supportive remarks and jokes. This general tendency of small groups to divide the leadership tasks between two people, according to Bales, was functional in the sense that the coexistence of both kinds of leadership contributed to a better performance by the group.

Parsons and Bales then leaped to the assumption that since the family was a small group, it was functional for one adult member to specialize in instrumental leadership and for the other to specialize in expressive leadership. Lo and behold, that was how the middle-class 1950s family was organized. The husband, they wrote, was the instrumental leader because his labor provided the financial support for the family; and the stay-at-home wife was the expressive leader because she provided emotional support to her husband and children. Consequently, Parsons and Bales argued that the breadwinner-homemaker family was well organized to fulfill the tasks that society assigned to it: providing the material goods necessary for a decent living, providing emotional support to adults, and raising children (Parsons & Bales, 1955). Although they never said it was superior to other ways of organizing families, by implication it was, for if wives worked outside the home there would no longer be a full-time expressive specialist.

But work outside the home they did. Although Parsons and Bales seemed to view the breadwinner-homemaker family of the 1950s as if it were timeless, it was, in fact, unusual in historical perspective. As married women poured into the workforce in the 1960s and 1970s, the breadwinner-homemaker family lost its dominant position (see Chapter 2). Much of the sociological writing about the family in the 1960s, 1970s, and 1980s was devoted to refuting Parsons's implicit conclusion that this change in the family was for the worse. This antifunctionalist viewpoint was congenial to the growing body of sociological research influenced by the resurgence of the feminist movement in the 1960s. Still, no single theoretical perspective has dominated the post–1950s literature. Rather, most writers have borrowed eclectically from several theoretical traditions, which are examined briefly.

THE CONFLICT PERSPECTIVE

One of these is **conflict theory.** Whereas functionalism focuses on stability and cooperation among members of a group, conflict theory focuses on inequality, power, and social change. Conflict theorists study how individuals, or groups of individuals, come to dominate others and the circumstances under which those who are dominated are able to reduce or eliminate the disadvantages they face. When analyzing the family, conflict theorists see men as more powerful and women as less powerful. For example, Randall Collins states that male dominance rests on two sources of coercion: physical force and control of economic resources. In societies in which men's use of physical force is curtailed by the state or by custom, men cannot be as dominant; nor can they be as dominant in societies in which women produce valuable goods and services outside the household (Collins, 1971). Conflict theorists have a much less favorable view of the 1950s family than did Parsons because of what they see as women's domination by men, due, in large part, to women's lack of economic resources.

Conflict theorists also see other groups as subject to domination. Marxist writers, for example, have emphasized the conflicting interests of capitalists—the

conflict theory a sociological theory that focuses on inequality, power, and social change

people who own factories and businesses—and the workers in those enterprises. The owners obtain their incomes by paying workers less than the value of the goods the factory or business sells and keeping the difference. Some Marxist-influenced writers on the family claim that women's unpaid work in the home benefits employers in two ways. First, the housework women do allows employers to pay workers less than what would be required if workers had to pay for household services. Second, the emotional support wives provide to husbands eases the burdens of the often alienating and monotonous work that employers require them to do (Zaretsky, 1986).

THE EXCHANGE PERSPECTIVE

exchange theory a sociological theory that views people as rational beings who decide whether to exchange goods or services by considering the benefits they will receive, the costs they will incur, and the benefits they might receive if they were to choose an alternative course of action

A third perspective is **exchange theory.** This sociological approach is similar to the model of human behavior that economists use. People are viewed as rational beings who decide whether to exchange goods or services by considering the benefits they will receive, the costs they will incur, and the benefits they might receive if they chose an alternative course of action. In the rational choice–based theory of the family that won Gary Becker the 1992 Nobel Memorial Prize in economics, women often choose rationally to exchange the performance of household and childcare services in return for receiving the benefits of a man's income. If men are more "efficient" at market production—meaning they can earn higher wages—and women are more "efficient" at home production—meaning they are better at raising small children—then both partners gain from this exchange, argues Becker (1991). Thus, Becker's model is consistent with the Parsonian analysis of the family.

But in the hands of others, exchange theory can shade into conflict theory and lead to very different conclusions. Many sociologists maintain that exchanges take on a different character if the two actors come to the exchange with unequal resources. Richard Emerson and his colleagues developed a version of exchange theory that is useful in studying families (Cook, O'Brien, & Kollock, 1990; Emerson, 1972). According to Emerson, if person A values goods or services person B has to offer, and if person A has few alternative sources of obtaining these goods or services, then person A is said to be dependent on person B. The degree of dependency is greater the more highly A values these goods or services and the fewer alternative sources A has. And the more A is dependent on B, the greater is B's power over A. When one person is more powerful than another, he or she may be able to shape the exchange so that he or she receives greater benefits and incurs fewer costs than does the other person. Husbands, many writers have suggested, are in a stronger bargaining position when they are the sole earners in their families because their wives have fewer alternative sources of income. According to exchange theory, when wives earn money on their own, their dependence decreases and therefore their husbands' power over them decreases (Scanzoni, 1972).

THE SYMBOLIC INTERACTIONIST PERSPECTIVE

symbolic interaction theory a sociological theory that focuses on people's interpretations of symbolic behavior

Less common but still important is the distinctive perspective of **symbolic interaction theory.** The major figure in symbolic interaction theory was philosopher George Herbert Mead, who taught at the University of Chicago early in the twentieth century.[10] Among all animals, only human beings, the symbolic interactionists point out, do not merely react instinctively to what others of their species do but rather *in-*

terpret what others do. We interpret symbols—gestures, words, appearances—whose meanings we have come to understand. This interpretation occurs in situations in which we interact with someone. It is this process of the interpretation of symbols during social interaction that the symbolic interactionists study. Some symbols are so clear and uniform that interpretation is straightforward; thus, we all know that the traffic officer's raised hand, palm facing the driver, means stop. But some symbols are harder to interpret. Symbols involving differences between women and men, it has been argued recently, are particularly problematic and in need of continual affirmation (see Chapter 3). For example, husbands who don't want to change their babies' diapers may make a grand display of fumbling at the changing table when called upon by their wives, thus exhibiting their male "inferiority" at the task. The interactionist perspective is also useful in analyzing situations where family relations seem less institutionalized, less set in concrete—such as in newly formed stepfamilies or dual-career marriages. It helps sensitize us to the ways in which people create shared understandings of how family members should act toward one another. These shared understandings become the bases of the social roles people play in families—spouse, parent, breadwinner, homemaker, child, and so forth.

THE FEMINIST PERSPECTIVE

Feminist theory, which has arisen from the feminist movement over the past two decades, is a theoretical perspective that differs from the other perspectives in that it is focused on a problem, rather than on a mechanism such as an exchange based on costs and benefits, coercion based on the threat of force, or the use of symbols to create shared understandings. The problem is the domination of women by men. Nevertheless, feminist theory shares with conflict theory an orientation toward relationships of power and inequality. The central concept in feminist theory is **gender,** which is usually defined as the social and cultural characteristics that distinguish women and men in a society (see Chapter 3). Feminist theorists argue that nearly all the gender differences we see in the roles of women and men are of cultural origin and have been socially constructed. By socially constructed, they mean arising not from biological differences but rather from culturally accepted rules, from relationships of power and authority, and from differences in economic opportunities. For example, the culture might include a rule that women should not work outside the home (as was the case among the American middle class from the mid-nineteenth to the mid-twentieth centuries). Or the opportunities for women might be limited to jobs that tend to pay less than comparable jobs in which most workers are men.

Moreover, feminist theorists assert that these cultural differences are constructed in ways that maintain the power of men over women (Thorne, 1992). For instance, feminist theorists criticize the idea that the breadwinner-homemaker family provided an exchange that was equally beneficial to women and men. Rather, they note that women's direct access to money through paid employment was restricted in this type of family, which maintained women's dependence on men. They also note that men's relationships with their children were often limited. The cultural belief that "women's place is in the home" and the lower wages paid to women employed outside the home compelled married women to give up

feminist theory a sociological theory that focuses on the domination of women by men

gender the social and cultural characteristics that distinguish women and men in a society

---

[10]For an account of Mead's viewpoint by his foremost interpreter in sociology, see Blumer (1962).

Feminist theorists would argue that a male-dominated social system has made it more difficult for women to combine work for pay with raising children.

the idea of paid employment. Under these constraints, their best strategy may indeed have been to trade household services for a male income; but it was a forced choice set up by a social system that favored men.

Sociologists have intensively studied gender roles, the patterns of behavior that typically occur among one gender but not the other. Many articles, for instance, document how parents, friends, and the media influence boys and girls to act in different ways. More recently, the study of gender roles has fallen out of favor among some feminist theorists (Ferree, 1990). Gender distinctions are such an integral part of our society, the theorists have claimed, that they can't be reduced to mere roles. Instead, the theorists have suggested that we analyze entire social institutions, such as the educational system or the labor market, to see how their organization maintains the inferior position of women.

Still, many sociologists think it is useful to examine social roles people play, such as mother, father, wife, or husband, and we will do so in this book. In addition, as stated earlier, a number of sociologists think there are some limited but potentially important biologically based differences in the ways women and men act in families. A minority of feminist social scientists are among those who believe it is important to explore biological differences and their implications for family life. "An ideology that does not confront this basic issue," writes one, "is an exercise in wishful thinking" (Rossi, 1984, p. 15).

Some feminist theorists maintain that the family is itself an artificial creation that has been organized to maintain male dominance. They would deny that there are any deep-seated predispositions among people that would lead to the formation of the kinds of families that we see. In fact, some would argue that we shouldn't even try to study the family anymore because to do so accepts as "natural" the inequalities built into it. Rather, we should merely study households and the relations among people within them. Needless to say, these critics would reject the contention that there is any biological basis for the ways in which men and women act in families. At the extreme, some maintain that even sexual intercourse, pregnancy, and giving birth are best viewed as, in the words of two anthropologists, "cultural facts, whose form, consequences, and meanings are socially constructed in any society" (Yanagisako & Collier, 1987).

Whether or not you think it's useful to study the family (as I obviously do), there is an important insight to be gained from feminist theory. It makes us aware that the experience of living in a family is different for women than it is for men. Arrangements that make men happiest don't necessarily make women happiest. A husband might prefer that his wife stay home to care for their children and do household work full time. His wife might prefer to combine a paying job with housework and childcare, and she might wish that he would share more of the household tasks. In other words, women's interests in the family are not necessarily the same as men's interests. The breadwinner-homemaker bargain may have been great for men (except for those who wanted an active role in raising their children), and it may have been great for women who wished to raise children and do housework full time, but it frustrated other women by restricting the possibility of developing a satisfying career outside the home. Feminist theory urges us to view families through a prism that separates the experiences of men and women rather than just considering what's best for the family as a whole. It is a view that I will take repeatedly in this book.

PERSPECTIVES FROM EVOLUTIONARY PSYCHOLOGY

The sociological perspective on the family does not provide a complete understanding. There is a vast amount of psychological literature on the family that focuses on the individuals involved. Whereas sociologists studying the family tend to look outward toward society, psychologists tend to look inward toward people's personalities and their interactions with other family members. They study how children come to understand the world around them and how they develop a sense of self. They observe how people's behavior is shaped by their family experiences. Several psychologists, for example, have observed in detail the effects on children of experiencing the breakup of their parents' marriages, as will be noted in Chapter 13. Moreover, as the next chapter will make clear, historians writing since about 1970 have greatly increased our understanding of how the contemporary family has emerged. Valuable work has also been done by economists who have applied their theories to family life. This book will draw upon these contributions from other social science disciplines, but it cannot provide a comprehensive account of them.

Nearly all sociologists believe that most of the differences in the roles men and women play and in the behaviors they show are social and cultural in origin. Yet some also think that the institution of the family has biological roots and, correspondingly, that the differences between women and men have both social and biological origins, and that it is likely that a person's sexual orientation (heterosexual or homosexual) has a substantial biological component. For example, a number of studies build a plausible case that the greater aggressiveness that men, on

Looking Back

1. **How do Americans feel about marriage and the family?** Many Americans seem to be ambivalent about marriage and the family. On the one hand, surveys show that most young adults plan to marry and to have children. On the other hand, young adults are postponing marriage. A number of factors, such as changes in women's participation in the paid labor force, increased cohabitation, greater acceptance of premarital sex, and improved contraception, underlie this postponement. Moreover, Americans increasingly value marriage for the personal fulfillment it can bring, rather than for the opportunity to play valued social roles such as spouse or parent.

2. **What do families do that is important for society? What do families do that is important for the individuals in them?** Families contribute to society by raising the next generation and caring for the ill and the elderly. On an individual level, families are settings in which people give and receive love, intimacy, and social support. This book proposes two definitions of the family—one for each of these questions. The public family perspective defines the family in terms of the presence of caregivers and dependents. The private family perspective defines the family in terms of an indefinite, intimate relationship between two or more individuals who live in the same household and share the fruits of their labor. These two perspectives constitute different views of the same reality; a given family unit might fit both of them.

3. **What are the grounds for being optimistic or pessimistic about the state of the family?** The optimists don't worry about recent changes in family life because they say it always has been changing. They note that recent changes have had positive effects such as providing greater opportunities for women who want to combine a career with raising a family. The pessimists tend to focus on children. They see more employed mothers, more divorce, and more childbearing outside of marriage as indications that children's well-being may be declining.

4. **How do sociologists go about studying the family?** Sociologists study the family as a social institution and the influences of the external social world on that institution. They observe real families and the people in them, and for the most part, they try to analyze their data objectively using the scientific method. Sociologists formulate hypotheses that can be tested, although there are limits to their use of the scientific method. The two most common research methods sociologists use are (1) the survey, a study in which a randomly selected group of individuals or families are asked a fixed set of questions; and (2) the observational study, in which the researcher spends time directly observing each participant in the study.

5. **What are the leading theoretical approaches to studying the family?** Sociologists have developed several theoretical frameworks for studying social institutions such as the family. These include functionalist theory, which emphasizes the functions, or uses, of the main ways that a society or a social institution, is organized; conflict theory, which analyzes the consequences of power, domination, and resistance; exchange theory, which considers individuals as rational beings who exchange goods or services on the basis of costs and benefits; and symbolic interaction theory, which emphasizes the ways in which people create shared understandings through social interaction. In addition, feminist theory has arisen as a way of understanding inequalities between women and men.

Thinking about Families

1. What are the boundaries of family life? Is any intimate relationship between two people a family? If not, what characteristics set apart families from other relationships?

2. How might the ways that sociologists study family issues differ from the ways that religious leaders or philosophers might study them?

3. Does it make sense to think of marriages and intimate relationships as settings in which people exchange goods and services and bargain with each other, as the exchange theorists do?

4. **The public family:** What are some of the ways that your family has carried out its "public" functions?

5. **The private family:** How has your family carried out its "private" functions?

Key Terms

Families on the Internet   www.mhhe.com/cherlin

Note: While all the URLs listed were current as of the printing of this book, these sites often change. Please check our web site (http://www.mhhe.com/cherlin) for updates.

 The Internet is a great source of information about family issues. Throughout this book, the "Families on the Internet" section will provide you with suggested World Wide Web sites. Keep in mind that web sites come and go on the Internet and that the contents of each web site change often. This flux means that you might occasionally not find a web site or specific piece of information within a site that is listed in this section. I will attempt, however, to suggest sites that are likely to be long-lived.

In addition, the publishers of this book have established a web site where up-to-date links to useful sites will be posted.

The first way to obtain information on the family is pure web surfing: Click the search button on your Internet browser and enter a phrase; the search engine will respond with corresponding links to web sites. As you know, the phrase can't be too broad: Entering "family" will cause the search engine to return a blizzard of links. But a more focused entry can be useful: Typing "civil union" or "domestic partnership" for example, should return a number of useful links about same-sex partnerships and marriage. It may also, however, return some not-so-useful links; and it can be difficult and time-consuming to distinguish the good sites from the bad, or simply irrelevant, sites.

Consequently, it helps to have some suggested links to broader web sites that provide issue-oriented information on a number of topics. For almost any public issue involving the family, two such "umbrella" sites are good places to start. The first is the Electronic Policy Network, **www.epn.org,** a site that provides links to many liberal and moderate organizations and publications. The second umbrella site is **www.townhall.com,** which has links to many conservative organizations and publications. Try to find a topic for which both sites have information and compare their perspectives.

The organizations that maintain the major national surveys have web sites. Information on the National Survey of Families and Households is available at **www.ssc.wisc.edu/nsfh/home.htm.** Information on the Panel Study of Income Dynamics is available at **www.isr.umich.edu/src/psid.**

chapter 2

The History of the Family

Looking Forward

1. What functions have families traditionally performed?

2. How did American families change after the United States was founded?

3. How have the family histories of major ethnic and racial groups differed?

4. How did the emotional character of the American family change during the early twentieth century?

5. What important changes occurred in marriage and childbearing in the United States in the last half of the twentieth century?

The serious study of the history of the family began in 1960, when the manager of a tropical fruit importing firm in France, a self-described "Sunday historian," published a book about the history of childhood (Ariès, 1960). Philippe Ariès, curious about family life in the Middle Ages, had examined works of art dating back 1,000 years. Any artist will tell you that children's heads are larger in proportion to the rest of their bodies than adults' heads. Yet many early medieval artists used adult proportions when painting children's heads and bodies, as if their subjects were, in fact, small adults. Moreover, the artists dressed children in the same clothes as adults. From such evidence Ariès concluded that the concept of childhood was a modern invention.

Of course, there always had been children, but until the 1700s, wrote Ariès, the long stage of life we call childhood wasn't recognized by most people. American historian John Demos put forth a similar argument about the Puritans in Plymouth Colony in the 1600s: "Childhood as such was barely recognized in the period spanned by Plymouth Colony. There was little sense that children might somehow be a special group, with their own needs and interests and capacities." (Demos, 1970). According to historians such as Ariès and Demos, parents withheld love and affection from infants and toddlers because so many of them died. The great French essayist Montaigne wrote in the late 1500s, "I have lost two or three children in their infancy, not without regret, but without great sorrow."[1] *Two or three*—Montaigne couldn't even remember how many. If children survived, wrote Ariès and Demos, they were treated as little adults. By age seven, boys and girls performed useful work—helping fathers in the fields or mothers at the hearth—and played the same games and attended the same festivals as adults. Ariès argued that it was only with the spread of schooling and the decline in child deaths—neither of which occurred on a large scale until the 1800s outside the noble and middle classes—that the notion of a protected, extended stage of childhood emerged.

Ariès's influential book launched a new generation of historians who studied ordinary families rather than royal families. His contribution is still respected even though many historians now believe that he underestimated parents' appreciation of childhood as a stage of life. For every Montaigne, the revisionist historians have found a Martin Luther, who wrote in the 1500s after the death of his infant daughter, "I so lamented her death that I was exquisitely sick, my heart

---

[1] From vol. 2, no. 8, of Montaigne's *Essais.* Quoted on p. 39 of Ariès (1960).

Marriage of Giovanni Arnolfini and Giovanna Cenami, Jan van Eyck's famous painting of the wedding vows of a wealthy couple in 1434, shows a late medieval view of marriage. Wives were valued primarily for their childbearing and domestic roles: The bride is shown holding her long gown over her womb, as if she were pregnant. In back of her is a statuette of St. Margaret, the patron saint of childbearing women. Arnolfini stands straight, his facial expression stern, as if ready to assume his role as head of the household. His wife's pose is more submissive: her head slightly bowed, her eyes slightly downcast. A dog symbolizes the faithfulness expected of the couple.

rendered soft and weak; never had I thought that a father's heart could be so broken for his children's sake."[2] When historian Linda Pollock located and read 68 diaries written by American and British parents in the 1600s and 1700s, she found that most of them were aware that children were different from adults and that they needed parental guidance and support. The diarists frequently referred to their children as "comforts" and showed pride in their accomplishments. "I doe not think one child of 100 of his age durst doe so much," wrote one proud father (Pollock, 1983). (For an overview of revisionist scholarship see Nicholas [1991].) Nevertheless, parents of this period did seem less saddened by the death of an infant than of an older child.

The family history industry that Ariès spawned has produced hundreds of volumes and thousands of articles. During the same period, a related field, the history of women, has grown just as fast. Together, these fields provide an anchor for the study of the contemporary family. They describe the context in which the contemporary family has developed. Among other things, they tell us that the public family is as old as human civilization but that the private family blossomed only during the past few hundred years. For the sociologist studying the contemporary family, the historical literature is a wonderful source of insights. This chapter will provide a brief guided tour of that literature. Of necessity, it will be a

[2]Quoted in Ozment (1983).

highly selective tour, one that provides a foundation for the detailed study of the modern family in the remaining chapters of this book.

First, we must go back even further in time than the historians have traveled in order to understand the origins of family and kinship. The we will look at what the colonial and American Indian families were like prior to 1776. Afterward, we will follow the changes in the American family that took place between 1776 and the start of the twentieth century. Finally, we will study the diversity of racial and ethnic American families in the twentieth century and the rise of what I call "the private family."

What Do Families Do?

THE ORIGINS OF FAMILY AND KINSHIP

We have all seen pictures of a new colt, minutes after birth, standing on its four legs. My local newspaper printed a photograph of a one-day-old dolphin swimming with its mother. In contrast, the average human baby cannot sit up until about six months and cannot walk until about age one. This difference in maturation time between humans and other animals is not an accident of nature; rather, it reflects the evolution of our species. Throughout most of their existence, human beings have been **hunter-gatherers:** They wandered through the forests in small bands, hunting animals and gathering edible plants. According to the theory of evolutionary biology, humans evolved from four-legged primates to beings that could walk upright and hunt or gather with two arms. Because those with greater thinking power were more likely to survive, the size of the human brain increased through natural selection.

These advances, however, came at a cost. The larger brain meant that babies' heads were larger at birth, but the shift to an upright posture limited the size of the pelvic opening through which the baby must pass. Consequently, humans are born smaller (relative to their adult size) than most other mammals and develop more after birth.[3] Infants need prolonged, intensive care in order to survive. In hunter-gatherer societies, as in nearly all other known societies, mothers provide most of the care during the first few years of children's lives. Anthropologists who have studied the few remaining hunter-gatherer societies report that mothers carry their young with them during the first year and continue to breast-feed them for several years (Howell, 1979). As a result, women specialize in finding plants and hunting small animals within a limited area, whereas men range farther afield in search of larger animals.

About 10,000 years ago, humans discovered the advantage of remaining in one place and planting crops. Settled agriculture revolutionized human organization because it allowed humans to accumulate surpluses of grain that could support larger kinship groups than was possible in hunter-gatherer societies. Indeed, human societies were often organized around large kinship groups. In societies in which a tribe ruled a territory and no other strong government existed, people often traced descent through either the father's or the mother's line, but not both. What resulted were kinship groups called **lineages: patrilineages** if de-

hunter-gatherers people who wander through forests or over plains in small bands, hunting animals and gathering edible plants

lineage a form of kinship group in which descent is traced through either the father's or the mother's line

patrilineage a kinship group in which descent is through the father's line

---

[3]For an overview, see Rossi (1977).

scent is traced through the father's line; **matrilineages** if traced through the mother's line. These groups seem odd, at first, to people in Western nations, who trace descent through both the father's and mother's line; but the structure serves a purpose. Among other virtues, lineages limit the number of people who are related to a person and with whom that person must share land, water, animals, and other resources. In a patrilineage, my sons will marry women from outside the lineage; then the couples will live near me (sometimes with me) and remain in my lineage. My grandsons will do the same. But my daughters and granddaughters will marry men from other lineages, move to their land, and leave my lineage. Consequently, I need to share my resources with, and to defend, only those persons related to me through my father, my brothers, and my sons. If a maternal uncle needs assistance, that's his lineage's problem; I am not my mother's brother's keeper.

Kinship, as one anthropologist has written, developed as "a weapon in the struggle for survival" (Fox, 1967). In tribal societies, family ties provide the structure that holds the society together: You are a member of the tribe not because you are a citizen (a concept that can't exist without a state) but rather because you are related to the other members. You obey rules set by the tribal elders, not laws set by a government. You tend farmland not because you purchased it but because the tribe lets you use it. Kinship groups ensure order, recruit members from outside the group (usually through marriage), defend against other outsiders, provide labor at harvesttime, and assist the less fortunate. Anthropologists who study social organization in tribal societies focus on family and kinship because, to a large extent, that *is* social organization.

In most societies, kinship groups are made up of smaller family units, consisting of a mother and children always, a husband usually, and other household members sometimes. In many of the Western nations [➡ p. 11] the larger kinship groups have been weak, and the smaller husband-wife-children unit has dominated. This smaller unit of husband, wife, and children is referred to as the **conjugal family** (the word "conjugal" is from the Latin term for joining together in marriage). If any other relatives—such as a grandparent or uncle—are present in the household, it is said to contain an **extended family.** Many Americans assume that most families in the past were like those in the television series *The Waltons,* with Grandma, Grandpa, Mom, Dad, and the kids sitting around the hearth, swapping stories, and enjoying one another's company. To be sure, there were substantial numbers of extended families in many European nations (Kertzer, 1991). But there were fewer families like that in the United States, England, and Northern France, for two reasons. First, young people in those areas typically waited until they could start a new household before they married. That might mean waiting for the father to retire and turn over his land or moving to the city to work for a merchant. Second, Grandma and Grandpa often didn't live long enough to share a household with their grandchildren, although most elderly people continued to live with one child, often unmarried at first, who remained at home (Ruggles, 1994). That child might marry after being granted the right to farm his or her parents' land. This arrangement, in which one and only one child remains in his or her parents' household even after marriage, is called a **stem family.** Life expectancy was so short, however, that the stem family was unlikely to last long.

In other parts of the world, larger family units have been more common. The traditional Chinese family was patrilineal, and the cultural ideal was for five male

matrilineage a kinship group in which descent is through the mother's line

conjugal family a kinship group comprising husband, wife, and children

extended family a kinship group comprising the conjugal family plus any other relatives present in the household, such as a grandparent or uncle

stem family a kinship group comprising parents plus one child who remains at home

In most American Indian tribes, families were organized into lineages in which descent was traced through either the father's or the mother's line.

American Indian the name used for a subset of all Native Americans, namely, those who were living in the territory that later became the 48 contiguous United States

based on lineages. (The term **American Indian** is often used for a subset of the original, indigenous people who had settled in North America thousands of years before Columbus, namely those who had settled in the territory that later became the 48 contiguous United States [Snipp, 1989]. Indeed, it was because Columbus mistakenly believed that he had reached India that he gave this aboriginal population the misnomer "Indian.") We do know that the American Indian population was devastated by diseases brought by Europeans, such as smallpox—diseases to which the native population had developed no immunities. Moreover, we know that large numbers of American Indians were killed in wars and massacres (Shoemaker, 1991). How these catastrophic events modified family and kinship is unclear. In the absence of direct evidence, scholars have assumed that the numerous accounts of American Indian societies in the 1800s and early 1900s can be generalized back in time. Although the assumption that present arrangements accurately reflect the past ignores the historical changes that occurred to American Indian societies after the arrival of the Europeans, the outlines of American Indian family and kinship seem clear.

Both patrilineal and matrilineal tribes existed. Related lineages were often organized into larger clans that provided the basis for social organization and governing. In matrilineal tribes such as the Hopi, for example, a person traced his or her relatives through his or her mother's line.[5] If you were a child, your father was a guest in your mother's home. Although strong bonds existed between wives and husbands, a woman's ties to her maternal kin—her mother, her mother's brothers, her maternal cousins—were generally stronger. Consequently, your maternal uncles played an important role in your upbringing. They, not your father, had to approve your choice of spouse. Still, if you were a boy, you did

[5]This account of Hopi kinship draws from Queen, Habenstein, and Quadagno (1985).

learn many of the skills of an adult male—growing crops, herding animals—from your father. It was as if you had two kinds of fathers: a biological father who taught you skills and an uncle-father who held greater authority over you. If you were a girl, you spent less time with your father.

When Hopi boys reached puberty, they moved out of the household, sleeping in the men's ceremonial house and eventually marrying into another clan. Girls, on the other hand, remained in or near their mother's homes throughout their lives, bringing husbands from other clans into their dwellings. In all tribal societies, the common requirement that individuals marry someone outside their clan forged alliances across clans. If clan A and clan B frequently exchanged young adults as marriage partners, the two clans would likely consider themselves as allies in any disputes with other clans in the tribe. Thus, the lineage and clan organization of American Indian societies served to strengthen the social order and to protect individuals against unfriendly outsiders.

Kinship was also matrilineal among the Apache of Arizona. Soon after a girl's first menstruation (which probably occurred several years later in her life than is the case today), her lineage held a four-day Sun Rise ceremony, after which she was eligible to marry (Joe, Sparks, & Tiger, 1999). Marriages were typically arranged by elders from the prospective bride's and groom's lineages. (Marrying someone from the same lineage was forbidden.) A series of gifts was exchanged by the bride's and groom's families, which culminated in the groom's family bringing him to the home of the bride. The bride's family then constructed a separate home for the couple. The gifts between families symbolized the importance of establishing an alliance with a family in another lineage. It's not that love between the young couple was necessarily lacking, but their marriage also served the larger purpose of tying together members of two lineages who could provide assistance in times of trouble or need.

EUROPEAN COLONISTS: THE PRIMACY OF THE PUBLIC FAMILY

Among the European colonists, there were no lineages. But the conjugal family of husband, wife, and children provided services that were of great value to the community. Consider education. In Plymouth Colony, children received their basic education from their parents, or if they were working as servants, in another family's home. Parents and masters were required by law to teach reading to their children and young servants, so they could at least "be able to duely read the scriptures" (Demos, 1970). Why weren't these children learning to read in school? Because there was no school—or rather, because the family *was* school. In addition to providing schooling, all Plymouth Colony families were expected to provide vocational training. Through apprenticeship and service, working next to an adult, children and youths learned the skills they needed to farm, trade, garden, cook, and make clothes. All families were also expected to supplement church services by engaging in "family worship," praying and meditating daily.

Selected Plymouth Colony families also functioned as

- *Hospitals* Some adults who supposedly had specialized knowledge took sick persons into their homes for treatment.
- *Houses of correction* Judges ordered some idle or criminal persons to live in the homes of upstanding families to learn how to change their ways.

total fertility rate (TFR)
the average number of children a woman will bear over her lifetime if current birthrates remain the same

Moreover, throughout the new nation, the birthrate began to fall sharply in the early 1800s. Demographers, the social scientists who study the growth, decline, marriage patterns, and movement of populations, often express the level of births through the **total fertility rate (TFR),** defined as the average number of children that women would bear over their lifetime if birthrates were to remain the same. At the birthrates prevalent among women at different ages in 1800, the average white woman would have had seven children. This TFR of seven was higher than the TFR of any western European country at the time (Coale & Zelnik, 1963). Births were higher because marriage tended to occur at earlier ages, and was more universal, than in western Europe. Observers such as Benjamin Franklin linked earlier marriage in the colonies to the greater availability of land in the New World, which allowed young couples to start their own families sooner (Haines, 1996).

By 1850, however, the TFR for white women had fallen to about five children. This fall in births occurred before there was much industrialization in the United States, so the growth of nonfarm work cannot have been a major factor. Rather, historical demographers have argued that decreasing land availability played an important role. In the eastern areas that had been settled the earliest, the amount of available farmland fell as population grew. Demographers think that the land shortage forced young adults to reduce their family size, in large part by delaying marriages until they could obtain land (Yasuba, 1962). In the more sparsely settled areas to the west of the original colonies, where land was more plentiful, birthrates remained high for a longer period.

At the same time, some historians believe that the idea of individualism gained greater currency during the 1700s. Lawrence Stone's influential account of British family history claims that individualism gained ground among the British middle and upper classes in the 1700s. Individualism, Stone wrote, had two meanings where the family was concerned. The first was a greater consideration of one's own self and, in particular, one's own sense of self-satisfaction. This led, in turn, to an increased emphasis on personal gratification in family relationships. The second meaning was of autonomy—individual freedom from constraints imposed by others. Consequently, Stone called this phenomenon the rise of **affective individualism,** meaning an outlook on personal relationships that emphasizes the emotional rewards to, and autonomy of, each individual more than that individual's obligations to care for and support others (Stone, 1977). Since the work of Stone, Ariès (whose theory of childhood was described at the beginning of the chapter) and other historians of what has become known as the "sentiments school" appeared, many historians have disputed the idea of a surge of sentiment in the 1700s (Cooper, 1999). These critics claim that as far back as they can push their investigations of British family life—even to the 1200s—the British were individualistic (Macfarlane, 1978; Pollock, 1983). Even on the European continent, the medieval family probably included affectionate relationships between spouses and between parents and children (Ozment, 1983). These critics suggest convincingly that the medieval family was not heartless or devoid of affection.

affective individualism
an outlook on personal relationships that emphasizes the emotional rewards to, and autonomy of, each individual more than that individual's obligations to care for and support others

Nevertheless, there probably was a movement toward greater individualism and sentiment in American family life in the 1700s and early 1800s. In 1776 Americans had begun a war of independence dedicated, as every schoolchild knows, to the values of "life, liberty, and the pursuit of happiness." That young adults successfully freed themselves from the control of their elders, and relations between husbands and wives and between parents and children became more affectionate, probably was not a coincidence.

Religion played a role in shaping these changes. Prior to the Revolution, the Puritan theology had strongly supported the authority of the father, but a wave of religious revivals that swept through many states in the early 1800s carried other values. If the Puritans saw children as depraved beings whose will needed to be broken, the revivalists viewed them as innocent beings who needed continual guidance and affection. And mothers, not fathers, were thought to be the parents who were better at this kind of childrearing (Ryan, 1981).

This new view of how to care for children elevated the position of women in the family, because they were to be entrusted with the major responsibility for childrearing. Consequently, married women's wishes and needs as individuals rose in importance (Degler, 1980). Women also had an interest in having fewer children, because the large families of the 1700s were difficult to provide for in terms of time and attention. In this way, the religious movements of the early 1800s promoted both the growth of individualism in the family and a fall in the birthrate.

FROM COOPERATION TO SEPARATION: WOMEN'S AND MEN'S SPHERES

Another spur to family change was the transition from the familial mode of production to the labor market mode of production. It began sometime in the 1700s and early 1800s, with the growth of commercial capitalism—an economic system that emphasizes the buying, selling and distribution of goods such as grain, tobacco, or cotton. Commercial capitalism created jobs for merchants, clerks, shippers, dockworkers, wagon builders, and others like them, who were paid money for their labor. The opportunity to earn money outside the home undermined the authority of fathers. Because sons had alternatives to farming, fathers no longer had a near monopoly on the resources needed to make a living. This greater economic independence facilitated the growth of individualism. The transition accelerated in the mid-1800s with the spread of industrial capitalism, which created factory work for the great masses of immigrants and their descendants.

The heart of this change was the movement of men's work out of the home. Instead of working together in a common household enterprise, husbands and wives now worked on separate enterprises—he exchanging his labor for wages, she maintaining the home and raising the children. Instead of working in close proximity, the two were physically separated during the workday. Moreover, wage work held no intrinsic value for most men, and in nineteenth-century factories it was frequently exhausting and dangerous.

The sharp split between a rewarding home life and an often alienating work life led to the emergence of the idea of "separate spheres": men's sphere being the world of work, and more generally, the world outside the home; and women's sphere being the home, relatives, and children. Whereas men's sphere was seen as being governed by the rough ethic of the business world, women's sphere came to be seen as morally pure, a place where wives could renew their husbands' spirituality and character. And whereas men's sphere was seen as providing no reward other than a paycheck, women's sphere was the center of affection and nurturing, the emotional core for husbands and children.

Thus developed a nineteenth-century ideology, a set of beliefs, which historian Barbara Welter named "the cult of True Womanhood" (Welter, 1966). The True Woman was, first of all, a pious upholder of spiritual values. She was also pure: She was to have no sexual contact before marriage—although men might try to tempt her—and none afterward except with her husband. Moreover, the True Woman was submissive to men, particularly her husband. And finally, she was domestic: Her proper place was in the home, comforting her husband, lovingly raising her children.

Woman's sphere at once limited women's opportunities and glorified their domestic role. It was a more restricted role than wives in the colonial era had experienced. To be sure, the Puritan wife was also home most of the day, but she was collaborating with her husband in the family economy; without her contribution, her husband might not have been able to feed and clothe their children. Then the movement to wage labor separated women from paid work. Men went out every morning into the wider social world, but their wives could not follow. In a culture that had begun to celebrate individualism, women were supposed to give up much of their individualism to care for their husbands and children. Seen from this vantage point, one might argue that women's lives were worse than they had been before the Revolution—more restricted, less productive, more dependent and more isolated. Indeed, many historians have argued as much.

But other historians, while acknowledging the restrictions and dependency inherent in the domestic sphere, argue that it nevertheless offered some benefits. Appointing women the guardians of moral values and giving them the major role in rearing children provided them with substantial influence. However circumscribed, it may have allowed wives to counter the authority of their husbands which had been so pervasive in the colonial period. Moreover, the ideology of women's sphere may have created a self-consciousness of, and an identification with, women as a group. Women established and maintained deep friendships with other women, reinforced by the segregation of their lives and by female rituals surrounding childbirth, weddings, illnesses, and funerals (Smith-Rosenberg, 1975). Some joined together in public associations to promote values consistent with domesticity, such as greater devotion to religion, assistance for the poor, or enlightened childrearing. These friendships and associations may have been a prerequisite for the development of feminist organizations in the nineteenth and twentieth centuries. Historian Nancy Cott captured the dual nature of women's sphere in the title of her book, *The Bonds of Womanhood* (Cott, 1977), for the bonds that tied women to the domestic sphere also bound them together in a subculture of sisterhood that prefigured their social and political movements decades later.

WORKING-CLASS FAMILIES

This was the picture for the white middle class. But life was different for the working class, especially for the tens of millions of immigrants who poured into American cities. Between 1850 and World War I, the scale of immigration was simply massive. Even in 1850, 10 percent of the population had been born in another country (U.S. Bureau of the Census, 1975). Then began a sustained increase in immigration. By 1900, 15 percent of the population was foreign born. The percentage then fell to 5 percent in 1960 before rising again to 10 percent in 1997 (U.S. Bureau of the Census, 1999).

The migrants to the country's growing cities from overseas or from rural America worked long hours for low wages and lived in crowded, often unsanitary conditions. In Homestead, Pennsylvania, in the 1890s, workers labored at one of Andrew Carnegie's steel mills from 7:00 A.M. to 5:30 P.M., six days a week, for less than $15 a week. Some worked longer night shifts or all seven days. According to one report, half of the African-American and Slavic workers in the town lived in one- or two-room shanties without indoor plumbing or toilets (Mintz & Kellogg, 1988).

Living between Modes
Working-class families may or may not have aspired to the breadwinner-homemaker model, but in either case, it was a style of life they could not afford. Instead, they needed to pool the economic contributions of more than one family member in order to subsist. Before stricter child labor laws were passed, children as young as 10 or 11 often worked alongside their fathers and older siblings at a factory. Unmarried sons and daughters contributed their wages to the family fund. To be sure, few wives worked for wages outside the home—just 2.5 percent of white married women (of all classes combined) did so in 1890 (Goldin, 1977). For a wife to work outside the home was such a sign of economic failure that white families avoided it unless there was no alternative except extreme hardship (Robinson, 1993). Instead, working-class wives made important economic contributions at home. Some earned money by doing laundry; others did piecework—literally, work for which they were paid by the piece—such as stitching shoes. Often they took into their households a kind of resident that has now almost disappeared—the boarder or lodger.

A boarder is someone who pays to live in a room and to eat meals in someone's household; a lodger is someone who pays for a room but does not eat in the household. Let me use the term "boarder" for both. In the nineteenth and early twentieth centuries, boarding was the most common living arrangement for unmarried adults who were not living with their parents. Very few people lived alone; as recently as 1900, only 5 percent of all households contained one person (Kobrin, 1976). Rather than live alone, unmarried people boarded for several reasons. First, few could afford to live alone, because wages were too low. Second, the surge of immigrants had created a housing shortage, which drove rents up further. Third, preparing meals required much more time and effort than is the case today. Since there were no refrigerators or freezers, people had to shop for food almost daily. There were no microwave meals, no TV dinners, no inexpensive fast-food restaurants. Fourth, having grown up in households larger than ours today, people may have preferred to live in the company of others. By one estimate, 15 to 20 percent of all urban households contained boarders at any given time (Modell & Hareven, 1973); the proportion of households that ever took in boarders was certainly much higher than that. In a sense, boarders were a replacement for grown children in the household's economy. When an older child who had contributed part of his or her earnings left home, a bed was freed and a hole was left in the family's budget. Families typically took in a boarder in response.

Working-class families did not correspond neatly to either the familial or the labor market mode of production. Like families operating in the familial mode, they pooled the efforts of several members in a common family enterprise: The husband and his teenage son might work for wages, the wife might take in boarders and do piecework and an unmarried older sister might contribute her wages so her brother could go to college. But unlike families in the familial mode, most members exchanged their labor for wages. More accurately, from the mid-1800s to the early 1900s, working-class families were living between modes—a phrase that has been used to describe most of the families that exist today in poor, less-developed countries (Caldwell, 1982). These families were still organized the old way, as if they were producing for their own use, even though some members worked for wages some of the time. Parents and children still contributed the fruits of their labor, be it cash or crops, to a common family fund. Individuals subordinated their own desires to the good of the family. And what was good for the family was decided by the parents, particularly the father.

Although living between modes was an admirable way for families to manage on limited resources, it was an unstable system. Once older children decided that they needn't turn over most of their earnings to their parents, the authority of the father eroded. Once the husband's wages increased enough that his wife could cut back on piecework and boarding, the family became heavily dependent on his wages. In such families, parents got smaller economic returns from children and were forced to expend more time and energy educating and rearing them. Families such as these were likely to decide that having fewer children and investing more in each was preferable to having many children. The result was a smaller, more isolated conjugal family—the kind we are familiar with today.

The Kinship Connection   Kinship ties to relatives outside the household were also beneficial to working-class families. Conventional wisdom used to hold that industrialization caused the breakdown of the large, extended family, but that generalization has been discredited. First, historical studies of western Europe showed that in some countries, extended families had never been as common as had been assumed, for reasons discussed earlier: higher death rates among adults and the expectation that young couples would start new households. Second, studies of early industrialization in England and the United States showed that in the early years of industrialization, the proportion of extended families actually increased and then declined in the twentieth century (Ruggles, 1987).

One explanation for the temporary rise in extended families is that ties with kin were an important means of finding a factory job or a place to live in a newly industrializing city. Historian Tamara Hareven studied French Canadians who immigrated to Manchester, New Hampshire, in the first two decades of the twentieth century to work in what was then the world's largest textile mill. The developments she described were similar to those in other industrializing cities in the late nineteenth century. Hareven found that workers were recruited through networks of kin. For example, the eldest son in one Canadian family with seven children migrated to Manchester in 1908, after his mother's death, and became a weaver in the mill:

> *He then brought his father and all his younger brothers and sisters. The father entered the same weaving room in which the son was working; subsequently, each child entered the mills upon reaching age 14 except for the youngest son, who became a barber and worked in the shop that his father set up after he left the mill* (Hareven, 1982).

Plants often hired relatives recommended by their workers. Hareven estimates that 76 percent of the French-Canadian workers had relatives working in the mill at some point, often in the same room. In Manchester and elsewhere, when factory work proved unstable, workers used family networks as sources of information and temporary shelter as they moved from job to job. In sum, family ties remained vitally important to working-class Americans during industrialization, and supposedly old-fashioned forms of kinship gained new purpose.

African-American, Mexican-American, and Asian Immigrant Families

Europeans, of course, were not the only immigrants to the United States. Three other groups were present early in the nation's history. Africans had been forced to immigrate—captured or bought in West Africa, transported across the ocean under horrible conditions that killed many, and sold as slaves upon arrival. Mexicans, in search of grazing land, had pushed north into the area that is now the Southwest. Asian immigrants first arrived in large numbers in the mid-nineteenth century, when they were used as laborers by the railroads and other enterprises. The family lives of all three groups differed from those of the Europeans.

AFRICAN-AMERICAN FAMILIES

An African Heritage?   As later chapters will document, African-American families have long been distinct from white families: Historically, they have maintained stronger ties to extended kin such as uncles, aunts, and cousins and have borne a higher percentage of children outside marriage. The extent to which these differences reflect the lasting influence of African culture has been hotly debated (Herskovits, 1990). But the similarities between the old and the new cultures are striking enough to consider whether some continuities may exist.

Traditionally, African society was organized by lineages, which I have defined as large kinship groups that trace their descent through the male or female line. Members of the lineage cooperated and shared resources with others, and adults carefully controlled and monitored courtship and marriage among the young. What mattered most was not the happiness of the married couple, but the birth of children who could be retained by the lineage. In the Western nations, we are used to thinking of marriage as an event that occurs at a particular time: On the appointed date, two people participate in a ceremony and register their intentions with the state government. But in Africa, marriage was much more of a process, a series of steps that occurred over a long period of time (Bledsoe, 1990). Childbearing could occur before the ceremony, but the clear expectation was that marriage would follow within a few years. (See *Families in Other Cultures:* The Process of Marriage in Sub-Saharan Africa.)

When Africans brought these cultural patterns to the United States, the institution of slavery stripped their elders of authority over the marriage process. Their lineages, as anthropologist Niara Sudarkasa (1980, 1981) has written, were reduced to extended families. In Africa, elders had had substantial authority over individuals because they controlled crucial resources, most notably land. An African who was disowned by a lineage faced a terrible future. But in the United States, the wider kinship group no longer controlled the allocation of land, livestock or jobs. Thus, among many African Americans, the extended kinship groups were limited to serving as social support networks. Extended families were important to individuals who belonged to them, but they had less control over their members' actions.

The Impact of Slavery   Until the appearance of new scholarship in the 1970s, in fact, most historians thought that the oppression and harsh conditions of slavery had destroyed most of the culture African slaves brought with them, leaving little in its place. The writings of both white and black scholars emphasized the losses imposed by slavery: the uprooting from Africa, the disruption of families through sales of family members to new owners, the inability of fathers to protect their families from the abuses imposed by masters. In an influential 1939 book, E. Franklin Frazier, a sociologist and an African American, argued that white masters had destroyed all social organization among the slaves. As a result, he wrote, slave family life was disorganized; the only stable bond was between mothers and their children:

> *Consequently, under all conditions of slavery, the Negro mother remained the most dependable and important figure in the family* (Frazier, 1939).

From Frazier and others, then, came the idea that both during and after slavery, most African-American families were headed by women, and that African-American men were relatively powerless in and outside the home. But in 1976, historian Herbert Gutman published a comprehensive study of plantation, local government, and Census records that suggested a much different picture (Gutman, 1976). Gutman found substantial evidence that whenever possible, slaves had married and lived together for life, and that they knew and kept track of uncles, aunts, cousins, and other kin. He cited letters such as one the field hand Cash sent to relatives on a Georgia plantation after he, his wife, Phoebe, and some of their children were sold away:

> *Clairissa your affectionate Mother and Father sends a heap of love to you and your Husband and my Grand Children. Mag. & Cloe. John. Judy. My aunt sinena . . . Give our Love to Cashes brother Porter and his Wife Patience. Victoria sends her Love to her Cousin Beck and Miley* (Gutman, 1976).

Moreover, Gutman argued, before and after slavery, in both the North and the South, most African-American families included two parents. These family ties were forged despite the frequent sale of husbands, wives, and children to other masters, despite the sexual abuse of slave women by owners, and despite high rates of disease and death.

Still, there were some differences, both before and after the Civil War, between black and white families. For example, young slave women often had a first child before marrying; if so, they were usually married within a few years, although not necessarily to the father (Jones, 1985). This pattern may have occurred in part because slave owners valued women who had many children, increasing the owner's wealth. Yet as we have seen, it is also consistent with custom in Africa. Another difference between black and white families was that after the Civil War, wives in rural black families worked seasonally in the fields, whereas white rural women didn't. According to 1870 Census figures for the Cotton Belt states, about 4 in 10 African-American wives had jobs, almost all as field workers. In contrast, 98 percent of white wives said they were "keeping house" and had no other job (Jones, 1985). Here again, the differences reflect a mixture

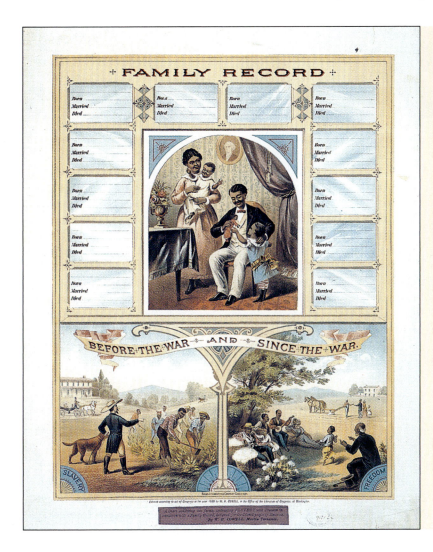

A family history chart from about 1880, "designed for the colored people of America" according to the artist, W. H. Cowell, shows scenes from before and after the Civil War.

of economic pressure and culture. The plots of land African-American sharecroppers farmed in the late nineteenth century provided such a marginal standard of living, men and women (and often children) were needed in the fields, at least at harvesttime. Historian Jacqueline Jones has also noted that "the outlines of African work patterns endured among the slaves" (Jones, 1985), in that African women often bore the major responsibility for cultivating food.

Moreover, although most black families still had two parents, black mothers were more likely to be living without a male partner than white mothers. This racial difference stemmed partly from the high mortality rates of black men; by one estimate, 42 percent of black wives were widowed by ages 45 to 50 around 1900 (Preston, Lim, & Morgan, 1992). But a difference still remains after mortality is taken into account (Morgan, McDaniel, Miller, & Preston, 1993). A much larger racial difference in household structure would emerge after about 1960 (see Chapter 5).

When black families migrated to Northern cities in the twentieth century, black women continued to work outside the home in larger numbers than white women. About one-third of married nonwhite women worked outside the home

The Process of Marriage in Sub-Saharan Africa

Historically, in the United States and other Western countries (and indeed, in many less-developed countries), a marriage started on the day when a civil or religious wedding ceremony took place. Before that day, the couple was not married; after that day, they were. Yet in much of sub-Saharan Africa, getting married has traditionally been a process that could take months or even years. Moreover, the process has been so ambiguous that outsiders had difficulty telling whether a couple was married or not. The prospective husband and wife could even redefine their marital status if their situations changed before the process was completed.

Among the Kpelle of Liberia, the process began with an initiation ritual for young women and men at roughly the time of puberty. This eventually was followed by betrothal to a future spouse; living together; a ceremony in which the woman was "turned over" symbolically to the man; a payment from the man's family to the woman's family; and the bearing of a child or two (Bledsoe, 1980). The process could occur rapidly or slowly, and the steps could occur in a different order. For example, a prepubescent girl could be betrothed to a man before her initiation ceremony, or the man's family might not make a payment to the woman's family until after the woman had borne a child.

The central reason for these customs was the very high value most African societies placed on bearing children. In many societies, land was held in common by tribal elders or the chiefs. They allocated land to adult men according, in part, to how many children they had (which depended, in part, on how many wives they had where polygyny was practiced). Thus, it was very important to a husband that his wife be capable of bearing children. Under these circumstances, some young men (and their parents) wished to wait until their partners gave birth to children before deciding that the marriage was final. Consequently, the final marriage ceremonies might not occur until the couple had cohabited and had a child. Alternatively, a man might begin to have sexual relations with his partner but not cohabit with her until she had borne a child (Little, 1973).

Moreover, families used their children's marriages to establish beneficial alliances or to obtain goods and services. For instance, a family might betroth their daughter before puberty to a powerful

---

in the 1920s and 1930s, compared with less than one-tenth of married white women (Goldin, 1977). Because of discrimination, black men were offered only low-paying, physically challenging jobs that couldn't support a family, such as stoking a blast furnace in a steel factory. Staying home simply was not an option for most black wives, who also faced discrimination and found work mainly as domestic servants. Not until the 1960s did black women break out of domestic service into occupations previously reserved for white women. Today, women of both races still lag behind men in earnings, and black men's employment situation, though improved, remains difficult.

MEXICAN-AMERICAN FAMILIES

Like African Americans, Mexican Americans established a presence early in the history of what is now the United States—although unlike African Americans, the descendants of these early residents are now vastly outnumbered by recent immigrants. In the early nineteenth century, well before migrants from the eastern United States arrived, Mexicans settled the frontier of what was then northern Mexico (Moore & Cuèllar, 1970). These pioneers crossed deserts and fought with American Indians to reach as far west as California and as far north as Colorado. Their early settlements generally included an elite landowning family and poorer farmer-laborer settlers. The landowning elite tended to be (or claimed to be) of nearly pure Spanish descent. Some owned vast tracts of land on which they

man who could provide access to land or other resources. Among the Kpelle, even when young people chose their own spouses, it was necessary that their parents agree to the match. Commonly, the groom's family might make a gift of money or cattle to the bride's family, a custom known as **bridewealth;** or the groom might agree to work for a time for the bride's family, a variant known as **brideservice.** Until the gifts were transferred, or until the agreed-upon labor was completed, the bride's family might not consider the marriage to be final. A dispute over the status of the marriage could occur should the terms of the agreement not be fulfilled to both sides' satisfaction.

Over the past few decades, these customs have been changing. Anthropologists report that young adults are choosing their own marriage partners for love and companionship now more than in the past, especially among the better educated (Harrell-Bond, 1975). Moreover, as women become better educated, they are less likely to wed men who already have wives. In Nigeria in 1990, 38 percent of young wives with no formal education were living in polygynous unions, compared with 16 percent of young wives with a secondary education or higher (Bledsoe & Cohen, 1993). Furthermore, as young adults have gained access to wage work, they have become more independent of their parents and in-laws. A young man with money has alternatives to relying on his parents for bridewealth or to performing brideservice. Anthropologist Caroline Bledsoe reports that one Kpelle man told her that young men who give their in-laws a lot of money don't have to work for them and can keep them at bay (Bledsoe, 1980). Still, compared with Western nations, marriage in sub-Saharan Africa is less of an event and more of a process.

Ask Yourself

1. Do you know anyone whose marriage has been more of a process than an event? Explain the circumstances.
2. In the United States, what current social trends suggest that marriage may be less of an event than it used to be? Are the cultural values that underline those trends similar to or different from the traditional cultural values of the Kpelle?

www.mhhe.com/cherlin

grazed cattle or sheep. They arranged their children's marriages with care and celebrated elaborate weddings and feasts, so as to preserve or merge their holdings with other wealthy families or with wealthy Anglo (non-Mexican) immigrants (Griswold del Castillo, 1979).

More numerous were the laborers who worked the great estates or farmed or grazed animals on their own smaller holdings. They tended to be *mestizos,* people whose ancestors included both Spanish settlers and Native Americans from Mexico. There is some evidence that informal marriages—those in which the couple never underwent a formal ceremony—were more common among this group (Griswold del Castillo, 1979). Informal marriages allowed couples to evade the control of their parents and other kin; and with fewer resources to protect than among the elite, the *mestizo* classes had less reason to control who married whom. These small landholders and laborers attempted to enlist the sponsorship and support of the well-to-do through the tradition of *compadrazgo,* a godparent relationship in which a wealthy or influential person outside the kinship group became the *compadre,* or godparent, of a newborn child, particularly at its baptism. The godfather and godchild were expected to retain a special relationship, and the godparent was supposed to assist his godchild, for example, by providing or finding a job (Camarillo, 1979).

This social structure was disrupted by a series of wars, revolts, and land grabs by U.S. troops and immigrants during the 1830s and 1840s. When it was over, the

bridewealth a custom in which a prospective bridegroom's family makes a gift of money or livestock to the bride's family

brideservice a custom in which a prospective bridegroom agrees to work for a time for the bride's family

mestizo a person whose ancestors include both Spanish settlers and Native Americans

compadrazgo in Mexico, a godparent relationship in which a wealthy or influential person outside the kinship group is asked to become the *compadre,* or godparent, of a newborn child, particularly at its baptism

United States had acquired, by conquest, the current Southwest. Soon thereafter, most of the Spanish elite lost their land to taxes, drought, and Anglo squatters. Instead of ranchers and farmers, Mexicans became more of a working-class community, employed by the growing numbers of Anglos (Camarillo, 1979). Census statistics for the Los Angeles district in the last half of the nineteenth century show a rising number of households headed by women (Griswold del Castillo, 1979). Some of these women were probably married to men who migrated from harvest to harvest, picking crops; others were informally married. But many were probably unmarried, their numbers reflecting the economic changes of the time. Mexican-American women, like African-American women, could find low-paying but steady work as domestics and launderers for wealthier Anglos, whereas Mexican-American men were losing their established positions as small ranchers and farmers.

> **barrio** a segregated Mexican-American neighborhood in a U.S. city

As the number of Anglo immigrants rose, Mexican Americans were forced into *barrios,* segregated neighborhoods in the city. Residents of the *barrios* faced high unemployment or low income if they provided low-wage labor to Anglo employers. During economic expansions, waves of new Mexican immigrants were drawn into the country, further depressing their wages (Camarillo, 1979). Mexican immigrant families often were highly male dominant: Husbands were supposed to be powerful, respected, and in charge; wives were supposed to submit to their authority (Queen et al., 1985). But the traditional male dominance eroded under the low wages of urban employment and the separation of migrant workers from their families. Today, Mexican-American families in the barrios still show the effects of poverty and unemployment. Yet they remain distinctive in other respects, such as their high birthrates (see Chapter 5).

ASIAN IMMIGRANT FAMILIES

The Asian Heritage   Before the middle of the twentieth century, most Asian-American families in the United States consisted of immigrants from China and Japan and their descendants. Family systems in East Asia (where China and Japan are located) were sharply different from those in the United States and other Western countries, although these differences are currently diminishing (Goode, 1963; Hong, 1999; Queen, Habenstein, & Quadagno, 1985). In the traditional East Asian family, fathers had more authority over family members than is true in the West. For example, fathers usually controlled who their children would marry and when. In addition, kinship was patrilineal, or traced through the father's line. In China, the ideal was that a man's sons (and eventually his grandsons) would bring their wives into his growing household. Daughters would be sent at marriage to live in their in-laws' households. When parents grew old, sons and their wives were expected to live with them and care for them. In Japan, the oldest son carried the main responsibility for the care of elderly parents. Thus, East Asian cultures placed a greater emphasis on children's loyalty to their parents than Western culture. For a son or daughter, happiness in marriage was less important than fulfilling obligations to parents and other kin.

> **remittances** cash payments sent by immigrants to family members in their country of origin

Asian Immigrants   Chinese immigrants first began to arrive during the California gold rush in the 1850s. After the Civil War, they were hired to build the railroads of the Southwest. Because the vast majority of these immigrant laborers were men, relatively few new families were formed. Many of the men fulfilled the obligations they felt toward kin by sending **remittances,** or cash pay-

Many Japanese–American families were sent to internment camps during World War II because of fears that they would be disloyal.

ments, to family members such as spouses or elderly parents in their country of origin. In California and most other western states, laws prohibited Chinese (and later Japanese) immigrants from marrying white Americans or becoming citizens. In fact, American sentiment against Chinese immigrants was so strong that in 1882 Congress passed the Chinese Exclusion Act, which virtually ended Chinese immigration until after World War II (Olson, 1979).

In the 1880s, significant numbers of Japanese immigrants began to arrive in Hawaii (which the United States would soon annex) and the mainland United States. The ratio of women to men was more balanced among the Japanese than among Chinese immigrants, so more families were formed. Both Chinese and Japanese families were patrilineal. The father's authority was strong, and ties to extended family members were important. Traditionally, parents or other relatives arranged their children's marriages (Wong, 1988). Since immigrants usually left their extended families behind, they developed other ways of building family-like ties in the United States. For example, people from the same region of China or Japan formed mutual aid societies, and wealthy merchants sometimes played the supervisory roles village elders had in Asia (Olson, 1979).

Like the Chinese, Japanese immigrants faced discrimination. After the war with Japan began in 1941, some Americans warned that Japanese immigrants might be disloyal, even though many had lived in the United States for decades. Bowing to these fears, the government rounded up Japanese immigrants, most of whom lived in California, and sent them to internment camps. Aside from the imprisonment, humiliation, and economic losses the Japanese suffered there, the camps eroded the traditional authority of Japanese parents (Kitano, 1988). They had little to offer children who were exposed to American activities such as dancing to the music of the latest bands. Young Japanese-American men could even volunteer to join a much-decorated U.S. Army unit that fought in Europe. After the war, the autonomy children had experienced in the camps contributed to sharp changes in Japanese-American marriage patterns. Whereas the older generation's marriages had been arranged by relatives who stressed obligations to kin and emotional restraint, the younger generation much more often chose their own spouses based on romantic love and companionship (Yanagisako, 1985).

1965 Immigration Act act passed by the U.S. Congress which ended restrictions that had blocked most Asian immigration and substituted an annual quota

Overall, Asian immigration was modest until Congress passed the **1965 Immigration Act,** which ended restrictions that had blocked most Asian immigration and substituted an annual quota of 170,000. Since then, the Asian population of the United States has expanded rapidly. The 1990 Census counted 6.9 million Americans of Asian origin—double the number in 1980. The two largest groups were Chinese (24 percent) and Filipinos (20 percent). Four other groups each constituted between 9 and 12 percent of the Asian population: Japanese, Asian Indian, Korean, and Vietnamese (U.S. Bureau of the Census, 1993g).

Filipino immigration began as a small stream of mostly students after the United States captured the Philippines in the Spanish-American War of 1898. After 1965, many Filipino immigrants were professionals, most notably nurses. Unlike Chinese and Japanese families, Filipino families trace descent through both the father's and mother's line, a system called **bilateral kinship** (the system followed in the United States). Such a system usually provides women more independence than patrilineal kinship, so Filipino-American women have been more likely to work outside the home than women in Chinese or Japanese families (Kitano & Daniels, 1988).

bilateral kinship a system in which descent is reckoned through both the mother's and father's lines

The Rise of the Private Family: 1900–Present

THE EARLY DECADES

An increase in premarital sex. A drop in the birthrate. A new youth culture rebelling against propriety, dressing outrageously, and indulging in indecent dance steps. And a rapidly rising divorce rate. Sound familiar? No, this is not a description of the present, or even of the 1960s and 1970s. Rather, these were the concerns of American moralists, politicians, and social scientists during the first few decades of the twentieth century. Premarital sex had become more common, although much of the increase occurred among couples who were already engaged (see Chapter 7). As for the flourishing new youth culture, it was exemplified in the 1920s by the "flapper" girls. Independent, often employed outside the home, and brazen enough to bob their hair and wear lipstick and eyeliner in public, the flappers patronized dance halls and movie theaters with their male companions. Perhaps the greatest source of concern, the divorce rate had risen to the point where a marriage begun in 1910 had about a 1-in-7 chance of ending in divorce. This may seem like a small risk today, but it represented a substantial increase over the 1-in-12 chance in 1880 or the 1-in-20 chance at the end of the Civil War (Cherlin, 1992b).

Yet the period from the 1890s through the 1920s was generally one of increasing prosperity—which raises the question of why an increase in divorce would occur. In part, it was made possible by the growing economic independence of women, who were now better educated, had fewer children, had likely worked outside the home before marrying, and therefore had greater potential to find work outside the home if their marriages ended (O'Neill, 1967). But that is not the whole story, for as historian Elaine Tyler May notes, the marriage rate kept rising right along with the divorce rate. What occurred in addition, she asserts, is that both women and men came to expect a greater amount of emotional satisfaction from marriage (May, 1988). More than ever before, they sought happiness, companionship, and romantic love in marriage. If they found their marriages fell short of their expectations, they became dissatisfied and asked for a divorce. (See *Families and Public Policy:* Divorce Reform: Have We Been Here Before? on page 64.)

And so women and men came to see marriage and family as central to their quest for an emotionally satisfying private life. Before the twentieth century, emotional satisfaction had been less important to both husbands and wives, but not because they were ignorant of the concept—no Ariès-like claim is made here that people of the twentieth century discovered happiness. Rather, before the twentieth century the standard of living had been so low that most people needed to concentrate on keeping themselves clothed, housed, and fed. Before 1900, pursuing personal pleasure was a luxury few could indulge in. Most were too busy just trying to get by.

Even after 1900, large segments of the American population—immigrants and racial and ethnic minorities—had little time to invest in private life. My grandparents immigrated from Eastern Europe just after the turn of the century, started a grocery store, and raised 10 children. Had I been around to ask them whether their marriage was satisfying, they would have said of course—they were raising a big family. They would not have answered in terms of companionship, romance, sexual pleasure, excitement, or personal growth. Yet these were the ways in which more and more Americans came to define a successful marriage in the twentieth century.

Still, Americans (and the citizens of other Western nations) were gradually enlarging the scope of the *private family*. They were defining marital success in emotional terms, not material terms; and beginning to derive their greatest satisfaction not from the roles they played (breadwinner, homemaker, father, mother) but from the quality of the relationships they had with their spouses and children. This process had certainly begun long ago among the more prosperous classes, and it continued throughout the twentieth century. But in some eras its ascendancy was more noticeable than in others, and the first few decades of the twentieth century was such an era.

As these developments were occurring the family was becoming less of a dominant force in people's lives. The many public goods the colonial family had provided gradually diminished: Compulsory schooling replaced education at home; hospitals replaced sickbeds; department stores replaced home crafts; and so forth. As marriage became less necessary economically and materially, it was redefined as a means of gaining emotional satisfaction. A well-known text on the family described this transformation as a shift "from institution to companionship" (Burgess & Locke, 1945). (See Chapter 8.) In this process, marriage became more fragile, for the bonds of sentiment were weaker than the ties forged by working a family farm or the unchallenged authority of the patriarch. Soon, an institution that had been designed to enhance survival and security began to creak under the weight of expectations that it provide so much emotional satisfaction. One result was a more or less continuous increase in the divorce rate, which reached a high plateau about 1980.

Privacy also increased after 1900. Two demographic trends contributed to this increase. First, the birthrate declined, which meant, among other things, fewer persons per room. Second, adult life expectancy increased due to advances in medicine and a rising standard of living. As a result of these trends, parents were younger when they finished the childrearing stage of life, and they lived longer after their last child left home. Consequently, a new stage of family life, the "empty nest" phase, became common. Before the twentieth century, far fewer married couples ever witnessed the departure of all their children (Cherlin & Furstenberg, 1992).

Greater prosperity also meant that more apartments were built, and more people could afford to live on their own. And the rise in individualism probably made more unmarried people *wish* to live on their own. Consequently, boarding and lodging went from commonplace to rarity during the first half of the century

Divorce Reform: Have We Been Here Before?

At current rates, about one out of two marriages begun in the United States today will end in divorce. As noted, the divorce rate has been increasing since at least the Civil War. The most recent burst occurred between the early 1960s and mid-1970s, during which time the probability that a marriage would end in divorce doubled. Since then, the rate has declined slightly (Cherlin, 1992b). Nevertheless, the rise in divorce has alarmed some commentators, who fear that it is undermining the institution of the family. (The effects of divorce will be discussed in detail in Chapter 13.)

Some writers have called for a toughening of divorce laws, which were relaxed in the 1970s and 1980s, when all states enacted "no fault" divorce legislation. One suggestion, for instance, is to require a longer waiting period before a person can obtain a divorce if children are involved (Galston, 1990/1991). Currently, in most American states, a person who wishes to obtain a divorce against the wishes of his or her spouse must wait a year or less after separating (Glendon, 1987). In 1997, Louisiana passed a law allowing couples who were marrying to choose "covenant marriage." In the event of a serious dispute

they would be required to undergo counseling and to remain married for at least two years if one spouse opposed a divorce (Jeter, 1997).

Yet this is not the first time a debate has emerged about the consequences of divorce, and restrictive legislation has been proposed. In fact, the divorce debates of the Progressive Era (1890–1930) bear an uncanny resemblance to the current discourse. As in the 1960s and 1970s, a rise in the divorce rate during that era caused concern. So did a fall in the birthrate among native-born whites. John Watson, a leading psychologist, voiced the fears of many when he predicted that "in fifty years there will be no such thing as marriage" (Mintz & Kellogg, 1988). Arthur Calhoun, the leading historian of the family, acknowledged the sweeping changes, but wrote approvingly that "we are in the midst of a social revolution" which would make a new, more democratic family "inevitable" (Calhoun, 1919).

Prior to the mid-1800s, a person could obtain a divorce in most states only by an act of the legislature. This requirement put divorce beyond the reach of all but the politically connected and the well-to-do. In

midcentury, however, many legislatures delegated the authority to grant divorces to the state courts. Persons of more-modest means could then obtain divorces from judges, who were more liberal than the legislatures had been in granting them. But in the 1890s and 1900s, rising divorce rates led many legislatures, especially in the eastern states, to tighten divorce laws. According to historian Elaine Tyler May, between 1889 and 1906 state legislatures enacted more than 100 restrictive marriage and divorce laws. For instance, 15 states forbade remarriage until one or two years after a final divorce decree, and 6 eliminated certain grounds for divorce. New York permitted divorce only in the event of adultery, and South Carolina prohibited it altogether (May, 1980).

The Progressive Era was also a time of great and varied action by groups seeking reform in order to increase democracy, governmental efficiency, and the quality of life. So-called "social progressives" sought improvements in industrial working conditions and in the lives of parents and children (Skocpol, 1992). Many social progressives, including those interested in the family, sought reform

(Laslett, 1973). In 1950, 9 percent of all households contained one person; by 1970 the figure was 17 percent; and by 1998 it was 26 percent (Kobrin, 1976; U.S. Bureau of the Census, 1999d). Even so, during the first few decades of the century, about two-thirds of young women and perhaps 40 percent of young men did not leave home until they married. If they did, it was often because their parents lived in rural areas, where young adults couldn't find jobs. Later, in the 1940s and 1950s, the age at which young adults left home fell sharply, both because of earlier marriage and because many young men left home to join the military during World War II and the Korean War (Goldscheider & Goldscheider, 1994).

The first few decades of the twentieth century, then, were an important time of change in the American family. The basis for marriage moved away from an economic partnership and toward emotional satisfaction and companionship. Men and women became more economically independent of each other. As a result of

through the passage of new laws. For example, an Inter-Church Conference led by Episcopal Bishop William Doane convinced President Theodore Roosevelt to order the Bureau of the Census to carry out a new study on marriage and divorce. In Roosevelt's message to Congress in 1905, he wrote:

> There is widespread conviction that the divorce laws are dangerously lax and indifferently administered in some of the states, resulting in a diminished regard for the sanctity of the marriage relation.[1]

To eliminate overly liberal state laws, Roosevelt called for uniform divorce legislation in all states.

Yet despite all this activity, despite numerous conferences on uniform divorce laws and attempts in Congress to tighten state provisions, little was accomplished, and the divorce rate continued to rise. Why did reformers have so little success? Historians who have studied the era argue that the reformers were fighting against powerful cultural changes in the nature of marriage. Marriage was becoming more of a companionship, more of a relation-

ship among equals. Increasingly, people sought personal satisfaction through marriage.[2] I would add that the rising standard of living in the early decades of the twentieth century allowed people to focus less on food and shelter and more on emotional satisfaction. Because of this new emphasis, people who found their marriages lacking in satisfaction were more likely to consider divorce (see Chapter 8). Moreover, the increasing employment of women decreased their economic dependence on men, making marriage less necessary.

Given the strength of these cultural and economic forces, the social progressives were unable to enact their program of divorce reform. Advances in one state would be stymied by setbacks in others. Resistance to more restrictive divorce legislation remained firm. The failures of the reformers may hold lessons for those who today urge public action to reduce the divorce rate. The same cultural and economic forces have continued to influence marriage and divorce throughout the twentieth century. Indeed, one could argue that they are more powerful now: The quest for personal fulfillment has led to widespread co-

habitation outside of marriage; the loosening of cultural constraints has led to a toleration of childbearing outside of marriage; and the economic independence of women has grown as a majority of wives now work outside the home. A look backward at the entire century, and particularly at the Progressive Era, suggests that today's divorce reformers have few promising strategies to follow. Lowering the divorce rate through political action and moral suasion is a very difficult task.

Ask Yourself

1. Think back over the last two or three generations in your family. Has the divorce rate increased from one generation to the next? What about marital happiness and personal fulfillment—does it seem to have increased?

2. What do you think of the idea of covenant marriage? From the family's point of view, what might be its advantages and disadvantages?

[1]Quoted in O'Neill (1967).
[2]Mintz and Kellogg, May, and O'Neill all present arguments along these lines.

www.mhhe.com/cherlin

these developments, the bonds of marriage became weaker, and divorce became more common. In addition, prosperity, lower birthrates, and longer life expectancy accelerated the trend toward privacy, as exemplified by child-free older couples and people living alone.

THE DEPRESSION GENERATION

The prosperity of the early decades of the century was interrupted by the Great Depression, which began in 1929 and continued until the late 1930s. In addition to its severe effects on family finances, the Depression also undermined the authority and prestige of the father. If he lost his job, his family might view him as having failed in his role as breadwinner. If his wife or his children were forced to find jobs, as many were, their labor was a constant reminder of his inability to

The hardships of the Great Depression strained many families in the 1930s. The family of farm laborer William Jones was photographed at "home"–blankets thrown over fence posts and containers–along a rural Missouri highway.

fulfill their expectations. We might expect that the divorce rate would have risen as a result of these difficulties, but instead it fell temporarily. Couples stayed together not because they were happier—many were less happy—but because they couldn't afford to get a divorce and live in two households. Years later, after the worst of the Depression was over, the divorce rate surged among couples who had married at the start of the Depression, had developed serious problems, but hadn't been able to separate until it was over (Cherlin, 1992b).

These economic hardships also forced many young adults to postpone marriage and childbearing. The Depression was so long and so severe that some couples never had the opportunity to have children. As a result, lifetime childlessness was more common among women who reached their peak childbearing years in the 1930s than in any other generation of women in the twentieth century: About one in five never had a child (Rindfuss, Morgan, & Swicegood, 1988). In contrast, only about 1 in 10 of the women who reached their peak reproductive years during the 1950s baby boom never had a child. [➥ p. 67]

As fathers and mothers struggled to make a living, their children helped out. Teenage boys took whatever jobs they could find; teenage girls took over more of the household work for mothers who were forced to work outside the home. The result was what Glen Elder, Jr., called "the downward extension of adultlike experience": Girls took on the role of homemaker; boys took on the role of breadwinner. Elder examined the records of a group of children who were first observed in 1932, at age 11, and then followed through adulthood. He found that when they reached adulthood, the men and women in the group who came from economically deprived families valued marriage and family life more highly than those whose families hadn't experienced hardship. Women from deprived fami-

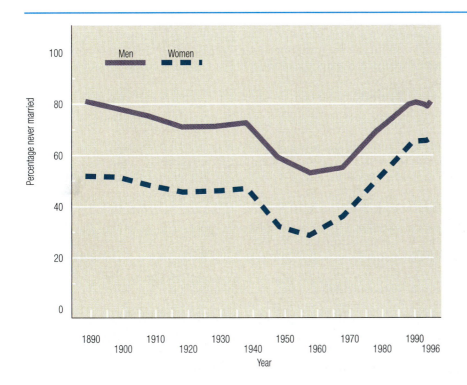

FIGURE 2.1
Percentage never married among men and women aged 20 to 24, 1890 to 1996. (*Sources:* for 1890–1960, U.S. Bureau of the Census, *Historical Statistics of the United States, Colonial Times to 1970*, pp. 20–21; for 1970–1996, U.S. Bureau of the Census, *Current Population Reports,* Series P20, "Marital Status and Living Arrangements," various issues.)

lies married at younger ages than other women. Perhaps the difficulties their families had faced when they were adolescents made the deprived group eager for a secure marriage; or perhaps they viewed families as an important resource in hard times. In any event, when they reached adulthood, these young men and women turned inward to build their own family lives.

THE 1950s

In fact, when the young adults of the Depression generation began to marry and have children after World War II, they created the most unusual and distinctive family patterns of the century. They married younger and had more children than any other twentieth-century generation. Figure 2.1 shows the percentage of 20- to 24-year-old men and women who had never been married, from 1890 to 1995. This is the age group that is most sensitive to variations in age at marriage. Note the percentage is highest at the beginning and end of this chart, indicating that young men and women were most likely to be single (and therefore to marry at an older age) in the late 1800s and late 1900s. The percentage who had never been married declined slowly during the first half of the twentieth century and then plunged to its lowest point during the 1950s. After 1960, it rose sharply especially for women, who by the mid-1990s were marrying later than at any time in the previous 100 years.

The years after World War II were also the time of the great **baby boom.** Couples not only married at younger ages, they had children faster—and had more of them—than their parents' generation, or as statistics would later show, than even their children's generation. Indeed, the late 1940s through the 1950s was the only period in the past 150 years during which the American birthrate

baby boom the large number of people born during the late 1940s and 1950s rose substantially. It spiked dramatically just after the war, as couples had babies they had postponed having during the war. After a few years it dropped, but then began to climb again, peaking in 1957. Women who married during the 1950s had an average of slightly more than three children, the highest fertility rate of the century (Evans, 1986).

Although the causes of the baby boom are not fully clear, a strong post–World War II economy and a renewed cultural emphasis on marriage and children were certainly contributing factors. One explanation focuses on the unique circumstances of the young adults who married during the 1950s. Since most of them were born during the Depression, when birthrates were low, they constituted a relatively small **birth cohort,** as demographers call all the people born during a given year or period of years. After the bad luck of growing up during the Depression and the war, they had the good fortune to reach adulthood just as the economy was growing rapidly. The Allied victory in World War II had left the United States with the strongest economy in the world. Employers needed more workers, but the small size of the cohort meant there were fewer workers to hire (especially given the widespread preference during the 1950s that married women forgo work outside the home). In this tight labor market wages rose for young men, allowing them to support larger families.[6]

This explanation, however, is incomplete. Birthrates rose not only among newlyweds in their early twenties but also among women in their thirties who had been married for years (Rindfuss et al., 1988). These older women belonged to larger cohorts, so that the small-cohort-size theory can't account for their behavior. Rather, the pervasiveness of the rise in births suggests that the preferred family size shifted during the baby boom. The cultural emphasis on getting married and having children seems to have been greater than was the case before or since— perhaps as a result of the trauma of the Depression and the war. The shift had a broad effect on women and men in their twenties, thirties, and even early forties.

Together, the strong economy and the marriage-and-childbearing orientation produced the high point of the breadwinner-homemaker family. The federal government helped by granting low-interest mortgages to armed forces veterans, allowing millions of families to purchase single-family homes in the growing suburbs. For the first time, the "American dream" of marriage, children, and a single-family home was within reach of not only the middle class, but many in the working class (Laslett, 1973).

The heyday of the breadwinner-homemaker family faded quickly, however. Figure 2.2, compiled from Census data by Donald Hernandez, shows the rise and decline of the breadwinner-homemaker family from 1790 to 1989, from the perspective of children aged 0–17. As the graph makes clear, the breadwinner-homemaker family is not the "traditional" American family. The figure divides all children into four groups. The first is the percentage who were living with neither parent—a small number at all times. The second is the percentage who were living in two-parent farm families. As noted earlier, farm families do not fit the breadwinner-homemaker model, because farm wives typically help to produce essential goods and services by tending livestock, growing vegetables, making clothing, harvesting, and so forth. Note that living on a farm was the experience of a majority of children until the mid-1800s.

birth cohort all people born during a given year or period of years

---

[6]The relative-cohort-size theory was expounded by Easterlin (1980).

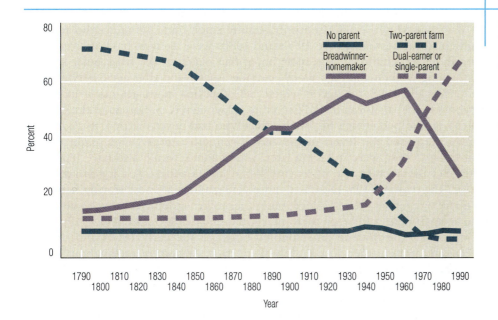

FIGURE 2.2
Percentage of children aged 0–17 living in each of four types of families, 1790–1989. (*Source:* Donald J. Hernandez, *America's Children: Resources from Family, Government, and the Economy,* New York: Russell Sage Foundation, 1993.)

The third group is the percentage of children living in breadwinner-homemaker families, defined here as two-parent, single-earner families not living on farms. This percentage was small early in the nation's history, but began to rise sharply in the mid-1800s, reaching a temporary peak in 1930. It fell briefly during the Depression, then peaked again in 1960. Data show that this family form was dominant only in the first half of the twentieth century, reaching its zenith during the 1950s. After 1960, as the figure shows, its dominance ended.

The fourth group is nonfarm families that do not fit the breadwinner-homemaker mold, either because both parents work or because only one parent is present in the home. Only about 10 percent of children lived in these kinds of families before 1900, but after 1940 the percentage rose dramatically. By 1989, the last year shown in the chart, these families were by far the largest group, greatly exceeding the declining breadwinner-homemaker group. The reasons for the rise in single-parent and dual-earner families, and the consequences of this rise, will be discussed extensively in later chapters. Still, the breadwinner-homemaker family has not disappeared; in 1989, about one-fourth of all children lived in such a family.

Moreover, overlooked during the 1950s because of all the attention given to the baby boom was a countercurrent that would loom large later in the century. Increasingly, married women went back to work outside the home after their children were of school age. They took jobs that had been typed as women's work—jobs that were relatively low paying, but still required some education, such as secretary, nurse, or salesclerk. As the service sector of the economy expanded, the demand for these pink-collar workers increased, and married women responded to the opportunities.

THE 1960s AND BEYOND

Just as social commentators confidently announced a return to large families, the roller-coaster car reached the top of its track and hurtled downward. The birthrate plunged from the heights of the baby boom to an all-time low in the 1970s, from which it has risen only slightly since then. Women who were in their childbearing years in the 1970s and 1980s were likely to have an average of only about 2.0 children.[7] The baby boom had begotten the baby bust. In addition, young women and men were marrying at later and later ages; between the mid-1950s and 1998, the age at which half of all first marriages occur increased by about four years for men and five years for women (U.S. Bureau of the Census, 2000f). So the percentage of young adults who had never married, as Figure 2.1 shows, surpassed the levels of the early twentieth century. One might expect that because they were marrying later, young adults would also have left home later. Yet the average age of leaving home has not increased much since the 1970s. The reason is that more and more young adults are now leaving home not to marry or even to attend college, but rather to live independently—to get a job, find an apartment, and be on their own (Goldscheider & Goldscheider, 1994).

Moreover, the divorce rate doubled between the early 1960s and the late 1970s, and has declined just slightly since then. At current rates, about one in two marriages will end in divorce (Cherlin, 1992). As at the beginning of the century, there is great concern about the consequences of this high divorce rate. At the beginning of the century, optimists could at least argue that the marriage rate was increasing right along with the divorce rate; but that was not the case during the 1960s and 1970s. Young adults postponed marrying, and divorced adults postponed remarrying, although **cohabitation**—the sharing of a household by unmarried persons in a sexual relationship—accounted for some of that postponement (Bumpass, Sweet, & Cherlin, 1991).

cohabitation the sharing of a household by unmarried persons who have a sexual relationship

There was one important continuity with the 1950s: Married women continued to work outside the home in ever larger numbers. Even women with preschool-aged children joined the workforce in large numbers. By the late 1990s, about three-fourths of all married women with school-aged children, and about two-thirds of married women with preschool-aged children, were working outside the home. Whereas in the 1950s, married women tended to drop out of the paid workforce when they were raising small children, today married women are much more likely to remain at their jobs throughout the childrearing years. This change in women's work lives has had a powerful effect on the family.

The most recent period in the history of the family—from about 1960 to the present—will be the main subject matter of this book. As a prelude to understanding the present, future chapters will examine in detail the recent history of marriage, childbearing, divorce, cohabitation, and women's labor force participation in the United States and elsewhere in the Western nations. These discussions will also be informed by studies of non-Western countries, which can deepen our understanding of the nature of contemporary family patterns.

THE CHANGING LIFE COURSE

We have seen that family and personal life changed greatly during the twentieth century. One way to understand these changes is to compare the experiences of groups of individuals who were born in different time periods.

---

[7]Evans (1986). The figure cited is an estimate for women born in 1956, who have not yet completed their childbearing years.

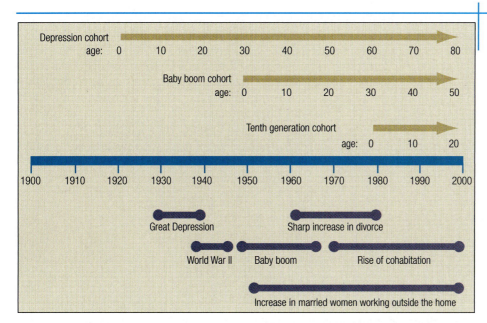

FIGURE 2.3
A life course perspective on social change in the twentieth century.

Consider Figure 2.3. In the middle of the figure is a time line for the twentieth century, divided into 10-year intervals. The top half shows the time lines for three different birth cohorts born 30 years apart. The first group was born in 1920; I have labeled them the "depression cohort" because they were nine years old when the Great Depression began in 1929. The second group, "the baby boom cohort," was born in 1950, at the start of the baby boom. The third group, born in 1980, is more difficult to label. Some social commentators have noted that people born in the 1980s and 1990s are very roughly the tenth generation of Americans born since the country was founded. I will call the third group the "tenth generation cohort." The bottom half of Figure 2.3 shows time lines for the occurrence of major historical events and trends that have changed family and personal life. For example, the Great Depression lasted from 1929 until about 1940, and the baby boom occurred from the late 1940s to the early 1960s.

One can think of the top and bottom halves of Figure 2.3 as showing two kinds of time. The top half displays what we might call "individual time": the passing of time in people's lives as they age. This is the usual way we think of time. The bottom half displays what might be called "historical time": the beginning and ending of key events and social trends that have influenced family life during the century. The figure's usefulness is that it allows a comparison of individual time and historical time; or put another way, it places the course of an individual's life in historical context.

For example, the figure shows that in 1950, as the baby boom started, members of the depression cohort were still in their childbearing years; therefore, they became the parents of the baby boomers. The figure also shows that by the time the baby boom cohort reached age 30 in 1980, a sharp rise in divorce had occurred. As a result, the baby boomers have had a much higher rate of divorce than the depression cohort. In addition, the figure shows that the tenth generation cohort is the first to have lived their early childhood years after the sharp rise in divorce. That is why far more tenth generation cohort members have experienced the break-up of their parents' marriages than have previous cohorts.

life-course perspective
the study of changes in individuals' lives over time, and how those changes are related to historical events

This way of looking at changes in family and personal life is an example of the **life-course perspective:** the study of changes in individuals' lives over time, and how those changes are related to historical events. Rather than study families as an undifferentiated group, sociologists and historians who use this perspective tend to study the lives of individuals within families. They examine how historical developments affect the course of these individuals' personal and family lives. Elder's work on the depression cohort (defined in his case as people born in 1921) is probably the most influential study of this genre (Elder, 1974). The life-course perspective is particularly attractive to scholars who wish to study social change over time. And as this chapter has made clear, the twentieth century was a time of great change in the kinds of family lives individuals lead.

WHAT HISTORY TELLS US

The history of the family tells us that Americans come from regions of the world that have different family traditions. To some extent, the American mixing bowl blends those traditions together and reduces the differences. The result is that the family lives of today's ethnic and racial groups have more in common than not. Still, the historical record can help us understand some of the variation we see today.

Americans of European ancestry hail from a system that has emphasized the conjugal unit of the married couple and children more than family systems in other regions of the world. In the nineteenth and early twentieth centuries, European-American conjugal families developed a sharp division of labor between the husband, who worked outside the home, and the wife, who by and large worked inside the home. That sharp division, however, broke down in the last half of the twentieth century as more married women entered the workforce. And during the twentieth century, European Americans placed increasing weight on personal satisfaction as the standard people should use in judging the quality of their relationships. European-American family traditions are important because they have been the basis for American law and custom. For example, American law gives parents nearly exclusive rights over children and gives far less authority to grandparents or other kin. (See Chapter 10, *Families and Public Policy:* Elián, the Troxels, and Parents' Rights.)

The family systems of American Indians and of Americans from other regions (such as Latin America, Asia, and Africa) have traditionally placed more emphasis on kin beyond the conjugal family. Sometimes these family systems consisted of tightly organized lineages. Think of the matrilineal tribes of the Hopi. At other times and places, they consisted of extended families in which grandparents, uncles, aunts, and others from both sides of a person's family might contribute to her or his well-being and even share a home. And as the Mexican tradition of *compadrazgo* showed, sometimes individuals without any ties of blood or marriage were recruited into a person's kin network.

Marriage was still central to most of these systems, although less so in Africa. But married couples were embedded in larger family structures that could provide assistance and support. This tradition of support is important because marriage declined among all American racial and ethnic groups during the last half of the twentieth century. The weakening of marriage left European-American families in a particularly vulnerable position because they had less of a tradition of extended family support to fall back on. The story of recent changes in marriage and family life, and their impact on Americans with different heritages, will be told in subsequent chapters.

Looking Back

1. **What functions have families traditionally performed?** Family and kinship emerged as ways of ensuring the survival of human groups, which were organized as bands of hunter-gatherers until about 10,000 years ago. Until the past 250 years or so, most families performed three basic activities: production, reproduction, and consumption. Most American Indian tribes were organized into lineages and clans that provided the basis for social organization and governing. Colonial American families performed functions such as education that are now performed by schools and other institutions. These kinds of families can be said to follow the familial mode of production. The colonial American family performed many activities that are now done mainly outside the family: educating children, providing vocational training, treating the seriously ill, and so forth.

2. **How did American families change after the United States was founded?** Between 1776 and about 1830, a new kind of family emerged among the white middle class in the United States, one in which marriage was based on affection rather than authority and custom. Over time, the primary role of women in these families became the care of children and the maintenance of the home. Children came to be seen as needing continual affection and guidance, which mothers were thought to be better at providing than fathers. As families became more centered on children, the number of children they raised declined. At the same time, a movement toward greater individualism weakened parents' influence over their children's marriage decisions and family lives. Working-class families, because of difficult economic circumstances, did not change as much.

3. **How have the family histories of major ethnic and racial groups differed?** Before the Civil War, African slaves married and lived together for life, wherever possible, and knew and kept track of other kin. After the Civil War, discrimination shaped their family lives. For example, out of economic necessity, rural black wives worked in the fields, and urban black wives worked for wages outside the home, more than white wives did. As for Mexican Americans, after U.S. troops and immigrants seized their land, they became more of a working-class community, increasingly confined to *barrios*. Over time, more and more women headed households, in part because their husbands often worked as migratory farm workers. Chinese and Japanese families also faced discrimination. Traditionally patrilineal, their authority over their children has declined over the generations. Filipinos, the second largest Asian immigrant group in the United States today, are descended mostly from people who immigrated in the twentieth century. Filipinos have a bilateral kinship structure more similar to the kinship system of Europeans.

4. **How did the emotional character of the American family change during the early twentieth century?** During the early decades of the twentieth century, rising standards of living allowed for greater attention to an emotionally satisfying private life. As the search for emotional satisfaction through family life became an important goal, the private family emerged. Eventually, the success of marriage came to be defined more in emotional terms than in material terms. People experienced more privacy in their personal lives through the increasingly common empty-nest phase of marriage and the rise in the number of individuals living alone.

5. **What important changes occurred in marriage and childbearing in the last half of twentieth century?** In the 1950s, young adults married at earlier ages and the birthrate rose to a twentieth century high. The baby boom was caused in part by the small cohort size and good economic fortune of the cohort that reached adulthood in the 1950s. In addition, a greater cultural emphasis on marriage and childbearing seems to have been present. The 1950s was the high point of the breadwinner-homemaker family, which was dominant only during the first half of the twentieth century. During the 1960s and 1970s, the trends in marriages, divorces, and births all reversed: Age at marriage increased sharply, the divorce rate doubled, and the birthrate reached its lowest level. Moreover, married women were increasingly likely to work outside the home even when their children were young.

Thinking about Families

1. Why was the family "a weapon in the struggle for survival," as one anthropologist has written, in hunter-gatherer and tribal societies?

2. How might the historical experiences of earlier generations of African Americans have influenced African-American family life today?

3. What are some of the ways that the life course of Americans born in the early twentieth century differed from the life course of those born toward the end of century?

4. **The Public Family:** Why were the American family's public responsibilities much broader in the colonial period than is the case today?

5. **The Private Family:** Why are emotional satisfaction, intimacy, and romantic love more important in American family life today than they were one hundred years ago?

Key Terms

1965 Immigration Act   62
affective individualism   50
American Indian   46
baby boom   67
barrio   60
bilateral kinship   62
birth cohort   68
brideservice   59
bridewealth   59

cohabitation   70
compadrazgo   59
conjugal family   43
extended family   43
familial mode of production   44
hunter-gatherers   42
labor market mode of
   production   45
life-course perspective   72

lineage   42
matrilineage   43
mestizo   59
patrilineage   42
polyandry   44
polygyny   44
remittances   60
stem family   43
total fertility rate (TFR)   50

Families on the Internet

Note: While all the URLs listed were current as of the printing of this book, these sites often change. Please check our web site (__http://www.mhhe.com/cherlin__) for updates.

Although it's the most modern of media, the Internet is also a resource for historians. For instance, the Library of Congress maintains a site entitled, "American Life Histories: Manuscripts from the Federal Writers' Project, 1936–1940." During the Great Depression, the government employed over 300 writers to gather life histories from 2,900 people in 24 states. You can view these documents and search them by keywords such as marriage, divorce, and children (**http://Lcweb2.loc.gov/ wpaintro/wpahome.html**). Enter "Haithcocks" in the search window to read a story of rural poverty among a family in Monkey Bottoms, a mill town in rural North Carolina. How had the Depression affected them?

The Women's Studies Section of the Association of College and Research Librarians maintains a list of women's history sites (**libraries.mit.edu/ humanities/womensstudies/history.html**). The University of Rochester has placed on-line several monthly issues of *Godey's Lady's Book* from 1850, one of the most popular magazines of the nineteenth century. You can view articles, poems, and engravings (**www.history.rochester.edu/ godeys**). Go to the February 1850, issue and read the story, "The Elopement," about a young woman whose father saves her from a tragic elopement at the last minute. What is the message to young women about obeying family versus their own hearts when choosing a husband?

chapter 3

Gender and Families

Looking Forward

1. How might biological influences affect the behavior of women and men?

2. How do sociologists distinguish between the concepts of "sex" and "gender"?

3. How do children learn the gender roles of women and men?

4. How does everyday life reinforce gender differences?

5. Are gender differences built into the structure of society?

6. What have been the contributions of gender studies to our understanding of the family?

The Berdache

berdache in Native American societies, a man or woman who dressed like, performed the duties of, and behaved like a member of the opposite sex

In 1841, the American traveler and artist George Catlin published his monumental *Manners, Customs, and Conditions of the North American Indians.* The result of his eight years of traveling among Native Americans in the West, it included about 300 engravings. One of them, entitled "Dance to the Berdache," is shown in Figure 3.1. It depicts warriors of the Sauk and Fox Indians dancing around a man wearing women's clothing. "For the extraordinary privileges he is known to possess," wrote Catlin of the man, "he is . . . looked upon as medicine and sacred, and a feast is given to him annually." Men like him, who dressed like women, performed women's occupations, and behaved like women, were called **berdaches** by French colonists. They existed in more than 100 Native American cultures (Callendar & Kochems, 1983).[1] In a smaller number of these cultures, female *berdaches,* who dressed and worked like men, were also found.

Most individuals became *berdaches* in one of two ways. First, some children displayed what their parents thought were *berdache*-like characteristics. In some of the Native American cultures, parents might develop a male child as a *berdache* if he showed "a gentle, androgynous [having characteristics of both sexes] nature" and showed great interest in the work of the other sex (Williams, 1986). Second, some men and women experienced spiritual visions at adolescence or even later, which they took as signs to become *berdaches.* These visions usually involved some supernatural intervention, such as instructions from the female moon deity. *Berdaches* were generally accepted members of adult society; anthropologists report that attitudes toward them "varied from awe and reverence through indifference to scorn and contempt" (Callendar & Kochems, 1983). In many cultures they were credited with supernatural powers and exceptional skill at carrying out the other sex's work. The dance at the annual feast that Catlin sketched indicated that the Sauk and Fox respected the powers of the *berdache.* As neither ordinary men nor ordinary women, *berdaches* could undertake special tasks that women and men could not perform as easily, such as negotiating a marriage bargain between a woman's family and a man's family or settling a dispute between a man and a woman.

---

[1]According to a commentary by Sue-Ellen Jacobs appended to this article, the word *berdache* came from the Arabic *bardaj,* which in turn came from the Persian *bardah,* meaning "kept boy" or "male prostitute." This term represented the colonists' preconceptions and was inappropriate; nevertheless, it became common usage.

George Catlin's "Dance to the Berdache, " from Catlin's *Manners, Customs, and Conditions of the North American Indians,* 1841. Original sketch at the National Museum of American Art, Smithsonian Institution, Washington, DC.

In many cultures, a *berdache* could marry a person of the same sex who was not a *berdache.* Male *berdaches* typically engaged in homosexual intercourse, while the sexual relations of married female *berdaches* were lesbian. But many *berdaches* also had heterosexual relations; the Navaho, for example, permitted male *berdaches* any form of sexual intercourse with either sex (Callendar & Kochems, 1983). Moreover, a male *berdache* could renounce his role and return to being an ordinary male. By some accounts, non-*berdache* males could have sex with a *berdache* without being considered primarily homosexual.[2]

Female *berdaches,* who were less common, were found in Native American cultures in which relationships between men and women were relatively egalitarian, and in which women owned and distributed the goods they produced. But in cultures with strong lineages, they were very rare. For instance, in matrilineal cultures, the children of a man's sister remained in his lineage under his control. Under these circumstances, females of reproductive age were too valuable to the men of the lineage to be allowed to take on the *berdache* role. But in less hierarchical cultures, some women could take on a male role without threatening the male social order (Blackwood, 1984). Put simply, female *berdaches* were more likely to be found in societies in which men had less control over women.

As the influence of European culture on Native Americans grew during the nineteenth century, the number of *berdaches* declined rapidly; by the end of the century there were very few. Nevertheless, the story of the *berdaches* can help to answer some important questions that will be addressed in this chapter.

[2]See the interpretation in Williams (1986).

sex the biological characteristics that distinguish men and women

gender the social and cultural characteristics that distinguish women and men in a society

1. *What is the difference between sex and gender?*   The social situation of the *berdaches* illustrates the distinction sociologists make between sex and gender. In most sociological writing, **sex** refers to the biological characteristics that distinguish women and men: sex chromosomes, reproductive organs, sex-specific hormones, and physical characteristics (Richardson, 1977). A very small number of people are born with ambiguous sex characteristics, but for the vast majority there is a clear sexual identification as either woman or man. **Gender,** in most sociological writing, refers to the social and cultural characteristics that distinguish women from men (Richardson, 1977). In our society, such characteristics include the different clothing that men and women wear or the expectation that boys shouldn't cry when they are hurt. Gender is said to be a social creation; sex is said to be a biological creation.

The distinction between sex and gender will be useful in examining many of the topics in this book. Nevertheless, drawing a line that separates the two is occasionally more difficult than this definition at first suggests. For example, the literature on the *berdaches* indicates that parents sometimes perceived qualities in their young sons that were more typical of daughters, and then raised them as *berdaches.* If sexual orientation is partly biologically determined, as evidence suggests (see Chapter 7), these parents may have recognized a predisposition in their sons toward a homosexual orientation. Indeed, some students of the *berdaches* phenomenon have advanced this interpretation. Walter Williams wrote:

> *Indian societies constructed an alternative gender and put their emphasis on the* berdache's *character and social role rather than on only sexual behavior. This is certainly a social construction. . . . Yet, the berdache does have an identity, which seems much more a reflection of the individual's innate character* (Williams, 1986).

If correct, this view implies that the gender parents chose for their sons—the *berdache*—was socially assigned on the basis, in part, of innate, biological characteristics. In other words, a *berdache*'s gender was influenced both by culture and by biology. In some real-world situations, separating sex and gender neatly may not be possible.

2. *How many genders are there?*   The story of the *berdaches* shows that gender need not be confined to two sexes. Just what gender were the *berdaches?* Did a male *berdache* who dressed, acted, and married like a woman take on the female gender? Not quite, for he could not give birth, often had greater physical strength, was sometimes taken along on hunts, and differed in other ways from women (Williams, 1986). Rather, the *berdache* appears to have occupied an intermediate position between male and female—a third gender, of sorts. He was called not a "man" or a "woman" but a "halfman-halfwoman," a "man-woman" or a "would-be-woman." Reflecting this mixture, the Zuni buried male *berdaches* in women's dress but men's trousers, on the men's side of the graveyard (Callendar & Kochems, 1983).

In the blurring of the difference between male and female, the status as an in-between gender, the *berdache* demonstrates how society and culture created gender categories. Recently, a number of adults who were born with ambiguous sexual organs have formed an organization, calling themselves **intersexuals** (Cowley, 1997). As children, most had surgery and long-term treatments with sex hormones to make their genitals and secondary sex characteristics more like

intersexual a person who is born with ambiguous sexual organs

those of males or females (see below). Their goal is to convince doctors and parents not to reassign a child's sex until the individual is old enough to make an informed choice.

Still, even though the *berdache*'s story and the emergence of intersexual activists show that female versus male is not the only possible gender distinction, the two-gender model is the typical manner in which people have made sense out of sex. Consequently, the assumption throughout most of this chapter will be that there are two genders.

3. *Can a person's gender identity be modified?* In some tribes Native American men were allowed to become *berdaches* in adolescence or even later if a supernatural event guided them to do so. They were also allowed to shed the status and return to the male gender. Clearly, under some cultural circumstances, gender identity can be established after middle childhood and modified in adulthood. Yet even in this extraordinary case, the modification is not from male to female, but rather from male to an in-between third gender. Research shows that most children develop a gender identity during their preschool years; that it is reinforced during middle childhood and adolescence; that it becomes a central part of the child's self-definition; and that it is altered in only a handful of exceptional cases.

A recent report illustrates the difficulty of completely overriding a biological predisposition toward being a woman or man. During infancy, a boy's penis was accidentally cut off during surgery. His parents accepted the recommendation of doctors that he undergo further surgery to feminize his genitals and be raised as a girl. Early medical reports indicated that the child was behaving in appropriately feminine ways, and the case was widely cited as showing that gender identity can be socially assigned (Colapinto, 2000; Money & Tucker, 1975). However, a 30-year follow up told a different story (Diamond & Sigmundson, 1997). As a child the boy rebelled continually against the clothing and play styles suggested to him, and as an adolescent simply refused to be a girl. After being informed of his history, he elected to have further surgery and hormone treatments in order to masculinize himself. He lived his adult life as a man, and has since married. In an editorial accompanying the medical journal report on the case, a physician writes, "the organ that appears to be critical to psychosexual development and adaptation is not the external genitalia, but the brain" (Reiner, 1997, p. 225). And the brain appears to form a gender identity in response to both biological and social cues.

4. *How much do gender differences reflect men's attempts to retain power over women?* We have learned that male *berdaches* were tolerated in many Native American cultures throughout Western North America, but female *berdaches* were more restricted. Women had the freedom to modify their gender only in cultures in which they had substantial resources relative to men, and in which the power of male-dominated lineages was weak. In cultures in which men had greater control over women, they blocked women's moves toward a male role. Do similar forces still operate today? As a social creation, notions of gender are likely to reflect the existing power relationships in a society. In fact, some scholars would restrict the definition of gender to sex-linked characteristics that reflect male power over women or would argue even more broadly that all gender differences reflect male power (Scott, 1986). Others would argue for a looser connection between gender and power. We will examine the connection between gender differences and male domination later in this chapter.

Overall, the story of the *berdaches* shows a flexibility and variability in gender that is unusual. Yet even in this unusual instance, as well as in the current controversy over sex reassignment, we can see evidence that both cultural norms and biological predispositions may influence a person's gender identity; that a shift in gender identity from male to female or vice versa occurs only rarely, and that gender differences can be influenced by the degree of power men have over women. Although the *berdaches* and the intersexuals show that alternative ways of organizing the culture and biology of sex and gender are possible, their rarity underscores how widespread is the familiar two-sex, two-gender model most of us take for granted.

The distinction between women and men, female and male, is basic to the study of the family because of the sharp differentiation, in nearly all societies, between what women and men do in families. Exactly what they do differs from one society to the next, but almost universally, they tend to do different things. To understand families, we must understand gender. And to understand gender, we must begin before birth, for the paths of male and female begin to diverge in the womb. The origins and consequences of gender differences in childhood, and their maintenance in adulthood through social interaction and male domination, constitute the subject of this chapter. (A more general examination of how parents raise their children will be the subject of Chapter 10.)

The Gestational Construction of Gender

When a sperm and an egg unite to form a human embryo, each contributes a sex chromosome—the genetic material that determines which sex the embryo will turn out to be. The egg always contributes an X chromosome. If the sperm also contributes an X chromosome, the embryo will normally develop into a girl. If the sperm contributes a Y chromosome, the embryo will normally develop into a boy. So at the moment of conception, the developing child's genetic sex is determined. But the story of sex and gender is far from over.

gestation the nine-month development of the fetus inside the mother's uterus

For the first several weeks of **gestation** (the term for the nine-month development of the fetus inside the mother's uterus), the external sex organs of soon-to-be girls and boys are identical. These primitive genitals can develop into either a clitoris, vagina, and ovaries or a penis, scrotum, and testes. But soon male embryos begin to develop testes. In the middle months of gestation, the testes in soon-to-be boys produce male sex hormones called androgens. These hormones cause the genitals to develop into the male form. In the absence of high levels of androgens, the genitals develop into the female form. After only a few months, then, the developing child's genital sex is determined by the level of male sex hormones.

HORMONAL INFLUENCES

So far the story is uncontroversial. But some scientists believe that the androgens that circulate in male fetuses do more than cause the genitals to take on the male form. They claim that parts of the fetus's brain develop differently depending on the level of androgen that is present. In other words, the brains of males and females may be organized somewhat differently because of the presence or absence of high levels of male sex hormones during the second trimester (the middle months) of gestation. If so, then some of the gender differences we recognize in women and men could be the result of differences in prenatal (before birth) hormone levels.

There is some evidence for this theory. Studies of girls who were exposed to abnormally high levels of male sex hormones while in their mother's wombs have found that they showed higher levels of interest in strenuous physical activity—climbing trees, biking, playing football—and lower levels of doll play and infant care than girls with normal hormonal histories. Similarly, boys who were exposed to abnormally high levels of female sex hormones showed lower levels of physical activity and more doll play and infant care than boys with normal hormonal histories. These findings suggest that prenatal hormone levels may influence behavior in ways consistent with gender stereotypes (Ehrhardt, 1985). Yet we cannot be sure that they reflect the effect of prenatal sex hormones on the brain. Skeptics note that the girls also had somewhat male-like genitals, which may have caused them to think differently about themselves, or their parents to treat them differently from normal girls (Bem, 1993).

Further support for the hormone/brain organization thesis comes from a 30-year study of mothers who gave birth between 1960 and 1963 and their daughters. Blood samples were taken from the mothers-to-be during each trimester of pregnancy and stored for later analysis. In 1990, the blood samples were tested for male and female sex hormones, both of which are normally present in women's blood. At the same time, blood samples were taken from the daughters, who were by then aged 27 to 30. Their sex-hormone levels were measured, and they were asked a detailed series of questions about gender-typed behaviors and values, such as the importance of a career and of marriage; the number of gender-typed activities they engaged in; whether they liked caring for babies; and the number of births they had had. The responses to all these indicators were combined into a single measure of "gendered behavior." The researchers found that the higher the level of male sex hormones in the mothers' blood in the second trimester of pregnancy (when hormones cause sexual differentiation) the more masculine was the gendered behavior of their daughters 27 to 30 years later. This was true even after adjusting for the level of male sex hormones in the daughter's own blood. Still, the researchers noted that hormone levels accounted for about one-fourth of the variation in gendered behavior; social and cultural influences could have accounted for most of the other three-fourths (Udry, Morris, & Kovenock, 1995).

In addition, the researchers had asked the daughters whether, when they were children, their mothers had encouraged them to behave in stereotypically feminine ways (such as wearing dresses or taking an interest in sewing) and stereotypically masculine ways (such as defending themselves physically or repairing things around the house). The standard parental socialization model, to be described in a few pages, would predict that daughters whose mothers had encouraged feminine behavior would act in more feminine ways as adults. In general, that is what the researchers found; however, they also found that the higher the level of male sex hormones in the mothers' blood, the weaker the effect of their encouragement on their daughters' behavior (Udry, 2000). In other words, daughters who were exposed to higher levels of male sex hormones before birth were less receptive to suggestions that they behave in feminine ways, while daughters who were exposed to lower levels were more receptive.

BIOSOCIAL INFLUENCES

biosocial approach (to gender differences) the theory that gender identification and behavior are based in part on people's innate biological differences

As this study suggests, gendered behavior may be a result not just of biological predispositions (e.g., prenatal hormone levels) but of social experiences as well (e.g., parents' pressure to behave in gender-typed ways). Sociologists who believe that both biology and society have important influences on gender differences are said to be taking the **biosocial approach** to human behavior (Rossi, 1977, 1984). The biosocial perspective does not suggest that hormones and chromosomes are destiny nor that biology always wins out over social influences. In fact, those who believe biological influences do affect gendered behavior would add two qualifications.

First biologically based differences in gendered behavior exist only "on average"; individuals can show a wide range of behavior. If we were to select a large group of women and another large group of men at random and measure the incidence of some biologically influenced behavior, we would find the behavior occurred more frequently among one group than the other. For example, if the behavior were aggression, we might find that, on average, aggression levels were higher among the men than among the women. But not all men, nor all women either, would show the same level of aggression. A modest number of women would be very aggressive, and a modest number of men not at all aggressive. To take another example, even if, on average, women are more predisposed than men to engage in nurturing behavior, as some observers suggest, in any randomly selected group, some women will not be very nurturing and some men quite nurturing.

Second, social influences can counteract biological predispositions. For instance, even if, on average, men are predisposed to be more aggressive than women, our society can control overly aggressive behavior through parental influences, moral education, public pressure, and for extreme aggression, law enforcement. Why, then, should biological predispositions matter at all? Because counteracting the influence of genes or hormones on human behavior is a bit like rolling a stone uphill: It can be done, but it takes continuing effort. If society were to decide that all biologically based gender differences in behavior should be eliminated, strong, deliberate steps would need to be taken to achieve that goal. And the stronger the biological predisposition, the stronger those steps would need to be. Understanding the biological bases of behavior, then, can help us estimate the ease or difficulty of bringing about social change.

EVOLUTIONARY INFLUENCES

If biologically based gender differences exist, how might they have emerged? Biosocial theorists apply the Darwinian evolutionary model. [➥ pp. 33–35] That is, like evolutionary psychologists, they note that the major part of the human evolutionary past was spent in hunter-gatherer societies. [➥ p. 42] Because infants were born relatively immature, and needed prolonged care to develop, the women in hunter-gatherer societies provided that care and gathered food, while men hunted and defended the group's territory. Evolutionary biology suggests that, over time, women may have evolved a greater capacity for the care of young children, and men may have evolved a greater capacity for aggressive territorial behavior.

It is, however, quite a leap from forest dwellers to city dwellers, from mothers carrying children while gathering edible plants to parents placing children in day care centers while gathering spendable wages. To what extent evolutionary biology is relevant to modern society is not clear. Many sociologists are reluctant to concede it any role, in part because social norms and behaviors, not evolution, are what they are trained to study. Some are also suspicious of evolutionary theory because biological explanations have been used in the past to deny equal opportunities to women. For instance, in the 1800s some doctors opposed higher education for women on the grounds that too much intellectual stimulation would diminish their ability to have babies (Freedman, 1990). Social scientists who advocate greater equality for women fear that biological explanations will again be used against their cause. Yet most social scientists who do believe that biology plays a role in shaping gender differences in behavior also concede that culture plays a crucial role. Historian Carl Degler (1990) wrote:

> *What social scientists who are interested in the biological roots of our actions are asserting is that our evolutionary past, like our cultural past, continues to influence us. Yet neither past is so controlling that we cannot seek ways to alter or modify its influences* (p. 43).

The Childhood Construction of Gender

Once born, children face multiple influences on their behavior. Sociologists, who have borrowed the concept of roles from the theater, often write about the social roles people play. A **social role** is a pattern of behaviors associated with a position in society (e.g., parent, teacher, supervisor, elected official).

The term **gender roles** can be defined as the different sets of behaviors that are commonly exhibited by women and men. Gender roles usually occur in pairs, one for each gender. For example, in many marriages during the first half of the twentieth century, men tended to play the gender role of "breadwinner," the person who earns all the income for the family, whereas women tended to play the role of "homemaker," the person who specializes in caring for the children and keeping house. Many sociologists think gender roles are entirely socially created, although a minority allow for biological influences. For example, in a book on gender roles, Jean Lipman-Blumen summarizes her view:

> *The family, and even gender roles, are social inventions, according to this perspective. More specifically, society magnifies biological sexual differences into artificially dichotomous gender roles. . . . These differences lead to the sexual division of labor, whose strict enforcement fosters the mutual, if unequal, dependence of men and women* (Lipman-Blumen, 1984).

Moreover, the gendered division of labor reflects men's interests more than women's:

> *Some observers have noted that the current structure of the sex-gender system represents a centuries-old power relationship—often a power struggle—that persists despite the erosion of its original social bases* (Lipman-Blumen, 1984).

This power relationship will be discussed later in the chapter.

social role a pattern of behaviors associated with a position in society

gender roles the different sets of behaviors that are commonly exhibited by women and men

As part of the socialization process, children learn appropriate gendered behavior from their parents.

PARENTAL SOCIALIZATION

socialization the way in which one learns the ways of a given society or social group so that one can function within it

socialization approach (to gender differences) the theory that gender identification and behavior are based on children's learning that they will be rewarded for the set of behaviors considered appropriate to their sex but not for those appropriate to the other sex

Researchers in the role theory tradition exemplified by Lipman-Blumen have argued that people first acquire gender roles through socialization during childhood. **Socialization,** according to the definition in one widely cited book, is "the process by which we learn the ways of a given society or social group so that we can function within it" (Elkin & Handel, 1984). It is how individuals learn to take on the attitudes and behaviors considered culturally appropriate for them. The emphasis in the **socialization approach** to gender differences is on conscious, social learning: Children are rewarded for behavior adults think is appropriate for their gender and admonished or punished for behavior that is not considered appropriate. By watching parents, teachers, television actors, and others, children learn the behavior of both genders, but they soon learn that they will be rewarded for one set of behaviors and not for the other (Mischel, 1966). For example, although at first little boys cry as much as little girls, they are admonished not to, so that as men they cry less often than women. Lipman-Blumen reminds us that in 1972, Senator Edmund Muskie of Maine, running for the Democratic nomination for president in the New Hampshire primary election, was widely perceived to have suffered a major blow when his eyes teared while denouncing a newspaper's criticism of his wife (Lipman-Blumen, 1984). (Muskie did worse than expected in the primary and did not win the nomination.) More generally, men are encouraged to be aggressive, competitive, and independent, whereas women are encouraged to be less aggressive, more nurturing to children and adults, and better at enabling and maintaining personal relationships.

A large number of studies support the theory that parents act differently toward boys than toward girls from birth onward. In the first 24 hours after birth, according to one study, parents described boys as more alert, stronger, and firmer and girls as less attentive, weaker, and more fragile—even though there were no actual differences between them, according to tests and observations (Rubin, Provenzano, & Luria, 1974). Other studies show that parents react more strongly to boys, giving them both more positive feedback and more negative feedback. Parents also seem to hold boys more and give them more freedom to explore. They offer boys toys such as blocks and tools, which allow for invention and manipulation; to girls they offer toys such as dolls, which encourage imitation. And when fathers play with their sons, they often engage in a rough-and-tumble style of play, while in playing with their daughters, they often role-play stereotypically female activities, such as having tea (Jacklin, 1984). With little conscious awareness, then, parents often teach girls and boys different ways of behaving. At an early age, children develop stereotypical conceptions of both genders, and they begin to use those conceptions to organize their knowledge and behavior (Bem, 1981).

THE MEDIA

Nor is gender socialization confined to parents; children learn lessons from books and television, among other sources. As recently as the 1960s, schools made little effort to balance the gender content in the books children were assigned to use. Publishers produced stories and histories that focused mainly on boys and men. Then, spurred by the feminist movement, school systems began to demand more balanced literature. Today, in most children's books, girls and boys receive much more equal treatment.

For instance, a 1972 study of books for elementary school reading classes found that boy-centered stories outnumbered girl-centered stories by a ratio of 5 to 2, and adult male characters outnumbered adult female characters by 3 to 1. A similar study conducted in 1989 showed "much more egalitarianism" (Purcell & Stewart, 1990). Girls appeared just as often as boys and were portrayed in a wider range of activities than in 1972. Women appeared more often than in 1972, but still not as often as men. Two-thirds of the photographs still featured male characters. Studies such as these suggest that substantial progress has been made in presenting gender-balanced portrayals in children's books, although some shortcomings remain.

Over the past few decades, however, books have lost ground to television and computer software as a source of information for children. A study conducted in 1986 and 1987 found that children aged 2 to 5 watched an average of nearly 3½ hours of television per day while 6- to 11-year-olds watched an average of 3 hours per day (Elkin and Handel, 1989). Studies have shown that at least through the early 1980s, more of the characters in children's programming were male than female, and the characters undertook mostly gender-stereotyped activities (Barcus, 1983). Moreover, the cable channels children and adolescents watch also show gender imbalances. A 1990 study of randomly selected music videos on Music Television (MTV) found that men appeared twice as often as women, and engaged in significantly more aggressive and dominant behavior. Women were shown engaging in more implicitly sexual and subservient behavior, and more often were objects of men's sexual advances (Sommers-Flanagan, Sommers-Flanagan, & Davis, 1993).

EARLY PEER GROUPS

peer group a group of people who have roughly the same age and status as one another

Researchers also suspect that much of the development of gender-specific behavior occurs from an early age in children's **peer groups**—similar-age children who play or perform other activities together. Between the ages of two and three, children begin to sort themselves into same-sex peer groups. Psychologist Eleanor Maccoby argues that these same-sex peer groups strongly influence the distinctive behavior patterns of boys and girls (Maccoby, 1998). In observing pairs of children who were on average 33 months old, Maccoby and her colleagues found that these youngsters were far more likely to show social behavior—offering or grabbing a toy, hugging or pushing, vocally greeting or protesting, and so forth—to children of the same sex than to children of the opposite sex. When girls were paired with other girls, they were just as active as boys who were paired with boys; but when girls were paired with boys, they frequently stood back and let the boys monopolize the toys. Observers suggest that the rough-and-tumble play style and focus on competition and dominance among boys are unattractive to girls. Moreover, they argue, young girls have difficulty influencing boys. Between ages three and five, girls increasingly attempt to influence other children by making polite suggestions, but boys increasingly make direct demands (Serbin, Sprafkin, & Doyle, 1984).

In another study, five- and six-year-olds were observed playing in groups of four. An adult woman sat at one end of the playroom, then shifted to the other end of the room halfway through the session. When the groups were composed of all boys or all girls, they changed positions to remain the same distance from the adult before and after she shifted seats. In fact, all-girl groups moved farther away from the adult than all-boy groups. But in mixed-sex groups the girls tended to stay close to the adult and to move with her, while the boys did not—as if the girls thought the adult might moderate the boys' rough, assertive play style. (Greeno, 1989).

Maccoby suggests that boys' peer groups reinforce a competitive, dominance-oriented interaction style that carries over into such adult male communication tactics as interrupting, boasting, contradicting, and threatening tactics that restrict conversation. Girls' groups, she suggests, reinforce a different style that carries over into adult female communication. Through expressing agreement or support, asking questions rather than making statements, and acknowledging other persons' comments, girls continue interactions rather than restricting them. These styles, Maccoby asserts, may influence adult, mixed-sex interactions in school, at the office, and in families. Same-sex peer groups emerge so early, she suggests, that both parental influence and biological predispositions may shape them (Maccoby, 1990).

CHILDREN'S PREFERENCES

The picture that emerges from this literature is of a barrage of messages, first from parents and then from peers, the media, and schools, that teach boys and girls different gender roles (Block, 1984).[3] Yet several studies suggest that these influences, although central, are not the whole story of early differences between girls and boys. Consider children's preferences for toys. Before their second birthday, boys and girls begin to choose different kinds of toys. In one British study, two groups of children 12 to 15 months old and 19 to 24 months old, respectively, were observed playing at home (Smith & Daglish, 1977). In both groups, boys played much more with cars and trucks than girls, while girls played much more with soft toys and dolls. Boys also engaged in more active and forbidden play, such as climbing on furniture or attempting to touch wall plugs.

Many sociologists would say that even by this young age, children's activities are influenced by their parents' beliefs about what kinds of play boys and girls should engage in. Indeed, Lenore Weitzman writes:

> *From the minute a newborn baby girl is wrapped in a pink blanket and her brother in a blue one, the two children are treated differently. The difference starts with the subtle tones of voice adults use in cooing over the two cradles, and it continues with the father's mock wrestling with his baby boy and gentler play with his "fragile" daughter* (Weitzman, 1979, p. 1).

The authors of the British study did ask the parents what kinds of play they thought appropriate for girls and boys. Not surprisingly, they found that some parents held strongly stereotypical views—boys should play with trucks, girls with dolls, and so forth. But the parents' views had no effect on their children's activities. That is, the sons of parents who didn't feel strongly that boys should play with trucks were just as likely to play with trucks as the sons of parents who did feel strongly that boys should play with trucks. Similarly, daughters of parents who didn't hold strong stereotypes were just as likely to play with dolls as daughters of parents who did hold strong stereotypes. The children's preferences seemed to evolve independently of their parents' preferences.

In another study, children aged 21 to 40 months were observed playing and were given a test to see if they could discriminate between genders: They were shown pictures of children and adults performing stereotypically male or female activities and were asked whether the person in the picture was a boy or girl (or man or woman) (Fagot, Leinbach, & Hagan, 1986).[4] Overall, the boys in the play groups engaged in more aggressive behavior (hitting, pushing, shoving, taking objects, yelling, calling names) and were more likely than girls to play with blocks, tools, cars, and trucks. Girls were less aggressive and somewhat more likely than boys to play with dolls, dance, or dress up. Were these children doing what they thought was appropriate for their own gender? Not so for the boys: Those who couldn't tell the genders of the people in the pictures were just as aggressive, and just as likely to play with stereotypically male toys, as those who "passed" the gender test. Their behavior seemed unaffected by their knowledge of the activities boys and girls were "supposed" to do. This finding suggests that boys' greater aggressive behavior may have a biological basis—although the boys in the study may already have been socialized to be aggressive. For girls, however, the gender

---

[3]The major exception in this literature is an overview by Eleanor Maccoby and Carol Jacklin (1974), which concluded that the extent of the differences in the way parents treat girls and boys had been exaggerated, as had differences in girls' and boys' behavior.

[4]On toy preferences preceding gender recognition, see also Weinraub, Clemens, Sockloff, Ethridge, Gracely, and Myers (1984).

recognition test made a difference. Even girls who "failed" the test were less aggressive than boys and played more with stereotypically female toys. Yet girls who "passed" the test showed a further drop in aggression—in fact, they showed virtually no aggressive behavior. The responses suggest the possibility of both a biological predisposition toward less aggressive behavior and a tendency to conformity to social expectations about how girls are supposed to behave.

LATER PEER GROUPS

Symbolic interactionists say that children develop a sense of self through activities such as peer group play—a "gendered" sense of self, in this instance. As a girl (or a boy) formulates what she will say or do in the group, she imagines how the others are likely to respond. This process of imagining how others will respond is what George Herbert Mead called "taking the role of the other" (Blumer, 1962). It is, interactionists say, how children develop an internalized sense of appropriate behavior.

Consider the same-sex peer groups that are formed in school settings by children somewhat older than the ones we have been considering. Children are socialized, in part, through playing games and sports in same-sex, school-age peer groups. In these groups, children learn the behaviors expected of them, try out these behaviors with their peers, get feedback on how well they are performing, and try again. Sociologists have studied how this interactive process produces and reinforces different behavior patterns in boys and girls. In a study of Little League baseball teams, Gary Alan Fine observed that boys were concerned with impression management—behaving in a way that met with approval from the other boys—as well as with winning or losing. They learned to control their emotions and not to cry; otherwise they would risk ridicule from their peers. They also learned to value competition. Once, when an opposing team showed up with too few players, a coach offered his first-place team the options of winning by forfeit or playing the game anyway and taking the small risk that they would lose. All the best players argued for taking the forfeit; only two players argued in favor of going ahead with the game because they were supposed to be playing for fun. When the team voted overwhelmingly to take the forfeit, the boys learned a lesson about valuing competition over cooperative play—a lesson that is consistent with the expected behavior of men (Fine, 1987).

At least until the recent expansion of athletic programs for girls, elementary school boys tended to play organized games more than elementary school girls (Lever, 1976; Thorne, 1993). More often, boys played competitive games with a set of rules and a goal. Their play involved larger groups with more mixing of different ages; occurred more often outdoors; and lasted longer than girls' games. In contrast, girls' play reinforced the relational and emotional skills women are expected to have. Girls tended to play indoors more; to engage more often in noncompetitive activities without a goal; and to play in smaller groups than boys. In these small groups, girls showed more affection than boys and learned to pick up nonverbal cues about their friends' moods. The traits that were reinforced by girls' play were consistent with an adult life that emphasizes home, family, emotional closeness, and cooperation.

Nevertheless, not all girls and boys follow these scripts. When Barrie Thorne (1993) observed children in elementary schools, she found that most play groups comprised either all girls or all boys. But a modest number of girls and boys played in groups with the other gender, and there was much crossing of the gender border—for example, when boys and girls chased one another or invaded the other gender's space. The degree of separation between girls' and boys' worlds, Thorne concluded, was overstated. Thorne's approach to her study reflects many of the principles of feminist research methods (see *How Do Sociologists Know What They Know?* Feminist Research Methods).

In sum, studies of young children's preferences and activities suggest numerous influences on the different behaviors of girls and boys. Society's expectations about how to behave are transmitted to children through channels such as parents, books, television, and peer groups. In these ways, cultural differences between women and men are reproduced in the next generation. Yet the evidence also suggests that children may have innate predispositions that affect gender differences in their behavior. These predispositions appear to be stronger for boys than for girls. Boys seem to prefer blocks, trucks, and rough play regardless of their parents' opinions about how they should play. Moreover, boys' toy preferences appear earlier than, and are more pronounced than, girls' preferences. Thus the influence of same-sex peer groups may reflect both socialization and biological predispositions.

UNCONSCIOUS INFLUENCES

Another perspective on the reproduction of gender differences has been developed by social scientists who don't think biology has much effect on gender, yet are puzzled by the tenacity of the gender stereotypes acquired in childhood, and surprised by how hard they are to change. For instance, Lillian Rubin writes:

> *Until recently I believed that we needed only to understand . . . socialization to explain stereotypic gender behavior. But more than a decade of watching women and men struggle to change—often with only limited success—has convinced me that there are differences between us that are not simply a product of role learning and socialization practices. . . . "Why?" I kept asking myself. "There must be something else necessary to explain the dogged persistence with which these ways of being resist our best efforts to change."*

Otherwise, Rubin reasoned, unlearning old ways of behaving wouldn't be so difficult, especially when we are intent on doing so.

> *The answer, I now believe, lies in some deep-seated psychological differences between women and men—differences, I hasten to add, that are not born in nature but are themselves a product of the social organization of the family* (Rubin, 1983, p. 40).

The answer Rubin favors is derived from psychoanalytic theory. Its foremost proponent in sociology is Nancy Chodorow, who draws on it to explain why women do the mothering in nearly all societies (Chodorow, 1978).

The **psychoanalytic approach** to gender differences is based on the psychoanalytic theory of children's development first put forth by Austrian psychiatrist Sigmund Freud at the turn of the twentieth century. Freud thought that children become like their same-sex parent by internalizing—unconsciously incorporating—a representation of that parent into their own personalities. So Freud's theory stresses unconscious mental processes, whereas the socialization approach stresses conscious processes. And whereas the central mechanism of the socialization approach is learning, the corresponding mechanism in psychoanalytic theory

psychoanalytic approach (to gender differences)
the theory that gender identification and behavior are based on children's unconscious internalization of the qualities of their same-sex parent

is internalization. Children become like a parent through a process that is beyond their conscious control and not even evident to them at the time.

The version of psychoanalytic theory borrowed by Chodorow asserts that the first several years of life are crucial to a person's gender identity and sense of self (Chodorow, 1978). After birth, the infant unconsciously experiences itself as merged and continuous with its first caretaker, who is almost always a woman. The young child, whether girl or boy, becomes deeply attached to the all-encompassing, comforting female figure and internalizes her image. There soon comes a time, however, when boys realize they must establish their gender identities as males. To do so, they must transfer their attachment and identity from their mothers to their fathers (or to other males, if the father is not present). This event is said to be a traumatic break for boys, who must do the difficult work of distancing themselves from their mothers to protect their gender identities. Consequently, the theorists argue, boys build psychological barriers between themselves and their mothers; they put fences around their gender identities. In the psychoanalytic language, they create rigid ego boundaries as a way of protecting their emerging identities. Girls, on the other hand, need not distance themselves from their mothers to establish their gender identities. They remain connected to their first attachment in life, and they enjoy a longer, more continuous period of attachment as they come to identify themselves as female.

As a result, Chodorow writes, "The basic feminine sense of self is connected to the world, the basic masculine sense of self is separate" (Chodorow, 1978, p. 169). Boys and men, she asserts, establish more rigid emotional boundaries between themselves and others; women, on the other hand, have more permeable boundaries. Therefore, Chodorow and others believe, women have more empathy, which my dictionary defines as "identification with and understanding of another's situation, feelings, and motives" (Copyright 1997 © by Houghton Mifflin Company. Reproduced by permission from *The American Heritage College Dictionary, Third Edition.*). Put differently, women are said to have a greater capacity for relating to others and an easier time establishing close relationships. And because they value so highly the connectedness they experienced with their mothers, according to Chodorow, women *want* to have children and mother them so they can recreate that fundamental attachment. They are also better, on average, at relating to infants than men, because of their greater ability to respond to a small being who cannot verbally express its needs.

And so, argues Chodorow, women mother because they were mothered by women themselves, and in the process developed a sense of self that not only makes them want to be mothers but also makes them better at it. If we wish to change this situation, she concludes, we must make a concerted effort to involve men in the parenting of young children on an equal basis with women; anything less will not work. This psychoanalytic model implies that girls grow up to become mothers not so much because of the kinds of toys they are given, as the socialization perspective would have it, but because of *who* gives them the toys—their primary caretakers, their mothers.

The psychoanalytic approach has been criticized for its reliance on clinical case histories.[5] On average, individuals who seek psychotherapy are likely to be

---

[5]This section draws from a review symposium on Chodorow's book in the journal *Signs* (Lorber et al., 1981).

more troubled than other people. Psychoanalytic theorists claim, nevertheless, that their patients' difficulties reflect differences in the population, albeit in exaggerated form. They argue that the deep insight that can be obtained from case histories far exceeds that which can be obtained from mere observation or large-scale sample surveys. Other critics have charged that Chodorow overestimates the extent of change that is possible in parenting roles. Judith Lorber asks about Chodorow's proposal that men and women share primary parenting:

> *If most men have developed nonaffective [low on emotion] personalities and strong ego boundaries, where are you going to find enough men with psychological capabilities to parent well and thus break the general pattern of the emotional primacy of the mother?* (Lorber et al., 1981, p. 485)

Critics, then, believe that Chodorow's system may be more resistant to change than she thinks.

The Continual Construction of Gender

Recently, much sociological research and writing on the construction of gender differences has focused not on socialization or predispositions in childhood, but rather on the continual construction and maintenance of gender differences in adulthood. In fact, some scholars have suggested that the concept of gender as a role should be dropped (Ferree, 1990). This rejection of the language of roles is in part a reaction to the 1950s structural-functionalist position that there are two natural roles in a family, breadwinner (instrumental leader) and homemaker (expressive leader). [➡ p. 28] Critics charged that the functionalists created the false impression that the breadwinner-homemaker division of labor was inevitable; that the two roles were equal in power; and that there were no ignored historical variations from it (Thorne, 1992).[6] They also argued that gender is a master identity, far too broad to be considered just one of life's roles (West & Zimmerman, 1987). A person's gender identity is so fundamental, for instance, that others are intensely uncomfortable unless they can determine what it is.

I think the attack on role theory also arose because research on early socialization into gender roles offered a distressing view for those who wished to change gender roles. As we have seen, this body of research suggested that gender roles emerge at an early age through an elaborate system that may include differential rewards and opportunities, differing biological predispositions, and unconscious psychoanalytic processes. Such a powerful mixture of influences might make later modification of gender roles difficult. A theoretical framework that viewed gender identities as more fragile, more fluid, and more in need of continual support would be more congenial to social change than gender role theory.

To develop such a framework, which is now known as the **interactionist approach,** a group of sociologists hearkened back to symbolic interaction theory (Blumer, 1962). [➡ p. 30] How they asked, do a wife and husband come to understand that she should do most of the housework? Socialization theory suggests that doing the housework is part of the gender role women learn

interactionist approach (to gender differences) the theory that gender identification and behavior are based on the day-to-day behavior that reinforces gender distinctions

---

[6]Yet by the 1980s, the functionalism of the 1950s was in full retreat and few writers used the term "role" in the strict functionalist sense; see Komarovsky (1992).

The interactionists suggest that gendered behavior is not only learned in childhood but reinforced day after day in adulthood.

beginning with the dolls and teacups they are given in childhood and the praise they get for helping their mothers wash the dishes. But the symbolic interactionists, while not denying that socialization occurs, emphasize that questions such as who does the housework are settled again and again in daily life. For example, in a study conducted by Sarah Fenstermaker Berk (1985), a woman who was asked "What household work does your husband do?" replied:

> *He tries to be helpful. He tries. He's a brilliant and successful lawyer. It's incredible how he smiles after he sponges off the table and there are still crumbs all over* (p. 206).

Here the husband's smile—the symbol—indicates to his wife that he is incapable of sponging all the crumbs off the table, despite having enough brains to be a brilliant and successful lawyer. It is a way for the husband to express a feigned helplessness, which he and his wife both interpret as meaning that she's the only one who can do a good job of cleaning up after dinner. Daily scenes such as this, Berk and others argue, not only produce clean tables; they also produce—and reproduce—gender distinctions. The interactionists focus on people's actions in concrete situations such as this one in order to determine how social meanings—in this case the shared understanding of who should do the housework—are produced.

Implicit in the interactionist view is the premise that gender distinctions are fragile enough that they need to be reinforced and reproduced day after day; otherwise, there would be no need to keep reproducing them. Is this premise valid? Socialization theorists and evolutionary psychologists would say no. However, adherents to the school of symbolic interaction known as ethnomethodology, and the gender theorists influenced by them, would say yes.[7] Ethnomethodologists claim that the social order we take for granted in everyday life is much more precarious, much more house-of-

---

[7] I am aware that many ethnomethodologists consider their perspective to be distinct from symbolic interaction; but I agree with Jonathan H. Turner (1986) that they are related.

Women still earn less than men in comparable jobs, on average, despite modest progress in the past decade or two.

cards–like, than we think. People must spend a lot of time, they assert, creating and re-creating a shared sense of social order in their everyday lives. Ethnomethodologists study how we create that shared sense. According to this line of reasoning, people must continually "do" gender—do the work of creating a shared sense of what the relations between men and women should be (West & Zimmerman, 1987). Gender becomes a verb, usually in the passive voice: Housework is gendered, work for wages is gendered, childcare is gendered, over and over in hundreds of situations. The household, in Berk's phrase, becomes a gender factory that produces the shared reality of gender relations along with crumb-free tables (Berk, 1985).

Gender and Male Domination

Another body of writing about the construction and maintenance of gender differences focuses not on social interaction or socialization, but on the very structure of society: its hierarchies of dominance and power and its economic system. According to this line of reasoning, gender differences are social creations deeply imbedded in the way society is organized (Risman, 1998). More specifically, in the United States and most other nations, inequalities between women and men are said to be built into their social systems through **patriarchy.** In most general terms, patriarchy is a social order based on the domination of women by men. But following some scholars, I prefer to reserve the term for conditions that are more common in agricultural societies, in which older men control their families and family groups are the main economic units. In industrialized societies, in which the family or lineage is no longer the main economic group, I prefer the simpler term "male domination" (Thorne, 1992; Orloff, 1993). But no matter which term one uses, the main point of this scholarship is that men exercise power over women in ways that are similar to how the wealthy exercise power over the poor and whites exercise power over blacks. Like class (see Chapter 4) and race (see Chapter 5), gender is said to be one of the basic ways in which a society is stratified into more and less powerful groups.

patriarchy a social order based on the domination of women by men, especially in agricultural societies

THE SEX-GENDER SYSTEM

Put another way, societies often take the biological sex differences between women and men and use them as the basis for a comprehensive social order in which men have advantages over women. Specific, limited sex differences become

How Do Sociologists Know What They Know?

Feminist Research Methods

Sociologist Barrie Thorne (1993) begins her book about children's play groups, *Gender Play: Girls and Boys in School,* by writing not about her subject but about herself. She recalls that the segregation of girls and boys on the playgrounds of the elementary school she attended was considered "natural." She tells the reader that her views on gender were transformed by the women's movement of the 1970s and 1980s, which argued that the differences between the genders is not natural but rather a social construction. She describes her commitment to raise her own children in a nonsexist way.

Thorne then discusses how, in her own research, she took pains to learn the terminology that the subjects themselves used: "kids" rather than "children." She explained, "I found that when I shifted to 'kids' in my writing, my stance toward the people in question felt more side-by-side than top-down" (p. 9). Using "kids" helped her to adopt the viewpoint of her subjects, as opposed to the viewpoint of an adult feminist scholar.

In fact, Thorne's entire first chapter consists of preliminary material about herself and her relationship with her subjects. The chapter illustrates a practice known as

reflexivity: a researcher's examination of the nature of the research process that she or he is undertaking (Fonow & Cook, 1991). The researcher *reflects* upon the beliefs (e.g., feminism) and statuses (e.g., college professor, woman) she brings to the project—and in particular, how those beliefs and statuses might affect the research project.

Reflexivity is part of a larger orientation that is called *feminist research methods.*[1] It emerged from the feminist movement of the 1970s and 1980s, and is linked to feminist theory. [➡ p. 31] A central tenet of feminist research methods is that scholars should conduct action-oriented research, meaning research that has the objective of advancing the liberation of women from oppression by men—and also ending the gender constraints placed on men (Fonow & Cook, 1991). Feminist researchers explicitly acknowledge this political agenda. More important, they argue that *all* social scientific research reflects the social and political beliefs of the researchers but that most social scientists hide their beliefs—sometimes even from themselves.

In contrast, most sociologists try to follow the *scientific method.* [➡ p. 24] A key as-

sumption of the scientific method as it is often practiced is that researchers are neutral figures who stand outside the phenomena they study. The researcher's point of view, it is said, should not influence the methods she or he uses or the conclusions she or he makes. In this way, the social scientist strives for objectivity—a way of viewing the social world that is independent of personal beliefs. [➡ p. 23]

But feminist researchers argue that objectivity is nearly impossible to achieve (Neilson, 1990). They argue that much supposedly "objective" social scientific research actually reflects male bias. They often criticize large-scale surveys and other forms of statistical research. For example, they note that not long ago, the U.S. Bureau of the Census, in its surveys, defined the husband as the "head of household" in a married-couple family, no matter what the family's situation was. Similarly, violence against women by husbands and partners was greatly underreported in crime statistics until feminists focused attention on the problem (Reinharz, 1992).

Scholars who use feminist research methods try to make connections to their subjects and to understand and take their

reflexivity a researcher's examination of the nature of the research process that she or he is undertaking

sex-gender system the transformation of the biological differences between women and men into a social order that supports male domination

the basis for pervasive gender differences. Gender theorists refer to this transformation of biological differences into a social order that supports male domination as a **sex-gender system** (Rubin, 1975).

Consider the economy, for example. In Western nations, people must purchase the goods they need with money (as opposed to making their own clothes and building their own houses). Western societies are organized so that men have access to more money than women: Men are more likely to work for pay, and when they do, most earn considerably higher wages and salaries than women (see Chapter 9). To be sure, men tend to have more education and work experience than women, in part because many women withdraw from the paid workforce to bear and rear children. Gender theorists argue, however, that the wage gap is far wider than differences in education

subjects' points of view. That is why Thorne sought to use language and methods that made her more of a "side-by-side" observer than a "top-down" (i.e., detached and objective) observer. Only by understanding the meanings that research subjects give their actions can the researcher provide a full account of an issue according to feminist research methods.

Proponents of feminist research methods frequently try to show that there is substantial variation from person to person in the ways in which women and men act. They do so because they oppose generalizations about women that might be used to restrict their independence and equality (for example, the belief, prevalent at mid-century, that the husband should earn the money and the wife should stay home and care for the children). They sometimes carry out research with the intent of demonstrating that generalizations about women are wrong. Thorne warns, for instance: "One should be wary of what has been called 'the tyranny of averages,' a misleading practice of referring to average differences as if they are absolute" (pp. 57–58).

So Thorne ventured out to the elementary school playground to disprove the idea that boys and girls are inherently different in their play styles—boys more aggressive, more concerned with dominance in groups; girls more concerned with relationships with a small number of friends. On the playground, girls and boys did separate, for the most part, in the ways the generalizations about them predict. They were not, however, completely separate. Thorne provided an insightful analysis of contact between girls and boys during the "border work" that maintained their separation, such as invading the other gender's spaces and chasing one another. She also found that a few children defied the stereotype, such as a boy who played jump rope and an athletic girl who played sports with the boys. And she documented occasional mixed games of dodgeball and the like.

From evidence such as this, Thorne concluded that gender "has a fluid quality" (p. 159) and that the claim that boys and girls have separate cultures "has outlived its usefulness" (p. 108). However, as one reviewer noted, the number of times that boys and girls cross the gender boundaries "are a tiny minority of her observations" (England, 1994, p. 283). Consequently, claiming that the average differences between boys and girls aren't important because some individuals cross the boundaries may be an overstatement.

Even if one is not always convinced by the conclusions of researchers like Thorne, one can find useful lessons in feminist research methods. Perhaps the main lesson is that researchers should pay more attention to where they are coming from: the reasons they choose to study a particular topic, the assumptions they have going into a research project, and the beliefs they hold that might influence their conclusions. Feminist researchers have made a convincing case that in the study of family and gender, objectivity has its limits.

Ask Yourself

1. Does your gender affect the way you react to Barrie Thorne's research? Explain.

2. What are the advantages and disadvantages of feminist research methods and of the scientific method? Why?

[1]The use of reflexivity pre-dates feminist research methods in sociology. Researchers working in the tradition of symbolic interactionism [➡ p. 30] incorporated it into their methods.

www.mhhe.com/cherlin

and work experience would predict—and recent economic studies suggest that their argument is correct. (See *Families and Public Policy:* The Earnings Gap.) In a number of ways—such as when parents encourage sons more than daughters to have careers, when employers discriminate against women in hiring or pay, and when long-established rules provide men with higher pay than women for comparable work—society creates and reinforces men's economic domination. Therefore, most women must depend on men if they wish to live in a household with a substantial income.

Just how men have achieved their dominant position in society is a subject of some debate. Many writers of this genre link male domination to capitalism—the economic system of the United States and most other nations (Shelton & Agger, 1993). **Capitalism,** which will be discussed (along with socialism) in detail in

capitalism an economic system in which goods and services are privately produced and sold on a market for profit

The Earnings Gap

*I*n the late 1990s, women who worked full-time as financial managers earned 69 percent as much as men who worked full-time as financial managers. Women bus drivers earned 74 percent as much as men who worked as bus drivers. And women computer programmers earned 81 percent as much as men made (U.S. Bureau of Labor Statistics, 1999g). Why in nearly all occupations did women earn less than men? And why were women workers concentrated in lower-paying jobs? Do employers discriminate against women workers? Or are other factors responsible for the earnings gap?

In the 1960s and 1970s, some labor economists argued that the earnings gap reflected the different social roles women choose. That is, they assumed that women preferred to devote a larger share of their lives to raising children than did men. Economists such as Solomon Polachek argued that women intentionally chose the kinds jobs they could leave for a period of time and then reenter, and they left voluntarily when they had young children (Polachek, 1979). Women earned less than men, according to this argument, because, on average, they had less work experience and invested less in their careers (for example, by taking fewer job training courses).

The evidence, however, has not supported this model—at least not as the sole explanation for the earnings gap. Numerous studies of the wage differences between women and men found that even after controlling for education, work experience, and other factors, a substantial portion of the gap remains. Robert Michael, a labor economist and chair of a National Academy of Sciences panel on Pay Equity Research, wrote in 1989:

> there exist sizeable and systematic wage differences between women and men that cannot be explained by measured differences in skill, experience, effort, job commitment, or most any other attribute of workers that has been studied. Some argue that the unexplained differences constitute a serious inequity that should be addressed by public and private policy (Michael, Hartmann, & O'Farrell, 1989, p. vii).

Why might the earnings gap still exist? One possibility is that some employers may engage in "statistical discrimination." They may note, accurately, that women have slightly higher rates of leaving jobs than men. Consequently, they may hesitate to hire

Chapter 6, is an economic system in which goods and services are privately produced and sold on a market for profit. Gender theorists have maintained that economic inequalities between women and men benefit capitalists, the owners of businesses, in at least three ways. First, employers save money by hiring women at lower wages than they would have to pay men. During the twentieth century, the sector of the economy that produces services, such as medical care, communications, insurance, restaurant meals, and the like, expanded faster than the factory sector. During this expansion, women—especially unmarried women—were hired as nurses (but less often as doctors), secretaries (but not managers), and telephone operators (but not supervisors), as well as for other service jobs (Oppenheimer, 1970). Their wages tended to be substantially lower than the wages of men with comparable responsibility, providing employers with considerable savings. Second, the lower wages paid to women tend to create divisions between male and female workers, which prevent them from joining together and organizing to protect their interests against the interests of capitalists.

Third, the unpaid work of housewives, gender theorists argue, allows families to subsist on the often modest wages men earn. Employers count on their male workers being married to women who will wash their clothes, cook their meals, and raise their children at no cost. Thus, employers gain greater profits by paying their workers less than the full cost of raising a family. Indeed, in the first half of the twentieth century, this division of labor was enshrined as the "family wage system," in which husbands were supposed to earn enough so that their wives did not need to work for pay (see Chapter 6). Wives' unpaid work was,

women for jobs that require expensive training and therefore tend to pay well. When they interview a woman, they may be wary of hiring her because they know that as a group, women have higher turnover rates—even though the specific woman they are interviewing might never quit (England & Farkas, 1986). Their statistical discrimination, in turn, can affect how parents socialize the next generation, and so on. Consequently, discrimination tends to linger, even though employers' attitudes toward women in the workplace may have become more positive.

A subtler issue is **comparable-worth discrimination:** a situation in which women and men in the same company do different jobs of equivalent value, but the women are paid less than the men. A remedy for this problem is to have an expert body classify jobs according to their

"worth," as defined by attributes such as skill, effort, responsibility, and working conditions. Then wages or wage guidelines would be set according to the job rankings, usually by a government body. To be sure, deciding how much value a given job produces relative to another is difficult. Yet in Australia and Great Britain, where government influence over wage levels is greater than in the United States, similar actions have reduced the earnings gap (Gregory et al., 1989).

Over the past decade or two modest progress has been made in closing the earnings gap. In 1980, the median weekly earnings of women who worked full-time were about 60 percent of men's earnings; in 1998 the figure had increased to 76 percent (Reskin & Padavic, 1994; Bowler, 1999). Still, women's earnings lag behind

men's in nearly every occupation. And some of the progress in narrowing the gap has occurred because the wages of men without college educations have gone down, rather than because the wages of women have risen (Bernhardt, Morris, & Handcock, 1995).

Ask Yourself

1. Have you ever compared notes with your coworkers and discovered that the women in your group were being paid less than the men? If so, how did you and the other employees interpret the earnings gap?

2. Besides statistical discrimination and comparable worth discrimination, what other explanations can you think of for the earnings gap?

www.mhhe.com/cherlin

and still is, invisible economically: Government statisticians do not count housework and childrearing as part of the gross national product—the annual accounting of the total amount of goods and services produced in the country. Yet wives' unpaid work is economically valuable. In recent decades, as more married women have taken jobs outside the home, millions of families have discovered how expensive it is to pay someone else to care for their children while they work.

Still, the nature of the connection between male domination and capitalism is unclear. Most feminist theorists have maintained that the two work well together, but are at least partially distinct. For example, some have described the social and economic organization of the United States as "patriarchal capitalism," arguing that male domination of women and capitalists' domination of workers are intertwined, with each reinforcing the other (Hartmann, 1976). Male domination is said to have emerged before capitalism, but to have broadened and strengthened once capitalism was established. An implication of this line of thought is that male domination would be reduced if capitalism were replaced by another economic system, such as socialism.

This implication, however, is undercut by cross-national research. Several scholars have studied the position of women in countries with a socialist economic system. Under **socialism,** the number and type of goods produced, and who they are distributed to, are decided by the government rather than by the market. Theoretically, a socialist system should eliminate the economic disparities between women and men, because there are no business owners who could

comparable-worth discrimination a situation in which women and men do different jobs of equivalent value in the same company but the women are paid less

socialism an economic system in which the number and types of goods produced, and who they are distributed to, are decided by the government rather than by the actions of a market

profit from paying women lower wages or from having unpaid housewives subsidize the wages employers pay men. In fact, in socialist countries such as the former Soviet Union and its Eastern European satellites, nearly all urban women worked outside the home. Yet most positions of power and advantage in these nations are held by men. Feminist scholars who have studied China, for instance, have been particularly disappointed by the continuing gender inequalities there, especially given the feminist rhetoric of the leader of the Communist revolution, Mao Zedong. Judith Stacey has concluded that sex-gender systems are "relatively autonomous" from economic systems, be they capitalist or socialist (Stacey, 1983). Men's domination of women, in other words, is not just a function of the economic system; it may even be largely independent of it. Although there are differences between the status of women in capitalist and socialist societies, male domination seems to be built into the social structures of most nations in ways that are compatible with either capitalism or socialism.

GENDER, CLASS, AND RACE

Rather than being reducible to class differences, then, many scholars argue that gender is a separate, distinctive way in which societies are stratified by power and advantage. A basic tenet of gender theorists is that gender should be thought of in the same way scholars think of class and race—namely, as a primary basis of social stratification. This viewpoint is especially useful when one is studying differences in occupations or earnings; it is also relevant to the study of families. For instance, women's and men's choices about whether and whom to marry can be influenced by how much they could earn if they were single and how much they can expect a spouse to earn. These earnings levels, in turn, are influenced by the sex-gender system of the society in which they live.

Still, let me suggest that in studies of the family, there is an important sense in which gender is not fully similar to either class or race. Sex differences in childbearing—the fact that women become pregnant, bear children, and can breast-feed them—may be relevant to the different family roles of women and men. I don't mean to suggest that the family roles of women and men are predestined by these sex differences, but I would argue that the sex differences cannot be ignored in studying the different behaviors of men and women. In her presidential address to the American Sociological Association, Alice Rossi said:

> Gender differentiation is not simply a function of socialization, capitalist production, or patriarchy. It is grounded in a sex dimorphism [the occurrence of two distinct sexes] that serves the fundamental purpose of reproducing the species.

Rossi argued that to some extent, the parenting styles of women and men build on biological differences between the sexes. If so, she stated, "This is where the sociological analogy so often drawn between race and sex breaks down" (Rossi, 1984, pp. 1 and 10).

The analogy breaks down, Rossi argued, because we could easily imagine a human society in which, as a result of intermarriage, there are no racial differences. We could even imagine (as Marx did) a society in which there are no class differences. Yet we cannot imagine a society in which there are no sex differences. That is because women and men have different biological roles to play in reproduction. Gender differences, then, may not be *wholly* socially constructed, and they may not always reflect male domination and power. Although male domination shapes

In the 1990s, the "Promise Keepers" movement promoted large rallies at which men pledged to be responsible fathers and husbands.

gender roles, it may not be the only force that does so. In this sense, the gender stratification perspective, although an important source of insight that I will draw on throughout this book, needs to be supplemented by other views.

GENDER: THE MALE POINT OF VIEW

Sociological writings on gender have commonly focused on the conditions under which women and girls live their lives. This orientation reflects the roots of gender studies in the feminist movement that began in the 1960s. Although men have not been absent from gender studies, they tended to be included mainly because of the ways in which they influence or control women. Beginning in the 1980s, however, both a scholarly and a popular literature emerged that was focused on men. This body of literature grew greatly in the 1990s, as social movements aimed at men gained strength. The main topic of these writings was **masculinity**—the set of personal characteristics that society defines as being typical of men.

The popular writings on masculinity have sought to define its essence and to build a more positive image of men. In part, the authors were reacting to what they saw as an overly negative feminist view of men. Poet Robert Bly (1990) became the best-known writer and movement leader through the publication of *Iron John: A Book About Men.* In it, Bly used a Grimm brothers fairy tale about a young man's encounter with a "wild man" to illustrate the need for men to get in touch with their forceful, hard, even fierce maleness. Unless men could find this inner essence, Bly and others argued, they were unlikely to be successful in their work or family lives. The leaders of this wing of the men's movement were careful to state that they were not encouraging violent or irresponsible behavior, however. "The kind of energy I'm talking about is not the same as macho, brute strength which men already know enough about," Bly told an interviewer (Thompson, 1991). "It's forceful action undertaken, not without compassion, but with resolve." Soon groups such as Promise Keepers filled sports stadiums

masculinity the set of personal characteristics that society defines as being typical of men

for rallies at which men were urged to be good, responsible fathers and husbands and to remain true to their masculinity.

Still, it was clear that in this version of masculinity, men were supposed to
bring their forcefulness to their family lives and to remain the dominant partners
in marriage. Male dominance in marriage, of course, is precisely what feminists
object to. Thus, a second, feminist-influenced branch of men's studies emerged
in opposition to the first. Although less prominent than the first in the popular
culture (but see Pollack [1998] on the problems of "real boys"), it is quite prominent in sociological writing. Writers in this feminist-influenced tradition of men's
studies accept the position that male dominance must be eliminated from marriage (and in the larger society as well) (Brod & Kaufman, 1994).

Moreover, these writers reject the idea that masculinity has a singular essence
(Coltrane, 1994). Instead, they argue that what we often think of as the "essence"
of masculinity—aggressiveness, attempts to dominate, emotional detachment,
aversion to homosexuality, and so forth—is merely a social construction. The
sex-gender system, these authors think, subordinates women in part by instilling
in men characteristics that lead them to dominate women. If the sex-gender system were changed, they argue, masculinity might take a different form: more
egalitarian, nurturing, and emotionally connected, and less exclusively heterosexual. These authors write not of masculinity but of *masculinities,* the title of an influential book R. W. Connell (1995) that implies that there is more than one way
to be masculine. Connell and others argue that the social influences that prop up
the Western version of masculinity are so pervasive they become invisible to us.
Consequently, we assume incorrectly that the current version of masculinity is
the way men naturally are.

Some writers are attempting to bridge the gap between the more traditional
brand of the men's movement and the feminist-influenced branch. Nock (1998)
argues that marriage is the setting in which men finally separate from their parents and do what is expected of successful men: provide for and protect a family.
Because most men rise to the challenge, he writes, marriage improves men's
lives. In a bow to the traditional branch, Nock concedes that conventional expectations of men and marriage are unlikely to change much. Yet he acknowledges
that those expectations have traditionally benefited men and disadvantaged
women. Nock's solution is to restructure the institution of marriage so that
women and men benefit equally from it. For instance, he favors reducing the economic dependence of wives on husbands. To stabilize marriage, he would give
tax credits to some married couples. Yet giving more benefits to married couples
would keep marriage in a privileged position compared to other family forms—a
move strongly opposed by many liberals and feminists. How (and whether) to
support both gender equity and marriage remains a contentious social issue.

The Contributions of Gender Studies

We have reviewed several approaches to the study of gender differences (see
Table 3.1). The socialization approach emphasizes conscious learning and interpretation by children of the world around them—their parents, peers, television,
and so forth. The lessons very young children learn allow them to construct a
sense of what society expects a girl or a boy to be like. The sex-gender system approach emphasizes the dominance men maintain over women through political

Table 3.1   Approaches to the Study of Gender Differences

APPROACH	HOW GENDER IS CONSTRUCTED	EXAMPLES
Socialization	Through learning from adults, the media, peers, and the like what kinds of behavior are expected of women and men.	Boys are given trucks and tools for birthday presents; girls are given dolls and stuffed animals. Boys are admonished not to cry; girls are allowed to cry.
Sex-gender system	Through the constraints of an economic and social system that restricts women's behavior in ways that favor men.	Women are paid less than men for working at the same job. Women who work outside the home are still expected to be the primary caregivers to children, even if they are married.
Biosocial	Through biologically based (e.g., genetic, hormonal) differences that have evolved over the history of the human existence.	Boys will sometimes insist on playing with trucks and tools even if they are given dolls and stuffed animals.
Psychoanalytic	Through relations with women caregivers early in life, which cause women to internalize a sense of connectedness to others and men to internalize a sense of separateness.	Women, on average, may find it easier to form close relationships with others; men may find it easier to be separate from others.
Symbolic interactionist	Through continual reinforcement of gender differences because of the everyday behaviors of women and men.	Husbands who are very competent outside the home will claim they're not good at washing dishes or changing diapers, and their wives will agree with them and do these tasks.

and economic systems, customs and traditions. (See *Families in Other Cultures: China's Missing Girls* on p. 104.) The biosocial and psychoanalytic approaches both suggest that girls and boys may have deep-seated predispositions toward certain types of behaviors. The biosocial approach emphasizes genetic and hormonal influences, while the psychoanalytic approach emphasizes the children's experiences with women caregivers. Finally, the interactionists argue that gender is too problematic to be created merely through childhood socialization; rather, it must be created and recreated in the everyday lives of adults. Throughout life, they argue, people construct and maintain gender differences through their everyday interactions with others.

Despite their different perspectives—or perhaps because of them—sociologists who have studied gender (along with their colleagues in anthropology, history, and psychology) have made important contributions to our understanding of the family. First, they have demonstrated that the roles men and women play in families are in part socially and culturally constructed. Indeed, many sociologists would argue that such differences are almost entirely constructed by conscious social forces. But even those who believe that there is a psychoanalytic or biological component to gender-role distinctions would agree that our society greatly exaggerates these distinctions. That is, even if one believes that on average women are predisposed to relate somewhat better to infants and small children than men, that does not explain why so few husbands share the care of older children. Biology cannot explain why a brilliant lawyer is unable to clean a table. Psychoanalytic theory cannot explain why the great 1950s liberal Adlai Stevenson told the 1955 graduating class of Smith College (a private liberal arts college for women) that their place in politics was to "influence man and boy"

Families in Other Cultures — *China's Missing Girls*

American fathers may have a slight preference for sons over daughters—studies show that married couples are somewhat less likely to divorce if they have boys than if they have all girls (Morgan, 1988). But most expectant couples are very happy if the woman gives birth to a healthy child of either gender. This is not as true in some other cultures. Consider China: Its families traditionally were patrilineal [➡ p. 42], defined as a kinship system in which descent is traced solely through the father. In such a system, a father transmitted his family line through his sons. His daughters, upon marrying, become part of their husbands' family lines. Moreover, China's families were also **patrilocal,** meaning that a young wife goes to live in her husband's parents' home. As a result, from the parents' perspective, daughters neither continue the family line nor contribute to the family's well-being as adults. Sons on the other hand, continue the family line, and are expected to remain at home to care for their elderly parents. Especially in rural areas where help with farm labor is highly valued, this patriarchal system created a distinct preference for sons over daughters. If a newly married man's wife gave birth to a girl, his relatives would console him with the saying that having a daughter brings in a son.

Many other cultures also have strong son preferences (see Das Gupta & Bhat, 1997, on India). But when the continuing preference for sons in China collided with the government's desire to reduce its rate of population growth, the consequences for girls—and for gender relations in general—were dramatic. China is the most populous nation on earth, making up one-fifth of humankind. In 1979, it instituted a "one-child policy," which limited urban families to one child and allowed most rural families only two. Because the state controlled people's access to jobs, housing, land, and consumer goods, it could—and did—penalize families that exceeded the limit.[1]

Under this rule, having a daughter precluded having a son. Consequently, the strict policy evoked resistance. In a normal population, women give birth to about 106 boys for every 100 girls. (Because males have higher death rates, these numbers even out as the boys and girls age.) In China the sex ratio was very close to 106 to 100 in the 1960s and 1970s, before the one-child policy (Zeng et al., 1993). The ratio in 1995, the latest year for which good information is available, was 117 boys for every 100 girls (Peng & Huang, 1999). Clearly, many fewer girl babies are being reported than would ordinarily have been born; they have become known as the millions of "missing girls" (Riley, 1996).

No one knows for sure what is responsible for this discrepancy. One factor is underreporting of girl babies who are hidden, sent to live with friends or relatives elsewhere, or given up for adoption (Zeng et al., 1993). Because these girls are unreported, they will have more difficulty obtaining state-controlled medical care, education, and later in life, housing and employment. In some cases, families abandon newborn girls, often in places where they can be found and placed in overburdened orphanages, brimming with girls but bare of boys. Recent reports also suggest the importance of sex-selective abortions. The number of sophisticated ultrasound machines, which can determine the sex of a fetus, increased greatly in China in the 1980s and early 1990s. Some parents are learning the sex of fetuses through ultrasound tests and then selectively aborting females (Riley & Gardner, 1997). And finally, a small number of parents may be allowing their infant daughters to die of neglect—not breastfeeding them as long as boys, for example—or even killing them.

The Chinese government argues that the sharp drop in birthrates will benefit women as well as men because women suffered more than men in previous economic crises (Riley, 1997). However, critics charge that the current policy reflects the lower value placed on women than on men. It places great pressure on Chinese women to bear sons at any cost.

patrilocal A kinship system in which newly married couples live with the husband's parents

through the "humble role of housewife" (Chafe, 1972). Moreover, biology can't explain the social changes in gender roles and family life that have occurred over the past few decades, or even the past few centuries, because evolutionary change is slow. Consequently, the biological and psychoanalytic approaches may not be very useful to a sociologist who is trying to explain social change—although they might be helpful in determining the difficulty of bringing about social change. In this book the social and cultural construction of gender will be relevant to discussions of changing conceptions of sexuality (Chapter 7), patterns

In a one-child system, Chinese couples are often happier if they have a boy than a girl.

Moral questions aside, the one-child policy has helped China's economic development by reducing population growth. But it is beginning to cause problems: As the first one-child generation reaches adulthood, young men are finding a shortage of young women to marry because of the sex-ratio imbalance. The elderly, who traditionally in China have relied on their children—especially their sons—for support, find they have fewer children, and often no sons, to care for them. The Chinese government is realizing that it will have to increase its support of the elderly greatly as a result. News reports suggest that it is easing up on enforcing the policy and allowing exemptions in some areas (Rosenthal 1998).

Ask Yourself

1. Has anyone in your family ever expressed disappointment at the birth of a girl? If so, what was the reason for desiring a boy?
2. Aside from the patrilineal nature of Chinese culture, what other reasons might account for China's missing girls?

[1]Market-oriented economic reforms in China have reduced the power of the government to enforce the one-child family policy because more people now obtain jobs themselves through the labor market.

www.mhhe.com/cherlin

of courtship, dating, and spouse choice, and the relationships between married or cohabiting couples (Chapter 8).

Second, sociologists of gender have taught us that gender distinctions sometimes (some would say *always*) reflect differences in power between men and women. Adlai Stevenson's speech was meant to convey to the Smith graduates how important their restricted political role was. But women whose only political influence is through their husbands are not equal in political power to men. After the rise of the feminist movement in the 1960s and 1970s and the increases in the number of women elected to political office, no male politician would make Stevenson's statement. Feminist scholars argue, moreover, that power differences do not stop at the family's front door; rather, the roles women play within marriages often reflect their husbands' greater power—in particular, his greater economic power. Said differently, the lesson is that families are not islands isolated from the rest of society; rather, the relations of power and inequality that hold outside the home can also extend within it. Differences in power and the allocation of work within the household will be examined in Chapter 9. Other chapters will include discussions of the effects of male domination on family law and policy (Chapter 6), domestic violence against women (Chapter 12), and the economic circumstances of divorced women (Chapter 13).

Looking Back

1. **How might biological influences affect the behavior of women and men?** There is some evidence that biological differences in the development of male and female embryos could account for some of the gender differences in children's and adults' behavior. Studies have found a correlation between gender-typical behavior and exposure to higher levels of male sex hormones before birth. Biologically based differences only exist "on average"; individuals can show a wide range of behavior. And social influences such as parental upbringing and education can counteract biological predispositions.

2. **How do sociologists distinguish between the concepts of "sex" and "gender"?** Sociologists use the term *sex* to refer to biologically based differences between women and men and *gender* to refer to differences that are social and cultural, and therefore constructed by society. Gender differences often reflect male domination over women. Nevertheless, in some instances social and biological influences on gender differences are difficult to disentangle.

3. **How do children learn the gender roles of women and men?** According to the socialization approach, young children learn stereotypical gender roles from parents, peers, teachers, and the media. The emphasis in this approach is on conscious, social learning. In general, children are taught to think that boys and men are aggressive, competitive, and independent, whereas girls and women are less aggressive, more nurturing, and better at enabling and maintaining personal relationships. From these lessons, children mentally construct the concept of gender. In fact, some scholars argue that gender is such

a broad and central identity it should not be considered merely a social role.

4. **How does everyday life reinforce gender differences?** Sociologists who take the interactionist approach believe that gender roles need continual reinforcement throughout life. In their view, everyday social situations, such as cleaning up the kitchen after dinner, recreate and reinforce gender distinctions. Starting in childhood, people create their own gender roles through interaction with others. In doing so, they "take the role of the other"— that is, they consider how others would react if they were to behave in a certain way.

5. **Are gender differences built into the structure of society?** Many gender theorists argue that gender differences are built into the structure of nearly all societies through patriarchy, a social order based on the domination of men over women. Society, they charge, turns limited sex differences into pervasive gender differences and enshrines them in a sex-gender system. Gender theorists argue that gender should be seen as a basic source of social stratification, as important as race and class.

6. **What have been the contributions of gender studies to our understanding of the family?** Sociologists who study gender have demonstrated that the roles men and women play in families are in part socially and culturally constructed. Indeed, many sociologists would argue that gender differences are almost entirely social constructions. Sociologists have also shown that gender-role distinctions often reflect differences in power between women and men.

Thinking about Families

1. Could there be more than two genders? An in-between gender?

2. Is the evolutionary past of humans likely to influence the behavior of women and men today?

3. If patriarchy is a system based on the domination of women by men, do Americans live in a patriarchal society?

4. **The Public Family.** Do parents, peers, and teachers prepare boys for success in the work world more than they prepare girls?

5. **The Private Family.** Does everyday life reinforce gender differences in families in ways we usually don't notice?

Key Terms

berdache   78

biosocial approach (to gender differences)   84

capitalism   97

comparable-worth discrimination   99

gender   80

gender roles   85

gestation   82

interactionist approach (to gender differences)   93

intersexual   80

masculinity   101

patriarchy   95

patrilocal   104

peer group   88

psychoanalytic approach (to gender differences)   91

reflexivity   96

sex   80

sex-gender system   96

socialism   99

socialization   86

socialization approach (to gender differences)   86

social role   85

Families on the Internet   www.mhhe.com/cherlin

*Note: While all the URLs listed were current as of the printing of this book, these sites often change. Please check our web site (**http://www.mhhe.com/cherlin**) for updates.*

Information on gender and on women's issues abounds on the Internet. On the liberal side, the Institute for Global Communications maintains WomensNet, which provides many links to sources of information (**www.igc.org/igc/womensnet**). On their web page, click on one of the links to news reports in the "Headlines" column. What types of issues is this organization most concerned about? A conservative perspective is available from Concerned Women for America (**www.cwfa.org**).

For an abundance of factual information on labor force issues such as earnings differences be-tween women and men, go to the home page of the Women's Bureau at the U.S. Department of Labor (**www.dol.gov/dol/wb**). The Women's Bureau is concerned with working conditions, including equal pay, for women employed outside the home. On their statistics and data page, look at their list of the leading occupations for women. In how many of these occupations are 90 percent or more of the workers women? For background on the issue of equal pay, download their report, "Equal Pay: A Thirty-Five Year Perspective."

Part Two

Race, Ethnicity, Class, and the State

F amilies are affected by the larger social structures in which they are embedded. Differences between the social roles of women and men are so fundamental to families that they were discussed in Part One. There are other important divisions in society as well. Social class differences—the ordering of individuals in a society according to power, prestige, and privilege—influence the ways that family life is organized. Racial and ethnic groups also differ in their family lives. In addition, the government has a substantial influence on families through its policies and programs. • Chapter 4 explores the differences in family life among social classes. It includes an examination of how trends in the economy have affected families. The kin networks of the poor, the changing attitudes toward gender roles among the working class, and the importance of the conjugal family among the middle class are also discussed. • Chapter 5 considers the consequences for families of the divisions in society along racial-ethnic lines. The distinctive family patterns of African Americans are discussed. The chapter also examines commonly used categories such as "Hispanic" and "Asian," which include groups that vary greatly in their family patterns. For example, the differences among Mexican-American, Puerto Rican, and Cuban families are described. • In modern nation-states such as the United States, the state itself exerts a strong influence on family life. It does so through the many programs that can influence individuals' decisions about whether to marry, to work outside the home, to buy a house in the suburbs, and so forth. Chapter 6 explores the influence of the state; in particular, it focuses on the political conflicts over measures that affect women's autonomy and that provide income assistance to poor families.

chapter 4

Social Class and Families

Looking Forward

1. What factors determine the social class position of families?

2. How have changes in the American economy since the 1970s affected families?

3. What do the kinship networks of many low-income families do for family members?

4. What are the characteristics of typical working-class and middle-class families?

5. What are the distinguishing features of upper-class kinship patterns?

At the end of the twentieth century, the American economy was a study in contrasts. For those in the upper class, times were very good. Consider the new Rolls-Royce Corniche convertible, which offers beauty and status for a mere $360,000. When Rolls-Royce introduced the car in the United States in 1999, it quickly sold out. Sales of the Jaguar XKR, a relative bargain at $80,000, were up 80 percent early in 2000. That year the Hinckley Company, a yacht builder in Maine, expanded production to reduce the waiting list for its sailboats, which cost from $400,000 to over $1 million (Walsh, 2000).

Even among the less-than-wealthy, Americans with a college education had recently seen an improvement in their economic position. But those Americans without a college education did not share in the end-of-century prosperity. Consider Kenny and Bonita Merten and their two sons, for example. This rather typical working-class family was profiled in the *New Yorker* magazine in 1995.[1] Kenny earned $7.00 an hour at his first job after marrying Bonita in 1972. His wage peaked at $11.80 an hour on a factory assembly line in 1993. But he was fired; his supervisors said he worked too slowly and his work was of low quality. Kenny said that factories can be choosy and prefer to hire young men. In 1995, working for a company that puts up barriers, sandbags, and signs on highways, he made $7.30 an hour.

In the time since Kenny and Bonita married, the cost of consumer goods more than tripled because of inflation. Consequently, Kenny would have to be earning over $24 an hour to match the buying power he had in 1972. Instead, by 1995 his buying power had declined by 70 percent. "I know I'll never be able to earn $11.80 again," he said. "The most I can hope for is a seven-dollar-an-hour job that doesn't involve swinging sandbags. Maybe if I come home less tired at the end of the day, I can handle an evening job."

Bonita worked the evening shift at a local nursing home. A recent raise had boosted her pay to $7.40 per hour. Even with two incomes, the Mertens were often unable to pay all of their bills. "1995 has been a pretty hard year in a pretty hard life," she said. "We had our water shut off in July *and* August, and we ain't never had it turned off even once before."

Kenny and Bonita married at the end of a period of great prosperity in the United States. In the 1950s and 1960s, the American economy was strong and

---

[1] See Sheehan (1995). The entire article is reprinted in Andew J. Cherlin. *Public and Private Families. A Reader,* 2nd ed.

wages were rising. In fact, the average income of full-time workers, adjusted for inflation, doubled. Many workers without college educations found jobs in the expanding factories of the nation. But the 1973 decision by oil-producing countries to sharply raise the price of oil sent the U.S. economy into a tailspin, and wages were stagnant until the late 1990s for workers without college degrees. Even after the United States adjusted to the oil price shock, it became clear that our employment base in manufacturing was not growing the way it had in the past. Corporations moved production overseas in order to take advantage of the lower wages paid to workers in the developing world. Computers and other technologies allowed employers to replace some workers with machines, such as the robots on automobile assembly lines. How recent changes in the economy may have affected families—and, more generally, how social class position, income, and poverty affect families—are the topics that will be addressed in this chapter. Let's discuss first, however, what sociologists mean by social class.

Defining Social Class

Class is a concept that is hard to define precisely but difficult to avoid using. It is used in two senses by sociologists. In the first sense, which derives from the writings of Karl Marx, a person's class position in a capitalist society, such as the United States, is determined by his or her relationship to "the means of production" (Marx, 1977). The latter term refers to the things necessary to produce goods and services, such as buildings, machines, and capital (money that can be used to buy equipment, place advertisements, hire workers, and so forth). Marx called those who owned the means of production the capitalist class. Those who traded their labor for wages paid by the capitalists he called the working class. Marx's basic, two-class model, however, is inadequate as a complete description of class in contemporary societies. It does not take into account, for instance, managers who are hired by business owners to supervise the work of others; independent professionals such as doctors in private practice; and owners of small businesses such as mom-and-pop grocery stores. As a result, many sociologists, some of them still working in the Marxian tradition, have developed multiclass models.[2]

Class in the second sense, for which the term **social class** is used, refers to an ordering of all persons in a society according to their degrees of power, prestige, and privilege. Whereas Marx's model focuses on economic factors, this definition is broader in scope. To be sure, wealthy people often have substantial power, prestige, and privilege, whereas poor people rarely do. Still, these three kinds of rewards are not tied solely to how much money a person has or to whether he or she owns a business. **Power** is the ability to force a person to do something even against his or her will. Most powerful people, however, are able to exercise their power most of the time without resorting to force or coercion. The president of the United States—who from 1992 to 2000 was Bill Clinton, a man without great wealth who did not even own a home—has perhaps more power than any other person in the world. He is the Commander in Chief of the world's most powerful military, and he has great political power as Chief Executive. **Prestige** refers to honor and status in a society. Supreme Court justices have prestige far greater

social class an ordering of all persons in a society according to their degrees of power, prestige, and privilege

power the ability to force a person to do something even against his or her will

prestige honor and status in a society

[2]See, for example, Wright (1976).

Middle-class families have a secure, comfortable income and can afford privileges such as a seashore vacation.

than their incomes alone would predict. A cardinal of the Catholic Church has great prestige and substantial power (by, for example, threatening excommunication) but little income. **Privilege** is a special advantage or benefit enjoyed by some individuals. It is more closely tied to income and wealth, for people with enough money can usually buy a privileged style of life, from beautiful homes to fine vacations to private schooling for their children.

In practice, a person's power, prestige, and privilege are heavily determined by her or his income, occupation, and education. Instead of a few distinct classes, this ordering might produce numerous layers, or "strata," in a society; consequently, some sociologists argue that, strictly speaking, one should not use the term "social class" in this second sense but rather speak of "social stratification."[3] However, the former term, which is more common, will be used in this book. This chapter will distinguish among families in four broad classes according to power, prestige, and privilege. In real life, there is considerable overlap among these four social classes, and not all families fit neatly into one category. Therefore they are meant as ideal types. Introduced by Max Weber, the term **ideal type** refers to a hypothetical model that consists of the most significant characteristics, in extreme form, of a social phenomenon. It is useful for understanding social life, even though any real example of the phenomenon may not have all the characteristics of the ideal type.

privilege a special advantage or benefit enjoyed by some individuals

ideal type a hypothetical model that consists of the most significant characteristics, in extreme form, of a social phenomenon

---

[3]A good discussion of how to define social class and social stratification can be found in Kohn and Slomczynski (1990).

FOUR SOCIAL CLASSES

The four social classes are upper class, middle class, working class, and lower class. When American adults are asked which of these four classes they belong to without any instruction about what these categories mean, they overwhelmingly choose either middle class or working class. For instance, in the 1998 General Social Survey (GSS), a biennial national survey, 4 percent of respondents said they were upper class, 46 percent said middle class, 45 percent said working class, and 5 percent said lower class (Davis & Smith, 1999). Both extremes apparently sound unpleasant to people, probably because of the stigma of being a "lower-class" person or the embarrassment of admitting to be "upper class." By most reasonable criteria, the lower class is larger than 5 percent. For instance, 10 percent of American adults had incomes below the poverty level in 1998 (U.S. Bureau of the Census, 1999c).

There is little consensus on the size of the upper class or on just how to define it. In general, **upper-class families** are those that have amassed wealth and privilege and that often have substantial prestige as well. They tend to own large, spacious homes, to possess expensive clothes and furnishings, to have substantial investment holdings, and to be recognized as part of the social and cultural elite of their communities. Upper-class husbands tend to be owners or senior managers of large corporations, banks, or law firms. Their wives are less likely to work for pay outside the home than women in other social classes. Some engage in extensive volunteer work, whereas others devote considerable time to entertaining and socializing with other couples to help advance their husbands' careers. There is little good research on the upper class, and this chapter will focus mainly on the other three social classes.

Middle-class families are those whose connection to the economy provides them with a secure, comfortable income and allows them to live well above a subsistence level. Middle-class families can usually afford privileges such as a nice house, a new car, a college education for the children, fashionable clothes, a vacation at the seashore, and so forth. The jobs that middle-class men and women hold usually require some college education and are performed mainly in offices and businesses. Middle-class men tend to hold higher-paying jobs such as lawyer, pharmacist, engineer, sales representative, or midlevel manager at a corporation. Jobs such as these usually have some prestige and include fringe benefits such as health insurance, paid vacations, paid sick leave, and retirement pensions. Women in general are underrepresented in the higher-paying professional and managerial occupations, although their numbers are growing. Women professionals still tend to be found in occupations that require a college education, such as nursing and teaching, but that don't pay as much as male-dominated professions. Relatively few women work at blue-collar jobs such as plumber or bricklayer, although again their numbers are growing in jobs such as assembler and bus driver. In contrast, a large number have lower-paying jobs in offices and businesses, such as secretary, department store clerk, and telephone operator. These clerical jobs came to be seen as "women's jobs" early in the twentieth century, and until recently nearly all the workers in such positions were women (Oppenheimer, 1970).

Working-class families are those whose incomes can provide reliably for the minimum needs of what people see as a decent life: a modest house or an apartment, a car, enough money to enroll children at a state or community college,

upper-class families families that have amassed wealth and privilege and that often have substantial prestige as well

middle-class families families whose connection to the economy provides them with a secure, comfortable income and allows them to live well above a subsistence level

working-class families families whose income can reliably provide only for the minimum needs of what other people see as a decent life

and so forth. Working-class men tend to hold manual jobs in factories, automobile repair shops, construction sites, and so forth. Layoffs are more common in manual occupations than in the office and business jobs middle-class men tend to have, so working-class men are more vulnerable to periods of unemployment. Moreover, working-class men and women are less likely to work a full week and have fringe benefits. Clerical jobs, such as secretary, or service jobs, such as cafeteria cashier or hospital orderly, are common among working-class women; a minority work in factories.

lower-class families families whose connection to the economy is so tenuous that they cannot reliably provide for a decent life

Lower-class families are those whose connection to the economy is so tenuous that they cannot provide reliably for a decent life, either because they work steadily at low-paying jobs (the so-called "working poor") or because they are frequently unemployed. They may live in deteriorated housing in neighborhoods with high crime rates. They may not be able to afford adequate clothing for winter, and they may need government-issued food stamps to purchase enough food. Lower-class men, who have little education and few occupational skills, can find jobs that pay only at or slightly above the minimum wage and that have few, if any, fringe benefits and little security. Lower-class women may work at low-paying service jobs; some are dependent on cash assistance from the federal and state governments to low-income families—commonly known as "welfare." A small minority of lower-class families are homeless. As their numbers grew in the 1980s and early 1990s, "homelessness" became a much discussed social problem. (See *Families and Public Policy:* Homeless Families: The Tip of the Iceberg, on pages 118–119.)

CHANGING CONCEPTIONS OF SOCIAL CLASS

These categories, although useful, cannot capture the full complexity of the social stratification of families. They date from the social scientific literature of the mid-twentieth century, when most families had two adults present and when relatively few married women worked outside the home. Most women at that time attained their class position through their husbands' occupations. Consequently, the categories work best in describing the position of two-parent, single-earner families. In contrast, when both spouses work for pay, the line between a middle-class family and a working-class family, or between a working-class and a lower-class family, becomes less clear. Suppose, for example, that the wife and the husband are both high school–educated factory workers, with a joint income that provides a comfortable standard of living. Is this family working class because of the occupations of both spouses and their lack of college education, or is it middle class because of their comfortable joint income? There is no clear answer to this question. Still, when married women are asked what class they belong to, they rely heavily on their husbands' jobs; but their own education and income also figure into their answers (Baxter 1994; Davis & Robinson, 1988).

Moreover, in the growing percentage of families in which a father is not present, the mothers' class position is not well defined. In these cases, the mothers' occupation, education, and sources of income (including child support payments, if any) must obviously be the criteria. A woman who works as a secretary might be comfortably middle class only as long as she is married to a man who earns substantially more than she does. If the marriage ends, her standard of living is likely to drop. Whether she necessarily becomes "working class" is unclear—she has less income, but she retains the same level of education and many of the same friends and interests. (More will be said about the economic situation of single-parent families below and in subsequent chapters.)

Families and the Economy

To return to the story of families and the changing U.S. economy, every old city has seen the closing of factories that had formerly provided full-time jobs at good wages to workers without college educations. For example, the Singer Sewing Machine Company dominated Elizabeth, New Jersey, from its founding in 1873 until it closed in 1982—its market reduced by ready-to-wear clothes and its competitive edge lost to plants in developing countries that paid workers far lower wages. One longtime worker told anthropologist Katherine Newman:

> *I worked there forty-seven years and one month. I was one of many people in my family. My niece worked there. My two brothers, my father. You see, Singer's in the old days, it was a company that went from one generation to the other* (Newman, 1988).

THE IMPACT OF ECONOMIC RESTRUCTURING

Young workers without a college education have been particularly hard hit by the changes in the U.S. economy. The growth of semiskilled and skilled manufacturing jobs has slowed because of two factors. The first is technological change, such as growing use of computers in offices and factories; the new technologies allow firms to replace workers with machines. The second factor is the movement of factory production to developing nations such as Taiwan and Mexico, where wages are much lower. Due to these changes, there is a growing shortage of full-time jobs, with fringe benefits, that pay substantially above the minimum wage and yet are available to persons without a college degree. These were the kinds of jobs that used to allow high school–educated young adults in this country to support a family. The strong economy of the late 1990s improved this situation, but the basic problem remains.

More and more, what's available to young workers without a college education are low-paying service and unskilled manual-labor jobs. In addition, the employment arrangements available to these workers are changing. The older, "standard" job that dominated American industry until recently involved full-time work that continued indefinitely and was performed under the supervision of the employer. But since the 1970s, there has been a sharp increase in **nonstandard employment:** jobs that do not provide full-time, indefinite work directly for the firm that is paying for it (Kalleberg, 2000). Nonstandard employment includes part-time work, work for temporary help agencies, work for subcontractors who perform services (such as maintenance) for larger firms, and short-term contract work. By the late 1990s, more than 20 percent of the workforce was composed of part-time or temporary workers (U.S. Bureau of Labor Statistics, 1999b). Most of these jobs offer low or moderate wages, but even middle-class jobs are not immune to the trend. As corporations downsize their managerial workforce to save money, middle-aged white-collar workers can find themselves replaced by temporary or contract workers.

In contrast, the 1950s and 1960s were prosperous times for American families. Between 1945 and 1973, the average income of full-time workers, adjusted

nonstandard employment
jobs that do not provide full-time, indefinite work directly for the firm that is paying for it

Homeless Families:
The Tip of the Iceberg

*I*t is one of the paradoxes of public debates about the family that the phenomenon of homeless families, which emerged in the 1980s, has received so much attention compared with the more general problems of poor families. To be sure, homelessness is worthy of public concern. Although few homeless families were visible in 1980, their numbers appear to have increased over the 1980s and 1990s (Rossi, 1994). By one recent estimate, more than one million children experience a spell of homelessness each year in the United States (Burt & Aron, 2000).

But these families are just a small share of the number with incomes so low that they face the same kinds of risks the homeless face. Several studies have examined why some families become homeless and others don't, and why the number of homeless families has increased.

To become homeless, a family must have both a low income and weak ties to other kin. That is to say, it must have too little money to pay rent and too few relatives to call upon for shelter. Single-parent families are vulnerable on both counts; their incomes tend to be low, and they cannot rely on the resources of a second parent and his or her kin. That is why the vast majority of homeless families are sin-

gle-parent families (Jencks, 1994). Yet most poor single-parent families are not homeless. Peter Rossi (1994) estimated that in the mid-1980s more than two million single-parent families had incomes that were less than half the poverty level. At most, about 5 percent of these families spent a night in a shelter during a given year.[1] The other 95 percent constitute what Rossi calls the "precariously housed," those who are especially vulnerable to homelessness through deep poverty and the lack of a second parent, but who manage to avoid it.

Why have a small but growing percentage of the poor appeared at the door of public shelters for the homeless since 1980? Several factors contribute. Rossi emphasizes the consequences of the restructuring of the economy, especially the worsening job opportunities for young adults without a college education. In an analysis consistent with this chapter, Rossi argues that the decline in manufacturing jobs has undercut the ability of many young adults to earn enough to marry. It may also have reduced the ability of other relatives to provide assistance. Moreover, marriage may have decreased among the poor and nonpoor alike for other reasons having to do with women's greater eco-

nomic independence or with cultural changes such as increased individualism. In any event, the growth of poor single-parent families was a key factor. According to Rossi's estimates, in the 1970s there were 1 million single-parent families with incomes less than half the poverty level but by 1991 there were 2.5 million.

Rossi and Christopher Jencks also note that the average value of welfare payments has dropped substantially since the mid-1970s because Congress and state legislatures did not adjust them for increases in the cost of living. So families with no other sources of income have been less able to afford housing. (Since the time limits on welfare were passed by Congress in 1996 there have been some reports suggesting increased homelessness; see Chapter 6.) Moreover, the supply of low-cost rental housing has declined since the 1980s, either through demolition, remodeling into high rent properties, or neglect and abandonment by slum landlords (Koegl, Burnam, & Baumohl, 1996).

The increases in very poor single-parent families in the 1980s and 1990s were real. It must be noted, though, that the increase in serious poverty affected many more "homed" families than homeless families, and yet public attention focused

for inflation, doubled (Levy & Michel, 1991). Young men and women growing up in the 1950s and 1960s expected that they would eventually earn more than their parents, just as their parents were earning more than their grandparents. In 1973, however, the Organization of Petroleum Exporting Countries raised the price of oil fourfold and the economies of the Western nations plunged into recession. Income growth stopped, and wages were stagnant until the late 1990s. Particularly hard hit were the kinds of entry-level jobs for which young parents tend to be qualified. The impact of the economic slump was so great that in 1996, the average 30-year-old husband with a high school degree earned

The number of homeless families seems to have increased during the 1980s and 1990s.

on the latter. Americans seemed far more sympathetic to families living in shelters than to the larger and growing number of poor families sharing cramped quarters with relatives or barely avoiding eviction from their own apartments.

The public reaction suggested that most Americans think every family ought to have a home, whether or not their poverty is in any sense their own making. Homelessness grabbed the guts of many Americans whose hearts were hardened against stories of hardship among the poor. But family homelessness is just the tip of the iceberg of serious poverty among families—an iceberg that grew ominously in the 1980s and early 1990s. Passengers aboard the Titanic learned the hard way that it's dangerous to ignore the rest of an iceberg. We would be wise to heed their lesson.

Ask Yourself

1. Has anyone in your family even been forced to move into a friend or relative's home, or perhaps into a homeless shelter? If so, what caused the crisis?

2. What can the government do to prevent families from becoming homeless? What can families themselves do?

[1]I derived this figure by dividing 100,000 by 2 million and converting the result to a percentage.

www.mhhe.com/cherlin

20 percent less than a comparable man in 1979 (Levy, 1998). Consequently, the gap between the wages of more-educated and less-educated male workers has widened considerably since the 1970s. To make matters worse, housing prices have risen substantially.

UNEQUAL DISTRIBUTION OF INCOME

Not only have wages failed to grow, but earnings have become more unequal. While the earnings of workers without a college education have been decreasing,

FIGURE 4.2
Percent of families with
children under 18 that had
incomes below the poverty
line, for whites, blacks, and
Hispanics, 1959–1996.
(*Source:* U.S. Bureau of the
Census, 1999i.)

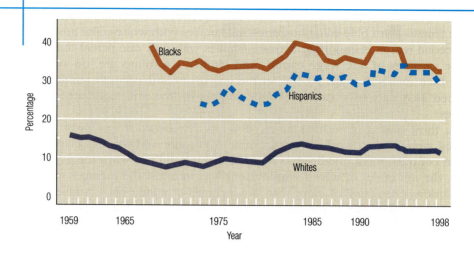

began to weaken in the mid-1970s, however, the percentage of families in
poverty began to rise for African Americans and whites and, by the mid-1990s,
had attained levels not seen since the 1960s. Since then, poverty rates have declined. Hispanic families showed a sharp rise in poverty between 1972 and 1982
and little change until a recent decline. In 1998, about one in eight white families
with children under 18, and about three in ten Hispanic and African-American
families with children under 18 were living in poverty, according to the official
definition, as were 19 percent of all U.S. children.

Not only did poverty increase until the late 1990s, it also became increasingly
concentrated in the growing numbers of households headed by divorced, separated, never-married, or widowed mothers. Whereas about one-fourth of all
poor families were headed by single mothers in 1960, more than one-half were
headed by single mothers in 1998 (U.S. Bureau of the Census, 1999c). These
single-parent families tend to remain poor longer than low-income two-parent
families, according to a national study, the Panel Study of Income Dynamics
(PSID), which is based on multiple interviews of the same families since the late
1960s. Economist Greg Duncan examined families in the PSID that were poor at
any time between 1969 and 1978 and isolated two groups of low-income families: the "temporarily poor," who fell below the poverty line only 1 or 2 years
during the 10-year period, and the "persistently poor," who fell below the line
at least 8 of the 10 years. Most temporarily poor families, he found, had an adult
male in the household, but 61 percent of the persistently poor families were
headed by a single woman. In addition to family structure, race also affected the
likelihood of being persistently poor. Regardless of family structure, most of the
temporarily poor were white, but 62 percent of the persistently poor were
black. Families in which the head was both black and a single woman made up
31 percent of the persistently poor (Duncan, 1984). (The connections among
race, family structure, and poverty are explored in the next chapter.)

Prospects for Dual-Earner Couples

During the 1970s and 1980s,
many families in the middle of the income distribution kept up with the cost of
living only because wives took jobs outside the home. Figure 4.3 shows the trends
since 1973 in the median incomes of three kinds of families. (The median is the

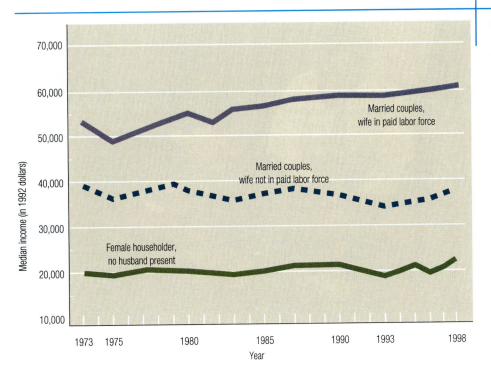

FIGURE 4.3
Median income of three types
of families, 1973–1996.
(*Source:* U.S. Bureau of the
Census, 1999k.)

midpoint in the distribution, the point at which as many families have higher incomes as have lower incomes. All dollar figures are expressed in 1992 dollars, adjusted for increases over time in the cost of living.) The bottom line shows that there was little change in the median incomes of families that were headed by women without husbands present. The middle line shows how married-couple families without wives in the paid labor force fared. The median income for this group also showed little change—a sharp break from the increases of the 1950s and 1960s. The only increase in income came for married-couple families in which the wife worked for pay, as shown by the top line. The gap between the median incomes of single-earner married couples and dual-earner married couples rose from about $11,000 in 1973 to about $26,590 in 1998 (U.S. Bureau of the Census, 1999b). With housing prices rising and young men's wages declining, families needed a second income to live the kind of lives they aspired to. An increasing number of them chose to have wives enter the paid labor force.

These income trends led economist Frank Levy, in his study of U.S. income distribution since the 1940s, to write, "The most striking development is in families' connection to the economy" (Levy, 1987). In the 1940s, Levy notes, most families had two parents and one earner, whether they were rich or poor. There wasn't much variation in family structure. Yet by the end of the century, more than half of the wealthier families had two earners, while most poor families had no earners or only one earner. In the 1940s, the key economic difference between families was how much the husband earned. Today, the key difference increasingly is whether or not there is a husband in the household at all. As the link between family structure and poverty grows stronger, persistent poverty is becoming the property of single mothers and their children and prosperity is becoming the property of dual-earner, two-parent families.

were raised primarily by their grandmothers because their teenage mothers were too young to assume the main responsibility for raising them. This alternating-generation pattern of childrearing also occurred in a low-income African-American neighborhood studied by Linda Burton (1990). In both communities, a woman's first experience as the primary caretaker for a new baby often did not occur until she became a grandmother. The two central roles in the women-centered kin networks, Harvey argued, were, first, the grandmother who is also a "mother" to her grandchildren and, second, the young mother who, still in the care of her own mother, is something of a sister to her own children. Marriage, wrote Harvey, was usually a "secondary alliance" compared with the grandmother-mother-child axis.[6]

The extended kinship ties of the women-centered network help its members survive the hardships of poverty. If the members of a household have little to eat or are evicted from their homes, relatives and friends in their network will provide whatever assistance they can. Sisters or aunts who are themselves poor will nevertheless give food or money because they know that in the future they may need emergency help. In this way, the kinship networks of the poor spread the burdens of poverty, cushioning its impact on any one household and allowing its members to get by from day to day. In a widely cited study of The Flats, a low-income African-American neighborhood in the Midwest, anthropologist Carol Stack found that individuals could draw upon a complex network of relatives and friends that extended over many households (Stack, 1974).

In fact, individuals actively cultivate these networks so that they will have assistance when they need it. For example, Stack writes of Lydia, a woman in The Flats who did not need assistance from kin as long as she was married and therefore did not want to be obligated to them. Instead of sharing with kin, Lydia used the money she and her husband were earning to buy a house and furniture. She

[6]Harvey (1993), quoted at 199. Instead of "women-centered," Harvey uses the term "uxoricentric," drawn from anthropological terminology.

generally refused to trade clothes or lend money, and on the few occasions when she and her husband gave something to a relative, they never asked for anything in return. Then, however, Lydia's marriage broke up. During the five-month period when the marriage was ending, Lydia suddenly began to give things to relatives. She gave some of her nice clothes to her sisters and nieces, a couch to her brother, and a television set to her niece (Stack, 1974).

By giving away these things, Lydia was attempting to create a kinship network that she could rely on when she was no longer married. Her actions are typical of how poor people actively construct extended kin networks by exchanging goods and services with others who are in need. Poor people cannot afford to rely solely on *assigned kinship*—the more restricted set of kinship ties that middle-class people acquire automatically at birth and when they marry: father, mother, grandparents, husband, wife, children. Rather, they make use of *created kinship* to recruit assistance wherever it can be found. [➡ p. 18]

The Costs of Kin Networks   Yet membership in such a kinship network is not without cost—which is why Lydia was reluctant to exchange resources with kin as long as she was married. Because an individual's meager income must be shared with many others, it is difficult for her or him to rise out of poverty. Stack described what happened when an older couple unexpectedly inherited $1,500. At first, they wished to use the money for a down payment on a house. Then other members of their network, upon learning of the windfall, asked for help. Several relatives needed train fare to attend a funeral in another state; another needed $25 so her telephone wouldn't be turned off; a sister was about to be evicted because of overdue rent. Moreover, the public assistance office cut their children off welfare temporarily. Within six weeks, the inheritance was gone. The couple acquiesced to these requests because they knew they might need assistance in the future. Even someone who finds a good job may not withdraw from a network unless she is confident that the job will last a long time.

Thus, these kinship-based sharing networks, admirable and necessary as a bulwark against destitution, can nevertheless serve to perpetuate poverty across generations. When another young woman in Stack's study decided to marry, the relatives and friends in her network tried to talk her out of it. Her contributions were valuable, and they did not want to lose her. Recognizing that she and her husband couldn't accumulate enough money to rise above poverty unless she left the network, the young woman married and then left the state that same night (Stack, 1974). In Potter Addition, a woman described how she and her husband moved to a farm outside town, only to see a stream of hard-luck relatives move in and out, eating their food. Of one relative who hoarded his food while eating hers, she said, "To this day, I can't figure out why I didn't throw him out." But then she recalled to the interviewer the many earlier times when she and her husband had received assistance from her guest (Harvey, 1993). Turning aside the demands of kin is a step poor people are reluctant to take unless they are sure they won't need help in the future. The problem is that unless a person denies some requests, it is difficult to accumulate any savings, and without savings it is difficult to leave the network.

WORKING-CLASS FAMILIES

How do sociologists view working-class families, perched above poverty although typically not by much? The predominant picture of working-class families still comes from several widely cited studies conducted in the 1950s, 1960s, and early 1970s. For example, after living in a working-class Italian-American neighborhood in Boston for eight months in 1957 and 1958, Herbert Gans reported that daily life centered around the family circle, a group of relatives and friends who lived near one another and who socialized largely with one another (Gans, 1982). Most households contained the conjugal family of husband, wife, and children, but conjugal families were embedded in the larger extended family and in many ways were secondary to it. Married couples tended to live near the wife's mother, who provided frequent assistance and emotional support. A study of working-class families in London in 1955 by Michael Young and Peter Willmott also found a strong bond between the wife and her "Mum," who tended to live nearby (Young & Willmott, 1986). When members of the family circle in Gans's neighborhood socialized, the women sat in one room and the men sat in another.

Gender-Role Segregation   In fact, women and men's worlds were highly segregated.[7] In the economic realm, it was seen as men's place to earn money and women's place to care for the children and the home. Even though low incomes often led wives to work at least part time outside the home, the ideal remained the breadwinner-homemaker family. Being the sole earner was a source of pride for men, an ideal to strive for. As one husband is quoted as saying in Lillian Rubin's study of working-class families in 1972:

> *She doesn't have to work. We can get by. Maybe we'll have to take it easy on spending, but that's okay with me. It's worth it to have her home where she belongs* (Rubin, 1992).

But this picture of working-class families is now out of date. Gans, Young and Willmott, and Rubin have reissued their books with new introductions and postscripts. All of them report that the distinctiveness of the working-class family has faded somewhat. The family circle is not as central to the sons and daughters of the Italian Americans Gans studied, he concluded in 1982, because greater affluence has reduced the need for mutual assistance, because migration to the suburbs has spread relatives apart, and because resistance has grown to the conformity that the family circle demands (Gans, 1982). In other words, the more-prosperous (compared with the 1950s) next generation did not need as often to borrow money, clothes, or food from their parents and siblings. Moreover, it is harder for the sons and daughters to socialize because they don't live as close to one another as family members of their parents' generation did. And the cultural drift toward individual fulfillment clashes with the pressure to maintain the same lifestyle as other members of the circle. According to Young and Willmott, writing in 1986, migration out of the working-class neighborhood of London they studied has loosened the bond between the daughter and her mum.

Gans and Rubin both also observe that the strict division of roles between wife and husband has weakened, although most men still do substantially less of the childcare and housework. Rubin notes that even when the women in her original study were working outside the home, they defined themselves primarily as wives and mothers. Paid work was something they did to help their families, but it was not an important part of their identity. Many shared their husbands' views that, ideally, they ought to stay home. By 1992, wrote Rubin in a new intro-

---

[7]See also Elizabeth Bott. *Family and Social Network* (London: Tavistock, 1957).

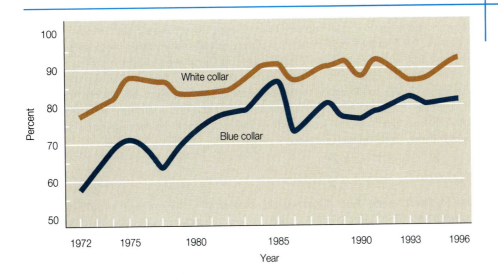

FIGURE 4.4
Percent approving of a married woman earning money in business or industry if she has a husband capable of supporting her, for married men under 50, by occupation, 1972–1996. (*Source:* Davis & Smith, 1996.)

duction to her book, these attitudes had changed: Women viewed employment as a proper activity, necessary to maintain their families' lifestyles and also a source of satisfaction and self-esteem (Rubin, 1992).

Changing Attitudes toward Gender Roles   The General Social Survey (GSS) provides further evidence of the changes among working-class families in attitudes about married women working outside the home. In most years since 1972, the GSS has included the question "Do you approve of a married woman earning money in business or industry if she has a husband capable of supporting her?" For each year in which the question was asked, Figure 4.4 shows the percentage who approved among married men under age 50, divided into two groups. The first group (top line) includes men with white-collar occupations: professionals, managers, sales, and clerical workers. These are the kinds of occupations that men in middle-class families are more likely to have. The second group (bottom line) includes those with blue-collar occupations, the kinds that men in working-class families are more likely to have: factory workers, people who operate machinery, and skilled and unskilled laborers. As you can see, in 1972, blue-collar husbands were substantially less likely than middle-class men to approve of a married woman earning money. Yet by the mid-1990s the gap between the two groups had narrowed greatly. Although both occupational groups grew more likely to approve of a married woman working for pay, blue-collar husbands had changed their opinions more. Thus, the figure supports the claim that working-class men have become more accepting of wives' employment probably because of the increasing economic importance of wives' earnings to working-class families.

At all times during the two decades covered by the GSS, most women said they approved of married women earning money in business or industry even if they had a husband capable of supporting them. In 1977, the GSS asked whether respondents agreed with the statement "It is much better for everyone involved if the man is the achiever outside the home and the woman takes care of the home and family." Among married women under 50, a majority of those who had worked last at clerical or blue-collar jobs said that they agreed—they thought it was better if the man were the achiever. Only among women professionals and managers did a majority disagree. These responses suggest that many married women in 1977 did indeed believe women, ideally, shouldn't work outside the home and that this belief was strongest among those who might be termed working class. By the early 1990s, however, clerical and blue-collar women were much more likely to disagree with the statement than they had been one and a half decades earlier: Only about one-third agreed. This change in attitude fits Rubin's report that women in working-class families have incorporated paid employment into their image of a wife's proper role.

MIDDLE-CLASS FAMILIES

The Primacy of the Conjugal Family   The core of middle-class kinship in the United States has been the conjugal family of wife, husband, and children (Schneider & Smith, 1973). Typically, the middle-class conjugal family is more independent of kin than the working-class version. The married couple is expected to spend their income on their children and themselves rather than to provide financial assistance to siblings or other relatives. Any assets or savings are passed from parents to children, rather than being spread throughout a kin network. Income sharing is not as necessary, to be sure, because the standards of living of kin tend to be higher than among the working class or lower class. Yet standards of living are higher in part *because* it is expected that the conjugal family will spend its savings on a down payment for a house rather than doling it out to relatives who need train fare to attend funerals or to pay bills and *because* it is expected that the family will move away from kin, if necessary, to pursue better job opportunities.

A clever survey of adults in the Boston area in 1984 and 1985 demonstrated people's beliefs about the restricted kinship obligations of the conjugal family (Rossi & Rossi, 1990).[8] Alice and Peter Rossi presented 1,393 people with a set of "vignettes": brief, hypothetical descriptions of relatives and friends who were experiencing crises that might require "some financial help" or "comfort and emotional support." For example: "Your unmarried sister has undergone major surgery and will be bedridden for a few weeks. This problem is straining her financial resources." From a list of relatives and friends (e.g., child, father-in-law, cousin, neighbor), eight crises (e.g., "run out of unemployment benefits and no job in sight"), and two obligations ("to offer some financial help," "to offer comfort and emotional support"), a computer program selected one relative or friend, one crisis, and one obligation at random and printed a vignette. The process was repeated until 26 crisis vignettes had been generated randomly to present to each of the survey respondents. We will focus on the vignettes for which the respondent was asked to rate "How much of an obligation would you feel to offer some financial help?" on a scale from 0 to 10, where 0 meant no obligation at all and 10 meant a very strong obligation.

The mean obligation scores for offering financial help, for 15 common relatives and friends, averaged across the various vignettes, was plotted by Rossi and Rossi on a "wheel of obligation," which is reproduced as Figure 4.5. The closer to

---

[8]Of the respondents, 94 percent were white, only 2 percent were unemployed, and over half were Catholic. The vignettes described here are a subset of a larger set of vignettes that the authors used.

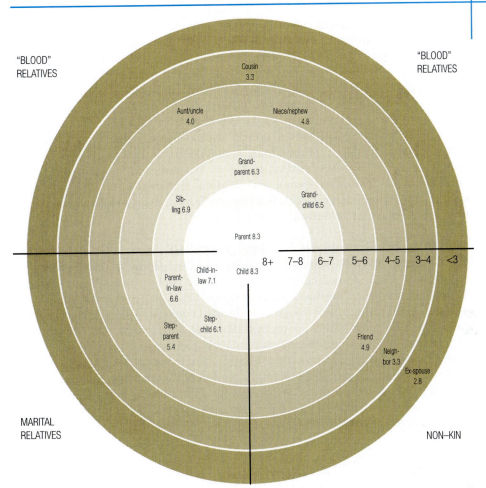

FIGURE 4.5
"Wheel of obligation": degree of obligation felt by survey respondents to various relatives and friends, for Boston-area adults, 1984–1985. (*Source:* Rossi & Rossi, 1990.)

the center of the wheel, the stronger the sense of obligation people felt: A mean score of 10 would be plotted at the hub of the wheel, whereas a mean score lower than 3 would be plotted in the outer circle. Note first that most of the mean scores are close to the hub, indicating that people felt a moderate to high level of obligation to most kin. Only neighbors and ex-spouses had mean scores lower than four. (Of course, these are hypothetical obligations; we don't know whether people actually would provide financial assistance this freely.) Since it did not make sense to ask these kinds of questions about a person's current husband or wife, there is no score for spouses. Other studies suggest that strong bonds of obligation exist between spouses (Schneider, 1980).

Note also that the highest levels of obligation were expressed toward a person's parents and children. Indeed, all the relatives in the two circles surrounding the hub are related to a person through a child, a parent, or a spouse. This pattern suggests that adults felt the most obligation to the members of the conjugal or single-parent families in which they grew up and to the conjugal or single-parent families in which they have had children. These vertical kinship ties—up and down the chain of generations from parents to children to grandchildren—engender the strongest feelings of obligation. They are created by direct descent and by marriage. Contrast the degree of obligation adults felt toward more distant relatives such as aunts, uncles, nieces, nephews, and cousins: None has an average score of five or above. Kinship ties from a person's marriage—even a second marriage—are stronger than kinship ties toward these more distant blood relatives. For instance, note that the adults felt more obligation toward a stepchild than toward a cousin or a nephew. Obligations to the conjugal family, and to one's parents, seem to take precedence over those to other relatives.

The image of kinship suggested by these findings is of a tall, solid tree trunk with skinny branches: The vertical axis is strong as one moves from parents to children to grandchildren, but the horizontal links are weaker as one moves from parents to uncles, or from children to nieces. Resources are passed from a person's parents to his or her spouse and children, and then to the grandchildren. Assistance to elderly parents is likely to be much more substantial and more common than assistance to elderly aunts and uncles.

The Role of Women in "Doing" Kinship   As will be discussed further in Chapter 11, it is women who do most of the helping of other kin. This is true even in middle-class families, which are more likely than lower- or working-class families to have a husband living at home. On average, women spend more time than men doing the work of kinship (di Leonardo, 1987). They are more likely to send cards and flowers on birthdays and holidays, to plan family get-togethers, and to help a frail elderly parent. Many men rely on their wives to keep these contacts alive and to provide assistance. "On topic after topic," wrote Rossi and Rossi at the end of their book, "we have found that ties among women were stronger, more frequent, more reciprocal [i.e., both giving and receiving], and less contingent on circumstances [i.e., not just given in a crisis] than those of men" (Rossi & Rossi, 1990).

UPPER-CLASS FAMILIES

Whereas the main economic task for families from other classes is to accumulate wealth, the main task for upper-class families is to preserve and increase their wealth. Traditionally, this has meant that upper-class parents take an active role in determining whom their children will marry. They know that their children will be highly desirable marriage partners, and they wish to obtain a good match: someone from a family that also has wealth or, at least, someone who is likely to help the children manage their wealth wisely. In England in the 1500s, rich families usually chose their child's spouse, creating what is termed an **arranged marriage.** When two wealthy families were involved, arranged marriages often seemed more like economic alliances than romantic partnerships. Indeed, historians suggest that there was little romance in many aristocratic marriages (Stone, 1977).

arranged marriage a marriage in which the parents find a spouse for their child by negotiating with other parents

However, by the 1600s, the ideals of companionship and intimacy in marriage spread and arranged marriages became less common. (They always had been uncommon among the poorer classes, who had less to gain by an arranged marriage.) Still, many parents strongly influenced their child's choice. Records from Hingham, Massachusetts, show that prior to 1700 families tended to marry their oldest daughters first, then their next oldest, and so on, suggesting substantial parent involvement (Smith, 1973). Records from Andover, Massachusetts, indicated that in the 1600s and early 1700s, sons tended to marry only when their fathers were ready to turn over control of their land (Greven, 1970).

Debutante balls offer upper-class parents the chance to introduce their daughters to young men from privileged backgrounds.

By the nineteenth century, parental influence over the timing of marriage and the choice of a partner had diminished substantially in the more prosperous classes. Even among the elite, it is likely that most children chose their spouse. Yet upper-class parents retained an indirect influence on their children's marriage partners through strategies that persist to this day. First and foremost was separate schooling. Wealthy children were much more likely to attend the nation's private boarding schools, where they met children from other wealthy families. John D. Rockefeller, Jr., heir to the most famous nineteenth-century fortune in the United States, met his future wife, Abby Aldrich, while attending Brown. Rockefeller certainly chose his wife; but he did so at an elite Ivy League university where, not coincidentally, the woman he chose came from a powerful Rhode Island family (Keller, 1991).

This pattern of separate education continued into the twentieth century. A study of marriage announcements in the Sunday *New York Times* from 1962 to 1972 found that 70 percent of the men and 84 percent of the women reported attending private schools, such as St. Paul's, Exeter, Andover, and Miss Porter's (Blumberg & Paul, 1975). Upper-class children were also more likely to attend elite universities: 52 percent of the men in the *Times* wedding announcements had attended an Ivy League college, and 29 percent of the women had attended one of the Seven Sisters colleges.

Until recently, at least, the vast majority of upper-class wives did not work outside the home. Still, wives of corporate executives and managers have had important roles to play in furthering their husbands' careers. The executive's wife was expected to host dinner parties, to attend charity events, to establish friendly relations with the wives of other executives, and to be ready to move to another city, should the executive be transferred. Not only her husband but also her husband's company expected that she would devote her efforts to his advancement. Hanna Papanek (1973) aptly labeled this phenomenon the "two-person career."

Kinship Networks among the Mexican Upper Class

It is well established that lower-class family members frequently belong to extended kin networks that share resources and provide support to one another. These networks enable individuals to survive the economic crises of poverty by turning to their relatives for aid. Among the middle class, extended kinship ties are less important. Yet among the upper class, the importance of kinship often rises once again (Goode, 1982). Anthropologist Larissa Adler Lomnitz has demonstrated the importance of kin in two studies of the extremes of poverty and wealth in Mexico City. First, she studied poor people living in shanty towns in the city—sprawling settlements made up of one-room shacks or brick cabins without running water. The residents of these neighborhoods survived by pooling their resources among a kinship network, much as the residents of Potter Addition or The Flats did (Lomnitz, 1977).

Lomnitz next studied kinship ties at the other end of the social spectrum, the Gómez family, which traces its roots back to Don Carlos Gómez, a nineteenth-century farmer and village trader (Lomnitz, 1987). In 1978, the Gómez family was a large, mostly wealthy network of business owners and their wives and children, comprising 360 people in five main branches. The businesses were privately held and family controlled, rather than being publicly held corporations. Prominent family members hired cousins, nephews, and brothers-in-law from their own branch, and sometimes from others, to work in their firms. It was expected that sons, who started to work for their fathers at an early age, would eventually take over the businesses. But as long as the father was alive, he retained control.

These economic arrangements, Lomnitz found, were supported by—or perhaps better said, made possible by—the structure of family and kinship. The basic unit was the grandfamily, a three-generation family composed of a father and mother, sons and daughters and their spouses, and grandchildren. Although married couples lived in their own households, the grandfamily members lived near one another and met often. For instance, once a week they went to their father and mother's home for a family dinner. The women of the grandfamily saw one another almost every day; moreover, the women kept in contact with women in other grandfamilies, maintaining the links of kinship. In each generation of each branch, at least one woman seemed to specialize in maintaining the links of kinship; Lomnitz called these **centralizing women.** Their conversations included not only personal news but also news about family businesses in their own branch and others. Frequent ritual events, such as christenings, first communions, marriages, and funerals, provided occasions for contact among members of different branches.

These extensive ties were useful for two reasons. First, wealthier family members were a source of employment and of money to invest in new business ventures. With so much wealth controlled by the family, individuals looked to their kin for economic opportunities. Second, kinship ties provided some protection against the risks of doing business. An individual could have trust, *confianza*, that a relative would abide by the terms of an agreement to produce, deliver, or sell goods. If a person broke a business agreement or was consistently unable to meet the terms of agreements, he would be subject to the ridicule and scorn of the other members of the family. Family ties thus enforced honesty and hard work.

Ask Yourself

1. Does your family participate in a close-knit kin network like those in Mexico? If so, for what reasons?
2. In the United States, wealthy families do not need the support of kin networks to do business. Why not?

www.mhhe.com/cherlin

---

centralizing women
Women who maintain the links among kin in large, extended families

Upper-class women are instrumental in maintaining ties among wealthy kin, as a study of a Mexican elite family demonstrated. (See *Families in Other Cultures: Kinship Networks among the Mexican Upper Class.*)

In sum, the upper class have historically sought to conserve their wealth and transmit it to their children first by arranging marriages, then by controlling access to land, and most recently by controlling whom their children meet. And in the twentieth century, they evolved a style of marriage in which wives' rewards came through supporting their husbands' careers. Let me caution, however, that we don't know the extent to which these patterns still hold as the twenty-first century begins. Starting in the 1960s, the elite universities enrolled more public school students and most of them became coeducational; consequently, the educational experiences of the children of the upper class may not be as distinctive as they were. Given the massive increases in the number of married women in the paid labor force—including increases in managers and professionals—it is not clear how many wives still devote themselves to the advancement of their husbands' careers. There is little current research on the upper class, in large part because sociologists are more interested in studying disadvantaged groups.

Social Class and the Family

Across all social classes, the changing economic roles of women and men over the past few decades have altered family lives. In the 1960s and 1970s, social commentators debated whether it was "necessary" for married women to work. After all, standards of living had been far lower in the first half of the twentieth century, and yet few married women had worked outside the home. However, the economic slide after 1973 more or less ended that debate. Among the working class, objections to married women working outside the home faded as decent-paying entry-level blue-collar jobs—the kind of jobs young husbands used to take—dwindled. Whereas in the 1970s wives' employment was seen by many working-class couples as a sign of a husband's failure to provide adequately for his family, now it is seen as a necessary and acceptable contribution.

Among middle-class couples with college educations, the employment situation has been better; still, as noted earlier, men's wages have stagnated until recently. Only two-earner couples have been beating inflation consistently. Moreover, the price of housing has risen far faster than wages, placing the American dream of homeownership out of reach of more and more single-earner couples. In the 1950s and 1960s, payments on a median-priced home required just 15 to 18 percent of the average 30-year-old man's income. That figure rose to 20 percent in 1973 and then doubled to 40 percent in 1987 (Levy & Michel, 1991). Consequently, for middle-class couples, too, wives' employment is seen as necessary and acceptable.

To be sure, there are other reasons for the increase in wives' employment over the past few decades. As birthrates declined after the baby boom, the number of years in which women have intensive childrearing responsibilities also decreased. Raising one or two children is simply not a full-time, lifelong job. Knowing this, many young women keep closer ties to the labor market before and even during the years in which they have small children. Having work experience is also prudent protection against the growing risk of a divorce and single motherhood.

Not all the forces for change have been economic. The rise in divorce, for example, has both economic and cultural roots (see Chapter 13). People's expectations about what constitutes a good life have also changed. Young middle-class couples could, in theory, aspire only to the standard of living of the late 1940s and early 1950s, which for many consisted of an apartment or a small, one-story home, one car, a clothesline in the backyard for drying the laundry, one telephone, no stereo system, few restaurant meals, no airplane travel, and of course no VCRs or computers, and still keep one parent home all day. This is not

Extended families are more important to the working class than the middle class.

an appealing prospect in a country where people have gotten used to a higher standard that is promoted by advertising and reinforced by the media.

It is hard to foresee, therefore, any scenario under which fewer married women would work outside the home. To the contrary, further increases are likely. Moreover, the rise is likely to widen the income gap between middle-class families, on the one hand, and working-class or lower-class families. Inequality will increase because better-off families have recently sent, and are now sending, large numbers of women into the workforce. In contrast, wives from lower-income families were the first to enter the workforce in large numbers beginning at midcentury, a trend that actually reduced family income inequality (Levy & Michel, 1991). Future growth in married women's labor force participation, however, will come increasingly from the middle class.

With regard to kinship, perhaps the most important difference among the lower-class, working-class, and middle-class families studied in this chapter is the relative autonomy of the parent-child unit from other kin. In lower-class families, ties between mothers and an extended network of kin are often a more important source of support to the mother than ties to the father of her children—even if the mother is still married to the father. In Potter Addition, a young mother's tie to her mother was usually stronger than her tie to her husband. In The Flats, mothers' ties to the fathers of their children commonly were weak, even nonexistent. Two-parent households are more often present in working-class families, yet ties to other relatives, particularly to the wife's mother, remain important sources of support. In contrast, the two-parent household of the middle-class family is typically independent of day-to-day support from other kin, in large part because family members and their kin have less need for economic assistance. Nevertheless, family members seem to retain strong obligations to assist relatives from whom they have descended—parents and grandparents—and relatives who descend from them.

Still, it is becoming increasingly difficult to speak of "the" social class position of a family anymore. The old way of measuring a family's social class, namely by considering only the husband's occupation and income, is inadequate, given the greater number of dual-earner and single-parent families. In addition, it may be that husbands have a firmer grip on their class position than their wives. As will be discussed in the chapter on divorce, women who gain a high-social-class position by marrying men with high-paying jobs can lose that position if their marriages break up. After a divorce many middle-class women experience downward mobility as they reenter the job market after a long absence, receive modest child support payments, and perhaps sell their family home and move to a less-expensive neighborhood.

Social class is not the only way American society classifies families. Rather, racial and ethnic distinctions are also frequently made. It is to racial and ethnic differences in family patterns that we now turn.

Looking Back

1. **What factors determine the social class position of families?** The degree of power, privilege, and prestige a family enjoys determines its social class position. There are four broad social classes in the United States: upper-class families, middle-class families, working-class families, and lower-class families. These classes are ideal types; in real life many families do not fit unambiguously into a single one of these categories. Because this social class structure developed in an era when most families had two parents but only the father worked outside the home, two-earner and single-parent families are particularly difficult to categorize.

2. **How have changes in the American economy since the 1970s affected families?** The restructuring of the U.S. economy since the 1970s has caused a shortage of well-paid semiskilled and skilled jobs that do not require a college education—the kind of jobs less-educated young men used to rely on to support their wives and children. Now many of these jobs no longer exist, or have been moved to other countries where wage rates are much lower. Since 1973, the year of the oil price rise, family incomes have increased only among the growing number of families in which both husband and wife work for pay outside the home. Persistent poverty has become concentrated among single-parent families.

3. **What do the kinship networks of many low-income families do for family members?** Lower-class families often depend on women-centered kinship networks, in large part because men cannot consistently earn enough to support their children. In these networks, poor people share what little they have with relatives and friends in order to cushion the hardships of poverty. But membership in a sharing network can prevent an individual from rising above poverty, because accumulating savings while at the same time providing financial help to others is difficult.

4. **What are the characteristics of typical working-class and middle-class families?** Working-class kinship patterns are more likely to involve two-parent households than lower-class kinship patterns, but the larger extended family is still important. Studies dating back a few decades suggested that working-class wives remained very close to their mothers, with whom they exchanged support, and that the worlds of working-class men and women were highly segregated. However, these distinctive qualities of the working-class family appear to have lessened substantially over the past decade or two. Middle-class kinship patterns are distinguished by a greater emphasis on the parent-child unit compared with ties to other kin. Middle-class families feel most strongly obligated to spouse, parents, and children. The result is a kinship structure with a strong vertical axis of support from parents to children to grandchildren, and weaker horizontal axes of support to other blood relatives.

5. **What are the distinguishing features of upper-class kinship patterns?** Upper-class kinship patterns are distinguished by greater parental influence over a child's choice of spouse, so as to preserve or enlarge the family's wealth and social position. Parents influence this choice by educating their children separately from the other social classes. Past studies have suggested that upper-class wives often work hard behind the scenes to advance their husbands' careers. How much of the traditional upper-class kinship patterns still exist today is not known.

Looking Forward

1. How is immigration changing the racial and ethnic balance in the United States?

2. How has African-American family life changed over the past several decades?

3. What are the family patterns of the major Hispanic ethnic groups?

4. What are the distinctive characteristics of the family patterns of Asian Americans?

5. How does the concept of "social capital" apply to immigrant families?

6. What has been the role of kinship ties in American Indian family life?

Hai Nguyen and Cuong Dan were high school students in New Orleans when Min Zhou and Carl L. Bankston, III (1998) studied them from 1993 to 1995. Both Hai and Cuong had fled Vietnam with their families as political refugees. Hai came from a refugee camp in Malaysia; Cuong left Vietnam in a boat. Both settled in a neighborhood of several thousand Vietnamese immigrants named Versailles Village, after the vacant apartment complex where relief agencies settled hundreds of Vietnamese families in 1985.

Hai told the two researchers that he planned to attend college. He hoped to enroll in one of two local universities, Tulane or Loyola, because friends from his neighborhood went there. Cuong said he had no intention of going to college. Despite their differing aspirations, both young men belong to what sociologists call "the **new second generation**": children who are either immigrants themselves like Hai and Cuong, or who were born to immigrants after their families arrived in the United States (Portes, 1996). Some members of the new second generation and their families are scattered across the nation; others, like Hai and Cuong, have settled in ethnic enclaves with other immigrant families.

new second generation
children who are either immigrants themselves or who were born to immigrants after their families arrived in the United States

The new second generation is on the leading edge of a great increase in racial and ethnic diversity projected for the United States over the next few decades. In 1965, a revision of the immigration laws allowed larger numbers of non-Europeans to enter the country. Since then, the number of Latin American and Asian immigrants to the United States has grown rapidly.

Already the new second generation is larger than most people think. By 1997, one out of five children in the United States was either an immigrant or the child of immigrants (Hernandez & Charney, 1998). According to Census Bureau estimates, if immigration rates and birth rates remain at current levels, by 2030 only 50 percent of American children will be non-Hispanic whites (U.S. Bureau of the Census, 1993d).

This chapter will examine the implications for family life of the growing racial and ethnic diversity of the American population. For the public family, the challenge is to socialize and educate a diverse generation of children so that they can be productive citizens. For the private family, the challenge is to understand the varying kinds of family relations among the many racial-ethnic groups. Clearly they differ from each other in some significant ways. Let's take a closer look at them.

These immigrants, shown taking the oath of U.S. citizenship, are among the large number of Latin Americans and Asians who have immigrated since the law was changed in 1965.

Racial-Ethnic Groups

All this, however, begs the question of what constitutes a racial or ethnic group. We generally think of racial groups as people with a common set of physical features that distinguish them from other groups. The boundaries of racial groups, however, vary from country to country and from the past to the present. For instance, in other New World countries such as Brazil, there is no sharp division between black and white but rather a continuum of skin color distinctions. As recently as 1910, the U.S. Census included a mixed black and white ancestry category labeled "mulatto." Yet during the twentieth century, the image of two distinct groups, black and white, became fixed in American culture, despite the mixed racial ancestry of many Americans.

Other racial categories remain more flexible, in part because none carries the long history of slavery and racial discrimination faced by African Americans. Consider the individuals in the United States who are descended from the original, indigenous peoples of North America. These peoples include American Indians, the name still often used for Native Americans in the contiguous 48 states, and Alaska natives, such as the Eskimo and Aleut. The 2000 Census questionnaire presented "American Indian or Alaska native" as one of 15 "race" categories. Of the 4.1 million people who chose it, 40 percent chose a second category, most often "white" (U.S. Bureau of the Census, 2001). Since the 1970 Census, the American Indian population has increased at a far higher rate than counts of births and deaths during the 1970s would suggest (Snipp, 1989; O'Hare, 1992). The increases in reporting were greater in California and the East than in traditional American Indian population centers. This pattern suggests that individuals residing in metropolitan areas far from tribal lands and having some Native American ancestry have become more likely to think of themselves as American Indians (Eschbach, 1993).

*H*ow can a child whose parents have different races have only one? Logically impossible, you might think; but until 1997, federal government statistical policy required that individuals check just one race for themselves or their children on official forms such as the Census of Population. And before 1997, the government recognized four races: (1) white, (2) black, (3) Asian and Pacific Islander, and (4) American Indian and Alaska Native. It also required its agencies, in a separate question, to ask about membership in one ethnic group: Spanish or Hispanic origin.

Interracial couples represent a small but growing share of all families. About 2.5 percent of married couples were interracial in 1998 (U.S. Bureau of the Census, 1999g). Their numbers are large enough, however, that they have become a visible presence and a reminder that the old categories may not fit much longer. In 1993, Representative Thomas Sawyer of Ohio, chair of the subcommittee of the House of Representatives that oversees the census and statistical policy, listened to the testimony of Susan Graham, an advocate for multiracial children and a mother of two of them. She told Representative Sawyer:

When I received my 1990 census form, I realized there was no race category for my children. I called the Census Bureau. After checking with supervisors, the Bureau finally gave me their answer, the children should take the race of the mother. When I objected and asked why my children should be classified as their mother's race only, the Census Bureau representative said to me, in a very hushed voice, "Because in cases like these, we always know who the mother is and not the father" (U.S. House of Representatives, Committee on Post Office and Civil Service, Hearings, 1994).

Ms. Graham said her son had been classified as white by the census but black by the school he attended. Her solution: Add a new category, "Multiracial," to the official government list and to the 2000 Census. Yet this seemingly logical step was opposed by many of the political leaders of the minority groups that would be most affected. They opposed a multiracial category because the statistics that agencies collect are used not just to describe the population but also to determine whether federal laws have been carried out. Congress and the courts use the information on race and ethnicity from the census to determine whether congressional districts are providing fair representation to blacks and Hispanics. Agencies that oversee banks use the information to determine whether banks are willing to loan money to members of racial-ethnic groups. Other agencies use the information from employers to determine whether employers are discriminating on the basis of race or ethnicity. Consequently, the political leaders opposed a multiracial category because they feared it would lower the number of blacks, Hispanics, or Asians counted in the census and would therefore dilute the political power that comes with greater numbers (Wright, 1994).

Faced with this dilemma, the government considered what, if anything, to do about Susan Graham's children and the many others like them when it fielded the 2000 Census of Population. In 1997, a government statistical committee decided that the 2000 Census (and all other government surveys) would allow individuals to choose more than one race; but it rejected a separate "multiracial" category. It also decided to place the question about Hispanic ethnicity before the question on race (rather than after it, which was the old policy), a change that probably increased the number of people who said they were "Hispanic." So when Americans filled out the 2000 Census, they saw the ethnic and racial questions shown in the figure. First they were asked whether they were "Spanish/Hispanic/Latino," and

the blue columns show, more than 80 percent of Asian-American family households were headed by a married couple, the highest percentage of any of the five groups. In contrast, just 44 percent of African-American family households were headed by married couples—the lowest percentage of any of the groups. Non-Hispanic whites, Hispanics, and Native Americans were in between. Correspondingly, African Americans had the highest percentage of family households headed by an unmarried woman and Asian Americans had the lowest. Few households in any group were headed by an unmarried male, as the middle columns show.[2]

[2](O'Hare, 1992). The data were taken from 1990 Census Summary Tape File 1C. By "unmarried," I mean never married, divorced, separated, or widowed.

United States Census 2000

→ **NOTE: Please answer BOTH Questions 7 and 8**

7. Is Person 1 Spanish/Hispanic/Latino? *Mark* ☒ *the "No" box if not Spanish/Hispanic/Latino.*

☐ **No, not Spanish/Hispanic/Latino**
☐ Yes, Mexican, Mexican Am., Chicano
☐ Yes, other Spanish/Hispanic/Latino – *Print group.* ↗
☐ Yes, Puerto Rican
☐ Yes, Cuban

☐☐☐☐☐☐☐☐☐☐☐☐☐☐☐☐☐

8. What is Persons 1's race? *Mark* ☒ *one or more races to indicate what this person considers himself/herself to be.*

☐ White
☐ Black, African Am., or Negro
☐ American Indian or Alaska Native – *Print name of enrolled or principal tribe.* ↗

☐☐☐☐☐☐☐☐☐☐☐☐☐☐☐☐☐

☐ Asian Indian   ☐ Japanese   ☐ Native Hawaiian
☐ Chinese   ☐ Korean   ☐ Guamanian or Chamorro
☐ Filipino   ☐ Vietnamese   ☐ Samoan
☐ Other Asian – *Print race.* ↗   ☐ Other Pacific Islander – *Print race.* ↗

☐☐☐☐☐☐☐☐☐☐☐☐☐☐☐☐☐

☐ Some other race – *Print race.* ↗

☐☐☐☐☐☐☐☐☐☐☐☐☐☐☐☐☐

then they were asked their race. There were 15 choices, and for the first time, Americans were allowed to check all the categories that applied to them. Overall, only 2.4 percent of the population checked two or more race categories. But 5 percent of those who checked "Black, African American, or Negro" also checked another category, as did 14 percent of those who checked one of the Asian categories, 40 percent who checked "American Indian or Alaska Native," and 54 percent who checked "Native Hawaiian" or "Other Pacific Islander" (U.S. Bureau of the Census, 2001). Clearly, many members of minority groups think of themselves as having more than one race.

Ask Yourself

1. Have you ever been frustrated by questionnaires that require you to select just one racial or ethnic group to describe yourself or a family member? If so, what do you think of the excerpt from the Census 2000 form shown here?

2. Relate the controversy over the wording of the Census questions to the concepts of the public and the private family. What was the private family's interest in this matter? The public family's interest?

www.mhhe.com/cherlin

African-American Families

The economic ups and downs of the last half of the twentieth century had a profound effect on African Americans. In the 1960s, as the economy boomed and the civil rights movement lowered barriers, African Americans made unprecedented gains in employment and income. But the post-1973 economic slowdown hit African Americans hard, especially the men (Levy, 1998), many of whom had moved into industrial jobs in the 1950s and 1960s. In the 1970s, as growth in manufacturing jobs slowed, African-American men who did not have a college education watched their economic prospects plummet. African-American women had established a position in the growing service sector, so the changing economy did not affect them as much.

Table 5.1 Indicators of the Decline of Marriage among African Americans and Whites		
INDICATORS OF THE DECLINE OF MARRIAGE	**AFRICAN AMERICANS**	**WHITES**
The percentage of young women who will ever marry has fallen more for African Americans than for whites[a]	88% in 1950s → 64% in 1990s	95% in 1950s → 93% in 1990s
The percentage of children born to unmarried mothers has risen for both African Americans and whites[b]	38% in 1970 → 69% in 1998	6% in 1970 → 26% in 1998
The percentage of family households headed by one parent has risen for both African Americans and whites[c]	33% in 1970 → 58% in 1998	9% in 1970 → 23% in 1998

[a]Rodgers & Thornton, 1985; Goldstein & Kenney, 2000.
[b]U.S. Bureau of the Census, 1991e; U.S. National Center for Health Statistics, 2000d.
[c] U.S. Bureau of the Census, 1998a.

These great economic changes, in turn, had a significant impact on lower-class and working-class black families. Without a stable economic base, some African-American men were reluctant to marry, for fear they could not provide for their families. And some African-American women were reluctant to marry them. In fact, William Julius Wilson argued in two influential books that the drop in semi-skilled and skilled blue-collar jobs—their flight to the suburbs or to low-wage nations such as Mexico or Taiwan—is the major reason for the sharp decline in marriage among African Americans (Wilson, 1987, 1996). Yet since the 1960s, a sizable black middle class emerged for the first time in American history.

THE DECLINE OF MARRIAGE

That there has been a sharp decline in the place of marriage in African-American family life is not in doubt. To be sure, the decline of marriage has also occurred among whites, but it has not been as great. Table 5.1 presents three indicators of the decline of marriage among African Americans and whites. The first row shows that the proportion of young adults who will ever marry has fallen more for African Americans than for whites since the 1950s. At current rates, about 64 percent of African-American young adults would ever marry. As will be discussed in Chapter 13, black women are less likely to marry, more likely to separate from their husbands if they do marry, and less likely to remarry than white women. The second row shows that for both groups, the percentage of children born to unmarried mothers increased sharply between 1970 and 1998. By 1998, 69 percent of all African-American births were to unmarried women. And the third row shows that the percentage of family households (meaning households containing parents and children under 18) that were headed by one parent rose for both groups between 1970 and 1998. A majority of African-American family households are now headed by one parent.

When we include cohabitation in the picture, the differences between blacks and whites are smaller but still substantial. Let me define **union formation** as the process of beginning to live with a partner either through cohabitation or marriage. The first unions formed by blacks are almost twice as likely to be cohabitations (rather than marriages) than is the case for whites. Therefore, studies that only examine the timing of first marriages produce greater differences between blacks and whites than do studies that examine the timing of first unions,

union formation the process of beginning to live with a partner either through cohabitation or marriage

either marital or cohabiting. In fact, racial differences in the timing of first unions are only about half the magnitude of racial differences in the timing of first marriages (Raley, 1996).[3]

The Impact of Economics   African-American women and men seem to weigh economic considerations more heavily than white women and men in deciding when to marry—as might be expected, given their more precarious economic situation. For instance, in the 1987–1988 National Survey of Families and Households, never-married African Americans were more likely than comparable whites to rate such factors as "having one's spouse established in a job" as important in making the decision to marry (Bulcroft & Bulcroft, 1993). As noted earlier, job losses in the 1970s and 1980s hit African Americans especially hard. Fewer young black men work at all now than in the 1960s. According to a recent study, for every three black unmarried women in their twenties, there is roughly one unmarried black man with earnings above the poverty line (Lichter et al., 1992). Greater benefits available to mothers through public assistance may also have increased women's independence and reduced the pressure to marry. Studies suggest that the effect of welfare on marriage behavior is modest but may have increased during the 1980s (Moffitt, 1990).

In addition to job losses—or perhaps as a result of them—there are other reasons why young black women may face a difficult time finding a suitable spouse. Consider the terrible toll that violence and drugs are taking on young black men. Homicide rates for young African Americans have risen to appalling levels over the past decade. If the rates in 1998 were to continue, about 2 of every 100 black 15-year-old boys would die violently before reaching age 44.[4] The rates of imprisonment and institutionalization of young black males are also strikingly high. The prison population grew rapidly during the 1980s and 1990s, and about half of all inmates are black. On any given day, about 3 of every 100 black men in their twenties are behind bars. Moreover, about 1 of every 100 black men aged 18 to 44 is admitted to state and county mental hospitals each year, and others are incapacitated by drug addiction or alcoholism (Cherlin, 1992).

Is the decline in marriage, then, due to the shortage of men who are "marriageable," as Wilson calls them, by virtue of steady employment? Recent studies suggest two conclusions: (1) the employment problems of black men are indeed an important factor in the decline in marriage, but (2) the racial difference remains substantial even after employment problems are taken into account. Several demographic studies have measured the relative numbers of employed black men in the local areas or states where black women live. The authors find that black women are more likely to marry if they live in areas with greater relative numbers of employed black men—thus supporting Wilson's hypothesis. Yet they also find that the drop in the availability of employed men cannot account for all—or even most—of the widening racial gap in marriage rates. Robert Mare and Christopher Winship, using Census data from 1940 through the mid-1980s,

---

[3]Still, black cohabiting unions are less likely to lead to marriage (and more likely to lead to a breakup) than are white cohabiting unions (Manning & Smock, 1995).

[4]Author's calculation from homicide rates for black males 15–24 and 25–44 in U.S. National Center for Health Statistics (2000c).

Marriage has declined among African-American young adults at all educational levels

reported that although men who were employed were more likely to marry, the "recent declines in employment rates among young blacks are simply not large enough to account for a substantial part of the trend in their marriage rates" (Mare & Winship, 1991). Another team of sociologists, using data from a national survey that followed young adults for several years, found that lower numbers of employed black males were "a significant factor contributing to delayed marriage—and perhaps nonmarriage—among black women." Yet even after marriage market opportunities were taken into account, the rate of marriage among the young black women in the survey was still just 50 to 60 percent of the rate for comparable young white women (Lichter et al., 1992).[5] Reviewing the evidence in his most recent book, Wilson (1996, p. 97) acknowledges that "even though the joblessness among black men is a significant factor in their delayed entry into marriage . . . it can account for only a proportion of the decline in marriages in the inner city, including postpartum marriages."

A similar pattern can be seen in a comparison of Census data on the percentage of black and white family households that are headed by a married couple (as opposed to an unmarried woman or man). Figure 5.2 shows this comparison for family households at different income levels. As the reader can see, for both African Americans and whites, the higher the family's income, the greater is the percentage that are headed by a married couple. Clearly, among both African Americans and whites, married couples are less commonly found in low-income households. Note also, however, that at each income level, white family households are more likely to be headed by a married couple than black family households. Even when there are no income differences between the families being

[5]Other similar studies are summarized in Cherlin (1992).

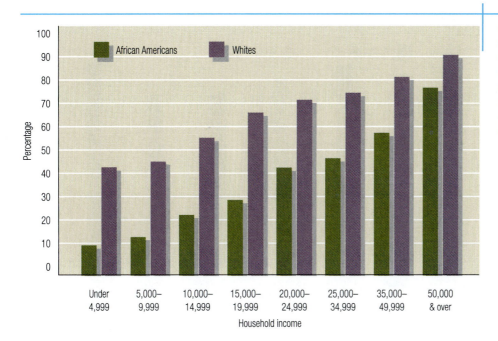

FIGURE 5.2
Percentage of family households that were headed by a married couple, by household income, for African Americans and whites, 1998. (*Source:* U.S. Bureau of the Census, 1999j)

compared, a racial gap still exists, and the gap is particularly pronounced among the poor and near poor. Economics, it seems, is part of the story of racial differences in family structure; but it is not the whole story.

The Impact of Culture   To more fully understand the differences in the family patterns of African Americans and whites, we must turn from economics to culture. There has been a resistance among liberal social scientists and activists to acknowledging the role of culture in shaping African-American family patterns. In part, this concern arises from the entirely negative way in which black families are often portrayed: problem-ridden, weak, overwhelmed. The strengths of black families are often overlooked. Figure 5.3, based on another comparison by Farley and Allen, helps to show where these strengths may lie. Graphed in Figure 5.3, across income levels from low to high, are the percentage of family households that are "extended"; that is, the percentage that contain relatives other than parents (or stepparents) and their children (Farley & Allen, 1987). Often the additional relatives are grandparents. Note that at all income levels—even among those earning more than $50,000 in 1980—black family households are more than twice as likely as white households to include a grandparent or other relative.

   In fact, grandparents play a stronger role in African-American families, on average, than they do among white families. In 1982, just before Frank Furstenberg and I carried out a national survey of grandparents, we visited a group of black grandmothers at a senior citizens' center in Baltimore. The grandmothers told us

FIGURE 5.3

Percentage of family households that are extended (contain relatives other than parents and their children), by family income, for African Americans and whites, 1980. (*Source:* Farley & Allen, 1987, Table 6.4)

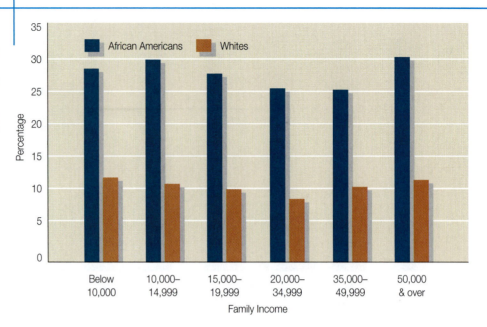

how involved they were with their grandchildren's upbringing. Most of them had lived at least temporarily with their grandchildren. One woman, for example, said about her grandchildren:

> *I was always named "sergeant"—"Here comes the sergeant." I loved them. I did for them, and gave to them, so that they had an education, so that they had a trade. I went to school regularly to check on them; they didn't know I was coming* (Cherlin & Furstenberg, 1992).

Very few white grandparents had this kind of hands-on involvement and authority. Our national survey confirmed that black grandparents, on average, were more involved in parentlike activities with their grandchildren than were white grandparents. Moreover, this racial difference still remained when we compared black and white grandparents of similar incomes. Even among working-class and middle-class families, black grandparents seem to play a stronger role than white grandparents.

More generally, in African-American families, ties to a network of kin are more important, compared with marital ties, than is the case in white families. When Alice and Peter Rossi measured the strength of people's feelings of obligations toward kin [➡ p. 130] they found that African Americans felt much stronger obligations to aunts, uncles, nieces, nephews, and cousins than did whites (Rossi & Rossi, 1990).[6] It follows, then, that when African Americans face adversity, they are probably more likely to seek help from kin than are whites. Moreover, African cultural patterns may still be influential [➡ p. 55]: In West Africa marriage is more of a process than an event, with childbearing sometimes occurring before the process is completed. In addition, poor white

[6]The comparisons controlled for the respondent's age, gender, and education.

families, such as those in Potter Addition [➡ p. 125], also show a pattern of re- lying less on spouses and more on parents and other kin (Harvey, 1993).

Recall that, in Potter Addition, the husbands were formally present in many households, even though they often had limited authority. In poor black fami- lies, husbands are less often present.[7] In fact, mothers' partners are often incor- porated into the kin networks on the basis not of whether they are the biologi- cal fathers of the mothers' children but rather whether they provide support to the children. Frank Furstenberg interviewed a group of low-income African Americans in an Eastern city who distinguished between "fathers" and "dad- dies." The former were biological fathers, whereas the latter were men who were providing support. A woman's current partner, for example, might be- come a daddy by helping with the care of a child from a previous relationship whose father provided little support. It was the daddies—the men who were providing assistance—not the fathers, who became members of the sharing net- works (Furstenberg, Sherwood, & Sullivan, 1992).

The chapter on class also discussed the strengths and weaknesses of relying on kin for support. Briefly, membership in a network of kin helps people subsist because it allows them to spread the burdens of poverty by borrowing when they are in need and lending when they are able. It also, however, makes escap- ing from poverty more difficult because it is difficult and risky for poor people to withdraw from the network. Moreover, not all poor black single-parent house- holds necessarily belong to strong networks. In a 1984 national survey, 68 per- cent of black single mothers, aged 19 to 26, lived in an extended-family house- hold, received half or more of their income from someone other than their husband, or received unpaid childcare assistance. The comparable figure for white single mothers was 54 percent (Hogan, Hao, & Parish, 1990). Still, 32 per- cent of the black single mothers in this study did not receive any of the three kinds of assistance.

The greater amount of help received by black single mothers than white single mothers is consistent with Stack's (1974) influential account of African- American kinship networks in "the flats" [➡ p. 126]. Yet statistical studies have found that black households, on average, don't receive more help from their social networks than do white households (Hofferth, 1984; Silverstein & Waite, 1993; Raley, 1995; Roschelle, 1997). In the 1987–88 National Survey of Families and Households, for example, black respondents did not report ex- changing more childcare and household help with kin living elsewhere than did non-Hispanic whites; in fact, on some measures non-Hispanic whites were more likely to exchange services (Roschelle, 1997). Another study of the same survey found that young black never-married adults were more likely to live with kin, see their mothers and siblings, and socialize with relatives than were comparable whites; but they were not more likely to receive assistance from kin (Raley, 1995).

Ever since Stack's work and subsequent ethnographic accounts (e.g., Mar- tin & Martin, 1978) appeared, most sociologists have accepted the premise

[7]Harvey did his fieldwork in Potter Addition in the early 1970s. In 1980, he reported, 56 percent of the poor families in the county were headed by a husband and wife, down from 71 percent in 1970. Still, the 56 percent figure is higher than that for poor black families nationwide in 1980, as Figure 5.2 shows.

that low-income black households give and receive more support from an extended network of kin than do white low-income households. Perhaps they do but statistical analyses of survey data just aren't rich enough in detail to substantiate the difference. There are, however, two other possibilities. The first is that the ethnographic studies, which were based on small samples and which usually lacked a comparison group of whites, overstated the differences between black and white families (Roschelle, 1997). The second is that poor people have fewer resources to share now than in the 1970s. We know, for instance, that the share of income going to the bottom fifth of the population has been declining. It may be that the poor are poorer than they were a generation ago, when widely cited studies of supportive kin networks were published. Some kin networks, therefore, may be overwhelmed by their members' needs.

In addition, studies of kin networks also show that support from kin tends to decline over time. In the 1984 national survey mentioned above, about two-thirds of the black single mothers were living with their own mothers at age 19, compared with about half of 21-year-olds and about one-third of 25-year-olds (Hogan, Hao, & Parish, 1990). This decline suggests that many single mothers move out of their mothers' homes as their children become older. Moreover, many of the grandmothers are themselves working outside the home and, therefore, are less available to their daughters. As the children enter adolescence, then, the support that kin provide to mothers may be substantially less than the support that was provided when the children were small. Several studies suggest that single mothers living without relatives provide less supervision and monitoring of their children's schoolwork and behavior than do mothers who live with a husband or other adult (Astone & McLanahan, 1991; Dornbusch et al., 1985). Despite their best efforts, many poor single mothers may have difficulty providing adequate parenting to their school-age children.

EXPLAINING THE DECLINE

How, then, can we explain the great decline of marriage among African Americans and the sharp increase in the proportion of children born to unmarried mothers? Although African Americans have had a higher proportion of single-parent households than whites since at least the beginning of the twentieth century [➡ p. 57], the difference has become more pronounced over the last few decades. There is no consensus as to why. Without doubt, changes in the economy are very important. In fact, some observers think the changes in families are entirely due to changes in the economy; others believe that culture may have played a role. In a previous book, I presented my interpretation. I will present it again here, with the caveat that no one can yet be sure exactly what mix of causes and effects was at work:

> *What happened in the last half of the twentieth century, I think, was that black families responded to two developments—one was a societywide shift in values and the other was a change in the labor market that was particularly damaging to blacks. The societywide shift was the weakening of the institution of marriage, [which was, in turn,] rooted in the increasing economic independence of men and women. [The decline of marriage] also reflected a cultural drift throughout the West to a more individualistic ethos, one which emphasized self-fulfillment in personal relations. It de-*

emphasized the obligations people have to others—including their spouses and partners. . . .

The second development also affected the entire nation, but it hit blacks especially hard: the economic restructuring described by Wilson and others. It appears to have decreased the growth of semiskilled manufacturing jobs, which can provide stable employment at adequate wages to people without a college degree. The greater growth of the service sector benefited black women more than black men because many of those jobs—secretaries, sales clerks, waitresses—had been labeled as women's work. The expansion of government social welfare programs may also have increased the economic independence of women and men. These changes in the labor market eroded the earning potential of black males, which in turn lessened their ability to support a wife and children.

The way that blacks responded to these broad-based cultural and economic shifts, I would argue, was conditioned by their history and culture. . . . Faced with difficult times economically, many blacks responded by drawing upon a model of social support that was in their cultural repertoire, a way of making it from day to day passed down by African Americans who came before them. This response relied heavily on extended kinship networks and de-emphasized marriage. It is a response that taps a traditional source of strength in African-American society: cooperation and sharing among a large network of kin. It was also a response consistent with the general movement away from marriage in the U.S. . . . Young black mothers relied heavily on their own mothers and other kin to help care for their babies. For most, a marriage followed several years later, and not necessarily to the father of their first child. Had these adaptations not been part of African-American culture, the retreat from marriage and the increase in the proportion of births to unmarried women probably would not have been as dramatic. The increased reliance on extended kin has allowed many poor blacks to have two or three children, pay their bills, and put food on the table—and obtain emotional support as well. But it is a response that also can have costs for parents and children (Cherlin, 1992b).

The costs, as described in the previous chapter, include the difficulty of escaping from poverty until *everyone* in your network escapes.

THE RISE OF MIDDLE-CLASS FAMILIES

Yet over the past few decades, some African Americans have managed to escape from poverty. Since the 1960s, a substantial black middle class has developed for the first time in U.S. history. A national study that followed for 15 years black children who were under age four in 1968 found that 13 percent of them lived in families whose incomes were always at least 50 percent over the poverty line. Another 8 percent lived in families that were never poor but whose incomes were close to the poverty line in at least one year (Duncan, 1991). Although these percentages are modest compared with those of white children (see Chapter 10), they are an overlooked social advance. Educational statistics also show great improvement. In 1998, 76 percent of African-American adults had graduated from high school, compared to 20 percent in 1960. During the same period, the percentage who had completed 4 or more years of college rose from 3 to 15 (U.S. Bureau of the Census, 1999l).

The newness of the black middle class means that most of its members have working-class or lower-class origins. Their parents typically did not accumulate

Since the 1960s, a sizeable middle class has emerged among African Americans. They are often ignored in the public focus on African-American poverty.

enough wealth to provide them with much of a nest egg or an inheritance. Consequently, they tend to have less money in assets (savings, investments, homes, cars) than comparable white middle-class people. For instance, a study in the mid-1980s found that black households had monthly incomes that were 62 percent of white incomes but that their median assets were only 9 percent of those of whites (Farley & Allen, 1987). As a result, their hold on middle-class status can be precarious. In words that only slightly overstate the case, Harriette Pipes McAdoo wrote that many black middle-class families are "only one paycheck from poverty" (McAdoo, 1988l).

In a study of the assets of respondents to the Census Bureau's Survey of Income and Program Participation in 1987 through 1989, Oliver and Shapiro (1995) also found much larger differences, on average, in wealth (assets) between blacks and whites than in income. Comparing college-educated blacks with college-educated whites, for instance, they found that whereas the blacks earned 76 cents for each dollar earned by the whites, blacks had assets of just 23 cents for every dollar of white assets. And if homes and cars were excluded from assets (leaving savings accounts, stocks, small businesses), black college graduates had *one cent* of assets for every dollar of white assets. Oliver and Shapiro ascribe the difference to three factors: (1) whites are more likely to inherit some wealth or borrow money for a down payment on a home or car from their parents; (2) whites can more easily obtain home mortgage loans from banks; and (3) homes in predominantly black neighborhoods don't appreciate in value as much as homes in white neighborhoods.

Moreover, many members of the new black middle class were able to move upward in part through the assistance of kin, such as siblings who helped pay for college or an uncle who provided a first job. These extended kinship ties tend to remain after a person has attained middle-class status, but the flow of assistance often reverses. The sister who has attained a job as a computer programmer may have an unemployed brother who needs a short-term loan to stave off his family's eviction from their apartment or a bright cousin from a poor family who needs financial help so he can go to college. Having benefited from the assistance of her kin on her way up the economic ladder, the computer programmer has a difficult time refusing their requests. Yet her salary may be insufficient to maintain her middle-class status as well as help all the relatives who are in need. The resultant financial pressure can create what Andrew Billingsley called "the mixed blessings of upward mobility" (Billingsley, 1992). Moreover, because of residential segregation, middle-class black neighborhoods tend to be closer to poor black neighborhoods, and in fact they usually contain some poor families. As a result, middle-class African-American parents may struggle to shield their children from the lure of street life, with its criminal behavior and drug usage. And middle-class African Americans must coexist with neighbors and relatives in the underground economy in ways most whites need not (Patillo-McCoy, 1999). Still, the growth of the African-American middle class is a success story that is too often lost in the understandable focus on the African-American poor.

Black churches have been a great source of social support to African Americans who have newly gained middle-class status. Throughout African-American history the church and the family have been the enduring institutions through which black families could gain the strength to resist the oppression of slavery, reconstruction, segregation, and discrimination (Berry & Blassingame, 1982). The church has served as a **mediating structure,** a midlevel social institution (other examples are civic groups, neighborhoods, and families themselves) through which individuals can negotiate with government and resist governmental abuses of power (Berger & Berger, 1983). It has been the greatest source of continuity, outside of the family, in the African-American experience. Today the church also serves as a link between the black middle class, many of whom have moved out of inner-city neighborhoods, and the black poor. Often by virtue of sanctuaries that are still in poor neighborhoods, churches provide a direct way for middle-class congregants to provide assistance to the poor (Gilkes, 1995). In some of the poorest black neighborhoods, which have lost both population and organizations over the past few decades (Wilson, 1996), churches are among the few nongovernmental institutions left.

mediating structures
midlevel social institutions and groupings, such as the church, the neighborhood, the civil organization, and the family

Hispanic Families

The label "Hispanic" covers groups that are so diverse with respect to family patterns that it makes little sense to combine them, yet that is the direction public discussions have taken. It lumps together recent immigrants with citizens whose families have been in the United States for generations, and white, middle-class political émigrés with darker-skinned, poorly educated laborers looking for work. The 2000 Census counted nearly as many Hispanics (35.3 million) as African Americans (36.4 million) (U.S. Bureau of the Census, 2001). Mexicans and Mexican Americans were by far the largest group, constituting about 65 percent of all Hispanics. Central and South Americans accounted for about 14 percent, Puerto Ricans for 10 percent, and Cubans for 4 percent (U.S. Bureau of the Census, 2000k).

MEXICAN AMERICANS

Mexican-American families occupy an economic level that is, on average, higher than that of Puerto Ricans and lower than that of Cubans. As was discussed in the previous chapter, Mexican poor and wealthy alike rely on kin networks for employment and support. In a country such as Mexico, where a strong central government has not always existed, kinship ties are also a way for the middle class to ensure trust and reciprocity in exchanges of money, goods, or property. Among the poor, kinship ties serve to help people shoulder the burdens of poverty. Recall that, according to anthropologist Larissa Lomnitz, the "grandfamily," the unit composed of parents, their children, their children's spouses, and their grandchildren, was the fundamental family unit in Mexico, rather than the nuclear family of parents and children (Lomnitz, 1987). Often the oldest generation lived separately but near their children and grandchildren.

Because the census does not measure kinship ties across households, we cannot directly test Lomnitz's claim. Nevertheless, the census data do show that Mexican-origin households are more likely than non-Hispanic white households to have at least three adults (Bean & Tienda,1987). Although we don't know exactly how these adults were related to one another, it's reasonable to assume that they often represented a married couple and their parents or, alternatively, an older married couple and their adult children.

total fertility rate (TFR) the average number of children a woman will bear over her lifetime if current birthrates remain the same

Mexican Americans also have more children than virtually any other large racial-ethnic group. Figure 5.4 shows, for racial-ethnic groups, the **total fertility rate (TFR)** in 1998. The TFR is the average number of children that women would bear over their lifetime if current birthrates were to remain the same. As can be seen, Mexican-American women would average just over three children, a substantially higher number than the TFR for non-Hispanic whites or blacks or other Hispanic groups, for that matter. In part, the higher fertility of Mexican women can be explained by their lower levels of education, relative to non-Hispanic white women. But the differential remains even after controlling for educational level (Bean & Tienda, 1987). Mexican Americans also marry at a younger age than other Hispanic groups, non-Hispanic whites, and African Americans (Bean & Tienda, 1987).

This picture of a marriage-based, multigenerational Mexican-American family is tempered somewhat by statistics on childbearing outside marriage and on marital instability. Figure 5.5 shows the percentages of unmarried women who gave birth in 1998 for racial-ethnic groups. The percentage was higher for Mexican Americans than for non-Hispanic whites although not nearly as high as among Puerto Ricans or African Americans. Still, Mexican Americans seem centered on high-birthrate, multigenerational families more than any other major racial-ethnic group in the nation. Some observers have suggested that the multigenerational households persist because older parents can provide childcare assistance or shelter to their economically pressed adult children, and this is no doubt true. Even so, the Mexican-American pattern of large, multigenerational families seems culturally distinctive. Perhaps the extensive communication and movement across the long, permeable U.S.–Mexican border keep the influence

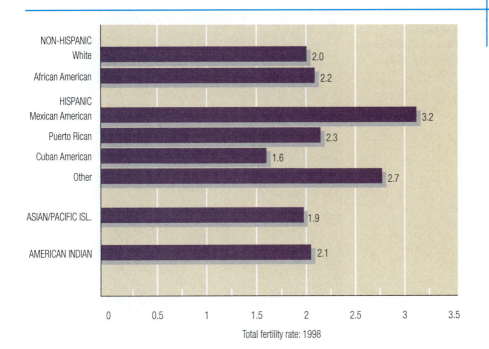

FIGURE 5.4
Total fertility rate for racial-ethnic groups in 1998. (*Source:* U.S. National Center for Health Statistics, 2000b)

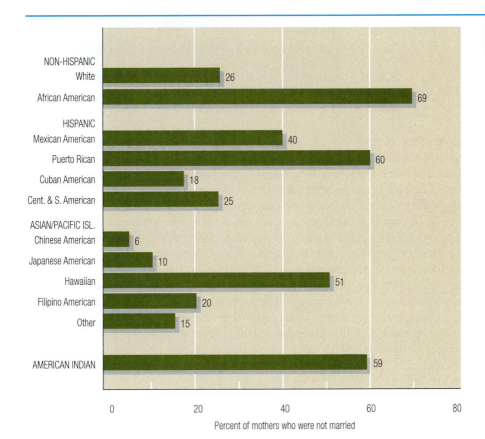

FIGURE 5.5
Percentage of women giving birth who were not married, for racial-ethnic groups in 1998. (*Source:* U.S. National Center for Health Statistics, 2000b)

Mexican Americans constitute about two-thirds of all Hispanics in the United States.

of the sending country stronger than is the case among some other immigrant groups. (See *Families in Other Cultures:* Transnational Families, on p. 161.)

There has been considerable change in the family lives of Mexican-American women. The traditional image of a Hispanic family is of a male-dominated household in which women do not work outside the home. Whether or not that image used to be accurate, it certainly isn't anymore. Between 1960 and 1990, the percentage of Mexican-origin women in the labor force increased from 28.8 to 52.9 (Ortiz, 1995). (The **labor force** is defined as all people who are either working outside the home or looking for work.) It is nearly as high as among non-Hispanic white women (57.5 percent). As non-Hispanic women have moved into the labor force, so have Mexican-American and other Hispanic women.

This change doesn't necessarily mean that the norms in Mexican-American and other Hispanic families have also changed greatly. In her study of dual-earner couples, Arlie Hochschild includes a case study of a Hispanic family in California, whom she calls Frank and Carmen Delacorte, in which the wife works outside the home and the husband does a substantial amount of housework (Hochschild, 1989). Yet Frank claims to believe that the man should be the head of the household, and Carmen agrees with him. Carmen doesn't want to work outside the home, she said, but the family needs the money: "I'm not working to discover my

labor force all people who are either working outside the home or looking for work

Families in Other Cultures — *Transnational Families*

In 2000, Mexico conducted the most openly contested Presidential election campaign in its history, one that unseated a political party that had held power for decades. During the campaign, Mexican politicians flooded the southwestern United States with Spanish-language advertisements. Why? Because of the large number of Mexican immigrants to the United States who remain Mexican citizens, take strong interest in Mexican politics, and are eligible to vote in Mexican elections. The phenomenon of immigrants who live in one country but maintain continuing ties with another is becoming more and more common as modern technology reduces the cost of international communication and travel. Increasingly, demographers are seeing what some call **transnational families:** families that straddle a sending country, such as Mexico, and a receiving country, such as the United States, by traveling frequently between them and maintaining continual contact across the borders (Baca Zinn & Wells, 2000).

Immigrants have long sent part of their earnings back to family members in their country of origin; indeed, that was the main reason why many people migrated. Today, families in developing nations still send members to work temporarily in a developed nation to earn higher wages and send some of their earnings back. But the transnational family goes beyond such financial transfer. Family members in the country of origin may continue to involve themselves in the immigrants' personal lives. For example, a study of Koreans in Los Angeles found that one-third of those who had married in the previous five years had flown back to Korea to obtain a spouse. There they were introduced to prospective partners chosen by parents and relatives (Min, 1993).

Sometimes immigrants return to their country of origin for services they cannot easily afford in their new country. For instance, the 1996 welfare reform law restricted immigrants' eligibility for social welfare benefits. In a study of the effect of welfare reform on families, my colleagues and I found one immigrant mother who returned home in part to obtain dental care for her children, which she could not afford in the United States.

What caused this change in the way immigrants relate to their families? The same technological forces that are allowing American families to keep in closer touch—cheaper long-distance calls, discount airline tickets, e-mail—also allow many immigrant families to keep in touch with kin in their countries of origin. Consequently, some immigrants may have begun to think of themselves as living in two (or more) countries at once. While in the past, immigrating often meant cutting off all contact with one's family, except for financial transfers and letters, that's not necessarily true anymore. For some immigrants today, the family transcends national boundaries.

Ask Yourself

1. Do you know a transnational family? If so, what is their country of origin, and how do they keep in touch with family members there?

2. To the people who belong to a transnational family, what might be the advantages and disadvantages of living in two or more countries at once? To the sending and receiving countries?

www.mhhe.com/cherlin

identity. No way!" (Hochschild, 1989, pp.62–63). Frank and Carmen believe that housework is women's work, but he "helps out" because of Carmen's supposed failings: Frank just happens to cook rice better than she does, he sews because she can't, he uses the ATM machine for her because she "always forgot" the password, and so forth. Thus, the Delacortes have moved toward more egalitarian gender relations without altering their beliefs in a more traditional division of labor. Other studies of Hispanic families confirm that even when husbands and wives hold traditional views they often expect that wives will work outside the home because the family needs their income (Hurtado, 1995).

transnational families
families that maintain continual contact between members in the sending and receiving countries

PUERTO RICANS

All Puerto Ricans are U.S. citizens because the island of Puerto Rico is a U.S. territory. Consequently, Puerto Ricans, unlike all other major Hispanic groups, are free to move to the mainland if they wish, and many have done so. In 1990, 2.7 million people who identified themselves as Puerto Ricans were residing on the mainland, whereas 3.5 million people lived in Puerto Rico. In other words, 44 percent of all people who claimed Puerto Rican ethnicity lived on the mainland. It is more difficult for individuals from other Hispanic groups to immigrate to the United States; they must either obtain visas, for which there may be a long wait, or find a way to enter and remain illegally. Demographers have long known that when the barriers to immigration are substantial, the people who manage to immigrate tend to have more education and skills than the average person in their home country. Immigration, in other words, is more selective when the barriers are high. People with greater skills are more confident that they can find decent-paying work in the United States, so they are more likely to take the trouble to immigrate. When the barriers are lower, on the other hand, immigration is less selective. We might expect, then, that Puerto Rican immigrants would tend to have less economic success, on average, than other Hispanic immigrants because Puerto Rican migration has been less selective.

Indeed, that is what the data show. Puerto Ricans are the most economically disadvantaged of the major Hispanic groups. (From here on I will be referring only to Puerto Ricans on the mainland, unless otherwise noted.) In 1999, 27 percent of all Puerto Rican family households had incomes below the poverty line, compared with 24 percent of Mexican-American family households, 19 percent of Central and South American family households, and 11 percent of Cuban-American family households (U.S. Bureau of the Census, 2000c). During the economic slow-down of the 1970s and 1980s, the economic well-being of Puerto Rican families deteriorated more than the well-being of Mexican-American families (Tienda, 1989). According to one summary, "Of all Hispanic-origin groups, Puerto Ricans have the lowest labor force participation rates, the highest unemployment levels, the highest incidence of poverty and of welfare utilization, and the lowest average levels of education" (Sandefur & Tienda, 1988). Some speculate that the economic decline among Puerto Ricans was heightened by their concentration in the New York City metropolitan area, which has undergone a loss of blue-collar jobs (Tienda, 1989).

Consistent with their lower economic standing, Puerto Ricans are second only to African Americans in the percentage of children born to unmarried mothers (see Figure 5.5). Yet many of the formally unmarried mothers are living in a partnership that they consider to be a marriage. In Puerto Rico and other Caribbean islands, a long tradition of **consensual unions** exists. These are cohabiting relationships in which couples consider themselves to be married but have never had religious or civil marriage ceremonies. From the viewpoint of the state and the Church, people in consensual unions are unmarried; but from the viewpoint of the couples and their peers, they are in a marriagelike relationship.

consensual union a cohabiting relationship in which a couple consider themselves to be married but have never had a religious or civil marriage ceremony

Among Puerto Ricans, then, there are three kinds of socially recognized unions: cohabiting unions, in which the partners do not consider themselves married; consensual unions, in which they have not undergone a marriage ceremony but still consider themselves to be informally married; and formal marriage, in which they have had a marriage ceremony and registered with the state. In a 1985 survey of Puerto Rican women aged 15 to 49 in the New York City area, the participants were asked:

> *As you know, there are various ways in which a man and a woman live in a union. Some couples legally marry, that is, they obtain a license; some couples consider themselves married but without a license; and some couples just live*

Like the majority of Cuban Americans, the dancers at this Miami block party chose to settle in the Miami metropolitan area.

together and do not consider themselves married, legally or informally. I would now like to ask you some questions about your marital history (Landale & Fennelly, 1992).

Among all women who had borne a child, 32 percent said they had ever lived in an informal marriage without a license, whereas just 13 percent said they had ever cohabited. The authors of the study report that whether or not a woman has borne a child in a union is a key factor in whether she defines it as an informal marriage or as a cohabitation. The birth of a child seems to change the social meaning of a union, making it more like a marriage (Landale & Fennelly, 1992).

Still, the tradition of consensual unions on the island of Puerto Rico cannot by itself be responsible for the increasing number of informal unions among mainland Puerto Ricans because consensual unions have been declining in frequency on the island. The deteriorating economic situation among mainland Puerto Ricans has played a major role. Among women in the same survey who had borne a child, those whose partners were employed and had at least a high school diploma were more likely to be in legal marriages (Landale & Forste, 1991). It would seem to follow that as the employment situation of Puerto Rican men has deteriorated, informal marriages and cohabitation have increased. I would speculate that—much as African Americans responded to tough times by drawing upon their tradition of strong, female-centered kin networks—Puerto Ricans have responded to tough times by drawing upon their tradition of informal marriage as a second-best substitute for formal marriage.

CUBAN AMERICANS

Most major immigrant groups today in the United States arrived in labor migrations: They came looking for higher-paying jobs. In contrast, the first waves of Cuban Americans came here in a political migration, fleeing the Communist government of Fidel Castro, who had led a successful revolution in 1959. The U.S. government allowed Cuban citizens to enter the country as political refugees. Indeed, the early migrants were drawn from the Cuban upper and middle classes, the elite that Castro's Communist party overthrew. These immigrants arrived with substantial amounts of education, skills, and capital. In addition, they were largely white in racial appearance. The U.S. government, sympathetic to their plight and wishing to isolate and embarrass Castro, welcomed them enthusiastically and provided assistance in retraining (Suarez, 1993).

Despite government efforts at resettlement, most Cuban immigrants chose to settle in the Miami metropolitan area, where a majority of the population is now of Cuban origin (Portes & Jensen, 1989). Classic sociological theories of immigration held that immigrants would adjust better and prosper more if they assimilated into the mainstream. (**Assimilation** means the process by which immigrant groups merge their culture and behavior with that of the dominant group in the host country.[8]) In the U.S. context, assimilation implies learning English, sending children to public schools, and dispersing geographically. Many Cuban immigrants chose, instead, to remain clustered in the Cuban neighborhoods of one metropolitan area, to listen to Spanish-language radio stations, to buy their food at markets owned by Cuban Americans, to eat at Cuban restaurants, and to send their children to private Cuban schools. They limited much of their lives to a large, dense, single-ethnic-group, almost self-sufficient community of the type that Kenneth Wilson and Alejandro Portes have called an **immigrant enclave** (Wilson & Portes, 1980).

According to classic immigration theory, then, Cuban immigrants should have suffered. Instead, they prospered. By 1970 the median income of Cuban-American families was higher than that of any other Hispanic group or of African Americans, at 80 percent of the median income of non-Hispanic white families; and by 1980 it had reached 88 percent of the median income for non-Hispanic white families (Bean & Tienda, 1987). Portes and other observers claim that Cuban immigrants successfully used the ethnically based connections of the enclave to obtain loans to start businesses when no Anglo bank would lend to them; they also used their connections to find jobs at Cuban enterprises. (See the section, later in this chapter, Social Capital and Immigrant Families.) He argues that the enclave strategy is a viable way for an immigrant group to achieve economic success.

Yet it must be remembered that these immigrants started out with a friendly reception from their hosts, arrived with substantial education and skills, received government assistance, and had white skin. These advantages were not shared by those who were part of a later wave of Cuban immigration that began in 1980, when Castro allowed a flotilla of small boats to depart from the port of Mariel. The Cuban government declared that many of the Mariel Cubans were criminals and undesirables; in addition, about 30 percent were nonwhite (Suarez, 1993). Unlike the first wave of Cuban immigrants, who arrived during an economic boom, the Mariel Cubans arrived at a time of stagnant wages and high unemployment. They were not welcomed enthusiastically or assisted, and they experienced discrimination from the earlier wave of immigrants. Later studies showed that only a small minority were criminals or otherwise socially undesirable; in fact, 14 percent of Mariel refugees interviewed in 1983 and 1984 had been managers or professionals in Cuba and another 24 percent had been skilled blue-collar workers (Portes, Stepick, & Truelove, 1986). By 1998, the median income of Cuban-origin families

assimilation the process by which immigrant groups merge their culture and their behavior with that of the dominant group in the host country

immigrant enclave a large, dense, single-ethnic-group, almost self-sufficient community

---

[8]A fuller definition of assimilation can be found in Gordon (1964).

had slipped to 77 percent of the median for non-Hispanic white families, reflecting the influx of Mariel refugees. Nevertheless, Cuban Americans remained by far the most prosperous Hispanic group, with a 1997 median family income 28 percent higher than among Mexican-origin families and 37 percent higher than that of Puerto Rican families (U.S. Bureau of the Census, 1999d).

The prosperity of Cuban Americans is derived in large part from business ownership. Cuban immigrants have become entrepreneurs, opening new businesses in far greater numbers than other Hispanic immigrants. The number of Cuban firms in the Miami area rose from about 900 in 1967 to approximately 25,000 by the mid-1980s (Portes & Jensen, 1989). The rate of business ownership among Cuban Americans in 1987 was three times higher than the rate among Mexican Americans and six times higher than among Puerto Ricans (O'Hare, 1992).

Many of the businesses were organized on a family basis. Married Cuban men were more likely to be self-employed, even after taking into account differences between married and unmarried men in education, work experience, citizenship, and English proficiency. If the men had children, they were even more likely to be self-employed (Portes & Jensen, 1989). Moreover, married men living with adults other than wives in their households were less likely to be self-employed, suggesting that the conjugal family of husband, wife, and children was most congenial to business ownership. Cuban immigrants appear to have used conjugal families as a means of pooling the labor and accumulating the capital necessary to start a business. Too many adults represented a drain on capital that could be used for the business; too few children or the absence of a spouse, on the other hand, resulted in insufficient labor or outside income (as from a wife's job) for starting a firm.

Asian-American Families

Much less has been written about Asian-American families than about African-American and Hispanic families because of their modest numbers prior to the 1965 immigration act. For example, the Korean population increased from an estimated 69,000 in 1970 to 350,000 in 1980 and to 980,000 in 1998 (Lee, 1998). In the 2000 Census, 11.9 million people checked one of the Asian racial categories (Asian Indian, Chinese, Filipino, Japanese, Korean, Vietnamese, or "other Asian") or wrote in entries such as Pakistani or Thai (U.S. Bureau of the Census, 2001). The family patterns in the many sending nations are diverse, but, in general, Asian cultures emphasize interdependence among kin more, and individualism less, than Western culture (Goode, 1963). Asian families place a greater emphasis on children's loyalty and service to their parents than do Western families.

These Asian ways can conflict with American ways. Two researchers, for instance, read a series of vignettes to a sample of Chinese-American immigrants from Taiwan and their parents in Chicago and Los Angeles. Here is one:

> *Wang Hong has to transfer three times on public transportation to get from where he lives to his office. Because of the time and inconvenience of taking public transportation, Wang Hong has tried very hard to save money to buy a car before winter. However, Wang Hong's parents have a need for money and ask Wang Hong to give them the money Wang Hong has saved.*

Both the parents and their adult children were asked to react to this vignette. The authors noted that when a similar vignette had been read to a general U.S. sample of

Asian immigrants, such as these Vietnamese in California, often pool their resources to start family-run small businesses.

the elderly and their caregivers, about three-fourths of both groups had thought that the child should buy the car. Yet a majority of the Chinese adult children and parents said that Wang Hong should give the money to his parents—placing obligation to one's parents over convenience of transportation (Lin & Liu, 1993).

Immigrants' families frequently pool economic resources to start businesses or to buy homes. Several Asian-origin groups have very high rates of business ownership, often accomplished by borrowing funds from kin and close friends. As for homeownership, shared residence and income pooling often help, as one Vietnamese immigrant told an interviewer:

> *To Vietnamese culture, family is everything. There are aspects which help us readjust to this society. It is easy for us because of [the] tradition of helping in the family.*
>
> *We solve problems because [the] family institution is a bank. If I need money and my brothers and my two sisters are working I tell them I need to buy a house. I need priority in this case. They say OK, and they give money to me. After only two years, I bought a house.*
>
> *Some Americans ask me, "How come you came here with empty hands and now you have a house?" I told them, it is easy for us because my brother and sister help with the down payment. Now I help them. They live with me and have no rent* (Gold, 1993).

This is not to say that all Asian immigrants adjust well and prosper. The first wave of Vietnamese immigration occurred in the immediate aftermath of the Vietnam War in 1975. Like the initial Cuban influx, it was a political migration of middle-class business and military personnel who were assisted on arrival. They have been successful as a group. Yet like the Mariel immigration, a later, less-educated stream of Vietnamese immigrants such as the families of Hai Nguyen and Cuong Dan, escaped in overcrowded boats to refugee camps in Southeast Asia. Those who have emigrated to the United States have fewer skills, have received less assistance, and have encountered a sluggish economy. A 1984 study of some of the later immigrants found that 61 percent had household incomes of less than $9,000 (Gold,

1993). In addition, as noted earlier, government statistics on the Asian-American population sometimes include Hawaiians or Pacific Islanders, who are among the poorest racial-ethnic groups in the United States. The median family income of Hawaiians is only slightly higher than that of African Americans. Nevertheless, Asian Americans are a prosperous group overall. In 1998, the median family income for Asian and Pacific Islander families was $52,826, which was 8 percent higher than the median for white families, an impressive achievement for a population that includes so many recent immigrants (U.S. Bureau of the Census, 2000i).

The extent to which Asian-style patterns will survive through the second and third generations of Asian Americans remains to be seen. Among Asian Americans whose families have been in the United States for a few generations, the traditional Asian patterns are less apparent. For instance, the relations between women and men are more egalitarian in third-generation Japanese-American families than in the older, immigrant generation (Ishii-Kuntz, 2000). And rates of interracial intermarriages are higher among the more established Asian groups, such as the Japanese and Chinese, than among more recent immigrant groups (Barringer et al, 1993). In fact, perhaps the most important fact about the new families being formed by Asian-American young adults is that about two-thirds of them involve non-Asian spouses. Consider the trends in marriages involving Asian-American women in their twenties: In 1980, 47.5 percent of these marriages were to an Asian-American husband; but by 1990 only 33.5 percent were to an Asian-American husband (Qian, 1997). Thus, the rate of intermarriage increased substantially during the 1980s; no data is available for the 1990s. Most of the intermarriages are to non-Hispanic whites, suggesting that Asian-American family patterns after the turn of the century may be more similar to the dominant U.S. patterns.

Social Capital and Immigrant Families

The recent literature on immigrants refers often to a concept developed by the French sociologist Pierre Bourdieu (1980) and expanded on by the American sociologist James S. Coleman (1988). **Social capital** is the resources that a person can access through his or her relationships with other people. To understand this concept, think about the social connections that might allow you to get a ticket to a sold-out concert (because your friend's cousin works in the box office), to be admitted to a competitive college (because your mother is an alumna), or to get your first job after college (because your roommate's father runs the company). In all these cases, the resources you would draw on would not be monetary (which social scientists refer to as "financial capital") or educational (which social scientists call "human capital"), but rather your social links to a network of people who can help you reach a goal you might otherwise fail to achieve.

That is the essence of the concept of social capital. In the literature on immigrants it is sometimes used more broadly to refer to a person's links to an entire immigrant community. The idea is that the community provides members with resources that help them to achieve goals they could not achieve alone, or even as families working together. For example, to explain why the children of Vietnamese immigrants in Versailles Village do better in school than their low social class would predict, Zhou and Bankston (1998) point to the social capital created by the close-knit Vietnamese community. They describe a Vietnamese Catholic church that offers after-school courses, and the Vietnamese Education Association,

social capital the resources that a person can access through his or her relationships with other people

a community group that holds an annual awards ceremony to honor high achieving students. Through these institutions, the authors argue, the Vietnamese community in Versailles Village provides social capital that boosts school achievement among Vietnamese students.

As I mentioned earlier, the literature on Cuban immigrants provides another example of the use of social capital. One reason for the growth in the number of Cuban-American-owned firms from the late-1960s to the 1980s was that immigrants could use their social standing in the Cuban community in Miami to obtain the initial loans needed to start a business. In the mid-1960s, according to Alejandro Portes and Julia Sensenbrenner, a few small banks owned by South Americans hired Cuban immigrant ex-bankers. The Cubans began to make loans to their fellow immigrants that other financial institutions would have thought risky. As one Cuban banker said:

> *At the start, most Cuban enterprises were gas stations; then came grocery shops and restaurants. No American bank would lend to them. By the mid-sixties we started a policy at our bank of making small loans to Cubans who wanted to start their own business, but did not have the capital. These loans of $10,000 or $15,000 were made because the person was known to us by his reputation and integrity. All of them paid back; there were zero losses. With some exceptions they have continued being clients of the bank. People who used to borrow $15,000 on a one-time basis now take $50,000 in a week. In 1973, the policy was discontinued. The reason was that the new refugees coming at that time were unknown to us* (Portes & Sensenbrenner, 1993).

Whereas American banks would have required more proof that an applicant would be able to pay back a loan, the Cuban bankers relied solely on the applicant's "reputation and integrity." That reputation was established through a network of ties within the Cuban enclave in Miami. The banker might have known someone who had married the sister of the applicant and could vouch for the applicant's character. To enforce the terms of the loan, the banker relied on the humiliation and, perhaps, ostracism that would befall a person who defaulted. In this way, Cuban immigrants were able to use their ties to a network of relatives and friends to obtain the money they needed to buy a grocery store or restaurant.

Beside the Vietnamese, many other Asian immigrant groups also have used their social capital to obtain the support they need to start businesses. Among some Chinese and Japanese immigrants, for example, a group of relatives and friends was formed in which each person invested a modest amount of money into a single credit fund. Subsequently, one member was allowed to borrow the entire amount in the fund to start an enterprise, and he was required to pay it back with interest. Then the fund was made available to another member of the group, and then another. The members trusted that their loans would be repaid because of the loss of face a person who did not repay would suffer from the other members of the group. These "rotating credit associations" provided their members with an advantage not shared by outsiders—an advantage based on close kinship and friendship ties (Light, 1972).

American Indian Families

Before the twentieth century, kinship ties provided the basis for governing most American Indian tribes. A person's household was linked to a larger group of relatives who might be a branch of a matrilineal or patrilineal clan [➡ p. 42] that

Despite a decline in the power of lineages, extended families remain significant for American Indians.

shared power with other clans. Thus, kinship organization was also political organization. Under these circumstances, extended kinship ties reflected power and status to a much greater extent than among other racial-ethnic groups in the United States. American Indian kinship systems allowed individuals to have more relatives, particularly distant relatives, than did Western European kinship systems (Shoemaker, 1991). Even today, extended family ties retain a significance for American Indians that goes beyond the sharing of resources that has been noted among other groups (Harjo, 1993). Kinship networks constitute tribal organization; kinship ties confer an identity.

Only 43 percent of the 1.9 million American Indians in 1990 lived on or near tribal lands—if we define an American Indian as someone who identifies him- or herself as such in the census. That figure is down from 53 percent in 1980.[9] As noted earlier, a substantial share of the growth of the American Indian population in urban areas in the East and on the West Coast reflects a rise in the number of people who considered themselves to be American Indians. In addition, migration from reservations to urban areas may have accounted for some of the drop in the percentage living near tribal lands. A large number of Americans have some American Indian ancestry because American Indians have a far higher intermarriage rate than racial-ethnic groups such as African Americans. In 1990, only about 40 percent of married American Indians were married to other American Indians (Sandefur & Liebler, 1997).

American Indians remain an economically disadvantaged population. Their median family income is comparable to that of African Americans (Snipp, 1989). Consistent with their high levels of poverty, the percentage of American Indian

[9]For 1980: Snipp (1989). For 1990: U.S. Bureau of the Census (1993d).

families headed by an unmarried woman is substantial: As Figure 5.1 shows, 31 percent of Native American families with children in 1990 (including Eskimos and Aleuts) were headed by an unmarried woman. Only African Americans had a higher percentage. Consistent with these figures, 54 percent of American Indian mothers who gave birth in 1990 were unmarried—a percentage comparable to Puerto Ricans and again exceeded only by African Americans. The percentage of adults who are divorced is also higher among American Indians than among the U.S. population as a whole (Sandefur & Liebler, 1997).

It's likely that many of the unmarried mothers were enmeshed in kinship networks that provided assistance. Little research, however, has been done on contemporary American Indian family patterns—especially among American Indians outside tribal lands. Beyond these lands, intermarriage and shifting conceptions of American Indian ethnicity make the study of families more complex. It is increasingly difficult to talk of the "American Indian family": There always has been diversity in family patterns among Indian tribes and among persons residing on reservations versus persons not on reservations, and now an American Indian family is often a multiracial family.

Race, Ethnicity, and Kinship

Family ties have been central to the successes and the struggles of racial-ethnic groups in the United States. All the groups that have been discussed in this chapter have relied on their relatives for support—whether that support be food for dinner or money to buy a restaurant. Their reliance on extended kinship contrasts with the nuclear family ideal among the non-Hispanic white middle class. To be sure, there are substantial differences among racial-ethnic groups in the kinds of family lives they tend to lead. Some of these differences reflect economic forces. Put another way, sometimes what we think of as ethnic or racial differences may, in large part, be class differences. For example, to compare Puerto Ricans on the mainland with Cubans on the mainland is to compare an economically disadvantaged group with a more economically privileged one.

Still in Chapter 4 and this chapter, we have seen similarities in the ways poor whites, African Americans, and Puerto Ricans organize family and kinship. Among these disadvantaged groups, the strongest family tie is often between a mother and her adult daughter. In what I have called women-centered kin networks, women organize exchanges of support that extend across households, linking networks of people who share their meager resources.

Nevertheless, the precise form of kinship varies from group to group, reflecting, in my opinion, long-standing cultural differences. For example, in Potter Addition [➡ p. 125], a majority of low-income white households included both a wife and a husband. Yet even though most men were married and living with their wives, it was women who, in practical terms, ran the households and provided most of the support for other kin. The distinctive characteristic of Puerto Rican households is the consensual union, although there are also many households headed by women without live-in partners. Single-parent households, or grandmother-daughter-grandchild households, are the common form among African Americans, with young mothers often residing with their own mothers for several years. For all these groups, assistance from family members other than one's spouse or partner is crucial for subsisting from day to day.

Among many immigrant groups, family ties provide critical assistance to individuals who wish to start small businesses. Most banks will not lend money to new immigrants because they are not sure they will be repaid. Immigrants tend not to have homes or other assets that they can use as collateral to secure a bank loan. Sometimes, however, they can obtain start-up loans from members of their kinship and community networks. Those who loan the money rely upon kinship and community ties as a form of moral collateral: A borrower puts his reputation and standing among his peers on the line when he or she obtains a loan. If the borrower were to default, he or she would be dishonored before family and friends. Thus, kinship ties provide a form of social capital that immigrants can use to obtain the financial capital—money, equipment, storefronts—needed to start an enterprise. These same ties also become recruiting networks through which members of the group can find jobs.

The immigrant entrepreneurs utilize what we might call marriage-centered kin networks. These exchanges tend to connect households that are headed by husbands and wives. It is the married couple that starts and maintains the business, although other relatives may work in it. Ties to a wider network of kin provide financial assistance that the married couple is allowed to manage largely for its own benefit. In contrast, women-centered kin networks require that any surplus be shared. In this way, the kin networks of the poor allow the maximum number of people to get the resources they need to avoid becoming destitute. Thus, the two kinds of kinship networks discussed in this chapter and the previous one have different functions: Marriage-centered networks allow for the accumulation of resources by the husband-wife household, whereas women-centered networks allow for the maximum sharing of resources across predominantly single-parent households.

I would suggest that these two forms of kin networks have different strengths and limitations. The women-centered networks are superior for easing the hardships of persistent poverty. They have allowed many poor individuals to subsist from day to day. Yet they make it difficult for network members to accumulate the resources necessary to rise above poverty. The marriage-based networks, on the other hand, are superior for allowing people to be upwardly mobile by accumulating enough resources to start a business or move to a better neighborhood. Yet they make it difficult for network members to provide assistance to all kin who need it. The differences between the two networks suggest, therefore, a tension that many people with low incomes may face: helping all of one's kin who need assistance versus accumulating enough money to better the position of one's own household. Different racial-ethnic groups resolve this tension in different ways.

This is not to suggest that whether a household escapes from poverty is solely, or even primarily, a matter of kinship networks. Entrepreneurial ethnic groups such as the Cubans and Koreans were drawn from the better-educated segments of the sending countries. In 1980, for example, 78 percent of the Korean-origin population had at least four years of high school, compared with 71 percent of the white population and 56 percent of the African-American population (U.S. Bureau of the Census, 1991e). As mentioned previously, most of the early Cuban immigrants were white and therefore did not face racial discrimination. A case could be made that, although there has been discrimination against Asian Americans, it has not been as institutionalized and as pervasive as has discrimination against African Americans. Moreover, the restructuring of the economy has had a major effect on the family lives of African Americans. Still, within these constraints, family and kinship patterns appear to make a difference in the life chances of the members of racial-ethnic groups, allowing many to survive and some to prosper.

Families, however, do not operate independently of government. Despite strong sentiment in the United States against government "interference" in family life, the state does intervene importantly. Let us next examine the relationship between the family and the state.

Looking Back

1. **How is immigration changing the racial and ethnic balance in the United States?** Since the immigration laws were modified in 1965, the proportion of all immigrants coming from Latin-American and Asian countries has increased greatly. One in five children in the United States is now an immigrant or the child of an immigrant. Within the Hispanic and Asian ethnic groups there is great diversity in family patterns.

2. **How has African-American family life changed over the past several decades?** African Americans have been adversely affected by economic changes that have reduced the number of semiskilled and skilled blue-collar jobs available to American workers. In part as a result of this economic transformation, the importance of marriage in African-American families has declined substantially relative to ties to extended kin such as grandmothers. The link between childbearing and marriage has also weakened; about two-thirds of black children are now born to unmarried mothers. African Americans have responded to these changes by drawing on the network of kin for mutual support. During the same period, however, a substantial African-American middle class has emerged.

3. **What are the family patterns of the major Hispanic ethnic groups?** The largest Hispanic group,, Mexican Americans, is characterized by high birthrates and large households. Nevertheless, Mexican-American women (and women in most other Hispanic groups) have entered the labor force in large numbers over the past few decades. Among Puerto Ricans, the poorest of the major Hispanic groups in the United States, a relatively high number of children are born to unmarried mothers. But some of these unmarried mothers live with partners, often in consensual unions that they consider to be like marriages. Cuban Americans are the most prosperous Hispanic group, although recent immigrants have reduced the group's economic standing. Most Cuban Americans settled in an immigrant enclave in the Miami area and many started family-based businesses.

4. **What are the distinctive characteristics of the family patterns of Asian Americans?** More than in any other group, including non-Hispanic whites, Asian-American families are headed by married couples. These families also have comparatively few children born outside of marriage and low divorce rates—characteristics that probably reflect a greater emphasis on the interdependence and mutual obligations of kin. Although some Asian subgroups are poor, Asian-American families as a whole have a higher median income than non-Hispanic white families. A majority of young adult Asian Americans now marry non-Asians, meaning that in the future Asian-American families will increasingly be multiracial.

5. **How does the concept of "social capital" apply to immigrant families?** Some Hispanic immigrant groups, most notably the Cubans, and many Asian immigrant groups use ties to others in their ethnic community to achieve certain goals, such as starting a business. This use of social connections to advance oneself is an example of what sociologists call social capital.

6. **What has been the role of kinship ties in American Indian family life?** Traditionally, kinship ties have been central to the political organization of American Indian societies. Even today, broad kinship ties provide American Indians with a sense of identity and belonging. American Indian family households have a low median income, reflecting the group's economic disadvantage. A relatively high number of family households are headed by unmarried women. Like Asians, American Indians have a high rate of intermarriage with other ethnic groups.

Thinking about Families

1. What defines an "ethnic group" or a "racial group"? Are these concepts useful or do they confuse more than enlighten?

2. Is there such a thing as relying too much on extended kin for support?

3. Can you think of an example of using social capital from your own family background?

4. **The Public Family.** Should more native-born Americans care for their aging parents the way many immigrant groups do?

5. **The Private Family.** Interracial and inter-ethnic marriages are widespread among Asian Americans and American Indians, common among Hispanics, and uncommon but increasing among African Americans. How might inter-group marriage change American families in the early decades of the twenty-first century?

Key Terms

Asian American   144
assimilation   164
consensual union   162
Hispanic   144
immigrant enclave   164

labor force   160
mediating structures   157
new second generation   142
non-Hispanic white   145
racial-ethnic group   144

social capital   167
total fertility rate (TFR)   158
transnational families   161
union formation   148

Families on the Internet   www.mhhe.com/cherlin

*Note: While all the URLs listed were current as of the printing of this book, these sites often change. Please check our web site (**http://www.mhhe.com/cherlin**) for updates.*

The U.S. Bureau of the Census collects detailed statistics through its monthly Current Population Survey, its Decennial Census of Population, and other studies. The information in this chapter on the growth of racial and ethnic minority families, household composition, and interracial families was obtained from the treasure trove of information at the Census Bureau's home page, **www.census.gov.** For instance, to find out the latest information on Hispanic families, select "H" in the "Subjects A to Z" box; then, on the next screen, find "Hispanic" and select the subcategory "People." You can then select and view the latest annual report on the Hispanic population in the United States. What percentage of the Hispanic population is now of Mexican origin?

The National Academy of Sciences convenes panels of experts to address scientific issues. Many of the panels publish their reports as books through the National Academy Press. Recently, the National Academy Press put the complete text of hundreds of these reports on-line at its web site, **www.nap.edu.** There you can read the report of the panel on the new second generation of immigrant children, *From Generation to Generation* (Hernandez & Charney, 1998). Go to the web page and then enter the title in the title-search box. When you have found the title, click on the "Open book, searchable, READ" button; you should see the table of contents. This report contains a number of tables on the conditions of immigrant children. Select Appendix B and examine the first table (starting on page 21), which shows the percentage of first- and second-generation children who are poor, by country of origin. Which country has the highest percentage of poor immigrant children? Which has the lowest?

chapter 6

The Family, the State, and Social Policy

Looking Forward

1. What is the "welfare state"?

2. What are some of the basic issues in the family policy debates?

3. Why was the 1996 welfare reform law a sharp break from earlier government policies toward low-income families?

4. What are the themes that conservatives and liberals stress in debating family issues?

5. What are the most important recent developments in family policy?

Consider two hypothetical families. In family A, a poor single mother struggles to raise two children. She receives cash assistance and food stamps from the government. When she or her children are sick, they visit the emergency room at the local hospital, where their care is paid for through Medicaid, the federal program of health insurance for the poor. She lives on the 15th floor of a publicly owned housing project that charges less for rent than she would pay if she rented an apartment privately. Her four-year-old goes to government-funded Head Start classes to learn skills that will be useful for school. It is obvious that family A receives a great deal of assistance from the government.

In family B, two employed, college-educated parents are raising two children. They are not receiving welfare, and they own their own home. It may seem as though they receive no assistance from the government, but they do. Their elderly parents in Miami Beach and Sun City receive Social Security checks, relieving family B of having to support them. Moreover, the couple deduct the interest payments for their home mortgage from their taxable income, which makes it easier for them to own a home. They take an income tax credit for part of the cost of the day care center their four-year-old attends, which makes it easier for both of them to hold jobs outside the home. In addition, when Mr. B was laid off from his job as a computer programmer for three months this past year, he collected federally funded unemployment compensation.

In truth, most American families, including most middle-class families, receive substantial government assistance. It has not always been the case that most families receive assistance. In the colonial era, almost no economic assistance was provided; rather, the family was viewed as an independent entity that ought not to be interfered with—a "little commonwealth" in Demos's phrase (Demos, 1970). In fact, there was relatively little government financial assistance to families throughout the nineteenth century. In the early decades of the twentieth century, however, labor unions gained enough strength to demand higher pay, shorter hours, old-age pensions, and unemployment compensation. Moreover, civic groups led by middle-class women pressed for programs to assist mothers and children in poverty, such as pensions for widows (Skocpol, 1992).

Then, in 1929 came the economic collapse of the Great Depression. The masses of unemployed workers looked to the government for assistance. Herbert Hoover, a Republican president who opposed most government involvement in the economy, was defeated in the 1932 election by Franklin Delano Roosevelt. Under Roosevelt, the federal government developed a number of programs to assist unemployed workers and their families. Among them was the **Social Security Act of 1935,** which cre-

Social Security Act of 1935 the federal act that created, among other provisions, Social Security, unemployment compensation, and aid to mothers with dependent children (later renamed Aid to Families with Dependent Children)

ated, among other provisions, Social Security (the system of pensions for the elderly), unemployment compensation (payments to workers who lose their jobs), and aid to mothers with dependent children. The latter program was subsequently renamed **Aid to Families with Dependent Children (AFDC).** It was the program of financial assistance to low-income, single-parent families that became commonly known as "welfare." For 61 years, AFDC was the heart of government assistance to poor mothers and children. Then in 1996 Congress passed, and President Bill Clinton signed, a bill that drastically changed the face of cash assistance to poor families. It is the ungainly named **Personal Responsibility and Work Opportunity Reconciliation Act of 1996,** which policy analysts refer to by its acronym, **PRWORA.**

In this chapter we will explore in detail the history of welfare programs between the Social Security Act and PRWORA, a period during which government assistance to poor families, and programs to compensate for families' alleged limitations, expanded greatly as the following examples reveal:

- In 1999, 7.2 million people received cash assistance through Temporary Assistance to Needy Families, the program that replaced AFDC in 1996.
- In 1998, 19.8 million people received food stamps, introduced in the 1960s to reduce hunger and malnutrition.
- In 1999, 568,000 children were living in foster care, most having been removed from their homes by government caseworkers.
- In 1999, 836,000 three- to five-year-old poor children were enrolled in Head Start, a program begun in the 1960s that attempted to provide early readiness for school.[1]

As the example of family B showed, government assistance is not limited to the poor. Consider as well the following data:

- In 1998, 27.5 million retired workers received Social Security payments, which eased their children's burden of support (U.S. Bureau of the Census, 1999d).
- In 1997, 7.3 million workers received unemployment compensation, enabling them to provide income to their families while looking for other jobs (U.S. Bureau of the Census, 1999d).
- In 1998, 24.9 million parents at all income levels deducted part of the cost of out-of-home childcare from their income taxes, a subsidy that made it easier for them to work outside the home and that cost the federal government 15.2 billion dollars in lost tax revenue (U.S. Internal Revenue Service, 2000).
- In 1996, 29.4 million federal income tax returns deducted the interest payments on home mortgages, a subsidy to homeowners that cost the federal government $54 billion in lost tax revenue (U.S. Bureau of the Census, 1996d, 1999d).

This list, which could be expanded, demonstrates that the government is far more involved in supporting families economically than was the case in earlier times. Extensive federal economic support began in the twentieth century. Most government involvement is based on a concern about the well-being of children (as in the cash assistance or foster home programs) or of the elderly (as in Social Security). In other words, most government programs that affect families do so out of concern about the proper caretaking and support of dependents—people

Aid to Families with Dependent Children (AFDC) a federal program of financial assistance to low-income families, commonly known as "welfare" until it was replaced by Temporary Assistance to Needy Families (TANF) in 1996

Personal Responsibility and Work Opportunity Reconciliation Act of 1996 (PRWORA) the federal welfare legislation that requires most recipients to work within two years and that limits the amount of time a family can receive welfare

---

[1]All figures in this paragraph are from U.S. House of Representatives (2000).

**Families in
Other Cultures**

Public Opinion toward Government Assistance for Working Parents

*O*ver the past 20 years, government benefits to working parents have increased in the United States. Parents with childcare expenses can now receive a partial reduction of their income tax. Low-income working parents can receive a substantial cash transfer through the Earned Income Tax Credit. And parents may take up to 12 weeks of unpaid leave from their jobs to care for a new baby or an ill child. Still, the United States provides less generous benefits to working parents than other developed nations.

The accompanying chart shows public opinion toward government assistance for working parents in the United States and four other nations. It is based on the results of surveys conducted in 1994 in 31 countries, as part of the International Social Survey Program (Smith, 1999). Random samples of adults in each country were asked two questions on this topic:

Do you agree or disagree . . .
A. Working families should receive paid maternity leave when they have a baby.
B. Families should receive benefits for childcare when both parents work.

As the charts indicate, Americans show substantially less agreement with these statements than people in the other four countries. They also show less agreement than people in nearly all the other countries in the study.

What accounts for this difference in public opinion? One key factor is that in many nations, family policy toward parents is driven by a national concern with keeping up the birth rate. The belief that

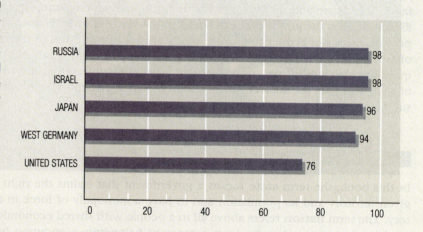

"Working women should receive paid maternity leave when they have a baby."
(percent agreeing)

RUSSIA — 98
ISRAEL — 98
JAPAN — 96
WEST GERMANY — 94
UNITED STATES — 76

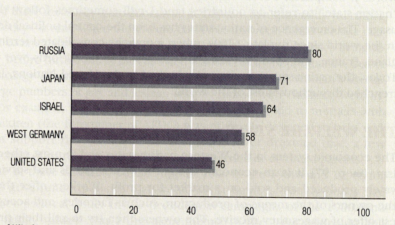

"Families should receive financial benefits for childcare when both parents work."
(percent agreeing)

RUSSIA — 80
JAPAN — 71
ISRAEL — 64
WEST GERMANY — 58
UNITED STATES — 46

*Attitudes toward government assistance for working parents in five nations, 1994.
(Source: Smith, 1999)*

In the United States, parents may take up to 12 weeks of unpaid leave from their jobs to care for a new baby or an ill child. In contrast, many countries in Europe and elsewhere offer several months of leave with partial pay.

government should encourage people to have more children is called **pronatalism.** Leaders in many nations have long worried that their populations will not grow as fast as the populations of neighboring and competing countries. The Germans historically have been concerned about the size of the French population (and vice versa); the Japanese have been concerned about China; the Russians hoped to make up the large losses they incurred in the twentieth-century world wars; the Israelis, to replace the Jews killed in the Holocaust.

What keeps the United States immune to pronatalist pressure is its receptiveness to immigration. Unlike most other nations, the United States has a long history of letting its population increase, in part, by accepting large numbers of immigrants. Japan, in contrast, has resisted immigra-

tion. So did West Germany[1] until it admitted "guest workers" in the latter part of the twentieth century to alleviate a labor shortage. Israel accepts Jewish immigrants but few others. So there is less pressure in the United States to maintain the size of the population by encouraging births.

There are other factors, of course. For example, the American political system has never supported government social programs as much as the Russian socialist (and post-socialist) system. In addition, attitudes seem to be changing in the United States. More Americans are accepting the idea of mothers working outside the home, and some political leaders have been promoting policies that assist working parents. Whether in the future, U.S. public opinion will remain distinctively unfavorable toward assistance to working parents is an open question.

Ask Yourself

1. Have you or a friend or relative ever had to go back to work sooner than desired after giving birth to a baby? If so, would a paid maternity leave have helped? In what ways?

2. The graph on the bottom shows significant differences in public opinion toward childcare benefits for working parents. What might account for these variations in public opinion from one country to the next?

[1]This survey was conducted before the Federal Republic of Germany, informally known as West Germany, expanded to include the former East Germany.

<www.mhhe.com/cherlin>

pronatalism the belief that public policies should encourage people to have children

It is but a short extension to argue that, according to capitalist economic theory, the government should not intervene in family affairs. To intervene is to disturb the workings of the invisible hand and therefore to risk doing more harm than good. For example, some critics of cash assistance to poor families argue that it discourages them from taking jobs, thereby reducing their standard of living in the long run.[2] (Others believe that the shortage of available jobs, or the need for some parents to care full time for their children, justifies cash assistance.) Yet not to intervene is to do nothing to help people in need or assist groups that might be unjustly disadvantaged in the labor market.

As noted earlier, the view that the government should not intervene in family affairs prevailed in the United States until the hardships of the Depression. Since then, the U.S. Congress has passed substantial legislation to protect workers and their families from the most harmful consequences of the labor market. In the social scientific literature on these laws and programs, authors refer to them as "social welfare" measures, and they write of the **welfare state,** by which they mean a capitalist government that has enacted numerous measures—such as Social Security, unemployment compensation, and a minimum wage—to protect workers and their families from the harshness of the capitalist system and to raise their standard of living above what wages paid in the labor market alone would do. Here the term "welfare" is used not in its common meaning of cash assistance to the poor but rather in the broader sense of the well-being of members of society. These social welfare measures expanded greatly in the 1950s and 1960s, as labor and minority groups pushed for them and as growing affluence allowed the government to raise taxes to support them. Still, Americans are less supportive of government assistance than are citizens in most other developed countries. (See *Families in Other Cultures:* Public Opinion toward Government Assistance for Working Parents.)

welfare state a capitalist government that has enacted numerous measures, such as Social Security, unemployment compensation, and a minimum wage, to protect workers and their families from the harshness of the capitalist system

The welfare state has treated husbands and fathers differently from wives and mothers. In the terms of feminist theory, the development of the welfare state has been "gendered" (Orloff, 1993). Beginning around the turn of the twentieth century, reformers campaigned, without much success initially, for laws that would require employers to pay male workers enough so they could support their families without their wives' (and children's) having to work for wages. During the same period, women's organizations and labor unions campaigned, with more success, for protective legislation: laws to limit the number of hours women could work for wages to "protect" them from having to work too long and hard outside the home (Skocpol, 1992). Together, these different objectives for women and men supported the **family wage system,** a division of labor in which the husband earns enough money to support his family and the wife remains home to do housework and childcare. This system, which was the "breadwinner-homemaker" family, is now in decline, but an examination of its development is useful for understanding the family policy debates occurring today.

family wage system a division of labor in which the husband earns enough money to support his family and the wife remains home to do housework and childcare

THE FAMILY WAGE SYSTEM

The moral vision behind campaigns for the family wage system specified that the family works best when men and women inhabit separate spheres

---

[2]See, for example, Murray (1984).

Franklin D. Roosevelt signed the landmark Social Security Act of 1935, which created the Social Security System, unemployment compensation, and aid to mothers with dependent children.

[➡ p. 51]: his, paid work outside the home; hers, unpaid homemaking and childrearing inside the home. This view, as has been discussed, gained in popularity in the nineteenth-century United States as industrialization moved the workplace out of the home. The family wage system was never a reality for many working-class and minority families, whose men could not earn enough to support a family. Nevertheless, it remained the dominant cultural view of the family throughout the first half of the twentieth century, and it still has advocates.[3]

The Social Security Act of 1935 followed the division of labor implicit in the family wage system. It provided old-age pensions only to persons who "earned" them by working a certain number of years in the paid labor force; originally only industrial and commercial workers were covered. The clear expectation was that these covered workers would overwhelmingly be men. In 1939, Congress passed an extension of the act that allowed widows of Social Security recipients to receive continued benefits after their husbands died. Women whose husbands were absent for other reasons, and who were still raising children, were eligible for the Aid to Dependent Children program—but only if their income was below a certain level. Congress did not anticipate that large numbers of women raising children might need assistance because they were divorced from their husbands or had never had a husband. It did not anticipate that large numbers of women would qualify for Social Security benefits themselves by working outside the home. The system presumed that, until the death of one spouse, families would consist of a husband who would *provide* for the family and a wife who would *care* for the family (Sapiro, 1990).

[3]See Carlson (1986).

The act set the tone for government policy concerning the family. Throughout the 1950s, the prosperous decade in which the breadwinner-homemaker family was much celebrated, the family wage system remained the cultural ideal. During the 1960s, policymakers paid little attention to the family per se. Rather, the 1960s was the decade of the War on Poverty. Under President Johnson, Congress initiated and enlarged numerous programs in aid of the poor. Nevertheless, some of these programs had important effects on families. Substantial increases in Social Security benefits and the creation of a health insurance system for the elderly (Medicare) greatly improved the economic well-being of older Americans, making them more independent of their children (see Chapter 11). The number of single-parent families on the AFDC rolls rose sharply in the late 1960s as benefit levels were increased and eligibility standards loosened. The 1964 Civil Rights Act and subsequent Supreme Court decisions banned discrimination against women in hiring and in wages, thus weakening the family wage system.

Family Policy Debates

Still, it was not until the mid-1970s that politicians began to talk specifically about "family policy." In the meantime, the face of the American family had changed. Between the early 1960s and the late 1970s, the divorce rate doubled; by 1980, about one of every two marriages was predicted to end in divorce. More and more married women were working outside the home: By 1980, three-fifths of married women with children under age six were employed.[4] The proportion of children born outside marriage had risen sharply to 11 percent among whites and 55 percent among blacks in 1980 (U.S. Bureau of the Census, 1991e). (These proportions have continued to increase; in 1998 they were 26 percent for whites and 69 percent for blacks [U.S. National Center for Health Statistics, 2000b].) This great growth in single-parent families and in two-earner, two-parent families—which continued in the 1980s and 1990s—undermined the breadwinner-homemaker ideal.

Sensing the anxiety these changes caused in some quarters, Jimmy Carter brought a family-strengthening theme to his 1976 campaign and to his presidency. Carter's defense of the family seemed as uncontroversial as endorsing Mom and apple pie. But family policy turned out to be a much more contentious topic than Carter had suspected, and it has remained a battleground ever since. For example, during the campaign, Carter promised to hold a "White House Conference on the American Family" to discuss "specific ways we can better support and strengthen our families."[5] But after a controversy over who would direct the conference, conservatives and liberals battled over whether it should be titled a conference on "the family" (meaning the breadwinner-homemaker family) or "families" (which would include dual-earner and single-parent families).

The battle over the White House conference illustrates the first of two kinds of conflicts that were not far beneath the surface of any major public issue concerning families: the conflict over women's autonomy and the conflict over income assistance. It is worth examining each of these conflicts.

---

[4]The statistics on divorce and women's labor force participation are from Cherlin (1992).
[5]Quoted in Steiner (1981).

THE CONFLICT OVER WOMEN'S AUTONOMY

The public debates about family issues have often been based on different visions of women's family roles. Under one vision, women should be relatively independent of men. They should have enough earning potential to support themselves if necessary. Laws should protect their right to make decisions about childbearing. Under the other vision, women should be more dependent on men. In their marriages, men should earn the money and women should specialize in housework and raising children. Difficult decisions about childbearing, such as whether to terminate a pregnancy, should be joint. Let us examine two forms this conflict over autonomy has taken: women's economic independence from men and women's ability to decide whether to abort a pregnancy.

Women's Economic Independence   What distinguishes the breadwinner-homemaker family from the kinds of families that were dominant both before it arose in the nineteenth century and after its demise began in the 1960s is the nearly complete dependence of wives on their husbands for the means of obtaining the family's needs. The means of obtaining these needs in an industrialized society is money, and in the breadwinner-homemaker family, men make it and women don't. Chapter 9 describes other kinds of families, such as the preindustrial farm family, in which both spouses worked together in a joint enterprise, and the contemporary dual-earner family. In these kinds of families, women are less economically dependent on their husbands because they help run the farm or work for wages at the office.

To be sure, full-time homemakers perform valuable labor—their washing, cooking, and sewing allow the family to get by on the husband's wages. (Put another way, their labor allows employers to pay men lower wages than they would need if they had to purchase housekeeping services.) Homemakers' care of children benefits their families and the larger society. In fact, men are dependent on women for these services, but this reverse dependence is masked by the off-the-books nature of the homemaker's work (Zaretsky, 1986). For instance, only now that many working parents have to pay someone else to care for their children do we realize how much childcare is worth. Nevertheless, male wage earners, having money, can buy services if they wish; female homemakers, lacking money, cannot—except with their husbands' consent.

Some of the advocates of the breadwinner-homemaker family believe it to be God-given or biologically designed. They argue that a strict division of labor and male dominance is natural. They believe that the moral worth of men and women depends on how well they each perform their distinct roles—husband as provider, wife as caregiver (Schlafly, 1978). Another group of advocates concedes that the breadwinner-homemaker family may not be natural in a religious or biological sense, but they nevertheless believe it to be the most preferable form. Although they acknowledge the historical variation in families, they argue that the breadwinner-homemaker family has been the backbone of capitalist prosperity and democracy. It is said to support prosperity, in part, because it provides a small, self-sufficient unit that can move to where the job opportunities are in an industrial society; it is not tied to one city by linkages to a network of extended kin (Baumgarth, 1986).[6] It is

---

[6]William Goode made the more general argument that the conjugal family fits the need of industrial societies in *World Revolution and Family Patterns* (New York: The Free Press, 1963).

also said to encourage prosperity by creating self-reliant individuals who can become entrepreneurs and managers. These valuable individuals, it is argued, can venture forth from the small conjugal family and then retire for rest and spiritual renewal into the domestic sphere of privacy it creates. Brigitte Berger and Peter Berger wrote that, far from being the product of the Industrial Revolution, the breadwinner-homemaker family was "one of the important *preconditions* of this technological cataclysm" (Berger & Berger, 1983).

Finally, writers such as the Bergers and others believe the breadwinner-homemaker family to be essential to democracy because it is a mediating structure [➡ p. 157] that can give individuals the support they need to resist the dictates of the nation-state. Without these mediating structures, it is argued, individuals would have loyalties only to the state. With them, individuals can join together, if necessary, to resist the great power of the national government, the freedom-limiting rules of the bureaucracy, the dictates of a totalitarian regime. In the United States, this idea can be traced back to the Bill of Rights, which protects mediating structures through "the right of the people peacefully to assemble" and the right to bear arms because "a well-regulated Militia" is "necessary to the security of a free State." Mediating structures, then, provide a setting for individual and social action. It is important that they have strong leadership in order to protect and support individuals. The two-parent family is said to be a mediating structure because the authority of the father and the emotional bonds among the members create a "countervailing power" (Glendon, 1989) that protects individuals from abuses of power by the state.

Until very recently, those who favor the breadwinner-homemaker family tended to oppose social welfare programs that they view as encouraging women's economic independence. For instance, many social conservatives have opposed legislation that would subsidize the cost of out-of-home care for the children of employed parents. They have argued that assistance to employed parents encourages more mothers to take jobs outside the home, which erodes the breadwinner-homemaker family (Gill, 1991). Some favor little or no further government action of any kind, in large part because many existing policies, as noted, were designed to support the breadwinner-homemaker family. Others support programs that would benefit families with stay-at-home wives as well as those with employed wives, such as an increase in the tax deduction any family can claim per child (Carlson, 1986).

But critics of the breadwinner-homemaker family read the tributes to the self-reliance and autonomy it produces and ask, Self-reliance and autonomy for whom? They note that the self-reliant young entrepreneurs who venture forth from this type of family are overwhelmingly male. Women, by and large, do not share equally in the autonomy this family form creates; their talents and desires for work outside the home are stifled. To be sure, there are other rewards that some women may find attractive, such as having close interaction with children and avoiding the stresses of a paying job; but in any case they are asked to sacrifice their individuality on behalf of the male members of their families. "This family ideal," writes Barrie Thorne, "denies women individualism, equality, and full access to economic and political resources" (Thorne, 1982).

The costs to women are apparent in the transcripts of interviews with 300 middle-class married couples in 1955—perhaps the height of the breadwinner-homemaker family's popularity. The wives, according to historian Elaine Tyler May, were twice as likely as their husbands to report that they were dissatisfied with their marriages. Moreover, twice as many said they would not marry the same person if they had to do it over again. Many stayed in their marriages despite substantial strain. One wife wrote:

> *One particular source of friction: My husband is a firm believer in "woman's place is in the home"—so it is, to a degree—but I have always felt the need for outside activities and interest in community affairs because I felt mentally stagnant by not taking part in outside programs and because I feel morally obligated to take part, in view of my education and some capabilities. He takes no interest in my interests and belittles most women's groups. . . . Whatever I have done has had to be at no inconvenience to him—and often with a scornful attitude on his part* (May, 1988, p. 198).

The argument that women's own individuality is lost in the breadwinner-homemaker family was popularized by Betty Friedan in 1963. Her influential book *The Feminine Mystique* (Friedan, 1963) helped to launch the contemporary feminist movement. Feminist writers challenged the idea that only the breadwinner-homemaker family can provide a balance of autonomy and community. More fundamentally, they challenged the claim that the breadwinner-homemaker family is natural. Rather, they noted that it is unusual in historical perspective and therefore very nontraditional. They cited anthropological studies of the great variety of family forms in various societies. In the more radical critiques, some feminists argued that there is little that is "natural" about any kind of small, husband-wife-children family structure; rather, family types were said to be socially constructed—usually, it was said, in ways that allow men to dominate women (Collier, Rosaldo, & Yanagisako, 1982).

The conclusion of this body of writing is that the defenders of the breadwinner-homemaker family are asking women to pay a high price in lost autonomy to maintain a family form that is neither more natural nor more desirable than other forms (Stacey, 1990). This stance translates into political support for measures that increase the economic equality of women and make it easier for mothers to work outside the home. For instance, critics of the breadwinner-homemaker family typically support laws which require that women and men who are doing comparable jobs be paid the same wages. Most would also favor greater subsidies to employed parents for their out-of-home childcare expenses and more generous work leaves to care for newborn children or seriously ill relatives (Pogrebin, 1983).

The Abortion Dilemma

Abortion has been one of the most bitterly contested and divisive of issues in our society. It starkly contrasts two visions of women's roles: one that emphasizes childbearing and mothering versus one that emphasizes autonomy and employment.

From the late 1800s to the early 1970s, access to abortion was restricted in the United States, generally available only when physicians certified that it was necessary to save the life of the mother. In the 1960s, feminist groups began to demand access to abortion as a woman's right—thereby making abortion a political issue. With the fertility rate falling to about two births per woman, on average, and with life expectancy lengthening, childbearing no longer lasted most of a woman's adult life. Pro-abortion-rights activists, who prefer to be called "pro-choice," sought to control the timing and numbers of the children they bore. They did so, in part, on behalf of poor women who simply wanted to limit how many children they would have. Yet the pro-choice advocates, as Kristin Luker (1984) has written, also shared

FIGURE 6.1

Percentage of persons in a 1994 national survey who supported different levels of government spending for two problems: "welfare" and "assistance to the poor." (*Source:* National Opinion Research Center, 1997)

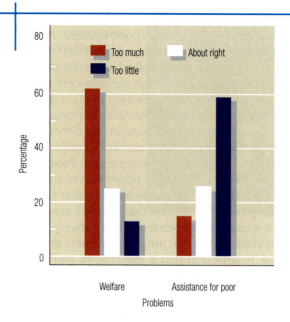

Public opinion in the United States favors assistance to the poor that enhances independence and self-reliance; there is much less support for cash assistance to people thought to be capable of working. A national survey carried out in 1994 illustrated this difference. People were asked whether they thought the country was spending "too much money," "too little money," or "about the right amount" on each of several problems. One-half of the sample was asked this question about "welfare," one-half was asked instead about "assistance to the poor." The results are shown in Figure 6.1. A majority thought the country was spending "too little" on assistance to the poor; but a majority also thought the country was spending "too much" on welfare, even though almost everyone who receives welfare is poor. As noted earlier, the use of the term "welfare" in the United States came to mean AFDC, the program of cash assistance to poor, single-parent families from 1935 to 1996. In fact, surveys from the 1930s onward show that never has a majority of Americans favored spending more on "welfare" or on "relief and recovery," as it was called during the Depression (Heclo, 1986). Instead, a majority believes that adults should be able to find jobs and manage economically on their own.

Since cash assistance such as AFDC was mainly available to single-parent families, critics of the program charged that it was an important cause of the growth of single-parent families over the past few decades. The evidence, however, is mixed. The most prominent critic in the 1980s, Charles Murray, noted that during the 1960s, AFDC benefit levels increased and so did the number of single-parent families. The implication is that more generous benefits encouraged more single-parent families to form. During the 1970s and 1980s, however, the value of the benefit package of AFDC plus food stamps stayed roughly the same; but the number of single-parent families continued to increase in number. Welfare, it seems, is not the whole story.

Still, it is possible that AFDC and related assistance programs reached a threshold by the end of the 1960s that supported a greater number of single-parent families. Several studies, however, suggest that these programs have probably not been the main force (Moffitt, 1990; Ruggles, 1997a). Another important contributor to the increase in single-parent families, as discussed in Chapters 4 and 5, is the growing scarcity of semiskilled manufacturing jobs that can provide people without college degrees enough steady income to support a family. Yet another, as also discussed, is the societywide cultural shift away from marriage that has occurred at all income levels.

Defenders of income assistance programs such as AFDC and food stamps argue that the social benefits of the programs exceed the costs. They note that cash assistance substantially improves the well-being of American children—one in five of whom lives in a family with an income below the poverty level. If cash assistance programs are not the main source of increases in single-parent families but are important sources of income for children, they reason, then the programs should be supported and even expanded. To do otherwise would be to punish poor children needlessly for the alleged sins of their parents (Grubb & Lazerson, 1988). It is also argued that some single-parent families are formed in circumstances—such as the end of an abusive marriage—that may improve the well-being of children. Moreover, providing single parents with enough support so that they can remain at home to spend more time caring for their children might be as good for children's well-being as compelling parents to work outside the home (Cherlin, 1995).

The 1996 Welfare Reform Law

As discussed earlier, AFDC was originally designed to support widows and their children, as part of the Social Security Act of 1935. Both AFDC and Social Security (the program that pays benefits to retirees) were created as entitlement programs by Congress. If a government program is an **entitlement,** the government is obligated to provide benefits to anyone who qualifies, regardless of the total cost of the program. For example, if I reach the official retirement age, walk into my local Social Security office, and ask to be signed up for benefits, they cannot say to me, "We're sorry, but we don't have any more money left this year. Come back next year." They *must* pay me the benefits I am entitled to. Not all government programs for low-income families are entitlements; housing subsidies, for instance, are limited: Only 31 percent of AFDC families also received housing subsidies (or lived in publicly owned housing) in 1995 (U.S. House of Representatives, Committee on Ways and Means, 1996). But starting in 1935, the government pledged to provide assistance through the AFDC program to any family that qualified (usually by having a low income, just one parent, and children under 18).

entitlement a program in which the government is obligated to provide benefits to anyone who qualifies, regardless of the total cost of the program

In 1950, Congress increased the AFDC benefit level in the hope that poor mothers would be able to stay home and care for their children. Starting about 1970, however, Congress passed a series of laws that encouraged, and later required, mothers receiving AFDC to take jobs and leave their children in the care of others. Yet "welfare" remained unpopular with the public. In a 1990 national survey, 70 percent of adults favored "reducing welfare benefits to make working for a living more attractive" (National Opinion Research Center, 1997). Bill Clinton, running against President George Bush in the 1992 election campaign, seized upon this unpopularity by promising to "end welfare as

FIGURE 6.2

Race and ethnicity of parents receiving Temporary Assistance to Needy Families (TANF) in 1997–1998. (*Source:* U.S. Administration for Children and Families, 2000)

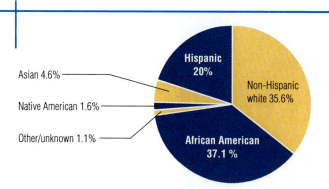

more so, the fathers of their children—as having chosen, in some sense, an irresponsible path to parenthood. Whether fairly or not, many Americans believe that people should refrain from having children until they can provide for them and are not willing to exempt the poor.

Moreover, there is another troubling subtext to the discourse about "deservingness." Not only the marital status but also the racial composition of the AFDC population had changed since the early days of the program. African-American single-parent families are heavily overrepresented among the persistently poor [➥ p. 122] and, therefore, among TANF recipients. Figure 6.2 shows the race of parents who received TANF in 1997–1998. African Americans, who constituted 37 percent of the TANF rolls, were overrepresented compared with their percentage of the total U.S. population in 1998 (13 percent) and even compared with their percentage of the total population with incomes below the poverty line (26 percent) (U.S. Bureau of the Census, 1999d). Observers of the welfare debate have suggested that racial animosity may underlie some of the public opposition to welfare spending (Grubb & Lazerson, 1988; Quadagno, 1994). Both Heclo and Katz argue that whites in the 1960s came to identify antipoverty policy with African Americans because of the civil rights movement, the activities of welfare rights organizations, the black urban riots in Watts and Northern cities, and the largely black bureaucracy that arose to administer the antipoverty programs (Heclo, 1986).

3.   *Concern about "dependency"*   The third reason for the policy reversal is the spread of the idea that the welfare-receiving poor had become too dependent upon public assistance. According to this line of reasoning, usually advanced by conservatives, people who receive public assistance for years and years often lose their initiative to find jobs. It is rational, Charles Murray (1984) argued, for welfare recipients to stay on the rolls: If they were to take a job, they would not only lose their benefits but also incur childcare, transportation, and clothing costs. Their new jobs probably wouldn't pay well and might not include health insurance (whereas AFDC/TANF recipients are covered by Medicaid). We have built a system, so this argument goes, that discourages people from moving from welfare to work (Kaus, 1992; Mead, 1992).

Moreover, the welfare critics state, children who grow up in this environment often become dependent on welfare themselves, thus perpetuating dependency from generation to generation. Drawing upon the work of anthropologist Oscar Lewis, who studied poor Puerto Rican families, critics claim that growing up on welfare fails to teach children the value of working hard, investing in the future, and waiting until marriage to have children. It also fails to provide them with successful role models to emulate. Of the culture of poverty, Lewis (1965) wrote:

> *Once it [the culture of poverty] comes into existence, it tends to perpetuate itself from generation to generation because of its effects on children. By the time slum children are age six or seven, they have usually absorbed the basic values and attitudes of their subculture and are not psychologically geared to take full advantage of changing conditions or increased opportunities which may occur in their lifetime* (p. xlv).

The supporters of PRWORA see it as a chance to break the cycle of dependency; hence the phrases "personal responsibility" and "work opportunity."[8]

Some social conservatives also argue that government agencies cannot do a good job of moving people from welfare to work because they are too impersonal and value-free. Rather, they maintain, religious organizations and other private agencies should take a greater role in assisting the poor, just as they did prior to 1935. (See *Families and Public Policy:* Who Should Help the Poor?)

This critical view of welfare is vigorously contested by others (mostly liberals) who believe that welfare usage is a *response* to poverty, not a cause of it. Yes, it is true, the defenders of time-unlimited welfare acknowledge, that children who grow up in families that receive welfare are more likely, as adults, to receive welfare themselves. (Although most adults on welfare did not receive it as children [Rank & Cheng, 1995]). But this association only shows that children who grow up in poverty are more likely to be poor as adults. What's being transmitted from generation to generation, according to this line of thought, is not a "culture of poverty" but rather social disadvantage: Children whose parents have less education and less income are themselves less likely to graduate from high school and obtain a good job (Rank & Cheng, 1995). In other words, poverty is the illness that public policy should treat, and welfare is only the symptom. Adults on welfare don't lack initiative, it is said; rather, they lack the opportunity to find steady jobs paying wages that can sustain a family (Handler, 1995). Ending cash assistance after five years, it is argued, is a cruel step that will further impoverish many poor children and their parents. In truth, no one knows how many poor children will be helped and how many will be harmed by the transformation of the welfare system under PRWORA.

Despite these different points of view, a Democratic president and many Democratic members of Congress joined with Republicans to enact the welfare reform law. Why did so many liberals and moderates support PRWORA? By the end of the 1980s, many liberal members of Congress had joined a new consensus that endorsed work outside the home with social support, rather than continued dependence on cash assistance, as the preferable goal for poor mothers. For one thing, they did so because so many nonpoor mothers were working outside the home. To some liberals, a program to help mothers receiving welfare obtain jobs seemed likely to increase their autonomy. In addition, many accepted the idea that persistent poverty was not just a problem of income but also of prolonged dependence on cash assistance. Finally, welfare remained deeply unpopular, and even liberal politicians were reluctant to oppose the 1996 bill, especially after it became clear that President Clinton would sign it.

---

[8]The word "Reconciliation" in the act's title just means that the final version was agreed upon by a House-Senate conference committee after the two bodies had passed slightly different versions.

and discourages the formation of two-earner marriages. If a man earns $50,000 and a woman earns nothing, they will pay less in taxes if they marry than if they stay single. On the other hand, if a man and a woman each earns $25,000, they will pay *more* in taxes if they marry than if they stay single (Crenshaw, 1994).

Support by conservatives for the programs and tax provisions described above demonstrates that they are not opposed to all government interventions into family life. Rather, conservatives were defending a particular set of interventions that were consistent with their vision of the family. The Depression-era and 1950s roots of these programs lie so far in the past that the government's role can seem almost invisible. It's understandable, then, that a politician might mistakenly believe that the government has had no role in shaping the contemporary family.

In fact, conservative groups have advocated government intervention when court rulings and legislation have undermined their vision of the family. After the 1973 *Roe* v. *Wade* decision on abortion, grassroots conservative organizations joined with religious groups to campaign for restrictive state laws and for a constitutional amendment banning abortion. The anti-abortion forces succeeded in passing legislation that prohibited the use of federal funds for performing abortions, thus restricting poor women's ability to obtain them (Tribe, 1990).

THE LIBERAL VIEWPOINT

As for the liberal *leitmotif,* it suggests a desire both to use government to assist families and to help all families equally. Actually, the kinds of measures advanced by liberals tend to help married couples in which wives are employed outside the home and single parents more than they help breadwinner-homemaker couples. This also is no coincidence. By and large, liberals, a political category in which there is a large overlap with feminists, believe that the breadwinner-homemaker family is at best no better than other family forms or at worst a form that unjustifiably restricts the autonomy of women.

In the 1980s, for example, liberals worked for the enactment of government programs that would provide employed parents with assistance in finding and paying for out-of-home care for their children. Many liberal advocates of childcare legislation recommended that the government make available vouchers that low- and moderate-income parents could give to their childcare providers, who in turn could exchange them for money. Also recommended were subsidies to childcare providers to improve the quality of care. Women who stay home full-time to take care of their own children would receive no benefits from these vouchers or subsidies.

In the family policy opera, liberals charge that conservatives, having set up the rules in their favor, are now saying that it's not fair to change them. Conservatives, in turn, accuse liberals of feigning support for all families while pushing measures that are unfair to breadwinner-homemaker families. Conservatives ask what the justification is for new spending programs that favor one kind of family over another. Liberals reply that the present set of programs already favors one form, and they are merely trying to restore a balance.

A PRACTICAL COMPROMISE

Yet in the late 1980s and 1990s, a pragmatic consensus was sometimes reached between conservatives and liberals that resulted in the enactment of significant legislation. Perhaps the foremost example of the consensus is the expansion of the **Earned Income Tax Credit (EITC).** Introduced in the 1970s, the EITC provides a refundable tax credit to low-income families with children in which at least one parent is employed. Even if the family earns so little that its members owe no taxes, they still receive a check for the value of the credit from the government if they file their tax returns. Essentially, the EITC is an income subsidy for parents who earn low wages. Conservatives like it for two reasons. First, it goes only to families in which a parent is employed; in the policy jargon, it targets the "working poor," those who earn barely enough (or not enough) to stay above the poverty line. (For a family of four, benefits are phased out at income in the low $20,000s.) An unemployed single parent is not eligible. Therefore, the EITC reinforces the obligation to work. Second, it applies not only to dual-earner, two-parent families but also to breadwinner-homemaker families because a family qualifies even if only one parent works outside the home. It therefore appears neutral toward wives working outside the home.

Liberals, on their part, like the EITC because it provides income assistance to many low-income families. Liberals also realize that there are relatively few breadwinner-homemaker families among the working poor (who can't afford a stay-at-home parent), so that, in reality, most of the money goes to two-earner families and to employed single parents. Finally, liberal members of Congress in this era realized that a program of tax credits for the working poor went as far as they could convince conservatives to move with regard to income assistance. The EITC was increased substantially as part of the 1988 welfare legislation and again in 1990. Then, as part of President Clinton's 1993 budget legislation, it was increased yet again and its upper income limit was raised so that more families were eligible. As of 2000, the EITC provided a maximum benefit of almost $4,000 to a family with two children and an income of $10,000 to $13,000.

With regard to gender and public policy, PRWORA also has moved conservatives and liberals closer together. Although PRWORA is certainly a public policy victory for conservatives, it has undermined their claim that government should not support mothers who work outside the home. In requiring work and providing childcare subsidies for TANF recipients, the Republican majority tacitly conceded that it is acceptable for the government to assist mothers who are employed. To be sure, the assistance is limited to poor, single mothers on welfare, but it will be hard for conservatives to hold the line. In 1997, at least two states with Republican governors announced plans to provide childcare subsidies to nearly all poor parents with jobs, whether they were on welfare or not.[9]

Moreover, an important childcare bill had passed Congress in 1990 only because a number of conservative members of Congress adopted a more pragmatic attitude than they had in the past toward women working outside the home. For instance, Republican Senator Orrin Hatch of Utah braved criticism from within his party to become a cosponsor of the childcare legislation. He told his supporters that, although he might wish otherwise, women were in the labor force to stay and their children needed assistance. In addition, in 1993, President Clinton signed into law a bill requiring large employers to provide their employees with 12 weeks of leave to care for newborns or deal with other family emergencies.

Earned Income Tax Credit (EITC) a refundable tax credit to low-income families with a child or children in which at least one parent is employed

---

[9]The two states were Illinois and Wisconsin.

These developments suggest that, at the turn of the century, the conflict over women's autonomy, so long a part of family policy debates, is moving toward a partial resolution: Many conservatives are reluctantly accepting the legitimacy of government programs to assist working mothers. So far this assistance has been limited to mothers with low incomes, but the general principle of government assistance to working mothers has been established. Given the large number of families with mothers who are employed, I think it is likely that such assistance will be broadened in the early twenty-first century. Many liberals, for their part, are reluctantly accepting the principle that assistance to the poor should not be unconditional but rather should be accompanied by attempts to make the poor self-sufficient. This is a significant retreat from their political position over the past several decades. It suggests that further assistance to low-income families is likely to take the form of services (e.g., job training, Head Start) and subsidies (e.g., childcare) rather than cash.

By September 1999, three years after PRWORA was passed, the number of families receiving TANF had fallen by a remarkable 44 percent (U.S. Administration for Children and Families, 2000). Passage of the law contributed to the decline, but so did the lowest unemployment rates in decades, and perhaps an expanded Earned Income Tax Credit as well. At any rate, the welfare rolls had fallen faster than most people had expected. Not yet clear, however, was how parents and children were faring in the brave new world of welfare reform once they were off the roles. Several studies are underway; over the next few years, observers concerned with family policy will be monitoring the results.[10]

---

[10]I have written a fuller update, "How Is the 1996 Welfare Reform Law Affecting Poor Families?" in Andrew J. Cherlin, *Public and Private Families: A Reader,* 2nd ed. (New York: McGraw-Hill, 2001).

Looking Back

1. **What is the "welfare state"?** In the twentieth century, the United States and other Western nation-states enacted numerous social programs to provide support to workers and their families. These "welfare state" measures softened the hardships of the labor market. In the United States, the programs were initially designed under the assumption that husbands would work full-time for wages, and wives would (and should) do full-time domestic work in the household. Congress did not anticipate that large numbers of wives would work outside the home, or that divorce and childbearing outside marriage would become more common.

2. **What are some of the basic issues in the family policy debates?** Two kinds of conflict characterize most debates about family policy. The first is a conflict over women's autonomy. Defenders of the breadwinner-homemaker family, which restricts women's economic independence, argue that it is the preferable family form. Critics note that the benefits of this family form go disproportionately to men, at a high cost in women's autonomy. Defenders and opponents of abortion rights differ on whether women should be able to decide whether to terminate a pregnancy. The second kind of conflict is waged over income assistance, specifically provision of assistance to the poor and near poor versus enforcement of their obligation to work. Critics of welfare programs such as AFDC and its successor, TANF, argue that they reduce work effort and contribute to the formation of single-parent families. Defenders of AFDC and TANF note that evidence of its harm is mixed at best, and it clearly lifts the incomes of poor children.

3. **Why was the 1996 welfare reform law a sharp break from earlier government policies toward low-income families?** The 1996 welfare reform law authorized states to set a time-limit of five years or less on the receipt of cash assistance in the new TANF program. After that, families would not receive benefits. The law also strengthened work requirements. Perhaps most important, the law eliminated the "entitlement" to cash assistance for low-income single-parent families. Before the law was passed, states had to pay benefits to any family that qualified for them. After its passage, states could limit the amount of funds they could spend in a given year.

4. **What are the themes that conservatives and liberals stress in debating family issues?** In debates over family policy, conservatives often claim that they want to keep the government from intruding into family life. But the government has already intervened in family life; social welfare legislation from the 1930s through the 1950s was designed to support the breadwinner-homemaker family. Liberals, on the other hand, tend to propose measures that would benefit single parents and married couples in which wives work outside the home more than they would benefit breadwinner-homemaker families. Conservative legislators tend to resist such proposals.

5. **What are the most important recent developments in family policy?** Recently, lawmakers have reached a pragmatic consensus and passed several pieces of legislation regarding families. Besides welfare reform (1996), Congress allowed several pieces of legislation to be enacted, including multiple expansions of the Earned Income Tax Credit, childcare legislation (1990), and family leave legislation (1993). Conservatives are reluctantly accepting the legitimacy of government programs to assist mothers who work outside the home. Liberals are reluctantly accepting the principle that assistance to the poor should not be unconditional.

Thinking about Families

1. What were the strengths of the breadwinner-homemaker families that predominated in the mid-twentieth century? What were their limitations?

2. Why is abortion such a bitterly contested family issue?

3. In what ways does the 1996 welfare reform law reflect the political conflicts over income assistance and women's autonomy?

4. **The Public Family** Many states now withhold part of a recipient's TANF benefits if she doesn't get her children inoculated against childhood diseases or if her children don't attend school regularly. Do you think this is a good policy?

5. **The Private Family** Is the government inappropriately invading private life if it tries to encourage people to form one kind of family—say, a married-couple family—rather than another?

Key Terms

Aid to Families with Dependent Children (AFDC) 177
block grant 192
Earned Income Tax Credit (EITC) 199
entitlement 191
family wage system 182
nation 179
nation-state 179
Personal Responsibility and Work Opportunity Reconciliation Act of 1996 (PRWORA) 177
pronatalism 182
Social Security Act of 1935 176
state 179
Temporary Assistance to Needy Families (TANF) 192
welfare state 182

Families on the Internet   www.mhhe.com/cherlin

*Note: While all the URLs listed were current as of the printing of this book, these sites often change. Please check our web site (**http://www.mhhe.com/cherlin**) for updates.*

For information on PRWORA and other welfare reform issues, the best place to start is **www.welfareinfo.org,** the home page of the Welfare Information Network, which describes itself as "a clearinghouse for information, policy analysis, and technical assistance on welfare reform." It contains links to the complete text of PRWORA (it's massive) and several summaries and analyses of the bill by both liberal (e.g., Children's Defense Fund) and conservative (e.g., Heritage Foundation) organizations. A page entitled "Selected Welfare Reform Related Data" provides links to a large amount of statistical data on poverty and welfare in the United States. A page entitled "Welfare Related Web Sites" provides links to over 100 other sites.

I am collaborating with several other researchers on a study of the consequences of welfare reform for parents and children in low-income families. Our study's web site is **www.jhu.edu/~welfare.** We have made available for downloading a number of policy briefs—short reports on a particular topic. To learn what welfare recipients know about changes in the welfare law and how they say they are responding, go to the publications page and read our policy brief, "What Welfare Recipients Know about the New Rules and What They Have to Say about Them."

Part Three

Sexuality, Partnership, and Marriage

n this part, we move from a focus on the effects of larger social structures—gender, class, race, ethnicity, government—on families to a consideration of how intimate family relationships are built from the ground up. These three chapters examine the emotional satisfactions and difficulties that people experience as they come to love someone and to form partnerships and marriages. They also examine differences in power and authority that emerge in these unions. In other words, the focus now shifts mostly to the private family. This is not to say that social structure disappears. On the contrary, family relationships are formed, maintained, and dissolved in a social context that must be considered. Nevertheless, the emphasis in this part is on how contemporary family relations provide intimacy, love, personal fulfillment, and cooperation but also sustain inequalities between wives and husbands. • **Chapter 7** discusses the emergence of the modern concept of sexuality, which is about a century old. It then traces the great changes in sexual attitudes and practices over the past few decades. It focuses on childbearing outside of marriage, which is a consequence of changing sexual practices. In addition, it examines the emergence of a gay and lesbian subculture. • Attention then shifts in **Chapter 8** to marriage and cohabitation. We will first study courtship, dating, and the marriage market. We will then examine cohabitation and its relationship to the process of becoming married. We will then review how marriage changed to a companionship in the early 1900s and how it has recently changed again to a more independent kind of partnership. • **Chapter 9** will examine the infuences that work life has on marriage. We will consider how differences in husbands' and wives' typical work arrangements can generate inequalities of power and authority. And we'll study the consequencses for family life of the great increase in dual-earner families.

Sexuality

Looking Forward

1. When did the idea of a sexual identity develop?

2. How has the relationship among love, sex, and marriage changed over time?

3. What is the nature of the teenage pregnancy "problem"?

4. How have views of homosexuality changed?

5. How has the AIDS epidemic developed, and what has been the public response to it?

Between 1882 and 1884, Isabella Maud Rittenhouse was courted by several suitors. Maud's diary, discussed by Steven Seidman, reveals that two stood out (Seidman, 1991). The first was Robert Witherspoon, a handsome, charming, educated, cultivated man, to whom Maud was powerfully attracted. The other was Elmer Comings, a rather plain-looking and socially awkward man who was, nevertheless, hard-working, reliable, and responsible. Today, the choice between them would be easy: 9 out of 10 Mauds would pick Robert, the object of romantic love, over unexciting Elmer. The real Maud, however, chose Elmer. Her reasoning shows how different was the relationship among sex, love, and marriage in the Victorian era than it is now.

To Maud and to most other nineteenth-century women and men, marrying someone because of strong romantic feelings was considered risky. Passionate, romantic love was thought to be a base emotion that faded away quickly, leaving little support for the couple. Far longer lasting was a spiritual love in which the partners joined together in a moral, uplifting marriage. The spiritual relationship rested upon a deep knowledge of each other and a sense of mutual obligation. Spiritual love was "true love," a union not only of the heart but also of the soul and the mind. Strong sexual attraction was equated with "romantic love," a dangerous emotional state that was hard to control. True love was much to be preferred.

There were practical reasons, rooted in the structure of nineteenth-century society, why people thought this way. The general standard of living was far lower than it is today, and most married women did not work outside the home. In order to have a comfortable life, it was crucial for a woman to marry an economically reliable, hard-working man. Correspondingly, a man needed to marry a woman who would raise children and manage a home competently. Feelings of romantic love could tempt a person to choose passion over partnership. Indulging in passion was a luxury most nineteenth-century people could not afford.

And so Maud decided that her romantic love for Robert was immature and that she could not overlook some lapses of character. She wrote that he had "beauty of feature and charm of tongue with little regard for truth and high moral worth"; whereas Elmer, "though not graceful . . . and handsome . . . [had an] inward nobility in him." Maud was well aware that she was rejecting romance when she rejected Robert: "If I do marry [Elmer] it will be with a respectful affection and not with a passionate *lover* love."[1] Moreover, Maud knew that, unlike Robert, Elmer did not share her knowledge of and interest in the arts and literature: "All

---

[1]All quotations are from Seidman (1991).

the time I am planning to bring him up to a standard where I *can* love him."
Thus, she girded for the task of marrying Elmer. Fortunately for her—although
not for Elmer—she broke off the courtship when Elmer entered into some suspicious business dealings that cast doubt on his character. But even in ending the
courtship, Maud relied on practical and ethical considerations rather than on her
feelings.

This separation between romantic love and sex, on the one hand, and marriage,
on the other hand, was typical of the cultural tradition of the Western nation-
states prior to the twentieth century. One historian studied the detailed writings
on marital sexual activity by 25 medieval theologians and found that only 2 of
them ever addressed the subject of love (Flandrin, 1985). Sexual relations that
were too passionate were thought to be immoral and to compete with a person's
worship of God. Sensual pleasures were for the love affairs a person had outside
of his or her marriage—never sanctioned by theologians but tolerated, in practice,
for men only. St. Jerome, quoting the Roman philosopher Seneca, wrote:

> *A prudent man should love his wife with discretion, and so control his desire and
> not be led into copulation. Nothing is more impure than to love one's wife as if
> she were a mistress. . . . Men should appear before their wives not as lovers but
> as husbands* (Aries, 1985a).

This separation between erotic love and marriage evaporated during the twentieth century. Both Seneca and Maud would be surprised to read the 1987 treatise
Super Marital Sex: Loving for Life, the author of which states, "Super marital sex
is the most erotic, intense, fulfilling experience any human being can have"
(Pearsall, 1987). More surprising still would be the increase in sexual activity outside the context of any kind of long-term relationship, the increase in childbearing outside of marriage, the emergence of an open homosexual subculture, and
the public display of sexually oriented goods, services, performances, and advertisements. How did we get from there to here? And what are the implications of
these changes for family and personal life as we enter the twenty-first century?
These are the questions to be explored in this chapter.

We will turn first to the emergence of sexual identities such as heterosexual or
homosexual—a more modern phenomenon than you might think—and the comparatively recent establishment of a relationship between romantic love and marriage. We will then focus on several important consequences of changes in sexual attitudes and behavior. We will examine the rise of childbearing outside of
marriage, particularly among adolescents. Then we will study the emergence of
an openly gay and lesbian sexuality, and the evidence on the origins of sexual orientation. Finally, we will look at the AIDS epidemic and the public response to it.

The Emergence of Sexual Identities

Although sex isn't new, sexual identities are. By a **sexual identity,** I mean a set
of sexual practices and attitudes that lead to the formation in a person's mind of
an identity as heterosexual, homosexual, or bisexual. Most people in our society
today could give a clear and immediate answer to the question "Are you heterosexual or homosexual?" Our sexual identity, in turn, becomes an important part
of our sense of who we are. Furthermore, we see this as "natural"—everyone, we
assume, has a sexual identity.

sexual identity a set of
sexual practices and attitudes
that lead to the formation in a
person's mind of an identity
as heterosexual, homosexual,
or bisexual

Yet the question "Are you heterosexual or homosexual?" would have stumped Americans until the late nineteenth century. Not only the terms "homosexual" and "heterosexual" but also the idea of "being" homosexual or heterosexual had not yet been invented. There were only two categories of sexual activities, the socially approved (sexual intercourse within marriage, in moderation, and undertaken mainly to have children) and the socially disapproved (all other activities, including acts between persons of the same sex, masturbation, oral sex regardless of the genders of the partners, and so forth). To perform any of the latter was sinful, but such behavior did not define a person as having a particular sexual identity. Moreover, one's sexual acts played a smaller role in defining one's sense of self. The concept of a sexual identity requires a self-consciousness and self-examination that was not prominent until the late nineteenth century.

That sexual identities only recently emerged as a concept suggests that they are socially constructed. The categories we use (for instance, homosexual versus heterosexual) are defined by the society we live in. This is not to say that biological predispositions play no role in sexuality; many believe them to be a part of the story, too (Schwartz & Rutter, 1998). But whatever predispositions do exist are shaped and labeled according to social norms and values. Moreover, as the story of Maud, Elmer, and Robert shows, these norms and values are, in part, a response to the way society is organized—such as how women and men divide their labor—and to economic factors such as its standard of living. The social norms and the organization of late-eighteenth- and nineteenth-century middle-class society in the United States, for example, may have supported more intimate same-sex friendships than is the case today. (See *Families in Other Cultures:* Was Alexander Hamilton Gay? And Other Irrelevant Questions.) The emergence of sexual identities is a key to understanding the changing relationships among sex, love, and marriage that have occurred during the late nineteenth and early twentieth centuries.

THE COLONIAL ERA TO 1890: SPIRITUAL LOVE AND SEXUAL RESTRAINT

Over the centuries, religious doctrine has powerfully shaped standards of acceptable sexual behavior. Prior to the American Revolution, religious authorities preached that sexual intercourse was appropriate only within marriage and only for the purpose of having children. The laws of the Massachusetts Bay Colony forbade, on penalty of death, most other sexual acts, including rape, adultery, and sodomy—which encompassed acts of penetration between two persons of the same sex, acts between men and animals, and acts other than vaginal intercourse between a man and a woman. Few people, however, were actually executed. One of the unfortunate was 18-year-old Mary Latham, hanged in 1645 after she admitted to having had sex with 12 men and calling her elderly husband a cuckold—someone whose wife has committed adultery. Another was William Hacketts, convicted of having sex with a cow, who was hanged in a public square just after he watched the execution of the cow (D'Emilio & Freedman, 1988).

Even among married couples who were trying to have children, sex was approved only in moderation. The Puritan minister Cotton Mather warned married couples of the dangers of "inordinate affection" (D'Emilio & Freedman, 1988). But after about 1750, young adults began to play a greater role in choosing their spouses. The growth of commercial capitalism provided sons with employment

Adultery was seen as a shameful act in the 1700s, although more so for women than for men. In Nathaniel Hawthorne's novel, *The Scarlet Letter*, Hester Prynne was forced to wear a scarlet "A" for adultery.

alternatives to the family farm; they no longer needed to wait to marry until they were given land by, or inherited it from, their fathers. As this change occurred, parents' influence over whom their children married declined. More so than parents, young adults tended to choose spouses on the basis of affection and mutual respect (although not necessarily passion or romantic love). Gradually, it became more acceptable for married couples to engage in sexual intercourse solely for the pleasure it gave them. But they were warned to exercise restraint; medical experts cautioned that excessive sexual activity caused illnesses ranging from depression to loss of vision to insanity. A widely read 1865 text by Dr. William Acton stated, "Too frequent emission of the life-giving fluid, and too frequent sexual excitation of the nervous system is . . . in itself most destructive" (Acton, 1865).

Then, in the nineteenth century, the growth of wage labor in factories separated the worlds of husbands, who typically worked outside the home, and wives, who typically didn't. The two domains came to be seen as "separate spheres": hers, the home and children; his, the wider world beyond. In the doctrine of separate spheres, women were said to be the guardians of virtue and morality. Consequently, women's sexual instincts were labeled as spiritual rather than carnal. It was part of the wife's role to limit the sexual passions of her husband and to balance the spiritual and physical sides of their union. By showing

Was Alexander Hamilton Gay?
And Other Irrelevant Questions

In April of 1779, Alexander Hamilton wrote to John Laurens, with whom he had served in the American Revolution:

Cold in my professions, warm in [my] friendships, I wish, my Dear Laurens, it m[ight] be in my power, by action rather than words, [to] convince you that I love you. I shall only tell you that 'till you bade us Adieu, I hardly knew the value you had taught my heart to set upon you.

In September, after almost giving up hope of receiving a letter from Laurens, Hamilton wrote of his joy at finally receiving one:

But like a jealous lover, when I thought you slighted my caresses, my affection was alarmed and my vanity piqued. I had almost resolved to lavish no more of them upon you and to reject you as an inconstant and an ungrateful—. But you have now disarmed my resentment and by a single mark of attention made up the quarrel (Katz, 1976).

Nor were famous American men the only ones who wrote intimate letters to other men. Karen Hansen tells the story of Brigham Nims, who lived for most of his life on his family's farm in New Hampshire, married, and had three children. In the 1830s, prior to marrying, Nims worked in a box factory in Boston for two years, where he struck up a close friendship with J. Foster Beal. They corresponded for a few years afterward. In one passage, Beal writes:

can not forget those happy hours [th]at we spent at G. Newcombs and the evening walks; but we are deprived of that privilege now we are separated for a time we cannot tell how long perhaps before our eyes behold each other in this world.

In a later letter, Beal reminds Nims of the time Beal nursed him through an illness:

I guess you have forgot all about you being at Boston last Sept. when you was so sick, and I took care of you, doctored you up, even took you in bed with myself; you will not do as much, as, to write me (Hansen, 1989).

Upon discovering these accounts, it is the instinct of the contemporary reader to immediately consider whether the relationships were homosexual. Yet historians argue that such a question represents the myopia of a person steeped in twentieth-century culture peering back at another time. The categories of homosexual and heterosexual did not yet exist, and therefore nineteenth-century people did not need to fit into them. Whether or not Hamilton's intimate friendship ever involved a sexual act was not its defining feature. As historian Jonathan Katz notes, even if many of the phrases in these letters were merely rhetorical flourishes, it is striking how easy it was for men to use language that today would be seen as indicating a sexual relationship.

In fact, what seems so different about these relationships is the seeming ease with which two same-sex individuals could engage in intimacies, such as sharing a bed or declaring their love for each other, without these acts marking the relationship as sexual or asexual. (Indeed, Hansen tells us that sharing a bed was not uncommon among the working class in nineteenth-century Boston because of the lack of space.) A broad range of af-

sexual restraint at the wife's request, the couple could focus on their love—for marital love was seen as a spiritual condition, quite separate from erotic desires. The common wisdom was that wives were better suited than husbands to maintaining sexual restraint because of their lesser desires. Dr. Acton wrote, "The majority of women (happily for them) are not very much troubled with sexual feelings of any kind. What men are habitually, women are only exceptionally" (Acton, 1865).

This denial of women's sexual feelings has been seen as a part of the sexual repression of the Victorian era (so named for Queen Victoria, ruler of Great Britain and Ireland from 1837 to 1901) (Marcus, 1964). It was not a natural condition but rather the result of the way young women and men were socialized. Yet the ethic of sexual restraint may have been useful to women. Historian Carl Degler argued that because childbearing was so dangerous, it was in wives' interest to limit the

fection and intimacy was open to same-sex friendships in a way that, for most men at least, it is not today.

The best-known study of same-sex intimacy in the late eighteenth and nineteenth centuries is Carroll Smith-Rosenberg's "The Female World of Love and Ritual" (Smith-Rosenberg, 1975). Smith-Rosenberg explored the "separate sphere" of middle-class women and found that they often formed deep emotional bonds of friendship with other women. Immersed in a network of female kin and friends, women helped one another in crises such as childbirth, helped to prepare one another for weddings, and spent long hours together talking. Some of their correspondence seems, by today's standards at least, to have a romantic and even erotic tone. Smith-Rosenberg writes of Sarah Butler Wister and Jeannie Field Musgrove, who first met as teenagers during a summer vacation, attended boarding school together for two years, and formed a lifelong intimate friendship. At age 29, Sarah, married and a mother, wrote to Jeannie, "I shall be entirely alone [this coming week]. I can give you no idea how desperately I shall want you." Jeannie ended one letter "Goodbye my dearest, dearest lover" and another "I will go to bed . . . [though] I could write all night—A thousand kisses—I love you with my whole soul."

The point of studying exchanges such as these, as Smith-Rosenberg herself argued, "is not whether these women had genital contact and can therefore be defined as heterosexual or homosexual." Rather, the point is that these women lived in a social context that allowed them the freedom to form a friendship that was quite intimate without the friendship's being labeled as anything more than that. Middle-class women's bonds could be loving and sensual without necessarily being sexual; it is likely that even if they were, the sexual acts would not be seen as the defining characteristic of the relationship. The social context allowed women more flexibility in creating intense emotional ties than is the case today, when we tend to think that close, sensual same-sex relationships must be "homosexual."

Smith-Rosenberg believes that the creation of a separate sphere for middle-class women established the conditions that allowed such close friendships to flourish. But the correspondence between Nims and Beal suggests that some men may also have established intimate friendships. How unusual Nims was we cannot know. Other than the two years he spent in Boston, he worked on the farm. Hansen argues that rural men, who did not leave home to work in a factory every day, did not experience as strict a split between the worlds of women and men. Perhaps, she suggests, they had a more fluid conception of gender that allowed them to be intimate friends with other men.

Ask Yourself

1. Have you ever hesitated to express affection for a friend of the same sex out of fear that others would think you were gay?

2. What do the twentieth-century concepts of hetero- and homosexuality say about the culture that created them?

www.mhhe.com/cherlin

frequency of intercourse with their husbands. Their supposed lack of erotic interest gave them some measure of control over pregnancy (Degler, 1980).

1890 TO 1960: ROMANTIC LOVE AND MARRIAGE

A series of economic, demographic, and cultural changes occurred during the early decades of the twentieth century. [➡ p. 62] Foremost among them was a rising standard of living. In more and more families, people earned enough money to meet their basic needs for food, shelter, clothing, and so forth. No longer facing crises of subsistence, they could focus on the quality of their emotional lives. Moreover, as industrialization and urbanization grew, married couples saw that children were costlier than in previous generations: Instead of laboring in the farm fields from an early age, children needed to stay in school so that they could obtain good jobs when they reached adulthood. Consequently, instead of benefiting from their children's labor, parents had to support them while they studied. As a result, couples had fewer children and invested more financial resources in each one (Stern, 1987). Women who reached adulthood in the late 1890s bore four children on average, whereas women who reached adulthood 20 years later bore about three (Cherlin, 1992). Declining birthrates meant that married couples would eventually enter a stage in which they were no longer caring for young children—a stage in which they could focus their attention on their personal lives.

Connecting Romantic Love and Marriage

These changes produced, among other things, the rise of the private family. Young couples began to see marriage as a means of self-fulfillment, to be obtained not through restraint and spirituality but through romantic love and sexual gratification. The notion began to spread that husbands and wives should be companions who attend unselfishly to each other's needs, including their sexual needs. In a major shift, women's sexual needs were acknowledged. Indeed, by the 1920s, young women were displaying their sexual nature publicly in ways that shocked their parents' generation. Cosmetics sales, for example, rose from $14 million in 1914 to $141 million in 1925 (D'Emilio & Freedman, 1988). The dance hall and the movie theater provided nighttime commercial activities that promoted romance.

Moreover, public discussion of sexual matters grew, as the writings of European and American intellectuals on the subject became popular. For instance, the British author Havelock Ellis challenged the Victorian ethic of sexual restraint in a widely read series of books published at the turn of the century. Ellis argued that sexual activity within marriage was "all that is most simple and natural and pure and good." He asked, "Why . . . should people be afraid of rousing passions which, after all, are the great driving forces of human life?" What the world needed, he wrote, was "not more restraint but more passion" (D'Emilio & Freedman, 1988). Sigmund Freud, the founder of psychoanalysis, put forth the stunning thesis that our sexual drives and needs are an unconscious, fundamental force that shapes our personalities from childhood onward.

All these developments strengthened the connection between sexual expressiveness and romantic love, on the one hand, and marriage, on the other hand, during the first half of the twentieth century. No longer was love within marriage primarily a spiritual ideal; rather, sexual gratification and romance became a central indicator of your love for your spouse, which became, in turn, an increasingly important indicator of the health of your marriage. Thus, an enjoyable sex life and a romantic attraction came to be seen as necessary components of a successful marriage. Prior to 1900 a marital sex life that was *too* satisfying was spiritually suspect. One hundred years later, there is no such thing as too much sexual satisfaction within marriage, as the readers of *Super Marital Sex* can attest.

The meaning of romantic love itself remains elusive. It is clearly bound up with sexual attraction, but it encompasses more than that. It usually leads to a desire for an intense, close relationship that will endure indefinitely. Some authors distinguish between **passionate love,** the sexually charged attraction at the start of many love relationships, and **companionate love,** the affection and partnership felt in a love relationship of long duration. Susan and Clyde Hendrick write:

passionate love the sexually charged attraction that occurs at the start of many love relationships

companionate love the affection and partnership felt in a love relationship of long duration

If passionate love is the flame that consumes two people at the beginning of their relationship, then companionate love is the glowing embers that endure when the dramatic flame has subsided. Sexual attraction, intense communication, and emotional turbulence early in a relationship give way (if the relationship is to endure) to quiet intimacy, predictability, and shared attitudes, values, and life experiences later in the relationship (Hendrick & Hendrick, 1992).

Gender Differences in Romantic Love   Women and men may experience romantic love differently. Several authors argue that women more often use practical criteria in addition to romantic love in choosing a spouse, whereas men rely more on romantic criteria such as physical attractiveness. In particular, women are said to pay attention to a man's potential for holding a steady job, earning a good salary, and remaining faithful and loyal. A national survey confirms this difference, in general, as will be noted in the next chapter. Unmarried women aged 19 to 35 in the survey were less willing than comparable men to marry someone who was unlikely to hold a steady job, who earned much less, or who was more than five years younger. Men, on the other hand, were less willing to marry someone who was not good-looking or was older (South, 1991).

Evolutionary psychologists [➡ p. 33] would argue that these differing preferences reflect the reproductive strategies that men and women have evolved: women valuing support and commitment in men; men valuing evidence (physical attractiveness, younger age) that women can bear children. Perhaps there are some echoes of our hunter-gatherer past in these patterns. But sociologists would also point to other reasons. Arlie Hochschild, for example, has argued that women have these preferences because they are financially dependent on men; even when married women work outside the home, they tend to earn less than men. Therefore, writes Hochschild, the choice of a spouse is more important to them in material terms. Yet because our culture places such an emphasis on love in marriage, and because of their own desire for love, women feel they must come to love the men they choose. In order to do so, according to Hochschild, women spend more time managing their feelings of love, by which she means being aware of one's feelings, working on them, and consciously shaping them. Women, she suggests, more often do the "feeling-work" of willing themselves to love someone (Hochschild, 1983). It is the kind of work Maud set for herself when she wrote of Elmer, "All the time I am planning to bring him up to a standard where I *can* love him."

1960 TO THE PRESENT

The ideological and material currents of the first half of the twentieth century also undercut the justification for limiting sexual activity to marriage. Before this century, when sex was viewed primarily as a way of producing children, it was important to limit it to the only socially approved arrangement for rearing children, namely marriage. Men guarded sexual access to their wives through a double standard that punished women more harshly than men for engaging in premarital sex and **extramarital sex**—sexual activity by a married person with someone other than his or her spouse. Yet as the idea of sex for personal pleasure spread during the twentieth century, the rationale for restricting sex to married couples weakened. Through the 1950s, moralists were successful in limiting sexual intercourse to engaged or married persons, especially among middle-class

extramarital sex sexual activity by a married person with someone other than his or her spouse

women. But beginning in the late 1960s, sexual activity prior to marriage rose to unprecedented levels. Moreover, in the 1970s, unmarried, middle-class young adults began to live together openly, a previously unheard-of arrangement except among the poor. Rates of cohabitation rose so high that more than half of young adults in the 1990s are likely to live with a partner before marrying.[2]

NONMARITAL SEXUAL ACTIVITY

The changes in the late 1960s and 1970s are reflected in the answers that women in a 1992 national survey of adults' sexual activity gave to the question of how many sex partners they had had by age 30. Among women who had entered adulthood in the 1950s, two-thirds had had only one partner. Clearly, having sex just with one's husband was the norm. Only a daring few had many sex partners: 3 percent reported five or more (Laumann, Gagnon, Michael, & Michaels, 1994). In fact, although there are few numbers in the historical record, virtually every historical study suggests that through the 1950s, a majority of American women had first intercourse only after they were engaged to be married (Rothman, 1984). Women's sexual needs still were thought to be less than men's, and women were still seen as the guardians of virtue—which in this case meant abstinence until marriage. Yet among women who entered adulthood in the 1960s, just 46 percent reported only one partner by age 30; and 18 percent reported five or more. The proportion reporting only one partner by age 30 fell further to 36 percent among women who entered adulthood in the 1970s, whereas the proportion reporting five or more rose to 22 percent.

[2]See Chapter 8 for evidence on the trends discussed in this paragraph.

FIGURE 7.1

Number of sexual partners in the past 12 months, for single (never-married) women and men in the United States, 1988–1991. (*Source:* Michael, Laumann, & Gagnon, 1992.)

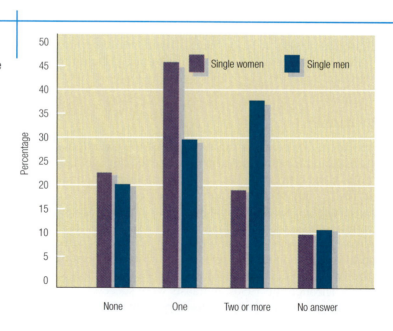

The changes have been less dramatic for men, reflecting the decline of the sexual double standard. This decline is evident from questions about sexual activity that were asked between 1988 and 1991 in the General Social Survey (GSS), an annual, national survey of the adult population of the United States. At the close of the interview, the interviewee was handed a three-minute supplementary questionnaire and envelope. The supplement noted the public health need for information about sexual partners and asked the interviewee to fill out the form and then to seal it inside the envelope. Figure 7.1 shows the number of sexual partners in the past 12 months reported by never-married women and men in the four annual surveys combined. Never-married women were just as likely as never-married men to report having had at least one sexual partner. Just 23 percent of never-married women and 21 percent of never-married men said they had not had sex in the previous 12 months. The major difference that remains is that men were more likely to report having two or more sex partners in the past year (Michael, Laumann, & Gagnon, 1992).

Marital and Extramarital Sex   Given the increases in sexual activity outside marriage, you might expect that married persons would be increasingly likely to have extramarital sex. Indeed, widely read books published in the 1960s and 1970s, such as *Open Marriage* (O'Neill & O'Neill, 1972) argued that marital relationships could coexist with, and perhaps even be enriched by, openly acknowledged extramarital affairs. Yet **sexual monogamy**—having just one sex partner—

sexual monogamy the state of having just one sex partner

Sexual activity prior to marriage rose greatly in the late 1960s and the 1970s.

is still the rule rather than the exception among married persons. Consider trends in public opinion. There is no doubt that the American public has become more tolerant of sexual activity among persons who have not yet (and may never be) married. Almost every year since 1972, the GSS has asked people their opinions about both premarital and extramarital sex. Between 1972 and 1998, the proportion who agreed that *premarital sex* was "always wrong" or "almost always wrong" declined from 48 percent to 36 percent. During the same period, however, the proportion agreeing that *extramarital* sex was "always wrong" or "almost always wrong" increased from 84 to 92 percent.[3]

Moreover, when the GSS in 1988 through 1991 asked its respondents about their sexual behavior, 98 percent of married women and 95 percent of married men said that they had had no sex partners other than their spouses during the previous 12 months (Greeley, Michael, & Smith, 1990). Clearly, most married couples adhere to the norm of monogamy almost all the time. Indeed, in the 1992 survey of adults' sexual activity, over 90 percent of women and over 75 percent of men said that they had never had another sex partner during the duration of their marriages, giving rise to wry newspaper headlines such as "Study Sees Marital Fidelity Rampant" (Laumann et al., 1994).

The emphasis on sexual gratification for both partners in marriage, new in the twentieth century, has provided wives and husbands with the potential for greater intimacy and emotional satisfaction. And access since the 1960s to modern methods of contraception, such as the birth control pill, has allowed individuals to separate sex-as-pleasure from sex-as-reproduction. Especially for women, whose sexual desires were often denied or ignored prior to the twentieth century, the legitimation of sexual gratification can be considered an advance. "Twenty years ago," wrote three feminist authors in 1986, "the woman dissatisfied with sex was made to believe she was lacking something; the woman who selfishly advanced her own pleasure was made to worry about being less than normal" (Ehrenreich, Hess, & Jacobs, 1986). Now it is taken for granted that both women and men should receive pleasure from sexual activity. The three authors praise the acceptance of "*pleasure*—perhaps especially sexual pleasure—as a legitimate social goal" (Ehrenreich et al., 1986). Yet observers have also noted that the emphasis on sexual satisfaction can create its own tyranny, since couples may believe that unless their sex lives are continually fulfilling there is something wrong with their marriages.

SEXUALITY AND MARRIAGE: AN OVERVIEW

In sum, there have been three eras in the attitudes toward sexuality and romantic love in the United States. Before about 1890, sexual attraction and romantic love were thought to be inappropriate bases for choosing a spouse. Moreover, even within marriage, sexual expression was thought to be an activity best done in moderation. From about 1890 to about 1960, in contrast, sexual attraction and romantic love were increasingly viewed as not only appropriate but, in fact, crucial criteria. Within marriage, people increasingly valued the emotional fulfillment they could obtain through sex and romantic love. The idea of a sexual iden-

---

[3]The question on extramarital sex was first asked in 1973; for both questions I have excluded "Don't know" and "No answer" responses (Davis, Smith & Marsden, 1999).

tity, based on one's attitudes and practices, passed into common usage. Still, sexual expression outside marriage continued to be seen as illicit.

In the most recent era, the positive value given to sexual expression and gratification has continued and even increased. In addition, sexual activity has become defined even more as a private matter. In 1965, for example, the Supreme Court ruled that a state law prohibiting the use of contraceptives violated marital privacy by allowing police to search the "sacred precincts of marital bedrooms" (*Griswold* v. *Connecticut,* 1965). In 1972, the Court, using similar reasoning, overturned laws prohibiting the sale of contraceptives to unmarried persons (*Eisenstadt* v. *Baird,* 1972). The rationale for these laws had been that sexual activity was carried out in order to have children and that the state had an interest in seeing that married couples did, in fact, have children and that unmarried persons did not. In this way, the state could promote and control the reproduction of the population. By the time of these court decisions, however, sex had become primarily a means of individual fulfillment. Therefore, the rationale for state intervention had weakened.

This changing view of sexual activity is part of the broader growth of individualism during the twentieth century. In the post-1960 era, cultural changes were spurred, in part, by the increasing economic independence of women, which made it possible for young adult women to postpone marriage without postponing intimate sexual relationships. In turn, young men were able to initiate sexual relationships with women without making a commitment to support them. (Women's economic independence will be discussed in more detail in Chapter 9.) The changes in sexual behavior were also guided greatly by the availability of more effective means of contraception, notably the birth control pill.

Within marriage, as noted above, the changes have increased the possibility of mutually and personally fulfilling sexual relations. Our culture has rejected Dr. Acton's old warning that too strong a focus on sexual activity is "most destructive" and has accepted instead Ellis's view that what the world needs is "not more restraint but more passion." Yet the cultural and economic changes of the past few decades have undercut the rationale for restricting this passion to marriage. It is no longer necessary to be married to have a regular, satisfying sex life. Consequently, the changes in sexual activity have weakened the role of marriage as the core of family life in the United States. Marriage must now compete with singlehood and cohabitation—an increasingly common form of sexual union that will be discussed in the next chapter.

Childbearing Outside of Marriage

One consequence of the cultural changes in sexuality is the rise in childbearing outside of marriage. Starting in the mid-1960s, young adults' sexual lives changed in two ways. First, having sexual intercourse prior to marriage, often many years before, became common. Figure 7.2 displays the findings of a series of national surveys of unmarried adolescent girls, age 15 to 19, since 1970. The percentage who had ever had sexual intercourse rose dramatically during the 1970s and then peaked in the late 1980s. Second, the incidence of early marriage decreased. In fact, between the mid-1950s and the late-1990s, the age at which half of all first marriages occur rose by four years for men and five years for women. Because of this enormous jump, the average age at marriage is higher today than at any time

FIGURE 7.2
Percentage of never-married, 15- to 19-year-old girls who had ever had sexual intercourse, 1971–1995. (*Sources:* U.S. National Research Council (1987); Forrest & Singh (1990); and U.S. National Center for Health Statistics (1997d), Table 19. For 1971, 1976, 1979, and 1982, percentages are for girls residing in metropolitan areas only. The 1988 and 1995 percentages are for all girls. However, the 1982 percentage, which is available for both groups, is nearly identical whether or not nonmetropolitan girls are included.)

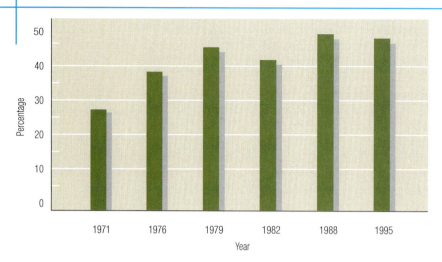

in the last 150 years (Fitch & Ruggles, 2000). The average first-time bride is now 25, and the average first-time groom, 27. Thus, far more young women and men now remain single throughout late adolescence and early adulthood.

Earlier sexual activity and later marriage have lengthened the stage of life when young adults can have a child outside of marriage. Figure 7.3 shows trends in first births to women age 15 to 29 in the period from the 1930s to the 1990s. The graph has one bar for each five-year period. The purple portion of each bar shows the percentage of first births to women who had not yet married. Note that until the early 1960s, 10 percent or fewer of all first births occurred to never-married women. But starting in the late 1960s, this proportion of first births to never-married women rose dramatically: By the 1990 to 1994 period, 40.5 percent of all first births fell into this category. (We will see in Chapter 8 that some of these mothers were living with the fathers of their children.) The reddish portion of each bar shows the percentage of first births that were conceived before marriage but born after marriage—colloquially, the shotgun marriages. The blue portion shows the percentage of first births that were conceived (and born) after marriage. Note that in the 1990 to 1994 period, less than half of all births in the United States fell into this category.

Making the transition to motherhood without a husband is now the predominant experience for African-American women: In 1998, 77 percent of first births to black women were to unmarried mothers. (Childbearing outside of marriage was also the majority experience among Hispanic women, at 52 percent.) But recently this has been rising more rapidly among whites: 34 percent of first births to white women were to unmarried mothers in 1998. Although media stories tell of middle-class women in their thirties having children on their own, or of lesbians having children, those kinds of first birth are still uncommon in the aggregate. Rather, unmarried first-time mothers tend to be young: In 1998 49 percent were teenagers and 33 percent were aged 20 to 24.[4]

---

[4]The figures in this paragraph are from unpublished tabulations provided by the U.S. National Center for Health Statistics.

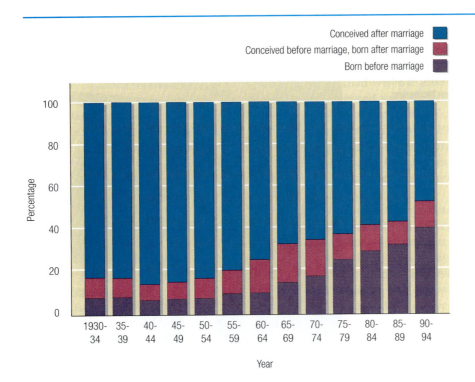

Conceived after marriage
Conceived before marriage, born after marriage
Born before marriage

FIGURE 7.3
First births to women 15 to 29 years old, United States, 1930–34 to 1990–94. (*Source:* U.S. Bureau of the Census, 1999e.)

ADOLESCENT SEXUALITY AND PREGNANCY

Adolescent sexual activity, however, appears to have declined slightly in the 1990s. Fewer never-married adolescent girls reported having had intercourse in 1995 than in 1988, as shown in Figure 7.2. Recent surveys of high school students suggest that the decline may have continued through the late 1990s. AIDS education may have been a factor: 90 percent of adolescents reported being taught about AIDS in school, and there was a sharp rise in the use of condoms (which effectively prevent the spread of HIV) among sexually active adolescents (U.S. Center for Disease Control and Prevention, 2000d). Still, sexual activity among unmarried adolescents remains much more common than in 1970.

Differences in sexual activity between adolescent boys and girls appear to have narrowed considerably. In the middle of the twentieth century, adolescent boys were more sexually active than girls (Darling, Kallen, & VanDusen, 1984). But by the end of the century, the gap had nearly disappeared, in part because in the 1970s and 1980s, the increase in premarital sex was greater for girls, and in part because in the 1990s, the decline in premarital sex was greater for boys (Santelli, Lindberg, Abma, McNeely, & Resnick, 2000). Class and racial differences in premarital sexual activity were also smaller at the end of the century because the rise in adolescent sexual activity had been greater among the middle class than among the poor, more noticeable among whites than among blacks (Forrest & Singh, 1989).

Summing up these trends:

- Adolescent sexual activity is much more common today than it was in the middle of the twentieth century.
- The greatest increase in adolescent sexual activity occurred in the 1970s and 1980s.

more than half of those who had received welfare had left the rolls; by the 22-year interview, two-thirds had left the rolls. In fact, at the 22-year reinterview their incomes varied widely: One-fourth were on welfare, one-fourth had family earnings of less than $15,000 (equivalent in purchasing power to about $19,000 in 1990 dollars), one-fourth had family earnings between $15,000 and $25,000 (equivalent to about $32,000 in 1990 dollars), and one-fourth had family earnings of $25,000 or more (Furstenberg et al., 1987).

Although teenage mothers are more likely to marry early than childless teenagers, their marriages are often brittle. In the Baltimore study, half of all the early marriages had dissolved by the 5-year reinterview, two-thirds by the 22-year reinterview. Most mothers had married at some point, and many cohabited with a partner, but the great majority of the marriages and partnerships had ended. Early marriages are, in general, less stable, perhaps because the spouses are less mature or because they cannot yet tell who will make a suitable long-term partner. The small minority of Baltimore teenage mothers who had managed to attain lasting marriages were in far better economic situations (Furstenberg et al., 1987). Because it usually brings a male worker's income to a family, marriage is one of the most important routes out of poverty for single mothers. It is, unfortunately, a difficult route for teenage mothers to follow.

To sum up what we know about teenage mothers:

- They are disadvantaged in education, income, and employment.
- Some, although not all, of their disadvantages are due to other factors in their lives, such as growing up in low-income families.
- There is much variation in the way their lives turn out.

Even with the selection effect and the variation in outcomes, having a child as a teenager still seems to diminish some young women's chances of an economically successful adulthood. It is also a potential problem for the children of the teenage mothers, a topic we will address in Chapter 10.

Gay and Lesbian Sexuality

The twentieth-century acceptance of sexual activity for reasons other than having children also weakened the justification for limiting acceptable sexual activity to opposite-sex couples. If sex was now a personal matter, the purpose of which was pleasure, then one might question why sexual acts between two men, or two women, shouldn't also be acceptable. During the 1950s, mainstream moralists supported the popular ideal of marriage and childbearing in part by harshly criticizing all the alternatives—especially homosexuality. Public vilification and persecution of homosexuals were intense in the 1950s before weakening in the 1970s.

A HISTORICAL OVERVIEW

In fact, Americans defined heterosexuality in part by mounting a public campaign against homosexuality beginning in the late nineteenth century. Recall that in the nineteenth century many women formed strong, deep friendships, reinforced by the separate sphere in which they lived. [➡ p. 52] (see also the *Families in Other Cultures* essay in this chapter) These friendships were assumed to be spiritual and carried no stigma, although some of them may have had a sexual component (Smith-Rosenberg, 1975). To a lesser extent, men were allowed to express love in a friendship without stigmatization (D'Emilio & Freedman, 1988). Certainly, there are examples from antiquity of attraction to the same sex without stigma: In much of ancient Greece and Rome, men were allowed, even expected, to desire sex with other men or boys as well as with women (Ariès, 1985b). The Greek biographer and historian Plutarch wrote:

> The noble lover of beauty engages in love wherever he sees excellence and splendid natural endowment without regard for any difference in physiological detail. The lover of human beauty [will] be fairly and equally disposed toward both sexes, instead of supposing that males and females are as different in the matter of love as they are in their clothes.[5]

Yet although the Greeks had words for specific sexual tastes, they had no general term comparable to "homosexuality" (Weinrich & Williams, 1991). In fact, no such term existed in Western societies until the nineteenth century.

Then, toward the end of the nineteenth century, an influential body of medical literature began to describe not merely homosexual acts but homosexual persons—distinctive individuals who were seen as suffering from a psychological illness that altered their sexual preference. Their supposedly unnatural condition was labeled "homosexuality," and it was said to pervade their personalities. They were no longer just men or women who engaged in sexual acts with a same-sex partner; they were homosexuals—seriously ill people (Foucault, 1980). In contrast to them, the same writers defined a "normal" sexual preference for the opposite sex as "heterosexuality." Heterosexuals were seen as mentally healthy as opposed to sick. This was the way sexuality entered our everyday language and our consciousness: as a means of organizing people into two contrasting sexual identities, one viewed as normal and one disparaged as diseased.

The medical model remained dominant until 1973, when the American Psychiatric Association removed homosexuality from its list of mental disorders (Silverstein, 1991). The model stigmatized homosexual people and served as a basis for prejudice and discrimination. But the very force of the critique also created a group identity for individuals who had previously had none. Much as the ideology of separate spheres created conditions that allowed for social and political action by women's groups, so the discourse on homosexuality as an illness created conditions that ultimately provoked social and political actions by homosexual persons. "Homosexuality began to speak in its own behalf," wrote Michel Foucault, "to demand that its legitimacy or 'naturality' be acknowledged, often in the same vocabulary, using the same categories by which it was medically disqualified" (Foucault, 1980). But that is getting ahead of the story.

In the early twentieth century, the growth of cities and the spread of wage labor allowed homosexual men and women to leave their families and communities and establish an underground sexual subculture. This anonymous, marginal world, however, was still small. Then, in 1948, Alfred Kinsey, a zoology professor at the University of Indiana, published the results of thousands of interviews with men about their sexual behavior. Kinsey's dry, statistical book with 173 figures and 162 tables, often referred to as the **Kinsey Report,** became an immediate bestseller. His findings on homosexuality shocked the country: Half of all men in his sample, he reported, acknowledged having had erotic feelings toward other men; one-third had had at least one sexual experience with another man; one out

Kinsey Report a 1948 book by zoology professor Alfred Kinsey detailing the results of thousands of interviews with men about their sexual behavior

[5]Quoted in Boswell (1982).

How Do Sociologists Know What They Know?   *Asking about Sensitive Behavior*

How do sociologists collect information on people's behaviors and attitudes? For the most part, they ask them. The most common way of doing so is through the random-sample survey. [➡ p. 25] Typically, a survey research organization will be hired to randomly select households and to ask the occupants a list of questions. In 1992, the National Opinion Research Center, one of the leading academic survey research organizations, asked a random sample of 3,432 adults detailed questions about their sexual activities and preferences. Researchers from the University of Chicago, who had written the questions, tabulated the results and published *The Social Organization of Sexuality* (Laumann et al., 1994). Several of their findings are presented in this chapter.

But can those findings be trusted? After all, the interviewers were inquiring about some of the most private and sensitive aspects of behavior. Biologist Richard Lewontin, writing in the *New York Review of Books* (Lewontin, 1995a), ridiculed the sociologists for believing the responses of their subjects. His scathing critique, and the subsequent exchange of letters between social scientists and him, addressed the limits of survey-based sociological research.

Lewontin's main objection is that sociologists can't be sure that people tell the truth when asked about their behavior, especially when the topic is as sensitive as sexuality. Some people may lie, while others may not even admit the truth to themselves. Lewontin also pointed to a discrepancy in the data: Men reported 75 percent more sexual partners in the previous five years than did women. A few complexities aside, the average number of sexual partners of men and women should be almost the same. The authors examine this discrepancy and conclude that the most likely cause is that men exaggerate or women understate the number of partners when asked. Writes Lewontin: "If one takes the authors at their word, it would seem futile to take seriously the other results of the study" (1995a, p. 29).

The authors responded that although they "readily admit that we were not always successful in securing full disclosure," they "spent a great deal of time worrying about how we could check the reliability and honesty of our respondents' answers" (Laumann et al., p. 43). They used techniques such as asking similar questions at different points in the interview to see if a person's responses were consistent. For some sensitive questions, the respondents were

given a form to fill out that they could return in a sealed envelope. The researchers asked their interviewers to evaluate whether the respondents appeared to be responding frankly, and 95 percent were judged to be frank. Then they compared the answers given by the "frank" respondents with the answers of the other 5 percent. They found few differences. For instance, less-than-frank women and men were just as likely to report having more than one sex partner in the past year (Laumann et al., pp. 564–68).

Lewontin was not appeased. For him, the sex survey is an example of sociology reaching for knowledge that is beyond its grasp. When they accept self-reports of sensitive behaviors and statistically analyze them, he argues, sociologists are trying too hard to imitate the natural sciences. Without adequate ways to measure information such as sexual behavior, and above all without the possibility of performing experiments, he maintains, sociology is limited:

[Sociologists] are asking about the most complex and difficult phenomena in the most complex and recalcitrant organisms, without that liberty to manipulate their objects of study which

Other American and European surveys have produced similar findings. In the GSS from 1989 to 1991, about 5 percent of men and 3 to 5 percent of women reported ever having a same-gender partner, and only about 1 percent of men and women reported sexual behavior exclusively with their own gender (Michael et al., 1992). In a 1991 survey of American men aged 20 to 39, 2 percent said that they had had any same-gender sexual activity during the previous 10 years (Billy, Tanfer, Grady, & Klepinger, 1993). European surveys have produced similar findings. A 1990–91 national survey in Great Britain found that 6 percent of men reported "any homosexual experience" (however the person defined it), and 4 percent reported one or more homosexual partners ever (Johnson, Wadsworth,

is enjoyed by natural scientists. In comparison, the task of the molecular biologist is trivial. . . . Like it or not, there are a lot of questions that cannot be answered, and even more that cannot be answered exactly. There is nothing shameful in that admission (Lewontin, 1995b, p. 44).

Lewontin's argument must be taken seriously by sociologists. There are indeed limits on how much sociologists can learn about human behavior; and random-sample surveys and statistical analyses can't surmount these limits. For some problems, sociologists might be better off abandoning surveys and turning to the kind of intensive, long-term field observations that anthropologists and some sociologists do—even though the findings from field studies aren't necessarily representative of the population under study.

Does it follow that we should reject all findings from the study of sexual behavior because it is likely that men exaggerated, or women understated, the number of partners? This is a matter of judgment. My answer would be no. For one thing, the results of the 1992 survey are likely to be more reliable than Kinsey's results, which have dominated discussions of sexual orientation for decades. As noted elsewhere in this chapter, Kinsey's sample is far less diverse and representative than is the Chicago researchers' sample.

In addition, some comparisons among different groups represented in the 1992 sample are likely to be valid even if the individual responses aren't entirely accurate. For instance, in one chapter the authors divide people into groups according to their responses to nine statements about sexuality (for example, "premarital sex is always wrong"). They find that, based on these statements, people's beliefs about sexuality can be classified into a few groups: "traditional," "relational," and "recreational." These groups differ greatly in their composition according to gender, race and ethnicity, age, and other characteristics. The researchers then discuss the implications of these social divisions for public debates on sexuality. (The chapter is reprinted in abbreviated form in the reader that accompanies this textbook [Cherlin, 2001].) These conclusions are likely to be valid unless people in some of the groups are more likely to reply truthfully than people in others. While this is a possibility, it seems unlikely to be a large enough problem to undermine the conclusions.

We should be wary of pushing survey research techniques beyond the limit of their usefulness. The 1992 survey pressed on that limit. The more sensitive the material and the more subjective the questions, the more skeptical readers should be. Nevertheless, we needn't dismiss the contributions of survey research to understanding sensitive issues. We should seek to supplement surveys with other, more intensive forms of data gathering. And we should recognize that there may be some questions about society that are beyond the capability of sociology to answer.

Ask Yourself

1. If you were asked to participate in a study of college students' sexual behavior, would you answer all the questions truthfully? Would you participate in the study?

2. Why is knowing about people's sexual behavior and attitudes important? Give a specific example.

www.mhhe.com/cherlin

Wellings, Bradshaw, & Field, 1992).[6] A 1991–92 national survey in France reported that 4 percent of men and 3 percent of women reported at least one occurrence of sexual activity with persons of the same sex during their lifetimes (Spira et al., 1992). To be sure, all these figures—including those in the 1992 University of Chicago survey—are likely to be minimum estimates, since some people probably did not divulge homosexual behavior, despite efforts to assure confidentiality.

Although the Kinsey Report badly damaged the model of homosexuality as an illness, the 1950s actually saw an increase in discrimination against homosexuals. Two factors contributed to this reversal. First, Americans turned inward toward

---

[6]No figures were presented for women.

marriage and childrearing after World War II, marrying younger and having more children than before or since in the twentieth century. The strong cultural support for the breadwinner-homemaker family also translated into renewed criticism of homosexuality—or any other reason for not marrying. Unmarried adults were sometimes suspected of being homosexuals and, implicitly, of being unable to live a proper adult family life. Second, the anti-Communist extremists of the late 1940s and early 1950s, such as Senator Joseph McCarthy, charged that homosexual people in government were security risks. According to their reasoning, homosexual people were vulnerable to blackmail by Communist spies, who would threaten to disclose their sexual identities unless they divulged government secrets. In 1950, a Senate committee investigating the employment of "homosexuals and other perverts" in government warned that homosexuals lacked "moral fiber." "One homosexual," the committee wrote, "can pollute a Government office" by enticing "normal individuals to engage in perverted practices" (D'Emilio & Freedman, 1988). Just after Dwight D. Eisenhower became president in 1953, he signed an executive order barring homosexual men and women from all federal jobs. This action spurred many states and localities to enact similar measures and fed something of a national panic about homosexuals (D'Emilio & Freedman, 1988). Overall, it was as if the increased emphasis on heterosexual marriage in the 1950s required defining and defaming its opposite—in this case, homosexuality. Moreover, homosexual people became lightning rods for the fear of communism.

The political liberalism of the 1960s improved the climate for homosexual people, and the civil rights movement and women's movement provided models for political organizing. Activists in the growing homosexual communities in cities such as New York and San Francisco urged the adoption of a positive, affirmative homosexual identity. The term "gay" began to be employed to mean not just a sexual orientation but an entire lifestyle, an open subculture with its own dress, social life, sexual mores, and community institutions. "Being gay," wrote the editor of a gay newspaper in 1975, "is more than just being attracted to members of the same sex. Being gay includes the affirmation and celebration of our varied lifestyles" (Seidman, 1991). The popularity of the term "gay" signified that homosexual women and men were transforming themselves from people labeled merely by their sexual preferences to a social group with its own subculture and its own claims to equal citizenship and equal treatment.

Many authors date the emergence of the gay political movement to the **Stonewall riot,** which occurred in the aftermath of a police raid on a gay bar, the Stonewall Inn, in the heavily gay Greenwich Village area of New York City in 1969. Influenced by other 1960s protest movements, a gay liberation movement formed in the aftermath of the riot. It urged homosexual people to develop a public identity, and it linked an end to discrimination against homosexual people with the radical social changes urged by other groups of the New Left. Lesbians found common ground with radical feminists in denouncing male dominance. By the mid-1970s, the movement had scaled back its more radical demands, but it continued to urge that homosexuality be defined as a positive, worthwhile style of life. Through encouraging gay individuals to "come out" to friends and relatives by announcing their sexuality and to be visible at public events such as gay pride marches, the movement helped to enhance the senses of selves of gay men and lesbians. It also had some success in overturning state laws and in the removal of homosexuality from the list of mental disorders. Yet, even in the early 1990s, nearly half the states had laws against sexual acts between two persons of

Stonewall riot the 1969 riot to which many writers date the emergence of the gay political movement

the same sex, although these laws were rarely enforced. In 1986, the Supreme Court affirmed the conviction of a Georgia man who was arrested in his bedroom while having consensual sex with another man. The decision, *Bowers* v. *Hardwick,* means that states may still enforce laws that declare gay and lesbian sex illegal (Rivera, 1991).

In the early 1990s, the rights of homosexual people remained a contentious political issue. Immediately upon assuming office in 1993, President Bill Clinton attempted to keep a campaign promise by ordering the military to allow homosexual people to serve. The order caused so much controversy that the president was forced by Congress to accept a compromise that allowed homosexuals to serve only as long as they did not divulge their sexual orientation or engage in homosexual behavior. Moreover, in a number of cities and states, citizens fought bitterly over ballot initiatives that would limit or expand the legal rights of homosexual people. In the latter half of the 1990s, controversy flared over the possibility of legalizing marriage for gay and lesbian couples. [➡ p. 4]

THE ORIGINS OF SEXUAL ORIENTATION

Some people believe that homosexuality is simply a lifestyle choice—one they themselves find objectionable. They use this belief to justify discrimination against homosexual individuals. Yet evidence is emerging that there may be a substantial biological component to sexual orientation (Bailey & Dawood, 1998). The evidence is somewhat stronger for men than for women. One study found that gay men had higher rates of gay maternal uncles and cousins, but not gay paternal uncles and cousins, than heterosexual men. This finding suggested that sexual orientation might be transmitted, in part, through a person's maternal line. The authors then decided to study the X chromosome—one of the two so-called sex chromosomes in the genetic material in every human cell—because men inherit their X chromosomes from their mothers. They examined the genetic material of pairs of gay brothers and found that most had identical material at the end of their X chromosomes, which supports the possibility of genetic transmission (Hamer, Hu, Magnuson, Hu, & Pattatucci, 1993). A similar study found more lesbian relatives among women who had experienced an early and exclusive sexual attraction to women, but not among women who had developed a later or nonexclusive lesbian orientation (Pattatucci, 1998).

Several other studies have recruited gay men and lesbians, each of whom had a same-sex sibling who was an identical twin, a fraternal twin, or an adopted sibling. The researchers then ascertained the sexual orientation of the subjects' twins or adoptive siblings. Identical twins have identical genetic material; fraternal twins share, on average, half their genetic material; and adopted siblings share no genetic material. Consequently, if homosexuality were partly biological in origin, one might expect the greatest similarity of sexual orientation among the identical-twin pairs and the least similarity among the adoptive-sibling pairs. If homosexuality were not at all biological in origin, one might expect no difference in the similarity of sexual orientation among the three groups of siblings, since both siblings in every pair had been raised in the same home by the same parents. In one such study, the authors found that, among the men, 52 percent of the identical twins, 22 percent of the fraternal twins, and 11 percent of the adoptive brothers were homosexual, which supports the biological model (Bailey & Pillard, 1991). Similarly, among the women, 48 percent of the identical twins, 16 percent of the fraternal twins, and 6 percent of the adoptive sisters were homosexual (Bailey, Pillard, Neal, & Agyei, 1993). A recent review of these sibling studies concluded that there are "almost certainly" genetic influences on sexual orientation for men and "somewhat less certainly so" for women (Bailey & Dawood, 1998).

These studies are not without limitations (Byne, 1994). Almost all of the researchers recruited subjects by placing advertisements in publications aimed at homosexual readers or in other places where homosexuals might see them. It is possible that the kinds of people who responded to the notices are not representative of the general population of lesbians and gay men. Moreover, the twin study assumes that parents treat fraternal twins (and adoptive siblings) as similarly as they treat identical twins. If parents treat identical twins more similarly, such as by dressing them alike, it is possible that their treatment accounts for some of the greater similarity in identical twins' sexual orientations. In addition, even if there are biological influences, it is unlikely that a trait as complex as sexual orientation would be determined at a single genetic site on a chromosome. Rather, several genetic sites, as well as levels of sex hormones, might be involved.

In addition, these studies suggest that sexual orientation is *not* completely genetically determined. After all, about half the identical twin pairs—who shared the same genetic material—had different sexual orientations in the studies cited above. Clearly, something about the twins' environments influenced them differently. As is the case with gender differences, any biological effects probably operate not by determining a person's sexual orientation but rather by creating predispositions toward one orientation or the other. Social and cultural factors then further influence sexual orientation. But unlike gender differences—where substantial evidence exists of the different treatment boys and girls receive from parents, peers, schools, and the like—there is little evidence that parents or peers treat children who will grow up to be gay or lesbian differently than they do other children. Moreover, the general failure of psychiatrists and psychologists to change the sexual orientation of gay and lesbian clients who wish to do so has undermined the credibility of the psychoanalytic explanation for homosexuality, which emphasizes unresolved issues of identification with one's parents (Haldeman, 1991). Nor is there much evidence that children and adolescents learn homosexual behavior from adults. So, although social and cultural factors clearly play a role in sexual orientation, no satisfactory theories have been advanced to explain their role.

The biological studies (including one in which autopsies showed that a region of the brain involved in sexual response was smaller in gay men than in heterosexual men [LeVay, 1991]) have been controversial, in large part because of their political implications. Some observers argue that if homosexuality is not a lifestyle choice but rather an inherent, immutable part of an individual's personality, there is little justification for restricting the legal rights of gay men and lesbians. Other gay advocates argue that the studies are less consequential because civil rights should not depend on whether a person's style of life is of cultural or biological origin. And some opponents of legal rights for homosexuals, noting that there is evidence of biological influences on behaviors such as alcoholism, argue that a person needn't give in to biological predispositions if they are undesirable or objectionable to others.[7]

_____

[7]Examples of the positions noted in this paragraph can be found in Angier (1993).

In sub-Saharan Africa, the region of the world with the most severe AIDS problem, the HIV virus has been transmitted primarily through heterosexual intercourse. These children in Zambia are among the 12 million African children who have been orphaned because their parents died of AIDS.

To be sure, research into the biological origins of sexual orientation need not have political significance. Rather, its purpose could be the same as that of most of the research discussed in this book—to increase our understanding of why people behave as they do in their family and personal lives. The great variation from society to society in the ways that sexual orientation is structured—the *berdache* tradition among Native Americans [➡ p. 78], the open acceptance of homosexual relations among the ancient Greeks and Romans, the mental illness model of the United States in the first half of the twentieth century, the recent emergence of an open lesbian and gay subculture—shows that social forces are an important part of the explanation for the behaviors and attitudes that emerge. But it seems likely that biological forces are also part of the story.

The AIDS Epidemic and Sexuality

The great changes in sexual behavior since the 1960s have increased the prevalence of sexually transmitted diseases (STDs). These diseases can be transmitted not only through intercourse but also through oral or anal sex. Indeed, reports suggest that in recent years more teenagers may be engaging in oral sex, mistakenly believing it to be "safe" from disease (Gates & Sonenstein, 2000; Remez, 2000). But let us focus on the STD that has posed the greatest public challenge, AIDS.

Gay men were the first group in the United States to be hit hard by the AIDS epidemic, but they are not the only group affected. **Acquired immune deficiency syndrome (AIDS)** is caused by the **human immune deficiency virus (HIV),** which can be spread through the exchange of blood or semen, typically during sexual contact or during the sharing of hypodermic needles by intravenous drug users. (It can also occur through blood transfusions, although the

acquired immune deficiency syndrome (AIDS) a disease, caused by the human immune deficiency virus (HIV), that leaves the body unable to fight against disease

human immune deficiency virus (HIV) the virus that causes AIDS

FIGURE 7.5

Number of deaths due to AIDS in the United States, for non-Hispanic whites, non-Hispanic blacks, and Hispanics, from 1985 and before, through 1996. (*Source:* For 1985 and before, and through 1990, U.S. Bureau of the Census [1996e]; For 1991–1996, U.S. Centers for Disease Control and Prevention [1997]. For 1997–1998, U.S. Centers for Disease Control and Prevention [2000b].)

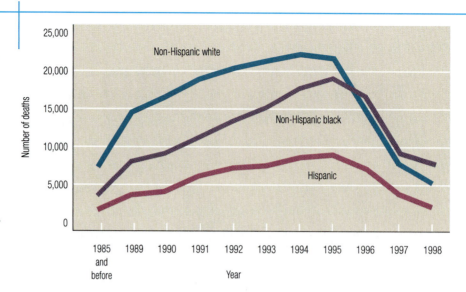

testing of donated blood has minimized the latter risk in the United States and many other countries.) Even though exchanges during heterosexual sex can also spread the virus, the primary source of sexual transmission in the United States has been between males. The reason for this predominance isn't clear; in Africa, in contrast, where almost 15 million people have died of AIDS (UNAIDS 2000) heterosexual sex has been the primary route of transmission.

Until the mid-1990s, the medical wisdom had been that people infected with HIV invariably progress to AIDS and then invariably die. Most medical treatment had aimed at prolonging the time from infection with HIV until AIDS symptoms appeared and then prolonging the period until death. But in 1996, the prognosis for people with HIV improved dramatically. A new class of drugs, called protease inhibitors, when used in combination with two (or more) older anti-viral drugs, vastly improved the medical condition of many people (Altman, 1997). As Figure 7.5 shows, AIDS deaths dropped 80 percent between 1995 and 1999. The new treatment has raised hope that many people with HIV will be able to live indefinitely with the infection. However, the treatment has not worked in every case, and it is too soon to know how long its beneficial effects will last. Moreover, it is expensive and requires close medical supervision (see *Families and Public Policy:* The Policy Response to AIDS in the United States, page 236).

SEXUAL BEHAVIOR AND AIDS

By the end of 1999, 725,000 cases of AIDS had occurred in the United States, and 425,000 people had died of the disease (U.S. Centers for Disease Control and Prevention, 2000b). The number of fatalities from AIDS is equivalent to the number of Americans who died in combat in all the major wars of the twentieth century: World War I, World War II, the Korean War, and the Vietnamese War. Gay men are heavily overrepresented in these statistics: 56 percent of all adult and adolescent AIDS cases in the United States can be traced to a category that the U.S. Centers for Disease Control and Prevention (2000b) calls "men having sex with men." Another 22 percent of cases can be traced solely to intravenous

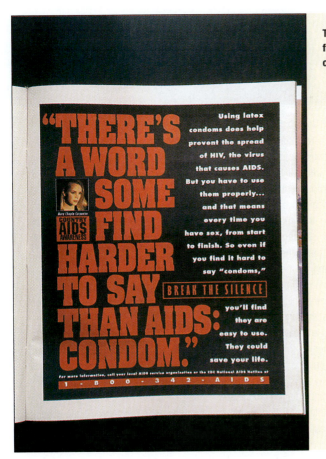

drug use, and an additional 8 percent to both homosexual behavior and intravenous drug use.

Figure 7.5 shows the shifting ethnic and racial patterns in deaths from AIDS. From the beginning of the epidemic through 1995, the highest number of deaths occurred among non-Hispanic whites, reflecting the early pattern of transmission through homosexual contact among whites. But the ethnic and racial composition of AIDS victims has changed greatly since then. By 1998, substantially more non-Hispanic blacks than non-Hispanic whites were dying of AIDS every year, a change that reflected the rising proportion of intravenous drug users among AIDS victims. Thus, during the 1990s, the largest group of people with AIDS shifted from gay white men to poor blacks and Hispanics, particularly drug users and their sex partners.

AIDS AND SEXUALITY

Beyond how, and to whom, the disease spreads, another question is what AIDS has done to sexuality—to our sexual identities, and to our attitudes and practices about sex. The AIDS epidemic has made sexuality more of a public issue

Families and Public Policy

The Policy Response to AIDS in the United States

In the United States, the public policy response to AIDS was slow in starting. Some activists believe that little was done because AIDS was perceived—inaccurately, it turned out—as a disease that affected only gay people. It wasn't until the late 1980s, by which time over 50,000 people had the disease and it had begun to infect heterosexuals, that a large-scale response began (Shilts, 1988).

Even then, there was much disagreement about how to respond. The dilemma is that AIDS places two sets of principles at odds: (1) individual freedom versus the collective interest; and (2) discouraging unpopular behavior versus trying to limit its consequences. As for the former, gay rights groups had fought for sexual freedom in the 1970s, had achieved something close to it in large cities, and were reluctant to give it up. In the 1970s, a growing number of bathhouses and sex clubs provided settings for impersonal gay sex. Moreover, an affirmative attitude toward gay sex became a centerpiece of the gay liberation political movement. Consequently, even when the link between unprotected sex and HIV transmission became apparent to public health officials, calls for the closing of the bathhouses were resisted by some gay political leaders and by the sex industry (Shilts, 1987).

Social conservatives and some public health professionals advocated widespread testing for HIV in the collective interest of identifying infected persons to prevent contact with them. Gay advocates argued, however, that mandatory testing would impose an unacceptable restriction on individual freedom because it would allow organizations such as the military or insurance companies to identify gay men and exclude them from membership or coverage. Nevertheless, Congress allowed the armed forces to institute HIV tests and exclude those who tested positive.

As for the second clash of principles, many social conservatives genuinely felt that homosexual relations—and even heterosexual relations outside marriage—were morally wrong and should not be condoned. Their response to the AIDS epidemic was to urge chastity for the unmarried and monogamy for the married (D'Emilio & Freedman, 1988). In contrast, other interest groups argued that, even though sex outside heterosexual marriage might be objectionable to some people, the threat AIDS posed to health required accepting its existence and urging people

than it has ever been. It is true that for several decades now, the commercialization of sex has made erotic images increasingly public. But AIDS has made the mechanics of sex itself—the organs and orifices involved, the same-sex and different-sex varieties, the kinds of contraceptives—a topic of unprecedented public discussion. As discussed earlier, as recently as the 1960s, some states had laws that prohibited even married couples from using contraceptive devices. Yet in 1988, just two decades after these laws were declared unconstitutional, C. Everett Koop, then the surgeon general of the United States, sent a brochure to every household in the nation explaining the connection between AIDS and sexual activity and urging everyone—not just married couples—to use condoms. In response to the spread of AIDS, adolescents were informed about anal intercourse, pieces on safe sex appeared regularly in the media, and condoms were advertised on television. In this discourse, sex was seen less as a means of personal gratification than as an issue of public health. Koop wrote:

> Some of the issues involved in this brochure may not be things you are used to discussing openly. I can easily understand that. But now you must discuss them. We all must know about AIDS. Read this brochure and talk about it with those you love (U.S. Centers for Disease Control, 1988).

Married couples who have no outside sex partners, however, are at virtually no risk of HIV infection. Therefore, by focusing attention on safe sex practices,

to limit risky behavior and to use condoms. By the late 1980s, the latter view had prevailed, as exemplified by the explicit brochure Surgeon General C. Everett Koop sent to every home in the United States in 1988.

The development of effective drug therapy has produced a new policy question: Should all persons with AIDS have equal access to the new drugs—and at what cost? They are very expensive—well over $10,000 per year—and they require expensive medical supervision and blood testing. Most middle-class people belong to health insurance plans through their employers that cover the expenses of treatment. But the United States has tens of millions of people who have no health insurance coverage; in 1997, 43.4 million were without coverage for the entire year

(U.S. Bureau of the Census, 1999d). Many are in working-class families where wage earners have jobs that do not provide health insurance. The cost of the AIDS treatment is far more than they could afford. Some of the poor—including families that are receiving what used to be called Aid to Families with Dependent Children and is now called Temporary Assistance to Needy Families [➡p. 192]—are covered by the government's Medicaid program of health insurance. But not all state Medicaid plans include sufficient funds for treating with the new drugs those who are infected (Groopman, 1997). As a result the poor and near-poor have limited access to the new treatments.

The response to AIDS shows that public health issues involving sexual activity often involve more than technical and medical

considerations. The social context of a sexual issue can determine what action, if any, the government takes. Prevailing moral values influence public opinion about whether the affected persons are worthy of assistance—whether they are blameless or, in some sense, to blame for their health problems. Concerns about individual freedom determine how restrictive the public response will be. These social and political conflicts influence the nature of the response.

Ask Yourself

1. Do you know anyone who has been denied treatment with expensive new AIDS drugs? If so, for what reason?
2. Should HIV testing be mandatory? What about health education that stresses limiting risky behavior?

www.mhhe.com/cherlin

health workers and educators have unavoidably communicated the message that sex outside marriage is acceptable, or at least tolerable, and can be publicly acknowledged—indeed, must be publicly acknowledged given the gravity of the risk to people's health.

Family planners have been urging for decades that we accept sexual activity outside marriage and encourage the use of contraceptives to avoid unwanted children and to stop sexually transmitted diseases. They have urged that contraceptives be made available to American teenagers to reduce pregnancies. Doing so, however, would require a tacit acceptance of teenage sexuality, a step many Americans have been unwilling to take. AIDS has broken this deadlock. The epidemic, said Marian Wright Edelman of the Children's Defense Fund, has accomplished "what one million teenage pregnancies couldn't do: get us talking about sex" (D'Emilio & Freedman, 1988). The talk has had results; national surveys reveal that the proportion of sexually active adolescents who used a condom at last intercourse rose from 46 percent in 1991 to 58 percent in 1999. (U.S. Centers for Disease Control and Prevention, 2000d). In fact, from the standpoint of family planning advocates, the small silver lining in the great gray cloud of AIDS may be the increased use of condoms by boys and unmarried men.

Moreover, the AIDS epidemic raised the profile of gay men and, by extension, lesbians. Public health campaigns demystified and explained homosexual sex. This explicit consideration implied a certain level of tolerance of homosexuality among the heterosexual majority. The origins of homosexuality and the political rights of lesbians and gay men were the subject of numerous feature stories in newspapers and magazines.[8] Yet until the mid-1990s, there was little change in the percentage of the population that accepted homosexual sex. In the GSS between 1973 and 1991, a constant 80 percent of the population, give or take one or two percentage points, agreed that homosexual sex is always wrong or almost always wrong (Davis & Smith, 1996). In the 1990s, however, the greater frankness and discussion about homosexuality seems to have led to greater public acceptance. In the 1994 GSS round, 71 percent agreed that homosexual sex is always wrong or almost always wrong; the percentage agreeing fell to 64 percent in the 1998 round (Davis, Smith, & Marsden, 1999).

Among the adult heterosexual population, AIDS has also brought a greater frankness about sex. Yet there have been only modest changes in sexual behavior. As noted earlier, for instance, condom use has increased; yet many people with multiple sex partners do not use condoms regularly. Perhaps the changes have not been greater because the spread of HIV through the non–drug-using heterosexual population, despite the apprehension of public health experts and the example of Africa, has been limited. For reasons not clearly understood, then, AIDS in the United States has largely remained a disease of gay men, drug users and their partners. The social composition of the victims AIDS has killed may explain why the public response to the disease was slow in coming and, some would argue, inadequate.

[8]See, for example, Gelman (1992); Henry (1993); Mathews (1993).

Looking Back

1. **When did the idea of a sexual identity develop?** The idea that individuals have a coherent sexual identity involving a preference for either opposite-sex or same-sex partners did not exist until the late nineteenth century. Before then, though religious doctrine and civil law forbade numerous sexual practices, a person who broke those laws was not thought to have a different personality from people who displayed conventional sexual behavior.

2. **How has the relationship among love, sex, and marriage changed over time?** During the nineteenth century, Americans distinguished between spiritual love, which they considered the proper basis for marriage, and romantic love, which they saw as a poor basis for marriage. Gradually sex for pleasure became acceptable, but only among married couples and in moderation. During the twentieth century, marriage came to be seen as a means of self-fulfillment through romantic love and sexual gratification. After about 1960, sexual activity by unmarried persons became more socially acceptable and much more widespread.

3. **What is the nature of the teenage pregnancy "problem"?** Over the past few decades, the proportion of teenage births that occur outside of marriage has risen sharply because of a decline in marriage among teenagers. Most such pregnancies are unwanted, but in some low-income neighborhoods, bearing a child—or fathering a child—may be one of the few ways a teenager can gain status and respect from peers and family members. Bearing a child as a teenager somewhat reduces a woman's chances of leading an economically successful adult life. Yet some of the disadvantages observed in these cases occur because teenage mothers tend to come from disadvantaged families, not solely because they had a child at a young age.

4. **How have views of homosexuality changed?** Until the 1970s, a medical model of homosexuality dominated thinking on this subject. According to this model, homosexuality was a psychological illness that pervaded the personalities of certain men and women, who were labeled homosexuals. But the illness model was undercut by evidence that to various degrees, homosexual behavior was widespread, and that it might have a biological component.

5. **How has the AIDS epidemic developed, and what has been the public response to it?** In the United States, the AIDS virus first spread through the gay male community, and then through the population of intravenous drug users and their sex partners. As a result of this pattern, more African Americans now die of AIDS each year than non-Hispanic whites. The public response included widespread HIV testing, despite some people's concerns that testing would restrict individual freedom, and frank public discussion of safe sexual behavior.

Thinking about Families

1. Did Maud Rittenhouse make the right decision in choosing Elmer over Robert?

2. Does it make any difference whether there is a biological component to homosexuality?

3. Would the public response to the AIDS epidemic have been different if it had affected primarily heterosexuals, as is the case in Africa?

4. **The Private Family** Has the contemporary American culture gone too far in accepting sex without romantic love?

5. **The Public Family** Should the government be involved in discouraging teenage pregnancy?

Key Terms

acquired immune deficiency
   syndrome (AIDS) 233
companionate love 212
extramarital sex 213
human immune deficiency virus
   (HIV) 233

Kinsey Report 225
nonmarital birth ratio 221
passionate love 212
selection effect 223

sexual identity 207
sexual monogamy 215
Stonewall riot 230

Families on the Internet   www.mhhe.com/cherlin

*Note: While all the URLs listed were current as of the printing of this book, these sites often change. Please check our web site (**http://www.mhhe.com/cherlin**) for updates.*

 The Sexuality Information and Education Council of the United States (**www.siecus.org**), an organization that favors the dissemination of information about sexuality and sex education through the schools, maintains a web site with a great deal of information about sexuality and sex education in schools. A search on the topic "homosexuality," for example, will return links to a number of fact sheets and articles. For a conservative perspective, consult the web site of the Traditional Values Coalition (**www.traditionalvalues.org**), which opposes gay rights and sex education that does not stress abstinence. Click on "issues" and you are likely to find several articles. Read an article or two about gay and lesbian issues at each of these sites. Can you understand the two organizations' basic positions, and how they differ?

The Alan Guttmacher Institute, a research center devoted to family planning issues, offers much relevant information about adolescent pregnancy and childbearing, birth control, and abortion at its web site (**www.agi-usa.org**). Click on "sexual behavior," and on the next page, select a report under "Latest statistics—facts in brief." What information can you find on recent trends in sexual activity, contraceptive use, or pregnancy?

chapter 8

Cohabitation and Marriage

But as wage labor spread, sons could find paying jobs away from the farm, and they gained greater independence from their parents. Sometimes the transformation in marriage practices can occur with startling speed. This has been the case in the rapidly industrializing nations of East Asia, where strong parental influence has been eroded over a generation or two. (See *Families in Other Cultures: World Revolution and Family Patterns*, in Chapter 15.)

ANGLO-AMERICAN COURTSHIP

In the American colonies, the influence of parents seemed to decline in the mid- to late 1700s. Historian Philip Greven found that prior to the late 1700s, sons in Andover, Massachusetts, married at later ages than their fathers. [➡ p. 49] The later marriage occurred, he argued, because sons had to wait until their fathers turned over control of the family farm. By the late 1700s, when commercial capitalism began to provide alternative job opportunities, the marriage ages of sons declined (Greven, 1970). Similarly, Daniel Scott Smith found evidence in the records of Hingham, Massachusetts, that, prior to 1700, daughters were more likely to have married in the order of their birth (i.e., the eldest married before the second eldest). This pattern suggested that parents were finding husbands for their daughters one at a time. After about 1750, marriages out of birth order became more common (Smith, 1973). Smith took this as evidence of a decline in parental influence.

By the 1800s, then, most young adults in the United States at least shared with their parents the responsibility for choosing a spouse. Indeed, young adults from the lower economic classes probably had substantial autonomy because there was little property for parents to worry about. (Among the upper classes, parents undoubtedly retained a stronger role.) Young people went about finding a spouse through courtship, a process that had been developed in Europe. **Courtship** is a publicly visible process with rules and restrictions through which young men and women find a partner to marry. The words *publicly visible* emphasize the important role of the community—and, in particular, parents—in watching over, and participating in, the courting a young adult does. For instance, in early modern Britain, the first stages of courtship occurred mainly outdoors, in plain view of peers and kin (Gillis, 1985). By and large, it was acceptable for casually acquainted young men and young women to be seen together only at public events such as festivals, games, or dances, and even then only in groups. At dances young people changed partners so frequently that no couple spent too much time together.

The words *rules and restrictions* emphasize the close adherence to well-established ways of acting. British courtship, for example, followed a carefully prescribed path from "talking" to "walking" in public places and then to "keeping company." Only when the couple became more serious did they begin seeing each other outside public, group settings. Typically, they moved on to night visiting, whereby a young man would call upon a young woman at her home. At first, there was little intimacy and privacy in these formal visits. Suitors often brought along a male friend to ease the potential awkwardness and embarrassment of the situation. The young woman's parents would be present in the home, although they might discreetly retire to bed. If the visits continued, a certain amount of kissing and fondling was permitted, but nothing more. Until a couple became betrothed (engaged), they were not allowed much privacy or sexual intimacy.

According to historical studies, American courtship, like British courtship, retained this basic character through the mid-1800s. (The historical studies, unfortu-

courtship a publicly visible process with rules and restrictions through which young men and women find a partner to marry

nately, tell us little about the poor, African Americans, or immigrants, who left few diaries and letters.) The first phase of courtship still took place at out-of-home events such as picnics, sleigh rides, and church socials. In a later phase, young men called at the homes of young women. Yet there were subtle changes over time. Most notably, the role of love increased. In the 1500s and 1600s, love had been an emotion people distrusted in selecting a spouse. To be sure, it was desirable to choose a partner whom you might grow to love after you were married, but more practical considerations—inheritance of land, strength, health—should guide your choice. By the 1800s, however, young adults wanted to love their partners before they married them (Rothman, 1984). Even so, love had a different meaning than it has today, as Maud Rittenhouse's diary showed. Young people were wary of passion, which was seen as wild and uncontrollable and therefore dangerous as a basis for a long-term relationship. Love was defined more in terms of sympathy, openness, candor, and understanding than of passion. Thus, Maud rejected her romantic love for Robert in favor of responsible Elmer.

This centuries-old system of courtship met its demise after 1900. Its decline in the United States was linked to great social and economic changes: migration from rural areas (and from overseas) to cities, the rise of industrial capitalism, higher standards of living, and the lengthening of adolescence. As more and more people moved to cities and worked in factories and offices, the number of potential partners and the places where they could meet grew. Consequently, it became harder for parents to monitor and oversee the process. And as standards of living rose, it became possible for young adults to keep some of their earnings or to receive allowances from their parents. Thus, young people began to accumulate a key resource: spending money. The city provided plenty of places to spend it, most notably the movie theater and the dance hall. Rising standards of living also allowed many families to buy an automobile. This marvel of technology let young couples wander far from home; it also gave them a private place for necking (kissing) and petting (touching below the neck). As a result, courtship, in the words of historian Beth Bailey, went from "front porch to back seat" (Bailey, 1988).

Finally, a new view of the teenage years arose: They were seen as a time during which teens needed to develop their personalities and capabilities free of the pressures of the adult world. In an influential 1904 book, psychologist G. Stanley Hall popularized the term "adolescence" for this newly recognized stage of life (Hall, 1904). Attention to adolescence emerged as child labor laws restricted how much younger teenagers could work and as more prosperous middle-class families no longer needed their children to work. Moreover, it arose as changes in the economy made it clear to parents that children needed at least a high school education in order to obtain better-paying jobs. Consequently, adolescence was embodied most clearly in the high school, which removed teenagers from the world of adults. Not until the early decades of the twentieth century did a majority of teenagers enroll in high school. College enrollments also increased early in the century and then skyrocketed after World War II. The high school and college years gave adolescents a protected time in which they could create and participate in their own subculture, relatively free of parental involvement.

THE RISE AND FALL OF DATING

What evolved, then, after the turn of the twentieth century was a new system of courtship based on dating. Although some might think that dating has been

The dating culture probably reached its peak in the 1950s.

around for a long time, it was rare until 1900 or so, and the term was not even used until then. The spirit of the change was captured in a 1924 short story in *Harper's* magazine. A man comes calling at the home of a young woman, expecting to spend the evening in her parlor. But when she opens the door, she has her hat on—a clear sign that she expects to go out.[2] As the story suggests, suddenly a young man was expected to take a young woman somewhere on a date—which meant he had to spend money. A firm rule of the dating system was that the young man paid the expenses. In return, he enjoyed the company of the young woman. Dating placed courtship on an economic basis. Young men provided goods such as movie tickets or restaurant meals in exchange for companionship and, often, necking and petting. Through these rules, argues Bailey, dating shifted the balance of power in courtship from women to men (Bailey, 1988). Under the old system, women received men in their own homes, at times they chose, and usually with their parents nearby. (During a girl's first season of receiving callers, her mother might initially invite the young men.) Now the evening was initiated and controlled by males, and it depended on cash earnings, which favored men over women.

Dating also shifted power from parents to teenagers and young adults. The movement of activity away from public gatherings and the home made it much harder for parents to influence the process. Rather, adolescents became oriented toward the dating system of their peer group—the other adolescents in the local school or neighborhood. With the triumph of dating, courtship moved from a parent- and other-adult-run system to a peer-run system where the participants made the rules and punished the offenders.

[2]This story is cited in both Rothman (1984) and Bailey (1988). It is cited by Bailey as Black (1924).

By the 1920s, sexual activity was more common, although intercourse was still rare. Some parents were alarmed at the apparent spread of necking and petting, which became a central part of the youth culture of dating. Popular accounts warned of the spread of "petting parties" among high school students, and adults sought unsuccessfully to stop them (Rothman, 1984). Colleges wielded parentlike authority through residence and visiting rules. Sometimes their efforts at control verged on the comic: In 1947, the dean of Northwestern University decreed that any mixed group of more than two people listening to the Michigan-Northwestern football game on the radio must register as a "party" and have an appropriate number of approved chaperons (Bailey, 1988).

Nearly all the efforts to control sexual activity centered on women. For although men initiated attempts at necking or petting (which they were expected to do in the dating culture), no one blamed them. Instead, it was seen as women's responsibility to stop them; if a young man wasn't stopped, it was his date's fault. Girls who complained of boys' advances were asked to consider whether they might somehow be encouraging them. Consistent with the cult of true womanhood, young women were seen as the repositories of virtue and morality; it was their responsibility to tame the wild impulses of men, who couldn't stop themselves. The author of a 1945 courtship manual for women wrote, "a man is only as bad as the woman he is with."[3]

The dating system probably had its heyday in the 20-year period—1945 to 1965—after World War II. Throughout the period, college enrollments rose sharply and most young adults at least completed high school. Postwar parents had grown up in the dating system, and so there was less parent-child disagreement about it than had been the case in the 1920s and 1930s. At the same time, young people in the 1950s may have started to date earlier than their parents.[4] In a national survey of high school students conducted in 1960, about two-thirds of all boys and three-fourths of all girls stated that they had begun to date by grade 9; virtually all had dated by grade 12 (Modell, 1989).[5]

What did alarm adults was the growth of "going steady," in which a boy and girl agree to date only each other. Previously common only among older, seriously involved couples, going steady was found in the 1950s among very young couples as well. According to the 1960 high school survey, a majority of 10th-grade girls and 11th-grade boys had gone steady at least once; two-thirds of the girls had done so by 12th grade (Modell, 1989). Adults, most of whom had not gone steady as adolescents, feared that adolescents were settling down too soon and that going steady, by withdrawing the couple from the dating competition, would prevent adolescents from finding an appropriate partner. They also feared it would lead to more premarital sex. Yet their fears proved groundless; rates of premarital intercourse did not rise sharply until a decade or two later. Whereas teenagers saw going steady as security, adults saw it as a premature commitment. And in the early-marrying postwar period, adolescents who went steady were, in fact, more likely to marry early—although their spouse was not necessarily a high school

---

[3]Quoted in Bailey (1988).

[4]Both Bailey and Rothman suggest that adolescents began to date at younger ages in the 1950s. But when a random sample of Detroit-area women in 1984 was asked to recall when they had begun to date, there was little difference in the responses of those who had married before the war versus after the war; see Whyte (1990).

[5]The data came from the Project Talent survey of 4,000 high school students nationwide.

sweetheart. When the 1960 national sample of high school students was reinterviewed in 1971, 59 percent of the girls who had gone steady by 12th grade had married before age 21 compared with just 27 percent of those who had not gone steady (Modell, 1989).

Many of these concerns about dating seemed less important by the 1970s and 1980s, for by then the dating system had become less closely connected to marriage. As the average age at marriage soared into the mid-twenties, steady dating in high school seemed more and more remote from serious attempts to find a spouse. What's more, cohabitation, perhaps a new stage of courtship, became a common event in young adults' lives prior to marriage. Also, the sharp rise in premarital intercourse for teenage boys and girls demonstrated that the dating system was increasingly ineffective in holding sexual activity to petting. Adolescents may have begun to socialize more often in larger, mixed-sex groups (Modell, 1989). To be sure, dating remained a part of youth culture, but it became less formal and less tied to marriage. And the old limitations on sexual activity were greatly weakened.

THE TREND TOWARD INDEPENDENT LIVING

The dating and courtship model assumes that most young adults will be living in their parents' homes and receiving at least some supervision from them. Historically, that was the case: At the start of the twentieth century, a lower standard of living, a shortage of housing for single people, and the predominant values of the time precluded almost all young adults from living independently of their parents until they married. Even at midcentury, many young adults did not leave home until they married. But since then, an increasingly larger percentage of single young adults have moved into apartments or homes, either by themselves or with roommates.

The trend toward independent living reflected the generally rising standard of living during the twentieth century. One hundred years ago, most single young adults helped support their families by turning over their wages to their parents; today it is common—even expected—for young adults to keep their wages. In addition, the rise in independent living was consistent with the broader growth of individualism in the twentieth century, which uncoupled sexual activity from marriage for young adults. [➡ p. 214] The increase in divorce also spurred independent living: Studies have shown that adolescents whose parents divorce, and in particular those whose parents divorce and remarry, leave home sooner than adolescents whose biological parents remain married (Cherlin, Kiernan, & Chase-Lansdale, 1995).

In addition, since midcentury the average age at first marriage has risen substantially. [➡ p. 67] Consequently, it has become common for young adults to set up an independent household years before they marry. But young adults who live independently are more likely to return to their parents' homes than are young adults who marry. (Usually, married young adults will only return if their marriages dissolve). Frances Goldscheider (1997) calculated that, since the 1950s, the odds that a young adult who left the parental home would return have increased by more than 50 percent. Parents whose children move out have learned to expect that the children may move back in if, for example, they lose their jobs. Some of the unmarried, independent young adults are, in fact, cohabitating, as will be discussed later in the chapter. But cohabiting relationships have higher rates of dissolution than do marriages, and young adults who end cohabiting relationships are more likely to return home than are young adults who end marriages (Goldscheider & Goldscheider, 1994).

Who Marries Whom?

At midcentury, for most young adults, dating and courtship led directly to marriage. Today, many will live with a partner before marrying. Others will have a child prior to marrying and then live with or marry someone else. It is still the case, however, that about 9 out of 10 whites and 2 out of 3 African Americans are projected to marry eventually (see Table 5.1). What kinds of people they marry, and how their social and economic environment affects their choices of spouses, has been a topic of much social scientific research. The literature describes the type of bargain that most prospective spouses used to make at midcentury: Men specialized in work for pay and women specialized in unpaid work at home. Among the poor, that bargain usually was not possible; rather, it was necessary to pool the earnings of both the husband and the wife (and often the children also) to obtain enough money to live on. Recent studies suggest that the bargain has now changed for the nonpoor too.

THE MARRIAGE MARKET

When sociologists and economists study who marries whom, they often make an analogy with the labor market, in which people seeking employment look for employers who will hire them at an acceptable wage. In the **marriage market,** unmarried individuals (or their parents) search for others who will marry them (or their children). Instead of an acceptable wage, the searchers require that a partner have an acceptable set of desired characteristics, such as a college education, good looks, a pleasant disposition, and so forth.

marriage market an analogy to the labor market in which single individuals (or their parents) search for others who will marry them (or their children)

There are three components to this market model of marriage. The first component is simply a group of people who are actively looking for a spouse at the same place at the same time. They constitute the *supply* of men and women who are in the marriage market. The second component is *preferences.* Each person has an idea of his or her own preferred characteristics in a spouse. Some people may care more about good looks, others more about personality or earning potential. A person will try to find a mate who ranks as high as possible on the characteristics she or he prefers. And that same person will probably have a minimum set of characteristics that she or he will accept. The third component is *resources.* These are the characteristics a person possesses that are attractive to others. In a sense resources are the flip side of preferences: Resources are what I have that a partner might want; preferences are what I want a partner to have.

So people who are looking for spouses, who have preferences about the qualities they want, and who have resources to offer create a marriage market. To be sure, it is difficult in real life to decide just who is looking for a spouse and who isn't. Moreover, this depiction of searchers as rational, calculating individuals who tote up the pluses and minuses of prospects is at odds with the popular image of people falling in love with each other. Clearly, the market metaphor can't explain everything about who marries whom. Nevertheless, in the aggregate, the behavior of unmarried persons resembles that of job searchers enough that the metaphor is useful.[6]

Sometimes preferences and resources are so incompatible that the market can't provide acceptable spouses for all who are looking. One explanation for the drop in the African-American marriage rate [➤ p. 148] is that decent-paying industrial jobs—making steel or cars or television sets—have moved to suburban plants or to firms in developing countries, so that men without college educations (and African-American men are less likely to have attended college) have a harder time finding a job that can support a family. Therefore African-American women, so this argument goes, can't find enough employed African-American men to marry (Wilson, 1987). Recent studies have indeed found that women's marriage rates are lower in areas where more men were unemployed, although the effect has not been large enough to fully explain racial differences in marriage patterns.[7] High levels of homicide, imprisonment, and drug use also remove some black men from the marriage market. [➤ p. 149]

In most marriage markets, men tend to be older than the women they marry. This custom was important in agricultural societies, in which children provided needed labor. Since a woman's capacity to bear children declines with age, it was advantageous for men and their relatives to prefer younger women, who could bear more children. In many preindustrial Asian societies, age differences were commonly 5, and sometimes 10, years. A family could make a better match for a young daughter; her value in the market decreased as she grew older. In preindustrial Europe, where land was more limited, very large families were not as advantageous. Consequently, young men and women both married later, and the age gap was perhaps three to five years, on average (Hajnal, 1982).

Now that the average married couple has only about two children, there is no longer a strong biological reason for wives to be younger than husbands. Single men still typically pay more attention to physical attractiveness, which may be a marker for the youth and health of a person, than single women.[8] This preference reflects the high value placed on women's attractive appearance in our society. Nevertheless, the age gap should be eroding, and government statistics suggest that it slowly is. In the United States in 1970, the bride was older than the groom in 16 percent of marriages; by 1990, 24 percent of brides were older.[9]

THE CHANGING MARRIAGE BARGAIN

In fact, over the past several generations, at least, men have placed a greater emphasis on the physical attractiveness of their spouses than women; conversely, women have placed a greater emphasis on the earning potential of their spouses (Buss, 1985). This difference fit the predominant marriage bargain at midcentury, in which men worked outside the home and women specialized in home work and

---

[6]The job search analogy has been carried furthest by Oppenheimer (1988).

[7]See, for example, Lichter, Le Clere, and McLaughlin (1991).

[8]See figure 8.1 and the associated discussion later in the chapter.

[9]For marriages in which neither the bride nor the groom had been married previously. Personal communication from Stephanie Ventura, U.S. National Center for Health Statistics.

emotional support. It is the bargain hailed in the writings of Parsons and his associates in the 1950s. [➡ p. 29] It is also the bargain implied by the theory of the division of labor advanced by economist Gary Becker, whose theoretical work since the 1960s pioneered the economic approach to studying the family.[10]

Becker drew his model from the theory of international trade, under which each country is said to have a "comparative advantage" in producing particular goods relative to other countries. For example, a poor, underdeveloped country with land and farmers but few schools and factories might be able to produce grain more "efficiently" (meaning cheaply) than tractors. In contrast, a developed country such as the United States, with its assembly-line factories and skilled workers, may be able to produce tractors (and other manufactured goods) more efficiently than grain. If so, according to the theory, each country will benefit if the underdeveloped country specializes in producing grain, some of which it can trade for tractors, and the developed country specializes in producing tractors, some of which it can trade for grain. Becker's application of this model to the family is straightforward: If women are more "efficient" at housework and childcare relative to earning money—either because they are better at caring for children or because they tend to be paid less than men—and men are more efficient at earning money rather than at housework and childcare, both will benefit if the wife specializes in housework and childcare and the husband specializes in paid work outside the home. Consequently, the model predicts that in the marriage market women will search for good providers and men will search for good homemakers. We might call this the **specialization model** of the marriage market.

Becker and his followers rarely examined any evidence on whether women actually are more efficient in housework and childcare than men. Nor did they explain why women might earn less in the labor force, except to suggest that women's wages are lower because they spend more time caring for children and therefore invest less in their careers. Rather, these social conditions—women are better at homemaking, men get paid more—were taken as given and not subject to much change; so was a cultural climate in which it was expected that married women with children should stay at home. In addition, Becker's theory assumes that the husband and wife are producers of a joint enterprise—their home and family—and that their preferences are identical. That is to say, a particular division of labor that makes the husband happier will make the wife equally happier.[11] Yet studies of the internal economy of the family suggest that husbands' and wives' preferences aren't identical.[12] Nevertheless, the predictions of the model fit the typical outcome of the marriage market at midcentury.

More recently, however, a number of studies have shown that the specialization model no longer fits the marriage market well. A set of questions in the 1987–1988 National Survey of Families and Households (NSFH) allows us to gauge the marriage preferences of women and men in the United States. Figure 8.1 displays the answers of unmarried white men and women aged 19 to 35, as analyzed by Scott South. Each person was asked to rate his or her willingness to marry

specialization model a model of the marriage market in which women specialize in housework and childcare and men specialize in paid work outside the home

---

[10]See Becker (1991).

[11]Some more recent work allows for different preferences among husbands and wives. See Thomas (1990).

[12]See Chapter 9.

FIGURE 8.1

Willingness to marry someone with a given characteristic, for unmarried women and men ages 19 to 35: (*A*) Older than you by five or more years. (*B*) Younger than you by five or more years. (*C*) Not "good-looking." (*D*) Not likely to hold a steady job. (*E*) Earning much less. (*Source:* South, 1991.)

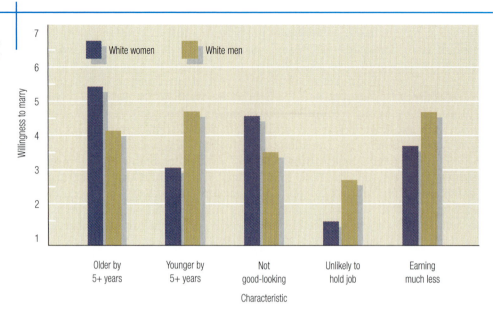

someone with a particular characteristic on a scale of 1 to 7, with 7 indicating the most willing. The average scores are shown for five characteristics. The gender differences are as one might expect: Women are more willing to marry someone five or more years older, whereas men are more willing to marry someone five or more years younger. Women are more willing to marry someone who is not good-looking. Men are more willing to marry someone who is earning much less.

But note that neither women nor men are especially willing to marry someone who is not likely to hold a steady job. To be sure, women are less willing than men; but even men are more willing, on average, to marry someone who is not good-looking or who is older, than they are willing to marry someone who is unlikely to hold a job. South's analyses also showed that black men were even less willing to marry a woman with poor economic prospects. Among African-American couples, low incomes have long made two-job marriages acceptable and often necessary (Cherlin, 1992).

The specialization model predicts that women with less education and lower earnings will be *more* likely to marry than better-educated, higher-earning women. The former group, it is said, has more to gain by marrying a man who will earn money while they specialize in housework and childcare. But several studies have now found evidence that, on average, women with less education and lower earnings are *less* likely to marry than better-educated, higher-earning women. In contrast to the specialization model, it is women with higher earning potential who have higher rates of marriage, other things being equal, for white and nonwhite women, poor and nonpoor women alike (Lichter, McLaughlin, Kephart, & Landry, 1992; Qian & Preston, 1993; Oppenheimer, Blossfeld, & Wackerow, 1995; Oppenheimer & Lew, 1995; McLaughlin & Lichter, 1997.) One study compares data for young adults in the 1970s and 1980s and finds that the specialization model was supported in the earlier decade but not the later one (Sweeney, 1997); so perhaps the model did hold as recently as the 1970s.

It appears, then, that the marriage bargain now includes the preference, for most couples, that both spouses will contribute to the family's income. Why has

Table 8.1 Changes in Union Formation Since the Mid-Twentieth Century

	1950s	1990s
When do sexual relations begin?	For a majority of women and many men, sexual relations began only after engagement or marriage.	Sexual relations typically begin many years before a union is formed.
What happens when premarital pregnancies occur?	Usually led to a hasty marriage because childbearing outside of marriage was highly stigmatized.	Much less likely to lead to marriage because childbearing outside of marriage is more acceptable. Still, many cohabiting couples marry when a pregnancy occurs.
Who cohabits?	Cohabitation is common only among the poor; it is not considered respectable among the nonpoor.	About half of all young adults will cohabit before they marry. It has become an important part of the process of finding a marital partner.
Who marries and when?	About 95 percent of whites and almost 90 percent of African Americans married; average age at marriage was younger than in any other decade.	90 percent or more of whites will marry, and only about two-thirds of African Americans will marry. Typical ages at marriage are several years older than in the 1950s.
What is the economic bargain?	Men typically exchanged their earning power for women's housework and childrearing effort. Middle-class and working-class married women rarely worked outside the home.	Men and women typically pool their earnings and achieve economies of scale (i.e., only one mortgage to pay for). Women with higher earning potential are more likely to marry.

this change occurred? In part, it reflects the greater acceptance of married women's work outside the home (see Figure 4.4). In addition, it reflects the prolonged stagnation of men's wages since the early 1970s. Valerie Oppenheimer has argued that the decline in the wage levels of young men without a college education [➡ p. 117] has reduced the willingness of young adults to marry. In one paper, she and her co-authors (Oppenheimer, Kalmijn, & Lim, 1997) present evidence that young men with low earnings and a pattern of what she terms *stopgap employment*—short-term, often part-time jobs (such as fast-food worker) that aren't part of a career path—are less likely to marry than are men with better economic prospects. Her article implies (although it doesn't present direct evidence) that an increase in stopgap employment—and the delay it causes young men in attaining steady work at higher wages—may be a factor in the rising age at marriage.

UNION FORMATION: A SUMMING UP

The process by which young adults find long-term partners has changed greatly since the middle of the twentieth century (see Table 8.1). In the 1950s, nearly everyone married, and they married at younger ages than before or since. Young single people spent less time searching for a partner than they do now. Cohabitation was held in such disrepute that it was not an option except among the poor. Childbearing outside of marriage was highly stigmatized, and a pregnancy often led to a forced marriage. Most young women and many men did not have sex until they were engaged or married.

It is much more socially acceptable now for a middle-class, single woman to adopt a child, as this mother did, than a few decades ago.

As we enter the twenty-first century, nearly all these conditions have changed. The typical age at marriage is much higher than at midcentury; and the proportion of people who never marry has grown. Young people typically spend more time searching for a partner. They do so in part because the earning potential of young men without college degrees has eroded and in part because cohabitation has emerged as an accepted, or at least tolerated, alternative living arrangement. About half of all young adults cohabit prior to marrying. It provides a way for them to enjoy some of the benefits of a partnership without committing to marriage. Childbearing outside of marriage is much less stigmatized, and far fewer nonmarital pregnancies lead to a hasty marriage. Most young adults begin to have sex many years before they marry; and better birth control technology and legalized abortion make it easier for them to do so.

Given all this change, one might reasonably ask: What *is* the marital bargain these days, and why do most people still eventually marry? The marital bargain is based more on a pooling of joint earnings than on an exchange of men's earnings for women's housework and childcare. Men are still required to be good, steady earners in order to be acceptable as spouses; but increasingly women are required to be good earners as well. Although women still provide more of the housework and childcare, the marital bargain typically calls for men to do more work at home than was the case at midcentury. Women with higher earning potential may be using their economic attractiveness to strike a bargain that results in a more equitable distribution of work in the home.

Why do most people still marry? Perhaps the only advantage marriage offers over cohabitation is that it requires a public commitment to a long-term, possibly lifelong, relationship. What's different about marriage, in other words, are social norms, such as the expectations of friends, relatives, and religious congregants about how married people will behave, and the legal rights and privileges reserved for spouses and married parents. This long-term public commitment is still attractive to most people. It allows individuals to invest emotionally in each other with less fear of abandonment. It also maximizes the chances that both parents will live together while their children are being raised—which is why pregnancy and childbirth are the events that lead many cohabiting couples to marry. Nevertheless, despite these advantages, it is clear that marriage does not hold as privileged a position in our family system as it did in midcentury. The gains to marriage, relative to alternatives, are perceived to be lower on average today than they were 40 or 50 years ago.

Cohabitation

One major departure from the old, marry-then-have-sex-then-have-children path for starting a family is cohabitation, commonly called "living together." By **cohabitation,** I mean a living arrangement in which two adults who are not married to each other but who have a sexual relationship share the same house or apartment. Before the 1960s, cohabitation was common mainly among the poor and near-poor. With little in the way of resources to share and little prospect of leaving money or possessions to their children, the poor have less reason to marry. For many, cohabitation has served as an acceptable substitute for legal marriage. But beginning around 1970, the proportion of all young adults who lived with someone prior to marrying increased sharply. By the early 1990s, a majority of first marriages were preceded by a period of cohabitation (Bumpass & Lu, 2000).

cohabitation the sharing of a household by unmarried persons who have a sexual relationship

In 1998, the Census Bureau estimated that there were about 4.2 million households in the United States maintained by two opposite-sex persons who were not married to each other and who had no other adults in the household. (There also were about 1.7 million such households maintained by two same-sex persons.) In contrast, there were only about a half-million such households in 1970 (U.S. Bureau of the Census, 1993c, 1999f). So great has been the increase in cohabitation that it has compensated in large part for the postponement of marriage. That is to say, far fewer young adults marry today by their midtwenties, but the proportion of young adults who live in either kind of union—marital or cohabiting—has declined much less. (Bumpass, Sweet, & Cherlin, 1991).

Cohabiting couples are more diverse than many people realize. Consider these facts:

- Although in many people's minds the image of a cohabiting couple is one of college-educated professionals living together, cohabitation continues to be more common among the less affluent and less well-educated. In a 1995

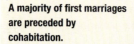

A majority of first marriages are preceded by cohabitation.

national survey of women ages 19 to 44, 59 percent of those without a high-school degree had cohabited, compared to 37 percent of those with a college degree (Bumpass & Lu, 2000). To be sure, cohabitation has increased greatly among the well-educated, but it has also increased among the less well-educated.

- Although we read more about young people living together before a first marriage, cohabitation is more common before a remarriage than before a first marriage. Indeed, the great majority of remarriages are preceded by a period of cohabitation (Smock, 2000).
- Although the common image is one of a childless couple, a surprising number of cohabiting couples have children: In the 1995 survey, 15 percent had children from the current relationship, and 35 percent had children from a previous relationship (Bumpass & Lu, 2000).

The last fact may be the most startling. About 40 percent of the births listed in official statistics as occurring outside of marriage are in reality births to cohabiting couples (Bumpass & Lu, 2000). One recent study of unmarried mothers who had just given birth found that 44 percent of them were living with the fathers of their children (Center for Research on Child Well-Being, 2000). In fact, over the past decade or so, most of the rise in childbearing outside of marriage has been the result of births to cohabiting couples, not births to women living alone (Bumpass & Lu, 2000).

More often the children who live in these families are from earlier relationships. In these cases the household is a like a stepfamily: a parent (usually the mother), her child, and a resident man who is not the father (Seltzer, 2000). We might call these households quasi-stepfamilies. We will discuss this topic more fully in Chapter 14, Remarriage and Stepfamilies. They are so numerous that, using this expanded definition, more children enter a stepfamily through cohabitation than through remarriage (Bumpass, Raley, & Sweet, 1995).

Why has this transformation in living arrangements occurred? The change has technological, economic, and cultural roots. The technological change is the improvement in birth control, especially the introduction of the birth control pill in 1960, and the legalization of abortion in 1973. These developments reduced the risks of unintended pregnancies and births. As for the economic change, young women are investing more time and effort in establishing job skills and experience. Consequently, an early marriage may interfere with their educational or career plans. In addition, the stagnant earning prospects for young men may encourage some to cohabit rather than marry because cohabitation involves less commitment and responsibility (Oppenheimer, 1994).

The cultural change involves the greater acceptance and practice of sex outside marriage and the reduced moral stigma of living with a partner without marrying. More generally, it involves the greater emphasis on self-fulfillment as the criterion for judging personal relationships. Happiness in marriage is now culturally defined more in terms of individual satisfaction and less in terms of how well one performs a role such as parent or spouse than was the case at mid-century. [➡ p. 9] This ethic of self-fulfillment also lends itself to cohabitation. By definition, either partner can leave a cohabiting relationship without legal approval if he or she is dissatisfied in any way. Cohabitation is a way of forming a union that minimizes a person's loss of independence.

Cohabitation is still evolving: Each year it becomes more common, and its role in the family system increases. States and localities have been implementing legal changes that give cohabiting couples more rights that once were reserved for married couples. (See *Families and Public Policy:* Domestic Partnerships.) Moreover, comparing cohabitation with marriage is difficult because as Smock (2000) notes in a recent review of articles on cohabitation, the meaning of marriage is changing, too. Nevertheless, we can examine two major perspectives on the meaning of cohabitation and see how well they fit: cohabitation as a substitute for marriage versus cohabitation as a part of the process of getting married.

COHABITATION AS A SUBSTITUTE FOR MARRIAGE

One perspective is that cohabitation is becoming a substitute for marriage. If that were the case, we could expect to see more long-term cohabiting relationships and more individuals who never marry, but do cohabit one or more times over their life course. Yet half of all cohabiting relationships last only a year or less, and only 1 out of 10 lasts as long as five years (Bumpass & Lu, 2000). The short duration of the typical relationship suggests that few people are having a single, long-lasting living-together relationship as a substitute for marriage. Moreover, if cohabitation were an acceptable long-term substitute for marriage, we would expect that few cohabiting women would marry when they became

Domestic Partnerships

*G*etting married is not only a way for couples to express their love and commitment to each other but also a way for them to obtain important practical and financial advantages not available to couples who cohabit or live apart. In most nations the law has long recognized marriage as a privileged relationship in which the spouses have special rights and responsibilities. Here is a partial list of rights and responsibilities that married couples have but cohabiting couples, in most jurisdictions in the United States, do not have:

- They can include each other as beneficiaries on pension and annuity plans offered by their employers, and they can purchase health insurance for each other through their employers.
- They can file a joint income tax return, which may reduce their tax liability.
- They can receive Social Security survivors' benefits if their spouse dies, and they can inherit from each other even when there is no will.

- They are jointly responsible for their children, and each can give legal permission to schools, doctors, and the like, for trips, operations, and so forth.
- They can adopt children together.
- In the event of a divorce, they are both normally entitled to either custody or visitation rights.

This list reflects the view, virtually unchallenged until a few decades ago, that marriage constitutes the only legitimate context for the raising of children. It also reflects the ideal, prominent in the first half of the twentieth century, that families should have one wage earner (the husband), who should be able to provide health insurance, survivors' benefits, and so on, to his wife.

Yet social changes have made the granting of rights solely to married couples debatable. For instance, about 12 percent of all births in the United States occur to women who are cohabiting with the fathers of their children.[1] Cohabitation itself is so

common that some observers question the rationale for denying cohabiting couples similar rights to those married couples have. They argue that there is little difference between a cohabiting couple raising children and a married couple raising children—and that the former ought to have the same rights and receive the same benefits as the latter. Others favor retaining the privileged place of marriage for any of several reasons: because of a moral or religious belief that heterosexual marriage is the only proper setting for having and raising children; because of a pragmatic belief that marriage provides a more stable two-parent setting than cohabitation; or because of a wish to avoid further spending by government or business that would be triggered by treating cohabitors like spouses.

Cohabiting heterosexual couples, at least, can avail themselves of these benefits by marrying. Lesbian and gay couples cannot. But over the past decade or so, a number of cities and counties have instituted ways for couples, whether heterosexual or

pregnant, because they wouldn't feel the need to. Yet studies show that a majority of cohabiting white women who become pregnant do marry before the birth of their child (Manning, 1993), suggesting that they don't think cohabitation is a satisfactory arrangement for raising children.

Among some African Americans, cohabitation may be more of a substitute for marriage. Black women who cohabit are much less likely to marry than are white women (Manning & Smock, 1995; Brien, Lillard, & Waite, 1999). Moreover, those who become pregnant are less likely to marry before the child's birth (Manning, 1993). And in the first month of a cohabiting relationship, black households are more likely to include children than white households. The weaker connection of cohabitation and marriage among African Americans is consistent with the weaker role of marriage, in general, in African-American family life. Studies also suggest that cohabitation is more of an alternative to marriage among mainland Puerto Rican women than among non-Hispanic whites (Landale & Fennelly, 1992; Landale & Forste, 1991).

The growth of cohabitation could also provide an alternative to marriage for men who do not highly value commitment, and a way for them to receive the benefits of a regular sexual relationship without having to marry. Akerlof,

homosexual, to register as "domestic partners," a kind of legal middle ground between marriage and cohabitation. In some places, domestic partners obtain minimal new rights, such as the right to visit an ill partner in a hospital (which was particularly desired by gay rights organizations due to the AIDS epidemic). In other places, such as New York City, municipal workers can obtain health insurance benefits for their domestic partners. Many of the companies and municipalities that offer benefits to unmarried partners restrict the offer to same-sex partners on the theory that heterosexual employees can marry if they wish to receive comparable benefits. So far, the costs of providing these benefits have been lower than expected because many gay or lesbian employees have partners who obtain benefits through their own jobs and because some employees find that coming out as gay isn't worth the extra benefits.

The extension of rights and recognition to gay and lesbian partnerships has often been controversial. A number of local and state initiatives have been on ballots in recent years. As noted in the opening pages of this book, Vermont in 2000 became the first state to create a form of domestic partnership for same-sex couples, which the legislature called a "civil union."

Social conservatives believe the benefits to be an unwarranted endorsement of a form of family life they morally oppose. Advocates of domestic partnerships, and of the more radical step of legalizing gay marriages, argue, in contrast, that these steps would allow gay men and lesbians to openly live the conservative lifestyles of committed, monogamous couples. The debate reflects the weakening role of marriage in the institution of the family. Although still dominant, heterosexual marriage is no longer the only acceptable way for couples to live together. Rather, heterosexual cohabitation is broadly tolerated. This toleration is so recent, however, that there is little consensus on the rights and responsibilities heterosexual partners should have toward each other and toward the children in their households. Toleration of gay and lesbian partnerships would seem to be a logical next step. Yet it is a leap that many heterosexuals still cannot make. The extension of legally recognized domestic partnerships—and even marriage—to lesbian and gay couples is likely to remain a contentious public issue into the beginning of the twenty-first century.

Ask Yourself

1. Are any of the couples you know cohabiting? If so, have their relationships reached the point at which legal considerations would be meaningful to them?

2. Should couples who are cohabiting have the same legal rights as married couples? Why or why not?

[1] About 30 percent of all births occur outside marriage. And of these 30 percent, about 40 percent occur to women who are cohabiting with the fathers of their children. (Bumpass & Lu, 2000).

www.mhhe.com/cherlin

Yellen, and Katz (1996) maintain that the introduction of effective birth control methods and legal abortion—coupled with the acceptance of sex outside of marriage—have benefited men because they can obtain a sexual relationship without the risk of an unwanted birth. This scenario only holds if men, on average, value long-term commitment in relationships less than women do (otherwise women would benefit just as much from nonmarital sexual relationships). The biosocial, or evolutionary, view of gender differences suggests that men may, on average, care less about commitment than women do. [➡ p. 34] Alternatively, gender theorists in sociology might argue that men are socialized into valuing commitment less. If either view is true, cohabitation may be to men's advantage in this regard.

COHABITATION AS PART OF THE MARRIAGE PROCESS

Some observers claim that cohabitation is a form of single life that doesn't have much to do with marriage. Rindfuss and VandenHeuval (1990) note, for example, that among college-age young adults, those who are cohabiting are nearly as likely to be enrolled in college as are those who are living without a partner. In

FIGURE 8.2

Percentage of cohabiting women and men under age 35 who agreed that each of the following statements was an important reason to them "why a person might *want* to live with someone of the opposite sex without being married": (*A*) It requires less personal commitment than marriage. (*B*) It is more sexually satisfying than dating. (*C*) It makes it possible to share living expenses. (*D*) It requires less sexual faithfulness than marriage. (*E*) Couples can be sure they are compatible before marriage. (*F*) It allows each partner to be more independent than marriage. (*Source:* Bumpass, Sweet, & Cherlin, 1991.)

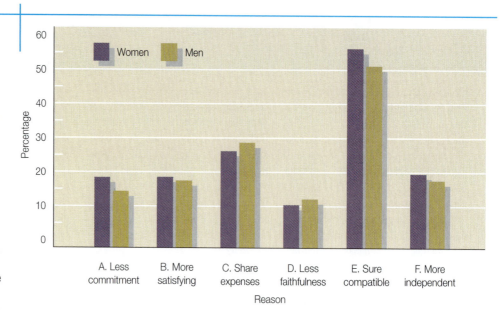

contrast, those who are married are much less likely to be enrolled. This pattern suggests that cohabitors behave more like singles when they make decisions about continuing their education. Moreover, neither singles nor cohabitors have made a long-term commitment to stay with their partners, but married persons have. Nor do cohabitors appear outwardly to be more committed to the institution of marriage than singles: In the 1987–1988 National Survey of Families and Households (NSFH), there was virtually no difference between the percentage of singles and cohabitors who agreed with the statement "It's better for a person to get married than to go through life being single" (Bumpass et al., 1991).[13]

Yet in other ways cohabitation does seem like a stage in the marriage process, even though the partners have not made a permanent commitment to each other. When never-married cohabiting persons in the NSFH were asked if they had marriage plans, 50 percent said they had "definite plans" to marry their partner and an additional 31 percent said they "think they will marry" their partner (Bumpass et al., 1991).[14] The cohabiting couples in the NSFH were also presented with a list of "reasons why a person might *want* to live with someone of the opposite sex without being married." They were then asked which of the reasons was important to them. The results are displayed in Figure 8.2. As can be seen, few cohabitors chose reasons pertaining to lower personal commitment, greater sexual satisfaction, less sexual faithfulness, or greater independence than in marriage. Rather, the only reason that was chosen by a majority was "Couples can be sure they are compatible before marriage."

One way to resolve the tension between interpretation 1 (it's like being single) and interpretation 2 (it's part of the marriage process) is to use the concepts

[13]Among persons under age 35, 36 percent of cohabiting, never-married persons agreed with that statement, compared with 34 percent of noncohabiting, never-married persons.

[14]Still, the partners disagreed about their plans in about one-fifth of the unions in which at least one person planned to, or thought he or she would, marry his or her partner.

of **manifest functions** and **latent functions.** Robert Merton first coined these terms to argue that social actions often serve two kinds of purposes: the publicly stated, acknowledged ones, which he called manifest functions, and the unacknowledged, unstated ones, which he called latent functions (Merton, 1968). The latter, he argued, may be as important as the former. One might argue that cohabitation has a manifest function that has little to do with marriage, namely providing a way to increase the emotional and sexual satisfactions to be gotten from intimate relationships. If you observe cohabiting couples who have recently moved in together, you will probably find men and women who devote little time to thoughts of marriage, except when a stray sociologist wanders in and asks about it. Nevertheless, if you pay a return visit a few years later, you are likely to find that they have married; and if they haven't, they probably won't be together any longer. The latent function of their cohabiting relationship was to assess the compatibility of a potential spouse. If the assessment proved positive, a marriage resulted; if not, a breakup occurred. That few would have acknowledged this function early on makes it no less real—it just makes it latent rather than manifest. Indeed, its latent nature may make it easier to perform: If cohabitors continually reminded each other that their every move was being evaluated, their relationship might become strained.

If the latent function of cohabitation is to be a part of the marriage process, as I am arguing, just what role does it play? Who makes use of it, and how? First, young women who are in a strong economic position seem to be using it to learn whether their male partners will be good earners—and possibly whether they will share equitably in the housework. A study that followed a national sample of high school graduates for 14 years showed that young single women with high earnings were more likely to cohabit than they were to marry. In contrast, young single men with high earnings were more likely to marry than to cohabit (Clarkberg, 1997). It is as if women with the highest—and therefore most attractive—earning potential were using these resources to establish a cohabiting relationship in which they could find out more about their partners. In particular, women can determine whether men seem to be steady wage earners and whether they will share the work at home. In this way, cohabitation may benefit the search process that young women with strong marriage market positions undertake.

COHABITATION AMONG GAYS AND LESBIANS

For gay men and lesbians, marriage is not an option, so cohabitation is the only form of partnership available. In the 1992 University of Chicago survey of sexual behavior (➡ p. 228), cohabitation was found to be common among individuals who said they had engaged only in homosexual sex the previous year: 44 percent of these women and 28 percent of these men reported they were living in such partnerships (Black, Gates, Sanders, & Taylor, 2000). Children are present in some of these same-sex partnerships. The 1990 Census allowed individuals who were living with someone of the same sex to indicate whether their housemates were partners. According to the data, 22 percent of women in same-sex partnerships and 5 percent of men in same-sex partnerships had children living with them (Black et al., 2000).

Some gay and lesbian couples register for domestic partnerships or hold commitment ceremonies to publicly affirm their commitment to one another. For these couples, cohabitation is a substitute for heterosexual marriage. But other

manifest function a publicly stated, acknowledged reason behind social actions

latent function an unacknowledged, unstated reason behind social actions

cohabiting gays and lesbians view their partnerships, whether short- or long-term, as different from heterosexual marriage. Indeed, some authors have argued that marriage should not be the model for gay and lesbian partnerships; rather, rights and responsibilities should be extended to all individuals, whether they have committed long-term partnerships or not (Polikoff, 1990). As is the case with heterosexual couples, there is substantial variation in the meaning of cohabitation among gay and lesbian couples.

Studies that have compared gay, lesbian, and heterosexual couples find no significant differences in love or relationship satisfaction (Savin-Williams & Esterberg, 2000). When a sample of homosexual and heterosexual couples were asked what were the "best things" and "worst things" about their relationships, a panel of raters who were given the written comments could not tell which comments came from homosexuals and which came from heterosexuals (Peplau, 1991). Kath Weston, an anthropologist who studied lesbian and gay couples in San Francisco in the 1980s, reported a concern about excessive "merging." Subsequent research suggests that this issue is more relevant for lesbian partnerships than for gay male partnerships (Savin-Williams & Esterberg, 2000). The problem, Weston wrote, is to avoid becoming so united with and dependent on your partner that you lose your independence and can't develop as a person. This language is similar to the way many married persons talk about the need to maintain a growing, independent self. Moreover, in their paid work and home lives, lesbian and gay couples fit the model of the independent marriage well: They tend to rely less on a division of labor than do heterosexual couples. Instead, they seem to split the domestic chores more equitably and flexibly, with partners sharing various tasks such as cooking and cleaning (Seidman, 1991).

The term "family" may carry different connotations for lesbians and gay men than for heterosexuals. Among married heterosexuals, the primary family unit is usually the wife, husband, and children—the conjugal family. "Family" can also mean the larger group of relatives including grandparents, brothers and sisters, and so forth; but these kin are usually of lesser importance than one's spouse. Weston argues that among gay and lesbian couples in San Francisco, the primary meaning of "family" encompasses not only one's partner but also a network of close friends. In fact, friends may be more central to your "family" than a partner because of the high likelihood that you and your lover will eventually dissolve your partnership. Weston cites a common adage that friends last, while lovers are simply "passing through" (Weston, 1991). The families of many of the people she studied consisted fundamentally of networks of friends and lovers who provided social and emotional support for one another. Family, she was often told, means having people you can count on—people who are "there for you." Thus the term "family" referred to a more or less stable group of people who served as a support network for one another. A partner might be integrated into this network, and he or she might remain in the network even if the partnership ended.

The relationships between gay people and their parents and siblings vary greatly, depending on whether they have come out and what the reactions of the blood relatives were to the announcement. What gay people must do is create a family from the relationships they can retain with biological kin, the close friends they have, and their present and former partners. One person told Weston, "Gay people really have to work to make family" (Weston, 1991). In contrast, most heterosexuals have a biological family they can take for granted and another family they acquire through marriage (although people in stepfamilies must also do the work of constructing a family—see Chapter 14). The families woven together by lesbians and gay men are another example of created kinship—the kind of kinship people must work to construct. [➡ p. 18] "There's a way of doing it gay," another person remarked to Weston about family ties, "but it's a whole lot harder, and it's less secure" (Weston, 1991).

COHABITATION: A SUMMING UP

Cohabitation is a diverse phenomenon that has different meanings for different couples. Most cohabiting relationships do not last very long; among heterosexuals, about half end in marriage (rather than a break-up). Particularly among whites, cohabitation often seems to be a stage in the marriage process. In these cases, cohabitation is an intermediate step that usually leads in short order either to a marriage or a break-up. Relative to whites, cohabitation is more often a substitute for marriage than a stage in the process among African Americans. Studies show that African Americans who cohabit are less likely to marry their partners, and black women who become pregnant while cohabiting are less likely to marry before the birth of the child than white women. Among Hispanic groups with a tradition of consensual unions [➡ p. 162], such as Puerto Ricans, cohabitation is also more of a substitute for marriage than among whites. Among gay and lesbian couples, it is sometimes a substitute for and sometimes an alternative to the unavailable option of marriage. Still, there is substantial variation within each group in how cohabiting couples view their relationships.

The link between cohabitation and marriage may be weakening. Fewer cohabitations end in marriage now than a few decades ago: In the 1970s, about 60 percent of cohabiting individuals married within three years compared to about 35 percent in the early 1990s (Seltzer, 2000). And from the 1980s to the 1990s, the percentage of cohabiting couples who had children together but did not marry increased. Cities are now providing cohabiting couples with some of the same legal rights and protections married couples have. Among all racial-ethnic groups, the meaning of cohabitation may be changing as the practice grows more common.

Marriage

As I suggested earlier in this chapter, not just the meaning of cohabitation, but the meaning of marriage in this society has been changing. In fact, it changed greatly over the course of the twentieth century. The most influential statement about the change that occurred during the first half of the twentieth century came from Ernest Burgess, a professor at the University of Chicago. In a 1945 textbook, Burgess wrote:

> *The central thesis of this volume is that the family in historical times has been, and at present is, in transition from an institution to a companionship. In the past the important factors unifying the family have been external, formal, and authoritarian, as the law, the mores, public opinion, tradition, the authority of the family head, rigid discipline, and elaborate ritual. At present, in the new emerging form of the companionship family, its unity inheres less and less in community pressures and more and more in such interpersonal relations as the mutual affection, the sympathetic understanding, and the comradeship of its members* (Burgess & Locke, 1945).

Burgess meant the family-as-institution and the family-as-companionship to be seen as ideal types. Introduced by Max Weber, the *ideal type* [➡ p. 114] is a hypothetical model that consists of the most significant characteristics, in extreme form, of a social phenomenon. *Ideal* is used not in the sense of best or perfect but rather in the sense of a pure, distilled form—so pure that it probably doesn't exist in reality. The ideal type is useful for understanding social life, even though any real example of the phenomenon may not have all the characteristics of the ideal type. Thus, Burgess cautions that purely institutional and purely companionship families exist "nowhere in time or space." Moreover, the companionship form "is not to be conceived of as having already been realized but as emerging" (Burgess & Locke, 1945).

Family life in preindustrial Western nations was, indeed, guided more by law and custom than by affection and emotional stimulation. The local government in Plymouth Colony, you will recall, kept a close watch over the conduct of family members. [➡ p. 48] Parents seem to have played a greater role in selecting a spouse for their children than was the case in later centuries. In general, husbands and fathers had greater authority than they do today: Religion and law certified the father as the head of the family, with broad powers over his wife (whose property he could sell) and his children (who remained with him in the event of divorce). In addition, the marginal existence of poor farm families and the modest standard of living of most urban families made the family's survival a higher priority than the personality development of the members.

In the twentieth century, an increasing proportion of men and women came to value family life for the personal, emotional satisfaction they could gain from it. Burgess's model reflects the rise of the private family—a process that began a few hundred years ago in the more prosperous classes but became widespread only after 1900. [➡ p. 15] Not until this century was the average standard of living high enough to allow family members to focus on their own personal fulfillment rather than on their daily subsistence.

THE COMPANIONSHIP MARRIAGE

In the late nineteenth and early twentieth centuries, companionship and sexual fulfillment became more important to a successful marriage. The sexual prudery of the Victorian era may have been overstated, but restraint of sexual passion seems to have been highly valued. For instance, the percentage of brides who became pregnant before their marriages decreased from 1800 to 1870 (Smith & Hindus, 1975). Until the twentieth century, sexual relations in marriage (and there was relatively little sexual activity outside marriage except among couples who were engaged) were seen more as a means of producing children than as a way to personal fulfillment. Historian Elaine Tyler May claims that nineteenth-century writers thought it immoral and dangerous for a married couple to have sexual relations more than once or twice a month (May, 1980). But after the turn of the century, progressive writers argued that an active sex life was central to a happy marriage. Birth control advocates, such as Margaret Sanger, fought for greater availability of contraceptives, an essential condition for removing the link between sexual relations and childbearing (Mintz & Kellogg, 1988).

In the 1920s, Robert and Helen Lynd conducted a famous study of life in Muncie, Indiana, which they selected as a typical American town and called

"Middletown" (Lynd & Lynd, 1929). The Lynds reported that, compared with the 1890s, young adults were more likely to view romantic love as the only valid basis for marriage. In this new romantic climate, they noted, women were more concerned with "youthful beauty." Throughout the country, mass production and rising incomes made fashionable clothing affordable. Advice columnist Dorothy Dix told her readers that "good looks are a girl's trump card." And she counseled, "Dress well and thereby appear fifty percent better looking than you are. . . . Make yourself charming" (May, 1980). This emphasis on sexual allure was new: Prior to the twentieth century, a young woman needed to convince a suitor that she could be a good partner, but it was less important that she be attractive. Although a young man expected that his wife would bear children and that their sexual relations would be pleasurable, he didn't necessarily expect much emotional fulfillment from sex. Nor did he necessarily expect a close friendship to develop with his wife. However, by the 1920s or 1930s, as May concluded, a young man wanted "both excitement *and* domesticity in a wife" (May, 1980).

companionship marriage a marriage in which the emphasis is on affection, friendship, and sexual gratification

institutional marriage a marriage in which the emphasis is on male authority, duty, and conformity to social norms

These changes ushered in what we might call, following Burgess, the **companionship marriage,** with its emphases on affection, friendship, and sexual gratification, in contrast to the **institutional marriage,** with its emphases on male authority, duty, and conformity to social norms. When looking back on Burgess's work, however, one must keep in mind that the "modern" companionship marriage that he saw emerging in the 1920s and 1930s was the single-earner, breadwinner-homemaker family that flourished in the 1950s—not the dual-earner family that emerged only in the last half of the twentieth century. Nineteen hundred thirty was the end of a three- to four-decade period during which companionship and emotional satisfaction had become central to more and more middle-class families. The husband and wife in the companionship marriage ideally adhered to a sharp division of labor (he working outside the home, she working inside the home). Nevertheless, they were supposed to be each other's companions—friends, lovers—to an extent not imagined a few generations earlier. Young women were seen increasingly as needing higher education, not so they could establish a career but rather so they could be stimulating conversationalists and adept homemakers. By midcentury, large state universities around the country enrolled hundreds of thousands of bright young women who majored in home economics or consumer science and joked that what they really hoped to get at college was an "MRS." degree.

Marriage patterns were somewhat different among African Americans in the first half of the century. Because of discrimination and lack of economic opportunity, African-American men often did not have the strong earnings record necessary to claim the authority and duty of a husband; consequently, the institutional marriage was never as strong. Statistics show that from the beginning of the twentieth century African Americans were more likely to end a marriage if there were serious difficulties than were whites (Preston, Lim, & Morgan, 1992). A comparison of the life histories of whites and blacks in the South in 1938 and 1939 collected by the Federal Writers' Project found that African-American women were more likely to leave abusive marriages than were white women (Pagnini & Morgan, 1996). Although the higher rate of divorce may reflect cultural differences, it also may reflect the lower economic benefits for African-American women of being married. Among African Americans, then, the transition from institution to companionship was less well defined.

THE INDEPENDENT MARRIAGE

In the 1960s, the breadwinner-homemaker marriage began to lose ground as both a cultural ideal and a demographic reality. It was gradually overtaken by family forms that Burgess had not foreseen, particularly marriages in which both the husband and the wife worked outside the home. Although women continued to do most of the housework and childcare, the roles of wives and husbands became more flexible and open to negotiation. Moreover, an even more individualistic perspective on the rewards of marriage took root. When people evaluated how satisfied they were with their marriages, they thought more in terms of individual satisfaction, as opposed to the mutual satisfaction gained through building a family. Recall the two national surveys of mental health [➡ p. 9], one of which was carried out in 1957 and the other in 1976 (Veroff, Douvan, & Kulka, 1981).

These surveys detected a shift in the criteria people use to evaluate whether they were satisfied with their lives. When people in the 1957 survey were asked to rate their life satisfaction, their thoughts turned to the social roles they played, such as spouse or parent. For example, in the 1950s, the editors of *McCall's* magazine wrote of a "new and warmer way of life," through which people would become fulfilled "not as women alone or men alone, isolated from one another, but as a family sharing a common experience" (Friedan, 1963).[15] Men who felt they were good workers and good providers tended to be more satisfied, as did women who felt they were good mothers and supportive wives. In other words, in 1957, people often used criteria external to themselves to decide how satisfied they were with their lives.

But by 1976, people were more likely to use internal criteria. When asked how satisfied they were, the people in the 1976 survey responded in terms of their own sense of personal fulfillment, emotional satisfaction, and self-development. It mattered less how well they were performing the roles society expected of them, such as earning money, raising children, or working hard on the job. It mattered more how much they enjoyed their jobs, how much emotional satisfaction they were getting from their marriages, how gratifying their sexual relationships were, and how pleased they were with the ways their lives were changing and developing. Being a good citizen or a responsible parent was less important; being emotionally satisfied was more important. Feeling that you were meeting your obligations to others was less central; feeling that you had opportunities to grow as a person was more central.

Francesca Cancian documented the changing beliefs about marriage by studying popular magazine articles offering marital advice in every decade between 1900 and 1979 (Cancian, 1987). She identified three themes that characterized beliefs about the post–1960-style marriage. The first was "self-development," the belief that each person should develop a fulfilling, independent self instead of merely sacrificing oneself to one's partner. Second, roles within marriage should be flexible and negotiable; and, third, communication and openness in confronting problems are essential. She then tallied the percentage of articles in each decade that contained one or more of these three themes. The results are presented in Figure 8.3. As the reader can see, the presence of these themes rose in the 1920s but then declined through the 1950s. After 1960, however, these themes rose to new heights. Assuming the content of these magazines reflects cultural beliefs about love and marriage, there is indeed evidence of a shift toward a more independent conception of marriage (Cancian, 1987).[16] (On the use of historical records by sociologists, see *How Do Sociologists Know What They Know?* Archival Research.) If the 1950s were the peak of the companionship marriage, we might then call the emerging post–1960 form the **independent marriage,** with its emphases on self-development, flexible roles, and communication about problems. Cancian called the change in meaning that accompanied the transition to the independent marriage a shift "from role to self" (Cancian, 1987).

independent marriage a marriage in which the emphasis is on self-development, flexible roles, and communication about problems

---

[15]Cited in Mintz and Kellogg (1988).

[16]Cancian also argues that a more interdependent style of marriage may arise, one which combines the mutual support of the companionship marriage with the greater equality and role sharing of the independent marriage.

Percentage of magazine articles containing at least one of three themes about marriage: self development, flexible and negotiable roles, and communication and openness, 1900–1979. (*Source:* Cancian, 1987).

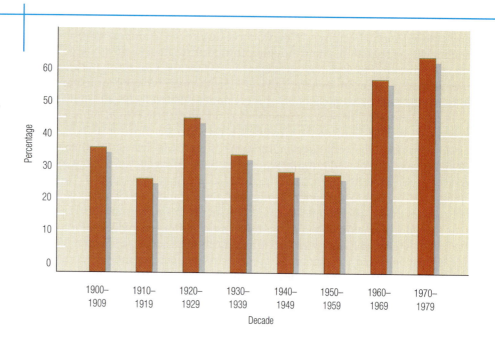

EXPLAINING THE CHANGE IN VIEWS OF MARRIAGE

Why, over the past century, did the shifts from the institutional marriage to the companionship marriage and then to the independent marriage occur? Both transitions—from institutional to companionship and from companionship to independent—were consistent with the long-term rise in the value Americans and citizens of other Western nations place on individualism. During the first transition, people were able to focus more on the satisfaction they derived from the small conjugal unit of spouses and children, as opposed to their membership in larger kinship groups or communities. Wives and husbands focused on the pleasures of companionship and affection and on the satisfactions of raising children together and performing their respective roles as homemaker or breadwinner. Yet there was little to prevent people from eventually pushing individualism one step further—to their own personal growth, to the development of their own adult personalities, to their own feelings of fulfillment. Once they began to do so in the 1960s, pressures rose to make marital roles more flexible and negotiable and to focus more on the individual concerns of the spouses. The second transition then ensued.

In addition, both transitions had economic roots. When most people's standard of living was so low that they had difficulty earning enough money for food and shelter, few had time for personal fulfillment. People needed to pool earnings and housework with spouses and children in order to subsist, and marriage was therefore more of an economic partnership. The rising standard of living during the twentieth century gave more people the luxury of focusing on their own feelings of satisfaction. They did so first in the context of the companionship marriage, focusing on the satisfactions of having one's spouse as a friend and raising children together. Moreover, the movement of women into the labor force during the century gave women more opportunities for independent living, even though their wages have remained well below men's. Their greater economic leverage could be used to demand more satisfaction from marriage. Their jobs also gave them a life outside the home. Women as well as men could now think in terms of their own individual development through adulthood.

To be sure, this description fits middle-class families better than others. Even among them, the companionship and independent marriages still represent ideal types, not fully achieved. For the poor, personal fulfillment has remained a luxury, and marriage of any kind has become less common and more brittle. Yet the sharply rising incomes of the 1950s and 1960s did bring a level of prosperity to the working class that it had not seen before. Assisted by veterans' benefits, millions of blue-collar workers and their wives and children were able to buy homes in the suburbs. Many of them followed the breadwinner-homemaker norm. Even in working-class families where wives worked for pay, it was common for the husband and wife both to think that it would be preferable for her to stay home if finances allowed (Rubin, 1976). Then, in the 1970s and 1980s, the incomes of young working-class men fell due to the restructuring of the economy. Having wives work for pay became an unavoidable necessity to most young couples. Whether this change caused a more independent form of marriage to emerge among the working class is unclear. On the one hand, more working-class wives have independent sources of income; on the other hand, growing financial pressures may have limited the focus on personal development that has characterized middle-class marriages.

MARRIAGE AND RELIGION

Organized religion in the United States has always supported marriage, and it continued to do so throughout the transitions to the companionship and independent marriages. In recent decades, one of the greatest changes in the influence of religion on family life has been the convergence in the practices of Catholic and Protestant families (Thornton, 1985). The numbers of Catholics surged in the United States during the late nineteenth and early twentieth centuries, as large numbers of immigrants from heavily Catholic countries in Southern and Eastern Europe (e.g., Italy, Poland) arrived. The teaching of the Catholic church is that marriage is a sacrament that can be dissolved only by annulment (a decree by the Church that a marriage was never valid). Moreover, the primary purpose of marriage, the Church teaches, is to bear and rear children, and all forms of artificial birth control and abortion are forbidden. In the first half of the twentieth century, Catholic families had more children, used birth control methods less, and had lower divorce rates than did Protestants. But by 1980, these differences had been greatly reduced. Among young Catholics aged 18 to 29 in a 1979 survey, 95 percent approved of birth control, and 89 percent approved of remarriage for divorced people (D'Antonio, 1985). Personal autonomy has replaced obedience to religious authority as the main determinant of family-related behavior among American Catholics.

Whereas Catholics have been changing greatly in their attitude toward religious authority, fundamentalist Protestants have changed much less (Thornton, 1985). They now constitute a distinctive subgroup in terms of family life: Compared with other religious groups, they are less likely to divorce, they have the highest birthrates, they have the lowest rates of married women working outside the home, and they have the most conservative attitudes toward gender roles (Ammerman & Roof, 1995). Although there is variation among fundamentalist families, they tend to hold to a more literal interpretation of the Bible, which leads them to view husbands as the authority in the home.

*B*oth Francesca M. Cancian's study of the changing content of women's magazines from 1900 to 1979 (Cancian, 1987) and Deanna L. Pagnini and S. Philip Morgan's study of biographies of African Americans and whites collected in the 1930s by the Federal Writers' Project (Pagnini & Morgan, 1996) are examples of **archival research.** This term refers to research that uses printed or written documents stored in libraries or other data archives. Historians rely on archival research of necessity because the written records of events are often the only information they have. Sociologists sometimes use this method, too, especially when they want to study social change by examining the past and comparing it with the present.

For each five-year period, Cancian selected eight articles listed in *Reader's Guide to Periodical Literature* under the heading "marriage," from large-circulation magazines addressed primarily to women, such as *Ladies' Home Journal, McCall's,*

and *Reader's Digest.* She recorded codes for each article according to its "dominant themes," and then tallied the codes by decade to see whether the themes had changed over time (see Figure 8.3). Pagnini read all 1,170 life histories that were collected by the Federal Writers' Project in 1938 and 1939 in the South and stored at the Southern Historical Collection at the University of North Carolina at Chapel Hill. Every time she encountered material on marriage or nonmarital childbearing, she prepared an excerpt that had no identifying information except an identification number. Later, Pagnini and Morgan analyzed the content of each excerpt (e.g., whether a woman who had an abusive marriage had left it) without knowing the race of the person whose excerpt they were examining. Only after the excerpts had been examined did they use the identification numbers to assign the proper race to each excerpt. (If you are interested in the biographies that the Federal Writers'

Project collected, you can view some of them through the web site of the Library of Congress [Lcweb2.loc.gov/wpaintro/wpahome.html] and search their contents through key words such as "marriage" or "divorce.")

Archival research presents many challenges. The best archival researchers know these limitations, face them squarely, and take pains to minimize them. First, it is difficult to know how representative the materials are. For instance, did the articles Cancian selected represent the views of American women at the time? Cancian forthrightly acknowledged this limitation:

The intended audience of the magazines seems to come from a higher social class in the earlier decades, and the content of the articles partly reflects the policies of editors and advertisers and the attitudes of the writers. Nonetheless, the magazines seem to provide a fairly

archival research
research that uses printed or written documents stored in libraries or other data archives

More generally, churches and synagogues remain strong supporters of marriage. (The link between church and marriage is less central among African-American churches because, while supporting marriages, these churches have historically reached out to the larger percentage of single-parent families [Gilkes, 1995].) And among married persons, those who are active religiously describe themselves as somewhat happier with their marriages, although it is not clear that religious activity causes the greater happiness (Booth, Johnson, Branaman, & Sica, 1995). In recent years, churches have been an expanding base for counseling, educational programs, and other attempts at "marriage-strengthening" (Stanley, Markman, St. Peters, & Leber, 1995). For example, some educational programs teach communication skills to engaged or recently married couples so that they will be better equipped to discuss and resolve problems that may arise.

Is Marriage Good for You?

Do individuals benefit from being married? A substantial body of literature shows that married men appear advantaged compared with unmarried men in many ways and that, to a lesser extent, married women seem advantaged as well. But it is difficult to know whether marriage *causes* these differences.

valid measure, since my findings are consistent with the other sources of data described in this chapter (pp. 173–174).

Pagnini and Morgan frankly noted that the life histories gathered in the South overrepresented poor whites and included many blacks:

While these could be termed limitations in that they do not statistically reflect the class, marriage, and geographical distribution of the Southern population, we would label them as strengths. So often in historical work we are not able to find materials about the working class or blacks; to have both is an advantage (p. 1702).

Another difficulty in archival research is determining how accurate the information is. For instance, the biographies of the Southerners are told through the words of the writers, who determined what questions

to ask and what words to write down. Moreover, the subjects were recalling events that took place, in some cases, decades earlier. Pagnini and Morgan claimed that they could make a virtue out of this necessity:

Thus, we must be aware that we are dealing with subjective perceptions and selected events . . . For those interviewed, we have memories and perceptions of what was important to these individuals and their families. We stress that for our purposes this is what we seek—there are superior sources that simply record the events themselves. Our goal here is interpretive . . . (p. 1702).

It is also difficult to know how to analyze the information. What categories should one use and how does one tell if a record fits in the category? For instance, how does a scholar reading women's magazines determine whether an article conveys a tone of self-sacrifice or self-fulfillment toward marriage? Cancian had pairs of people read

and code each article independently. She set rules for interpreting the content of the magazines and refined the rules until both coders in each pair agreed on 85 percent of the coding for a particular article.

Archival research does not necessarily provide a representative picture of social history. But it is one of the only tools we have. If social scientists recognize the limitations of archival research, inform their readers about them, and take care to minimize them, the written record can provide an enlightening window on the past.

Ask Yourself

1. Do popular magazines present an accurate picture of present-day attitudes toward love and marriage? A hundred years from now, what might sociologists think when reading them?

2. What other documents could sociologists examine to see how Americans' views of marriage have changed over time?

www.mhhe.com/cherlin

For example, married men and women live longer, on average, than do unmarried men and women. A recent study estimated that married men and women who are age 48 have a greater-than-80-percent chance of reaching age 65, whereas never-married and divorced men and women have a less-than-70-percent chance of living that long (Waite & Lillard, 1995). A number of studies have found evidence that married men have substantially better health then unmarried men, in terms of general life satisfaction, depression and anxiety, and treatment for psychiatric difficulties. The same relationships hold for women, but the differences between the married and the unmarried are smaller. (See Gove, Style, & Hughes, 1990, for a review.)

There are two possible reasons for these findings:

1. *Being married actually causes people to feel better and live longer.* Waite (1995) suggests two ways that marriage might be good for one's physical and mental health. First, it may deter people from undertaking risky behavior. Married men and women are less likely to drink and drive, abuse alcohol or drugs, and get into serious arguments (Umberson, 1987). Marriage may provide people with a sense of responsibility to children and spouses that leads them to take fewer risks. In addition, marriage may provide a partner who monitors a person's health closely and urges a healthier lifestyle. Second, married people have higher

incomes and more wealth (Smith, 1994), in part because of economies of scale (two people can share a home or a car). A higher standard of living eases stress and makes people less likely to abuse alcohol or drugs.

2.   *Mentally and physically healthier people are more likely to get married and to stay married.*   As women and men choose partners, we would expect them to favor the healthy and the happy over the troubled and the ill. So there should be *positive selection into* marriage: People with positive qualities are more likely to enter into it. Recall the discussion of the selection effect on teenage childbearing: Young women who have children as adolescents are not a random sample of all adolescents. [➡ p. 223] Similarly, people who marry are not a random sample of all adults; rather, they represent the most attractive 90 percent of the population in the marriage market. Moreover, people with poorer mental health have marriages that are more troubled and are therefore more likely to divorce. So as couples age, there is *negative selection out of* marriage: People with negative characteristics are more likely to leave it. Because of selection into and out of marriage, we would expect currently married individuals to be physically and mentally healthier even if what goes on in a marriage has nothing to do with it.

Because sociologists cannot randomly assign some people to marry and others to stay single and then study them, we cannot say definitively whether being married actually causes people's health and mood to improve or whether we are merely witnessing a selection effect. But the findings for men, at least, are so strong and consistent across a number of studies of different domains of life as to suggest that some of the advantages shown by married men are caused by the marriage relationship itself. And it is quite possible that there are some benefits for women as well. If the effects of marriage were purely due to selection, we would expect that as people get older, the difference between the married and unmarried would increase—because the unmarried group would be composed more and more of unhealthy individuals who never married or who divorced. But data on death rates and treatment for mental illness do not show a gap between the married and the unmarried that increases with age (Gove et al., 1990).

A recent book by Waite and Gallagher (2000) goes further, claiming not only that the benefits of marriage are real, but that women gain about as much from marriage as men. Compared to current alternatives for women, the claim of equal benefits for each gender is probably true in some respects. For instance, women typically earn less than men, so wives tend to gain more in household income than husbands (because their husbands tend to earn more than they do). But as England (2000) argues, husbands typically gain greater bargaining power in the household than wives, because husbands can threaten to leave the marriage and take their higher incomes with them. (More will be said about earnings and bargaining power in the next chapter.) Waite and Gallagher also claim that marriage benefits women because it protects them from domestic violence. How so? Married women are less likely to be victimized than cohabiting women. But women who are neither living with a man nor married have an even lower risk, so a woman who is concerned about avoiding domestic violence might reasonably decide to avoid heterosexual unions altogether, rather than to marry. Nevertheless, even if the presumed benefits to women are inflated, Waite and Gallagher do convincingly refute an older literature which held that marriage lowers a woman's well-being (Bernard, 1972).

Marriage might benefit men more than women because unmarried men have fewer social resources to draw on. As Chapter 11 will show, women are enmeshed in support networks with other women—mothers, sisters, grandmothers—much more than men are. In contrast, men tend to rely heavily on their wives for social support; and they therefore have more to gain from marrying. In addition, marriage has played a crucial role in defining what it means to be an adult male in our society (Nock, 1998). One theory of gender suggests that men define themselves by separating from their birth family more than women do. [➡ p. 92] Marriage has been the culturally approved way for men to achieve this separation in adulthood. It leads to noticeable changes in their public behavior: Married men spend more time with relatives or at religious services and events, and less time with friends and at bars or taverns, than they did before they married (Nock, 1998). It is the way that men in American society have taken on the culturally prescribed roles of wage earner, father, and public citizen.

Marriage as an Ongoing Project

Perhaps the most fundamental change in marriage is this one: Whereas in earlier times what mattered most in a marriage was how well you and your spouse carried out your duties, now what matters most is whether the marriage helps you to achieve a more fulfilling sense of self, to grow as an individual, or to experience a greater level of personal satisfaction. Ann Swidler writes of changes in idealized views of love in Western society, which she calls "love myths." The nineteenth-century myths defined love as a spiritual, moral matter in which sexual restraint was valued—the kinds of myths that made Maud choose Elmer. But the current love myths, Swidler argues, define love as part of a quest for fulfillment and identity (Swidler, 1980). Unlike in the past, the quest doesn't end when you find a marriage partner; on the contrary, it involves a continuing effort to find a better personal life through an evolving relationship. It also implies a new model of adulthood. In the old model, you developed an identity in young adulthood, found a partner compatible with that identity, got married, and then further personality development stopped. Now there is a cultural imperative to keep changing and developing your identity throughout adulthood in order to maintain or, better yet, increase your sense of personal fulfillment.

Developing a satisfying sense of self through love and sexual expression, then, becomes an ongoing project throughout adulthood. To carry out this project, a married person must be able to communicate openly and honestly with his or her spouse about thoughts and feelings. Consequently, communication and understanding become highly valued qualities in today's love myths. But suppose one partner isn't satisfied and then decides he or she can't develop his or her sexual life adequately within the relationship. Or suppose one partner feels he or she has gotten all the personal benefits out of the relationship that are possible. Then, given the new emphasis on self-fulfillment and self-development as the standards by which to judge intimate relationships, there is little reason for the unsatisfied partner to stay in the relationship. On the contrary, the emphasis on self-fulfillment encourages him or her to leave.

In this way, the new love myths devalue qualities such as commitment, trust, and permanence (Swidler, 1980). And herein lies an important reason for the sharp rise in the divorce rate in the United States and other Western nations in the 1960s

Keeping a marriage intact requires communication and flexibility as life circumstances change.

and 1970s and the continued high rates since then (see Chapter 13). The cultural changes surrounding love and marriage have made it more acceptable for a person to leave a relationship if he or she feels personally dissatisfied. One is no longer expected to keep a marriage together for the sake of the children—although the presence of young children does lower the odds that a couple will separate (Cherlin, 1977). This emphasis on self-fulfillment and development in marriage has placed high expectations on the relationship. Only in the twentieth century has marriage had to bear such a heavy responsibility for personal happiness, and the institution may not be able to match the expectations spouses now have. To be sure, there are other important causes of the post–1960 rise in divorce, foremost among them the increasing economic independence of women. (This topic will be examined in detail in Chapter 13.) Nevertheless, the cultural changes in the way people evaluate love and marriage have certainly played a significant role.

The increased emphasis on self-development in marriage has been criticized as creating shallow, potentially exploitative relationships in which each partner seeks what is best for his or her own development—but not what's best for the marriage and for their children. Yet there is also a positive side to this form of marriage. Communication and negotiation may allow couples to attain greater intimacy than if they were forced to retain their initial way of relating. Although it is easy to criticize the excesses of the search for a more fulfilling personal life, the ability of couples to increase their satisfaction through communication and openness may revitalize some marriages. Until recently, argues Swidler, our culture of love suggested that the only problem was finding someone to marry— that, once married, there was nothing else to worry about. It was as if adult life were unchanging and unproblematic once you married and found a job. But that is not so. Adult life today, for many, does involve changes in one's experiences outside the home. The recent cultural shifts, Swidler writes, allow for "a search for models of self and models of love that are compatible with continuing growth and change . . . rather than giving moral meaning only to the dramatic moment of the shift from youth to adulthood" (Swidler, 1980).

In the independent marriage, wives and husbands need not be locked into roles that are set when they marry. The emphasis on communication and flexibility allows them to renegotiate the marital bargain if they wish. In contrast, the roles of wives and husbands in the companionship, breadwinner-homemaker marriages were restrictive and, to a much greater extent, nonnegotiable. Husbands were often opposed to their wives' having an active life outside the home. They frequently refused to do housework and childcare. Although the husband's role relieved him of work in the home, it also denied him the opportunity to be deeply involved in his children's lives. The more flexible roles of the independent marriage allow men to develop greater involvement with their children. They also allow women to pursue a rewarding work life outside the home. In these ways, the independent marriage holds out the possibility of a fuller life for both spouses and a more equal partnership. Whether the emergence of the independent marriage is favorable for children is another issue, which will be examined in Chapter 10. Moreover, even for the spouses, the possibilities are not always realized: Few fathers share childcare and housework equally, and power imbalances remain a feature of many marriages, as the next chapter will show.

Looking Back

1. **What is the history of courtship and dating?** In the United States and other Western nations, for centuries young adults went about finding a spouse through the publicly visible process of courtship. The practice declined in the United States after 1900 due to migration to large cities, growing affluence, and the emergence of adolescence as a protected time between childhood and adulthood. The rise of dating after 1900 placed courtship on an economic basis and transferred power from young women (and their parents) to young men. The heyday of dating was probably 1945 to 1965; during the 1970s and 1980s, as the average age at marriage rose and cohabitation became more common, the practice became less closely connected to marriage.

2. **How does the marriage market work?** The marriage market—a model that is widely used by social scientists—consists of individuals who are searching for a spouse in a particular geographic area, who have a set of preferences concerning the type of person they wish to find and a set of resources to offer in return. The predominant marriage bargain at mid-twentieth century, based on the specialization model of marriage, involved a husband who traded his earnings in return for childcare and housework by his wife. This model of marriage no longer fits the present-day marriage market. In particular, evidence suggests that both men and women now prefer partners with good earnings potential.

3. **What is the role of cohabitation in the American family system?** Prior to 1970, cohabitation was found largely among the poor. Since then the practice has expanded greatly at all income levels. In the United States today, a majority of marriages are now preceded by a period of cohabitation. These unions tend to lead within a few years either to marriage or a break-up. Cohabitation is a diverse phenomenon that includes not only childless young adults, but couples with children. A substantial share of the children who are officially born outside of marriage are actually born to two cohabiting parents. For some people (particularly non-Hispanic whites), cohabitation is part of the marriage process; for others (particularly African Americans and mainland Puerto Ricans), it is a substitute for marriage.

4. **How has marriage changed over the past century?** The institutional marriage was held together by community pressure and the authority of the family head. But

by the mid-twentieth century, it had been eclipsed by the companionship marriage, which was held together more by mutual affection and intimacy. The ideal type of companionship marriage was the single-earner breadwinner-homemaker family that flourished in the 1950s. Beginning in the late 1960s, this model was overtaken by the independent marriage, in which both spouses were increasingly concerned with personal growth and self-fulfillment. In the independent marriage, the relationship between spouses tends to be seen as an ongoing project that is open to negotiation and change.

5. **Do women and men benefit from marriage?** A substantial body of literature shows that in many ways married men appear to be advantaged compared to unmarried men, and that to a lesser extent, married women seem better off than unmarried women. There are two possible reasons for these findings. First, being married may actually cause people to feel better and live longer. Second, mentally and physically healthier people may be more likely than others to get married and stay married. Both explanations are plausible, but some of the advantages shown by married men and women are likely to be caused by the marriage relationship itself.

Thinking about Families

1. If the systems of courtship and dating have faded, what has replaced them, particularly for adolescents?

2. Is the change in the typical marriage bargain between women and men over the last half century a good one?

3. Why do most cohabiting relationships last only a few years or less before leading to either marriage or a break-up?

4. **The Private Family** Do people expect too much emotional satisfaction from a cohabiting partner or spouse?

5. **The Public Family** Should the public be concerned about the rise of cohabitation and childbearing outside marriage?

Key Terms

archival research   274
cohabitation   259
companionship marriage   270
courtship   248

independent marriage   271
institutional marriage   270
latent function   265
manifest function   265

marriage market   253
specialization model   255
union   245

Families on the Internet   www.mhhe.com/cherlin

*Note: While all the URLs listed were current as of the printing of this book, these sites often change. Please check our web site (**http://www.mhhe.com/cherlin**) for updates.*

To investigate the market in Russian women who are willing to marry an American man, visit one of the many web sites maintained by matchmaking firms like the one Randy Heisey used. Scanna International (**www.scanna.com**) has on-line booklets of eligible Russian women. When I opened the page for **www.russianconnection.com,** a blinking headline read "Meet the most beautiful educated women with traditional values!" For information on the modern mail-order bride industry, go to **www.bridesbymail.com,** which includes an on-line resource library. What kinds of marriages are these sites marketing to American men?

In recent years, a loosely knit "marriage movement" has arisen to promote marriage. Visit the web site of the Coalition for Marriage, Family, and Couples Education, **www.smartmarriages.com,** to obtain information. What is the case this group is making for marriage?

chapter 9

Work and Families

Looking Forward

1. How do sociologists think about power and authority within marriage?

2. How did the introduction of wage labor affect families?

3. How has married women's work changed over the past half-century?

4. How has the amount of housework and childcare done by husbands and wives changed over the past half-century?

5. What are some of the strains working parents can experience?

6. How is the workplace responding to the needs of working parents?

"After I started earning money," a billing clerk who was married to a forklift operator told a sociologist, "my husband showed me more respect" (Hochschild, 1989). She was not alone. A woman who earned less than her husband for years noticed a sudden difference when she took a high-paying job. One evening she told her husband she was tired, and he replied, "Well, you work as hard as I do." He had never said that before, she told a reporter (Goldstein, 2000). "A little light went off in my head: 'Oh, now I make what you do, I work as hard as you do,'" she said. Unasked, her husband started to do the laundry. "I'd say, 'I need to vacuum today' and the next thing I know, he'd be doing the vacuuming."

Another woman who earned far less than her husband complained to interviewers:

Gordon still has to have the last word on everything. We get annoyed with each other over that, but when I start to push back, he reminds me just who supports me and the children. He doesn't always bring that up, but if I start to win an argument or make more sense about something we should do, I think he gets frustrated and so he gives me his big final line which is something like, "If you're so smart, why don't you earn more money?" or how dumb I am 'cause if I had to go out and support myself I'd be a big fizzle (Blumstein & Schwartz, 1983).

As the marriages of these women demonstrate, and as numerous studies have shown, wives have less power when they earn substantially less money than their husbands.[1] To be sure, lower earnings are not the only reason wives typically have less power in their marriages. Both wives and husbands may have been socialized to expect that the husband should be the head of the household, the person who makes the final decisions. This expectation certainly was one of the tenets of the breadwinner-homemaker family, and some couples still endorse it today.

Nevertheless, earnings and employment are an important determinant of relations between wives and husbands. In this chapter we will explore differences in power and authority between wives and husbands, and the consequences of those differences in daily life. For perspective, we will compare the contemporary state of affairs with family power prior to the twentieth century. As we will see, in the twentieth century large numbers of married women moved into employment outside the home. That change has both altered and failed to alter wives' and husbands' roles in the family in fundamental ways.

[1]For a review, see England and Farkas (1986).

Moreover, earnings and employment are an important influence on the time parents and children spend together and apart. The movement of married women into the paid workforce has greatly changed the daily routines of families with children. This chapter will examine how families deal with the rushed schedules that often result when both parents (or the lone parent present) work outside the home. It will conclude with a discussion of the ways in which business and government are responding to these developments.

Power and Authority

THE MEANING OF POWER

A large research literature exists on marital power, in which the word "power" is used loosely in two different senses. These parallel the distinction that sociologists make between two ways in which a person or group of people can dominate others: power and authority (Gerth & Mills, 1946). *Power* [➡ p. 113] is the ability to force a person to take an action—or to accept another person's actions—even if he or she doesn't want to and resists. It is the "possibility of imposing one's will upon the behavior of other persons" (Bendix, 1960), whether or not one actually exercises this power. For example, in some societies a man can take a second wife even if his first wife objects.

Sometimes widespread cultural beliefs and values lead some people to accept the domination of others. When a group of people acknowledges the right of others to supervise and control their behavior, sociologists say that those in command are in **authority.** In distinguishing between power and authority, the key words are "acknowledged" or "accepted." I have authority over an aspect of your life if you acknowledge and accept it. The great sociologist Max Weber wrote of "patriarchalism" (most people now use the term *patriarchy)* [➡ p. 95]—meaning a social system based on the domination of husbands and fathers over wives and children—in so-called traditional societies. Here, wrote Weber, the right of the husband to be dominant is supported by long-standing, widely held norms and values that both women and men accept. Therefore, Weber asserted, the patriarch rules through "traditional authority." A farm wife might accept the authority of her husband as part of the natural and correct order of society. But male authority isn't just a preindustrial phenomenon. When Adlai Stevenson told the Smith graduates in 1955 that their place in politics was to influence men through the role of housewife [➡ p. 103], he was repeating a widespread cultural belief that even many educated women themselves agreed with at the time. Many women in the audience that day must have accepted Stevenson's statement as part of the natural order of family life.

In practice, however, it is often difficult to distinguish between power and authority. Your power over me may be latent—under the surface, hidden—most of the time, but it may be real nonetheless. For instance, if you have power over me, I may refrain from doing something I know you don't like—which means that you will obtain the results you want without having to flex a muscle or withhold a penny (Komter, 1989). If a wife knows her husband adamantly opposes her working outside the home and if she fears his anger, she may not even raise the issue of taking a job. An observer might not notice the wife's latent desire to work outside the home and the husband's power over her.

authority the acknowledged right of someone to supervise and control others' behavior

Moreover, persons in power may grant limited authority to their subordinates. I would argue that this often occurs in family life. During the nineteenth century, men accepted—even promoted—the authority of wives over moral and domestic matters. Yet wives' access to opportunities in the emerging world of paid work was limited. Today, wives often have substantial authority in the home because husbands—who do less domestic work—accept their wives' authority in this sphere. Still, most husbands retain substantial power, based on their greater earning power, and they still retain substantial authority, based on widely held, though changing, beliefs about what is proper behavior for women and men.

THE FAMILY'S INTERNAL ECONOMY

We also tend to assume that, although income is earned by individual husbands, wives, and children, it is used for the benefit of the whole family. In our own thinking about families, and in much of the academic literature, we usually ignore how income is distributed once a family member earns it. In economic writing about family income, for example, it is almost always assumed that everyone in the family has the same preferences about how to spend their income—as if

In the famillal mode of production, family members jointly produce many of the goods they consume or sell. Pictured here is a Pakistani family gathering apricots.

the family were a single person with one set of preferences and earnings.[2] In contrast, a growing number of sociologists who study family power and authority write of the **internal economy** of the household. They mean the study of what happens to income inside the household: how much income gets allocated to meet each member's needs and whose preferences shape how income is spent.

For example, in a study of British married couples in 1983, Jan Pahl found that if the incomes of the wife and husband increased by the same amount, 28 percent of the wife's increase would be spent on housekeeping expenses, on average, compared with 16 percent of the husband's increase. The husbands were more likely to spend part of their income on leisure, most commonly drinking and gambling (Pahl, 1989).

The ability of husbands to hold back more income for personal consumption would seem to be a clear example of male power over women concerning family finances. But often this power shades into authority; that is to say, most wives accepted the idea that their husbands were entitled to more leisure spending because the men were steadily earning most of the family's income. "You can't deny a man when he's earning," one English woman told an interviewer (Pahl, 1989). Yet when wives had their own earnings, they were more likely to protest.

> **internal economy** the way in which income is allocated to meet the needs of each member of a household, and whose preferences shape how income is spent

Power and Modes of Production

With these ideas in mind, what can be said about the power and authority wives have historically had relative to husbands in different modes of production? The evidence is inconsistent at times, making it hard to draw definitive conclusions for every situation. Men's power has exceeded women's power—and has often far exceeded it—in almost every historical setting. That is to say, family and kinship systems are run by males almost everywhere. This discussion, then, addresses the issue of relative levels—of the degree of authority and power in family matters that wives in one society have relative to wives in other societies.

THE FAMILIAL MODE OF PRODUCTION

With the development of settled agriculture, perhaps 9,000 years ago, the familial mode of production [➡ p. 44] emerged as a way of life in which families produced most of the food and goods they needed to survive. Consider, for example, the family of Jean-Baptiste and Rosalie, who were studied in 1861 by an associate of the French sociologist Frédéric Le Play.[3] They lived on a 10-acre farm in the province of Aisne with their 15- and 13-year-old sons. Two older daughters had already married and left home. The family produced most of the food they needed and grew a cash crop, hemp, the fibers of which they sold to ropemakers. During the planting season, Jean-Baptiste and his sons spread manure, plowed, and sowed the land. In the harvesting season, the whole family (including the two daughters before they were married) helped to cut, gather, and thresh the rye grain that the family used for bread and to cut and separate the hemp fiber from the stem. In the winter the family prepared the hemp fiber for

[2]That is to say, the husband and wife have a single, joint utility function. See Becker (1991).

[3]The report on this family is presented and discussed by Meyering (1990).

sale: Jean-Baptiste cleaned and straightened it while Rosalie rolled the coils and assembled them into 5-kilogram bundles.

Rosalie also had primary responsibility for preparing the family's food, washing clothes, tending the vegetable garden, and caring for the barnyard animals (two cows, two pigs, eighteen chickens, and six rabbits). When Rosalie's children were young, her mother cared for them when she worked in the fields. When they were old enough to work in the fields, Rosalie cut back on fieldwork. Nonetheless, she still spent so much time in the fields that, unlike many other wives, she bought the family's clothes rather than making them. In addition, she sold excess food produce at local markets.

As Jean-Baptiste and Rosalie's family illustrates, in the familial mode of production there is always a clear difference in the tasks men and women do. Nevertheless, there is no question that both the wife and the husband are doing valuable, productive work. Jean-Baptiste couldn't get along without Rosalie's labor—which is why many widowers remarried quickly after their wives died. No one would think of calling Rosalie a "housewife"; no teenager would ask her sons "Does your mother work?" Yet today in common English, we often restrict the word "work" to mean working for a wage or salary outside the home, which excludes what's done in and around the home. We restrict the definition of work to mean **production for exchange value**—work for wages outside the home, or production in the home of goods or services that can be sold—rather than **production for use value**—work that produces goods and services used within the home, such as cooking food and caring for children. Yet this is a rather time- and place-bound usage, most applicable to the middle-class families in the nineteenth- and twentieth-century West who invented the housewife. It obscures the fact that important work always goes on in the household, whether or not it brings in cash.

Still, farm wives such as Rosalie had less power and independence than their husbands. Granted, they typically managed the provision of food and all or part of the family budget (Tilly & Scott, 1978). Thus, they had considerable authority within the family over daily food consumption and expenditures. Of their economic role, Thomas Tusser wrote in 1562: "husbandrie weepeth, where huswiferie sleepeth" (Pahl, 1989).[4] Yet overall control of family finances usually remained in the husband's hands. What's more, the farm wife was legally subordinate to her husband. For instance, under English law until 1882, a husband had complete control over the income and personal property of his wife, and he could dispose of it any way he wished. At the time of their marriage, the husband and wife became one legal person—and that person was effectively the husband. A married woman could not enter into a business partnership or make contracts without her husband's participation (Hall, 1990). The law also punished women more heavily than men for committing adultery and tolerated physical beatings of wives. A wife was important enough to the household that it would be unwise for her husband to alienate her or to go too far in mistreating her; nevertheless, he had substantial, if latent, power over her.

THE LABOR MARKET MODE OF PRODUCTION

The introduction of the labor market mode of production [➡ p. 45] changed the nature of the Western family. Initially, husbands and older children worked for

production for exchange value work for wages outside the home

production for use value work that produces goods and services used within the home

---

[4]By "husbandrie" Tusser here means husbandry, the management of domestic affairs on a farm by men.

wages and contributed them to a common family fund, under the control of the male head. In 1862, another of the French families studied by LePlay's associates—Constant, his wife, Madeline, and their five children, aged 6 to 20—lived in the province of Upper Rhine (Meyering, 1990). Constant and his two sons, both teenagers, worked in the same small factory weaving cotton cloth 13 hours a day. Nearly all the boys' earnings—30 to 40 percent of the family's total income—went into the family fund. Constant's earnings accounted for about 40 percent of the family's total income. The eldest daughter was a domestic servant in another local household, which relieved her parents of the burden of supporting her; the two youngest daughters, aged 10 and 6, were in school. The family also rented a room in their house to a weaver they knew.

Until 1858, when her sons were old enough to work in the factory, Madeline had worked at home winding bobbins (reels of thread) on a piece-rate basis. Now her contribution consisted of unpaid but essential work preparing food, caring for the children, cleaning the house, and making, mending, and washing the family's clothes. Like Madeline, most wives specialized in production for use value, although some earned money for work done at home such as taking in lodgers or doing laundry for wealthier families. Most husbands specialized in production for exchange value.

A number of writers have proposed that greater power accrues to family members who produce for exchange value than to those who produce primarily for use value. This proposition is, in fact, the core of Friedrich Engels's analysis, more than a century ago, of the source of inequality between women and men; and related propositions have been stated frequently by others since then. Whereas men are compensated with money for their work, women's valuable work of raising children, which creates the next generation of the labor force, is unpaid. Under socialism, Engels wrote, childcare would be performed by public agencies and all women would work outside the home. Once this happened, Engels (and presumably his collaborator Karl Marx, who wrote nothing directly on the subject) believed, male domination would fade away: "The supremacy of the man in marriage is the simple consequence of his economic supremacy, and with the abolition of the latter will disappear of itself" (Engels, 1972). (Socialist nations have not, however, eliminated male domination.)

In nearly all societies, wives' ability to produce goods and services for exchange is limited because they must also carry out household and childrearing tasks. England and Farkas (1986) have argued that the investments of time and effort that a wife typically makes in the home—raising the children, providing emotional support to her husband, keeping in touch with the husband's relatives, and so forth—cannot easily be transferred to a new marriage. Rather, they are **relationship-specific investments,** efforts that are valuable only in a person's current relationship. That is to say, if a wife initiates a divorce, keeps custody of the children (as is usually the case), and wishes to remarry, she will likely find that the children—in whom she has invested much time and effort—lower her attractiveness to prospective husbands. Her efforts to nurture and support her first husband and her ties to his family also won't do her any good in the marriage market. If she doesn't wish to remarry, her income will probably be lower than before she divorced. Husbands, in contrast, tend to invest time and effort in their jobs, accruing, if they are fortunate, seniority, promotions, and wage and salary increases. These job investments can more easily be transferred to another marriage, because prospective wives will value the increased earnings (England & Farkas, 1986).

relationship-specific investment time spent on activities such as childrearing that are valuable only in a person's current relationship

In other words, husbands and wives who work outside the home make investments in earning power that could be used in any marriage, whereas household investments can be used only in their current marriages. Wives who do not work outside the home would consequently have fewer alternative partners than their husbands, should they divorce and wish to remarry. According to social exchange theory [➡ p. 30], if person A needs the income partner B provides and values being married, and if person A has fewer alternative sources of partnership (because her investments of time and effort aren't as transferable), then A is said to be dependent on B. The degree of dependency is greater the more A needs the income and the fewer her alternatives are—which implies, in this case, that wives with little job experience and lower earning potential are more dependent. And the more A is dependent on B, the theory states, the greater is B's power over A (Emerson, 1972). He can use his greater power to shape his family's daily life and to control key decisions.

Even when wives do work for pay, they may be required to turn over their income to their husbands or fathers. But where wives have control over earnings from production for exchange, so the argument goes, they have more power. Their earnings give them the stature to speak their grievances. (See *Families in Other Cultures:* "I Also Have Some Rights," on pp. 292–293.)

From Single-Earner to Dual-Earner Marriages

By the mid-twentieth century, the wives in most working-class and middle-class families, who did not work outside the home, had also withdrawn from informal sources of income such as keeping lodgers or taking in laundry. They had withdrawn because of increases in men's earnings and because of reduced demand for home services such as lodging. Teenage and young adult children stayed in school longer and worked fewer hours, often keeping for personal use most of what they did earn. The two-parent family usually had only one paid worker—the husband. The 1950s were probably the high point of the single-earner, two-parent family in the United States. [➡ p. 67] Many commentators refer to this breadwinner-homemaker family as the "traditional" family, but the history of women's work demonstrates how atypical the single-earner family was.

MARRIED MOTHERS ENTER THE LABOR FORCE

Figure 9.1 shows the low levels of married women's work outside the home at the middle of the twentieth century and the great changes since then. The two lines show the percentage of married women with children who were in the labor force for every year since 1948. Government statistical agencies consider someone to be in the labor force if he or she is working for pay outside the home or looking for such work. In 1948, only about one-fourth of married women whose youngest children were at least six years old (and therefore in school) were in the labor force, as were only about one-tenth of married women with children under age six. The graph shows the steady increase in labor force participation since then. The expansion of the service sector of the economy caused an increase in the demand for workers to fill the kinds of jobs that had been gender-typed as women's work: secretaries, salesclerks, nurses, and so forth (Oppenheimer, 1970). As a result, the wages of these jobs increased, attracting more women to take them (Butz & Ward, 1979; Smith & Ward, 1985).

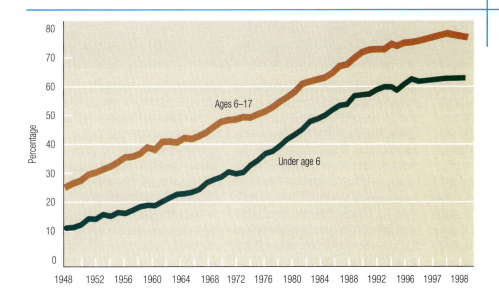

FIGURE 9.1
Labor force participation rates of married women with children under age 18, by age of youngest child, 1948–1998. (*Sources:* U.S. Bureau of Labor Statistics [1988]; and U.S. Bureau of the Census, Statistical Abstract of the United States, various years.)

At first, the rate of participation increased faster among those whose children were in school. Because women began childbearing at relatively younger ages in the 1950s and early 1960s and rarely had more than three or four children, they were still in a prime working age when all their children reached school age. With school to use as a childcare center and less childrearing effort necessary at home, many women with school-aged children reentered the labor force. Since the 1970s, the rate increased faster among those with at least one preschool-aged child. As a result of these changes, 77 percent of all married women with school-aged children, and 64 percent of those with preschool-aged children, were in the labor force in 1998, although a majority were working part-time (Cohen & Bianchi, 1999). In fact, the increase has been greatest in recent years among mothers of very young children, so much so that 62 percent of all married women with children under age two were in the labor force in 1998 (U.S. Bureau of the Census, 1999d).

Several factors contributed to the increase in married women's labor force participation. During the twentieth century, the service sector of the economy expanded greatly. The **service sector** consists of the workers who provide personal services such as education, health care, communication, restaurant meals, legal representation, entertainment, and so forth. Many of the jobs in the service sector had come to be stereotyped as women's work; these jobs usually required some education but paid less than men's work. Examples include secretary, nurse, and elementary school teacher. As the demand for these kinds of jobs increased, wages increased (although they remained lower than men's wages) and more married women were drawn into the labor force (Oppenheimer, 1970).

In addition, as the population shifted from farms to cities, each generation (except for the parents of the baby boomers) had fewer children. There was no longer a need for lots of child labor to help on the farm; moreover, the rising wages of women in the labor force meant that women who stayed home were passing up more and more income (Butz & Ward, 1979). As a result, parents' preferred strategy was to have fewer children and to invest more resources in each—to pay for college education or job training courses, for example. This strategy reduced the number of years in which young children would be present in the

service sector workers who provide personal services such as education, health care, communication, restaurant meals, legal representation, entertainment, and so forth

Married women's movement into the labor force has greatly changed family life.

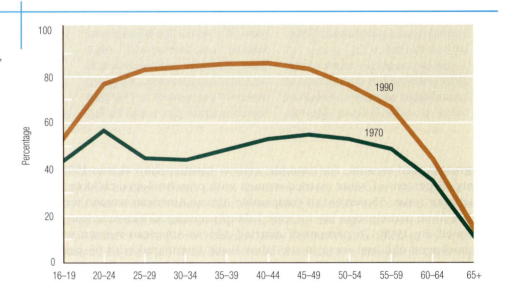

FIGURE 9.2

Labor force participation rates for U.S. women by age, 1970 and 1990. (*Sources:* Bianchi & Spain [1986], Figure 5.1; U.S. Bureau of Labor Statistics [1991].)

percentage of women in the labor force was higher for women in their early twenties than for teenagers; but then it dropped among women in their mid-twenties and early thirties, which are the most common years for having small children at home. The percentage then rose again to a second peak among women in their forties, whose children tend to be older. Therefore, the second peak reflects women who returned to the labor force after their children entered school. This double-peaked pattern typifies a society in which many women enter the labor force before marriage, drop out while raising young

"Bring Your Daughter to Work Day" allows mothers to interest their daughters in jobs and careers.

children, and then enter again. Yet by 1990 the dip between the peaks is gone; rather, the graph has a single, high plateau for women between about 25 and 50, reflecting women's higher and more-continuous levels of work outside the home throughout the prime working years of adulthood.

Despite women's increased attachment to the labor force and rising wages, it is still the case that they earn substantially less, on average, than men. From 1960 to about 1980, the average woman who worked full-time, year round, earned about 60 cents for each dollar earned by a comparable man.[5] To be sure, women have worked outside the home less, on average, than men have during their adult lives, so they have accrued less seniority, on-the-job training, and so forth. Yet differences in job experience appear to account for only about one-fourth to one-half of the gap (England & Farkas, 1986). A substantial proportion reflects a more complex process involving employer discrimination and the resultant way that parents socialize their daughters. (See *Families and Public Policy:* The Earnings Gap on p. 98)

Since 1980, however, women's average earnings have increased faster than men's, reaching 74 cents for each dollar a man earned in 1996 before dropping to 72 cents in 1999 (U.S. Bureau of the Census, 2000d). Women's earnings rose relative to men's in the 1980s and 1990s because some women workers were doing better economically and some men were doing worse. As for women doing better, demographers Daphne Spain and Suzanne Bianchi note that in the 1980s, women born during the baby boom were finishing school and entering the labor force. Conversely, the mothers of the baby boomers were exiting the labor force

[5]This figure represents the ratio of women's median earnings to men's median earnings, for year-round, full-time workers; U.S. Bureau of the Census (1997f).

to retire. Since the mothers had married at early ages and had children soon after marrying, they had received less education than their daughters and spent less time working outside the home prior to having children. As a result, their earning potential had been limited. In contrast, their daughters had received more education, postponed marriage and childbearing, and spent more time in the labor force before having children—all of which had increased their earning potential. Well-educated women moved into professional occupations in unprecedented numbers: Women's share of law school degrees rose from 5 percent in 1970 to 44 percent in 1996, and their share of medical school degrees rose from 8 percent to 41 percent during the same period. So in the 1980s and 1990s, as the baby boom daughters replaced their mothers in the labor force, the average earnings of college-educated women increased (Spain & Bianchi, 1996; U.S. Bureau of the Census, 1999d).

Yet that is only half the story. Earnings did not rise much for baby boom daughters without college educations, most of whom were clerical and service workers such as secretaries, bank tellers, or cafeteria workers. The men they tended to marry—baby boom sons without a college education—saw their incomes decline as skilled blue-collar jobs became scarce. Therefore, the ratio of women's earnings to men's earnings rose among the less-well-educated not because women were earning substantially more but rather because men were earning substantially less. The rising ratio demonstrates how important wives' earnings have become in maintaining the standard of living of working-class and lower-class married couples (Bianchi & Spain, 1996).

Among African Americans, the ratio of women's earnings to men's earnings has long been higher than among whites. In the first half of the twentieth century, discrimination severely limited job opportunities for both black women and men, but black women were hired as household workers for white families—jobs that may have been demeaning but were at least available and steady. In 1940, 60 percent of all black women in the labor force were private household workers. Beginning in the 1960s—a decade of civil rights legislation and economic prosperity—employment opportunities for African Americans improved. The improvement, however, was greater for black women, who took advantage of the expanding opportunities in service sector occupations, than for black men. By 1990, just 2 percent of black women were household workers (Bianchi, 1995). What is more, young black women were earning virtually as much, on average, as young white women. Because black men's economic progress (like the progress of less-well-educated white men) lagged behind, the median earnings of black women rose to 84 cents for every dollar earned by black men in 1999, compared with 76 cents for every dollar among whites (U.S. Bureau of Labor Statistics, 2000a).

WORKING WIVES' POWER AND AUTHORITY: THE STALLED REVOLUTION?

The increased labor force participation of married women, and the growth of women's incomes relative to men's, should translate into increased marital power for wives—at least according to the theory outlined at the start of this chapter. In the vast majority of two-parent families with mothers who are employed, the husband is also working outside the home. The most famous American study of wives' employment and marital power was conducted in 1955. The authors, Robert Blood and Donald Wolfe, asked a sample of married women in

Historically, African-American married women have worked outside the home more than white married women; but the percentage who work has incresed further in recent decades.

the Detroit area "who usually makes the final decision about" each of eight common household decisions, including what car to get, whether to go on a vacation, and how much the family can afford to spend on food. Wives who were employed were more likely to make the final decisions themselves or to jointly make the decisions with their husband than wives who were not employed (Blood & Wolfe, 1960).

Daily decisions of the kind Blood and Wolfe studied may reflect authority more than power. Consider information from a study of more than 3,000 married couples in the late 1970s by Philip Blumstein and Pepper Schwartz. The higher the wife's income, the more likely she was to have "more say about important decisions affecting [their] relationship" and the more likely she was to see herself as "running the show in [their] relationship." But a wife's income did not have as much effect on whether her husband was more likely to "give in to [her] wishes when one of us wants to do something the other does not want to do." As the authors note, the last measure is closer to the sociological definition of power than the first two (Blumstein & Schwartz, 1991). Their findings, then, suggest that wives' earnings may boost their authority to make daily economic decisions more than their power to win disputes with their husbands.

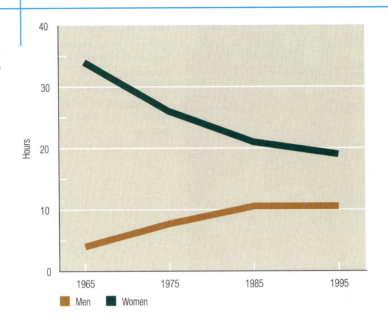

Moreover wives still do more of the housework than their husbands, though there has been some change over the past few decades. Figure 9.3 presents the results of studies done in 1965, 1975, 1985, and 1995, in which national samples of adults were asked to keep diaries of the amount of time they spent on various activities during a week (Bianchi, Milkie, Sayer, & Robinson, 2000). The figure displays the average weekly hours spent on housework by married women and married men. (Major categories included cooking, meal cleanup, cleaning, laundry, outdoor chores, repairs, and paying bills.) The green line shows that over the 30-year period, the average time spent by married women dropped substantially, from 33.9 hours to 19.4 hours. As the orange line shows, during the same period, the average time spent by married men increased from 4.7 to 10.4 hours.

Overall, these trends suggest the following conclusions:

- The total amount of housework done by married couples has declined, because women have reduced the time they spend doing housework more than men have increased theirs. Married couples probably have replaced some of the housework they used to do by purchasing services, such as restaurant meals or paid housecleaning. They may also have become accustomed to slightly dirtier homes and slightly more wrinkled sheets and clothing than married couples of the past.
- The relative amount of time married women and men spend on housework has become less unequal. In 1965, women's average hours of housework were seven times greater than men's; by 1995, they were two times greater. Again, this trend is due more to women reducing the time they spend on housework than to men increasing theirs.

The authors of this study also reported that employed women and men do less housework than those who are not employed. This finding is consistent with the-

Married couples do less housework today because wives have reduced their hours more than husbands have increased them.

ories of marital power, as well as with the sheer lack of time available to employed parents. Several other findings, however, cannot be explained as easily. For example, other things being equal, the presence of children in a family increases housework more for women than for men. And marriage seems to increase women's housework more than it does men's. Perhaps marriage and childbearing encourage some couples to adopt traditional gender roles.

To some extent, the amount of progress toward equality that has been made depends on who researchers ask. In a 1992 national survey of employed women and men, 43 percent of men in dual-earner marriages or partnerships reported that they shared childcare equally with their wives or partners, but only 19 percent of women in dual-earner families reported equal sharing. As for cooking and cleaning, men in dual-earner marriages or partnerships did more than men whose partners were not employed, yet women still did far more, on average, than men. Eighty-one percent of women in dual-earner families said they took major responsibility for cooking, and 78 percent said they took major responsibility for cleaning. Even according to men's reports, their employed wives and partners took major responsibility for cooking 69 percent of the time and cleaning 63 percent of the time. Moreover, women who earned more than half the household's income still took responsibility for cooking, cleaning, and shopping more often than their husbands or partners (Galinsky, Bond, & Friedman, 1993). Employed wives still do substantially more of the housework than their husbands.

Nor are there pronounced social class differences in the proportion of household work done by husbands. There is a certain image of the working-class husband as doing less around the home, perhaps exercising more power in the household to compensate for having less power in the workplace. But a comparative study involving national surveys of dual-earner couples in the early 1980s in both the United States and Sweden found no difference in the proportion of housework done by husbands in different social classes in the United States and little difference in Sweden (Wright, Shire, Hwang, Dolan, & Baxter, 1992).

What often differs by class is how couples talk about the wife's and husband's contribution (Hochschild, 1989). It is common in working-class families for the couple to define what the husband does around the house as "helping out" the wife, whereas middle-class couples talk about husbands' taking responsibility for household tasks. In addition, it is common for working-class couples to define the man as the main earner, even if his wife's wages are an important source of income. This way of thinking allows couples to retain the breadwinner-homemaker ideal even as their actions contradict it. The husband can continue to consider himself a successful earner who merely needs his wife's help. Similarly, he can view his housework and childcare as merely helping his wife do her tasks. A factory worker told Ellen Israel Rosen that she needs to "help out her husband" financially. In addition, she said, "My husband helps me a lot too. That's one thing I told him. If you want me to help you out then you'll have to help me. That way we can help each other. So far it's been working pretty good" (Rosen, 1987).

Figure 9.3 shows that men did not increase their housework hours from 1985 to 1995. Married women still do twice as much housework as men. The slow pace of change among men in dual-earner families has puzzled and disappointed many observers. Arguing that the current period is a transitional phase in American family life, Arlie Russell Hochschild wrote of a "stalled revolution," in which wives have moved into the labor force but husbands have not yet adjusted. The result, she asserted, is that employed wives work a "second shift" of household tasks and childcare. In addition to the burden this situation imposes on wives, she wrote, the stalled revolution may hurt men, whose wives "cannot afford the luxury of unambivalent love for their husbands" (Hochschild, 1989).

Yet recent evidence suggests that men may be doing more housework and childcare than before. Certainly, men's involvement at home is becoming more culturally acceptable. In 1979 and 1989, national samples of men were asked the question "Would you respect a man more, less, or about the same if he decided to stay home and take care of the children while his wife worked?" In the 10-year period between surveys the proportion of men who said they would respect a man *more* increased from 6 to 17 percent, while the proportion who said they would respect a man *less* decreased from 39 to 19 percent (Pagnini & Rindfuss, 1993). At the start of the twenty-first century, a substantial change in husbands' and wives' housework and childcare may be underway.

Overload and Spillover between Work and Family

role overload the state of having too many roles with conflicting demands

The growth of dual-earner families and employed single parents has raised concerns that parents may be performing too many roles with conflicting demands— a condition that is sometimes called **role overload.** The roles these adults play can include worker, spouse, parent, and sometimes caregiver to other relatives. A 1997 survey of employed women and men found that 85 percent lived with family members and had daily responsibilities at home. Forty-six percent had children under age 18 at home, and 13 percent were providing care to an elderly or other adult relative (Families and Work Institute, 1998). Clearly, most employed adults have to juggle the demands of home and work.

However, research has *not* found a clear relationship between the number of roles a person must manage and the degree of distress she or he experiences (Thoits, 1992). In fact, there is some evidence that people with multiple roles (including nonfamily roles such as being involved in the activities of a religious organization) may in some cases have better mental health than people with fewer roles (Thoits, 1986). It may be that multiple roles increase a person's sense of meaning and purpose in life and therefore improve mental health. Or it may be that mentally healthier people join more organizations, are more likely to marry, and have busier lives. One researcher suggested that a combination of roles may cause distress mainly when it differs from the normal, expected combination for a person of a particular gender and age (Menaghan, 1989). For example, being a mother who works outside the home may have been more stressful in the 1950s and 1960s, when there were fewer social supports for such people, than it is today. Rather than role overload, some Americans may be suffering from too much paid work.

OVERWORKED AND UNDERWORKED AMERICANS

Some observers have suggested that balancing work and family has become more difficult for Americans because they are working longer hours. This was the thesis of the best-selling book *The Overworked American* (Schor, 1992). Yet a closer look reveals that while some Americans are overworked, others are underworked. Jacobs and Gerson (2001) compared Census data from 1970 and 1997 and found two very different trends. College-educated people with professional and managerial jobs were indeed working longer hours in 1997 than in 1970. Most of these people received weekly salaries that remained the same no matter how many hours they worked. Consequently, employers had an incentive to pressure them to work longer hours, especially given the downsizing of the workforce in many firms. In contrast, workers without college educations were working fewer hours in 1997 than in 1970. These workers tended to receive hourly wages, which meant their employers had to pay them more for every extra hour worked. Instead of encouraging these sales and these service workers to work longer hours, employers have tended to hire more part-time workers. Often part-time workers are not eligible for fringe benefits such as health insurance, which provides further savings to employers. In sum, the labor market seems to be moving in opposite directions at the top and bottom, toward longer hours among the college-educated and shorter hours among the less-well-educated.

Still, workers can *feel* overloaded, even if they are not working longer hours than they used to. Today, fewer families include a wife who devotes all her time to housework and childcare. More families now feel the faster pace of combining paid employment with raising children. But again, people's feelings about this trend may differ according to their education and occupation. More than half the college graduates in the 1992 survey of employed women and men said they would prefer to work fewer hours than they currently worked. Yet less than one-third of those without a high school degree said they would prefer to work fewer hours (Jacobs and Gerson, 2000). At the top of the labor market, workers are feeling overloaded but economically secure; at the lower end, they are feeling underemployed and economically insecure.

SPILLOVER

spillover the fact that stressful events in one part of a person's daily life often spill over into other parts of her or his life

Another motif in the research literature is that stressful events in one part of a person's daily life often spill over into other parts of her or his life. **Spillover** can occur whether or not the person experiences role overload. In other words, a bad day at even an enjoyable job can cause a parent to come home and behave angrily toward his or her children. In the 1997 survey, 26 percent of employees said they had not been in a good mood at home because of their work over the past three months; 28 percent said they did not have enough energy for their families and other important people (Families and Work Institute, 1998). In an influential article in the late 1970s, Joseph Pleck argued that spillover involving work and family operates in opposite directions for employed men and employed women. The demands of family life—a school vacation, an ill child—are permitted to intrude into women's jobs more than into men's jobs, he wrote, because supervisors and coworkers expect that when a family emergency arises, mothers rather than fathers will be called upon to deal with it. In contrast, according to Pleck, the stresses of work are permitted to intrude on family life more for men than for women. Because men's jobs are often seen as more demanding and more central to the family's well-being than are women's jobs, it is more acceptable, for example, for husbands to miss school concerts because of business trips than it is for employed wives to do so (Pleck, 1977).

It may also be more acceptable for husbands to come home from work irritable or preoccupied than it is for wives. Wives are often cast in a more supportive role, even though their daily lives may be stressful. One woman talked about her husband to two researchers:

> He takes a lot of crap [at his job]. He gets very few rewards for what he does, and people are not very facilitating there. So it's up to me when he comes home to try and fill that need and make him feel good about himself. And yet, I am not getting any reverse back (Pearlin & McCall, 1990).

Wives may serve to buffer husbands from further stress at home more than husbands do for them. One woman in the same study said that when she sees her husband come home troubled, she tells her children, "Dad has a lot on his mind. If you want to ask him for something, wait until later" (Pearlin & McCall, 1990).

Men also appear more likely to withdraw from their families in reaction to a stressful day at work. One author suggests that the male professionals he studied view displays of stress at home as signs of failure in meeting work responsibilities. Men may instead act weary, which is more acceptable because it can be seen as a sign of hard work, or they may tune out their wives and children. But worries are hard to hide, and withdrawal can lead to irritability and anger, as in this case:

> A situation that is perfectly normal and next to nothing—something happens with a kid—I may go into a tailspin over it. I might boil up or boil over. Norma will then fly up and say, "You are not treating them fairly." And then it will come out that at that particular point I was up to my eyebrows with the damned business and I just wasn't relaying that. In fact, I was keeping it in (Weiss, 1990).

The stresses of work can spill over to the home lives of married couples.

For many blue-collar workers, other causes of stress may be low pay, dirty or dangerous work, or dehumanizing treatment by supervisors. Blue-collar men, some studies show, bring their troubles home in ways similar to middle-class men who have had a bad day at the office. Tired and irritable, blue-collar men sometimes withdraw from their wives and children in the evenings (Mortimer & London, 1984). Low-wage jobs also increase a couple's need for a second income. Consequently, a higher proportion of working-class wives than middle-class wives work outside the home (although the difference is narrowing).

CHILDCARE

One surprisingly common way in which dual-earner couples manage childcare is to work different shifts. In one study, one-third of all dual-earner couples with preschool-aged children had at least one spouse working an evening, night, or rotating shift (Presser, 1999). Husbands who were home when their wives were working did more cooking, cleaning, and washing than husbands who were never home when their wives were working (Presser, 1994). The increase in nonday-shift and weekend work isn't due solely to couples' childcare needs. The growth of the service sector of the economy is also responsible. Nevertheless, when asked why they were working evening or night shifts, a majority of married women in a Census Bureau survey said the main reason was that their hours made it easier to care for their children or other relatives (Presser, 1989).

In fact, it appears that wives and husbands in many of these split-shift couples are sharing the childcare (Presser, 1989). How best to care for the children of employed parents is a topic that will be discussed in later chapters. Some observers view staggered-shift parent care as a good solution to the childcare problem. Other things being equal, parents arguably provide better care in most instances than nonrelatives. But split-shift childcare sharing is not without its difficulties. Employed wives, who still tend to accommodate their working hours to their spouse's needs more than their husbands do, may be forced to turn down better jobs or work fewer hours so that they can be available when their husbands aren't home. Couples working different shifts may have little time for each other, and their marriages may suffer. In a national sample of recently married couples with children who were followed for five years, divorce was six times more likely among husbands who worked a night schedule rather than a day schedule (Presser, 2000). One repair worker told Lillian Rubin:

> *I usually get home about forty-five minutes or so before my wife has to leave for work, so we try to take a few minutes just to make contact. But it's hard with the kids and all. Most days the whole time gets spent with taking care of business— you know, who did what, what the kids need, what's for supper, what bill collector was hassling her while I was gone—all the damn garbage of living. It makes me nuts* (Rubin, 1994).

Single parents, of course, do not have the luxury of relying on a spouse to provide care, regardless of when they work. Yet never-married, separated, or divorced mothers are even more likely to work nonday, weekend, or rotating shifts than married mothers, perhaps because of their more limited education or work experience (Presser, 1989). With few commercial childcare providers offering evening, night, or weekend care, single mothers must often rely on their own mothers or other relatives. Here again, one could argue that, as caregivers, grandmothers are superior to nonrelatives. Many of the grandmothers, however, are themselves working or are caring for their own aging parents (see Chapter 11); providing care may be a strain on them. Some single mothers, with no one to rely on, attempt to care for their children themselves while working. Nationally, 8 percent of all preschool-aged children with employed mothers were cared for by the mothers themselves. For example, a mother might earn money by caring for the children of several other employed mothers as well as her own children.

More generally, single parents often have no one with whom to share the burdens of the day, and unless they live with their mothers or other relatives, there is no one to buffer them from the demands of their children when they come home from their jobs. Moreover, employed single mothers are sometimes in a precarious financial situation. I will describe in Chapter 13 how the economic status of many women plummets after a divorce. The lack of money may force them to reduce their standard of living, move to a new neighborhood, or otherwise disrupt their daily lives. Single parents are sometimes successful in constructing new support networks made up of other single parents, friends, and kin. Still, it seems likely that overload and spillover are a greater problem for employed single parents than for employed married parents.

UNEMPLOYMENT

Most of the studies of spillover between work and family assume that adults in the family who want to work outside the home can find and keep a job. Yet unemployment also creates stress. Research dating back to the Great Depression suggests that unemployment is more likely to cause marital problems among couples whose marriages were already shaky before the husband or wife lost a job (Komarovsky, 1971). More recently, a Boston area study of 82 families in which the husband had recently lost his job found that spouses who rated their marriages as satisfactory prior to the job loss were less anxious and depressed afterward (Liem & Liem, 1990). The Boston study, an Iowa study of 76 rural families, and a few others like them provide some insight into the process by which job loss leads to family problems. At the first interview, the unemployed husbands in the Boston study were more depressed and anxious than a matching group of employed husbands, but their wives were not more depressed or anxious than the wives of employed husbands. Four months later, however, the wives were experiencing more depression and anxiety. The authors speculate that many husbands become upset soon after the job loss and begin to act irritably and angrily toward their wives and children. Most wives are not as upset initially, but as their financial concerns grow and their husbands' behavior worsens, they often develop psychological symptoms. The Iowa study showed similarly that economic strain leads husbands to behave in a hostile way toward their wives—as well as to reduce their warm, supportive behavior. The husbands' hostility and lack of warmth, in turn, lead wives to feel less positively about their marriages. If the wives then respond with hostile behavior, their husbands' satisfaction with the marriage also declines (Conger et al., 1990).

On the whole, the available studies suggest that it is not as much the absence of supportive behavior as the presence of angry, irritable, hostile behavior that triggers these declines in the quality of the marriage. The results are consistent with laboratory observations that cycles of negative behavior from husband to wife and back are central to escalating marital conflict (Gottman, 1979). The studies also suggest that spouses with fewer prior psychological problems and more social support from kin and friends are more likely to weather the storm of unemployment. Finally, working-class and middle-class families show similar distress when a parent loses his or her job, despite their differing economic circumstances. Working-class families, who typically have few financial reserves, experience the more immediate economic consequences, but they report receiving more support from kin and friends than do middle-class families. Among the latter group, losing a job, as has happened to executives during the recent waves of corporate "downsizing," means losing status and social identity (Liem & Liem, 1990).

Toward a Responsive Workplace?

To judge by the concerns of workers and, increasingly, of corporate managers, the strict separation of paid work and family life—to the extent that it ever existed—is breaking down. When employed women and men in the 1992 survey who had been at their current jobs for less than five years were asked how important various factors were in their original decisions to take their jobs, 60 percent said that the job's effect on personal and family life was very important and 46 percent said that family-supportive policies at the job were important. In contrast, only 35 percent said that wages and salary were important. Moreover, one-quarter to one-third of those without access to flexible working hours said they would switch jobs or sacrifice advancement in their companies to obtain flexible hours. About half without access to time off to care for sick relatives said they would trade salary or other benefits to obtain it (Galinsky et al., 1993). Clearly, family responsibilities are on the minds of many workers. Congress has been paying more attention, too. (See *Families and Public Policy:* Putting Work-Family Issues on the Agenda.)

Half a century ago, the breadwinner-homemaker family was at its peak. Few married women with young children worked outside the home, and few members of Congress favored assistance for employed mothers. But today several laws provide benefits for working parents, and Congress seems poised to pass more legislation. When and how did this change?

Sociologist Paul Burstein and his colleagues examined this question by counting the number of members of Congress who sponsored (officially supported) various kinds of work-family bills between 1945 and 1990 (Burstein & Bricher, 1997; Burstein, Bricher, & Einwohner, 1995; and Burstein & Wierzbicki, 2000).

The results are presented in Figure 9.4, which shows the number of sponsors for three different types of legislation over the 45-year period. Though most of the bills did not become law, their content is informative. The first type, "separate spheres" bills, contained proposals that would support families in which the husband worked outside the home and the wife did not. An example was legislation that would have limited the number of hours women could work, to protect their ability to be good mothers. Unthinkable today, such bills were commonplace in the first half of the twentieth century. The black line in the chart shows a modest but steady number of sponsors for these bills throughout the 1945–1990 period.

The second type of legislation, "Equal opportunity" bills, was based on the premise that working women were entitled to the same opportunities as working men. For instance, they might require employers to pay equal wages to women and men doing the same job. Such an idea might seem obvious, but before the 1960s many employers paid women less than men, on the theory that men were the main earners for their families and so deserved more than women. The green line in Figure 9.4 shows a modest number of sponsors for equal-opportunity bills until the mid-1960s, after which sponsorships rose sharply. Not coincidentally, the mid-1960s were the era of the civil rights movement and the birth of the modern feminist movement.

Most recently, legislators have supported "work-family accommodation," including an income tax credit for child care expenses. These bills attempt to help parents combine paid work with childrearing. The white line in Figure 9.4 shows that sponsorship of this type of bill was rare through most of the period, but rose dramatically over the last 10 years. Had the study continued into the 1990s, it undoubtedly would have shown further growth. In 1993, for example, Congress passed the Family and Medical Leave Act, which allows workers to take time off to care for newborns and seriously ill children or to handle other family medical emergencies.

During the 1980s and 1990s, corporations began to address these concerns. They did so largely out of self-interest. The Census Bureau estimates that 62 percent of the new entrants to the labor force between 1998 and 2006 will be women, many of whom will have family responsibilities (U.S. Bureau of the Census, 1999d). Employers who wish to recruit and retain good workers realize that they must make their jobs attractive to people who are caring for children—and to the growing number who are caring for elderly parents. Most large firms now have some personnel policies to help employees with family responsibilities (Glass & Estes, 1997). Small firms are much less likely to offer family-friendly policies for several reasons:

- They typically do not invest as much time and money training new workers, so they don't have as much to lose if employees quit because of family-related problems.
- They don't have the volume of workers necessary to make services such as on-site childcare cost-effective.
- Because of their lower sales revenues, they cannot pass along the costs of the policies to consumers as easily as large firms can.

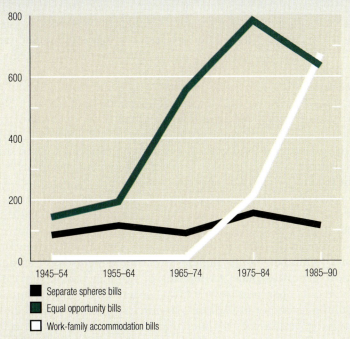

Separate spheres bills
Equal opportunity bills
Work-family accommodation bills

FIGURE 9.4

Sponsorship of Work-Family Legislation, 1945–1970. (*Source:* Burstein, Bricher, & Einwohner, 1995.)

Why have work-family accommodation bills been proposed only recently? Not until the 1980s did a majority of married mothers of young children take jobs outside the home (see Figure 9.1). In other words, not until that time did members of Congress face a large constituency of working parents clamoring for help in accommodating their children as well as their jobs.

Ask Yourself

1. Do you know any couples who are trying to raise a family while both of them work full time? If so, what is their major problem? Could a change in public policy help to solve it?

2. Should American workers receive paid parental leaves, like workers in some European countries?

www.mhhe.com/cherlin

Consequently, a two-tiered class system is developing: Larger firms, which tend to have better-paying, steadier jobs and better-educated workforces, offer better policies to help workers achieve balance between the demands of work and family; smaller firms, which tend to have lower-paying, less-steady jobs and less-well-educated workforces, provide less help. So middle-class, well-educated managers and professionals and better-paid blue-collar factory workers are much more likely to be offered assistance with family demands than are less-advantaged workers, such as the part-time and temporary workers or low-paid service workers (Kingston, 1990). In fact, many of the part-time or temporary jobs that are being created lack any fringe benefits such as health insurance, pension contributions, sick leave, and vacation days.

Even among large firms, much of the assistance is limited, such as establishing information and referral offices to match parents with childcare openings. Cash benefits are usually limited to salary reduction plans that allow workers not to pay taxes on the part of their earnings (up to a limit) they spend on childcare. Yet these plans are of more value to higher-paid employees—who can afford to have the extra earnings withheld from their paychecks by their employers and who pay a greater percentage of their incomes in taxes—than to working-class employees.

flextime a policy that allows employees to choose, within limits, when they will begin and end their working hours

One of the most common, and most widely used, employee benefits is **flextime,** a policy that allows employees to choose, within limits, when they will begin and end their working hours. For example, a company might allow its employees to begin work anytime between 7:00 and 9:00 A.M. and to leave anytime from 3:00 to 5:00 P.M., as long as they work eight hours. Studies suggest that this is the family-friendly policy workers use the most (Galinsky, 1992; Hochschild, 1997). In the 1997 survey, 45 percent of employees said they could choose, within a range of hours, when they began and ended their workdays (Families and Work Institute, 1998). Again, middle-class employees benefit more than working-class employees: The more prestigious the occupational category, the more likely workers are to have flextime (U.S. Bureau of the Census, 1993f). Employed parents use flextime to match their work schedules to the school or day care schedules of their children. Flextime doesn't necessarily increase the amount of time parents can spend with their children, but it does allow them to avoid stressful conflicts between childcare and job responsibilities.

parental leave time off from work to care for a child

To be able to spend more time with their children, especially when they are infants or when they are sick, employed parents need other options. One of these is **parental leave,** time off from work to care for a child, with a guarantee that the employee can have her or his job back when she or he returns. Many employers have been reluctant to grant parental leave automatically because they have feared it would hurt their productivity and cost too much. Most Western European nations require corporations to provide parental leave; yet in this regard, as in many family policies, the United States lags behind. Sweden has the most generous plan: 15 months of leave at partial pay (Moss & Deven, 1999). A modest parental leave bill was enacted by Congress and signed by President Clinton as one of his first acts in office in 1993. It required companies with 50 or more employees to offer unpaid leaves of up to 12 weeks to employees with newborn babies or seriously ill children or other relatives. Employers must allow employees to return to their jobs at the end of the leave.

Other innovations are as yet less common. These include part-time work with fringe benefits and job sharing. Whether significant numbers of part-time jobs with fringe benefits will be created remains to be seen. In job sharing, two people split the time and duties of a full-time position usually held by one person. Unlike part-time positions, which are often in low-status occupations, shared jobs presumably can be on a higher level—and therefore more appealing. The small number of existing shared jobs tend to be in such professions as teaching, psychology, and social work. Few have been created in for-profit corporations (Kamerman & Kahn, 1987).

But even when innovations such as part-time jobs with benefits and job-sharing are offered, most workers don't take them. Hochschild (1997) studied the employees of a large corporation and found that family life is so hectic for working parents that some of them retreat into their work. Especially for women, who do the majority of housework and childrearing, combining work with family life makes for a busy home life. Ironically, then, some workers are finding the workplace to be a haven from overburdened home lives. But others work long hours because they are afraid of being laid off or passed over for promotions. Even at Hochschild's plant, downsizing and restructuring led to the layoffs of many workers and expectations of faster production for the remaining workers.

Overall, there has been progress in making the workplace more responsive to workers' family needs. The least progress, however, has occurred in occupations that don't pay well. Yet workers in low-paying jobs need assistance *more* than those who are better paid. For instance, a 1990 survey showed that, among mothers who were paying for care and had a child under age 5, those earning less than $15,000 spend 23 percent of their incomes for childcare, whereas mothers earn-

...nt of their incomes for childcare (Hof- ...of work could widen the gap between ...as the economy turns to information ...mputer-assisted communication could ...eir jobs from home.[6] Such a shift, it is ...aretakers to mesh the demands of fam- ...n the 1997 survey said they were regu- ...s such as these are easier to imagine in ...er-paying part-time service jobs such as ...a challenge, therefore, to provide a re- ...w end of the occupational distribution

...will become more of a reality only if ...childcare and domestic work. Unless ...nue to be seen as primarily a "woman's ...f corporations will pay attention to the ...culture is recognizing that many men ...eir families. By the 1990s, even a staid ...d publish an issue with a man and his ...ne "Can Your Career Hurt Your Kids? ...nts—and Flexible Companies—Won't ...cover story would have been unthink- ...hanges in men's attitudes toward house- ...ave so far outstripped changes in what ...hat men will soon drop their resistance

...g and important, are unlikely to meet ...e in caring for children and the elderly. ...nefit middle-class employees and those ...ss employees or those in small firms. ...e so-called **responsive workplace**— ...onditions are designed to allow employ- ...es more easily—to urge that corporate ...ment assistance targeted at low-income

workers. In the 1990s, pressure from working parents prompted Congress to enact legislation providing childcare assistance, beginning with a 1990 bill. The 1996 welfare reform law [➡ p. 191] also included childcare assistance funds for parents who left the welfare rolls to take jobs. In 1997, President Bill Clinton held the first White House Conference on Child Care. It seems likely that government will do more to help working parents find and pay for childcare in the years ahead.

responsive workplace a work setting in which job conditions are designed to allow employees to meet their family responsibilities more easily

[6]Galinsky (1992), for example, writes of the "anytime-anyplace office."

Looking Back

1. **How do sociologists think about power and authority within marriage?** By power, sociologists mean the ability to force someone to take an action against her or his will; by authority, they mean the acknowledged right to supervise other people or to act on their behalf. The kinds of work women and men do are related to wives' and husbands' authority and power in the family. In general, working for pay outside the home increases a person's power in the family; therefore, wives who work outside the home tend to have relatively more family power.

2. **How did the introduction of wage labor affect families?** With the introduction of wage labor, men's and women's work roles changed, although men's changed more than women's. Husbands began to work for exchange value, trading their labor in factories or shops for wages. Wives worked mainly for use value in the home, although they often earned money at home by producing goods on a piecework basis, by taking in lodgers, or by doing laundry. Where wives produced for exchange and controlled their earnings, as in the Mexico City study, they tended to have more power in the family.

3. **How has married women's work changed over the past half-century?** In the second half of the twentieth century, married women entered the labor force in large numbers. A majority of married women with young children are now employed outside the home. The rise of the service sector and the long-term decline in fertility are two important reasons for women's increase in labor force participation. Women still earn less money than men, in part because they have less labor market experience, but also because employers tend to pay women less than they pay men for comparable work. Women's earnings rose relative to men's in the 1980s and 1990s, because well-educated women workers were faring better and less-well-educated men were faring worse than they had in the past.

4. **How has the amount of housework and childcare done by husbands and wives changed over the past half-century?** Wives have greatly reduced the amount of housework they do, while husbands have increased theirs. As a result, the relative amount of housework done by husbands and wives has become less unequal, although wives still do twice as much as husbands. Overall, the total amount of housework being done has declined; couples are buying more services, such as restaurant meals, than they used to.

5. **What are some of the strains working parents can experience?** Working parents may suffer from overload due to their multiple roles as workers, parents, caregivers, and spouses. Difficulties at work can spill over into their home lives, leading to their emotional withdrawal from the family or to irritable, angry exchanges. One increasingly common way for dual-earner couples to manage childcare is to work split shifts, a practice that provides children with parental care but can strain a marriage to the point of divorce.

6. **How is the workplace responding to the needs of working parents?** Workers are concerned about meshing their jobs with their family responsibilities, and corporations and government are responding. Large corporations are increasingly providing limited assistance such as childcare information and referral offices and flexible hours. So far, these and other reforms have benefited middle-class workers and employees of large corporations more than low-paid workers and employees of small corporations. In response to worker demands, government childcare assistance has increased.

Thinking about Families

1. If a husband earns substantially more money than his wife, should he expect her to do more of the housework and childcare than he does?

2. How many different family roles might a worker be called on to play during his or her adult life?

3. What are the pros and cons of parents caring for children by working different shifts?

4. **The Public Family** Are benefits such as family leave or tax credits for childcare unfair to workers without children?

5. **The Private Family** Might couples' feelings toward each other be different if they shared the housework and childcare equally?

Key Terms

authority   285
flextime   308
formal sector   292
informal sector   292
internal economy   287
parental leave   308
production for exchange
   value   288
production for use value   288
relationship-specific
   investment   289
responsive workplace   309
role overload   300
service sector   291
spillover   302

Families on the Internet   www.mhhe.com/cherlin

*Note: While all the URLs listed were current as of the printing of this book, these sites often change. Please check our web site (**http://www.mhhe.com/cherlin**) for updates.*

 To get a sense of the concerns of working parents, go to one of the web pages designed especially for parents by a major search engine, such as **www.excite.com/guide/family/parenting/working_parents.** There you will find links to information sources, on-line magazines, advice, message forums, and the like. After examining some of the links, list the topics that seem most important.

Shift work (evening, night, weekend, or rotating work schedules) has become such a common strategy for handling work and childcare that at least one web site is devoted to it: **www.shiftworker.com.** What are the particular challenges this site focuses on?

Dealing with the family issues of employees has become a speciality for some managers. A clearinghouse for information on work-family issues and problems is **www.workfamily.com.** Read the tip of the month, scan the list of important studies, and explore other features of this site. If you were an employer using this site, what would you learn about managing workers with work-family conflicts?

Part Four

Links across the Generations

In this section, we shift from same-generational relations of spouses and partners to intergenerational relations between parents and children. How adequately parents are meeting their overall responsibilities for raising children is a topic of much discussion and concern. In addition, working-age adults bear most of the responsibility for supporting and taking care of the elderly. The increasing number of elderly persons raises the question of whether family care will continue to be adequate. In the terms of this book, the issue is whether the public family is meeting its caretaking responsibilities for children and the elderly and, if it isn't, then why not. • Chapter 10 examines the care of children by their parents. No public issue involving the family has received more attention in recent years than the well-being of children. The chapter begins by asking two questions: What are parents supposed to do for children? And what might prevent parents from doing what they are supposed to do? It then evaluates the complex question of whether children's well-being has declined. • In Chapter 11, the focus shifts from the young to the old. The chapter first reviews the substantial changes that have occurred in the lives of the elderly during the twentieth century. It subsequently examines levels of contact, affection, and assistance between the elderly and their adult children. Then it discusses whether changes in health, income, and intergenerational relations have led to greater or lesser well-being among the elderly.

Children and Parents

Looking Forward

1. What are the main goals in socializing children, and how do parents differ in the way they fulfill their role?

2. How does the socialization of children vary by ethnicity, class, and gender?

3. What difference do fathers make in a child's socialization?

4. What barriers must parents overcome in socializing their children?

5. How has the well-being of American children changed over time?

On her midyear report card, Crystal Rossi, then a seventh-grader in Brooklyn, New York, got a 65 in social studies and failing grades in English, math, science, foreign language, and physical education. She was 12 years old, white, and lived with her mother and stepfather. Her father lived a few blocks away. "The classes are boring," she told a *New York Times* reporter (Manegold, 1993). "Kids who study are all nerds. Who'd want to be like that? Everybody makes fun of them." An assistant principal told the reporter, "We have already sent the family an 'at risk' letter. She's on a decline."

Crystal said she wanted to be a lawyer because "you get to talk back to people" and "you make a lot of money." But she had never met one. In fact, if Crystal were to graduate from high school, she would be the first person in her family to do so. Her mother told her to do her homework but conceded to the reporter that she rarely checks to see if it is done. Threatening to send Crystal to her room didn't do much good: She and her sister shared a television, VCR, radio, Nintendo system, and their own telephone line.

On the streets—and even in the school's halls—Crystal faced crime, violence, and drugs. She had tried alcohol and cigarettes but not, she said, marijuana, LSD, or crack. Still, she knew kids who had tried them all: "Everybody drinks," she said. "They drink and do acid in the park." She had friends who had joined one of the two girls' gangs, Bitches on a Mission and Five Million Hoodlums. "They can protect you," she told the reporter. "They can keep you safe."

Crystal talked tough but was vulnerable underneath. "I'm always nervous," she confided. "I get nervous over nothing. And then I'll get a really big headache. . . . Sometimes I can't even sleep. I stay up all night and then I'm too tired to get up in the morning."

Lafayette Rivers was 10, and his brother Pharoah 7, when a reporter first met them in a largely black public housing project in Chicago (Kotlowitz, 1991). Their high-rise building sat in a neighborhood vacated by middle-class whites and blacks alike. Their parents had separated, and their father—steadily employed but addicted to drugs—rarely showed up. Shootings were an almost daily occurrence; sometimes children were killed in the crossfire. When the reporter asked Lafayette what he wanted to be, he replied, "If I grow up, I'd like to be a bus driver." *If* I grow up—Lafayette wasn't sure he would.

Given the horrible violence in his neighborhood, his fear was perfectly understandable. His mother certainly thought so—she had recently begun paying $80 per month out of her public assistance check for burial insurance for

Crystal Rossi laughs with friends outside her junior high school in Brooklyn, New York.

Lafayette, Pharoah, and her younger triplets. Her three eldest children had already been in drug-related trouble with the law. A 20-year-old daughter worked occasionally as a prostitute to support her drug habit. A 19-year-old son had been imprisoned for burglary. A 17-year-old son had been selling drugs since he was 11.

When they heard gunfire outside their first-floor apartment, Lafayette and Pharoah knew to run into the hallway and dive onto the floor. During the summer of his ninth year, Pharoah developed a stammer that worsened as the shooting wore on. He listened to classical music on the radio, he said, because it relaxed him. During one incident, as bullets whizzed by the apartment, a stuttering Pharoah asked his mother to make them stop. Then he fainted. In his quest for safety and peace, he would sit on the lawn of a calm condominium three blocks from the project until someone shooed him away.

Rachel, 14, lives a life of privilege that Crystal, Lafayette, and Pharoah see only on television. She resides in an exclusive neighborhood of an Eastern city and attends an expensive private school. It is taken for granted that she will attend college. Yet she is drifting toward trouble. Some nights, she sneaks out of the house where she lives with her mother, a lawyer, and her stepfather, a pharmacist, to rendezvous with boys. She and her girlfriends smoke marijuana and drink together, occasionally stealing liquor bottles from their parents' cabinets. She has a difficult relationship with her biological father, whom she visits once a month. Her grades aren't good, and her teachers are worried about her.

The Crystals, Lafayettes, Pharoahs, and Rachels are all too common in the United States. More than one in five children lives in poverty (U.S. Department of Health and Human Services, 1997). One in nine 15- to 19-year-old girls becomes pregnant every year (U.S. Department of Health and Human Services, 1997). Firearm homicide is the leading cause of death for black teenage males (Federal Interagency Forum on Child and Family Statistics, 1997). About 4 in 10 children will witness the breakup of their parents' marriage before they reach 18, and perhaps 1 in 10 will witness a divorce, a remarriage, and a second divorce (Bumpass, 1984). Grim statistics such as these have led to a growing sense of concern about the well-being of American children. Is their quality of life deteriorating? Is our society failing to meet their needs?

Much of that concern centers on the family. Some critics charge that the institution of the family is not providing children with the care, supervision, and discipline they need to become well-adjusted, productive adults—that it is failing in perhaps the central responsibility of the public family. If one agrees with that charge (and not everyone does), it leads to another important question: To what extent are larger social forces such as the restructuring of the economy, racial discrimination, and the cultural drift toward individual autonomy and self-fulfillment undermining the ability of the family to raise children well? These are difficult questions, about which observers have strong, conflicting opinions. Although this chapter can't provide definitive answers, it can introduce you to the extensive social scientific evidence that scholars and policymakers have produced in recent years.

What Are Parents Supposed to Do for Children?

First, however, we need to ask what it is that parents are supposed to do for their children. For the first several years of life, at least, families provide the main setting in which children's fundamental needs are met. In the United States, parents are given broad powers to shape their children's lives. (See *Families and Public Policy: Elián, the Troxels, and Parents' Rights.*) What are the lessons children need to learn from their families, and how are those lessons shaped by social forces such as ethnicity, class, and gender? What behaviors by parents provide the best foundation for children's development?

First and foremost, parents, and sometimes other adult relatives, supply most of the love, nurturing, and care that children need in order to develop a basic sense of trust in other human beings. They also train young children in the skills they need to become more autonomous, such as walking, dressing, and feeding themselves. Later they provide the guidance, support, and discipline children need in order to become competent members of their society. In other words, family members socialize their children. [➡ p. 86] Indeed, families are the major source of primary socialization—the settings for the first lessons children learn about their society.

SOCIALIZATION AS SUPPORT AND CONTROL

As parents socialize their children, they act in two broad ways (Peterson & Rollins, 1987). First, they provide emotional support—love, affection, warmth, nurturing, or acceptance. Emotional support shows children that parents care about their actions. It makes children feel more positively about themselves. Because children want to continue receiving such support, they try to act in ways they think will please their parents. Second, parents exercise control—they seek to limit or change children's behavior. Sometimes parental control is coercive, consisting of the use or threat of punishment or force. But control also may be inductive, that is, based on setting consistent limits, explaining the reasons for

Elián, the Troxels, and Parents' Rights

In November 1999, the U.S. Coast Guard rescued a six-year-old boy floating on an inner tube off the coast of Florida. Like many Cubans before them, Elián González and his mother had attempted to reach the United States by crossing the sea in a small boat. When the boat capsized, Elián's mother drowned.

After his rescue, Elián's relatives in Florida attempted to take custody of him, arguing that he should be granted political asylum in the United States rather than be sent back to communist Cuba. But Elián's father, still in Cuba, asked that the boy be returned; he had not given permission for Elián to leave the country. The United

The U.S. Department of Justice ruled that Elián González's father had the right to take custody of him even though relatives objected.

States Department of Justice agreed, ruling that parents have a fundamental right to custody of their children that supersedes the claims of other relatives, even when political considerations might dictate otherwise. The decision infuriated anti-Communist Cuban immigrants, who mounted a fierce campaign to prevent the boy's return. When Elián's Florida relatives refused to relinquish the boy, Federal agents raided the house where he was staying and returned him to his father.

At about the same time, another struggle over parents' rights, this one in the state of Washington, made the headlines. The state legislature had recently passed a law allowing anyone to petition the court for visiting rights on the grounds that they would be in a child's best interest. Grandparents Jennifer and Gary Troxel had asked the court for overnight visiting rights to the children of their late son and Tommie Granville Wynne. The children's mother, whose fitness as a parent was not in question, had offered more limited visits. When the family court ruled in favor of the Troxels, Wynne appealed.

On appeal, the Washington State Supreme Court declared the law unconstitutional, ruling in favor of Wynne. The Troxels appealed to the U.S. Supreme Court, but in June 2000 the Court sided with the Washington State Supreme Court by a six to three margin, agreeing that the law was unconstitutional.[1] Those justices in the majority reasoned that Wynne was, by all accounts, a fit parent, and that fit parents are presumed to act in their children's best interest. The state, they reasoned, should not interfere with parents' ability to make decisions for their children.

In both the González case and the Troxel case, the winning argument was that parents have close to a fundamental right to direct their children's upbringing—at least as long as their decisions do not greatly harm the children. In cultures that place a greater value on extended family ties, grandparents and other kin might be granted more extensive custody and visitation rights. But in the American legal system—and probably in American public opinion as well—parents' rights prevail.

Ask Yourself

1. Has anyone in your family been involved in a child custody dispute? If so, were parents' rights, as opposed to other relatives' rights, an issue?

2. Besides the issues of custody and visitation, what other ways can you think of that the government limits parents' rights in order to ensure the well-being of their children?

[1] *Troxel* v. *Granville*, No. 99-138, 2000.

www.mhhe.com/cherlin

these limits to the child, requesting that the child comply, and praising her or his compliance. Parents may also exercise control by threatening to withdraw their love if the child does not behave well.

Numerous studies have examined the ways in which parents combine various aspects of support and control. In what is probably the most influential analysis, psychologist Diana Baumrind distinguished among three styles of parental behavior (Baumrind, 1971). In the **authoritative style,** parents combine high levels of emotional support with consistent, moderate control. Children are provided with warmth and affection and with firm, consistent discipline. But the discipline is moderate and is based on requests and explanations rather than on the use of force or punishment. Baumrind and others claim that authoritative parenting produces children who are more socially competent—meaning that they have higher self-esteem, cooperate better with others, develop a better moral sense, and are more independent (Peterson & Rollins, 1987). The two other styles of behavior, it is claimed, produce children who are less competent and who may show more behavior problems, anxiety, or depression. In the **permissive style,** parents provide support but exercise little control over their children by any means. And in the **authoritarian style,** parents combine low support with coercive attempts at control. The implication of this research tradition is that children are socialized best when parents set clear standards, enforce them consistently but without harsh punishment, and provide substantial emotional support. One can spare the rod without spoiling the child, it seems, but setting no limits on children's behavior is virtually as bad as relying solely on the stick.

SOCIALIZATION AND ETHNICITY

The three-category classification of parenting styles is still widely cited, and the authoritative style is generally seen as more effective than the authoritarian style. Yet recently, some scholars have questioned whether the model can be applied to racial and ethnic minority families. African-American parents, for instance, are somewhat more likely than white parents to use physical punishment; and Asian-American parents are more likely than white parents to insist on discipline and obedience (McLoyd, Cauci, Takeuchi, & Wilson, 2000). Within African-American or Asian-American culture, according to critics, these actions may not have the negative meaning that whites, especially middle-class whites, attach to them (Chao, 1994). In fact, some studies suggest that they do not lead to poorer outcomes in racial and ethnic minority families (Deater-Deckard, Dodge, Bates, & Pettit, 1996). While discarding Baumrind's classification would be premature, researchers must be careful in extending it to racial and ethnic minority parents.

One of the primary tasks in socialization, in fact, is to familiarize children with the culture in which they are growing up. Consider the acquisition of language. Learning to talk not only allows children to communicate with others, it also carries important lessons about their society. A French child learns two words for *you:* Siblings and friends are called *tu,* and parents and other adults are called *vous.* Thus the child learns which relationships are characterized by equality and intimacy and which are characterized by respect and social distance. A Japanese girl learns to show deference to men by addressing them differently than she does women. At a conference I attended in Tokyo, a female Japanese professor was criticized by a male colleague—in Japanese. She replied to him in English. When asked later why she responded in English, she said that, had she chosen Japanese,

authoritative style (of parenting) a parenting style in which parents combine high levels of emotional support with consistent, moderate control of their children

permissive style (of parenting) a parenting style in which parents provide emotional support but exercise little control over their children

authoritarian style (of parenting) a parenting style in which parents combine low levels of emotional support with coercive attempts at control of their children

Japanese children are taught to be loyal to the group, wheras American children are taught to be more independent.

she would have had to use the "respect language" a polite woman must employ when addressing a man. In English, she could fight back as a linguistic equal.

Socialization also involves teaching children norms and values. **Norms** are widely accepted rules about how people should behave. **Values** are goals and principles that are held in high esteem by a society. The norms and values may be those of the dominant culture in the society, of a subculture, or of both. Families begin this process; schools, churches, peer groups, and even the media carry it on. For example, Japanese children learn to place a higher value on loyalty to the group in situations where an American child would learn to value independent action. Their greater dependence on others begins in the first few years of life. Japanese mothers tend to wean their children from breast-feeding later than American mothers. They also carry their children on their backs when they go shopping and often sleep with them (Preston & Kono, 1988). Childrearing manuals in Japan urge parents to emphasize the child's dependence on the family. A leading manual discounts the importance of teaching a baby to eat vegetables or any particular kind of food; rather, its author stresses the importance of teaching the baby to eat with the family and to share the same food (Boocock, 1991). Japanese preschool teachers seem to be more lenient than American teachers in allowing rough play and noise, but the Japanese teachers treat a child's reluctance to participate in group activities as a more serious problem. A reluctant child will experience more pressure to join the group in a Japanese setting than in an American preschool (Boocock, 1991).

norm a widely accepted rule about how people should behave

value a goal or principle that is held in high esteem by a society

SOCIALIZATION AND SOCIAL CLASS

Several studies show strong differences between working-class and middle-class parents in how they socialize their children. Social class was defined as an ordering of all persons according to their degrees of power, privilege, and prestige. [➡ p. 113] Middle-class families were defined as those with secure, comfortable incomes that allow them to live well above subsistence, whereas working-class families were defined as those whose incomes provide only for the minimum needs for a decent life. In much of the literature on social class and socialization, class is defined according to the occupation of the father. Families are said to be working class if the father (or the mother, if no father is present) holds a blue-collar job such as a laborer, mechanic, factory worker, or truck driver. Correspondingly, families are said to be middle class if the father holds a white-collar job such as office worker, manager, accountant, or lawyer. As Chapter 4 noted, this focus on the father is an oversimplification; nevertheless, the literature is well worth examining.

Social Class and Parental Values   Beginning in the 1960s, Melvin Kohn pioneered a line of research showing the connections between the conditions a person experiences on the job and his or her childrearing values (Kohn, 1969). Working-class employees, for the most part, are closely supervised, work with physical objects (trash, trucks, bricks), and perform simple tasks repetitively (as on an automobile assembly line). It is important for workers in these jobs to obey their supervisors and to accept the discipline of doing repetitive tasks. In contrast, middle-class workers are less closely supervised, usually work with data (e.g., as would computer programmers) or people (as would personnel managers), and perform a variety of tasks (as would physicians). Middle-class jobs encourage more independence than working-class jobs and often reward creativity and individual initiative.

When working-class and middle-class parents are asked to select the most important characteristics that children should have, their preferences reflect their occupational positions. Working-class parents are more likely to select obedience to authority, conformity, and good manners, whereas middle-class parents are more likely to select independence, self-direction, curiosity, and responsibility (Alwin, 1990). Working-class parents emphasize the kinds of characteristics their children would need if they were to enter blue-collar jobs. To work on an assembly line for 40 years requires obedience and conformity; someone who is creative and independent might have a harder time tolerating the job. In contrast, to be a successful manager requires independence and initiative.

Thus, each class socializes its children to fill the same positions their parents have filled. Because of his or her conformist upbringing, a child from a working-class family may be less successful as a manager than a self-directed child from the middle class. In this way, socialization by parents both is influenced by and helps to perpetuate the social class divisions in the United States and similar developed societies. Some authors believe that schools often fulfill a similar function. Working-class children, it is argued, are more likely to be assigned to nonacademic tracks in which discipline and rote learning are emphasized, whereas middle-class children are assigned to college preparatory tracks in which creativity and initiative are emphasized (Bowles & Gintis, 1976).

Kohn's model assumes that occupational conditions affect people's values and ways of thinking. It is possible that the effects run in the opposite direction: People who value independence may try harder to find jobs that provide independence. Or some underlying characteristic—such as intellectual ability—may influence both a person's preference for independence and the type of job she or he obtains. Kohn's later research, in which people were monitored over time, suggests that the effects run both ways: Job conditions affect people's ways of thinking, and their ways of thinking affect the kinds of jobs they obtain in the future (Kohn & Schooler, 1978).

Historical Trends in Social Class Values   These social class differences in childrearing values have existed since at least the early decades of the twentieth century. Nearly half a century after the Lynds took up temporary residence in Muncie, Indiana, to write *Middletown* (Lynd & Lynd, 1929), a team of sociologists returned to Muncie to see what had changed and what had not (Caplow, Bahr, Chadwick, Hill, & Williamson, 1982). The Lynds had asked 143 married mothers to select, from a list of 15 qualities of children, the three qualities they thought most important in childrearing. In 1978, the study team asked the same questions of 333 married mothers in Muncie. The list included qualities reflecting both conformity (strict obedience, loyalty to church, good manners) and self-direction (independence, tolerance, curiosity). Figure 10.1 shows the results, which were tabulated by Duane Alwin, for "strict obedience" and "independence"; the other qualities showed a similar pattern (Alwin, 1988).

The figure shows the percentage of mothers who selected each characteristic as one of the three most important. For instance, more than 40 percent of both the working-class and "business-class" mothers interviewed in 1924 selected "strict obedience" as one of the three most important characteristics. (The Lynds' "business class" is similar to the "middle-class" definition used in this chapter.) Two conclusions can be deduced from the figure. First, in both the 1920s and the 1970s, business-class mothers were somewhat less likely to think obedience was important and, by larger margins, were more likely to think that independence was important. So the class differences in childrearing values do exist; moreover, they seem to be long-standing and not just the result of recent social change.

Second, between the 1920s and the 1970s, *both* working-class and business-class mothers have come to place less importance on obedience and more on

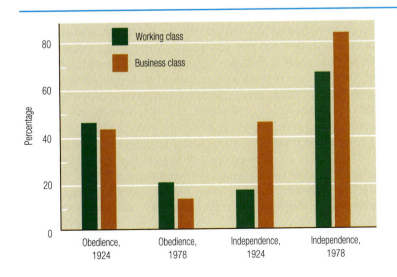

FIGURE 10.1

Percentage selecting characteristics as one of the three most important emphases in childrearing, by class, Middletown data, 1924 and 1978. (*Source:* Alwin, 1990.)

independence. In other words, during the twentieth century there has been a shift in emphasis among all mothers away from encouraging conformity and toward encouraging self-direction.[1] We know that educational levels in the population increased during the century; in the 1920s, a typical blue-collar worker would not have finished high school; by the 1970s, he or she probably would have. The typical white-collar worker would have gone from being a high school graduate to a college attender. As the level of education increased, it may be that parents became more adept at manipulating data and mastering complex logic—the kinds of skills that are said to lead toward a greater emphasis on self-direction. Kohn wrote that "education provides the intellectual flexibility and breadth of perspective that are essential for self-directed values and orientation" (Kohn, 1969).

Alternatively, I would add, the rising value that American (and, more generally, Western) culture has placed on individual autonomy in the twentieth century may explain the historical trend. As noted elsewhere in this book, the rise in divorce, the increase in cohabitation, and the decline in fertility are among the trends that suggest an increased cultural emphasis on individualism. Alwin makes a similar argument: He suggests that secularization—the decline of moral values linked to religion—may have affected parents across class lines and therefore caused the historical drift away from conformity. In support of the latter proposition, he reports that the percentage of mothers who selected "loyalty to church" also declined among both the working class and the business class between the 1920s and the 1970s.

These studies and others like them show that there are indeed social class differences in the ways in which parents socialize their children. These differences affect, and are affected by, people's occupational experiences. Parents stress values that are consistent with the occupations of people in their social class. In this way, they transmit the class inequalities of their generation to their children's generation. Nevertheless, during the last century, parents in both working and middle classes have drifted toward a greater emphasis on the importance of autonomy and self-direction.

SOCIALIZATION AND GENDER

Chapter 3 presented evidence that parents socialize their daughters differently than their sons [➡ p. 89]; here that discussion will be briefly summarized. Although an early review suggested that the differences were smaller than many observers had thought (Maccoby & Jacklin, 1974), many studies have since claimed that parents do indeed treat their daughters and sons differently (Block, 1984). The distinctions parents make may reflect, in part, biologically based differences between girls and boys (Rossi, 1984); yet parents' actions also tend to magnify and exaggerate gender differences. The emphasis in sociological studies of this process has been on the conscious social learning children do as they are rewarded for some behaviors and punished for others—and as they watch and imitate adults of the same gender. In addition, girls and boys may also develop different senses of self because of unconscious, psychoanalytic processes of merging and separating from those who were their primary caretakers as infants,

---

[1]Alwin (1988) provides further evidence of this shift.

who are nearly always women (Chodorow, 1978). Schools, peer groups, and the media further exaggerate gender differences, so that adult gender roles are far more distinctive than any biological differences might warrant. The stereotypical adult gender roles leave men with substantially more economic power than women (Lipman-Blumen, 1984).

WHAT'S IMPORTANT?

Social class and gender differences do exist, then, in how children are socialized. Nevertheless, it is possible to make some general statements about what parents are supposed to do. First, they should provide support to their children. This includes material support such as food, clothes, and shelter, as well as emotional support such as love and nurturing. The need for the former is obvious: Without material support, the child is in physical danger. Yet without emotional support, she or he is likely to grow up without a sense of security or a capability for trusting and loving other people. Second, parents should provide control. They must supervise and monitor their children's behavior not only to help them avoid physical harm but also to teach children the limits of acceptable behavior. This control, developmental psychologists state, needs to be consistent, rather than varying and unpredictable, and firm but moderate, rather than explosive and punitive.

One could supplement this basic list according to one's values. Some might stress the importance of religious and ethical training—an upbringing that teaches children about the spiritual and moral side of life. Those who believe that people of both genders should undertake a wide range of behaviors that are now stereotyped as masculine or feminine—who believe, for example, that men should provide more care for children and women should have better opportunities for careers—might add that parents should encourage more **androgynous behavior** (i.e., behavior that has the characteristics of both genders) in their children. From this perspective, boys should be encouraged to be more nurturing and girls more aggressive. Similarly, those who believe that the values passed along to working-class children limit their occupational achievements might add that parents of all classes ought to encourage autonomous behavior in their children.

> **androgynous behavior**
> behavior that has the characteristics of both genders

WHAT DIFFERENCE DO FATHERS MAKE?

Most of the literature on parenting focuses on mothers rather than fathers—an understandable emphasis, since mothers do more childrearing than fathers in nearly all societies. But during the 1980s and even more so in the 1990s, scholars conducted a great deal of research on the role of fathers in childrearing. Although the quality of these studies is uneven, the best of them suggests that fathers do make a difference in their children's lives (Marsiglio, Amato, Day, & Lamb, 2000). For example, Mosley and Thomson (1995) examined information on two-parent families from the 1987–1988 National Survey of Families and Households. They found that in both white and African-American families, when fathers were more involved with their children (reading to them, helping them with homework, or restricting their television viewing), the children had fewer behavior problems, got along better with others, and were more responsible. This relationship held even if researchers controlled for the

Fathers' influence on sons may be more important before adolescence; their influence on daughters may be more important during adolescnce.

mother's involvement with the children and the family's racial and class background. Other research suggests the following conclusions:

Fathers Relate to Young Children Differently Than Mothers   Fathers relate to young children in part through a vigorous style of play that is often labeled "rough and tumble" in the literature. Picture a father throwing his toddler up in the air and catching her, or rolling on the floor with her, and you have the idea. Psychological studies suggest that these active play sessions help children learn to regulate their emotions (Parke, 1996). Children learn the limits of excitable behavior (e.g., no biting or kicking) and how to bring their emotions back down when it is over. These lessons, it is thought, lead them to be better playmates, to have more friends, and, in adolescence and adulthood, to have more self-control in highly charged situations.

Fathers' Influence Is Often Indirect   Fathers' influence often works through mothers rather than directly to the children. Fathers exercise this indirect influence in part through providing emotional support to mothers or backing up the mothers' authority. The better the quality of the father and mother's relationship, the better is the child's behavior and school achievement, on average (Amato, 1998). Fathers also provide income to the family—in fact, that has often been seen as their major contribution—although studies suggest that income by itself doesn't help children as much as does parental input (Mayer, 1997). Frank Furstenberg and I have speculated that one reason why some divorced fathers have difficulty relating to their children is that they are not used to interacting directly with them in a context where mothers are absent (Furstenberg & Cherlin, 1991).

Fathers' Influence on Children Is Long Term As Well As Short Term   Because mothers tend to be the more hands-on parent in everyday life, fathers' influence is likely to be more subtle and long-term. Consider a study of over 200 Boston-area men, who were first interviewed as schoolboys in the late 1940s and reinterviewed periodically for about 40 years. In the 1980s, John Snarey (1993) reinterviewed the men and their adult children to study the long-term effects of fathers' **generativity**—a term coined by psychologist Erik Erikson (1950) to mean concern about guiding and shaping the next generation. Using information from past interviews, Snarey rated each father's parental generativity—caring activities with children that developed or shaped their capacities, such as rocking to sleep or reading to younger children, or taking an older child to an art gallery or teaching him or her how to fish. He then asked the (now grown-up) children about their education and occupation. He found that in families where fathers had been more generative, the children had had greater educational and occupational success, even when he took into account other important characteristics of the parents and children.

> **generativity**   a feeling of concern about, or interest in, guiding and shaping the next generation

Fathers' Influence on Daughters May Be Different from Their Influence on Sons   Some studies suggest that fathers' involvement with daughters may be more consequential when they are adolescents than when they are younger (Hetherington, 1972). The theory is that adolescent girls' task is to separate from their mothers and learn to manage heterosexual relations. Involved fathers, it is said, help that process by providing safe (i.e., nonromantic) role models for their daughters (Parke, 1996). As for boys, father involvement may be more important when they are preadolescents, since this is the time in which they must separate from their mothers and identify as male. Indeed, Snarey (1993) found in the Boston study that fathers' generative activities prior to adolescence were important for their sons' achievements, whereas generative activities during adolescence were important for their daughters' achievements.

How Nonresident Fathers Act toward Their Children, Not How Much Time They Spend with Them, Makes a Difference   A large proportion of children experience their parents' divorce or are born to single mothers (see Chapter 13). Most of these children live with their mothers. One might think that the more time these children spend with their fathers, the better their development would be, but a majority of studies on this topic do not show a strong link between the frequency of a father's visits and child development (Marsiglio et al., 2000). What studies do show is that children whose nonresident fathers have an authoritative parenting style (for example, who encourage their children and discuss their problems) tend to develop better than children whose visits with their fathers are purely recreational (Amato & Gilbreth, 1999). Within limits, then, the way nonresidential fathers behave as parents seems to make more of a difference than how often they see their children. (A father who rarely sees his children has little influence on them.)

An Appraisal   This list is far from exhaustive; many other studies report effects of fathers on children. However, there are also many studies which have failed to find effects of fathers. For example, studies that also control for mothers' influences and that interview both generations yield weaker evidence of the effects of fathers (Amato, 1998). This newly emerging research literature leaves the reader with two impressions: (1) fathers do have significant effects on children's development, but (2) fathers' effects are, in general, weaker than mothers' effects—especially in terms of the day-to-day behavior of children. As for the latter impression, it is hard to see how it could be otherwise: Mothers do far more of the childcare in the typical two-parent family than do fathers. One might predict that fathers' influence would be stronger in families where both parents shared the childcare responsibilities equally, but that topic remains to be studied.

Another unresolved question is whether any second adult in the household—a grandmother, a lesbian lover—can provide the same benefits to children or whether a father is needed. Some observers argue that men and women have evolved differing approaches to childrearing—as evidenced, for example, by fathers' rough and tumble play and mothers' greater nurturing—and, therefore, that a mother and father are needed (Popenoe, 1996). Many other sociologists would disagree and claim instead that fathers' behaviors aren't programmed by evolution but rather are learned from parents and peers; they would argue that the benefits of having a father rather than a different second caregiver are not proven. Unfortunately, the research evidence isn't sufficient to provide a clear answer; it may be that both evolutionary psychology and socialization contribute to shaping fathers' caregiving behaviors (Parke, 1996).

What Might Prevent Parents from Doing What They Are Supposed to Do?

Yet even parents with the best intentions sometimes cannot care for their children and socialize them as well as they would like to. The larger society sometimes interferes, as when a parent loses a job or a family cannot climb out of poverty. The transformation of the U.S. economy over the past two decades [➡ p. 117] has hurt many parents and made childrearing more difficult. Social change also may interfere: Some observers have argued that recent changes in the organization of families make successful parenting more difficult. Among the changes causing these alleged difficulties are the great increase in the proportion of children who are cared for by someone other than a parent because their parents work for pay, the doubling of the divorce rate since the 1960s, and the increasing proportion of children born outside marriage. Newer arrangements, such as surrogate motherhood and children who live with lesbian or gay parents, have also generated interest and concern. In this section, the effects of these developments on the quality of parenting will be examined.

UNEMPLOYMENT AND POVERTY

The literature on socialization ignores, for the most part, the family's income. "Support" in this literature means emotional support in most cases; it is as if the socialization theorists assume that all families provide children with an adequate level of income support. Of course, that is not true. On the most basic level, low income means fewer clothes and less food. It can mean being evicted from your apartment. It can mean that your children's bedroom has peeling, lead-filled paint. The effects of poverty on children can start before they are born. Pregnant, poor women are more likely to receive inadequate prenatal care and to engage in behaviors harmful to the fetus—such as smoking (which reduces birth weight), using drugs, and eating an unhealthy diet (Halpern, 1993).

Unemployed fathers, like this out-of-work carpenter, can become depressed and act irritably toward their partners and children.

In addition, the consequences of unemployment and poverty can be more subtle. They can change the ways parents act toward each other.[➡ p. 304] They can also change the way parents and children interact. Consider the declining fortunes of agricultural communities in the American Midwest. In 1987, sociologist Glen Elder, psychologist Rand Conger, and several collaborators studied 76 families in a rural Iowa county (Elder, Conger, Foster, & Ardelt, 1992). All were white, a majority were middle class, and each consisted of a married couple and at least two children, one of whom was in seventh grade. After obtaining background information from the family members, the research team set up a video camera. While the tape rolled, they asked the parents to spend 30 minutes reviewing the history and present status of their marriage. Then they taped a 15-minute discussion in which the parents attempted to solve a problem in their marriage. They then taped one of the parents and the seventh-grader in two discussions: talking about a family activity and talking about a family problem such as doing chores or getting along with a younger sibling. Finally, they taped the other parent and the seventh-grader in the same two discussions. Over the next several months, trained raters viewed and reviewed the videotapes, coding the kinds of behaviors each person displayed, such as warmth, affection, or anger.

Unemployment   Nineteen of the fathers had lost their jobs, had had their hours cut back, or had been demoted in the preceding year. Other families had experienced a drop in income or very little growth. The researchers combined these events into a measure of how much "economic pressure" each family was facing. (Even though most of the mothers were employed outside the home, the researchers focused on fathers, who were still the main earners in nearly all the families.) Studies of families during the Great Depression had shown that men who had lost their jobs were tense and irritable in their relations with wives and explosive and punishing in their relations with their children (Liker & Elder, 1983). The tapes showed similar behavior: Fathers in families under economic pressure were more irritable and hostile toward their wives and children. Their wives often replied in kind. One daughter said that at dinnertime "we are kinda cautious, like walking on hot ground or something" (Elder et al., 1992). The interviews revealed that fathers under economic pressure tended to be depressed, lacking energy and interest—more so than their wives. One father said, "There would be some good days, but there would be more bad ones than good ones. Kind of lethargic. Oh, I know it's gotta be done, but I'll do it tomorrow. We kind of floated." Moreover, during the taped discussions, children whose fathers were more hostile and irritable were themselves more sullen, angry, and abrasive. In their interviews, these children admitted to more symptoms of depression (e.g., feeling lonely, hopeless, no interest) and aggressiveness (e.g., I am tempted to break a rule if I don't like it; I do the opposite of what a bossy person says; I yell back if I'm yelled at).

The study suggests a chain of events running from economic difficulties to children's behavior problems. The loss of a job or a drop in income causes psychological distress for the husband, who is still expected to be the family's main earner. The distress in turn leads to depression and to angry, explosive exchanges with his wife and children. And the children then become more depressed, hostile, and aggressive. It is possible, however, that causation could run the opposite way: Men who are depressed and hostile may be more likely to lose their jobs and to have children with similar characteristics. Still, the sequence proposed by the Iowa researchers is plausible and is supported by other studies (Kessler, House, & Turner, 1987).

Poverty   Studies of poor urban families show similar dynamics (Seccombe, 2000). A parent in poverty may be depressed about job prospects, anxious about paying the bills, or angry about crime and drugs in the neighborhood. One mother receiving public assistance payments in New York City said, "Every month I have to decide which bill to pay, which doesn't give you a clear mind. You're always depressed" (Halpern, 1993). Such a parent has few psychological resources left to devote to her or his children. Instead of reasoning with the child or explaining why a certain behavior is good or bad, a depressed and anxious parent may respond to perceived misbehavior simply by threatening harsh punishment—but may then give in if the child refuses to obey. Thus, the child obtains little emotional support and receives discipline that is inconsistent, harsh, and punitive. As noted earlier, this style of parenting has been associated with diminished social competence among children, although some scholars question its application to racial-ethnic minority groups. A recent set of studies suggests that low income has more of an effect on children's school achievement than it does on their behavior; moreover, low income seems to be more detrimental to younger children than to adolescents (Duncan & Brooks-Gunn, 1997).

Since such a large proportion of African-American children live in persistently poor, single-parent households, the distress their mothers often experience is particularly consequential for their development. One research review suggests that poor black single mothers may be more vulnerable to psychological distress than white single mothers with comparable incomes because of the former's chronic economic difficulties (McLoyd, 1990). A higher proportion of black single mothers have never married, whereas a higher proportion of white single

Grandmothers typically play a larger role in childrearing in African-American families than they do in other families.

mothers are divorced. The divorced mothers are more likely to have avoided economic problems prior to the breakup of their marriages; the never-married mothers are more likely to have lived persistently in poverty.

In addition, it is more common among poor black children than among poor white children to be raised by a grandmother—particularly among children whose mothers (and often grandmothers) were teenagers when they gave birth. In these families, teenage childbearing compresses the generations, producing grandmothers who are in their thirties and forties rather than their fifties and sixties (Burton, 1990). To be sure, many young grandmothers provide crucial support and excellent childcare. Moreover, the role of the grandmother in African-American families is stronger, in general, than in European-American families. [➡ p. 152] Nevertheless, some grandmothers may not be at a life stage at which they expect to be caring for grandchildren, and they may be holding jobs themselves. Psychologist P. Lindsay Chase-Lansdale and her colleagues videotaped interactions between young African-American mothers and their children, and between grandmothers and the same children, in two kinds of families: those in which the three generations lived in the same household and those in which the grandmother lived in a separate household (Chase-Lansdale, Brooks-Gunn, & Zamsky, 1994). To the research group's surprise, the quality of parenting—by both the mother and the grandmother—was *lower* when the three generations lived in the same household. The only exception occurred when the mother had given birth in her early teens. It seems likely that a selection effect [➡ p. 223] is at work: Young mothers who have the financial and psychological resources to live on their own probably are more competent, on average, at raising a child. Mothers who have fewer resources are more likely to live with grandmothers. Joint residence is an arrangement often born of necessity. It has mixed effects on children in poor families (McLoyd et al. 2000).

DIVORCE AND REMARRIAGE

The most common way in which children come to live with a single parent is when their parents divorce. Chapters 13 and 14 will examine the effects of divorce and remarriage on children, so I will only summarize the findings here. In the first two years or so after the separation, most children are distressed. The custodial parent, usually the mother, often sees her income go down as the father withdraws much of his support; she may be forced to sell the family home and move to a new neighborhood. She may be so depressed and angry that she cannot provide the consistent support and supervision her children need. The children may be caught in the middle of continuing contact between the former spouses. This "crisis period" is typically a difficult time for both children and parents. Yet some of the problems that children display after a separation were present before the parents split up—suggesting that they might have occurred even had the parents stayed together.

Moreover, over the long term, as Chapter 13 will note, most children do not seem to suffer substantial harm because of their parents' divorce. To be sure, their risk of experiencing outcomes such as dropping out of school, having a child as a teenager, or receiving public assistance increases. The remarriage of a custodial parent, as Chapter 14 will note, does not appear to lower these risks—the well-being of children in stepfamilies is similar to that of children living with unmarried, divorced parents. These increased risks should be troubling to those who are concerned with children's well-being. Still, most children do not experience these undesirable outcomes; rather, most appear to enter adulthood without serious divorce-related problems. It is likely, then, that the increase in divorce has produced short-term trauma for most children and has, on average, reduced their long-term well-being moderately. I think the most prudent conclusion is that divorce is neither a benign event nor an automatic disaster for children. Over the years, most children appear to cope adequately with it and do not suffer serious harm. Yet it deserves to be a source of public concern because it adversely affects most children in the short run and a minority of children in the long run (Cherlin, 2000).

SINGLE PARENTHOOD

What of the effects of single parenthood itself, apart from any effects of poverty or of divorce? What if, say, an unmarried middle-class woman decides, in the style of early-1990s television character Murphy Brown, to have a child? Some critics have claimed that, regardless of their income levels, single parents are hindered by the absence of a second parent. These claims are controversial because defenders of single parents counter that, given the appropriate resources, they can provide care that equals the quality of care by two-parent families (Young, 1994). There is little doubt that many of the problems single parents face can be traced to low incomes or to continuing conflicts with former spouses—and therefore could be eased by greater income support from ex-spouses or the government and a lessening of postmarital tensions. In this sense, single parents per se are capable of adequate parenting much more than critics contend.

Even so, the presence of only one parent is sometimes a handicap, even after lower income is taken into account. An analysis of four national surveys found that low income, and declines in income, could account for about half the disadvantages of living in a single-parent family, such as the higher risk of dropping out of school or having a birth prior to marriage; yet half of the higher risks remained (McLanahan & Sandefur, 1994). Several studies show that single parents do not monitor and supervise their children as well as married or cohabiting parents. For instance, in a national survey of high school students, those in single-parent families were less likely to report that their parents kept close track of how they were doing in school than students from two-parent families. They were also less likely to report that their parents almost always knew where they were and what they were doing. These differences remained even after controls for the socioeconomic status of the families (Astone & McLanahan, 1991). Other studies of adolescents have found that single parents engaged in less consistent parenting and more arguments (Hetherington & Clingempeel, 1992; Dornbusch et al., 1985).

An influential 1977 study claimed that when a single mother lived with another adult, typically her own mother, the two adults could provide childrearing virtually as well as two-parent households (Kellam, Ensminger, & Turner, 1977). Yet the recent work reviewed earlier in this section suggests that mother–grandmother homes are not necessarily better than single-parent homes. In addition, far fewer single mothers are still living with their own mothers by the time their children are adolescents, even though this is the period when supervision is most difficult (Parish, Hao, & Hogan, 1991). Overall, I would draw two conclusions: First, single parents, if they have adequate incomes, usually provide good care for children. Second, it is nevertheless the case that, other things being equal, it is better for children to be raised by two parents than by one.

NONPARENTAL CHILDCARE

Because of the great increase in the proportion of mothers working outside the home, more than half of all preschool children today are regularly cared for by others while their parents work or attend school. Figure 10.2 shows the childcare arrangements parents who were working or studying used for their preschoolers in 1995, according to a government survey (U.S. Bureau of the

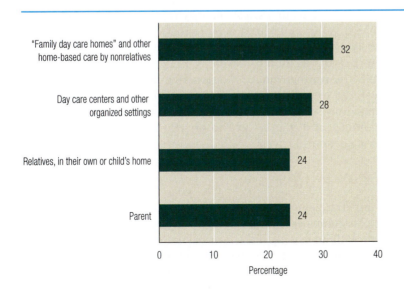

FIGURE 10.2
Childcare arrangements for children under five, 1995. (*Source:* U.S. Bureau of the Census, 2000g.)
Note: Percentages add to more than 100 because some children had more than one arrangement.

Census, 2000g). (The percentages add to more than 100 because some children had more than one arrangement.) The most common arrangement was so-called family day care homes, in which a person cares for other people's children, usually in her own home. The second most common was day care centers or other organized settings, such as Head Start programs. A bit less common was care by relatives, such as a grandmother. Finally, 24 percent of preschool children were cared for by a parent. (Many dual-earner couples manage childcare by working different shifts. [➡ p. 303])

The increase in so-called day care has alarmed some observers, who worry that out-of-home care will be inferior to the care parents can provide at home. The problem is framed in terms of "working mothers," even though fathers are working outside the home, too, because in most societies women have provided more of the care of young children than men. And it is framed as a "day care" problem, even though some children need care while their parents work evenings or nights. Yet recent evidence suggests that in general, children are not harmed by out-of-home care (Perry-Jenkins, Repetti, & Crouter, 2000). To be sure, a grossly overcrowded center or a neglectful family day care provider can cause problems, but typical arrangements do not seem to do much harm. Very few studies have shown any negative effects for children older than age one.

As for infants, the leading study was conducted by a research network organized by the National Institute for Child Health and Human Development (NICHD). Researchers studied 1,000 infants in eight states, visiting the children's families several times and observing their childcare settings. At age 15 months, they assessed the children to see if they had a secure attachment to their mothers, which is important in developing a basic sense of trust in others. (In this context, a secure attachment meant that the child used the mother as a secure base for exploring the environment and a haven of safety to return to when distressed.) Researchers reevaluated the children at ages 24 and 36 months.

The NICHD investigators found that use of childcare was not associated with an insecure attachment to the mother except when her quality of parenting was poor. The investigators suggest that when infants receive adequate parenting, their attachment is not affected by childcare; but when they do not receive adequate parenting, their attachment can be damaged (NICHD Early Child Care Research Network, 1998). The investigators also reported that children in kindergarten who had been in childcare for more than 30 hours per week, on average, were more likely to be rated as aggressive (acting mean, bullying) toward other children (Belsky, Weinraub, Owen, & Kelly, 2001). Still, almost all children were within the normal range of aggressive behavior. We can conclude that it is unjustified to proclaim that nonparental care is generally harmful to children. It may, however, be harmful to infants who do not receive adequate parenting at home, and it may lead to an elevated risk of aggressive behavior upon entering school.

LESBIAN AND GAY PARENTHOOD

There are other living arrangements, more recent in their emergence and less common, that have consequences for children. One of the newest arrangements for children is to live with an openly lesbian or gay parent and, often, that parent's partner. It is only since the 1960s that circumstances have allowed more than a rare occurrence of this kind of family. Those circumstances, which are discussed elsewhere in this book, include the following: the sharp, post-1960 rise in

The number of children raised in lesbian and gay families is still small, but it is growing.

divorce, which encouraged more homosexual men and women who were in heterosexual marriages (often with children) to end their marriages; the emergence of an openly gay subculture in large cities, which provided a supportive environment for lesbian and gay couples; and the greater tolerance of childbearing outside marriage and single parenting in general. There are two main types of gay and lesbian families with children (Patterson, 2000). In the first type, the children were born to a married parent who later came out as lesbian or gay, obtained a divorce, and retained custody of the children. Because women retain custody of children much more often than men after a divorce, most of these families include a lesbian mother, her children, and often her new partner. Children in this type of family have experienced the transitions and difficulties associated with a parental divorce (see Chapter 13). The second type of gay and lesbian family, less numerous but growing, consists of existing lesbian or gay couples who have either adopted a child or conceived one through **donor insemination**—the insertion of donated semen into the uterus of an ovulating woman.

donor insemination a procedure in which semen is inserted into the uterus of an ovulating woman

Questions Raised by Researchers   There are some theoretical reasons to expect that children raised in either type of lesbian or gay family might differ from children raised by heterosexuals in their sexual identities, attitudes, and behaviors (Bailey & Dawood, 1998). As we will see in Chapter 13, writers influenced by Freud have theorized that a boy will have difficulty adopting the adult male role if he cannot see how his father behaves and is not subject to his father's authority. If this view is accurate, and if lesbian and gay parents provide boys with even fewer opportunities to interact with a heterosexual father figure than do heterosexual single parents (an assumption that has not been demonstrated), growing up with gay parents should disrupt the process of heterosexual identification even more. In addition, social learning theory (Mischel, 1966), an influential perspective in social psychology, has been applied to sexual development. The basic idea is that children learn their sexual identities (and almost everything else) by imitating the adults they see. It follows, then, that the less contact a boy has with heterosexual male role models, or a girl with heterosexual female role models, the less likely it is that they will develop heterosexual identities. Moreover, social learning theory implies that children who are exposed to examples of homosexual intimacy—such as a parent and same-sex partner sharing a bed—would be more likely to manifest a homosexual orientation when they reach adulthood.

Studies of Children in Gay and Lesbian Families

Many studies have attempted to compare children living with lesbian parents and children living with heterosexual parents—mostly heterosexual single parents.[2] Most of the studies have been of lesbian families of the first type: children born to mothers who were married and who subsequently divorced and began living openly lesbian lives. Consequently, most of the children had spent at least a few years living with their fathers in early childhood. Virtually all the mothers studied have been white, well educated, and middle class. Moreover, the studies have all been based on nonrandom samples of lesbian mothers, which means that the subjects either volunteered to be studied or were recruited through acquaintances and organizations known to the authors. They may not, therefore, be representative of lesbian mothers in general. And there are few studies of children being raised by gay fathers and their partners.

Since they volunteered to talk, it is likely that the lesbian mothers in these studies are more comfortable with their identities and more open about their lesbian lifestyle than a random sample of lesbian mothers would be. If having a lesbian mother influences a child's psychosexual development through processes such as identification and imitation, the effects should be apparent in these families, if anywhere. Yet the studies show little or no difference in the psychosexual development and behavioral adjustment of children in lesbian families, compared to children in heterosexual families (Patterson, 2000). The few studies of lesbian families of the second type—those in which a partner became pregnant through donor insemination—have reported similar findings (Chan, Raboy, & Patterson, 1998).

Consider a long-term study by three respected British researchers, which began in 1976 (Golombok, Spencer, & Rutter, 1983). Initially, they compared 37 children in lesbian households with 38 children in heterosexual, single-mother households in 1976 and 1977. The children were all between 5 and 17 years of age, with an average age of 9.5. The researchers examined three aspects of psychosexual develop-

---

[2]For a review, see Patterson (1992).

ment. The first was gender identity—the concept children had of themselves as males or females. All the children they studied reported that they were glad to be the sex they were and none said they would prefer to be the other sex. The second was what the researchers called "sex-typed behavior," activities that stereotypically differentiate boys and girls. They asked the mothers how often each of their children performed 14 such activities—including typically male activities, such as playing with construction toys, playing cops and robbers, and playing soccer, and typically female activities, such as playing with dolls, playing pretend games such as tea parties, cooking, and sewing. They also asked the children directly to name their favorite toys, hobbies, books, sports, and so forth. The result showed no significant differences between boys in lesbian households and boys in heterosexual households, nor between girls in the two kinds of households. Regardless of their mothers' sexual orientation, boys were far more likely to engage in the male activities and girls were far more likely to engage in the female activities.

The third aspect was the sexual orientation of the children. Most of the children were too young for a definitive judgment to be made, but the researchers still obtained some evidence on friendship patterns. Among the younger children, nearly all reported a best friend of the same sex. Children who were beyond puberty were questioned about romantic crushes or friendships. Six of the nine such children in lesbian families showed heterosexual interests, two showed no definite interests, and one showed homosexual interests (a girl reported a crush on a female teacher). Among 11 such children in heterosexual single-parent families, 4 showed heterosexual interests and 7 showed no definite interests. The researchers judged that both patterns seemed typical for these age groups. Moreover, there were no significant differences in behavior problems (as assessed by both parents and teachers) and in the quality of relationships with other children (as assessed by parents' reports) for children in lesbian versus heterosexual homes.[3]

In 1991 and 1992, one of the original researchers and a collaborator located and reinterviewed 46 of the children, who were now 17 to 35, with an average age of 23.5 (Tasker & Golombok, 1995). They found that the children who had grown up in lesbian families were more open to the possibility of same-gender sexual relationships but that few of them identified as gay or lesbian. The greater openness was observable in two ways: First, 6 of 25 children from lesbian families reported at least one same-gender relationship, ranging from a kiss to cohabitation; but none of the 21 children from heterosexual families reported a same-gender relationship. Second, 14 children from lesbian families said they had considered the possibility of a same-gender relationship, compared with 3 of the children from heterosexual families. Nevertheless, only two of the children from lesbian families were currently in a same-gender relationship and identified as lesbian (both were women). In other words, growing up in a lesbian family seems to have expanded the sexual possibilities that the children considered and to have led to some short-term, same-gender sexual relationships, but it does not seem to have altered the basically heterosexual orientation of the vast majority.

Tentative Conclusions   It is hard to know how much confidence to place in these nonrandom studies. But the evidence so far, such as it is, supports the

---

[3]See also Kirkpatrick, Smith, and Roy (1981); Hoeffer (1981).

conclusion that children in lesbian homes look very much like children in hetero-sexual single-parent homes, although they may be more open to the possibility of same-gender relationships. Most children from lesbian homes who were studied showed the kinds of behavior that one expects in children who will grow up to have a heterosexual orientation. These children also showed no greater symptoms of mental health problems than the children from heterosexual single-parent homes. In their earlier article, the British researchers concluded, "Perhaps it is the quality of family relationships and the pattern of upbringing that matters for psychosexual development, and not the sexual orientation of the mother" (Golombok et. al, 1983). I would add that the small number of children who identify as gay or lesbian, despite their upbringing in lesbian families, suggests that psychosexual development unfolds, in part, from biological predispositions that children carry with them from birth.

The Well-Being of American Children

Now that we have studied what parents should do for their children and how social changes may have aided or hindered parents' tasks, we are ready to confront what is probably the most critical question to be asked about the public family in the 1990s: Has the well-being of children declined? This is a question that, in recent years, has often been posed and answered affirmatively by national commissions, politicians, and editorial writers. (We should also examine how children's well-being is studied by sociologists and other participants in this debate: See *How Do Sociologists Know What They Know:* Measuring the Well-Being of Children.) The answer to the question depends on two further questions: (1) Compared with when? and (2) Which children?

COMPARED WITH WHEN?

The reality of children's lives in the past was harsher than the nostalgic picture that is sometimes drawn. In the early 1930s, my Aunt Rose gave birth to a son, William, who caught strep throat as an infant. Half a century later, when the pediatrician told me that *my* son had strep throat, I trudged to the drugstore, bought an antibiotic, and nonchalantly spooned it into him. Within two days, he was fine. But antibiotics such as penicillin had not yet been isolated when William took ill, and sulfa drugs, their precursors, were not yet in general use. William died, a victim of an illness that today is hardly more serious than the common cold. The death of an infant, though tragic, was not an unusual event in 1935; 1 in 18 babies died before its first birthday. Nearly 1 in 10 died before reaching age 15 (U.S. Bureau of the Census, 1975).

We tend to forget how much lower the typical standard of living was in the first half of the twentieth century than it is today. One-third of all homes in the 1940s had no running water, two-fifths had no flush toilets, half had no refrigerators, and three-fifths had no central heating. The average person ate half as much beef and one-third as much chicken as has been the case in recent years.[4] Thousands of children contracted polio each year. The infant mortality rate—the

[4]These statistics are cited in Levy (1987).

proportion of children who die in their first year of life—was three times higher than it is today (U.S. Bureau of the Census, 1975; U.S. Bureau of the Census, 1999d). Just 53 percent of persons in their twenties had graduated from high school, compared with 87 percent today (U.S. Bureau of the Census, 2000b). I could go on; the point is that a nostalgic picture of a carefree childhood in the "good old days" is inaccurate. Even as late as the 1940s, life was far tougher for children in many respects than is the case now.

Consider, for instance, trends in the income of families with children. Whether the economic situation of children has become worse or better over time depends on when you start looking. Figure 10.3 shows the percentage of children living in families with incomes below the official government poverty line from 1949 to 1999. By this standard, as the figure shows, nearly half of all children in the country were poor in 1949—a far higher percentage than is the case now. But the great economic boom of the 1950s and 1960s changed all that. [➥ p. 68] By 1969, as Figure 10.3 shows, just 15.6 percent of children were living in families below the poverty line. Childhood poverty had declined for whites, blacks, and Hispanics—a rising tide of prosperity had lifted all boats. Then the post-1973 economic decline, which particularly affected the kinds of entry-level jobs for which young parents tend to be qualified, reversed the trend. By 1993, the poverty rate had risen to 22 percent—higher than in 25 years— before dropping to 16.9 percent in 1999. It was far higher among children of Hispanic origin—30.3 percent in 1999—and black children—33.1 percent in 1999 (U.S. Bureau of the Census, 1999i).

This evidence suggests that, to answer the question about the declining well-being of children, we must ask, compared with when? The well-being of American children in the first half of the twentieth century cannot be judged to be better overall than their well-being today. The period in which children's well-being was at its peak was not in the distant past but rather in the third quarter of the twentieth century—and particularly in the 1950s and 1960s. This was the era when baby boom children grew up. In many ways, neither their parents nor their children

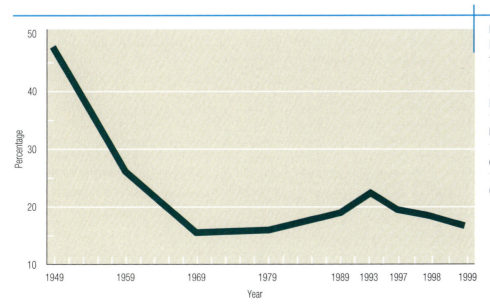

FIGURE 10.3
Poverty rates for children in the United States, 1949 to 1999. (*Sources:* for 1949–1969, Smolensky, Danziger, & Gottschalk, 1988; for 1979 and 1989, U.S. Bureau of the Census, 1993e; for 1993, U.S. Bureau of the Census, 1997f; and for 1999, U.S. Bureau of the Census, 1999i.)

The troubling trends in the lives of many American children have created a demand by policymakers, journalists, and other observers for better information about the well-being of children. Until the 1980s, the federal government collected relatively little information about children. Family sociologists were focused on the conjugal family of husband, wife, and children—but paid little attention to the children themselves. The rise in divorce and in childbearing outside of marriage in the 1960s and 1970s increased the demand for better knowledge about the consequences for children, and academic researchers and government agencies began to respond.

The first questions they had to consider were the following: How do you measure children's well-being in the large-scale surveys that the federal government tends to fund and that sociologists study? And what aspects of children's lives are important for well-being? The most obvious areas are basic needs such as a child's standard of living and health. The Bureau of the Census gathers information annually about income levels and poverty of households with children. In 1981, the government fielded the first child health supplement to the National Health Interview Survey, a large, ongoing survey of Americans' health. The data from these and other government surveys are made available (with names and addresses deleted to ensure confidentiality) to sociologists who wish to analyze them.

But these indicators only tell part of the story. Sociologists and psychologists are interested in two other important domains: *cognitive* indicators of what children are learning and *socioemotional* indicators of how they are feeling and behaving. Cognitive indicators are relatively straightforward; sociologists studying random samples of children and their families can ask permission to talk to children's teachers and to obtain test scores from their schools. For preschool-aged children, of course, there are no test scores to obtain. As a result, survey researchers interested in young children sometimes administer short tests directly to them. For example, a child might be shown a progressively more difficult series of pictures and asked to identify each one.

More difficult to measure are the socioemotional aspects of well-being. For younger

have had it so good. In this period, as Figure 10.3 showed, rates of childhood poverty declined to lower levels than before or since (although recent declines are nearing the all-time low).

Moreover, children were less likely to spend time in a single-parent family in the 1950s and early 1960s than before or since. At the turn of the century, almost one-fourth of all children saw one of their parents die by the time the child was 15 (Uhlenberg, 1980). When this figure is added to the divorce rate, which was much lower at that time, perhaps one in three children spent time living in a single-parent household. By the 1950s, however, death rates had fallen substantially and the divorce rate was still much lower than it is today; as a result, fewer children—perhaps one in four—spent time in a single-parent family than was the case at the turn of the century. Yet by the 1970s and 1980s, the continuing decline in death rates had been overwhelmed by the sharp rises in divorce and childbearing outside marriage; consequently, the proportion of children spending time in a single-parent family reached a high in the 1990s of about one in two (Furstenberg & Cherlin, 1991) and has stayed at that level.

WHICH CHILDREN?

Yet it is important to note that not all children are doing worse today than in the 1950s and 1960s. For during the 1970s, 1980s, and 1990s, the distribution of income in the United States became more unequal. [➡ p. 120] Figure 10.4 shows

children, the best strategy for survey researchers is to ask parents questions about their children's behavior. Following the work of developmental psychologists, sociologists ask parents questions about two kinds of behavior problems: externalizing problems (acting out, aggressive behavior) and internalizing problems (feelings kept inside, such as anxiety and depression).

Older children can be asked directly about problematic behavior. For instance, since 1991 a federally funded national study, Monitoring the Future, has annually asked nationwide samples of 8th, 10th, and 12th graders about drug use. To be sure, we cannot determine whether students are being fully truthful in their responses (See *How Do Sociologists Know What They Know?* Asking about Sensitive Behavior.

[➡ p. 228] But even so, changes in their responses from year to year are likely to represent real increases or decreases. For example, between 1991 and 2000, the surveys showed a doubling of the percentage of 8th graders who reported ever using marijuana (Johnston, O'Malley, & Bachman, 2001.) Other surveys have tracked trends in sexual behavior and pregnancy among adolescents. [➡ p. 218]

Overall, far more information on children's well-being is available from survey research today, compared with two decades ago. In recent years, interest in indicators of children's well-being has been so high that federal government agencies have coordinated their data gathering. The U.S. Department of Health and Human Services publishes an annual volume entitled *Trends in the Well-Being of America's Children and Youth,* filled with graphs and tables. It provides very useful information for sociologists and for students writing papers on the well-being of children and is available on the Internet. (See "Families on the Internet" at the end of this chapter.)

Ask Yourself

1. Have you ever responded to a survey of children's well-being? If so, were you truthful in your responses?

2. Which measures of children's well-being—income and health, cognitive achievement, or socioemotional status—do you think are most critical? Explain your viewpoint.

www.mhhe.com/cherlin

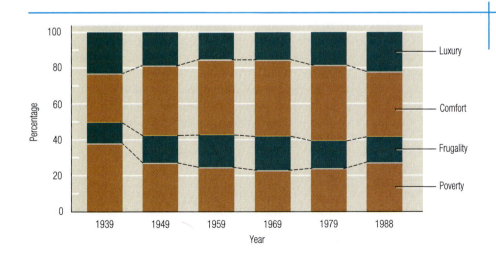

FIGURE 10.4

Percent of U. S. children who were living in "poverty," "frugality," "comfort," and "luxury," 1939–1988. (*Source:* Hernandez, 1993.)

what growing income inequality has meant for children. Demographer Donald Hernandez divided all children into four groups according to their family's income:

Relative poverty: A family income less than one-half the median family income. (The median is the point in the income distribution at which as many families have higher incomes as have lower incomes.)

Frugality: A family income above the relative poverty level but less than three-fourths of the median family income.

Comfort: A family income above the frugality level but less than 50 percent above the median family income.

Luxury: A family income at least 50 percent above the median family income.

Children by Socioeconomic Status

Although these divisions and their labels are arbitrary, they can be used to follow trends over time. Using census data, Hernandez calculated the percentage of children in each group in 1939, 1949, 1959, 1969, 1979, and 1988. Each bar in the figure shows the distribution in one of these years. For example, the left-most bar shows that nearly 40 percent of children were in the "poverty" group in 1939, at the end of the Great Depression. Yet, moving down from the top of the same bar, we can see that more than 20 percent of all children were in the "luxury" category. Not all children suffered during the Depression; some were in families that weathered the storm well. It was the middle categories that were squeezed. During the next 30 years, the percentage in both the "poverty" and "luxury" groups declined, as the middle expanded. Yet since 1969, the middle has once again been squeezed: The proportion of children in the "poverty" group and in the "luxury" group *both* increased between 1969 and 1988. Children at the top of the income distribution in 1988 were doing better than they were in 1969, whereas children at the bottom were doing worse.

A more recent study reached a similar conclusion. Two economists studied data on American children in the years 1976 and 1996, and divided the children into three rough categories:

1. Children were classified as having poor prospects for adulthood if they had three of the following four characteristics: an unmarried mother, a teen mother, a mother without a high school degree, and a family income below the poverty line.
2. Children were classified as having good prospects for adulthood if they had three of the following four characteristics: a married mother, a mother who was 26 or older when they were born, a mother who had completed college, and a family income at least four times the poverty level.
3. Children who fell between these two groups were classified as having average prospects.

Like Hernandez, the authors reported a good news, bad news story. Over the 20-year period, the percentage of children with good prospects rose from 9 to 26 percent—a substantial increase. However, the percentage with poor prospects rose from 8 to 12 percent. Both groups grew in size, and the average group shrank from 83 to 62 percent. In sum, the size of the group of children who have been doing better has increased, as has the size of the group of children who have been doing worse. The size of the middle-income group has been shrinking.

The bars in Figure 10.4 are like photographs: They present a snapshot of all children in the United States at six different points in time. Whether those same

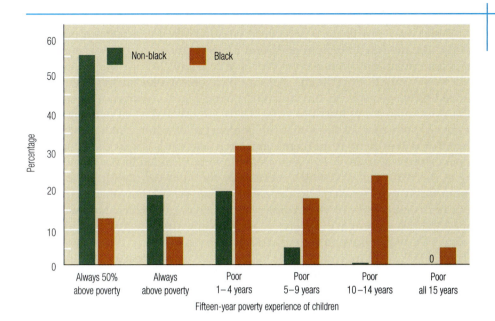

FIGURE 10.5
Fifteen-year poverty experiences of children who were under the age of four in 1968, by race. (*Source:* Duncan, 1991.)

children will be poor or comfortable or wealthy the next year cannot be determined from the snapshots. In fact, a national study that has followed thousands of children and their families for more than 30 years shows that the snapshots conceal great movements of children and their families in and out of poverty over the course of childhood. Many children experience poverty for a short period. Among whites, relatively few experience it throughout their childhood; but among blacks, persistent childhood poverty is common.

Children by Race and Ethnicity Figure 10.5 shows the experiences of children in the Panel Study of Income Dynamics (PSID), who were under the age of four in 1968 and whose families were reinterviewed in each of the next 15 years—a period when poverty rates were similar to those of the late 1990s (Duncan, 1991). The first set of bars on the left shows the percentage of non-black children (whom I will call "white" for the sake of simplicity since most were, indeed, white) and black children whose families had incomes that were always at least 50 percent above the poverty line in each of the 15 years. A majority (56 percent) of white children fell into this category, compared with 13 percent of black children. The next set of bars represents children whose families were always above the poverty line but were close to the line in at least one year. Combining these two categories, we see that 75 percent of white children and 21 percent of black children never experienced poverty. The racial difference is great. Still, the figure demonstrates that a substantial number of black children were never poor. These children are often overlooked in articles about the economic situation of African Americans.

The next set of bars represents what we might call "temporary poverty": those who were poor 1 to 4 years out of 15. About one-fifth of white children—a substantial number—experienced temporary poverty. It was common to be poor for a few years. Among black children, it was even more common. But the racial differences are most dramatic in the final three sets of bars, which represent what we might call "persistent poverty," that is, being poor at least 5 of the 15 years. By this measure, only about 6 percent of white children experienced persistent poverty. The modest amount of persistent poverty among whites was a great social accomplishment of the post–World War II era; before then, persistent poverty was much more likely. Yet any pleasure at that accomplishment is matched by displeasure at the situation among black children, 47 percent of whom were poor for at least five years. There are other ways of defining persistent poverty, but they all show that the percentage of white children who were affected was less than 10 percent, and often less than 5 percent (Duncan & Rodgers, 1991). Moreover, Hispanic children were included in the "white" category of the PSID analyses, which means that the rates for non-Hispanic whites were probably even smaller. The alternative definitions all show that the percentage of persistently poor black children was 30 percent or higher. Although many white children experience poverty at some point, then, persistent childhood poverty is far more common among African Americans.

The PSID further indicated that children who were persistently poor were much more likely to live in single-parent families. [➡ p. 122] According to the PSID study, the average black child who lived with one parent spent more than seven years in poverty—nearly half of her or his childhood (Duncan, 1991). This is not to say that family structure is the only cause of the high rates of persistent poverty among children. Many poor single mothers were poor *before* they gave birth to their children. In addition, black single parents tend to live in racially segregated neighborhoods with high concentrations of poverty. These neighborhoods often have high levels of crime and drug abuse, few social services, and few jobs. One study found that the absence of affluent neighbors was associated with higher rates of childbearing and school dropout among teenagers, even after attempts to control for family structure and race (Brooks-Gunn, Duncan, Klebanov, & Sealand, 1993).

Information on poverty trends for Hispanic children is sketchier because government statistics were very limited until the 1970s. Even today, most tabulations display data on all Hispanic children combined; yet, there is great diversity within the Hispanic category. [➡ p. 157] With this caveat, one can examine recent trends in the annual poverty rate. Between 1980 and 1995, the rate for Hispanic children increased from 33 to 39 percent, a larger increase than among either African Americans or non-Hispanic whites (U.S. Bureau of the Census, 1997g; U.S. Bureau of the Census, 1997f). It is likely that the sharp increase reflected, in part, the continuing immigration of individuals and families from low-income backgrounds. But by 1999, the rate had fallen to 30.3 percent (U.S. Bureau of the Census, 1999i).

A SUMMING UP

Overall, I think that comparisons of the "average" child now and in the past can be misleading. As Figure 10.4 suggests, the percentage of children who are in prosperous families has increased in tandem with the percentage who are in poor families. This trend holds for blacks as well as for whites. Persistently poor children are the group that has fared the worst since the 1950s and early 1960s and that seems most distinctively and gravely deprived of a decent childhood today. The PSID data showed that persistently poor children are disproportionately black. Indeed, the racial difference is so great that, by most reasonable definitions, a majority of all persistently poor children today are African Americans, even though African Americans constitute only about 16 percent of all children. The U.S. government provides less assistance to children in low-income families than almost any other Western nation. It may be that the racial polarization between the heavily black population in deep poverty and the white majority prevents Americans from reaching out to the poor. (See *Families in Other Cultures: U.S. Children in International Perspective*, on pp. 346–347.)

Poor and Wealthy Children   Persistently poor children are more likely to live in single-parent families than were similar children in the 1960s (Duncan & Rodgers, 1991). To the extent that living in a single-parent family makes it more difficult to escape from poverty, poor children may be experiencing hardships for a longer period of their lives. To the extent that single parents have more difficulty supervising and monitoring teenagers, children may be receiving less supervision than they need. Yet it's simplistic to blame single parents for persistent poverty. As noted earlier, many poor single mothers were poor before they became mothers. Becoming a single parent didn't make them poor—they already were. In addition, the past two decades have seen a great deterioration in the labor market prospects of young adults without college educations, which made it more difficult to start and maintain a two-parent family. One recent study estimated that, even if there had been no increase in single-parent families since 1960, about 80 percent of today's poor children would still be poor; moreover, the gap between white and black child poverty rates would still be large (Hernandez, 1993). The growth of single-parent families hasn't helped matters for poor children, but it is probably not the major cause—and certainly not the sole cause—of the problems of poor children.

Among children from families that are not poor, I submit, the decline in well-being since the 1950s and 1960s has not been as great. A fortunate, growing minority of children live in relatively wealthy families. Although they too face an increased risk of parental divorce or teenage pregnancy, the risks are lower than among the less fortunate. (Many studies demonstrate, for example, that the higher a family's income, the lower the likelihood of divorce.) It's not at all clear that their well-being has declined; in fact, it may have improved.

Children in the Middle   It is among children from families in the narrowing middle, neither poor nor affluent, many of which have been hard-pressed to maintain their standard of living, that a judgment about trends in well-being is most difficult. My own sense is that, on average, the children in the middle have experienced a moderate downward drift in well-being since the 1960s. They are less likely to live with two parents, due mainly to increases in divorce. They have grown up during a period of economic belt tightening by the working and middle classes. Their rates of births outside marriage are higher, their suicide rates are higher, and their SAT scores are lower.

Probably the two greatest changes in the family among this middle group have been the increases in the number of mothers who work outside the home and in divorce rates. Little was said about divorce in this chapter because it will be discussed in Chapter 13. Nearly all children are intensely upset when their parents separate, and their risk of dropping out of school, having a child as a teenager, or experiencing other undesirable consequences rises. These effects are troubling and worthy of serious concern. It appears, however, that most children do not

U.S. Children in International Perspective

*T*he decline in children's well-being raises the question of how well U.S. children are doing compared with children in other developed countries. The answer is not very well. U.S. children learn less about mathematics and science. They must cope with the highest rate of divorce of any Western nation (although if the breakup of cohabiting parents is included, Sweden's overall rate of family dissolution might be higher). Rates of adolescent homicide (and also adult homicide) are far higher than anywhere else. The percentage of teenage girls who give birth is higher, even among white Americans, than anywhere else. And so forth. No nation presents as pale a statistical portrait of children as the United States.

Consider information about child poverty collected from 25 countries between 1987 and 1995. For each country, the figure on page 347 shows the percentage of children who lived in low-income families, defined as families with incomes less than half of the median (or middle) family income. Russia, its post-socialist economy in shambles, barely exceeded the United States high percentage of poor children. No other country came close. Why do so many U.S. children live in low-income families? One possibility is the high rate of poverty among racial-ethnic groups in the United States. Yet even when childhood poverty among U.S. whites is compared with that of whites in other Western countries, Americans still show higher rates. Another possibility is the large number of single-parent families in the United States. But

even when the comparisons are restricted to children living in single-parent families in other countries, U.S. children are poorer than those almost anywhere else.

What really account for the difference are the more generous social welfare programs in most other countries. The governments of most other countries provide more benefits to all families, regardless of income. For example, most have a child allowance that is paid to parents solely on the basis of how many children they have. Most have unemployment benefits that are more generous and are paid for a longer period of time than in the United States. Most provide payments to parents who take a short-term leave from their jobs following childbirth. These universal benefits are popular with citizens of other countries because they are seen as aiding everyone, not just the poor.

In contrast, the United States relies more on so-called means-tested benefits, which are given only to families that fall below an income threshold. These benefits are not as generous as in the other countries. For example, the main cash benefit available to families with children is Temporary Assistance to Needy Families, which was known as Aid to Families with Dependent Children before the 1996 welfare legislation, and which is provided primarily to single-parent families in poverty. AFDC was so unpopular that most states did not increase it to keep up with inflation; consequently, its real value declined after the mid-1970s.

Because means-tested benefits are usually less popular with voters, they tend to be less generous than universal benefits. For example, Social Security is a universal benefit in the United States because it is available to all elderly persons regardless of income. In contrast to AFDC/TANF, Social Security benefits have risen dramatically over the last few decades. The lack of universal benefits for parents of young children in the United States seems to reflect the strong individualistic ethos in this country. In the American myth, each person is supposed to make it on his or her own. The poor are often viewed as "undeserving" of help—of having failed at the task of providing for themselves and their children.

Children in Scandinavian families, such as this one in Norway, are less likely to be poor than children in most other countries because of generous social welfare programs.

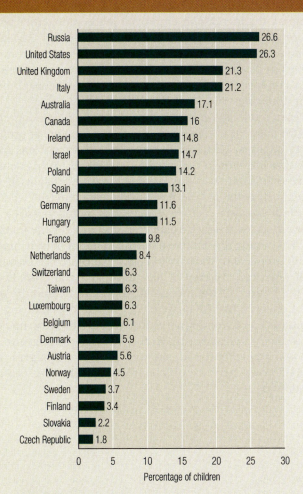

Country	Percentage of children
Russia	26.6
United States	26.3
United Kingdom	21.3
Italy	21.2
Australia	17.1
Canada	16
Ireland	14.8
Israel	14.7
Poland	14.2
Spain	13.1
Germany	11.6
Hungary	11.5
France	9.8
Netherlands	8.4
Switzerland	6.3
Taiwan	6.3
Luxembourg	6.3
Belgium	6.1
Denmark	5.9
Austria	5.6
Norway	4.5
Sweden	3.7
Finland	3.4
Slovakia	2.2
Czech Republic	1.8

*Poverty is defined as percent of children living in families with adjusted disposible incomes less than 50 percent of adjusted median income for all persons. Income includes all transfers and tax benefits.

Percentage of children living in families with incomes less than half of the median income for all families, 1987–1995. (*Source:* Bradbury & Jäntti, 1999.)

When I travel in Western Europe, I find that people have a greater sense that their fellow countrymen are deserving of assistance purely because they are citizens. The French, for example, seem to believe that every French person has a right to a minimally adequate standard of living. I find a greater sense of "we-ness," a feeling that we are all French (or British or German) and must assist the less fortunate—especially children. In the United States, I see a greater split between "us"—the middle class—and "them" the undeserving poor. This split may well be aggravated by the ethnic and racial differences in the United States between the poor and the better off.

Lingering prejudice and discrimination encourage some middle-class whites to see black or Hispanic poor people as different from them and therefore less worthy of their support. The split between us and them and the strong belief in individual initiative result in less support to poor children than in any other developed country.

Ask Yourself

1. Do the statistics shown in the graph surprise you? In your opinion, is a 26.3 percent child poverty rate acceptable in the richest nation in the world?
2. What are the long-term implications for American society when more than a quarter of all children grow up in poverty?

www.mhhe.com/cherlin

suffer long-term harmful effects from divorce. Moreover, some of the problems that we blame on divorce are visible in children before their parents even separate, which suggests that some of the problems might have occurred even if the parents had stayed together.

I have argued in this chapter that having both parents (or one's only parent) work outside the home has little effect on children. Consequently, there is little justification for lumping the increase in employed mothers together with clearly problematic developments such as childbearing among unwed teenagers or increased deaths by homicide and suicide. To be sure, the greater economic independence of women has facilitated divorce. Yet there is no evidence suggesting that the increase in employed mothers is a major cause of teenage pregnancy, drug use, suicide, or homicide.

Nevertheless, even a moderate deterioration in well-being among children in the middle is cause for concern to those who believe in the idea of progress—the idea that our society ought to be improving the lives of its citizens rather than backsliding. I think that changes in the family contributed to this deterioration, but I'm not convinced the family was the major actor. The family itself was acted upon by larger forces such as the restructuring of the economy and a cultural shift toward ever-greater individualism. Yet parents are not merely passively acted on by social forces; they must be assigned some responsibility for the consequences of their actions, such as getting divorced and having children outside marriage.

And although I am skeptical of those who claim that there is a pervasive crisis in the well-being of American children, I do think that a real crisis is occurring among children at the bottom of the income distribution. Behind the dismal statistics lie the lives of children like Lafayette and Pharoah Rivers, diving for cover during the daily gunfights and wondering if they will get to grow up. When the reporter proposed to their mother that he write a book about Lafayette, Pharoah, and other children in the neighborhood, she thought that was a great idea. Still, she warned, "But you know, there are no children here. They've seen too much to be children" (Kotlowitz, 1991).

Looking Back

1. **What are the main goals in socializing children and how do parents differ in the way they fulfill their role?** By socializing their children, parents equip them to function well in society. Among other things, parents teach children norms (widely accepted rules about how to behave) and values (goals and principles that are held in high esteem in a society). Parents provide both material and emotional support to their children and exercise control over them. A combination of high levels of emotional support and consistent, moderate discipline, called an authoritative parenting style, seems to produce children who are most socially competent, at least among white families. Authoritarian (strict) and permissive parenting styles seem less successful.

2. **How does the socialization of children vary by ethnicity, class, and gender?** In racial and ethnic groups such as African Americans and Asian Americans, parents rely more on strong discipline than white parents. Working-class parents stress obedience and conformity more than middle-class parents; conversely, middle-class parents stress autonomy and self-direction more than working-class parents. Members of each social class emphasize values that are consistent with the kinds of jobs they perform. Parents also socialize boys and girls differently, so that any preexisting differences are exaggerated in childhood and adult behavior.

3. **What difference do fathers make in a child's socialization?** Growing evidence suggests that fathers do make a difference in their children's lives. Fathers often play vigorously with young children, which may help children learn to regulate their emotions. They also influence their children indirectly, through the emotional support they give their wives. The caring activities fathers engage in with their children may have a long-term effect on their children's educational and occupational attainment, even if they do not live with their children.

4. **What barriers must parents overcome in socializing their children?** Unemployment and poverty can affect the way parents act toward each other and toward their children. Job loss or low earnings can cause a parent to become depressed and angry; fathers in these situations are likely to have angry, explosive exchanges with their wives and children. Single parenthood also raises the risk of some adverse consequences, such as a child dropping out of school. There is little evidence, however, that children are harmed by one or both parents working outside the home. And the evidence on children who grow up with lesbian parents suggests that they do not differ much from children with heterosexual parents.

5. **How has the well-being of American children changed over time?** Comparisons between the "average" child today and the "average" child a few decades ago can be misleading. Economic inequality has increased since the early 1970s: The percentage of children at both the bottom and the top of the income ladder has risen, whereas the middle group has decreased in size. The growing proportion of children who live in relatively wealthy settings tends to be doing well. At the other extreme, persistently poor children appear to have suffered greatly. Children in the shrinking middle group may have suffered a moderate reduction in well-being over the past few decades, a trend that eroded some of the gains of the 1950s and 1960s.

Thinking about Families

1. Is raising a child more difficult today than it was a few decades ago?

2. Does our society provide enough assistance to parents?

3. How much of a difference does having a father in the household make to children?

4. **The Public Family** What are the crucial duties society expects of parents in raising their children?

5. **The Private Family** What kind of satisfaction do parents get from raising children?

Key Terms

androgynous behavior   325
authoritarian style
  (of parenting)   320

authoritative style
  (of parenting)   320
donor insemination   335
generativity   327

norm   321
permissive style
  (of parenting)   320
value   321

Families on the Internet   www.mhhe.com/cherlin

Note: While all the URLs listed were current as of the printing of this book, these sites often change. Please check our web site (__http://www.mhhe.com/cherlin__) for updates.

 A great deal of information on children—especially disadvantaged children—is available on the Internet. For instance, a report mentioned in the "Measuring the Well-Being of Children" essay in this chapter, *Trends in the Well-Being of America's Children and Youth, 2000,* issued by the Office of the Assistant Secretary for Planning and Evaluation of the U.S. Department of Health and Human Services, was available in 2001 at (**http://aspe.hhs.gov/hsp/00trends/index. htm.**) A more recent volume may be available. Other resources include the National Center for Children in Poverty at Columbia University (**http://cpmcnet.columbia.edu/dept/nccp**),

which maintains a web site with several well-done reports about child poverty (click on "Child Poverty Facts"). Browse some of the fact sheets and tables at these sites to get a sense of recent trends in child poverty.

Monitoring the Future (**www.monitoringthe future.org**) is an annual survey of 8th, 10th, and 12th grade students, undertaken by the University of Michigan's Institute for Social Research. The survey includes information about drug and alcohol usage and cigarette smoking (click on "Data Tables and Figures"). What were the trends in drug usage by teenagers in the 1990s, according to this study?

chapter 11

The Elderly and Their Families

Looking Forward

1. How has grandparenthood changed over the past century?

2. How has the standard of living of the elderly changed?

3. Are the elderly isolated from their kin?

4. How much support do the elderly provide to, and receive from, their kin?

5. Who cares for the frail elderly?

In 1985, when Frank Furstenberg and I were finishing our research for a book on grandparents (Cherlin & Furstenberg, 1992), we visited a senior citizens' center in a Jewish neighborhood in Baltimore. There, we talked with a group of grandparents who told us that the new development in the neighborhood was the immigration of many families from Russia. With some envy, they described to us the relationships the Russian grandparents had with their grandchildren. One woman said:

> We have quite a few Russian friends. Now these friends, invariably the mothers are living with the sons, the daughters, with grandchildren—they're all together. I have noticed such a difference with our Russian friends, who have only been in this country four or five years—these are new immigrants. The grandchildren have great reverence for the grandparents; they live together. When they go on vacation, they take the grandparents with them! I'm just shocked! When they go out eating, they take the grandparents with them! . . . And this is such a new experience because we don't go eating with our children. They go their way, we go our way. It's a special occasion when you go out with your children—an anniversary, a birthday.

Her husband added:

> The [Russian] grandparents are very much involved with the families of their children. They assume such a responsibility. We know a woman who was a famous surgeon in Russia, she's here in America, and she has that same feeling that she has to take care of her grandchild if the mother goes away. She's always obligated to that little girl. Now, you wouldn't find the same thing in America.

The grandparents in the room contrasted this great degree of togetherness, respect, and mutual obligation with the weaker ties they experienced with their own children and grandchildren. After a number of these comparisons between the fullness of the grandparent–grandchild relationship among the Russian immigrants and the thinness among the Americans, one of us asked whether anyone in the group would trade places with the immigrants in order to have their type of relationship. The question was met with immediate cries of "No way!"; "No"; and "I'm satisfied." The questioner pursued the point further: "Why wouldn't you trade places? There are all these strong family ties." A woman replied, "I don't think I could live with my children," and a chorus of "No" and "No way" followed.

These American grandparents don't want to live with their children because if they did, they would lose some of the independence they prize. As will be noted later, they belong to the first generation of elderly Americans in which most persons have the opportunity for a reasonably long, healthy, comfortable, independent life. Previous chapters have shown that the kind of intimacy Americans value increasingly consists of love and affection between two independent individuals,

Adults live much longer, healthier lives than a century ago.

each acting to maximize his or her own sense of self-fulfillment. This combination of affection and independence wasn't available to most elderly persons a generation or two ago—too many died prematurely or lacked the money to live on their own. In the second half of the twentieth century, however, the lives of the elderly changed dramatically for the better. Now the grandparents in Baltimore want just what their middle-aged children want: close, warm, satisfying family ties but also independence from kin. They want affection and respect from their children and grandchildren, but they do not want to be obligated to them. The price paid for strong family ties by the Russian immigrants—and by family members in developing countries around the world—is a substantial loss of independence. It is a price most Americans, old or young, are unwilling to pay.

This is not to say that all elderly persons are healthy, well-off, and independent. As the elderly population has expanded, so has the number of frail persons in need of care. The cost of the technology-driven health care provided to the increasing numbers of frail elderly has risen dramatically in recent years and has become a major problem for the nation. In addition, although the proportion of elderly persons who have incomes below the government poverty line is less than the proportion of poor among the nonelderly, it is still the case that, as of 1999, 9.7 percent of elderly persons were poor (U.S. Bureau of the Census, 2000e). Moreover, a disproportionately large part of the elderly population sits precariously just above the poverty line—not poor, but not by much.[1] The incidence of poverty is greater for elderly women than for men, as we shall see.

This chapter will focus on the family lives of the elderly—their interactions with spouses, children, grandchildren, and other relatives. As birthrates and death rates both decline, there are relatively more older people and relatively fewer

[1]Figures will be given later in this chapter.

younger people in the population. Whether society will be able to adequately meet the needs of the elderly is an issue of great importance from the perspective of the public family. Spouses and relatives, as will be demonstrated, provide most of the assistance to the elderly. Providing adequate assistance is likely to be more difficult when the huge baby boom generation begins to retire. Other changes in family life, such as the increase in women's work outside the home and the rise in divorce, may also complicate the task of caring for the elderly.

In addition, the quality of family life for the elderly is an important issue from the perspective of the private family; and here the news is heartening. The recent trends in the well-being of children are lamentable, as noted in the previous chapter, but the recent trends in the well-being of the elderly deserve at least two cheers. Programs for the elderly have been the one indisputable success of U.S. social welfare policy since the Great Depression. In fact, so successful have the programs been, and so far have both death rates and birthrates fallen, that most people fail to realize how new is the kind of life most elderly Americans are leading today—a longer, healthier life in which the elderly provide substantial assistance to their family members. In order to understand what has happened, we need to begin by looking back in history.

The Modernization of Old Age

We tend to associate grandparents with old-fashioned families—the large, rural, three-generation kind that can be seen on reruns of *The Waltons*. We have a nostalgic image of Grandma, Grandpa, Aunt Bess, Mom, Dad, and the kids sitting around the hearth, baking bread and telling stories. Correspondingly, many observers think that the role of older people in families has become less important since the farm gave way to the factory. According to this view, industrialization meant that older people could no longer teach their children and grandchildren the skills needed to make a living. Moreover, older people no longer controlled the resources—such as farmland—that gave them influence over the lives of the young. There is some truth to this perspective. But the historical facts suggest that grandparenthood—as a distinct and nearly universal stage of life—is a post–World War II phenomenon. To be sure, there have always been grandparents around, but never this many and never with so few of their own children left to raise.

MORTALITY DECLINE

The Statistics   First of all, a century ago—even 50 years ago—far fewer people lived long enough to become grandparents. Much of the decline in adult **mortality** (the demographers' term for deaths in a population) from preindustrial levels occurred in the twentieth century. Only about 37 percent of all women born in 1870 survived to age 65; in contrast, about 77 percent of women born in 1930 reached age 65 (Uhlenberg, 1979; Uhlenberg, 1980). The greatest declines occurred in midcentury, especially for women. The number of years that the average 40-year-old white woman could expect to live increased by four between 1900 and 1940, by seven between 1940 and 1980, and by one since then. For white men the increases have been smaller: a gain of two years between 1900 and 1940, four between 1940 and 1980, and 2.5 since then (U.S. Bureau of the Census, 1999d). The trends for nonwhites are similar, but in every decade the

mortality the number of deaths in a population

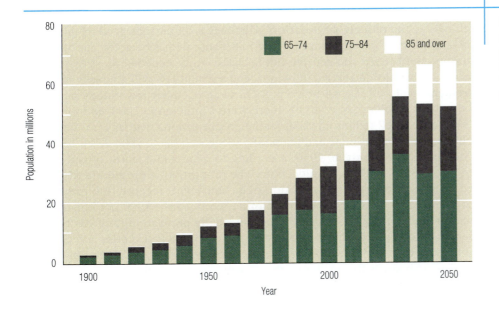

FIGURE 11.1
Actual and estimated population 65 years old and over in the United States: 1900–2050. (*Source:* U.S. Bureau of the Census, 1983.)

life expectancy of nonwhites has been lower than that of whites. In 1997, white babies had a life expectancy of 77.1 years, compared with 71.2 years for black babies (U.S. Bureau of the Census, 1999d).

A more difficult question is whether the gains in life expectancy that have been occurring recently have added healthy years or infirm years at the end of life. Have modern medicine and improved standards of living allowed the elderly more years of activity or merely more years in which they are ill or disabled? The answer appears to be that during most of the added years of life expectancy, older people have chronic illnesses that limit their activity but do not make them bedridden. They are neither fully healthy nor in need of care in a hospital or nursing home. For instance, between 1970 and 1980, life expectancy increased by 2.7 years for white women (and 4.6 years for black women), but there was no increase for white women (and an increase of only 1.1 years for black women) in the length of life expected without any disabilities (Crimmons, Saito, & Ingegneri, 1989).[2]

The Social Consequences   The decline in mortality during the twentieth century has had two consequences. First, both women and men can expect to live much longer lives than was the case several decades ago. Second, women tend to outlive men. In 1997, the average female baby could expect to live 79 years, the average male baby 74 years (U.S. Bureau of the Census, 1999d). A century ago the sex difference was much smaller because many more women died in childbirth. So it is the case today that (1) there are many more older people in the population than there used to be, and (2) 6 out of 10 older people are women. Figure 11.1 shows the growth of the U.S. population aged 65 and over

---

[2]It is possible, as the authors note, that older people were more likely to report themselves as disabled in 1980 than in 1970 because of the growth of government programs that provide disability benefits.

elderly population the group of people aged 65 years and over

since 1900 and projections to the year 2050. Under the usual convention, which I will follow, the **elderly population** is defined as all persons aged 65 and over. This is an arbitrary cutoff point that is used because 65 has been the age at which a person could retire and receive full Social Security benefits. Most 65-year-old persons are healthy and active, however, and a recent law will gradually raise the retirement age to 67. As can be seen, there were relatively few elderly people in 1900—about 3 million. In contrast, there were 35 million in 2000, and there will be an estimated 67 million in 2050 (although projections that far into the future should be seen only as educated guesses).

Moreover, as recently as 1950, according to Figure 11.1, most of the elderly were aged 65 to 74. Then, in midcentury, the proportion of the elderly who were aged 75 to 84 began to grow more rapidly, and more recently the proportion who are aged 85 or older has risen. In other words, since 1900 not only has the elderly population increased greatly but the elderly population itself has become older and older, increasingly top-heavy with those in their seventies and eighties. As the older elderly population expanded, **gerontologists** (social and biological scientists who specialize in the study of aging) invented the following terms to differentiate among the aged: **young-old** for those 65 to 74, **old-old** for those 75 to 84, and **oldest-old** for those 85 and over.

gerontologist a social/biological scientist who specializes in the study of aging

young-old the group of elderly people 65 to 74 years of age

old-old the group of elderly people 75 to 84 years of age

oldest-old the group of elderly people 85 years of age and over

The sharp decline in mortality has caused a profound change in the relationship between older persons and their children and grandchildren. For the first time in history, most adults live long enough to get to know most of their grandchildren, and most children have the opportunity to know most of their grandparents. The chances were only 50-50 that a child born at the beginning of the twentieth century would still have two living grandparents when he or she reached the age of 15. In contrast, the comparable chances rose to 9 in 10 for a 15-year-old in the 1970s (Uhlenberg, 1980). Currently, then, nearly all children have the opportunity to get to know at least two of their grandparents—and many get to know three or four. But children born at the beginning of the century were not nearly as fortunate.

FERTILITY DECLINE

fertility the number of births in a population

The decline in **fertility** (the demographers' term for births in a population) is the second reason why grandparenthood on a large scale is a recent phenomenon. As recently as the late 1800s, American women gave birth to more than four children, on average (Ryder, 1980). Many parents still were raising their younger children after their older children left home and married. Under these conditions, being a grandparent took a backseat to the day-to-day tasks of raising the children who were still at home. Today, in contrast, the birthrate is much lower, and parents are much more likely to be finished raising their children before any of their grandchildren are born. When a person becomes a grandparent now, there are fewer family roles competing for her or his time and attention. Grandparenthood is more of a separate stage of family life, unfettered by childcare obligations—one that carries its own distinct identity. It was not always so.

The combination of falling mortality and fertility rates has also altered the bonds of kinship that people have. Because birthrates have fallen, younger people tend to have fewer brothers and sisters than their parents and grandparents. So the horizontal bonds of kinship—those to relatives in the same generation as you—have tended to shrink. In contrast, lower mortality means that you have a much greater chance of having living parents well into your middle years than your parents or grandparents. Vertical kinship ties—those to relatives in preceding or following generations—have tended to grow. The result is a kinship structure with growing links up and down the generations and withering links across them (Bengtson, Rosenthal, & Burton, 1990). A number of gerontologists have argued that lowered mortality rates are making the four- and five-generation family (e.g., my grandparents, my parents, me, my children, and my grandchildren) common.[3] Yet although there are more of these linkages than there used to be, they are still the exception rather than the rule. A survey in the Boston area showed that at no stage of the adult life course up through age 70 did more than 20 percent of the respondents belong to more than a three-generation linkage of kin. And the number in five-generation linkages never topped 2 percent. At all ages, the most common generational depth was three. In young adulthood, the three generations were typically my grandparents, my parents, and me; in middle age the three were my parents, me, and my children; and at older ages they were me, my children, and my grandchildren.

The authors of the Boston study, Alice and Peter Rossi, conclude:

> *The truly remarkable demographic change over the twentieth century is the impact of increased longevity on the number of years when the majority of the population may still have at least one living parent* (Rossi & Rossi, 1990).

The watershed age, they argue, is 50. Prior to age 50, there is little drop-off in the percentage of adults who have at least one living parent; at about age 50 the percentage declines sharply. (And at about the same age, the percentage who have grandchildren increases sharply.) Thus, the lives of most parents and children now overlap by about 50 years. These long, potentially rich co-biographies are the product of lower mortality.

RISING STANDARD OF LIVING

Older people also have more money, on average, than they did a few decades ago. As recently as 1960, older Americans were an economically deprived group: 35 percent had incomes below the poverty line, compared with 22 percent of the total population. Now they have more than caught up: 9.7 percent were poor in 1999, compared with 11.8 percent of the total population (U.S. Bureau of the Census, 2000e). The main reason they are no longer disadvantaged is Social Security, the federal government program that provides retirement benefits to persons aged 62 and over. Beginning in the 1950s and 1960s, Congress expanded Social Security coverage, so that nearly all workers, except some who are employed by government, are now covered.[4] And since the 1960s, Congress has increased Social Security benefits far faster than the increase in the cost of living. As a result, the average monthly benefit has doubled in value since 1960, even after taking inflation into account (U.S. House of Representatives, 1993). Today's elderly benefited from the societywide rise in economic welfare in the 1950s and 1960s,

---

[3]See, for example, Shanas (1980).

[4]Persons between ages 62 and 65 are eligible for partial benefits if they retire; persons aged 65 and over are eligible for full benefits. However, the minimum age for full benefits will be raised gradually to 67 over the next two decades. See Clark (1990).

when they were working; then, as they reached retirement, they benefited from the increase in Social Security benefits.

Variations by Age, Race, and Sex   Still, there are sharp variations by age, race, and sex in the proportion of the elderly who are poor. Overall, older elderly persons are more likely to be poor than younger elderly persons, elderly women are more likely to be poor than elderly men, and African-American and Hispanic elderly persons are more likely to be poor than white elderly persons. For example, in 1997, 9.2 percent of persons aged 65 to 74 were poor, compared with 12.2 percent of those aged 75 and over (U.S. Bureau of the Census, 1999d). Only 6.9 percent of elderly men were poor, compared with 11.8 percent of women. And 9.0 percent of the white elderly were poor, compared with 26.0 percent of the black elderly and 24.4 percent of the Hispanic elderly (of any race) (U.S. Bureau of the Census, 1999d).

Moreover, a larger percentage of the elderly than of the nonelderly have incomes that place them just above the poverty level. In 1999, 13 percent of the elderly had incomes between 100 and 150 percent of the poverty level, compared with 12 percent of all persons under the age of 65 (U.S. Bureau of the Census, 2000e). This nearly poor group is in some ways more vulnerable to economic and health crises than the poor elderly. Economist Timothy Smeeding has named them the **'tweeners** because they fall between the poor, who can qualify for additional public assistance, and the middle class, who can supplement their Social Security checks with savings and pensions (Smeeding, 1990).[5] Although nearly all elderly persons are covered by **Medicare,** the government program of health insurance for the elderly, Medicare pays for less than half of the health expenditures of the elderly. Moreover, it pays nothing for nursing home care. Persons with incomes below the poverty line are also eligible for **Medicaid,** the government health insurance program for the poor of all ages, which does pay for nursing home costs. Middle-class elderly persons can afford to purchase private health insurance to pay the bills Medicare doesn't cover. But the 'tweeners typically have too much income for Medicaid and too little to buy private insurance.

It is also uncertain whether the Social Security and Medicare systems will provide the elderly of the future with the same level of benefits that today's elderly receive. Low birthrates today mean that there will be fewer workers in a decade or two to pay Social Security taxes for the growing number of elderly. In addition, the increases in the old-old and oldest-old may strain the already costly Medicare system. (See *Families and Public Policy:* Financing Social Security and Medicare, on pp. 362–363.)

Social Consequences   Nevertheless, because of the general rise in their standard of living, older parents and their adult children are less dependent on one another economically. Family life in the early decades of the twentieth century was precarious; lower wages, the absence of social welfare programs, and crises of unemployment, illness, and death forced people to rely on their kin for

'tweeners the group of elderly people who have incomes that place them between the poor, who can qualify for public assistance over and above Social Security, and the middle class, who can supplement their Social Security checks with savings and pensions

Medicare the government program of health insurance for all elderly people

Medicaid the government program of health insurance for people with incomes below the poverty line

---

[5]Smeeding defines the 'tweeners as elderly persons with incomes between 100 and 200 percent of the poverty line, but the precise cutoff is not important. By his definition, the 'tweeners constitute 20 percent of all elderly persons—and 40 percent of all elderly persons living alone.

support to a much greater extent than is true today. There were no such things as unemployment compensation, welfare checks, food stamps, Medicare, Social Security benefits, or government loans to students. Often there was only your family. Some older people provided assistance to their kin, such as finding a job for a relative, caring for the sick, or minding the grandchildren while the parents worked. Sometimes grandparents, their children, and their grandchildren pooled their resources into a common family fund so that all could subsist. Exactly how common these three-generational economic units were, we do not know; it would be a mistake to assume that all older adults cooperated with their children and grandchildren at all times. Still, historical accounts suggest that intensive intergenerational cooperation was more common than it is today because it was needed more.[6]

SEPARATE LIVING ARRANGEMENTS

The increased independence of the elderly is clearly shown in the great changes in their living arrangements over the past half century. Figure 11.2 on page 364 displays trends in living arrangements between 1940 and 1980 for persons aged 60 and over, and it also displays living arrangements in 1994 for persons aged 65 and over.[7] Living arrangements are grouped into four categories: (1) living alone, (2) living with their spouse, (3) living without a spouse but with other relatives, or (4) living with nonrelatives only. The upper panel is for women, the lower for men. Among women, there was a sharp increase in the percentage who were living alone—as you can see from the increasing size of the uppermost section of each bar, moving from left to right. Conversely, there was a sharp fall in the percentage who were living without a spouse but with other relatives (such as a daughter or son). By 1994 it was nearly as common for an elderly woman to live alone as to live with a husband.

This shift toward elderly women's living alone has occurred for two reasons. First, women have been outliving men by a greater and greater margin each decade, so that the number of elderly widows has grown much larger. About 7 in 10 wives survive their husbands (Treas & Bengtson, 1987), and few widows remarry because of the imbalance between the sexes. Second, an elderly widow today is much more likely to live alone than an elderly widow 40 or 50 years ago. In a Los Angeles survey, elderly persons were asked, "Would you prefer to live with your own children or in a separate residence?" Ninety-eight percent of the non-Hispanic whites, 83 percent of the blacks, and 72 percent of the Mexican Americans replied that they would prefer to live on their own.[8] The increases in the income of the elderly have allowed more of them to attain this desire. Overall, 1 of every 10 households in the United States in 1998 was maintained by an elderly person living alone (U.S. Bureau of the Census, 1998a). This represents an enormous change from midcentury, when such households were rare.

---

[6]See, for example, Anderson (1971); Hareven (1982).

[7]Figure 11.2 excludes elderly people who were living in nursing homes. Data for 1994 are taken from a published report from the Census Bureau's Current Population Survey, which presented information for people aged 65 and over (U.S Bureau of the Census, 1996b).

[8]The study was carried out by Vern Bengtson and collaborators and is cited in Treas and Bengtson (1987).

*T*he *Chicago Sun-Times* photograph published in newspapers around the country on August 19, 1989, was startling. A band of angry elderly persons, shouting and carrying placards, surrounded a car carrying their U.S. representative, Dan Rostenkowski, then the chairman of the House Ways and Means Committee. His offense had been to sponsor new legislation that *increased* the elderly's protection against long-term hospital stays by limiting the cost to individuals to a maximum of $1,370 per year (Soldo & Agree, 1988). Why were the protesters mad? Because the legislation required that the wealthiest 40 percent of the elderly pay for part of this new benefit through a surtax on their income tax liabilities. A leader of the protesters told a reporter that he did not believe that the elderly should have to pay anything for the new program ("House panel leader," 1989). Fed by questionable opposition from some advocacy groups for the elderly, the protests grew so strong that a stunned Congress repealed the legislation. The incident reinforced a stereotype—overdrawn, as most stereotypes are—of the elderly as demanding ever-greater retirement and medical benefits but refusing to contribute more to the costs of them.

That the benefits paid to the elderly have increased greatly is well known. Social Security benefits accounted for 23 percent of the federal budget in 1999—$116 billion more than all expenditures on national defense. Benefits under Medicare, the government health insurance program for the aged, constituted another 12 percent (U.S. Bureau of the Census, 1999d). The long-term worry is that, as the proportion of the population that is elderly increases, paying for the benefits will become a serious burden on the nonelderly, working-age population. The problem could become severe after 2010, when the large baby boom generation begins to retire.

There are actions that could ease this burden. Although the public pays more attention to the cost of Social Security than to the costs of Medicare, Social Security is actually in better shape. In 1983, Congress passed legislation that greatly strengthened the long-term financial status of the system. Among other things, the legislation increased the payroll taxes that workers and their employers pay into the government's Social Security trust fund. The legislation also raised the age at which people can retire and receive full benefits from 65 to 67 in 2027 (Soldo & Agree, 1988). (Although a two-year increase may seem modest, it will save money because 3 to 4 percent of 65-year-olds die within two years.) Due to the increased payroll taxes, the Social Security trust fund is collecting large surpluses that theoretically should be saved to pay for future costs. Unfortunately, politicians are finding it difficult to resist the temptation to use the surpluses to balance the federal budget today rather than to save it for the next century. Consequently, the surpluses may not provide as much help as they should.

Little has been done, however, to control the spiraling growth of Medicare payments. Three factors are contributing to the growth: the increase in the elderly population, the growing share of the elderly population that is in the old-old and oldest-old categories (and therefore at greatest risk of serious illness and disability), and the increasing cost of health care. According to one projection, Medicare expenditures will increase from about 2 percent of the gross national prod-

Gender Differences in Living Arrangements   Nevertheless, Figure 11.2 shows a very different pattern for elderly men than for elderly women. To be sure, the percentage living alone has increased, as indicated by the top section of the bars, but the increase has been modest. At all times since 1940, the vast majority of elderly men have been married and sharing a household with their wife. Moreover, the proportion who were married *increased* between 1940 and 1994—as you can see by the increasing size of the next-to-the-top section of each bar. This marriage bonanza for elderly men was the flip side of the spouse drought for elderly women. Men had a higher risk of dying than women, but if they managed to live longer than their wives, their remarriage prospects were better than were elderly women's. The current generation of elderly men has been cared for by women throughout their lives—by their mothers when they were growing up and by their wives (many of whom did not work outside the home after marriage) in middle age. They continue to be cared for by women in old age. Most elderly widows, on the other hand, must continue to care for themselves or to rely on relatives living mostly in other households. And so the older years have

uct (the value of all goods and services produced by the nation) in 1990 to between 4 and 8 percent of the gross national product by 2025 (Palmer, 1988). There are several options that could help contain the costs of health care. The government could raise the payroll tax that pays for Medicare, as has been done with the Social Security payroll tax. Workers see one combined deduction on their paychecks for Social Security and Medicare; given the recent increases in this deduction, there could be substantial opposition to further hikes. The government could also raise the age of eligibility for Medicare and instead cover the youngest elderly through a national health insurance program. Gerontologist Robert Binstock proposed in congressional testimony in 1992 that elderly people who are better off economically could be charged larger deductibles (the amount an individual must pay for a service before Medicare pays anything) or larger copayments (the percentage of the cost of a service that the individual, not Medicare, must pay after the deductible is met) (U.S. House of Representatives, 1994). Binstock and others note the wide range of incomes among the elderly and urge that those who are better off be required to pay more of the costs of their medical care. He argued that elderly voters are not more self-centered than any other group and that they would be willing to support "sensible policy changes." Some survey research supports his view: In a 1988 random sample of area residents of Albany, New York, the elderly were less likely to support spending on retirement pensions than were middle-aged Americans (Logan & Spitze, 1996). Yet the crowds around Dan Rostenkowski's car suggest how difficult it may be to pass any bill that increases costs for even the financially fortunate elderly.

Ask Yourself

1. Do you have elderly relatives who receive Medicare benefits? If so, how important is government health insurance to them? If the government did not offer Medicare benefits, would your relatives, or their children, be able to afford their medical care?

2. Should Medicare beneficiaries be charged according to their ability to pay? Explain your reasoning.

www.mhhe.com/cherlin

Elderly Americans, their numbers expanding, have become an important political interest group.

taken on an increasingly different character for women than for men—women more likely to be living apart from kin, men more likely to be living with their wives. (The rise in divorce in early and mid-adulthood has also separated the worlds of men and women; more on that in a few pages.)

Cultural Underpinnings   The notion that older parents should retain their independence is deeply rooted in the culture of the Western nations. Historical studies suggest that the preference for heading one's household until as late in life as possible has long been entrenched in Western Europe (Laslett & Wall, 1972). In many areas, the households were formed and maintained under the stem family system. [➡ p. 43] The father eventually gave ownership of the farm to the one son who remained home (and thus formed the "stem"); he then brought in a wife. Ordinarily, the son was not allowed to marry until he was given control of the property. But older parents were often in no hurry to turn over their house and land to their son and heir, as demonstrated by the

FIGURE 11.2

Living arrangements of women and men 60 years old and over in the United States, 1940 to 1980, and for women and men 65 years old and over, 1994. (*Source:* Sweet & Bumpass, 1987; U.S. Bureau of the Census, 1996b.)

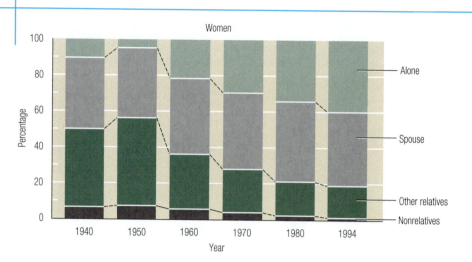

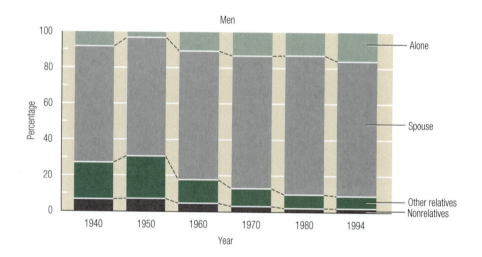

eighteenth-century Austrian folk song [➡ p. 247]: "Father, when ya gonna gimme the farm?" A U.S. historian has documented the reluctance of first-generation settlers in Andover, Massachusetts, to turn over control of their property to their sons. As in the Austrian case, the young men in Andover needed their own farmland in order to marry. The reluctance of fathers to part with their land sometimes meant that sons were forced to postpone marrying until relatively late ages (Greven, 1970).

Today, of course, most children do not wait to inherit their parents' land but rather leave home to work for wages. Consequently, older parents' households are usually devoid of adult children. Still, the preference for retaining an independent household is strong. Like our Baltimore informants, most elderly persons in the United States, Canada, and Western Europe want to see their children and grandchildren often but not to live with them. What they want, according to a famous phrase, is "intimacy at a distance" (Rosenmayr & Kockeis, 1965). This trade-off between intimacy and independence has probably reduced the amount of contact the elderly have with their kin. For example, three of five elderly persons in

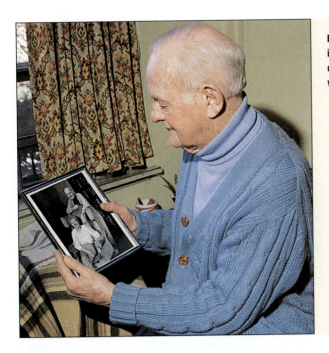

Elderly widowers often find it difficult to manage the daily household tasks their wives did.

the United States in 1900 were living with at least one (usually unmarried) child (Smith, 1979), and until recently few were living alone. But the preference that today's elderly express for living alone is genuine, and it is consistent with deeply held values of individualism in Western culture. It is not merely a rationale that the modern elderly have invented to mask disappointment at living apart from kin.

DYING AND DEATH

Changes in life expectancy and living arrangements have altered the ways in which families experience dying and death. The death of a child or a mother during childbirth is no longer common. Rather, grandparents usually die before their children and grandchildren. Although the death of a spouse is difficult for either partner, studies suggest that elderly men may have more difficulty adjusting to being widowed than elderly women (Quadagno, 1999). Elderly men, many of whom entered breadwinner-homemaker marriages in the 1950s and 1960s, typically have not done much cooking, cleaning, or other household tasks. On losing their wives, some of them find daily household management difficult. Elderly widows, in contrast, more often have financial problems. Because they tend to have less work experience, their Social Security checks are often smaller, and they may not ever have balanced the family checkbook or paid the bills.

Despite their financial problems, elderly women have better mental and physical health after widowhood than elderly men. One study found that on average, widowers were more depressed than widows following the loss of their spouses (Umberson, Wortman, & Kessler, 1992). Other studies have reported that men are more likely than women to die in the first few years after widowhood (Quadagno, 1999).

As we have noted, most adult children are in their fifties when they first experience the death of a parent. Even if their parents were no longer providing much assistance, losing them can still be emotionally difficult. In general, middle-aged adults who have lost a parent show greater psychological distress and poorer physical health than other adults in their age group. But not always: If the parent had mental health, alcohol, or other problems, their children's functioning may improve after their death (Umberson & Chen, 1994). An adult child's experience in losing a parent varies according to the parent-child relationship.

The Quality of Intergenerational Ties

Beyond these demographic developments, what can be said about the quality of the relationships between older people and their kin today? What does it mean that so many elderly women live alone and so few elderly persons of either sex live with their children? Are they lonely and isolated? Are they a part of their children's and grandchildren's lives? Do they provide much support to their kin and receive much in return? Sociologists studying these issues often define the subject as "intergenerational solidarity." The concept is a broad one, and, fittingly, *solidarity* is a word with many connotations. When asked, a word processor pops up the following synonyms: cooperation, fellowship, harmony, unity, stability, and reliability. An unabridged dictionary defines solidarity as "an entire union of interests and responsibilities in a group," and it quotes a phrase from Joseph Conrad: "Solidarity knits together innumerable hearts" (*Webster's Third New International Dictionary,* 1976). We might say, after Conrad, that **intergenerational solidarity** refers to the characteristics of family relationships that knit the generations together.

> **intergenerational solidarity** the characteristics of family relationships that knit the generations together

With respect to the older parents and their adult children, three broad characteristics of intergenerational solidarity have received the most attention from social scientists. They have been given slightly different names and definitions (Rossi & Rossi, 1990; Roberts, Richards, & Bengtson, 1991; Silverstein & Bengtson, 1997). Here are the names and definitions I will use:

- *Contact*   How frequently parents and children see each other and are in touch electronically through telephone calls or e-mail messages.
- *Affinity*   How emotionally close parents and children feel and how much they agree on values, attitudes, and beliefs.
- *Assistance*   The amount of assistance, in either time, goods, or money, that parents and children provide to each other.

Contact and affinity are relevant for judging whether the elderly obtain the closeness and emotional support they wish—and whether they provide closeness and emotional support to their children and grandchildren. These are the kinds of questions included in under the umbrella of the private family. [➡ p. 15] Assistance, on the other hand, is relevant to the kinds of questions that arise from the perspective of the public family [➡ p. 14]—specifically, who will care for the frail elderly and who will help young or middle-aged parents with problems such as amassing a downpayment for a house or coping with a divorce? Let us examine these three characteristics of intergenerational relations.

CONTACT

It might seem logical to infer that, in a society in which 1 in 10 households contains an elderly person living alone and in which few elderly persons live with their children, the elderly must be isolated from their children and grandchildren. Indeed, many observers have concluded as much. "Isolated" is a value-laden term, however, and what might seem like isolation to a Japanese grandparent [➡ pp. 378–379] might seem like a surfeit of contact to an American grandparent. Statistics cannot settle a matter such as this, but they can describe the patterns of contact between the elderly and their kin.

Among elderly persons in one national study who were living alone and who had living children, three-fourths lived within minutes of a child and two-thirds saw at least one of their children weekly (U.S. National Center for Health Statistics, 1986). In another national survey, about half of the elderly with children had seen at least one of them that day or the day before; four-fifths had seen a child in the last week (Shanas, 1980). Similarly, in our survey, we interviewed the grandparents of a national sample of children and asked them "When was the last time you saw any grandchild?" About half of the grandparents had seen at least one grandchild that day or the day before, and 70 percent had seen a grandchild within the last week. Just one in six had not seen a grandchild within the previous month (Cherlin & Furstenberg, 1992). Elderly persons living alone who don't have children (about 3 in 10), of course, have much less frequent contact with relatives. But overall, the amount of contact that the elderly have with their children and grandchildren is surprisingly high.

What affects the amount of contact? In our grandparent study, we found one dominant factor, so strong that it alone accounted for nearly two-thirds of the variance in contact among the families: distance (Cherlin & Furstenberg, 1992). Almost invariably, grandparents who lived near their grandchildren saw them regularly—no matter what their social class was or whether the grandparent was on the mother's or father's side. If the grandparents lived within a mile, they typically saw their grandchildren twice a week. If they lived 1 to 10 miles away, they typically visited about once a week; and at further distances the number of visits fell off rapidly.

Geographical Distance Between Generations   The dominance of

distance illustrates both the strength and the vulnerability of the grandparent–parent–grandchild relationship. As for its strength: When grandchildren live close by, grandparents see them regularly, except under unusual circumstances. Parents and children, with few exceptions, make sure they visit the grandparents. The pull grandparents exert when they live nearby shows how strong is the sense of obligation among adult children to keep in touch with their parents and their in-laws. This sense of obligation is usually overlaid with love, concern, and assistance, but even when it is unsupported by these props, it is often still honored. The uniformly high frequency of visiting among nearby kin suggests that the bond among grandparents, their adult children, and their grandchildren is still strong.

On the other hand, when adult children move away, grandparents' access to their grandchildren drops dramatically. To be sure, adult children who have weaker ties to their parents may be the ones who tend to move from their hometowns. Job possibilities, marriage, and many other events also enter into the decision to move. Still, from the grandparents' point of view, whether or not adult children live close by involves a large element of luck. When a son takes a job in another state or a daughter-in-law moves away after a divorce, the grandparent is rarely able to overcome this impediment to regular contact.

Mother–Daughter Relationships and Family Culture   In ad-

dition to living close by, the grandparents in our study saw their grandchildren more frequently if they had a close relationship with the mother of the grandchild—their daughter or daughter-in-law. Middle-aged women do the work of "kin keeping" more often than middle-aged men, and studies show that their ties with older and younger generations are stronger and more consistent, on average, than men's (Rossi & Rossi, 1990). [➡ p. 132] Finally, family culture—shared values and traditions—seems to influence contact. We found more contact among families that reported traditions of family songs, recipes, jokes, and so forth, and the Boston study reported that adults raised in more cohesive families established families in adulthood that also were more cohesive (Cherlin & Furstenberg, 1992; Rossi & Rossi, 1990).

AFFINITY

Hand in hand with the demographic and economic changes in the lives of the elderly have come great changes in the emotional content of their relationships with their children and grandchildren. During the twentieth century, there appears to have been an increasing emphasis on bonds of sentiment: love, affection, and companionship. There is no evidence that the emotional ties between parents and children have grown weaker. When Furstenberg and I asked grandparents whether grandparenthood had changed since they were grandchildren, we heard stories of their childhood that differed from the idyllic *Waltons* image. Their grandparents, we were told, were respected, admired figures who often assisted other family members. But again and again, we heard them talk about the emotional distance between themselves and their grandparents:

The only grandmother I remember is my father's mother, and she lived with us.

INTERVIEWER: What was it like, having your grandmother live with you?
Terrible [laughter]! She was old, she was strict. . . . We weren't allowed to sass her. I guess that was the whole trouble. No matter what she did to you, you had to take it. . . . She was good, though. . . . She used to do all the patching of the

The ties between grandparents and grandchildren are increasingly based on love and affection, rather than authority and discipline.

pants, and she was helpful. But, oh, she was strict. You weren't allowed to do anything, she'd tell on you right away.

INTERVIEWER: So what difference do you think there is between being a grandparent when you were a grandchild and being a grandparent now?
It's different. My grandma never gave us any love.

INTERVIEWER: No?
Nooo. My goodness, no, no. No, never took us anyplace, just sat there and yelled at you all the time.

INTERVIEWER: Did you have a lot of respect for your grandmother?
Oh, we had to whether we wanted to or not, we had to.

Grandma may have helped out, and she certainly was respected, even loved; but she was often an emotionally distant figure. This is not to say that affection was absent from the relations between young and old. But there has been a shift in the balance between respect and affection. For example, we asked grandparents who knew at least one of their own grandparents "Are you and [your grandchild] more friendly, less friendly, or about the same as your grandparents were with you?" Forty-eight percent said "more friendly"; only 9 percent said "less friendly." Similarly, 55 percent said their relationship with grandchildren was "closer" than their relationship had been with their grandparents; just 10 percent said "not as close."

Demographic and Economic Change
Granted, it is hard to judge the accuracy of these recollections of two generations ago. But the story that the grandparents consistently told us fits with the demographic and economic developments that have been discussed. It is easier for today's grandparents to have a pleasurable, emotion-laden relationship with their grandchildren because they are more likely to live long enough to develop the relationship; because they are not still busy raising their own children; because they can travel long distances more easily and communicate over the telephone; and because they have fewer grandchildren and more economic resources to devote to them. Earlier in the nation's history, the generations were often bound up in economic cooperation that took precedence over affection and companionship. In fact, there may be a trade-off between bonds of obligation and authority, on the one hand, and bonds of sentiment. Historian David Hackett Fischer, in his book on the history of aging in America, noted the following differences between the nation's early and later years:

> *Even as most (though not all) elderly people were apt to hold more power than they would possess in a later period, they were also apt to receive less affection, less love, less sympathy from those younger than themselves. The elderly were kept at an emotional distance by the young* (Fischer, 1978).

Conversely, in modern America:

> *As elders lost their authority within the society, they gained something in return. Within the sphere of an individual family, ties of affection may have grown stronger as ties of family obligation grew weak* (Fischer, 1978).

This increasing emphasis on affection appears to be continuing among the elderly and their children and grandchildren today. Nearly all studies report a high level of warmth and emotional closeness among the different generations in a family (Treas & Bengtson, 1987). Nevertheless, the degree of emotional closeness between parents and children varies over the life cycle. It will come as no surprise to parents that closeness and intimacy decline as children move into adolescence. That is the life stage when children must establish their autonomy. As the children reach adulthood, closeness improves again, and it improves further as the parents enter old age and their children enter middle age (Rossi & Rossi, 1990). Moreover, there appear to be substantial gender differences in closeness. The Boston study found that in mid and later life, mother–daughter relationships are the closest, mother–son relationships are second, father–daughter third, and father–son fourth. These differences suggest once again that it is women who invest more in family ties.

Shared Values   The second component of affinity is agreement between the generations on values, attitudes, and beliefs. Most studies show substantial agreement between older parents and their adult children. In a 1990 survey of 1,500 adults, individuals with living parents were asked how similar their opinions were to those of their mothers and fathers. Sixty-nine percent said that their opinions were "very similar" or "somewhat similar" to their mothers' opinions. Agreement with fathers was not quite as high: 60 percent said their opinions were "very similar" or "somewhat similar" (Silverstein & Bengtson, 1997). Substantial agreement between parents and children is to be expected for two reasons (Roberts et al., 1991). First, parents socialize their children in their own values while raising them—both at home and at the family's place of religious worship. Second, parents and children often share the same social class position and therefore have similar kinds of jobs and leisure activities. As noted in the previous chapter, a person's social class position can influence her or his opinions about independence, conformity, and other values.

Nevertheless, the experiences of parents and children do diverge in ways that can cause differences of opinions. Studies suggest that individuals' beliefs are affected by the social context during their adolescence and young adulthood and that these beliefs, once formed, tend to remain throughout adulthood. For example, growing up during an economic depression may make a person frugal for a lifetime. Consequently, if the social context in which children grow up differs from the context when their parents grew up, some differences in beliefs are likely. This process is called the **cohort replacement model** of public opinion because it presumes that each successive *birth cohort* [➡ p. 68] experiences a different social environment and retains distinctive opinions throughout adult life (Alwin, 1996).

cohort replacement model a model of changing public opinion in which each successive birth cohort experiences a different social environment and retains distinctive opinions throughout their adult life

ASSISTANCE

In middle and old age, as in childhood, most people in need of assistance turn to their kin. The majority of help that the elderly and their adult children receive comes from one another. And because of lengthening life expectancy, this stage of mutual assistance lasts longer than ever before. At current rates of fertility and mortality, according to one widely cited demographic estimate, the average person can expect his or her life to overlap slightly longer with a parent over the age of 65 than with children under the age of 18 (Watkins, Menken, & Bongaarts, 1987). Here again a striking demographic statistic found its way to the cover of *Newsweek,* which announced that "the average American woman spends 17 years raising children and 18 years helping aging parents" (*Newsweek,* 1990). But *Newsweek* didn't get it quite right: Yes, adult children will provide assistance during the years when they have aging parents, but most of them also will *receive* substantial help from their aging parents as well. Until their last years, most aging parents are relatively healthy and economically independent.

Mutual Assistance   In fact, until they are very old or very ill, the elderly typically give more assistance to their adult children than the children provide them (Soldo & Hill, 1993). Assistance is episodic rather than continual: Parents or children help out or give money when there is a particular need. For instance, grandparents spend much more time providing assistance to their adult children when their grandchildren are in their preschool years than when they are adolescents. Indeed, in 1995, grandparents were the primary source of childcare for 19 percent of preschool children whose mothers worked outside the home (U.S. Bureau of the Census, 2000g). As will be mentioned in Chapter 13, it is common for a divorced daughter to move back in with her parents temporarily after her marriage breaks up. Financial assistance also tends to occur in lump transfers rather than continual flows. Older parents might provide a child with a few thousand dollars toward the down payment on a home, or they might help a child pay for a grandchild's college tuition.

These patterns of giving assistance only when there are specific needs imply that, at any given time, most older parents and adult children are not providing much assistance to each other. In a national survey of adults with living parents, only 17 percent of the adults reported getting $200 or more from their parents, and only 4 percent reported giving $200 or more, within the previous five years—excluding help with mortgage payments. Childcare is more common: About 13 percent had received baby-sitting or childcare assistance from their parents in the previous month. Giving and getting advice and support are more common still: 27 percent had received, and 25 percent had given, advice or emotional support in the previous month (Eggebeen & Hogan, 1990).

African-American and Hispanic elderly persons, who tend to have lower incomes than whites, are more likely to reside with a relative (other than a spouse) than are whites, but among those who do not coreside, there is little difference in the amount of assistance. That is to say, black or Hispanic adults and their parents who live apart are not more likely to exchange goods and services than similar whites—despite what studies of low-income people's sharing networks might lead one to expect. The researchers who have uncovered this finding speculate that many elderly poor people are not enmeshed in effective sharing networks—or else that the poor have fewer resources to share today than when many of the observational studies of kinship networks were undertaken (Eggebeen & Hogan, 1990).[9]

The kind of assistance the two generations provide to each other is complementary. According to the Boston study, adult children tend to provide more personal support, such as comfort or care during an illness, whereas older parents tend to provide more material help: a loan, part of a down payment on a house, or help with finding a job (Rossi & Rossi, 1990). This pattern allows the older generation to maintain a sense of independence, so central to American values. In reality, however, adult children also provide substantial financial support to their parents—but in such a way that no one need notice. The hidden subsidy is Social Security, the role of which in raising the living standard of the elderly was discussed earlier. I pay thousands of dollars a year in Social Security taxes, and the program sends thousands of dollars a year to my elderly parents. Yet the genius of the system is that my parents and I don't have to acknowledge this connection; we can both maintain that, as good American parents and children should be, we are economically independent of each other.

[9]See also Hofferth (1984).

FIGURE 11.3
Relationship of informal caregivers to disabled elderly recipients of care. (*Source:* U.S. Senate, Special Committee on Aging, 1988.)

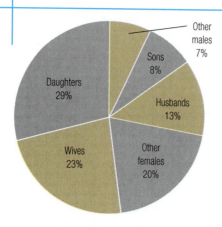

FIGURE 11.3
Relationship of informal caregivers to disabled elderly recipients of care. (*Source:* U.S. Senate, Special Committee on Aging, 1988.)

Care of the Disabled   *Newsweek* was right, nevertheless, in using the word *woman* instead of *adult* to describe the caregiver. For here again, women are the kin keepers, providing most of the care for elderly husbands and parents. Figure 11.3 shows the relationship of the persons providing "informal"—that is, unpaid—care to disabled elderly persons in 1982; 72 percent of them were women, most often daughters or wives. Moreover, there is a rough hierarchy of caregivers. If the elderly person's spouse is alive and reasonably healthy, she or he will normally become the primary caregiver; if the spouse is not alive, an adult daughter is usually next in line; and if there is no daughter who can manage the care, another relative, such as a son or a sister, may be called upon (Gatz, Bengtson, & Blum, 1990). Since a majority of elderly women survive their husbands, this hierarchy means, in practice, that elderly women are likely to be cared for eventually by their daughters. For an unmarried elderly person, having a daughter is the key to receiving support. In a 1984 national health survey, elderly respondents were asked if they needed help with any of 13 activities of daily living and home management. If they answered affirmatively, they were asked whether or not they received help from one of their children. Among those who were unmarried and not living with a child, persons who had at least one daughter were more likely to receive help than those who had just a son or even two sons (Spitze & Logan, 1990b).

These mostly female caregivers not only assist their relatives but also perform a critical public service. Without the care that they provide, our already expensive government health care programs would be much more costly. Since Medicare does not pay for nursing home care, individuals must pay nursing home costs by spending their own money first. Only when individuals have spent most of their savings—and therefore meet the government requirements for being poor—are they eligible for Medicaid, which will then step in and pay the bills. Typically, persons of modest means who enter nursing homes—the costs of which average more than $40,000 per year—"spend down" their assets in several months and then turn to Medicaid (Palmer, 1988).[10] Public spending for nursing home care totaled about $51 billion in 1997. Individuals in care spend another $30 billion out of their own pockets (U.S. Bureau of the Census, 1999d).

---

[10]In 1995, nursing home care for 1.55 million residents cost $75.5 billion, an average of $48,700 per resident (author's calculation from U.S. Bureau of the Census, 1999d).

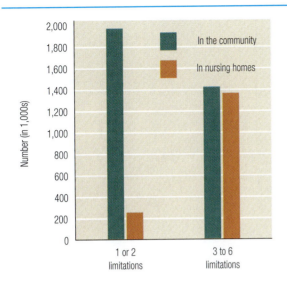

FIGURE 11.4
Elderly persons in the community and in nursing homes, by number of limitations in activities of daily living. (*Source:* National Aging Information Center, 1996.)

Four percent of the elderly in the United States resided in nursing homes in 1995 (U.S. National Center for Health Statistics, 1997c). It is not hard to grasp the implications of the growth of the elderly population for the future demand for nursing home care. As was noted in the discussion of Figure 11.1, the oldest-old, those aged 85 and over, are the fastest-growing segment. Their numbers virtually doubled from 2.2 million in 1980 to 4.3 million in 2000, and are still increasing rapidly (U.S. Bureau of the Census, 2000d). Perhaps 40 percent of them, at current rates, will reside in a nursing home at some point during their last years (Soldo & Agree, 1988). From the public standpoint, it is crucial to hold down the number of persons who will need institutionalized care. That is precisely what family members do now.

You might think that most seriously impaired elderly persons are cared for in nursing homes, but that is not so. More are living in the community (that is, in private homes or apartments, not in institutions) than in nursing homes. Figure 11.4 illustrates this fact. In order to measure physical impairment, gerontologists have developed standard questions about the activities a person needs help with. The most common set, **activities of daily living,** or ADLs, refers to personal care, including bathing, dressing, eating, getting into and out of bed, walking indoors, and using the toilet (U.S. National Center for Health Statistics, 1987). These questions have been asked of national samples of elderly persons both in the community and in nursing homes (National Aging Information Center, 1996), allowing us to make a comparison of their degrees of impairment. Figure 11.4 compares the number of elderly persons in nursing homes with the number of elderly persons in the community who had at least one ADL limitation that lasted for six months or more in 1989. Both populations are divided into two groups: those with one or two limitations in ADLs and those with three to six. The graph then shows:

- Among those with one or two ADL limitations, far more were living in the community than in nursing homes in 1989.
- Even among the most seriously impaired elderly—those with three to six limitations—slightly more were living in the community than in nursing homes in 1989.

activities of daily living (ADLs) personal care activities, including bathing, dressing, getting into and out of bed, walking indoors, and using the toilet

Adult daughters and other female relatives provide much of the care for the frail elderly.

Women in the Middle?   About four-fifths of the care of the disabled elderly who are living in the community is provided by relatives, most of them women.[11] If these caregivers went on strike tomorrow, nursing homes would be flooded with new patients and Medicaid would pay out billions more. For instance, let us return to Figure 11.4 and suppose that most of the caregivers of the 850,000 non-institutionalized persons with five or six limitations in ADLs quit. If, say, 500,000 of these elderly persons were forced to enter nursing homes, the bill, at about $40,000 per person, would be $20 billion per year. Of course, it is absurd to imagine that so many caretakers would quit because most are relatives who love the persons they care for and feel a sense of obligation to help. There is reason, nonetheless, to be concerned about the future availability of caregivers. The informal care system has depended on the availability and goodwill of middle-aged women. A few decades ago, most married women were not employed outside the home; presumably, they had more time to devote to caring for an aging parent. But a majority of married women now work outside the home, and the proportion will likely increase further in the next decade or two. Sons and daughters who are employed full-time give less help to, and receive less help from, their parents (Rossi & Rossi, 1990). In addition, the fall in birthrates since the 1950s means that there are proportionally fewer adult daughters per elderly parent.

Moreover, some of these caregivers may also face requests for help from their own children. A daughter, for example, might separate from her husband and wish to return to the parents' home temporarily with the grandchildren. Or the woman herself, having postponed childbearing until her thirties, might still be raising children. The specter of double demands up and down the generational ladder has led to much concern about the caregiving burden for "women in the

[11]U.S. Senate, Special Committee on Aging (1988).

middle" (Brody, 1981). Although concern may be warranted, few women, and fewer men, are faced with demands for care from children and parents at the same time. Most older people do not need extensive care until late in life; by that time their children are usually through raising the grandchildren. So, for a middle-aged adult, the peak years for the care of young children typically occur before the peak years of the care of older parents (Uhlenberg, 1993).

For example, a survey in the Albany-Schenectady-Troy, New York, metropolitan area found that women and men in the middle were most commonly in their early forties; even so, just 17 percent of women and 14 percent of men were spending three or more hours per week caring for children as well as three or more hours per week caring for parents. An even smaller percentage of men and women in their fifties and sixties was caring for older and younger kin (Spitze & Logan, 1990a). Being caught in the middle, then, is a brief period for most caregivers. Some people will experience it in early middle age, when they are still raising children and their parents are still alive. A few may experience it later in middle age, when divorce or unemployment produces a crisis for their adult children.

It would seem obvious that being caught in the middle would be highly stressful, as the caregiver seeks to fulfill what is expected of her as wife, employee, mother, and daughter. Some studies have indeed found a high stress level among such caregivers (Brody, Kleban, Johnson, Hoffman, & Schoonover, 1987). But it may also be the case that having a job takes a person's mind off her caregiving responsibilities, making it easier to provide care. Some recent studies have noted this "buffering" effect of one role on the stress provoked by another. One study found that caregivers with multiple roles—spouse, employee—experienced less stress than those mainly engaged in providing assistance (Stoller & Pugliesi, 1989).[12] The stress felt by caregivers in the middle may stem only from the care they give to frail parents, not from an overload of responsibilities. If they are employed, their jobs may provide them with a sense of fulfillment and excitement rather than strain (Epstein, 1988). This is not to minimize the difficulty of caring for an ailing parent, nor to diminish the social importance of care that adult children provide. If multiple roles do produce strain for women, who provide much of the care, one solution would be for men to assume more of the responsibility.

THE VARIABILITY OF INTERGENERATIONAL TIES

Not all families, of course, have strong intergenerational ties. Silverstein and Bengtson (1997) examined the variation in solidarity reported by adult children in a 1990 national survey. Adult daughters and their mothers were more likely to have high levels of all indicators of solidarity—contact, affinity, and assistance—than were daughters and fathers or than sons and either fathers or mothers. This finding confirms once again the central role of the mother–daughter bond in intergenerational relations. At the other extreme, adult children in the study reported low levels of all indicators of solidarity when their parents were divorced. The lack of solidarity was particularly strong between adult children and their divorced older fathers.

---

[12]See also the discussion in Spitze and Logan (1990a).

The Effects of Divorce and Remarriage

     Other studies also show that older divorced fathers and their children, on average, have relationships that are far less close than the relationships of fathers and children from families with no divorce. In the National Survey of Families and Households, conducted in 1987 and 1988, adults were asked who, among persons not living with them, they would turn to for assistance in three situations: an emergency in the middle of the night, the need to borrow $200 for a few weeks, and the need to talk to someone about a problem. Two researchers tabulated the answers given by men aged 50 to 79 who had living adult children. About half of all the men who had been divorced did not even mention a child as someone they would turn to in any of the three situations. In contrast, less than one-fourth of never-divorced men failed to mention a child. Moreover, only 50 percent of the divorced fathers had weekly contact with their children, compared with 90 percent of never-divorced men (Cooney & Uhlenberg, 1990). Another study using the same survey found that adult children from divorced families rated the quality of their relationship with noncustodial fathers no more positively than adult children who had never lived with their fathers since birth (Aquilino, 1994). Yet another study found that if the custodial parent had remarried, thus providing the children with a stepparent, relations between adult children and the noncustodial parents were weakened further (Lye, Klepinger, Hyle, & Nelson, 1992).

     The same survey indicated that adult stepchildren saw their stepfathers less often than adult biological children saw their fathers and that adult stepchildren rated the quality of their relationship with their stepfather lower. Moreover, if the marriage between the natural parent and the stepparent had ended, either because of a divorce or because the natural parent had died, the ties between an adult stepchild and stepparent often ended as well: 57 percent of the adult stepchildren in stepfamilies ended by divorce never saw their stepparent, and 46 percent of adult stepchildren in stepfamilies ended by death never saw their stepparent (White, 1994). Thus, the relationship between adult stepchildren and stepparents, which in any case seems less close than between adult biological children and parents, may not even survive a divorce or death. Consequently, some elderly stepparents may not receive as much support from their stepchildren as they may need.

Implications for the Future

     It seems doubtful, then, that the daughters and sons who provide so much of the care for the frail elderly will provide as much care for noncustodial fathers, never-married fathers, or stepfathers as for biological fathers they lived with continuously while growing up. As Chapter 13 will note, the divorce rate doubled in the 1960s and 1970s, and the proportion of children born outside marriage rose during (and after) those decades as well. The men who reach the age of 65 after the year 2000 will be part of the first generation to have lived most of their adult lives after the great increases in divorce and childbearing outside marriage. Many fathers have little contact with their children after a divorce or a separation from the children's mother.

     Elderly men will have to rely even more heavily on their main source of support today: their current wives. It is possible, however, that this strategy won't work as well in the future either. The women who will be reaching old age will belong to the first generation to have extensive employment histories throughout adulthood. They may have more financial resources when they retire, and some may keep working at least part-time after reaching age 65. Frances Goldscheider speculates that fewer widowed and divorced women may find it attractive to remarry an elderly man: They will have less need for financial support, and they may prefer other activities to caregiving. If divorced men aren't remarried in old age, and if they can't rely on their children, they may have no one to help them in their last, frail years. In fact, the percentage of elderly men who live with their wives, after increasing from 1940 to 1980 (see Figure 11.2), has now leveled off.[13] Research on divorce, Goldscheider writes, "has focused on women and children as the 'victims'" because of the loss of the father's income. Yet in old age, when kinship ties matter, "it is males who are at risk" (Goldscheider, 1990).

Elderly gay men and lesbians may also face challenges in obtaining support in old age. Their ability to call on others for assistance will depend on how well they have been able to construct a network of friends, partners, and biological relatives. The effectiveness of these networks is likely to vary widely. In addition, many of their ties are likely to be with people in the same generation; consequently, their access to younger adults who could provide help may be limited (Kimmel, 1992).

But Are They Really Happy?

I have on several occasions given lectures about the American family to audiences of Asians, who are used to a family system in which elderly parents are expected to live with their adult children. (See *Families in Other Cultures:* The Elderly and Their Families in Japan.) Some members of the audience are surprised and dismayed to learn that most older persons in the United States, and throughout the Western nations, live apart from their children. Hands go up and I am politely asked how Americans could do such a cruel thing to their parents. I then explain, as I have in this chapter, that the vast majority of older persons in the United States prefer it that way. Hands go up again, and it becomes clear that many in the audience don't believe it.

Here in the United States, as well, some observers don't believe that the elderly really are happier living apart from their children. The skeptics acknowledge that the elderly say they prefer to live apart but question whether deep down this preference is real. Hasn't there been a loss in family feeling, the skeptics ask, since the time when most elderly were living with their children? Haven't modern grandparents, in their rush to retirement villages in the Sun Belt, abandoned their bonds to their grandchildren?[14] In endorsing their independence from their busy, self-absorbed children, aren't they making a virtue out of necessity?

There is a grain of truth to these charges. There probably has been some weakening of the bonds among the generations as the elderly and their children have established separate residences. But the multigenerational households of the past were held together in part by economic hardship. Older parents and their adult children had to cooperate in order to make ends meet. As they worked for the common good, no doubt strong bonds of obligation and loyalty and trust developed. Given the chance to live separately, however, most older parents and

---

[13]For a comparison of 1980 and 1990, see U.S. Bureau of the Census (1991d).

[14]See for example, Kornhaber and Woodward (1981).

The Elderly and Their Families in Japan

In North America and Western Europe, people are used to a family system in which most of the elderly live apart from kin. The family system in Japan, until recently at least, could hardly have been more different. In the traditional Japanese household, all children except the eldest son left home when they reached adulthood. Until their deaths, the parents lived with the eldest son and his wife in the household. Japanese culture emphasized the importance of filial piety—obeying and serving one's parents throughout one's life. As recently as 1970, 77 percent of the elderly in Japan lived with their children.

But this system is being tested by the most rapid aging of any population in the world and by Japan's continuing economic development. By world demographic standards, the Japanese birthrate plummeted overnight. As recently as 1947, the average Japanese woman bore 4.5 children; 10 years later, the average was down to 2.0. And since World War II, life expectancy in Japan has risen to the highest level in the world (Preston & Kono, 1988). This sharp fall in births and sharp increase in longevity has quickly given Japan one of the highest proportions of elderly persons of any country. And, as is well known, the Japanese economy has grown by leaps and bounds over the past few decades.

Under these changed circumstances, the proportion of the elderly who live with their children has declined. Between 1980 and 1990, for example, the proportion living with a married child decreased from 53 to 42 percent (Morioka, 1996). Although a majority of Japanese still tell pollsters that they believe it is good, in the abstract, for children to take care of their elderly parents, fewer are counting on it. For example, the proportion of married women under the age of 50 who say they plan to depend on their children in old age dropped from 65 percent in 1950 to just 18 percent in 1990 (Ogawa & Retherford, 1993). Japanese demographers are now predicting that by 2010 a majority of the widowed elderly will be living alone (Hirosima, 1997).

And many three-generation households are now formed because of a specific condition rather than because of a general commitment to filial piety. Japanese sociologists are reporting an emerging pattern of "eventual coresidence," in which the older parents live separately as long as their health allows them to; only after frailty or illness sets in do they coreside with a child (Oda, 1991). Moreover, some urban young adults are finding that coresidence with parents is economically advantageous given the very high cost of housing in metropolitan areas. Grandmothers can also provide childcare for the growing (although still modest) number of mothers employed outside the home. So the old family forms are being retained for some new reasons.

In fact, the commitment to filial piety appears to be eroding rapidly. The figure shows the responses, in surveys from 1963 to 1990, of married women under age 50 to the question "What is your opinion about children caring for their elderly parents?" As can be seen, the percentage responding that it is either "unavoidable" or "not a good custom" increased sharply from 12 percent in 1963 to 34 percent in 1990, whereas over the same period the percentage responding that it is either "a good custom" or "a natural duty" declined from 80 percent to 50 percent. Most of the change occurred in the 1980s. Japanese women have moved toward the view, which predominates in the Western nations, that assistance to the elderly is something to be given for specific needs rather than out of a general sense of obligation.

Moreover, the proportion of Japanese elderly who are being cared for in institutions is not as different from that in the United States as one might expect. As noted earlier in the chapter, about 4 percent of the elderly in the United States reside in nursing homes. In Japan, the figure is about 2 percent. But the average length of a hospital stay for elderly Japanese is much higher than in the United States; these long stays have been labeled "social hospitalization." On any given day, 2.6 percent of elderly Japanese are in a hospital, compared with just 0.8 percent in the United States; some of the long stays in Japan may be a culturally acceptable alternative to nursing home care.[1]

The family lives of the Japanese elderly, then, are a mixture of persistence and change. Many—although no longer a majority—live with their children, sometimes with a younger son or even a daughter. General support for the cultural ideal of coresidence is still widespread. In a 1986 comparative survey, 58 percent of the elderly in Japan said it was better to live with their children than merely to meet to eat and talk, whereas in the United States only 3 percent of the elderly thought it was better to live with their children (Martin, 1989). Nevertheless, the proportion of the Japanese elderly living apart from their children has been growing, and younger parents' confidence that their children eventually will support them has been slipping. To an increasing degree, coresidence is a response to an expensive housing market, a lack of available childcare services, or an illness, rather than to the norm that parents ought to live with their children whatever the circumstances. If the housing market improves or childcare becomes more widely available, coresidence could decrease further. I think it likely that the family lives of the elderly in Japan will continue to evolve toward greater independence from their children, although older parents will probably remain more dependent on their children than in the West.

Ask Yourself

1. Do any of your elderly relatives live with their children? If so, do they do so by choice or necessity?

2. Compare and contrast relations between parents and children in Japan and the United States. Which are more significant, the similarities or the differences in intergenerational relations?

[1]The figures for Japan are from Martin (1989). I calculated the 0.8 percent figure for the United States from data in U.S. Bureau of the Census (1991e).

www.mhhe.com/cherlin

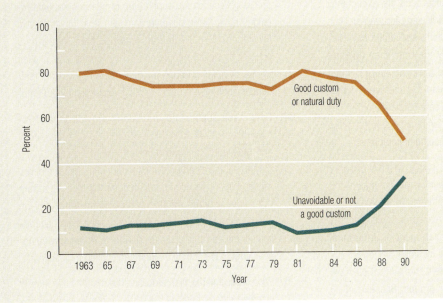

Responses of married women under 50 in Japan to the question, "What is your opinion about children caring for their elderly parents?" Orange line: percent responding either "a good custom" or a "natural duty." Green line: percent responding either "unavoidable" or "not a good custom." (*Source:* Ogawa & Retherford, 1993.)

adult children have chosen to do so. In addition, despite the growth of retirement communities in the South, there's little evidence that the elderly, as a group, live farther from their adult children than they used to (Uhlenberg, 1993).

When we asked the Baltimore grandparents why they wouldn't trade places with the Russian immigrants in order to have strong ties to their children and grandchildren, one grandmother said, simply, "It's too late." What she meant was that, given the opportunity for independence, most American grandparents had already seized it and couldn't give it up. To live with their children, they would have to adjust their daily schedules to fit their children's busy lives. It's easy to look at current living arrangements and criticize the elderly for emphasizing autonomy and personal satisfaction in their daily lives. But they are merely engulfed in the same flood of self-fulfillment that has washed over their children and grandchildren. To ask grandparents to lead a retreat to a family system that emphasizes cooperation over companionship, obligations over independence, duty over love, is perhaps unfair. This is the first generation in which most older Americans have had a choice in these matters; should they be criticized for making the same choices as everyone else?

Looking Back

1. **How has grandparenthood changed over the past century?** Today most adults live long enough to get to know their grandchildren because adult life expectancy has lengthened substantially, particularly for women. And because birth rates are lower, and most adults have finished raising their children by the time they become grandparents, grandparenthood is now a more distinct stage of life. Declining births mean that the average person has fewer links to kin in the same generation; but because of declining mortality the average person has more links to kin in preceding or succeeding generations.

2. **How has the standard of living of the elderly changed?** Over the past half-century the incomes of the elderly have risen dramatically, thanks to the expansion of the Social Security rolls, increases in Social Security benefits, and the growth of private pension programs. Still, many elderly persons have incomes just above the poverty line, and elderly women and minorities have higher poverty rates than other groups. Because of an improved standard of living and a preference for independent living, the number of elderly persons living alone has risen sharply—especially among women, who tend to survive longer than their husbands.

3. **Are the elderly isolated from their kin?** The elderly value both their independence and contact with their kin. Most have frequent contact with at least one child, especially with those who live nearby. There is a greater emphasis on affection and companionship, and a lesser emphasis on economic cooperation, in intergenerational relations now. Some observers suggest that the quality of intergenerational relations has declined, but others counter that older people and their children have chosen a style of relating to one another—that is, separate residences and fairly frequent contact—that suits them both.

4. **How much support do the elderly provide to, and receive from, their kin?** Most of the help that the elderly and their adult children receive is mutual. Except when they are ill, the elderly provide more help than they receive. Among those who need care, most elderly men get it from their wives, while most elderly women must rely on daughters and other relatives. Older men who have divorced and had little contact with their children may be unable, later in life, to rely on their adult children for support.

5. **Who cares for the frail elderly?** The majority of seriously disabled elderly persons are cared for in their homes by family members, rather than in a hospital or nursing home. The most common family caregiver other than a spouse is an adult daughter. In the future, fewer adult daughters may be available as caregivers, both because more of them will be employed and because the elderly will have fewer adult children. Whether family members will continue to provide as much care as they do now is unclear.

Thinking about Families

1. How valuable have your relationships with your grandparents been to you?

2. How different must family life have been a century ago, when death rates were higher for both adults and children?

3. Why are the lives of elderly women typically so different from the lives of elderly men?

4. **The Private Family** Should we be surprised that American grandparents want to live near their grandchildren, but not with them?

5. **The Public Family** Together, the federal and state governments spend twice as much money on Social Security and Medicare as the federal government spends on the entire defense budget. Is government spending too much money on the elderly?

Key Terms

activities of daily living (ADL) 373
cohort replacement model 370
elderly population 358
fertility 358
gerontologist 358
intergenerational solidarity 366
Medicaid 360
Medicare 360
mortality 356
old-old 358
oldest-old 358
'tweener 360
young-old 358

Families on the Internet   www.mhhe.com/cherlin

*Note: While all the URLs listed were current as of the printing of this book, these sites often change. Please check our web site (**http://www.mhhe.com/cherlin**) for updates.*

The Ameristat web site, (**www. ameristat.org**), offers a number of interesting charts and graphs about the elderly population in the United States. Most of the data can be downloaded in tabular form. Click on "older population" to answer the following questions. What happens to the marriage gap between elderly women and men as they age? What percentage of the elderly population has health insurance coverage? Which states have the largest percentage of older people? How are the social characteristics of the elderly likely to change in the near future?

The U.S. Bureau of the Census (**www.census. gov**) maintains a number of publications about the elderly that can be downloaded to a personal computer. In early 2001, they included a wall chart, "Aging in the Americas into the XXI Century." Click on the letter "O" in the subject index, and then on "older (55+) population data." How does population aging differ in Latin American countries and the United States?

Part Five

Conflict, Disruption, and Reconstitution

Conflict between women and men has a public significance beyond the immediate family context. It spans both the private family, where it affects the quality of emotional support, intimacy, and cooperation, and the public family, where its social consequences are played out on a larger scale. Conflict between spouses can also lead to separation, divorce, and remarriage. • Chapter 12 considers violence between spouses and partners and by parents against children. After a brief review of the history of domestic violence, the chapter summarizes current knowledge. The most important theories of domestic violence are presented, followed by an examination of sexual aggression and violence in dating relationships and a discussion of public policies. • Marital conflict, these days, often leads to divorce. About one of every two marriages in the United States, at current rates, would end in divorce. Chapter 13 probes the causes and consequences of this high level of marital dissolution. It examines the process that divorcing couples experience and the consequences for both children and adults. • A majority of divorced persons remarry. Yet remarriage, as Chapter 14 shows, can bring difficulties for adults and children. The chapter describes the new kinds of family relationships and kinship networks that form after remarriages. Then it discusses why children whose parents are remarried seem to fare no better than children in single-parent families.

chapter **12**

Domestic Violence

Looking Forward

1. When did domestic violence become a social issue?

2. What is the extent of violence against women by intimate partners?

3. What is the extent of child abuse?

4. What do we know about sexual aggression by dates or acquaintances?

5. Why does domestic violence occur?

6. What are the public policy debates concerning domestic violence?

In 1996, the body of 4-year-old Nadine Lockwood was found in her mother's apartment in New York City. She had been starved to death. Prior to her death, a police detective and a city caseworker, acting on tips that the child was being abused, had separately visited the home. Neither found any evidence of abuse. Consequently, the case was closed, even though Nadine's mother had been known to the city's child protective agency since 1989, when her first child was born addicted to cocaine, and then two years later, when Nadine was born addicted to cocaine. Nadine's death—and the death in 1995 of six-year-old Elizabeth Izquierdo, who was beaten to death by her mother after several visits by caseworkers—led to demands that child protective service workers be more aggressive in removing children from potentially abusive parents ("Starving a Child to Death," 1996). Yet removing children from their homes has its own risks, as when children separated from their families drift through the foster care system.

The problem is that the public hears about child abuse or marital violence mainly through sensational cases, such as Nadine's and Elizabeth's deaths or O. J. Simpson's trial for the murder of his former wife. A few decades ago, even social scientists ignored **domestic violence,** which will be defined in this chapter as violent acts between family members or between women and men in intimate or dating relationships. Not a single article on the topic appeared in *Journal of Marriage and the Family,* the major scholarly journal in the field, between its founding in 1939 and 1969 (O'Brien, 1971). Now, however, hardly an issue appears without one. In fact, the increase in research has been so sudden and so massive that it requires an explanation. It wasn't spurred by an increase in domestic violence, because there isn't much evidence of an increase, at least until recently, as will be noted later. Rather, its rise reflects the increased political power of the feminist movement, which views domestic violence as an important barrier to women's equality, and the increasing cultural emphasis on individualism in marriage and family life. To appreciate what has occurred, it is necessary first to examine the history of domestic violence as a social problem.

domestic violence
violent acts between family members or between women and men in intimate or dating relationships

Domestic Violence in Historical Perspective

The recent attention to highly publicized cases of child abuse and wife battering is not the first outpouring of public concern about domestic violence. Rather, the history of domestic violence in the United States shows short periods of public attention separated by longer periods of neglect. The periods of attention have had less to do with the prevalence of violence than with the power of various political and social groups (Pleck, 1987).

EARLY HISTORY

In the New England colonies, the Puritans believed that it was the responsibility of the government to enforce moral behavior, even if that meant intervening in the affairs of the family. And moral behavior excluded violent acts by husbands against their wives. The well-known minister Cotton Mather told his congregants that for "a man to Beat his Wife was as bad as any Sacriledge. Any such a Rascal were better buried alive, than show his Head among his Neighbours any more" (Pleck, 1987). Friends, neighbors, and fellow churchgoers watched over a family's conduct in ways we would view today as nosy, if not meddlesome. In 1641, the Massachusetts Bay Colony enacted the first law against wife beating in the Western world, according to historian Elizabeth Pleck; it also prohibited parents from exercising "any unnatural severitie" with their children (Pleck, 1987).

How strictly this law was enforced, however, is unclear because the number of persons actually charged with wife beating was small. The Puritans must have felt the tension between respecting the integrity of the family and intervening to protect women and children from abuse. After the Puritans, government officials in most eras were even more reluctant to intervene. Indeed, the history of the

"Spare the rod and spoil the child. —P. 121.

Ichabod Crane flogs a disobedient student in a late-nineteenth century edition of *The Legend of Sleepy Hollow*. Corporal punishment in schools was acceptable until the twentieth century.

issue of domestic violence is, in large part, a story of conflict between the goals of preserving the family unit and of protecting women and children. When intervention was seen as shoring up the family (as among the Puritans), it received broader support; when it was perceived as undermining men's authority and contributing to divorce, it received less.[1]

A peak of concern occurred in the late 1800s, when the child protection movement arose. In 1874 the first society for the prevention of cruelty to children was founded; 40 years later there were 494 of them. Pleck argues that the growth of these societies, usually started by leaders of the local social elite, reflected a desire to control the behavior of the unruly, growing immigrant and working-class populations. In addition, I think, the growth came at a time when attitudes toward children were evolving from seeing them as economic assets to seeing them as emotionally rewarding beings to be nurtured (Zelizer, 1985). Still, leaders of the movement were careful to reassure parents that their authority to discipline their children, even by occasional physical punishment, was not in question. The founder of the New York Society for the Prevention of Cruelty to Children assured nervous supporters that he favored "a good wholesome flogging for disobedient children," although he wished to protect children from "undue parental severity" (Pleck, 1987). And the few organizations that sought to help battered wives had to fight suspicion that they were encouraging the breakup of the family.

THE TWENTIETH CENTURY

The Political Model of Domestic Violence   During the twentieth century, two ways of thinking about domestic violence have emerged. The first is what might be called the *political model* of domestic violence—political not in the sense of Democrats and Republicans but rather in the sense of the relations of power and authority between men and women. Historian Linda Gordon has argued that domestic violence has been a politically constructed problem in two senses:

> *First, the very definition of what constitutes unacceptable domestic violence, and appropriate responses to it, developed and then varied according to political moods and the force of certain political movements. Second, violence among family members . . . usually arises out of power struggles in which individuals are contesting real resources and benefits. These contests arise not only from personal aspirations but also from changing social norms and conditions* (Gordon, 1988).

The struggles are usually about men's power to control the behavior of women. Resorting to force is a way for a husband to compel his wife to behave as the husband wishes. Traditionally, social structure has supported men's control over women through law and social custom. Laws that allowed husbands to use physical force against their wives are an example: The term "rule of thumb," for instance, comes from a rule in old English law that a husband was allowed to hit his wife with a stick no thicker than his thumb (Gelles & Cornell, 1990). The political model implies that domestic violence is deeply rooted in laws and customs that reinforce male dominance and is unlikely to be ended without political action by women's groups and their allies.

---

[1]This paragraph, and the next several, draw heavily from Pleck (1987).

The Medical Model of Domestic Violence The second way of thinking is the *medical model,* under which domestic violence is seen as an illness and a source of injuries. In contrast to the political model, the main concern is not with relations of power but rather with illness and well-being. Health and social welfare professionals who have campaigned against child abuse, for example, have focused attention on the physical and mental harm that children suffer from physical and sexual violence. Some have argued that both the victims and the perpetrators of violence suffer from various "syndromes," illnesslike complexes of symptoms, injuries, and attitudes, that need to be treated. The professionals point to links between being violent and such personal problems as a history of abuse as a child, alcoholism, or mental illness. The medical model therefore conceives of the problem as though it can be solved by the intervention of health and social welfare professionals, much as they might attack schizophrenia or tuberculosis.

The first two decades of the twentieth century were a time when domestic relations courts, which treated family disputes more as social welfare cases than as criminal cases, were established throughout the states. But the issue of domestic violence was relatively quiescent until 1962, when pediatrician C. Henry Kempe and his colleagues, troubled by X-ray pictures of broken bones in children and reports of maltreatment, published an article entitled "The Battered Child Syndrome" (Kempe, Silverman, Steele, Droegemuller, & Silver, 1962). Kempe and his colleagues brought the medical model of domestic violence to the public's attention. In their view, child abuse was centered on a "syndrome" of repeated violence and inadequate parenting. This perspective created sympathetic concern not only for the blameless victims but also for the abusers, who seemed to be fighting a mental illness that needed treatment. In these ways the "syndrome" attracted broad public interest; within five years, every state had enacted laws that required medical personnel to report suspected cases of child abuse.

Still, there was little attention paid to wife beating until the mid-1970s, when feminist groups succeeded in making violence against women into a political problem. A decade earlier, the feminist movement had undergone a major revival, boosted by the parallel growth of the civil rights movement and the anti–Vietnam War movement. Some feminist groups focused on combating rape. Part of their strategy was the formation of services for rape victims, such as hot lines, crisis centers, and legal support. The issue of rape led organizers to the issue of sexual and physical violence directed toward married women. The movement's fundamental goal was not to treat the injuries of the victims or ease the personal problems of the perpetrators—valuable as those steps might be—but rather to remove the social supports for male violence, such as a reluctance to prosecute alleged offenders. Consequently, activists worked for changes in the law, funds for crisis centers and shelters for battered women, and the rejection of social norms that tolerated violence directed at women. With feminist influence at a high point in the 1970s, political pressure for action grew. By the end of the 1970s, nearly every state had enacted laws to protect women from violence through a mixture of support services, requirements that physicians report suspected cases, and tougher criminal procedures.

The increased emphasis on individualism in family life in the 1960s and 1970s—part of the growing focus on the private family—also helped the victims of domestic violence (Carp, 1991). The individualistic ethic justified efforts to support battered wives who wanted to end their marriages and to support the removal of children from abusive parents. It undermined the legitimacy of allowing husbands to control their wives' behaviors by the use of force. Nevertheless, the tension between preserving two-parent families and helping victims of abuse soon reemerged. In 1980, liberals in Congress proposed legislation to provide support services for victims of domestic violence. Conservatives argued that the bill would wrongly commit the federal government to intervene in private, family matters, and they maintained that its remedies, by assisting women who wanted to leave their husbands, would hasten the breakdown of the two-parent family. Despite this opposition, supporters of the bill were able to secure modest funding in compromise legislation. Meanwhile, President Reagan closed the newly founded Federal Office of Domestic Violence. The debate over how the government should help spouses and children cope with domestic violence continues to this day; I will return to it at the end of the chapter.

What Do We Know?

In this mixture of concern, apathy, and debate, one important question often gets lost: How much domestic violence is there? We know little about how much violence there was in the past. The official records of court proceedings can tell us only about the rare instances when abuse came to the attention of the legal system. Consequently, it's impossible to know whether domestic violence has increased, decreased, fluctuated, or stayed the same over the past few hundred years—or even over the past 50 years. In the 1980s and 1990s, however, a series of national surveys gathered information about violence between adults in intimate partnerships and also about child abuse. The results of these surveys can help us to determine the scope of the problem.

WHAT CONSTITUTES DOMESTIC VIOLENCE?

But first we must have a set of criteria about exactly what acts constitute domestic violence. Unfortunately, there is little consensus about those criteria among either the public or academic researchers. Consequently, it's not possible to state a single, precise definition. It's not even clear how to define the term *domestic*. Most early studies of adult domestic violence focused on married and cohabiting couples, but many recent studies have focused on the broader concept of "intimate partners," or boyfriends and girlfriends.

From the perspective of the medical model, the main criterion that defines domestic violence is injury, in the case of physical abuse, and sexual penetration, in the case of sexual abuse. Domestic violence, according to this viewpoint, is relatively clear-cut: It is synonymous with the broken bones in Dr. Kempe's X-rays or the cuts and bruises a woman displays as she enters a hospital emergency room. From a political perspective, however, violence can be defined more broadly as including minor injuries or even the threat of serious injury. That is to say, a slap in the face may not injure a woman, but she may see it as a threat that harsher blows will follow if she does not accommodate her husband's or partner's wishes. Even a verbal threat of physical harm may make her submit to an unwelcome demand or an unwanted sexual advance. Under this broader definition domestic violence could include not just serious injuries but also attempts to coerce women through minor violence such as slapping or through the threat of injury.

It also could include stalking—repeatedly following or spying on someone in a way that frightens the victim—even if actual violence does not occur. Critics of this kind of definition would suggest that it confuses serious harm with much less serious consequences and makes the problem so broad as to be unmeasurable. Supporters of this definition would suggest that the narrow medical model misses the point, which is to work toward ending men's domination over women through the use or threat of superior physical force.

INTIMATE PARTNER VIOLENCE

Rather than defining intimate partner violence, most surveys of adult domestic violence ask about a range of assaults from not-so-serious (pushing or shoving) to very serious (threatening with a gun). Survey researchers then publish a list of the percentage of respondents who report experiencing each type. In an article on surveys conducted in 1975 and 1985, the authors focused on what they called "serious violence" such as kicking, hitting with a fist or an object, beating up, or threatening or using a knife or gun (Straus & Gelles, 1986). They reported that severe violence by husbands toward their wives declined over the period from 4 to 3 percent of couples. Yet the number of serious incidents was so small that it is hard to judge whether the decline was real. In any case, the surveys do not support the idea of a growing "epidemic" of severe violence. Most likely, what has changed over time is not the prevalence of intimate partner violence but the amount of attention we have paid to it. (See *How Do Sociologists Know What They Know?* Advocates and Estimates: How Large [or Small] Are Social Problems?)

Prevalence The best estimate of current prevalence comes from a survey of 8,000 women and 8,000 men conducted between November 1995 and May 1996 by the National Institute of Justice and the Centers for Disease Control and Prevention. In the National Violence Against Women Survey, adult respondents were asked whether they had been victims of various types of physical assault or stalking by "intimate partners," defined as current or former spouses, cohabiting partners, and boyfriends or girlfriends. Figure 12.1 displays the women's responses to the physical assault questions. The top bar shows that 22 percent of the women reported having been victimized by physical assault of any kind at the hands of intimate partners. The other bars show that the most common types of physical violence were the less serious ones: being pushed, grabbed, or shoved, slapped or hit. (Women could answer positively to more than one type.) Smaller but still disturbing numbers of women reported more serious assaults. For example, 9 percent of female respondents had been beaten up, and 4 percent had been threatened with a gun.

Overall, women reported substantially higher rates of intimate partner violence than men; Figure 12.2 shows this gender difference. Only about 7 percent of men reported a physical assault of any kind by an intimate partner (compared to 22 percent for women); and less than 1 percent report ever having been raped or stalked. In contrast, 8 percent of women reported an actual or attempted rape by an intimate partner, and 5 percent reported a stalking. The gender difference even carried over into same-sex couples. Men who had lived with male partners were more likely to have experienced violence than men who had lived only with women, while women who had lived with female partners were less likely to have experienced violence than were women who had lived only with men

Advocates and Estimates: How Large (or Small) Are Social Problems?

In February of 1997, the U.S. Department of Justice released studies showing that (1) the number of rapes reported to police had dropped in 1995 to the lowest rate per person in a decade; and (2) the number of people who said they were raped or sexually assaulted in the annual National Crime Victimization Survey had dropped by 44 percent from 1993 to 1995 (Butterfield, 1997). This was good news—except to some advocates for victims of rape and sexual abuse. Professor Mary Koss told the *New York Times* that reports showing a decrease in rape "upset me because it lessens the sympathy for rape victims" and makes them even less likely to come forward (Butterfield, 1997, p. A1). She disputed the new figures: "The Justice Department looks at the incidence of rape year by year, but

many mental health experts believe it is common sense to look at prevalence, over a lifetime," as if this criticism somehow meant that a sharp decrease in the annual rate was meaningless.

Professor Koss was acting no differently than many advocates for (and against) social causes when they describe the scope of the problem they care about. As a general rule, advocates for social causes tend to use the broadest definition of the problem, whereas opponents tend to use the narrowest. Consider homelessness. [➡ p. 118] In the 1980s, advocates for the homeless repeated an estimate by activist Mitch Snyder that two to three million people were homeless. When government officials or academic researchers produced far lower estimates, they were sharply criticized. Then Snyder was asked

about the basis of his estimate in a television interview, and he replied:

> *Everybody demanded it. Everybody said we want a number . . . We got on the phone, we made a lot of calls, we talked to a lot of people, and we said, "Okay, here are some numbers." They have no meaning, no value* (Jencks, 1994, p. 2).

Nor is the tendency to define the magnitude of a problem in a way that's consistent with one's view of the problem limited to liberals and feminists. In 1995, three conservatives published an analysis of welfare benefits in every state. Welfare benefits, they argued, were so generous that they destroyed the incentive to work; therefore, welfare benefits should be sharply limited (Tanner, Moore, & Hartman,

FIGURE 12.1

Percentage of women who reported having been physically assaulted by an intimate partner, by type of assault. (*Source:* U.S. National Institute of Justice, 1998.)

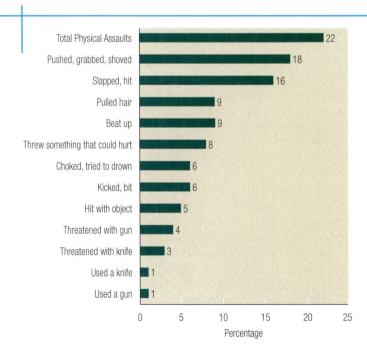

1995). The benefit levels they reported were startlingly high. For example, in Maryland, the "full package" of welfare benefits was equivalent to $22,000 per year—so high that a worker would have to earn $11.00 per hour to match them. But the "full package" included $5,864 of housing assistance, even though only one-fourth of welfare recipients in Maryland received such assistance; $1,028 for the value of the food given to pregnant and nursing mothers and their young children under another program that most recipients don't receive; and other such benefits. When the package was restricted to Aid to Families with Dependent Children, food stamps, and Medicaid, it was reduced to $12,124.

This is not to say that any of the advocates described here are distorting the data or lying. There is more than one way of defining most social problems. It is probably true, for example, that rape and sexual assaults are still underreported in government surveys, as advocates would claim. So the problem is larger than official statistics show. It is difficult to find all of the homeless, who hide themselves in the abandoned buildings and alleyways of low-income neighborhoods. And housing assistance is worth money to those welfare recipients fortunate enough to receive it. So just focusing on cash benefits to the poor is too restrictive.

My point is only that, as a consumer of social statistics, you should always ask yourself what the biases are of the people who are presenting you with the numbers. If they have a strong stake in convincing you that the problem is large in scope, they will probably choose an expansive definition of it. If they want to convince you the problem is not serious, they'll usually choose a much narrower definition. Evaluate not only their numbers but also their social and political arguments with this tendency in mind.

Ask Yourself

1. In doing student research or observing local politics, have you noticed dramatic differences in the statistics people quote to support their positions? If so, give an example. Did you understand the reason for the discrepancy?

2. What other reasons besides bias might help to explain conflicting statistics on social problems?

www.mhhe.com/cherlin

(U.S. National Institute of Justice, 2000a). All in all, the survey suggested that men are much more likely than women to perpetrate violence on their partners.

Responses to the National Crime Victimization Survey of 1999 also suggest that women are victimized by domestic violence far more often than men (U.S. Bureau of Justice Statistics, 2000a). The survey asked a national sample of adults whether they had been the victims of rape, robbery, or assault and, further, whether the perpetrator had been an intimate partner (spouse, ex-spouse, boyfriend, girlfriend). Women reported that 20 percent of the rapes, robberies, and assaults they had experienced were committed by an intimate partner, whereas among men, intimates had committed just 3 percent. Moreover, women who had been victimized by intimates were more likely to have been injured than were men who were victimized. For instance, 10 percent of women who had been victimized by intimate partners reported receiving medical or hospital care, compared with 5 percent of men (U.S. Bureau of Justice Statistics, 2000b). The statistics paint a picture in which women face a higher risk of being injured by someone they know well than men.

As Figure 12.2 showed, almost 8 percent of women in the National Violence Against Women Survey reported being raped or experiencing an attempted rape by an intimate partner. Only 18 percent of them, however, reported the incident to the police. Attention to rape by intimates—especially by husbands—is fairly new. Until recently, laws against rape have specifically excluded sexual relations

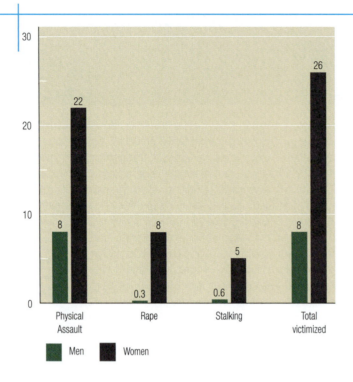

between husband and wife; in the 1980s, several states even broadened that exclusion to cover cohabiting couples (Frieze & Brown, 1989). The long-accepted legal principle is that by marrying, wives give their consent to sexual intercourse, so their husbands may demand it by force if necessary.

Some advocates of family privacy and the traditional authority of the husband still agree with that position. But as attitudes toward physical violence in marriage have changed, forced sexual acts among married couples have come into question. In fact, the typical partner rape does not take place in a happy home, in which an otherwise nonviolent man forces his partner to have sex. Rather, it appears to take place in a troubled, violent home. Thirty-six percent of the women who reported being raped by an intimate in the 1995–1996 National Violence Against Women Survey also reported being injured in the most recent rape. Although most of the injuries were minor, one out of six injured women reported lacerations or knife wounds.

Marital Status   Some intimate partnerships are more likely to lead to violence than are others. A few older studies suggested that married couples had lower rates of domestic violence than cohabiting couples (Stets & Straus, 1989). The 1995–1996 survey confirmed that difference: Married women had a 57 percent lower risk of experiencing violence than women who were cohabiting (U.S. National Institute of Justice, 2000). The lower risk for married women could be a selection effect [➡ p. 223], because women may refuse to marry men who seem violent. Alternatively, becoming a husband could make some men curb their violent tendencies.

Social Class   Although domestic violence affects all social classes, several studies report substantially higher rates of domestic violence among low-income

Domestic violence may not have increased, but the attention society pays to it has.

couples than among higher-income couples.[2] Part of this difference, however, may reflect a greater reluctance of middle-class individuals to admit to violence or a greater vigilance toward poor families by social welfare agencies. Still, it appears that there is at least a modest association between lower social status and violence against spouses and partners (Stark & Flitcraft, 1988). There are theoretical reasons to expect this association: More than three decades ago, William Goode suggested that men with more income and education have additional resources besides force that they can use to control the behavior of their wives (Goode, 1971). This relationship between social class and violence against wives also holds in developing countries: A Bangkok, Thailand, survey found that men with more income, education, and prestigious occupations were less likely to have hit, slapped, or kicked their wives (Hoffman, Demo, & Edwards, 1994). In addition, the frustrations of poverty and unemployment create stress that may lead some men to beat their wives. Studies show that unemployed men have rates of assault on their wives that are nearly double the rates for men who are employed (Gelles & Cornell, 1990).

CHILD ABUSE

Hitting children is the most tolerated form of family violence. Indeed, the vast majority of parents have spanked or slapped their children (Steinmetz, 1987). Although

[2]For a summary, see Stark and Flitcraft (1988).

Although there is widespread support for parents' right to spank or slap children, most people probably view beating or punching as child abuse.

it is difficult to make historical comparisons, the use of physical force against children may have been more prevalent in colonial times than ever since. The Puritans believed children were born tainted with sin, and expressed their diabolical nature through stubbornness, willfulness, and disobedience. Consequently, good parents had a moral duty to defeat such expressions of sin. When two- and three-year-olds first began to act contrary, the task of the father was to "break the child's will" and instill obedience through stern discipline. Even a century ago, physical force was probably more common than it is now. No one today could imagine the head of a children's welfare organization announcing his support for flogging.

Even if we grant parents the right to spank or slap, at some point physical force shades into physical abuse. As with violence between spouses and partners, there is no single definition of exactly what constitutes **child abuse.** The definition that earns the greatest consensus among child welfare professionals is serious physical harm (trauma, sexual abuse with injury, or willful malnutrition) with intent to injure—although it is difficult to determine whether there has been intent to injure (Starr, 1988). There is less consensus about other possible forms of abuse, many of which adults would find disturbing, such as sexual abuse without injury or various forms of neglect (e.g., leaving young children home by themselves all day). The 1985 national survey of married or cohabiting adults with children found that 2 percent had kicked, bitten, punched, or beaten up their children during the previous year. (This percentage excludes parents who had hit their children with an object such as a stick or a belt.) I think that most people would view repeated kicking, punching, and beating as child abuse (Straus & Gelles, 1986).

child abuse serious physical harm (trauma, sexual abuse with injury, or willful malnutrition) of a child by an adult, with intent to injure

Prevalence   Further information comes from several national surveys of child welfare professionals. In 1980, 1986, and 1993, the National Incidence

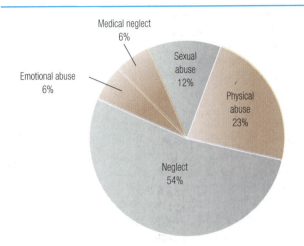

Emotional abuse
6%

Medical neglect
6%

Sexual
abuse
12%

Physical
abuse
23%

Neglect
54%

FIGURE 12.3
Substantiated cases of child abuse and neglect, 1998. (*Source:* U.S. Department of Health and Human Services, 2000.)

Study of Child Abuse and Neglect (NIS) interviewed a broad range of professionals who serve children; they were asked whether they had seen children who appeared to be abused or neglected (Westat, Inc., 1981; Sedlak, 1991; Sedlak & Broadhurst, 1996). In a separate 1998 study, child protection officials in each state were asked about the numbers and characteristics of cases of child abuse and neglect that had been reported to them. Although all of these surveys miss children who were not seen by professionals or reported to state agencies, they still provide some of the best recent information. Figure 12.3 shows the percentage of substantiated cases (i.e., verified as accurate by state or local agencies) in 1998 that fell into each of five categories, according to the reports of the state child protection officials.

More than half the reports were of parental neglect rather than abuse. The NIS surveys of professionals found that more than half of the neglect cases referred to educational neglect, which typically means that the children weren't attending school regularly and that their parents were not making much effort to have them attend. The remainder of the cases of neglect referred to physical neglect, which usually means that children were left unattended or poorly supervised by their parents. Note that about one-third of all cases referred to physical or sexual abuse, the kinds of child-related domestic violence that are of greatest public concern.

The surveys also suggest that child abuse was not equally likely in all families. Rather, it was more likely to occur in low-income families, in single-parent families, and in families in which the husband did not have a full-time job (Sedlak & Broadhurst, 1996; Steinmetz, 1987). The 1993 NIS found that, compared with children in families with incomes of $30,000 or more per year, children in families with incomes below $15,000 were 22 times as likely to experience some form of maltreatment (Sedlack & Broadhurst, 1996). To be sure, some of this social class difference could merely reflect a greater tendency of doctors, nurses, social workers, and neighbors to report poor families for suspicion of neglect or abuse (Hampton & Newberger, 1985). Even so, a review article concludes, "Child abuse *is* class related" (Starr, 1988).

As was the case with spouse abuse, there is good theoretical reason to think that the hardships of poverty might lead distressed parents to have less patience with their children or at least to be more neglectful. In fact, neglect appears to be more closely associated with poverty than does abuse: Low-income families were nine times more likely to have been involved in educational or physical neglect than other families, according to the professionals' reports, compared with three to five times more likely to have been involved in physical or sexual abuse (Besharov & Laumann, 2001). It is poor families that are more often forced to leave a child unattended while adults work or who have little faith in the present system of education and therefore don't make sure their children attend school.

Sexual Abuse and Its Consequences
The state child protection officials' reports indicate a low prevalence of child sexual abuse, but social surveys find a higher rate. In the 1992 survey of sexual activity, the adult subjects were asked, "Before you [reached puberty] did anyone touch you sexually?" (Laumann et al., 1994). Seventeen percent of the women and 12 percent of the men said yes. Among the women, nearly all the touching had been done by men (63 percent) or adolescent boys (28 percent) rather than by women. Men, however, were most likely to report touching by adolescent girls (45 percent), followed by men (23 percent) and adolescent boys (15 percent). Nearly all the incidents for both sexes had involved touching genitals, with a minority reporting vaginal, oral, or anal sex.

The interviewers also asked who did the touching (Laumann et al., 1994). Among women, the most common responses were an older relative (29 percent) or a family friend (29 percent); even more men named a family friend (40 percent). As for cases of sexual abuse that would fit the usual legal definition of **incest**—sexual relations between a child and her or his parent, brother, or sister—16 percent of women who had been touched named a father or brother. Thus, our best estimate is that, overall, about 3 percent of adult American women (that is, 16 percent of the 17 percent who reported touching by anyone) had experienced incest as children. As for abuse at preschools or schools, only 3 percent of the women who were touched and 4 percent of the men reported that a teacher had done the touching. Despite attention in the media to alleged incidents of sexual abuse of children in day care centers, less than 1 percent of all substantiated cases of child abuse in 1992 occurred in day care or foster-care settings (McCurdy & Daro, 1994).

Studies also suggest that women who are abused sexually before puberty have earlier and riskier sexual careers. Women in the 1992 survey who reported that when they were children they were sexually abused by a person at least four years older than they were were more likely to have first intercourse before age 16, to have 11 or more sexual partners as adults, to acquire a sexually transmitted infection in their lifetime, and to report a later experience of forced sex (Browning & Laumann, 1997). A survey of over 10,000 adolescent girls in a midwestern state found that girls who had been sexually abused had twice as many sexual partners during the past year than did girls who had never been abused (Luster & Small, 1997). Christopher Browning and Edward Laumann argue that sexually abused girls absorb a model of sexual relationships, a "sexual script" (Gagnon & Simon, 1973), on which future sexual relationships may be based; lacking alternative models, they may be "eroticized" to be more receptive to early sex and may associate sex with power inequalities or social isolation. "Adult-child sexual contact, for women," the authors write, "seems to provide access to sexuality without cultivating the emotional and cognitive skills to manage sexual experiences" (Browning & Laumann, 1997, p. 557).

Rising Abuse or Rising Reports?
In 1998, according to the state child protection officials, 2.8 million reports of suspected cases of child abuse

incest sexual relations with one's child, brother, or sister

and neglect were made to state or local government officials (U.S. Department of Health and Human Services, 2000). This compares with slightly over one million reports in 1980 and about 150,000 reports in 1963 (Besharov & Laumann, 2001). No one, however, believes that there is 19 times as much child abuse and neglect now as in 1963. In fact, it's not clear whether there has been any increase. The state laws passed after the Kempe article was published clearly increased the number of cases of suspected abuse that doctors and nurses reported to government authorities. In the 1980s, the expansion of reporting requirements to include other professionals such as teachers, as well as a general rise in public consciousness about child abuse, resulted in further increases in the number of reported cases. People seem to be increasingly likely to report a family to the authorities if they suspect maltreatment. Of the 2.8 million cases that were reported in 1998, enough evidence existed to substantiate only about 800,000 (U.S. Department of Health and Human Services, 2000). (States now investigate each reported case to see whether there is evidence of maltreatment.) Even the latter figure includes repeat reports on the same child; when repeats are eliminated, about 640,000 substantiated reports remain.

Still, there may have been an increase in child abuse and neglect in the late 1980s and early 1990s, followed by a leveling off in the mid-1990s. The 1993 NIS survey reported a 42 percent increase in the number of physically abused children and an 83 percent increase in sexually abused children since the 1986 NIS (Sedlak & Broadhurst, 1996). An increase of this magnitude between 1986 and 1993 would be significant and troubling—if it really reflected more abuse. But experts caution that it is impossible to tell whether this is the case (Donnelly, 1994; Besharov & Dembosky, 1996). Between 1986 and 1993, reporting systems continued to broaden in many states. It is possible that the increase occurred solely because professionals were looking ever more closely at children for signs of abuse and were more likely to file reports. Nevertheless, the period from the mid-1980s to the early 1990s was one in which the percentage of children living in poverty rose. [➡ p. 339] It could be that an increase in abuse and neglect also occurred.

Poverty or Abuse?   Not surprisingly, studies show that children who are physically or sexually abused often experience greater emotional problems, including depression, aggression, low self-esteem, troubled relationships with peers, and many others. Not all abused children, of course, show all—or even any—of these problems. Furthermore, it is unclear what proportion of the problems these children display are the result of their abuse, as opposed to other difficulties (Emery, 1989). Many abused children, for example, grow up in families that are troubled by poverty and unemployment. Consequently, some of the problems that abused children show would probably have occurred even if they hadn't been abused. In fact, Douglas Besharov, the first director of the National Center on Child Abuse and Neglect, argues that child protective workers sometimes overreact to families in which the real problem is poverty, not maltreatment. When they remove a child from his or her parents in cases of neglect without physical or sexual abuse, Besharov maintains, workers often make his or her problems worse. Such children are usually sent into the foster-care system, which has its own problems and is not a clear improvement over living at home. (See *Families and Public Policy:* Foster Care, on pp. 402–403.) Besharov and Lisa Laumann advocate, instead, that more social services be focused on assisting the parents of these children (Besharov & Laumann, 2001).

Physical or sexual abuse of children can lead to emotional problems such as depression.

Is there a "cycle of abuse," in which adults who were abused as children are more likely to abuse their own children? One review of the literature estimated that about 30 percent of persons who were abused as children become abusers when they reach adulthood, compared with about 5 percent among persons who were not abused. Those who were abused as children but managed to avoid repeating the behavior were more openly angry about the abuse, were more likely to have been abused by just one parent, and were more likely to have had a supportive relationship with the nonabusing parent (Kaufman & Zigler, 1987). If this estimate is accurate, two conclusions can be drawn: (1) Adults who were abused as children are indeed more likely to become abusers; but (2) most adults who were abused as children do not become abusers. The effect of abuse on children is to raise the risk of undesirable consequences, including becoming an abuser, yet many children do not experience these consequences.[3]

ELDER ABUSE

elder abuse physical abuse of an elderly person by a nonelderly person

Another kind of domestic violence that has drawn public attention is **elder abuse.** It is, however, a problem without a clear definition. One definition, which reflects the emphases in public discussions, is physical abuse of elderly persons by nonelderly persons—typically their children or other caretakers in their children's generation. Yet a large, random-sample survey on the topic found that the most frequent abusers of the elderly were their spouses. In this study of 2,020 elderly persons in the Boston area, 2 percent reported that they had been

---

[3]The literature on domestic violence (e.g., Gelles & Cornell, 1990) also discusses so-called "hidden" victims, such as parents, siblings, and elders. Yet, by definition, it is difficult to accurately estimate how many such people are victimized.

the victims of physical abuse at least once since they had reached age 65. In three-fifths of these cases, the abuser had been the elderly person's spouse (Pillemer & Finkelhor, 1988). Although spouse abuse is as regrettable among the elderly as among the nonelderly, there's no need to characterize the elderly version as a separate problem. To be sure, a small number of elderly persons are assaulted by their children or other younger adults. The victims of this kind of abuse tend to be mentally or physically impaired persons who are dependent on their caretakers (Gelles & Cornell, 1990). Although public programs to reduce such assaults may be worthwhile, there is no convincing evidence that such assaults are as common as assaults against spouses or children. In the Boston-area survey, only nine elderly persons, or less than 0.5 percent, said a son or daughter had ever abused them physically.

Sexual Aggression and Violence in Dating Relationships

Partner, child, and elder abuse are not the only aspects of violence between men and women that have received attention of late. As courtship and dating have changed, so have attitudes toward the use of coercion to obtain sexual intercourse. During the 1980s, researchers and clinicians introduced the study of sexual aggression by men against women whom they were dating and against acquaintances. Studies of physical assaults by acquaintances also became more common.

SEXUAL AGGRESSION

There are at least two reasons for the lack of attention to this problem before 1980. First, the rates of sexual activity among unmarried young persons were substantially lower prior to the 1970s; consequently, the incidence of acquaintance rape was probably lower also (although there are no satisfactory data). Second, young women tended to be blamed for their dates' improper sexual advances. [➡ p. 251] As the practice of blaming the victim began to weaken and as rates of sexual activity increased, researchers brought forth study after study showing significant amounts of sexual coercion, including forcible rapes that were rarely reported to the police.

Prevalence   Yet adequate national data on the prevalence of sexual aggression among acquaintances still do not exist. Twenty-two percent of all adult women in a 1992 University of Chicago survey of sexual activity said they had been forced to have sex by a man at least once in their lives (Laumann et al., 1994). Acquaintances (defined as "someone you knew but not well" or "someone you had just met") were named in 19 percent of the incidents of forced sex reported by these women. Overall, then, we can estimate that 4 percent of all adult American women (that is, 19 percent of the 22 percent who reported forced sex by anyone) have experienced forced sex by an acquaintance. Most other studies of sexual aggression by acquaintances have focused on college students. For example, in the spring semester of 1997, interviewers contacted by telephone a random sample of 4,446 women in two- and four-year colleges (U.S. National Institute of Justice, 2000b). They asked detailed screening questions about types of sexual victimization the women might have experienced in the seven months, on

*F*oster care—the removal of children from their parental home and their placement in another home—is a program with few admirers and many critics. Like abortion policy, foster-care policy involves a difficult choice between two worthy goals, in this case protecting the integrity of the family unit and protecting children from physical and mental harm. In most circumstances, the children are removed without their parents' permission after a child protective worker investigates a report of abuse or neglect. Consequently, foster care embodies the most severe form of state interference between parents and children—seizing the children against the parents' will. Because child protective workers tend to be middle-class and the affected children tend to be poor, it is sometimes criticized as a class-based intrusion into family life (Liss, 1987). Because it substitutes state-directed care for parental care, it is sometimes criticized as antifamily (Berger, 1986). Because it fails to return many children to their families in a timely manner, it is criticized for warehousing children from problem families, rather than helping the parents provide better care (Steiner, 1981). Yet few would disagree that children should be protected from some parents—the drug-addicted, the physically or sexually abusive, for instance—who are not fit to raise them.

In the late 1970s, when about 500,000 children were living in foster care, a policy consensus formed: Alarmed by the numbers of children in care, both conservatives and liberals agreed that child protective workers should place a higher priority on helping troubled parents keep their children and care better for them. If a foster-care placement was needed, greater efforts should be made to return the children to a permanent home—either by sending them back to their parents or, if absolutely necessary, by putting them up for adoption. Congress codified this consensus in the Adoption Assistance and Child Welfare Act of 1980.[1]

The new consensus worked as intended for several years. The number of children in foster care declined to about 275,000 in 1983 through 1985 (*The Crisis in Foster Care,* 1990). Then, suddenly, it rose sharply to 340,000 in 1988 and to 442,000 in 1992 (Toshio, 1993).[2] By 1999, it was back over the 500,000 mark (U.S. House of Representatives, 2000). The new law, it appears, was overwhelmed by a huge, unexpected wave of children at risk of harm. The wave was greatest in large cities such as New York and Chicago, and the largest percentage increases in foster care occurred among newborns and infants, many of whom were low-birthweight or otherwise impaired babies born to mothers who had had little or no prenatal care (Wulczyn & Goerge, 1992).

Many observers speculated that at least some of this rise was the result of the rapid spread of crack cocaine usage during the same period (U.S. House of Representatives, 1993). Women in poor neighborhoods used crack more than they had used earlier addictive drugs such as heroin. The legacy of crack appears to include much larger numbers of babies born with drug-induced impairments or abandoned at birth in hospitals. It is unlikely, however, that crack is the whole story. A rise in homelessness among families also occurred during the late 1980s and early 1990s. Consequently, some parents were not able to provide basic shelter and security to their children, and child protective workers are more likely to remove a child from a homeless family than from one in a home (Rossi, 1994; Jencks, 1994).[3]

Coupled with the rise in reported cases of child abuse, the surge in abandoned and

foster care the removal of children from their parental home and their placement in another home

average, "since school began in fall, 1996." As Figure 12.4 shows, 1.7 percent reported a "completed rape," which the study defined as sexual penetration of various kinds (e.g., penile-vaginal, oral-genital, digital-vaginal) by force or the threat of force; and 1.1 percent reported, by this definition, an attempted rape. The authors calculated that, using their definition and projecting these rates to an entire four-year college career (which assumes these rates would not change over time), one-fifth of college women might be victimized by an attempted or completed rape.

Only about half of the women categorized as experiencing a completed rape answered "yes" when asked, "Do you consider this incident to be rape?" Does this mean the study, with its graphic questions, overestimates the prevalence of rape? Not necessarily. Some women may be reluctant to define an incident as rape because of embarrassment or because they don't want to define themselves as victimized.

drug-impaired infants led some experts to call for seizing more at-risk children from parents (Ingrassia & McCormick, 1994). More important, highly publicized cases such as the deaths of Nadine Lockwood and Elizabeth Izquierdo, described at the beginning of the chapter, caused a public outcry against child protective workers who were seen as too slow to remove children from potentially abusive families (Sexton, 1996). Thus, the pendulum of professional and public opinion has swung back to the 1970s, before the movement toward keeping families intact reached its peak.

Yet neither option—vigilance and early removal of children perceived to be in danger, or increased efforts to help troubled parents so that they can keep their children—has worked well. The foster-care system was designed on the basis of assumptions about families that no longer hold. It assumed that the family problems leading to foster care were temporary—as when a mother became ill with a disease such as tuberculosis and needed six months or a year to recuperate. It assumed that large numbers of mothers who did not work outside the home could be found to care temporarily for children whose parents couldn't care for them. It didn't anticipate

the shortages, now occurring, of suitable and willing foster parents (*The Crisis in Foster Care,* 1990). It didn't foresee families sleeping in homeless shelters and drug-addicted newborns abandoned in nurseries. In addition, it probably ignored levels of child abuse that today would be unacceptable.

The heart of the problem is that there still are no good alternatives to parental care for children. Long-term foster care, with children frequently shuttled from family to family, is problematic. Yet abusive or neglectful parents also harm children. One recent innovation is to place children in the homes of relatives and pay them. This so-called "kinship care" option preserves some of the child's family bonds and seems preferable to care by nonrelatives, but it is not without problems. Relatives may have more difficulty than strangers in restricting visits by abusive parents. Moreover, they tend to keep children for a longer period of time than other foster parents; yet they are sometimes reluctant to adopt the children for fear of angering the parents (Wulczyn & Goerge, 1992). Thus, kinship care can conflict with the goal of finding a permanent home for foster children. Moreover, foster parents typically receive substantially more money per child

than parents do under Temporary Assistance to Needy Families (the newly renamed cash welfare program), [➡ p. 192] creating a possible incentive for families receiving TANF to place the children in kinship foster care. The only real, long-term hope is to prevent more children from being abused and neglected. That would require an assault on poverty, unemployment, and family breakup. Meanwhile, the quandary of what to do about abusive and neglectful parents and their children continues.

Ask Yourself

1. Do you know anyone with experience as a foster parent? If so, what was that person's opinion of the foster care system?

2. Which do you think is more important, protecting a family's integrity or protecting children from abuse?

[1]Public Law 96-272.
[2]The APWA's estimate for 1993 is 464,000.
[3]A small but growing number of children in foster care, estimated at about 1,000 in 1990, were born to mothers with AIDS and have tested positive for the HIV virus that causes AIDS. See *The Crisis in Foster Care.*

www.mhhe.com/cherlin

Some may not know that the legal definition of rape in most jurisdictions includes not only vaginal intercourse but also forced sexual penetration of other kinds.

In addition, as Figure 12.4 shows, 1.7 percent reported a completed incident, and 1.3 percent an attempted incident, of "sexual coercion," defined as unwanted sexual penetration with the threat of nonphysical punishment, promise of reward, or pestering or verbal pressure. So about as many women experience sexual coercion as experience rape under these definitions. Slightly higher percentages reported unwanted "sexual contact" such as touching or fondling of breasts or kissing by force or the threat of force. Overall, women who reported frequently drinking enough to get drunk, who were unmarried, and who had been a victim of sexual assault before the current school year were more likely to have been victimized.

FIGURE 12.4

Percent of college women
reporting completed or
attempted rape or sexual
coercion in seven months, on
average, "since school began
in fall, 1996." (*Source:*
U.S. National Institute
of Justice, 2000b.)

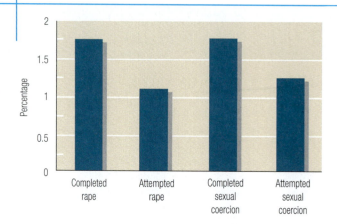

Perpetrators   College men are far less likely to report initiating a rape or an
attempted rape. The lower figures probably represent a mixture of underreporting, multiple rapes by some, and rapes committed by nonstudents. In one study of
students in 32 colleges, most (88 percent) of the men who answered affirmatively
to questions about forced intercourse that seemed to indicate a rape responded
that it "definitely was not a rape"; moreover, these men perceived the woman's
refusal as less clear than the women in the sample perceived it. Seventy-four percent said they had been drinking alcohol or using drugs, and 75 percent said the
woman had been. Forty-seven percent said they expected to engage in similar behavior again (Koss, 1988).

Nationally, 46 percent of all the rapes and sexual assaults reported in the 1999
National Crime Victimization Survey were committed by a friend or acquaintance
of the victim (U.S. Bureau of Justice Statistics, 2000a). The younger the rape victim
(and the victim is under age 18 in more than half of all rapes), the more likely the
rapist is to be a family member. One Justice Department study of rapes that were
reported to the police in several states found that 16 percent of the rapes had occurred to girls under age 12, and virtually all these rapes had been committed by
family members or acquaintances ("Report Cites Heavy Toll," 1994).

Other studies suggest that young men who commit sexual aggression against
acquaintances are more likely to show hostility toward women and to believe
that men are supposed to be more dominant and women more subordinate
(Lundberg-Love & Geffner, 1989). The men also show greater physiological
arousal when presented with rape scenarios in psychology experiments, are
more likely to consider violence against women acceptable, and are more sexually active than men who don't commit sexual aggression. In contrast, there are
relatively few differences between women who have been victims of sexual aggression and those who haven't (Cate & Lloyd, 1992).

The circle of friends a person has also makes a difference. At one large university,
researchers found three distinct peer groups. In the first, neither the women nor the
men had initiated or been victimized by sexual aggression; in the second, some of
the women had been victimized but the men in the group had not been the aggressors; and in the third, women had been victimized and men had been aggressors.
The peer groups in this latter category included students who used alcohol and
drugs more often, tended to live in dormitories, fraternities, and sororities (as opposed to at home), and placed a higher value on the social aspects of going to col-

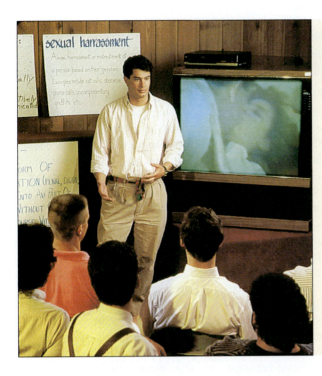

Awareness of sexual aggression in dating relationships is much greater on college campuses than a generation ago.

lege (Gwartney-Gibbs & Stockard, 1989). What can't be determined from these studies is whether belonging to an aggressive group changes a young man's behavior or whether young men who are already aggressive for other reasons join such groups.

PHYSICAL ASSAULT

Physical assault, whether or not sexual aggression occurs, also appears to be common among dating couples. A national sample of 250 never-married persons who had dated someone six or more times in the past year was asked about the incidence of physical violence in that dating relationship. The interviewer read a list of nine types of violence, ranging from "minor aggression" ("threw something," "pushed, grabbed, or shoved," "slapped") to "severe aggression" ("kicked, bit, or hit," "beat up," "used a gun or knife"). Thirty percent chose answers showing that they had inflicted minor aggression on their dating partners at least once in the previous 12 months, and 11 percent reported inflicting severe aggression. Violence was more likely to be inflicted, the survey demonstrated, by persons who reported trying to control their partners' actions ("I make him/her do what I want," "If I don't like what s/he is doing I make him/her stop"). Moreover, the survey suggested that people who were better at what sociologists have called "taking the role of the other" experienced reduced levels of violence. Specifically, persons who said they could imagine the other person's point of view and put themselves mentally in the other person's place ("When something affects him/her, I feel it too," "I understand his/her feelings quite well") were less likely to inflict violence or to have violence inflicted on them (Stets, 1992).[4]

---

[4]The subjects were between the ages of 18 and 30.

Families in Other Cultures

Wife Beating in the Developing World

$\mathcal{D}$omestic violence is not limited to developed nations such as the United States. In 1998, a man in India justified wife beating as a way of correcting improper behavior: "If [she makes] a great mistake, then the husband is justified in beating his wife. Why not? A cow will not be obedient without beatings." In a 1995 survey, 80 percent of rural Egyptian women agreed that wife beating was justified under some circumstances, such as refusing a husband's request for sex. Across the developing world, violence toward wives is justified for many reasons, including disobeying one's husband, talking back to him, or failing to care adequately for one's children or home (Heise, Ellsberg, & Gottemoeller, 1999).

What determines whether domestic violence is common in a society? Anthropologist David Levinson studied field reports from 90 preliterate and peasant societies. He found that the extent of economic inequality between the husband and the wife made a difference. Wife beating was more likely to occur in societies in which men controlled the allocation of food or cash to the members of the household; it was more likely where women could not amass or control wealth, as by earning an independent income or owning a dwelling; and it was more likely where men had the final

say in household decision making. Where men's economic power over women was greater, they had little to lose by alienating a wife or her kin through excessive violence because the wife controlled fewer resources. Therefore, husbands had less incentive to restrain their violent impulses (Levinson, 1988). In addition, wife beating was less common where female work groups, which could provide support to abused wives, existed.

What of the larger societies that have undergone economic development and urbanization in recent decades? Several authors have suggested that urbanization and development might increase levels of domestic violence initially. The increase supposedly would occur because traditional social controls would break down as urbanization and industrialization proceeded; then, as newer social controls were developed, domestic violence might decrease again. This line of reasoning implies that levels of domestic violence should be lower in rural societies untouched by industrialization than in industrializing societies (Gelles & Cornell, 1990). Yet evidence for this proposition is slim. A study compared responses of rural and low-income urban respondents to a survey in Papua New Guinea, one of the few developing coun-

tries that has relevant survey data (Morley, 1994). Samples of rural villagers and urban dwellers were asked whether they had hit their spouses, as well as other questions about their attitudes toward domestic violence. In contrast to the idea that development boosts violence, hitting was slightly more common among the rural villagers. Moreover, fewer urban residents thought that it was a "husband's right" to hit his wife. Rebecca Morley, the author of the Papua New Guinea study, suggests that wife beating may emerge as a clearly defined "social problem" in urban areas, in contrast to its greater acceptance in rural areas (Morley, 1994). This greater awareness and attention may create the perception of an increase, even if the underlying rates of wife beating remain the same.

Ask Yourself

1. Are you familiar with a developing country or with immigrants to the United States from a developing country? If so, have you noticed differences in the treatment of women in that country?
2. Why might wife beating be considered a more serious social problem in cities than in rural villages?

www.mhhe.com/cherlin

Another study compared rates of physical assault in a college student sample to national figures for cohabiting and married couples. The authors reported that dating couples had rates of physical assault (15 percent in the previous year) that were a bit lower than for married couples (20 percent), but that cohabiting couples had noticeably higher rates (35 percent) than either dating or married couples. The authors speculate that disagreements about controlling the other partner's behavior may be important. In dating relationships, they argue, the partners expect to have less control, so they may not become as angry about a lack of control. On the other hand, married couples may agree to a high level of control. In the middle, say the authors, are cohabiting relationships, where there may be more disagreement about the amount of control a partner can expect (Stets & Straus, 1989). Their argument is intriguing, but it may also be that people who choose to cohabit have personalities and backgrounds that predispose them to violence more than those who don't cohabit.

Explanations

Why do people abuse their spouses, partners, or children? According to the political model of domestic violence, assaults against spouses and partners arise, in part, from power struggles between men and women. Men have an advantage in these struggles because of their greater physical strength, on average, and because of a social system that often reinforces male dominance. During the many thousands of years humans spent as hunter-gatherers, male strength was central to the life of bands. Men defended the band's territory against intrusions by other bands, and men armed with spears hunted animals. It is likely that men used their strength to compete for women and to dominate them. Later, in larger social groups, men were often able to shape laws and norms—such as the belief that the husband should be the head of the household—to their advantage so that they didn't need to use force to achieve their ends. The system of male dominance that still appears to some extent in virtually every society today is based in part upon the use of, or the threat of the use of, force against women.

But most men, despite their advantage in strength and despite cultural beliefs, don't hit their wives. In addition, both men and women abuse their children. Consequently, the general notion of male dominance isn't useful in explaining why some husbands are violent and others are not or why parents abuse their children. Many other explanations have been proposed, most of which have some plausibility. These explanations are often referred to as "theories" of domestic violence, although most of them are just collections of related propositions. Some of these perspectives emphasize psychological factors, whereas others emphasize social structural factors. At the present time, we don't know enough to tie them together into a single, coherent explanation. When Richard Gelles and Murray Straus, two leaders in the field, were asked to write an essay integrating theories of domestic violence, they presented propositions and outcomes from 13 so-called theories (Gelles & Straus, 1979). Instead of mechanically discussing all 13, let me focus on the ones I think are the most important.

SOCIAL LEARNING PERSPECTIVE

The explanation that is probably cited the most draws upon the **social learning perspective** developed by social psychologists. According to this perspective, individuals learn behavior they will later exhibit by observing what others do and seeing the consequences of these actions. Thus, children from violent homes are said to learn by observation and personal experience that aggressive or violent behavior is an acceptable and often successful way of controlling others and getting what you want (Bandura, 1973). In fact, a number of studies do show that children who grow up in homes characterized by domestic violence are more likely, as adults, to act violently toward their spouses and children. (All children may, to some extent, learn that violent behavior is acceptable through watching the pervasive violence in television programs and films.)

For example, respondents in the 1975 national survey were asked whether, as children, (1) they had ever observed either of their parents hitting the other and

social learning perspective the theory that individuals learn behavior they will later exhibit by observing what others do and seeing the consequences of these actions

(2) whether their parents had hit them as teenagers. Among men who had neither seen hitting nor been hit, 1 percent committed acts of severe violence against their wives. Among men who had been hit by their parents, the corresponding figure was 3 percent. It was 6 percent among men who had observed their parents hitting each other, and it rose to 12 percent among men who had both observed their parents hitting each other and had been hit themselves (Kalmuss, 1984).

This pattern of findings can be interpreted in two ways. The glass-half-empty interpretation is that men are far more likely to beat their wives if they have witnessed hitting or been hit by their parents. This interpretation shows why the social learning perspective does help us to understand why some men are violent. The glass-half-full interpretation is that the vast majority of men who have witnessed hitting or been hit by their parents do *not* beat their wives. This second interpretation shows the limitations of the social learning perspective as an explanation for violent behavior: It doesn't explain why most people who have been exposed to violence are not themselves violent.

FRUSTRATION-AGGRESSION PERSPECTIVE

frustration-aggression perspective the theory that aggressive behavior occurs when a person is blocked from achieving a goal

An alternative explanation is derived from the **frustration-aggression perspective.** Here the central idea is that aggressive behavior occurs when a person is blocked from achieving a goal, such as when economic inequalities cause men and women to work for low wages, high unemployment rates make it hard to find a job, or racial discrimination limits the opportunities of people from racial-ethnic groups. When these conditions occur, it is said, the person may displace his or her frustration and anger onto a safer target—such as his or her spouse or children. These targets are safer than employers or strangers because there is less chance of being arrested, being hit hard in return, or losing one's job. In contrast to the social learning approach, violent behavior is not viewed as directed toward a specific end, such as dominating a wife. Rather, violence is seen as an emotional outburst of displaced anger, usually by a man. So this perspective suggests that, regardless of what people have learned about violence as children, they will be more likely to act violently if they are frustrated by forces they feel are blocking their ability to get a job, move out of a dangerous neighborhood, or attain other important goals. Consequently, the frustration-aggression approach helps us to understand why domestic violence is somewhat more common among the lower social classes, whose members are more likely to be blocked from attaining their goals (but who may also be more likely to have grown up in violent homes).

The frustration-aggression approach raises the question of where a person's basic tendency to act violently (when blocked or frustrated) comes from, other than social learning. Some evidence suggests that men's greater aggressiveness, compared with women's aggressiveness, may be partly of biological origin. [➡ p. 90] Gelles and Straus argue, however, that aggression is learned behavior; in fact, they reject the idea that there is any biological influence on domestic violence.[5] Yet a national study of armed services veterans found that husbands who had higher levels of testosterone—the male sex hormone—were more likely to have hit or thrown things at their wives (Booth & Dabbs, 1993). The possibility of biological influences is not presented here to excuse

[5]See Gelles & Straus (1979), footnotes 7 and 8.

the behavior of violent men. Most people can (and do) control their urges and predispositions. Even in the testosterone study, 71 percent of men in the group that had the highest levels of the hormone did *not* hit or throw things at their wives—just as most men who come from violent homes do not beat their wives. Still, men with a greater biological predisposition toward aggression might be more likely than others to beat their wives and their children if they are frustrated and angry about events occurring outside the home.

SOCIAL EXCHANGE PERSPECTIVE

A third explanation draws upon the **social exchange perspective.** This explanation proposes that people calculate whether to engage in a particular behavior by considering the rewards and costs of that behavior and the rewards of alternatives to it. The model here is that of the rational actor. It suggests that a man may decide whether to beat his wife by considering the rewards (he can control her; he can let out his anger and frustration at the rest of the world) against the costs of violence (she might seek a divorce) and the rewards of not being violent (she will continue to do much of the childcare and contribute the paycheck from her job). This approach helps to explain why wives are more likely to be the victims of violence if they don't work for wages; in that case, the costs of violence to the husband (she might seek a divorce) are lower and the rewards of not being violent (she will contribute earnings) are lower because the wife is not employed. The social exchange perspective is also consistent with cross-cultural evidence that severe violence against women is less common in societies in which women have more economic independence. (See *Families in Other Cultures:* Wife Beating in the Developing World.) Moreover, it also helps to explain the greater violence against women among the lower social classes. Men with more income can influence their wives' actions by exchanging money for the desired behavior. With money they can get the same rewards poorer men must use force to obtain, but without incurring the high costs of force—such as the possibility that the wife will seek a divorce.

social exchange perspective the theory that people calculate whether to engage in a particular behavior by considering the rewards and costs of that behavior and the rewards of alternatives to it

Domestic Violence and Public Policy

In the epilogue to her book on U.S. social policy against domestic violence since the Puritans, Pleck wrote:

> *The history of social policy against domestic violence has been one of persistent, even inherent conflict between protecting the victim and preserving the family, and the gradual development of alternatives within and outside the family for victims of abuse* (Pleck, 1987).

Since the mid-1970s this often dormant conflict has surfaced again. Yet there is a subtext to the protect-the-victim versus preserve-the-family discourse. Public policies that protect the victim restrict men's use of their superior physical force and therefore decrease the power of men over women. That is why feminist groups have worked so hard to bring the problems of battered women to the public's attention, to create crisis centers, shelters, and support services, and to modify the law in nearly all states. Wrote Gordon, "Defining wife-beating as a social problem . . . was one of the great achievements of feminism" (Gordon, 1988).

THE POLICY DEBATE

Because liberals tend to favor equality between men and women more than conservatives, more liberals than conservatives favor policies such as the following: state intervention in marriages in which husbands use severe physical or sexual violence against their wives; continued growth of support services for victims in crisis; and more assistance for battered women who wish to leave their marriages (such as childcare, job training, and tougher child support enforcement). But although the liberal, protect-the-victim activists have been succeeding recently, a conservative, preserve-the-family movement has also emerged since the mid-1970s. Conservatives are more likely than liberals to support male-headed two-parent families. Since this family form has traditionally been dominant (although it is becoming less so), conservatives have an interest in preserving the family status quo. That is one reason why many conservatives disapprove of state intervention in families, except in the most extreme cases, and why, in part, they believe that what occurs in a family is the private business of its members. Conservatives have not had much success on these issues recently; their most notable triumph was delaying and reducing federal funds in the early 1980s. They did not have much success in the 1990s in part because of legislation that was passed in the wake of the O.J. Simpson case. For example, within days of Simpson's arrest in 1994 on charges of murdering his former wife, the New York State Legislature passed a bill that required the police to arrest suspected perpetrators of domestic violence whether or not the victim is willing to press charges. Within two months, the U.S. House of Representatives had approved nearly all the provisions of the Violence Against Women Act, which had first been introduced, without success, six years earlier.

SOCIAL PROGRAMS

Other recent developments, mentioned earlier, also seem to have assisted the liberals. For instance, the cultural emphasis on independence and self-fulfillment implies that an unhappy spouse should be able to leave her or his marriage. These values are inconsistent with the notion that a woman should stay in an abusive marriage. Moreover, the increasing economic independence of women provides them with earning power that they can use to gain more authority in marriage or to live independently of men. In addition, the deteriorating earnings of young men, especially those without a college education, reduce their attractiveness to women and therefore make it less likely that women they abuse will remain with them. Unless there is a reversal of these trends, liberal policy positions seem likely to continue to prevail.

Still, it can be challenging to translate the protect-the-victim policy into effective programs. Consider the spread since the early 1980s of mandatory arrest policies in domestic violence complaints. This approach was influenced by an experiment conducted by the Minneapolis police force in 1981 and 1982. When responding to domestic violence complaints, the police randomly assigned the offender to one of three treatments: arresting him, ordering him to leave the home for eight hours, or trying to mediate the dispute. The results, based on subsequent arrest records and interviews with the victims, showed that arresting the suspect resulted in the lowest level of repeat violence (Sherman & Berk, 1984).

Intrigued officials at the Department of Justice decided to support replications of the experiment in other cities. But many state governments—eager to

Many jurisdictions make an arrest mandatory when police are called to a domestic violence dispute.

take action against the problem—legislated mandatory arrest policies without waiting for the results of the replications. Unfortunately, when the experimental results from the other localities were published in 1992, they showed that arrests were effective only for suspects who were employed. Arrests of suspects who were unemployed did not reduce subsequent violence; in fact, in some localities unemployed suspects were more likely to commit subsequent attacks if they had been arrested. The experiments seem to show that arrest deters only men who have something to lose by going to jail—namely, their jobs and their incomes. For men with little to lose, the arrest may do little good and may even spur the suspect on to further violence.[6] If these results are valid, there is no uniform policy conclusion to be drawn from them: A suburb with a low unemployment rate might find a mandatory arrest policy effective in combating domestic violence, but a central city police force in a high-unemployment area might find mandatory arrests counterproductive.

Even so, the results certainly don't suggest dropping arrests as an option for police officers. Rather, they suggest that mandatory arrest policies, such as New York State's post-Simpson law, may impose rigid practices that don't work as well as more flexible programs. Altogether, these recent results illustrate the difficulty of designing programs to address spouse abuse. Still, in the current period of high divorce rates, greater gender equality, and rising individualism, the image of the bruised and battered woman has led most Americans to approve of government efforts to help her escape her husband. It is hard to imagine returning to a time when men could hit their wives with impunity or parents could boast of giving their children a good wholesome flogging.

---

[6]Three articles reporting the results of the replications were published in Sherman and Smith (1992), Pate and Hamilton (1992), Berk, Campbell, Klap, and Western (1992). See also the comments and replies in the December 1993 issue (vol. 58, no. 6), of *American Sociological Review*.

1. **When did domestic violence become a social issue?** Domestic violence has been a social issue at various points throughout U.S. history. The Puritans, who took a strong stand against wife beating, passed the first laws against it. A period of renewed interest occurred in the late 1800s, and another in the 1960s. Two theoretical models, a medical model and a political model, have been applied to this social problem. The current interest and activity are largely a result of political and social action by feminist groups and by health and social welfare professionals.

2. **What is the extent of violence against women by intimate partners?** Although some women engage in violence, evidence suggests that women are far more often the victims than the aggressors in domestic violence. In a recent survey, 22 percent of women said they had been the victims of physical assault by an intimate partner at some time in their lives. Eight percent of women in another study said they had been the victims or rape or attempted rape by an intimate partner. Sexual violence is often linked to physical violence; studies show that forced sexual acts tend to occur in violent marriages. Domestic violence is more common among cohabiting couples than among married couples, and more common among low-income families than higher-income families. Cross-cultural studies show that wife beating occurs in most societies. Societies with less violence against women tend to be more egalitarian than others and to encourage intervention in family disputes.

3. **What is the extent of child abuse?** Though the physical abuse of children has probably decreased over the long term, surveys continue to show disturbing levels of child abuse by parents. More than half the reported cases refer to educational or physical neglect; about one-third, to physical or sexual abuse. Child neglect, and to a lesser extent, physical abuse are somewhat more common among low-income families than others. Some cases of neglect may reflect the constraints of poverty more than abuse by parents. Though reports of child neglect and abuse have risen greatly in recent decades, the increase may reflect more complete reporting rather than an actual increase in the rates of neglect and abuse. Severely neglected or abused children are sometimes placed in foster care. In the late 1980s and 1990s, the number of children in foster care rose dramatically. There is a continuing debate about whether government social programs should emphasize the preservation of families or the protection of children.

4. **What do we know about sexual aggression by dates or acquaintances?** Although adequate data do not exist, studies suggest that men commit substantial amounts of sexual aggression and violence against women they are dating and other female acquaintances. According to one national survey, about 4 percent of adult women in the United States have been forced into sex by an acquaintance. In one national study, 11 percent of dating couples reported severe physical aggression. Men who commit sexual aggression are more likely than others to show hostility to women, to be easily aroused by rape scenarios, to be sexually active, and to belong to sexually aggressive peer groups. People who try to control the other partner's behavior or are less able than others to imagine another person's point of view are more likely than others to be physically abusive. Physical assault may be more common among cohabiting partners than among couples who are dating or married.

5. **Why does domestic violence occur?** Assaults against spouses and partners arise in part from power struggles between men and women. Men have an advantage in these struggles because of their greater physical strength, and because of a social system that often reinforces male dominance. But most men do not hit their wives, so other explanations are needed for domestic violence. According to the social learning approach, children from violent homes will learn that violent behavior is an acceptable and often successful means of controlling others; consequently, they will be more likely as adults to use violence against spouse and children. The frustration-aggression approach emphasizes that individuals who are blocked from attaining a goal may displace their frustration and anger onto their spouses and children. The social exchange approach suggests that people calculate the rewards and costs of violent behavior and the alternatives to it. According to this approach, women who have some economic resources are less likely than others to be victimized, as cross-cultural studies show.

6. **What are the public policy debates concerning domestic violence?** Liberals and conservatives disagree about the desirability of early and extensive state intervention in cases of domestic violence. The fundamental

issue is the conflict between preserving the family and helping the victims. Liberals, who tend to emphasize helping the victims, generally favor more equality between men and women. Conservatives, who tend to emphasize preserving the family, generally favor the continued dominance of the male-headed two-parent family. Recently, liberal activists have been more successful than conservatives in pushing their agenda.

Thinking about Families

1. Why wasn't the problem of domestic violence taken seriously until the middle of the twentieth century?

2. When, if at all, are parents justified in hitting their children?

3. Which of the most important explanations for violent behavior against intimates makes the most sense to you?

4. **The Public Family** Should child protective workers leave children with parents who have not been violent, but who seem likely to be violent in the future, or should they take children away from potentially violent parents?

5. **The Private Family** Is rape a concept that should be applied to married couples?

Key Terms

child abuse   396
domestic violence   386
elder abuse   400
foster care   402

frustration-aggression
   perspective   408
incest   398

social exchange
   perspective   409
social learning perspective   407

Families on the Internet   www.mhhe.com/cherlin

*Note: While all the URLs listed were current as of the printing of this book, these sites often change. Please check our web site (**http://www.mhbe.com/cherlin**) for updates.*

 Several sites offer information and links on the topic of child abuse. The National Clearinghouse on Child Abuse and Neglect Information (**www.calib.com/nccanch**) provides statistics, reports, and answers to frequently asked questions. The National Committee to Prevent Child Abuse (**www.child-abuse.org**) offers information on steps people can take to prevent child abuse. Several fact sheets are available under "publications"; select and read one or two of them.

The Family Violence Prevention Fund (**www.fvpf.org**) maintains a web site with stories of victims of domestic violence and people who have made a difference in reducing domestic violence. In addition, the Yahoo web site maintains a page with comprehensive links to numerous organizations and articles on domestic violence (**www.yahoo.com/society_and_culture/crime/types_of_crime/domestic_violence**). Explore a few of these to get a sense of the different points of view among the organizations listed.

Divorce

Looking Forward

1. What is the history of divorce in the United States and other Western nations?

2. What social and individual factors are associated with a greater likelihood to divorce?

3. What happens to parents during the divorce process?

4. What are the short-term effects of divorce on children?

5. What are the long-term effects of divorce on children?

Introduction

What if you and your spouse-to-be had to sign a pledge, enforceable in court, to undergo marriage counseling before you wed and to undergo more counseling if you ever wanted a divorce? And what if you waived the right to divorce without your spouse's consent, except after a 24-month waiting period? Would that lower the chances that you would ever divorce? The Louisiana legislature hoped that it might. In 1997, legislators passed a bill creating a new, optional form of marriage called "covenant marriage." When applying for a marriage license, couples who chose covenant marriage would sign a document in which they pledged to follow these restrictive rules (Jeter, 1997).

Covenant marriage hasn't been the success its supporters hoped it would be. Only about 3 percent of couples who have married in Louisiana since 1997 have adopted it. One study suggests that the court clerks who issue marriage licenses sometimes fail to tell couples about the option, which requires more work on their part than a standard marriage license. But even when couples do learn about covenant marriage most opt for a standard marriage license. The few couples who have chosen it tend to be much more religious and a bit more politically conservative than others (Nock, Wright, & Sanchez, 1999).

Still, covenant marriage stands as a symbol of public concern about the high levels of divorce in the United States. It represents a reaction to the introduction in every state of "no fault" divorce laws, which allow one partner to obtain a divorce after a short period, even if the other partner doesn't want one. But, as will be noted below, it's not clear whether the liberalized divorce laws helped cause the high level of divorce or whether the laws were a reaction to it. What is clear is that the United States has the highest rate of divorce of any developed country. The probability of a marriage ending in divorce doubled between the early 1960s and late 1970s. At current rates, about half of all American marriages begun since the late 1970s will end in divorce (Cherlin, 1992). (See *How do Sociologists Know What They Know?* Measuring the Divorce Rate.)

The young adults who entered college in the 1990s and early 2000s are members of the first cohort to grow up after this latest great surge of divorce. (About 40 percent of American children who grew up in the 1980s and 1990s experienced the breakup of their parents' marriages [Furstenberg & Cherlin, 1991].) When two childless adults divorce, the breakup, although emotionally painful, is straightforward. Having concluded their legal business, the ex-spouses need not, and often do not, see each other again. When children are involved, however, a clean break is not in their interest. Even though divorce severs the family ties between the husband and wife, it does not sever the ties

Henry VIII (1491–1547), King of England, broke with the Catholic Church so he could divorce Katherine of Aragon and marry Anne Boleyn.

between each parent and the children. In the majority of cases, the mother keeps custody of the children, forming a single-parent family that may endure for years. The father's relationship—typically reduced to regular visits, or less—is problematic. Indeed, many divorced fathers fade from their children's lives. Nevertheless, a modest but growing number of fathers are obtaining custody of their children, either by themselves or jointly with their wives.

Moreover, for many adults and children, a divorce does not signal the end of the changes in their family lives. A substantial proportion of parents will remarry, often after a period of cohabiting with their spouse-to-be. Remarriage after divorce further complicates adults' and children's lives. It introduces a stepparent into the child's family but doesn't subtract a biological parent—unlike remarriage after a parental death. It can bring a bewildering network of quasi relatives that extends over several households. In short, it necessitates another major adjustment for adults and children who may have struggled to adjust to postdivorce, single-parent life. In addition, almost half of all children whose custodial parents remarry will witness a *second* divorce before they reach the age of 18 (Bumpass, 1984).

These developments have greatly altered American family life. They have also been a source of concern. What do we know about the causes and consequences of the recent rise in divorce? About the effects of remarriage on stepparents and stepchildren? How are divorce and remarriage altering the nature of the family? These are the questions to be pursued in this chapter, on divorce, and in the next chapter, on remarriage and stepfamilies.

Three Eras of Divorce

Far from requiring an act of Parliament or permission from a state legislature, divorce is now easy to obtain in most Western nations. It was not always so. The law and public opinion have changed dramatically over the past two centuries, greatly altering the way in which marriage is viewed. It is useful to think of three historical eras of divorce.

How Do Sociologists Know What They Know?

Measuring the Divorce Rate

A newspaper reporter calls a sociologist who does research on divorce and asks, "What's the most recent statistic for the divorce rate in the United States?" "In 1998," the sociologist replies, "about 19 out of every 1,000 married women divorced." "Nineteen out of a thousand," she responds, "No way! That's tiny. The divorce rate has got to be much higher than that."

"Well," says the sociologist, "another way of saying it is that about half of all marriages would end in divorce at current rates." "Great," the reporter replies, "and what year is that for?" "It's not for a year," the sociologist tries to explain, "it's a projection based on this year's rates . . ." But he can tell that the reporter is losing patience fast. She wants a figure and a year, not a lecture in demography, and she's writing a story on a deadline.

In fact, it's hard to answer the question, "what's the current divorce rate?" in a way that is both precise and meaningful. The difficulty is that the most meaningful statistic describes the proportion of all current marriages that will end in divorce, but it's impossible to know that proportion until everyone who is now married has grown old and died. So sociologists try to estimate this lifetime figure, but their estimates are just educated guesses. The precise statistic is based on the number of divorces in the most recent year for which data are available, but it doesn't tell us much about people's experience with divorce.

The 19-out-of-1,000 rate is the precise statistic; it represents the number of divorces in the United States divided by the number of married women. It includes women who have been married for many years as well as those who married only recently. It gives the probability that a married woman would have become divorced in 1998: 19/1,000, or about 2 percent. So in 1998, 2 percent of married women obtained divorces.

This does indeed sound like a very low figure, given all of the public concern about divorce. No wonder reporters are unhappy with it. It is a *cross-sectional rate,* meaning a rate at one point in time. It provides a snapshot of the experiences of married American women during a single year. In 1999, the 981 of every 1,000 married women who didn't divorce in 1998 were still at risk of divorcing, and another 19 or so did. In 2000, yet another 19 obtained divorces, and so on, year after year, into the future. So although the average woman married in 1998 had a 2 percent chance of becoming divorced *in 1998,* she had a far higher chance of becoming divorced *over the rest of her married life.*

Just how high her lifetime chances are, we cannot know with certainty. But let us

THE ERA OF RESTRICTED DIVORCE

era of restricted divorce the time of a restrictive approach toward divorce, until about the middle of the nineteenth century; divorces were usually granted only on the grounds of adultery or desertion, and generally only to men

annulment a ruling that a marriage was never properly formed

One approach to divorce, taken during what I will call the **era of restricted divorce,** characterized the Western nations until the middle of the nineteenth century. In nearly all the countries, according to historian Roderick Phillips (1991), it was very difficult to obtain a divorce.[1] Still, the European countries differed from one another in how restrictive their divorce laws were according to what religion was most prominent in each country. Catholic countries, such as France, followed the Catholic Church's position that divorce was forbidden. Only if Church officials granted an **annulment**—a ruling that a marriage had never been properly formed in the first place—could a couple dissolve their marriage. Annulments could be granted only in situations such as a marriage between relatives of too close a degree or one in which the spouses had never had sexual intercourse. Protestant countries (except for England) were more liberal, typically granting divorces in cases of adultery or desertion. Several of the American colonies were more liberal still. Most of the colonies recognized the grounds of adultery and desertion; some also allowed divorces on the ground of extreme violence by a husband.

[1]The historical material in the next few paragraphs draws upon Phillips (1991). The eras and their titles are mine.

conduct the following thought experiment: Suppose the risks of divorce in 1998 were to stay the same, for every age group, for the next few decades. That is to say, suppose that a woman in her thirties 10 years from now would have the same risk of divorce as did women in their thirties in 1998 and that a woman in her forties 20 years from now would have the same risk as did women in their forties in 1998, and so on. Now think of a hypothetical young woman in her mid-twenties who married in 1998. We could fast-forward her through time and calculate her risk of divorce at every age throughout her lifetime—because we are assuming that these risks will remain the same as those observed in 1998. Then we could sum these risks. The result would be a measure of her lifetime probability of divorce.

When sociologists do this calculation, they find that the lifetime probability of divorce for a young woman marrying today is about 50 percent. I write "about" because the exact answer depends on some of the technical assumptions in the calculations, and different sociologists make different assumptions. It's important to recognize that this figure is just a projection of current risks into the future. In fact, it is unlikely that divorce risks will stay the same for the next few decades. It is true, as Figure 13.1 suggests, that the risks of divorce have not changed much since 1980. But as the figure shows, the 1950s, 1980s, and 1990s are the only decades since the Civil War in which divorce risks have remained more or less stable. They could start changing again tomorrow.

The utility of the lifetime estimate, then, is not that it will prove accurate 40 years from now—it may not—but rather that it indicates the underlying force of divorce that is implied by the behavior of married people today. The lifetime estimate, in other words, answers an important *what if* question: What if the risks of divorce at each age stayed the same as they are now; what lifetime level of divorce would these current risks imply? This is the question most newspaper readers want an answer to, even if the answer is necessarily uncertain.

Ask Yourself

1. How many couples in your family have divorced in the past year? In the past 10 years? The past 20? Is your family's divorce rate similar to the divorce rate for the country as a whole?

2. In general, do news reporters do a good enough job of explaining the significance of social statistics such as the divorce rate? What are the dangers of misreporting such statistics?

www.mhhe.com/cherlin

Nevertheless, divorce remained rare everywhere. Its rarity, in large part, reflected the strong male dominance in marriage. Most divorces were granted on grounds of the wife's adultery, but very few wives were granted divorces on grounds of the husband's adultery. In fact, as mentioned earlier, few divorces were granted to women at all. Adultery was the main ground used by men for divorce not just because of sexual jealousy but also because of men's concern about who would farm their land and inherit their property. If, for example, a farmer's wife gave birth to a child fathered by another man, the child might have a claim on the farmer's land—especially if the farmer was unaware that he was not the father. Thus, divorce in this era was very difficult to obtain and, when obtained, was usually invoked because a man wished to ensure that his wife would not bear a child by another man. Marriage, for both men and women, was primarily an economic partnership—a means of pooling labor in order to grow enough food, or to make enough money, to subsist. Its romantic aspects were decidedly secondary, if only because making a living took so much effort. One reason why wives were valuable to husbands was that they could bear children, who were a major source of labor. In fact, fathers took custody of children after divorces in colonial America.

It is inconceivable, however, that marital breakup in this era was as rare as the low frequency of divorce implies. Although divorce was usually unavailable to the landless and the poor, separation without divorce must have been commonplace.

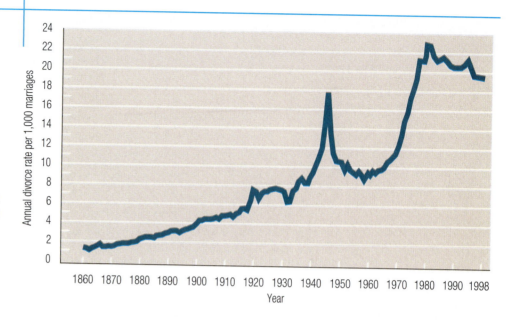

Contemporary studies of families around the world demonstrate that the legalities of coupling and uncoupling—obtaining a legal marriage or a legal divorce—are less important in the poorer classes, where little money or property is involved (Goode, 1982). Cohabitation without marriage and separation without divorce are much more common. Moreover, the African slaves in the American colonies, as noted in previous chapters, were denied access to legal marriage or divorce. Thus, a considerable amount of separation and desertion must lie hidden beneath the history of formal divorce in the era of restricted divorce as well.

THE ERA OF DIVORCE TOLERANCE

era of divorce tolerance
the time of a tolerant approach toward divorce, from the middle of the nineteenth century until, in the United States, 1970; the grounds for divorce were widened, and divorce was made more accessible to women

The middle of the nineteenth century marked the beginning of the **era of divorce tolerance,** which lasted in the United States until 1970. During this period, it gradually became easier to obtain a divorce. As the doctrine of separate spheres, with its emphasis on domesticity for women, became more widespread, legislatures and courts grew more sympathetic to cases in which husbands' conduct toward their wives was reprehensible. Most jurisdictions in the United States added as grounds for divorce behaviors such as habitual drunkenness or failure to provide for one's wife. In the twentieth century, legislatures added less specific offenses such as "mental cruelty." These new grounds made divorce more accessible to mistreated wives.

Just as the doctrine of separate spheres was important to changes in divorce laws, so too was the shift in how marriage was viewed. Marriage in the nineteenth and twentieth centuries underwent a gradual change from an economic partnership first and foremost to an emotional partnership based on love and companionship—from an institution to a companionship, in Burgess's memorable phrase. As this transition was made, the failure of a marriage to involve love and companionship came to be seen as a valid reason for divorce. Figure 13.1 shows the annual divorce rate for the United States from 1860 (the earliest year for which statistics exist) until 1998. It shows, for example, that about 2 of every

1,000 married couples in 1880 obtained a divorce that year, whereas about 19 or 20 of 1,000 couples obtained a divorce in each of the most recent years.

The divorce rate rose substantially in the late 1800s and early 1900s. According to demographic estimates of lifetime divorce experience, 8 percent of all marriages begun in 1880 eventually ended in a divorce, compared with 12 percent of marriages begun in 1900 and 18 percent of marriages begun in 1920 (Preston & McDonald, 1979). Divorce was transformed from a rare privilege granted mainly to wealthy men, in the previous era, to a common, if still frowned upon, occurrence increasingly available to women. In fact, Phillips reports that more than two-thirds of divorces in the United States between 1880 and World War I were granted to women. During the same period, divorce caused great concern among social reformers in the United States—not unlike the concern expressed today (O'Neill, 1972). Organizations such as the National Divorce Reform League encouraged legislatures to make divorce laws more restrictive. [➡ p. 64]

Still, the annual rate of divorce kept rising, as can be seen in Figure 13.1. The steady rise through the first half of the twentieth century was broken only by two spikes in the years after World Wars I and II and a dip during the Great Depression years. The spikes were caused by the disruption and pent-up demand for divorce that had built up during each war. The dip occurred not because marriages were happier during the depths of the Depression but rather because many unhappy couples couldn't afford to get divorced. After World War II the annual rate of divorce fell somewhat, reflecting the home- and family-oriented ethos of the 1950s baby boom years. Then, in the early 1960s, a sharp rise began. By the late 1970s, about 21 or 22 of every 1,000 married couples were getting divorced each year—a rate that has not changed much since then (Cherlin, 1992b, Goldstein, 1999). (There have long been some non-Western societies with even higher divorce rates than ours. See *Families in Other Cultures:* Divorce among the Kanuri.)

As recently as the 1960s, in order to obtain a divorce, a person had to prove that her or his spouse had done something wrong—and not just anything wrong, but rather one of a short list of specific wrongs: adultery, desertion, nonsupport, mental cruelty, and so forth. In truth, however, an increasing number of people were seeking divorces not because the other spouse had committed a terrible act but rather because the divorce seeker was unfulfilled by the marriage, unsatisfied emotionally, and trapped in a relationship that no longer seemed worth maintaining. Often, the other partner, feeling angry and alienated, consented to the divorce. Self-fulfillment, as has been discussed in earlier chapters, has become a dominant, perhaps *the* dominant, criterion for evaluating marriages. As a result, a divorce hearing was often a sham, in which one partner would "prove," with the tacit cooperation of his or her spouse, that some nonexistent or overblown wrong had occurred. In reaction to this situation, sentiment grew for eliminating altogether the idea that one spouse had to be at fault for a divorce to be granted.

THE ERA OF UNRESTRICTED DIVORCE

The first major laws to eliminate fault were implemented in the United States in 1970, ushering in the **era of unrestricted divorce,** in which a divorce has been available virtually without restriction, except for a waiting period, to any married person who wants one. In that year California became the first jurisdiction anywhere in the Western world to eliminate fault grounds for divorce and to replace

era of unrestricted divorce the time of a virtually unrestricted access to divorce, from, in the United States, 1970 to the present; divorces are usually granted without restriction to any married person who wants one

Families in Other Cultures

Divorce among the Kanuri

*W*hat if a society had a divorce rate that made ours look low? What if every marriage ended in divorce and some individuals divorced many times? What would such a society look like, and how would it function? It turns out that there have been many societies in which divorce was more common than it is in the United States and other Western countries today. Some of the recent ones were Islamic societies, for, under traditional Islamic law, divorce was easy for a man to obtain. He needed only to say "I divorce thee" three times and he and his wife were thereby divorced. Now, a wise man did not abuse this power, and social pressure may have existed to settle disputes short of divorce. It was much more difficult for a woman to obtain a divorce, but if she was really unhappy, she could often provoke her husband into giving her one.

The Kanuri of northeastern Nigeria were a high-divorce-rate Islamic society until the 1960s, at least (Cohen, 1971). When anthropologist Ronald Cohen studied six different sites, he found that 68 to 99 percent of all marriages had ended in divorce. Men would say "I divorce thee" only once to establish a divorce because they believed it possible for a man to remarry a woman whom he had divorced, and that could not happen if the declaration had

been repeated three times. Men were allowed to have up to four wives, although only the wealthier half had more than one and few had more than two.

Although frequent, male-initiated divorce among the Kanuri was part of a system of strong male dominance, divorce also served the interests of women at times. Girls' first marriages were arranged by relatives shortly after puberty. A young girl was frequently sent to be the wife of an older, prosperous man, whom she was expected to obey. A divorce allowed her to escape this marriage. Moreover, divorced women had much more independence than married women. The latter were often secluded in the household, whereas divorced women could move about freely. Cohen writes of the divorced woman, "she can entertain lovers, visit with relatives, and no man has a right to order her about."

In this patriarchal system, children remained with the husband after a divorce. Consequently, most children experienced being separated from their mothers. The Kanuri dealt with this problem in part by enlarging the role of the father's sister. Because Kanuri kinship is patrilineal (descent is reckoned along the male line only), the father's sister is part of his kinship group. It was believed, therefore, that she might treat the man's children better than a new

wife brought into the household to replace the departed one. As a result, many children were raised for a time by their paternal aunts. In cases of frequent, rapid divorce, the paternal aunt might be the only stable female figure in the lives of the children of the household.

It was no accident, then, that the sister of the emir, the ruler of the society, was one of three female relatives who had a noble title (the others were his mother and his senior wife). She had a warm, maternal image. For example, she was the head of an organization that provided hospitality to strangers who came to town. Her membership in the royal family served to institutionalize the role of the paternal aunt as mother surrogate. In this way, the Kanuri managed the problem of mother loss that was inherent in their high-divorce-rate society.

Ask Yourself

1. What aspect of divorce among the Kanuri most resembles divorce in contemporary American society?

2. If you were a sociologist doing a follow-up study on divorce among the Kanuri, what long-term effects of divorce would you particularly want to examine? Why?

www.mhhe.com/cherlin

---

no-fault divorce the granting of a divorce simply on the basis of marriage breakdown due to "irreconcilable differences"

them with **no-fault divorce,** the granting of divorce simply for marriage breakdown due to "irreconcilable differences" (Glendon, 1987). Coming several years after rising divorce rates had begun to clog the courts, no-fault divorce was hailed as the way to bring the law into line with changes in societal attitudes toward divorce. It reflected the belief that a person should not be forced to continue in a marriage that she or he found to be personally unacceptable. Such an individualistic view of the marriage bond would have outraged the American colonists and their Western European contemporaries; yet in 1970 it carried the day. It was consistent with the shift from the companionship marriage to the independent marriage. [➡ p. 271] England, where a century earlier only Parliament could authorize the end of a marriage, also added no-fault grounds to its divorce law in

1969. By the end of the 1980s, virtually every Western nation and every state in the American union had adopted some form of no-fault legislation. England, France, Germany, and other countries required that if only one partner wanted the divorce, and children were involved, he or she had to wait several years before it was granted. In contrast, the typical U.S. state required a waiting period of one year or less (Glendon, 1987). Divorce had changed from a way for wealthy men to protect their property from heirs fathered by other men to a way for the average person to improve her or his own sense of well-being. In the most liberal no-fault states and nations, it had become something close to an individual right.

Factors Associated with Divorce

Given the current high level of divorce, two questions arise about its causes: First, on an aggregate level, why did the divorce rate virtually double in the 1960s and 1970s? Second, on an individual level, what factors place a person at greater risk of experiencing a divorce? Let us examine these questions in turn. Table 13.1 on page 424 provides a summary of the factors associated with divorce.

THE SOCIETYWIDE RISE

You might think that the introduction of no-fault divorce would boost the divorce rate. There is some evidence that a surge of divorces occurred during the first few years after a state enacted no-fault legislation (Nakonezny, Shull, & Rodgers, 1995). The surge may have been a "backlog effect" (Rodgers, Nakonezny, & Shull, 1997) of couples in unhappy or troubled marriages who were quick to take advantage of the new, liberalized rules. It is unclear whether, after the initial surge, no-fault divorce had a lasting effect on the number of divorces; several studies suggest that it did not (Schoen, Greenblatt, & Mielke, 1975; Wright & Stetson, 1978; Peters, 1986).[2] Whereas no-fault laws began to spread through the 50 states in the 1970s, the divorce rate, as Figure 13.1 shows, had begun to increase substantially several years earlier. These facts suggest that no-fault divorce was more a consequence of the trend toward more divorce than a cause. Its introduction is an example of how changes in family law in the contemporary United States have often followed, rather than preceded, changes in behavior and values. In this instance, the social changes were the greater emphasis on personal fulfillment as a criterion for whether a marriage should continue and the greater economic independence of women from men.

Cultural Change   Previous chapters have examined the growing place of personal fulfillment in marriage, and an extensive discussion will not be presented here. Cultural critics claim that this emphasis erodes bonds of obligation and trust. As a framework for thinking about relationships, it is alleged, the emphasis on personal fulfillment results in a vocabulary that is rich in ways of thinking about individual well-being but impoverished in ways of thinking about commitment (Bellah, Madsen, Sullivan, Swidler, & Tipton, 1985). For instance, numerous books, articles, lecture series, courses, and support groups exist on self-actualization or

---

[2]For similar findings from the Netherlands, see van Poppel and de Beer (1993).

Table 13.1 Factors Associated with Divorce	
SOCIETYWIDE FACTORS	
No-fault divorce legislation	State no-fault divorce laws produced an initial surge of divorce in the 1970s, but it is unclear whether no-fault laws have had a lasting effect.
Cultural change	A greater emphasis on personal fulfillment made divorce a more acceptable option for people who felt unfulfilled by their marriages.
Women's employment opportunities	Women's growing employment opportunities led to a rise in the number of wives working outside the home. Employment gave wives greater economic independence, which made divorce a more attractive alternative to an unhappy marriage.
Men's employment opportunities	As young men's economic opportunities decreased since the early 1970s, their reduced earning potential may have caused stress in marriages.
INDIVIDUAL FACTORS	
Low income and unemployment	Divorce is more common among people with lower incomes. Lack of money can cause strain and tensions in a marriage.
Age at marriage	People who marry as teenagers have a higher rate of divorce. They may not choose partners as well as those who marry later.
Race and ethnicity	African Americans have higher rates of separation and divorce than most other groups. Low income and unemployment, as well as a lesser emphasis on marriage in African-American kinship, may contribute.
Cohabitation	People who cohabit prior to their marriage have a higher rate of divorce. They may have a weaker commitment to marriage than do people who marry without cohabiting first.
Parental divorce	People whose parents divorced are more likely to end their own marriages in divorce. They may model their behavior on their parents' marriages, or they may have a genetic tendency toward having problems in intimate relationshps.
Spouse's similarity	People who marry people who are similar to them in characteristics such as religion have a lower rate of divorce. Such couples may be more compatible in their values and interests.

self-development or human potential, but much less intellectual activity is centered on maintaining personal responsibilities and obligations to others. Put another way, a focus on personal fulfillment represents a shift toward the concerns of the private family as against the concerns of the public family. Under these circumstances, divorce becomes a more acceptable option for people who feel personally unfulfilled; indeed, *not* divorcing in the face of personal dissatisfaction comes to need justifying. Still, there's little direct evidence to show just how large a factor cultural change has been in the rise in divorce since the 1960s.

Women's Employment   In most cases, women do not earn as much as men nor do they typically earn enough to fully support themselves and their children. Nevertheless, the average wages earned by women rose substantially between 1950 and 1980; this rise, in turn, spurred the great increase in married women's movement into the paid labor force (Smith & Ward, 1985). Wives' employment theoretically could have contrasting effects on divorce.

- *Income effect.* Women's employment could lower the likelihood of divorce because the increase in the family's income could relieve financial pressures

The movement of married women into the work force was one factor in the twentieth-century increase in divorce.

and thereby reduce tension in the marriage. Moreover, the job could increase the wife's self-esteem and make her more satisfied with her life in general.

- *Economic opportunity effect.* On the other hand, employment could raise the likelihood of divorce by providing an opportunity for the wife to support herself independently of her husband. This opportunity would make divorce a more attractive alternative for women who were unhappy with their marriages. The economic opportunity effect would even operate for wives who were not themselves working outside the home. They might be more likely to divorce if they lived in areas in which the employment prospects for women were good.

Research suggests that the economic opportunity effect is more powerful than the income effect. Historian Steven Ruggles (1997b) examined the individual records from the censuses of 1880, 1910, 1940, 1980, and 1990. In each census, he found that women were more likely to be divorced or separated if they lived in areas where it was common for married women to work outside the home. He interprets these findings to mean that women who have greater opportunities for paid employment are more likely to be divorced or separated. And he notes that between 1880 and 1990, employment opportunities for women have increased dramatically. Numerous studies show that married women who work outside the home are more likely to divorce than married women who do not, although it is unclear whether this association is due to the mere fact of working outside the home, to the number of hours worked, or to the level of wages earned (Greenstein, 1990). Commentators throughout the twentieth century have noted the relationship between women's paid employment and divorce.[3]

---

[3]For a review of these studies, see Cherlin (1992b). Some recent studies have not found strong associations of women's employment and divorce (Tzeng & Mare, 1995).

Nevertheless, women by no means initiate all divorces; a wife's income might also make a husband feel less guilty about asking for a divorce. A woman's independent income facilitates divorce; equally unhappy couples in which the wife is not employed might not be able to divorce as easily. It is also possible that the chain of cause and effect works the opposite way; at least one study suggests that a woman who thinks her marriage is in trouble may be more likely to take a job outside the home in case the marriage fails (Johnson & Skinner, 1986). Moreover, the cultural change toward self-fulfillment could be the driving force behind both the greater number of women working outside the home *and* the greater number of divorces.

Men's Employment   Since the early 1970s, the employment opportunities for men without college educations have been declining. [→ p. 117] Oppenheimer (1994) argues that the economic opportunity effect has worked in reverse for men. That is, divorce has risen not just because women's economic opportunities have *increased* but rather because young men's economic opportunities have *decreased,* leading to greater stress in marriages and more divorces. Despite the increase in married women's employment, our society still expects that husbands earn a steady income. When they do not, Oppenheimer argues, their marriages are subject to greater stress and a higher risk of divorce. Still, Oppenheimer's view cannot explain the long-term rise in divorce rates prior to the early 1970s because men's economic opportunities were improving during most of the late nineteenth and early twentieth centuries (Ruggles, 1997a).

INDIVIDUAL RISK FACTORS

There are many other social and economic factors that seem to increase or decrease an *individual's* likelihood of ever experiencing a divorce but have not contributed to the recent, *societywide* increase. Consider teenage marriage: As will be noted below, people who marry as teenagers have a greater likelihood of divorce than those who postpone marriage. Yet the societywide average age at marriage has been increasing since the 1960s. Consequently, we can rule out teenage marriage as a cause of the societywide rise in divorce. The list of individual risk factors includes the following.

Low Income and Unemployment   Divorce is more likely if the husband is unemployed. In fact, it is more likely among families with low incomes, regardless of employment, than among families with higher incomes. Some middle-class observers, aware of the sharp rise in divorce among middle-class families, are surprised to learn this. During the 1960s and 1970s, the divorce rate rose sharply among families in all social classes, but at all times the rate has been greater among families with lower incomes (Cherlin, 1992). The simple reason is that lack of money can cause problems and tensions in any marriage. Also, recall evidence from Chapter 9 [→ p. 304] on the strain that unemployment places on a marriage: It can lead to depression and then to hostile and irritable behavior by the husband, who is failing to fulfill his traditional responsibility as a provider. His behavior, in turn, can provoke anger and depression in his wife and children.

Age at Marriage   In addition, as noted above, people who marry as teenagers have a higher likelihood of divorce than people who wait until their twenties. Teenagers probably cannot choose partners as well as older persons can. In part, they are not mature enough. Compared with people in their twenties, teenagers may not know as well what kinds of persons they will be as adults and what their needs in a partner will be. Even if they do have a good sense of their emerging selves, they will have a more difficult time picking an appropriate partner because it is hard to know what kind of spouse an 18-year-old will prove to be over the long run. Moreover, teenage marriages are sometimes precipitated by an accidental pregnancy, and it is known that a premarital birth raises the likelihood of divorce. It does so partly because it brings together a couple who might not otherwise have chosen to marry each other. It also may be more difficult, on a practical level, for a couple to make a marriage work if a young child is present from day one. Still, earlier marriage cannot be an explanation for the post-1960 rise in divorce because age at marriage increased after 1960.

There is some evidence that the divorce rate is also higher for people who marry for the first time at an unusually late age, such as over 35 (Sweet & Bumpass, 1987). Late first marriage could be a sign of some personality factors that make them less attractive as marriage partners, or it could be that people who marry late (especially women, who tend to marry men who are older than they) have a restricted pool of eligible partners and must compromise in their selection. In either case, most of the evidence is based on data from 1980 or earlier, when marriage ages were generally lower than in the 1990s. As more and more people postpone marriage until their thirties, the distinctiveness of late marriers will fade and the association between late marriage and divorce may diminish.

Moreover, people with less education have a greater probability of ending their marriages in divorce. Yet much of this effect occurs because people with less education tend to marry earlier—soon after high school, for example, rather than soon after college (Sweet & Bumpass, 1987). After taking into account age at marriage, the most distinctive group is high school dropouts, who in some studies show the highest probability of divorce. Demographers have speculated that dropouts may be less persevering in marriage as well as schooling, but the evidence is slim (Glick, 1984).

Race and Ethnicity

Race and Ethnicity   African Americans have substantially higher rates of marital separation than most other racial-ethnic groups; about one-half of the marriages of black women end within 10 years (Sweet & Bumpass, 1987). Although lower income, unemployment, and lower educational level are important sources of this racial difference, these factors alone cannot account for it. For example, among college graduates in 1980 (and divorce rates haven't changed much since 1980), 44 percent of black women who had married 10 to 14 years earlier had already separated or divorced, compared with 23 percent of comparable non-Hispanic white women (Sweet & Bumpass, 1987). Indeed, at every level of education, black women are more likely to have separated. It is likely that the lesser emphasis in African-American culture on marriage, relative to extended kinship ties, also plays a role. [➡ p. 152] African Americans, who can rely more heavily on mothers, grandmothers, and other kin, have less need to stay married; they also have an alternative source of support if a marriage ends (Orbuch, Veroff, & Hunter, 1999).

In addition, black women who separate from their husbands are considerably less likely to obtain a legal divorce, and again the differences are not due solely to economics or education. Within three years of separating, 55 percent of black

FIGURE 13.2
Percentage of women who
had separated or divorced by
1980, among all women who
had married for the first time
10 to 14 years earlier, by
racial-ethnic group. (*Source:*
Sweet & Bumpass [1987].)

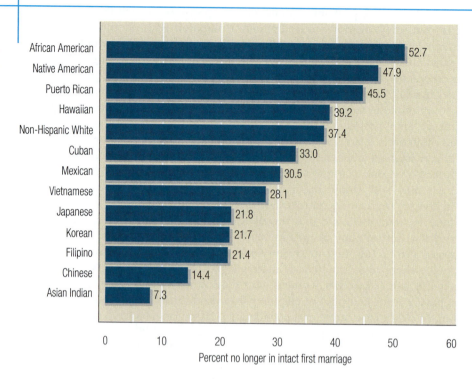

women had obtained a divorce, according to the 1980 Census, compared with 77 percent of Mexican-American women and 91 percent of non-Hispanic white women. What these statistics imply is that black women have a higher likelihood of separating from husbands, but they turn these separations into divorces at a much slower pace. Perhaps their lower expectations of remarrying, which will be discussed in the next chapter, provide less motivation to obtain a legal divorce.

Figure 13.2 compares the prevalence of divorce among 13 racial-ethnic groups in the United States, according to the 1980 Census. Comparisons this fine-grained can be made only by using the computer files from the large, decennial census, and no one has yet constructed a similar chart from the 1990 or 2000 data. For women who had married for the first time 10 to 14 years prior to 1980, the bars show the percentages that had separated or divorced by the 1980 Census. As can be seen, Native Americans have the second-highest percentage of couples who had separated or divorced. To what extent this reflects their high levels of poverty versus other factors is not clear. The figure also demonstrates the great diversity of the ethnic groups often lumped together as Hispanic. Puerto Ricans have the third-highest percentage of separated or divorced couples. Yet Cubans have a lower percentage than non-Hispanic whites, and Mexicans have a lower percentage than any other major racial-ethnic group except Asians. The Asian groups are still made up heavily of recent immigrants from countries with low divorce rates; whether they will retain their distinctively low rates of dissolution in subsequent generations remains to be seen.

Personal and Family Background   The personal and family histories people bring to a marriage also matter. Since married couples who live together

prior to marriage have already had, in a sense, a trial run at marriage, we might expect that they would have a lower divorce rate than couples who did not live together before marrying. Just the opposite, however, is true: Couples who cohabit have higher divorce rates. Researchers have found that people who will not cohabit before marriage often have a stronger commitment to marriage and family life than those who will. Consider a study in which a national sample of high school seniors in 1972 was asked a series of questions about personal and family values and then was followed through 1986. Those who responded in 1972 that "finding the right person to marry and having a happy family life" was "very important" were substantially less likely to cohabit prior to marrying than those who responded that it was "not important." So were those who responded that "living close to parents and relatives" was important. Individuals who participated actively in church-related activities were also substantially less likely to cohabit prior to marrying (Clarkberg, Stolzenberg, & Waite, 1993; Waite & Gallagher, 2000).

Results such as these suggest that people who cohabit prior to marrying are a self-selected group who differ from noncohabitors in their attitudes toward personal relationships and family life. The cohabiting individuals carry these values with them when they marry, and, as a result, they are more likely to divorce than married people who did not cohabit. In addition, some evidence suggests that the experience of cohabiting itself, with its lower level of commitment than marriage, may change an individual's values and contribute to a higher likelihood of divorce (Thornton, Axinn, & Hill, 1992).

A number of studies show that persons whose parents divorced while they were growing up are more likely than others to become divorced themselves (Amato, 1996; White, 1990). Yet persons who lost a parent through death while they were growing up are *not* more likely than others to become divorced (Diekmann & Engelhardt, 1999).[4] These contrasting findings suggest that more than a parent's absence must be involved, because otherwise the effect of a parental death would be the same as the effect of a parental divorce. Rather, something about growing up in a divorced family must be associated with a higher risk of divorce as an adult. One possibility is that living through a parental divorce somehow diminishes a person's ability to sustain a successful marriage. For example, children of divorce may witness more parental conflict than other children, and may adopt a conflict-laden style of relating in their own marriages. A second possibility is that children in divorced families may share characteristics inherited from their parents (such as a tendency to become seriously depressed) that make a lasting marriage difficult for both generations (McGue & Lykken, 1992). But even if there were a genetic mechanism, it could not account for the nineteenth- and twentieth-century increases in the nation's divorce rate because, as noted in earlier chapters, evolutionary genetic changes occur far more slowly.

Finally, people who marry people who are similar to them are, in general, less likely to divorce, probably because the couples are more compatible in their values and interests. For example, Catholics married to Catholics and Protestants married to Protestants are both less likely to divorce than Catholics married to

---

[4]The association between growing up in a divorced family and being at higher risk of divorce as an adult may be weakening because growing up in a divorced family is less stigmatizing and less difficult now that divorce has become common (Wolfinger, 1999).

Protestants (Lehrer & Chiswick, 1993). People who are far apart in age also have higher divorce probabilities than people who are closer in age, particularly if it is the wife who is much older (Carter & Glick, 1976). (If the wife is older, the marriage goes against the social norm of older men marrying younger women.) We don't know exactly why; it may be that a large age difference, especially if the wife is much older, indicates that one or both of the partners had personal characteristics that made them less desirable on the marriage market.

The Process of Divorce

The unmaking of a marriage occurs in many stages over a period of time that often begins well before the couple separates and that extends well after they are granted a divorce. A number of observers of the process of divorce have attempted to describe its different aspects.[5] Here are the four major aspects.

THE EMOTIONAL DIVORCE

Separating from a spouse is a difficult process for nearly all the people who go through it, notwithstanding the fact that at least one spouse initiated the process and is presumably better off because of it. In instances of clear fault, such as wife battering, drunkenness, or desertion, the cause is obvious and both spouses are usually aware of it. In the many more instances in which one or both spouses are unhappy and unfulfilled, the causes are murkier, and neither spouse, at first, may be aware of the true situation. Typically, though, one person becomes dissatisfied first and begins the process of ending the marriage. Diane Vaughan, who interviewed people about the process, calls this person the **initiator** (Vaughan, 1990). The initiator has the advantages of being the first person to know that there is a chance of separation, of preparing emotionally for it, and of using the threat of leaving in order to demand change. The threat is similar to what Willard Waller, writing in the 1930s about courtship, defined as the "principal of least interest": the party that is less interested in maintaining the relationship has the advantage in bargaining (Waller, 1938).

> **initiator (of a divorce)** the person in a marriage who first becomes dissatisfied and begins the process of ending the marriage

Early Warning Signs The initiator begins to express discontent, but without clearly and directly stating that he or she is unhappy with the marriage. Instead, the initiator may try to change the other partner's behavior or the relationship—as by having a baby or urging the partner to change jobs or take up a new interest. One person told Vaughan:

> *Somehow I had misjudged her—who she was and what she was capable of. Maybe I thought she was someone she was not. . . . She needed something of her own, some friends of her own. . . . I encouraged her to get out in the world and get involved* (Vaughan, 1990).

If these efforts are unsuccessful, the initiator begins to invest more energy and emotion outside the relationship. At some point, the initiator declares his or her

---

[5]See, for example, Bohannan (1971b). Bohannan also writes of the "community divorce" involving changes in friends and community and the "psychic divorce" involving regaining autonomy; these aspects are included elsewhere in the discussion.

dissatisfaction with the relationship to the partner. Only then, in many cases, does the partner realize the seriousness of the situation. The confrontation can bring about efforts by the spouses to reconcile their differences or to alter the relationship to their joint satisfaction.

> *I was very upset, hurt, crying, but at the back of my mind I thought well, maybe this too will pass if I continue to play—play, that's an interesting choice of words—play this open, warm, loving type of person, that maybe I'll get her back, still, and not be too angry or hostile at her* (Vaughan, 1990).

Sometimes these efforts, perhaps aided by marital counseling, succeed and the separation is averted. If they fail, it is likely that the couple will separate, sometimes with the thought that it is temporary.

Separation

Often, however, the initiator has decided by that time that he or she doesn't want the marriage to continue.

> *Even at that point, at initial separation, I wasn't being honest. I knew fairly certainly that when we separated, it was for good. I let her believe that it was a means for us first finding out what's happening, and then eventually possibly getting back together* (Vaughan, 1990).

The "temporary" separation announces the breakup to the couple's world. There may be an attempt to reconcile, but by this time the initiator's heart is usually not in it. Even if the initiator is making a good-faith effort, it may not be possible for the partner to regain a sense of trust in the initiator (Weiss, 1975). A final separation then occurs.

In his studies of newly separated persons, Robert Weiss noticed the persistence of their feelings of attachment to their partners, even among initiators. **Attachment,** a concept Weiss borrows from the literature on infants, is a bonding to another person that produces feelings of security, comfort, and ease when the other person is present or nearby. Weiss found that feelings of attachment persisted for months—sometimes years after a person separated, long after feelings of anger had replaced feelings of love. The persistence of attachment caused "separation distress": the person focused his or her attention on the estranged spouse and experienced discomfort that the spouse was no longer accessible (Weiss, 1975).

Weiss estimated that it took his subjects two to four years to recover fully from the separation. The first phase of recovery—after the old pattern of life had been destroyed but before the separated person had successfully integrated a new pattern—was a time of stress, often accompanied by disorganization and depression. Another writer called this first phase "crazy time" (Trafford, 1982). According to Weiss, it lasts about a year, after which time there is a longer period in which the person has put together a new pattern of life but is still vulnerable to setbacks. One man who had been the initiator of his separation told Weiss:

> *I had quite a bit of guilt over the whole thing happening, and as a result of that I was really bogged down with it. . . . I can remember the first four months of separation were just horrendous. . . . It was four months of bouncing off the walls. I couldn't eat. I couldn't sleep. I could not work. . . . And a friend of mine said, "Hey, get hold of yourself. Get some sleep." I saw a doctor who prescribed some antidepressants or something. I started to eat again, started sleeping. And then once I started eating and sleeping I started to rebuild. The first thing was my job. And then all the other things just fell into place* (Weiss, 1975).

attachment a bonding to another person that produces feelings of security, comfort, and ease when the other person is nearby

Eventually, most people adjust emotionally to the separation. As life moves on, people become less preoccupied with their former spouses. In fact, one study of divorced persons found that their adjustment was significantly higher when they were less preoccupied with their ex-spouses. Those who were more likely to disagree with statements such as "I can't stop thinking about my ex-spouse," "I am curious about what my ex is doing," and things "trigger thoughts about my ex-spouse" answered positively to questions about emotional well-being (Masheter, 1997).

THE LEGAL DIVORCE

Property and Assets   In addition to ending their emotional relationship, the couple must end their legal relationship. If there are no children, the separation agreement mainly specifies any continuing payments that one agrees to make to the other and divides up their property and assets. In the past, the important property, if any, has consisted of savings, homes, automobiles, and so forth. Increasingly, though, the most valuable property a person owns is intangible. This "new property," as it is sometimes called, consists of personal intangible assets, created during the marriage, from which one spouse will continue to benefit. It may include a professional license or educational credential, such as a medical school degree that allows a person to practice as a physician. Or it may include retirement benefits that one spouse has accrued for old age. As long as the couple remain married, they will share the rewards of these assets, but if they separate, only one spouse will benefit from them.

Consider a 1979 case in Kentucky, *Inman* v. *Inman*. The couple met when they were both undergraduates planning to attend medical school. After their graduations, Ms. Inman took a job as a biologist to pay for Mr. Inman's medical school expenses, with the understanding that after he received his medical degree she too would attend medical school. Instead, the couple separated a year after Mr. Inman graduated. Ms. Inman asked the court to award her compensation for her husband's medical degree, arguing that she had financed it in the expectation of joint benefits but that now the benefits would accrue only to him. The court ordered Mr. Inman to reimburse her for the costs of medical

Most married couples need legal assistance to complete their divorces. The procedure is more complex if the couple has children.

school plus inflation and interest (Weitzman, 1985). Still, there is no consensus in legal rulings about what exactly constitutes marital property, how to value it, and how to distribute it. In the event of a divorce, asks legal scholar Robert Levy, is the wife of an inventor entitled to a share of his future royalties on patented inventions? If so, how much? To date, the law has provided little consistent guidance, Levy concludes, on matters of marital property such as this (Levy, 1989).

Although wives may request maintenance payments—known as **alimony**—from their ex-husbands, few couples now agree to it and few judges order it. As women have moved into the paid labor force, the legal system has come to assume that they can be self-supporting following a divorce, perhaps after some temporary financial assistance from the ex-husband. This assumption, however, may not hold for wives who have been out of the labor force for many years—a point I will return to shortly.

Child Custody   When children are present, the legal situation is more complex. There is first the matter of custody: Who will have responsibility for the children, and where will they live? **Legal custody** refers to having the right to make important decisions about the children and to having legal responsibility for them. **Physical custody** refers to where they actually live. In the United States in the past, the two kinds of custody were usually merged; the father typically had custody in both senses prior to the mid-nineteenth century, the mother, after that. Family law throughout much of the twentieth century was based on a presumption that maternal custody was better for young children; indeed, custody was awarded to the mother in about 85 percent of the cases (Weitzman, 1985). In most states, however, that presumption has been replaced with the rule that the court should decide according to the "best interests of the child"—a standard that formally favors neither parent. Nevertheless, it is still the case today that in the majority of divorces, mothers have both legal and physical custody. (It is also the case that in a majority of divorces, fathers do not want physical custody.)

Some states are moving toward a presumption in favor of **joint legal custody,** which means that both parents retain an equal right to make important decisions concerning the children (as opposed to sole legal custody, in which one spouse can make the decisions without consulting the other) (Bartlett, 1999). A decree of joint legal custody is essentially a decree that the parents' responsibilities toward their children have not changed; despite the divorce, they both remain responsible. In California, which has led the move toward this kind of custody, two-thirds of a sample of more than 1,000 divorce cases in the mid-1980s resulted in joint legal custody. In practice, however, joint legal custody didn't mean much in this sample; legal scholar Robert Mnookin and psychologist Eleanor Maccoby found that fathers who had joint legal custody didn't see their children more often than fathers whose ex-wives had sole legal custody, nor were the fathers more involved in decisions about their children. The researchers concluded that joint legal custody is valuable mainly as a symbol of the father's continuing responsibility for his children (Maccoby & Mnookin, 1992).

In a growing but still small number of cases, divorcing couples are agreeing to **joint physical custody,** under which the children spend substantial time in each household—perhaps alternating on a weekly basis. Joint physical custody, however, requires a great deal of cooperation between the ex-spouses, who must

alimony maintenance payments from an ex-husband to an ex-wife

legal custody (of children after a divorce) the right to make important decisions about the children and the obligation to have legal responsibility for them

physical custody (of children after a divorce) the right of a divorced spouse to have one's children live with one

joint legal custody (of children after a divorce) the retaining by both parents of an equal right to make important decisions concerning their children

joint physical custody (of children after a divorce) an arrangement whereby the children of divorced parents spend substantial time in the household of each parent

After divorce, mothers typically retain custody of the children. Some non-custodial fathers take them for regularly scheduled overnight visits.

transport children back and forth, share clothing, coordinate schedules, and so forth. Many—perhaps most—divorcing couples cannot manage this much cooperation. To jump ahead briefly to the effects on children, the California study shows that joint physical custody can work very well for the children when the parents voluntarily choose it and can cooperate. But if the parents are still angry and warring with each other, the children tend to feel caught in the middle. For example, a parent may attempt to extract information about the private life of the ex-spouse from the children, which often causes stress and anxiety. The researchers urge judges not to impose joint physical custody on parents who don't want to undertake it (Buchanan, Maccoby, & Dornbusch, 1991).

THE COPARENTAL DIVORCE

Regardless of state laws, the reality is still that most children remain in the care of their mothers most of the time. This imbalance persists because it carries forward the typical childcare situation in two-parent families—namely, the wife does most of the care. It is difficult to get fathers involved in care after the divorce because most of them were not intensively involved before. In fact, the level of contact between fathers and their children after divorce is very low. Figure 13.3 shows the amount of contact between children and their fathers, for children who were living with their mothers and whose fathers were living elsewhere. The pie charts are based on responses of the mothers of these children in the 1987–88 National Survey of Families and Households (Seltzer, 1991). More recent data are not available. There are separate pie charts for children whose parents were married when they were born—the group of main concern in this chapter—and children whose parents were not married when they were born. About one-third of the children of previously married parents had seen their father either once in the past year or not at all. Among the children of never-married parents, the comparable figure climbed to about half. Only about

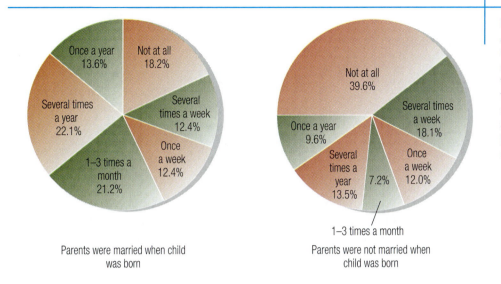

FIGURE 13.3
Amount of contact between children and fathers, for children who were living with their mothers and whose fathers were living elsewhere, according to the National Survey of Families and Households, 1987–1988. (*Source:* Seltzer [1991].)

one-fourth of the children of previously married parents had seen their fathers once a week or more often during the past year.

Why do so many fathers fade from their children's lives after a divorce? For some, visits to the children may be a painful reminder of the life they left behind, triggering feelings of guilt or sadness. Others may be investing their emotional energy in new families formed by remarriage. In addition, Frank Furstenberg and I have speculated that many fathers, when they were married, may have related to their children only indirectly, through their wives. They tend to see parenting and marriage as a package deal; when the wife is removed, they have difficulty connecting directly to their children (Furstenberg & Cherlin, 1991).

Even when fathers do remain involved, conflict between the parents tends to diminish over time. Still, the parents don't necessarily cooperate in rearing the children. Advocates of joint legal custody had hoped it would encourage more ex-spouses to practice **coparenting,** in which the divorced parents coordinate their activities and cooperate with each other in raising the children. Coparenting does occur, but more commonly the parents gravitate toward a more detached style: They talk as little as possible, avoid meeting each other, send messages through their children, rendezvous at restaurant parking lots to exchange them, and go about their parenting business separately. Rather than coparenting, this dominant style might be called **parallel parenting,** in recognition of the separate tracks the two parents follow in their dealings with the children (Furstenberg & Cherlin, 1991). One and a half years after they had filed for divorce, the California couples' most common style of parenting was conflicted: lots of arguments, threats, and distress (although there were many cooperative parents, too). When the parents were reinterviewed two years later, the most common style was "disengaged": little conflict and little cooperation; in short, parallel parenting (Maccoby & Mnookin, 1992).

coparenting an arrangement whereby divorced parents coordinate their activities and cooperate with each other in raising their children

parallel parenting an arrangement whereby divorced parents gravitate toward a more detached style, going about their parenting business separately

THE ECONOMIC DIVORCE

Many fathers seem to fade from their children's lives in part because they will not or cannot contribute to their children's support. Figure 13.4 displays the sad

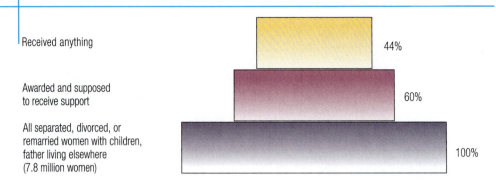

FIGURE 13.4
The child support pyramid: award and receipt of child support payments to women with children under the age of 21 living in their households who have fathers living elsewhere, 1997. (*Source:* U.S. Bureau of the Census [2000a].)

Received anything — 44%

Awarded and supposed to receive support — 60%

All separated, divorced, or remarried women with children, father living elsewhere (7.8 million women) — 100%

story of the child support pyramid. The figures are from a Bureau of the Census study of the 7.8 million separated, divorced, or remarried mothers who in 1997 had children under the age of 21 who were living with them and whose fathers were absent from the household. The base of the pyramid represents all these women. Moving up the pyramid, we can see that less than two-thirds had been awarded child support payments and were supposed to receive them in 1997. (Most of the rest had not been awarded child support payments for various reasons, such as inability to find the father.) Less than half had actually received any child support money in 1997. Among those who had received anything at all in 1997, the average amount was about $341 per month (U.S. Bureau of the Census, 2000a). (The situation was even grimmer for the 3.8 million mothers who had never married the fathers of their children; just 22 percent had received any child support payments in 1997, and the average amount they received was about $164 per month.)

Many mothers, therefore, are hit with a financial double whammy when they divorce. First, they lose their husbands' income, which typically exceeds theirs by a substantial margin. Second, less than half receive any money in child support payments. As a result, the average mother's standard of living is reduced by about 30 percent in the first year after she separates from her husband. In contrast, the average father's standard of living *rises* about 15 percent—because usually he is supporting only himself (Hoffman & Duncan, 1988).[6] One woman told Terry Arendell:

> *My husband really liked good food and always bought lots and the best. So when he left, it was really hard to cut the kids back. . . . Now there's often no food in the house, and everybody gets really grouchy when there's no food around. . . . We've lost $150 a month now because my husband reduced the support. It gets cut from activities—we've stopped doing everything that costs, and there's nowhere else to cut. My phone is shut off. I pay all the bills first and then see what there is for food. . . . I grew up playing the violin, and I'd wanted my kids to have music lessons—piano would be wonderful for them. . . . But lessons are out of the question* (Arendell, 1986).

Sometimes women and children fall into poverty because of the breakup. For instance, a government survey followed thousands of households for 28 months

---

[6]Hoffman and Duncan demonstrate convincingly that the widely cited figures in Weitzman (1985)—namely, that women's standard of living falls 73 percent and men's rises by 42 percent—are almost certainly too high and, in fact, are inconsistent with other figures in Weitzman's book.

beginning in 1984, including many in which fathers left the household during the study. Among the children whose fathers left the household, 19 percent had been living below the poverty line even before the breakup had occurred. But the loss of a father nearly doubled the proportion of children who were living in poverty to 36 percent by the end of the study. Moreover, the proportion whose mothers relied on Aid to Families with Dependent Children doubled from 9 to 18 percent just after the separation, and the proportion whose mothers were receiving food stamps jumped from 10 to 27 percent just after the separation (U.S. Bureau of the Census, 1991a). Because of statistics such as these, there have been several attempts to increase the amount of child support fathers pay. (See *Families and Public Policy:* Enforcing Child Support Obligations.)

Breadwinner-Homemaker Couples The inequity is worst for older women who have been out of the labor force for many years and whose husbands initiated their divorces. They married their husbands under the terms of the breadwinner-homemaker bargain: They were to raise the children and do the housework while their husbands worked for pay outside the home. Over the years, whatever skills they had developed that might land them a paying job deteriorated. Then, after perhaps 15 or 20 years of marriage, their husbands left.

These women turn to a legal system that, in an effort to treat men and women equally, expects divorced mothers to become self-supporting soon after their marriages end. It is a system that increasingly allows either spouse to end the marriage unilaterally, that rarely grants alimony, that often orders husbands to pay only modest levels of child support, and that, until recently, did a poor job of enforcing its support orders. It is a system that seems to assume it is dealing with upper-middle-class dual-career families in which wives have well-paying professional or managerial jobs. But even in upper-middle-class families, most women's earnings are substantially lower than their husbands' incomes. No wonder that, in one national study, 31 percent of women whose families had above-average incomes before their separations saw their standard of living drop by more than half in the first year (Duncan & Hoffman, 1985).

Single-Father Families Although most single-parent families are headed by mothers, the number of single-father families has been growing rapidly. Between 1980 and 1998, the number of single fathers living with their own children under 18 almost tripled from 616,000 to 1,798,000. These families now constitute 19 percent of all single-parent families with children (U.S. Bureau of the Census, 1999d). In addition, there are perhaps 800,000 custodial fathers who have remarried and therefore are not counted in the single-father total (Meyer & Garasky, 1993).[7] Adding in the remarried fathers would bring the total number of custodial fathers, single and married, to about 2.6 million. Single fathers tend to have higher incomes than single mothers because men's wages are typically higher than women's. However, single fathers tend to have lower incomes and less education than married fathers. A 1989 Census Bureau survey of single fathers found that 18 percent had incomes below the government poverty line and

---

[7]The authors, using another government survey, estimate that remarried, custodial fathers constitute about 40 percent of all custodial fathers. The remaining figures in this paragraph are all taken from Meyer and Garasky.

Children in single-parent families would benefit if every absent parent knew he or she would have to pay child support. This has been the goal of several new laws that were enacted in the 1980s and 1990s. Since 1994, for example, all parents who have been ordered by the courts to pay child support have had their payments deducted automatically from their paychecks. Moreover, states are now required to adopt guidelines for the amount of child support a parent should pay, according to income and number of children; judges must follow these guidelines or state in writing why they didn't (Cherlin, 1993).

The 1996 welfare reform act [➡ p. 191] contained a number of additional measures to strengthen the system. For instance, it provided more support for programs to establish paternity in hospitals at the birth of the children, and it penalized welfare recipients who failed to cooperate. It required employers to send the names of newly hired employees to state and federal agencies that will match the names against lists of parents who have not paid child support obligations. It allowed states to deny occupational and driver's license renewals to parents who fail to pay (U.S. Administration for Children and Families, 1996). In fact, toughening child support enforcement has been one of the most popular family policies among both conservatives and liberals. Conservatives favor tougher enforcement because making fathers pay is consistent with their belief that parents should take responsibility for the well-being of their children. (Although the law applies equally to absent mothers who owe child support payments, in practice the vast majority of payments are collected from fathers and distributed to mothers.) The new measures send a message to fathers that they can leave their marriages, but they can't leave their children. Conservatives hope that the measures will deter men from fathering children they can't, or don't intend to, support. Liberals favor tougher measures because increased collection of child support payments will provide more economic support to children in low-income single-parent families.

There is evidence that these measures are producing results. Between 1993 and 1997, the proportion of custodial mothers who reported receiving the full amount of child support they had been awarded increased by 30 percent (U.S. Bureau of the Census, 2000a). However, most of the measures help middle-class single parents more than poor single parents and their children. Most middle-class single mothers are divorced, and can obviously identify the fathers of their children. Moreover, most middle-class fathers are employed and can make some child support payments. Many poor single mothers, in contrast, were never married to the fathers of their children. Even when the fathers can be identified and located, they may not be employed, and thus may not be able to pay much in child support. Consequently, some experts warn that child support programs that stress enforcement of divorce decrees will not work for poor families. Rather, these experts advocate programs to increase the earnings capacity of single fathers, so that they can afford to pay child support (Meyer, 1999).

Ask Yourself

1. Do you know anyone who has had difficulty collecting court-ordered child support payments? If so, was the problem caused by the absent parent's inability to pay or simply an unwillingness to pay?

2. Besides the measures described here, what other steps could government take to improve the economic well-being of children in single-parent families?

www.mhhe.com/cherlin

another 21 percent had incomes less than twice the poverty line. Yet few single fathers are granted child support awards, since most have higher incomes than their ex-wives. Nevertheless, some single fathers with low incomes may need assistance from their former wives.

About 4 percent of all children in 1998 lived in single-father families (U.S. Bureau of the Census 1998b). Our mental image of the single-father family is the divorced dad living alone with his children. However, only one-fourth of single-father families consist of divorced men living alone with their children. Of the rest, most are sharing their households with mothers, sisters, or new girlfriends, who may be doing much of the childcare (Eggebeen, Snyder, & Manning, 1996). Yet the census counts them as "single-father families" as long as the mother of the child is not in the household.

The number of single-father families has been growing.

The Effects of Divorce on Children

At least one partner chooses to divorce in every case of marital disruption. Presumably, then, at least one partner's well-being is enhanced by the divorce. But children do not choose that their parents divorce. It isn't necessarily true that their well-being is enhanced by their parents' divorce. In fact, there are good reasons to think that their well-being should be, in many cases, diminished. They lose the benefit of having both of their parents living in the same household with them. They must go through an emotionally difficult process of adjusting to the breakup. Frequently, they must cope with continuing, bitter conflict between their parents. They often feel the consequences of a sharp fall in family income. Here is a description of their experiences.

THE CRISIS PERIOD

Psychologists P. Lindsay Chase-Lansdale and E. Mavis Hetherington have written that the first year or two after the parents separate is a **crisis period,** during which both the custodial parent and the children—nearly all of whom are intensely upset when they learn of the separation—often experience difficulties (Chase-Lansdale & Hetherington, 1990). After the breakup, the custodial parent (typically the mother) is often angry, upset, and depressed. One consequence, according to observers, is the "diminished parenting" that often occurs during the crisis period (Wallerstein & Kelly, 1980). Distracted, distressed parents may have difficulties providing the daily mixture of emotional support and moderate, consistent discipline that psychologists called "authoritative parenting." [➡ p. 320] Instead, parents seem to be emotionally distant and preoccupied, prone to ignore misbehavior or to lash out with harsh discipline. For example, a child misbehaves, prompting the harried, depressed parent to respond angrily.

crisis period a period during the first year or two after parents separate when both the custodial parent and the children experience difficulties in dealing with the situation

Her response can set off more negative behavior: A toy is thrown on the floor or a bowl of cereal is knocked off the table. The parent responds even more angrily, further provoking the child.

In this way, the parent and child are drawn into what Hetherington and others call "coercive cycles," in which the parent's and child's responses aggravate the situation. Hetherington found that acting-out behavior and coercive cycles are more common among boys than girls (girls show fewer outward problems, although they may be holding in feelings that will erupt years later). After a year or two, however, many custodial parents have reorganized their lives and begun to manage their anger and depression enough to provide a more supportive and structured routine for their children (Hetherington, M. Cox, & R. Cox, 1978).

Moreover, as discussed earlier, the frequent decline in the family's standard of living, brought about by the withdrawal of the father's income and partial or nonexistent support payments, creates an additional source of distress for the recently separated parent and her children. In a study of families with young children, interviewed before a separation and about one year afterward, boys were showing more behavior problems in families whose incomes had dropped below the poverty line (Morrison & Cherlin, 1995). A number of studies do show that children's distress is greater during the crisis period than afterward, as parents begin to adjust to the divorce.

Several other factors are at work in making life difficult for children after the breakup, increasing the chances that they will be upset and misbehave. The situation of each child usually involves some combination of the following factors.[8]

Loss of a Parent   Most of the early articles on the impact of divorce on children addressed the consequences of having the father leave home. Following a Freudian model, the writers theorized that a boy would have difficulty adopting the adult male role if he could not see how his father behaved and if he was not subject to his father's authority. However, a major review of the research literature in 1973 found little evidence to support this viewpoint (Herzog & Sudia, 1973). Nevertheless, many observers believe that the loss of a parent, of either gender, will make the tasks of the remaining parent more difficult for other reasons. For instance, if a teenager protests when a parent tells him he can't go to a party Friday night, it helps if a second parent is around to back up the first one. In other words, the tasks of monitoring and supervising the behavior of children may be more difficult if only one parent is present. Several studies do show that if a second adult, such as a grandmother, is present in the household, children seem to behave better and do better in school.[9]

Parental Conflict   Continuing conflict between the parents harms their children's well-being, especially if the parents use the children as pawns in their battles. When parents fight, children tend to become fearful and distressed—whether the parents are married or divorced. In fact, studies show that children in two-parent families wracked by intense conflict are more depressed and show more behavior problems than children in divorced families (Peterson & Zill, 1986). After the breakup, children have fewer problems if their parents can cooperate or at least engage in parallel parenting. A study found evidence that if parents are still fighting after a divorce or separation, their sons show *more* behavior problems if they see the nonresident parent regularly than if they see him or her less often. Conversely, if there is little conflict between the parents, the

---

[8]This list draws upon (but is not identical to) the categories in Amato (1993).
[9]See for example, Dornbusch et al. (1985).

sons show *fewer* behavior problems if they see the noncustodial parent regularly. (No differences were found for daughters (Amato & Rezac, 1994).)

It's important to recognize that the conflict that harms children can begin before the breakup. Divorce is not just an event that happens the day a parent moves out; rather, it is a process that typically begins much earlier. In a research project that I carried out with several collaborators, we examined the records of thousands of British and American children who had been followed from age 7 to age 11 (Cherlin et al., 1991). We focused on children whose parents had been married at the beginning of the study and watched as they split over time into two groups: those whose parents divorced and those whose parents stayed together. Not surprisingly, the children whose parents divorced were showing more behavior problems and were doing worse in school. But then we looked back to the start of the study, before anyone's parents had been divorced. We discovered that children whose parents would later divorce were *already* showing more behavior problems and doing worse in school than children whose parents would remain together. This finding suggests that some of the trauma of divorce begins before the separation, as unhappy parents begin to move apart. In addition, it suggests that the problems that children exhibit after a divorce might have occurred to some extent even if their conflicted parents had remained together.

Multiple Transitions   Apart from exposure to the parents' distress and conflict, the breakup forces children to adjust to jarring transitions. The first, of course, is the departure of a parent from the home. This is not necessarily the last transition, however. The financial settlement between the parents frequently requires that the family's house be sold. As a result, children must often move to a new neighborhood, begin classes at a new school, and make new friends. One study found that two-fifths of divorced mothers move during the first year after the divorce—a majority of them because they are forced to do so by a falling income (McLanahan, 1983). Many divorced mothers move in with their parents temporarily while they make the transition to single parenting (Goldscheider & Goldscheider, 1994).

Other adults will probably move in and out of the child's household. A majority of single parents remarry, and, as will be discussed in Chapter 14, two-thirds of remarriages are preceded by a period of cohabitation. Moreover, as noted earlier, half of all children whose parents remarry will witness a second divorce before they reach age 18. More will be said about remarriage shortly; for now I will suggest that the cumulative stress of these multiple transitions may cause difficulties. For instance, one national study found that the number of family transitions a young woman had experienced was a stronger predictor of whether she would bear a child before marrying than the number of years she had spent in a single-parent family (Wu & Martinson, 1993).[10] Similarly, a large study in New Zealand found that both children whose married mothers had stayed married *and* children whose single mothers had stayed single had fewer behavioral problems than children whose mothers had changed partners (Najman et al., 1997).

AFTER THE CRISIS PERIOD

After the crisis period, the majority of children resume normal development (Emery, 1999). Still, a study by Hetherington and W. Glenn Clingempeel found that, five years after the disruption, about 25 to 30 percent of young adolescents

---

[10]See also Capaldi and Patterson (1991).

Being exposed to continual conflict between their parents can harm children, whether the parents are married or divorced.

were displaying serious behavior problems, as opposed to less than 10 percent of young adolescents who were still living with both parents.[11] The researchers found that the problems of some boys in the crisis period had persisted; in addition, girls were now displaying as many problems as boys. Early adolescence is a time when tension between parents and children can increase as the children try to become more independent. It is possible that this task is more difficult for children whose parents have divorced. According to the Hetherington and Clingempeel study, single mothers monitored their children's behavior less closely and engaged in more arguments with them than did married mothers. Moreover, the researchers speculated that children who are just coming to terms with their own burgeoning sexuality may have a more difficult adjustment when they must confront intimate relationships between a parent and that parent's new boy- or girlfriend or spouse.

LONG-TERM ADJUSTMENT

The Sleeper Effect   How do children of divorced parents fare over the long term? The psychologist Judith Wallerstein followed a group of such children

---

[11]By "serious" behavior problems, I mean scores on a checklist of behavior problems that were high enough to indicate that some clinical help might be needed. See the commentary by Maccoby (1992a).

for 25 years. Her books about their well-being after 10 years (Wallerstein & Blakeslee, 1989) and 25 years (Wallerstein, Lewis & Blakeslee, 2000) report widespread, lasting difficulties in personal relationships. At the 25-year mark, a minority had managed to establish successful personal lives, but only with great effort. The legacy of divorce, Wallerstein claims, doesn't fade away:

> *Contrary to what we have long thought, the major impact of divorce does not occur during childhood or adolescence. Rather, it rises in adulthood as serious romantic relationships move center stage. When it comes time to choose a life mate and build a family, the effects of divorce crescendo.* (p. xxix)

Because these young adults didn't have the chance to observe successful marriages, Wallerstein maintains, they didn't learn how to create one. Faced with the choice of a partner or a spouse, their anxiety rises; they fear repeating their parents' mistakes. Lacking a good model to follow they are more likely to make bad choices. Overall, Wallerstein states, only about half the women and one-third of the men in the group were able to establish successful personal lives by the 25-year mark.

Yet Wallerstein's study is based on just 60 families who voluntarily came to her clinic for counseling and therapy soon after a divorce. Although she screened out children who had seen a mental health professional, many of the parents had extensive psychiatric histories.[12] Troubled families can produce troubled children, whether or not the parents divorce, so blaming the divorce and its aftermath for nearly all the problems Wallerstein saw among the children over 25 years may be an overstatement.

In contrast, consider a long-term study of the effects of parental divorce on the mental health of over 10,000 British children born in 1958 (Cherlin, Chase-Lansdale, & McRae, 1998). At age 33, the mental health of persons whose parents had divorced was somewhat worse, on average, than that of persons whose parents had stayed together. However, the majority of persons from divorced families were not showing signs of serious mental health problems. In addition, some of the differences in mental health between the two groups had been visible in childhood behavior problems at age seven, before any of the parents divorced. Some of the seeming effect of divorce at age 33, then, probably reflected long-term difficulties that would have occurred even without a divorce.

In light of this British study, what can we draw from Wallerstein's research? I suggest that it is a valuable description of the lives of children from *troubled* divorced families, one that reveals what can happen to children when conflict or mental health problems accompany a divorce. And many divorcing parents do face the kinds of difficulties Wallerstein saw in her study. Moreover, her basic point that the effects of divorce can sometimes last into adulthood, or even peak in adulthood, is valid. Wallerstein was the first person to write about children who seemed fine in the short-term, but experienced emotional difficulties later, in adolescence or young adulthood. In her book on the 10-year follow-up (Wallerstein & Blakeslee, 1989), she called this delayed reaction the "sleeper effect."

But the negative effects of divorce probably are not as widespread as Wallerstein claims. Some portion of what she labels as the effects of divorce on children probably weren't connected to the divorce. And the typical family that experiences divorce won't have as tough a time as Wallerstein's families did. Parents

---

[12]See the appendix to Wallerstein and Kelly (1980).

with better mental health than those in her sample can more easily avoid the worst of the anger, anxiety, and depression that comes with divorce. They are better able to maintain the children's daily routines at home or in school. And their children can more easily avoid the extremes of anxiety and self-doubt that plagued the children in Wallerstein's study.

Education and Employment   Rather than Wallerstein's gloomy picture, the long-term view seems to encompass both a glass-half-full and a glass-half-empty perspective. When parents divorce, or when single parents raise children outside marriage, their children run a higher risk of experiencing undesirable events (such as dropping out of school) in young adulthood and beyond. Nevertheless, most children from single-parent families will not, as a consequence, experience such problems (Amato, 1999). Consider studies based on national surveys by Sara McLanahan which show that, even after adjusting for parents' education, race, number of siblings, and place of residence, children who live in a single-parent family (whether with a divorced parent or a never-married parent) are more likely to drop out of high school, to have a child as a teenager, and to be "idle"—out of school and out of work (McLanahan, 1994). Her estimates imply, for instance, that 29 percent of those who grow up in single-parent families may drop out of high school compared with 13 percent of those who grow up in two-parent families. How large is this difference? On the one hand, it implies that the chance of dropping out of high school more than doubles for children from single-parent families—a substantial effect that seems worthy of concern. That's the glass-half-empty perspective. On the other hand, 7 in 10 children from single-parent families *do not* drop out of high school. That's the glass-half-full perspective.

It is possible that some of these long-term difficulties are due to the poor quality of the parents' marriages, rather than to the divorce itself. A study by Paul R. Amato and Alan Booth (1997) attempted to disentangle these two possibilities. The study began as telephone interviews with a nationally representative sample of married couples in 1980. The interviewers asked their respondents multiple questions on marital quality, including marital happiness, marital interaction (e.g., "How often do you eat your main meals together?"), marital conflict ("How many serious quarrels have you had in the past two months?"), and divorce proneness (e.g., "Has the thought of getting a divorce or separation crossed your mind in the last three years?"). The researchers divided all of the families into two groups, low conflict and high conflict, using all of the information. Then in 1992 all of the children who had lived with their parents in 1980 and who were now age 19 or older were interviewed.

The investigators report that offspring who experienced high marital conflict in 1980 were doing *better* in 1992 if their parents had divorced than if they had stayed together; on the other hand, offspring from low-conflict families were doing worse if their parents had divorced. This finding confirms the oft-stated but rarely substantiated belief that if family conflict is severe, children may benefit from a divorce. But the researchers caution that only a minority of the divorces that occurred were in high-conflict marriages (such as marriages with physical abuse or frequent serious quarrels). For that minority, the consequences of experiencing continuing conflict between their parents probably would have been worse than the consequences of the divorce. But the majority of offspring who experienced parental divorce probably would have been better off if their parents had stayed together.

Marital Happiness   Do the effects of a parental divorce carry over to an individual's own marriage? Information from the National Survey of Families and Households suggested the following picture: People whose parents divorced seemed just as happy with their marriages, on average, as did people whose parents did not divorce. However, people whose parents divorced were more likely to think that their marriages were in trouble, as if they were more sensitive to signs of marital strain. And among all people who reported their marriages as less than very happy, persons from divorced families were more likely to argue frequently and to shout or hit while arguing, as if repeating the conflictual style they may have learned or inherited from their parents (Webster, Orbuch, & House, 1995).

In Sum   Overall, the research literature on the effects of divorce on children suggests the following conclusions:

- Almost all children experience an initial period of intense emotional upset after their parents separate.
- Most resume normal development without serious problems within about two years after the separation.
- A minority of children experience some long-term problems as a result of the breakup that may persist into adulthood.

From the glass-half-empty perspective, we can conclude that divorce may cause a substantial percentage increase in the number of individuals who may need the help of a mental health professional or who may not obtain as much education as they should or who may be unemployed more often than they should. As a society, we should be troubled by this development. From the glass-half-full perspective, however, it seems that most individuals do not suffer serious long-term harm as a result of their parents' divorce. We need to keep both perspectives in mind when considering the effects of divorce.

As noted, a divorce is not the end of the changes faced by many single parents and their children. A majority of the parents will either live with another partner, marry one, or do both. The next chapter explores the determinants and consequences of remarriage. I will postpone an overall discussion of the effects of divorce until the end of that chapter.

Looking Back

1. **What is the history of divorce in the United States and other Western nations?** There have been three eras in the history of divorce in modern Western nations. During the first era, which lasted until the middle of the nineteenth century, divorce was very difficult to obtain. It was granted mainly to wealthy men who owned land, usually to ensure that an adulterous wife would not bear a child who would have a claim on the man's property. During the second era, divorce became increasingly available in cases of reprehensible conduct, but was still frowned upon. The third era began in 1970, when the state of Cal-

ifornia eliminated the need to prove a spouse was at fault to obtain a divorce. Divorce became available on demand, with few restrictions other than a waiting period.

2. **What social and individual factors are associated with a greater likelihood of divorce?** The two most important causes of the rise of divorce in the twentieth century were the increased emphasis on self-fulfillment as the central criterion for judging marriages, and the growing economic independence of women. Other factors that are associated with divorce include income,

age at marriage, race and ethnicity, cohabitation, and personal background. Couples with low incomes are more likely to divorce than couples with higher incomes. People who marry as teenagers are more likely to divorce than those who marry as adults. African Americans, Native Americans, and Puerto Ricans have a higher rate of divorce than non-Hispanic whites, Cubans, Mexicans, and Asian Americans. People who cohabit before marrying have a higher risk of divorce than people who do not cohabit first. Children of divorced parents are more likely to divorce than other adults. Finally, couples who share similar characteristics, such as age and religion, are less likely than others to divorce.

3. **What happens to parents during the divorce process?**
A divorce begins when one spouse initiates the separation. When it occurs, both spouses typically experience great distress. Legally, couples must divide up their tangible and intangible property, and agree on custody arrangements for their children, if any. States have been moving toward joint legal custody of children; in a small but growing number of cases, parents also share physical custody. Nevertheless, many fathers see their children infrequently after a divorce. In families in which the father does remain involved, the dominant style of parenting is a detached, low-conflict, low-cooperation mode that can be described as parallel parenting. Economically, the income of mother and children usually falls after a divorce, both because of the mother's lower wages and because most men pay little in child support.

4. **What are the short-term effects of divorce on children?** Divorce has several effects on children. First, one parent, usually the father, leaves the household, depriving the children of a role model, and the remaining parent of a source of support and help in monitoring and supervising the children's behavior. Second, during the crisis period following the separation, the custodial parent is often upset and angry; consequently, maintaining the children's daily routine and providing emotional support and consistent, moderate discipline can be difficult. In addition, the custodial parent must often cope with a substantial drop in family income. Third, the child may suffer if he or she is caught up in continuing conflict between the two parents, though the conflict and its negative effects may have preceded the separation. Finally, the sheer number of transitions involved, each requiring adjustment on the children's part, may overwhelm their ability to cope.

5. **What are the long-term effects of divorce on children?** Long-term studies suggest that parental divorce raises the risk of undesirable outcomes in their children, such as dropping out of high school, bearing a child before marrying, or suffering from mental health problems as an adult. But some of the problems that children from divorced families show probably preceded the divorce, and might have occurred even if the parents had not separated. Studies suggest that a majority of children whose parents divorce will not experience serious long-term problems.

Thinking about Families

1. Should getting a divorce be more difficult? Is "covenant marriage" a good idea?

2. What effect, if any, is the current high divorce rate likely to have on American society and culture in the future?

3. Why do so many divorced fathers see their children only infrequently?

4. **The Public Family** Should parents in unhappy marriages stay together for the sake of their children?

5. **The Private Family** Why is a divorce so emotionally difficult, even for the person who initiated it?

Key Terms

alimony 433
annulment 418
attachment 431
coparenting 435
crisis period 439

era of divorce tolerance 420
era of restricted divorce 418
era of unrestricted divorce 421
initiator 430
joint legal custody 433

joint physical custody 433
legal custody 433
no-fault divorce 422
parallel parenting 435
physical custody 433

Families on the Internet   www.mhhe.com/cherlin

*Note: While all the URLs listed were current as of the printing of this book, these sites often change. Please check our web site (**http://www.mhhe.com/cherlin**) for updates.*

 There are numerous web sites about divorce, most devoted to practical information for people who are about to divorce, in the process of obtaining a divorce, or dealing with postdivorce issues, such as modifying the legal agreement. Balanced overviews are hard to find. In addition to dispensing practical advice, **www.divorceonline.com** reprints many articles on divorce-related topics. See also **www. divorcecentral.com** or **www.divorceinfo.com** for a sense of the issues of greatest concern to people going through a divorce.

Over the past several years, a "marriage movement" has developed among professionals and academics who believe that the benefits of marriage are underappreciated, and that too many marriages end in divorce. A key web site is **www.smartmarriages.com,** which offers information about upcoming conferences, recent books and articles, and news reports. How might the resources available at this web site help to strengthen marriages?

chapter 14

Remarriage and Stepfamilies

1. What are the basic characteristics of remarriages and stepfamilies?

2. How can we define "family" and "kinship" in the case of stepfamilies?

3. How do stepparents, parents, and children go about building a stepfamily?

4. How does the well-being of children in stepfamilies compare to the well-being of children in other kinds of families?

5. How have increases in divorce, remarriage, and related trends altered family life?

In 1979, when Danny Henrikson was a year old, his parents divorced. Danny's mother, Nancy, was awarded custody of his eight-year-old brother, Jay; his three-year-old sister, Joie; and him. Nancy soon married James Gable, and then in 1982 she died. The children's father, Gene Henrikson, agreed that Gable would retain custody of the children. Henrikson moved from Michigan to New York and rarely visited or called his children. Gable, on the other hand, was a devoted stepfather who worked continually with Danny to overcome a learning disorder. In 1983, Jay, who was then 12, visited his father in New York. Upon his return, Jay told Gable that he wanted to live with his father. Gable consented and transferred custody of Jay to Henrikson in New York. Then, at the end of 1985, Henrikson filed a court action seeking custody of Danny and Joie.

At this point, Danny was seven and had lived in Michigan with Gable since he was one. Gable fought the transfer, arguing that it was in Danny and Joie's best interests to remain in the home where they had been, by all accounts, raised well. The trial judge ruled in Gable's favor, writing, "the length of time the children have lived in a stable, satisfactory environment and [the] desirability of maintaining continuity . . . is weighed very strongly on behalf of the Gables." Henrikson, however, appealed to a higher court. In 1987, the Michigan Court of Appeals reversed the decision and awarded custody to Henrikson. Yes, the appeals court judges wrote, an established custody arrangement shouldn't be changed unless doing so is in the best interests of the child. However, another presumption also applied:

> *When the dispute is between the parent or parents and . . . a third person, it is presumed that the best interests of the child are served by awarding custody to the parent or parents (Henrikson v. Gable, 1987).*

After seven years of being Danny's dad, James Gable was not a parent, in the eyes of the court; rather, he was a "third person." Gene Henrikson, who had moved to New York and had hardly stayed in contact with Danny, was the parent. The appeals court clearly felt that the biological parents remain the legal parents, even if they have little to do with their children; whereas stepparents, even if they have raised the children since infancy, are still the legal outsiders.

The Incomplete Institution

David Chambers, the legal scholar who unearthed this case, notes how little standing the law gives to the relationship between stepparents and stepchildren. In most states, the stepparent has no legal obligation to contribute to the support of the stepchildren, even if he has lived with them for years and the nonresident biological parent has paid nothing. And if the stepparent and the custodial parent get divorced, the stepparent has no further obligation to support the stepchildren, even if he had been supporting them informally for years. When judges must choose between stepparents and biological parents, observes Chambers, their decisions vary widely from case to case and jurisdiction to jurisdiction:

> *The incoherent pattern of outcomes and the murky and inconsistent discussions of the governing rules almost certainly reflect our society's conflicting and unresolved attitudes about stepparents* (Chambers, 1990).

(See *Families and Public Policy:* The Rights and Responsibilities of Stepparents, on pages 452–453.)

The conflict and lack of resolution are even broader. More than 20 years ago, I published an article entitled "Remarriage as an Incomplete Institution" (Cherlin, 1978). Curious about the complex families formed when divorced people remarry, I had reviewed the research literature and interviewed a number of remarried couples in Maryland. In all of them, at least one spouse had children from a previous marriage living in the household. Sometimes both did, but more often the father's children, if any, lived with his former wife. Some of the families also had a mutual child from the new marriage. What I found were people who were working hard to create a coherent family life. Every day they faced issues and problems that people in first marriages never dream of, such as, Does a stepfather have the authority to discipline his stepchild if the child does something wrong? What should a child call the woman his father married after he divorced the child's mother? Where is the "home" of a child who spends four days a week living with his father and three days living with his mother?

These daily problems often cut to the heart of more fundamental questions: What is a family, and what are its boundaries? Who is a relative and who is not? What obligations do adults and children sharing the same household owe to one

Stepfamilies must create their own rules and shared meanings through discussion and negotiation.

The Rights and Responsibilities of Stepparents

Until recently, the legal rights and responsibilities of stepparents with regard to their stepchildren in American and English law could be summed up easily: There weren't any. Even if stepparents had resided with their stepchildren for many years, they had no obligation to support them or to care for them in any way. And even if a stepparent had provided most of the care of the stepchildren for years, the biological parent would still retain custody of the children if the marriage ended. The lowly status of the stepparent extends back hundreds of years in English common law. Under common law, a remarriage did not create any legal link between the stepchildren and their stepparent. "It was as if," British legal scholar Stephen Cretney writes, "the remarriage had never happened" (Cretney, 1993).

As noted elsewhere in this chapter, 9 in 10 remarriages are formed as a result of divorce rather than widowhood. Children typically reside with a custodial parent, usually their mother, and a stepparent, while a second biological parent resides elsewhere. Consequently, the traditional body of law gives the biological parent who resides outside the home legal priority over the stepparent who lives with the children. So sweeping is this priority that the judge in the Henrikson case was only following standard legal precedent when he gave Danny's biological father in New York custody over the objections of a stepfather who had lived with him for years.

The judge's decision stems from a time in which the custody of children was treated fundamentally as a matter of the ownership of property. For children were indeed seen as property a few centuries ago—not because they were unloved but rather because they were valuable sources of labor for a family. A man who remarried after his wife died wanted to protect his children from the claims of his new wife's family. His children were an important asset. Today, however, our conception of children has changed, and we view them primarily in terms of the emotional and financial investments parents make in them and the emotional gratification parents receive. When courts consider custody and support cases, they usually base their deci-

sions on the standard of what is in the best interests of the child. And it is not clearly in the best interests of children to be removed from homes in which they have been given good care, even if the caregiver was not a biological parent. This is why many people find judges' decisions in cases such as *Henrikson* v. *Gable* troubling.

Slowly, the law concerning stepparents is changing. In England, the Children's Act of 1989 allows stepparents to assume some responsibilities and gives them the right to petition the court under a number of circumstances (Cretney, 1993). Although the stepparent does not have legal responsibility for the child, if he or she is caring for the child, he or she may do what is reasonable to promote the child's well-being. If the marriage between the parent and the stepparent ends, the stepparent may request that the children live with him or her. (The judge, of course, need not grant this request.) Should the biological parent die, the surviving biological parent has the right to take the children, as happened in the Henrikson case, but the stepparent may ask the court to let the children

another? People in first marriages rarely think about these questions because our culture provides us with a set of social roles (patterns of behavior associated with positions in society—in this case, parent, spouse, and child) and social norms (widely accepted rules about how people should behave) that address them. These roles are so ingrained that we take them for granted—we know, for example, who our relatives are; we know what a parent is. The widely accepted, taken-for-granted character of the roles and rules of family life is what makes the family a social institution. Recall that a social institution is a set of roles and rules that define a social unit of importance to society. [➡ p. 19]

But stepfamilies create situations in which the taken-for-granted rules and the well-established roles don't apply. Consequently, stepfamilies must create their own rules, their own shared meanings, through a long and sometimes difficult process of discussion, negotiation, and trial and error. In other words, as I argued in my article, life in stepfamilies is incompletely institutionalized in our society.

remain with him or her. Still, the stepparent has no recognized legal status.

In the United States, the practices of the courts seem to be evolving slowly in the direction of recognizing some rights and responsibilities for stepparents. With respect to custody, all states give biological parents priority, but many states allow a third party, such as a stepparent, to obtain custody if parental custody would be detrimental to the well-being of the child.[1] In some states, it is now easier for a stepparent to adopt a stepchild, even over the objections of the noncustodial parent. Adoption can occur if, for instance, the noncustodial parent hasn't made child support payments or visited the child for a year or more.[2] Stepparents even have won custody in a few special circumstances. In one case, upon the breakup of the marriage of a stepmother and a biological father, the stepmother was given custody of a child who had lived with them. The child was deaf, and the court was impressed by the educational efforts made on his behalf by the stepmother during the marriage.[3]

In another case a stepmother, Mary, was granted custody of her stepson, Brendan, over the objections of the biological mother, following the death of the biological father. Brendan, age 12, had been living with Mary and his biological father prior to the father's death. Although residing in a different state, Brendan's biological mother had visited him regularly. Nevertheless, he told the court he wished to continue to live with his stepmother. The court found that a "mother-son relationship developed" between Brendan and Mary. Furthermore, it held that "the superior right of a natural parent to custody of his or her child is not absolute but only one of several factors looked to in determining best interests of the child."[4]

I think it is likely that this slow evolution will continue, as parenthood comes to be defined partly in terms of what parents actually do for children, not just whether they are biologically related. This is not to say that the claims of resident stepparents should always win over the claims of biological parents living elsewhere. Yet, given the number of stepparents who are caring

for children, it seems time to recognize the importance of their contribution and to provide them with some of the rights and responsibilities that until now have been reserved for biological mothers and fathers.

Ask Yourself

1. Do you know anyone who has been involved in a child custody dispute between a biological parent and a stepparent? If so, in whose favor was the dispute resolved, and on what grounds?

2. Should stepparents be given more rights and responsibilities? What might be the consequences of such a change for stepchildren? For biological parents? For society as a whole?

---

[1]See, for example, California Code, Section 4600, and Massachusetts Code, Section 208.28. I thank Elizabeth Scott for providing me with much of the information about recent case law in this and subsequent paragraphs.

[2]*In the Matter of J.J.J.*, 718 P. 2d 948 (Alaska 1986).

[3]*In re Marriage of Allen*, 626 P. 2d 16 (Wash. App. 1981).

[4]*In re Marriage of Carey*, 544 N.E. 2d 1293 (Ill. App. 2 Dist. 1989).

www.mhhe.com/cherlin

The lack of shared meanings can create problems for parents, stepparents, and children. Negotiation and bargaining take time and effort and can cause bruised feelings. To be sure, stepfamilies offer the possibility of creating useful new roles that have no counterparts in first marriages (such as the trusted "intimate-outsider" roles some stepparents play—see below). Still, institution building is difficult work and takes its toll on stepfamilies.

There are other reasons why we might expect the tasks of family life to be more difficult for stepfamilies than for families formed by first marriages (White, 1994). In terms of social networks, individuals in stepfamilies have ties to different sets of individuals, such as biological parents living elsewhere or children living with another parent (see below). The pull that these networks exert can undermine attempts to strengthen the unity of the stepfamily. In addition, stepparents who join families well after the stepchildren were born do not have the investment of time and effort that the parent already has made; therefore, the role of stepparent may be less central to their identities. Finally, evolutionary psychologists would note that parents pass on their genes to children, whereas stepparents do not pass on genes to stepchildren (Popenoe, 1994). Therefore, they would predict that stepparents would express less warmth and support toward stepchildren, on average, than biological parents, as research on stepfamilies confirms (Hetherington & Jodl, 1994). Despite these limitations, many stepfamilies are successful. How parents and stepparents put their families together, what these families look like, and how they are changing the very nature of family and kinship are the subject of this chapter.

The Demography of Remarriage and Stepfamilies

There's nothing new about remarriage per se, but until recently most remarriages followed the death of one of the spouses. The decline in adult death rates in the twentieth century and the increase in divorce, however, have changed the balance: Currently in the United States, 9 in 10 of all remarriages follow a divorce rather than a death (U.S. National Center for Health Statistics, 1991a). Widows and widowers tend to be older persons, not parents caring for young children, and the probability of remarrying is lower for widows and widowers than it is for divorced persons. For the balance of this chapter, the term "remarriage" refers to remarriage after divorce. Because of the increase in divorce, more than 4 in 10 weddings in the United States involve a remarriage for the bride, the groom, or both (U.S. National Center for Health Statistics, 1991a).

DECLINING MARRIAGE RATES

Eighteenth-century poet and critic Samuel Johnson once said that remarriage is the triumph of hope over experience. Recently, the triumph has been occurring less often. Until the 1960s, the remarriage rate and the divorce rate went up and down in parallel—when the divorce rate increased, so did the rate of remarriage. It seemed that divorced people weren't rejecting the ideal of being married, they were just rejecting their own first marriages and trying again. Starting in the 1960s, however, the annual rate of remarriage (the number of remarriages in a given year divided by the number of previously married persons aged 15 and older in the population) fell even though the divorce rate began to rise. The fall has continued ever since. At current rates, only about two-thirds of separated and divorced women will ever remarry; the corresponding figure for men is about three-fourths.[1]

Remarriage Rates   Some divorced persons are more likely to remarry than others. Some have a greater desire to remarry. For example, one study found that women who married in their teens or early twenties are more likely to remarry than women who married later. The authors speculate that women who

---

[1]Based on the 1985 data, Bumpass, Sweet, and Martin (1990) estimated that 72 percent of recently separated women would remarry. But remarriage rates have declined further since then. A 1992 Census Bureau report suggests that the true figure may be closer to two-thirds (U.S. Bureau of the Census, 1992c). The most recent estimate for men—78 percent remarry within 10 years—is from 1980 Census data and is probably too high now (Sweet & Bumpass, 1987).

married young may have less experience in, and less of a preference for, living independently.[2] Other women may be less attractive to potential spouses. Women who have three or more children, for instance, have a lower likelihood of remarrying, probably because they have a harder time finding a partner who would want to move into their household. Given the norm that wives should be younger than their husbands, older women face a shrinking marriage market. They are expected to marry from the diminishing pool of older single men, whereas men can choose from the expanding pool of younger women. Consequently, women who divorce at a younger age are more likely to remarry than those who divorce at an older age. What is more, the greater financial independence of some older divorced women, who may be more established in their jobs, may make them less interested in remarrying.

In addition, remarriage is far more likely among non-Hispanic whites than among Hispanics or African Americans. According to one estimate from 1980 Census data, about half of all non-Hispanic white women will remarry within five years of their separation, compared with one-third of Mexican-American women and one-fifth of African-American women.[3] These differences occur, in part, because remarriage rates are lower for the poor than for the nonpoor. With few assets or little property to pass on to children, people with low incomes have less need for the legal protection marriage brings. Yet lower incomes don't account for the entire difference. The low remarriage rates for African Americans are also consistent with the lesser place of marriage in the African-American family. Recall that fewer African Americans ever enter a first marriage and that they take longer to do so than whites. This explanation doesn't apply to Hispanics, whose rates of first marriage are more similar to those of non-Hispanic whites. It is likely that the Catholic Church's opposition to remarriage influences the behavior of this heavily Catholic group.

Divorce Rates among the Remarried

Remarriages are somewhat more likely to end in divorce than first marriages. Among women, about 37 percent of remarriages have dissolved after 10 years, compared with about 30 percent of first marriages (Sweet & Bumpass, 1987). The difference is concentrated in the first several years, during which time people in remarriages have substantially higher rates of divorce than people in first marriages. In my article, I hypothesized that the lack of institutionalized rules and roles might cause conflict in remarriages that would lead to divorce. Such conflict would be more likely, I thought, in remarriages in which stepchildren are present because of the increased complexity they bring to the family unit. Frank Furstenberg, Jr., and Graham Spanier, among others, have suggested an alternative reason for the difference in divorce rates. Remarried people, they argued, have demonstrated that they are willing to resort to a divorce when their marriages are unsatisfactory, whereas some people in first marriages may be very reluctant to do so. Consequently, these authors assert, remarriage involves a select group of people who may differ from first-time marriers in their propensity to divorce (Furstenberg & Spanier, 1984). Their argument is an example of a

---

[2]All the findings in this paragraph are from Bumpass, Sweet, and Martin (1990).

[3]Sweet and Bumpass (1987). More recent statistics are not available, but it is unlikely that the racial-ethnic differentials have changed much.

Remarriage rates are higher among non-Hispanic whites than among African Americans and Hispanics.

selection effect [➡ p. 223]: the idea that two groups differ because certain kinds of people select (or are selected into) one group more than the other. For example, the claim here is that people who are prone to divorce tend to select the remarried group, whereas people who are averse to divorce select the first-marriage group.

Another variation of this selection argument is that persons in remarriage may not be as skilled in choosing a compatible partner or holding a marriage together. For example, Teresa Castro Martin and Larry Bumpass found that a majority of remarried people had begun their *first* marriages as teenagers (Martin & Bumpass, 1989). They speculate that a teenage first marriage may be a sign of personality characteristics or other difficulties that make it harder for a person to select a good spouse or maintain a marriage. (We know that first marriages begun in the teenage years have a high divorce rate.) In any case, they found that the greater number of teenage first-time marriers in the remarried population accounted for much of the higher divorce rate among the remarried. Another recent national study reported that a teenage first marriage (a measure of the selection of particular kinds of people into remarriage) accounted for portions of the higher divorce rate among the remarried as did the presence of stepchildren (a measure of stepfamily complexity) (Booth & Edwards, 1992).

Increasing Cohabitation

The overall decline in remarriage, however, is deceptive. As remarriage rates have declined, cohabitation among the formerly married has increased. Consequently, the number of cohabiting couples in which at least one partner was formerly married has increased. Figure 14.1 illustrates the change. The bars on the

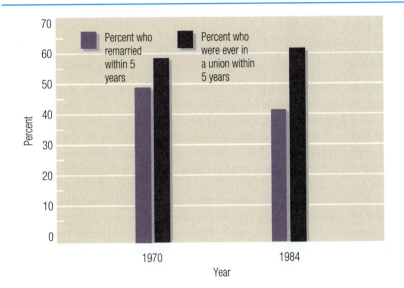

FIGURE 14.1
Percent who remarried within five years, and percent who were ever in union within five years, for persons separating around 1970 and around 1984, according to the National Survey of Families and Households. (*Source:* Bumpass, Sweet, & Cherlin [1991].)

left-hand side represent the situation around 1970. Forty-nine percent of persons had remarried within five years after they separated from their spouses. In addition, some had cohabited with a partner without marrying. When those who cohabited without remarrying are added to those who remarried, the sum is the number who were ever in a union—marital or cohabiting—within five years of separating. As can be seen, 58 percent had ever been in a union in 1970. By 1984, the pattern had changed. Only 42 percent had remarried within five years of separating, reflecting the drop in the remarriage rate. But the percentage who had ever been in a union had *increased* from its 1970 level to 62 percent in 1984. In the interim, cohabitation had become so widespread among the previously married that its increase had more than compensated for the decrease in remarriage (Bumpass, Sweet, & Cherlin, 1991). Divorced persons, in other words, are not less inclined to live with someone; rather, they have substituted cohabitation for remarriage. At least 60 percent of remarried people live with a partner—usually, but not always, their future spouse—before they remarry (Bumpass & Sweet, 1989).

In some postdivorce cohabiting relationships, children from previous marriages are present. In the past, households such as these have not been counted as stepfamilies because the potential stepparent is not married to the biological parent of the would-be stepchild. From the child's perspective, however, it may not matter whether his or her parent and live-in partner are married. In both cases, the child's relationship with his or her parent's partner is similar to that of a stepchild and stepparent. Nor may it make a difference to the child whether his or her parent was ever married previously. Suppose that a never-married woman gives birth to a child and several years later cohabits with a man other than the father. Suddenly her child must live in the same household as a man who is like a stepfather.

REDEFINING STEPFAMILIES

The rise of cohabitation among parents with children from previous relationships has led some sociologists to suggest that the definition of stepfamilies be

stepfamily a household in which two adults are married or cohabiting and at least one of the adults has a child present from a previous marriage or relationship

enlarged to include cohabitation as well as remarriage. Let us, then, define a **stepfamily** as a household in which:

1. Two adults are married or cohabiting, and
2. At least one adult has a child present from a previous marriage or relationship.

This definition does not require that the adults be married. Data from the 1987–1988 National Survey of Families and Households shows that under this broad definition, one-fourth of stepfamilies involved cohabiting couples (Bumpass, Raley, & Sweet, 1995) rather than remarried couples. In fact, a majority of children first entered stepfamily life through cohabitation rather than marriage; in many instances, the cohabiting parent subsequently married the live-in partner.

This definition also does not require that the child's parents ever have married. It allows for the increasingly common case in which a woman gives birth to a child outside of marriage and later lives with or marries someone other than the father. This path is particularly common among African Americans: About two-thirds of African-American stepfamilies, under this definition, were preceded by a nonmarital birth rather than a divorce (Bumpass et al., 1995). So this definition encompasses the kind of stepfamily, formed with little connection to marriage, that has become widespread among low-income and minority populations.

This way of conceptualizing stepfamilies is still new. Nearly all of the research on stepfamilies has been conducted within a framework based on divorce and remarriage. In part, that is because most of the research has been conducted on middle-class families. We know little about stepfamily life among the poor and near-poor. Throughout most of this chapter, then, the discussion will pertain more to stepfamilies formed by divorce and remarriage than to stepfamilies formed by nonmarital childbearing and cohabitation.

The New Extended Family

Mother, father, children: These are the building blocks of the conjugal family—the family unit based on first marriage. One of the taken-for-granted aspects of family life in the Western nations is that children are born into conjugal families and that the parents and children in the conjugal family live in the same household until the children grow up. Until the last few decades, that assumption was justified. More recently, the increases in divorce, childbearing outside marriage, and remarriage have rendered it problematic. Divorce splits the conjugal family into two households—one that typically contains a custodial parent (usually the mother) and the children and a second that contains the noncustodial parent (usually the father). In the case of a nonmarital birth, the conjugal family is never even formed.

Remarriage can bring a multitude of ties across households, creating what Furstenberg has called "the new extended family" (Furstenberg, 1987). Consider one set of family ties studied by Anne Bernstein (1988) and diagrammed in Figure 14.2. It is centered on the marriage of Carin and Josh, who reside in household 2. They have a mutual child, Alice. Josh used to be married to Peggy, with whom he had two children, Janet and Tim, who live with Peggy in household 3. Carin used to be married to Don, with whom she had two children, Scott and Bruce, who still live with her. Her former husband, Don, then remarried Anna and had two more children, Ethan and Ellen, who live with Anna and him in

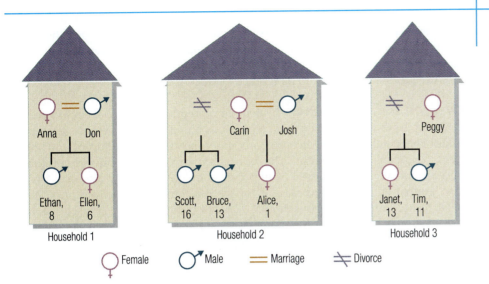

FIGURE 14.2
Bruce's stepfamily.
(*Source:* Bernstein, 1988.)

A stepfamily is a household in which two adults are married or are cohabiting and at least one has a child present from a previous marriage or relationship.

household 1. Here is how 13-year-old Bruce described his family (you are allowed to look at the chart while reading this):

> *Tim and Janet are my stepbrother and sister. Josh is my stepdad. Carin and Don are my real parents, who are divorced. And Don married Anna and together they had Ethan and Ellen, my half-sister and -brother. And Carin married Josh and had little Alice, my half-sister* (Bernstein, 1988).

SOME DEFINITIONS

How are we to make sense of this admixture? How many families are involved? What are their boundaries? The relationships spill over the sides of households, with children providing the links from one to the next. Let me suggest that there are two ways to define families in this context. The first is to focus on a household, even though ties extend beyond it. The advantage of this strategy is that we are used to thinking of families as being synonymous with households because we are used to thinking about first-marriage families.

Households   I have previously defined a stepfamily as a *household* that contains a parent with children from a previous union and that parent's current partner. The children from the previous union are the stepchildren, and the current partner is a stepparent. The household can be even more complex: Both partners may have children from previous unions, and they also may have a new, mutual child from the current union. But the defining criterion is that they all reside in the same household. Although there are three households in Figure 14.2, only household 2 contains a stepfamily according to our definition. Household 1 has no children from previous unions living there, and household 3 has children from a previous union and their biological parent but no current spouse or partner.

Remarriage Chains   The second way to define families is to ignore household boundaries and to focus instead on the human chains that extend from one household to another like intertwined strands of DNA. The bonds of the chains, the forces that hold the strands together, are children from previous unions. They link a divorced woman and her new partner with her ex-husband and his new wife. Anthropologist Paul Bohannan called these pathways "divorce chains" (Bohannan, 1971a). But if our interest is the links to quasi relatives that stepfamilies bring, it is probably more accurate to refer to them as **remarriage chains,** paths that link individuals across households through the ties of disrupted unions and new unions. Bruce was describing his remarriage chain. On one end, it begins with Anna, his father's current wife, and their children, Ethan and Ellen. Bruce sees them when he goes to Anna's house to visit his father, Don. Through Don and then Bruce, the chain continues into household 2, where it comprises Bruce's brother, Scott, his mother, Carin, his stepfather, Josh, and their mutual child, Alice. In addition, Josh's children from his first marriage, Janet and Tim, are included because they come to Bruce's house to visit their father. So Bruce's chain extends from Anna to Tim. Note, however, that Bruce doesn't mention Peggy, whom he rarely sees because he has no parents to visit in Peggy's household. In contrast, if Tim were asked about his family, he would obviously include Peggy. On the other hand, he probably doesn't see anyone in household 1 very often and wouldn't include them.

In fact, if you asked the people in the figure who was in their family, you likely would get a different answer from almost every one of them. To be sure, Bruce and Scott would probably name the same chain, as would Janet and Tim, and Ethan and Ellen. Otherwise, each person has his or her own distinctive chain. Consequently, the only way to specify the members of a remarriage chain is to define it in reference to a particular person—not a household. The stepfamily becomes a node, a switching point, that routes the chains to their various destinations.

Remarriage chains can serve as support and exchange networks, as ex-spouses and new spouses give and request favors. Family therapist Jamie Keshet describes the chain of a single mother named Marge, whose mother needed surgery. Marge

remarriage chain a path that links individuals across households through the ties of disrupted unions and new unions

wanted to spend two weeks with her mother, who lived in another state, after the surgery (all parenthetical material is in Keshet's account):

> *She called her former husband, Peter, to see if he could take the children for that time (Peter is a resource for her). Peter talked with his second wife, Jessica, and they agreed. . . . Jessica had two children from her first marriage. She called her ex-husband, Ron, to see if he could switch his visitation weekend so it would come after Peter's kids had gone, rather than in the middle of their stay. (Ron is a potential resource for Jessica and Peter in helping them have time alone together.) Ron agreed but found himself thinking, "I am expected to change my plans because my ex-wife's second husband's ex-wife's mother is ill"* (Keshet, 1988).

This system depends on the cooperation of all involved and can easily be disrupted. In extended-kin networks centered on conjugal families or "blood" relatives (see below), people might extend favors based on goodwill and a sense of shared purpose. In remarriage chains that sense of goodwill is limited, and decisions are more likely to be made using the calculus of self-interest. Ron is annoyed, but he will agree this time because he may need to ask Jessica for a similar favor in the future.

DOING THE WORK OF KINSHIP

Some links in the chains are weaker than others, and some fail entirely to form. When Americans think about kinship, they think about people related either through "blood" or through marriage. **Blood relatives** are people who share common ancestors: parents and children, uncles and aunts, nephews and nieces, grandparents and grandchildren. In theory, this network of blood relatives spreads out to an almost limitless number of people: second cousins (two people whose parents were first cousins), third cousins, and so forth. It spreads out on both the maternal and paternal sides, which is why anthropologists classify the Western countries as having **bilateral kinship,** a system in which descent is reckoned through both the mother's and father's lines (as opposed to kinship systems in which relatives are counted only on the mother's side or only on the father's side). Yet if I were to draw my family tree, I would include very few second cousins and no third or higher-order cousins because I don't know them. A friend of mine whose mother was estranged from her family never saw many of her maternal kin; her family tree includes many more relatives on her father's side than on her mother's side.

As these examples suggest, the mere existence of a blood tie does not make a relative. In American kinship, people must establish a relationship to consider each other kin. Having a relationship means seeing each other regularly, corresponding, and/or giving or receiving help—somehow making repeated connections. If there is no relationship, even a blood relative may not be counted as kin. Now, it's true that almost everyone considers their parents and their children to be relatives even if they haven't seen them in a long time. But you would understand what someone meant if she said, "My father left home when I was three and I never saw him again; I don't consider him part of my family." And you might not consider a cousin whom you last met when you were a child to be a relative.

To be a relative, then, you must do the work of creating and maintaining kinship. Among parents and children, this happens almost automatically—so much

blood relatives people who share common ancestors: parents and children, uncles and aunts, nephews and nieces, grandparents and grandchildren

bilateral kinship a system in which descent is reckoned through both the mother's and father's lines

so that we rarely think about it. But among stepparents, it does not happen automatically. For one thing, a stepparent in a remarriage or cohabiting union that has followed a divorce or a nonmarital birth does not replace the stepchild's nonresident parent, as was the case when most remarriages followed a death. Rather, the stepparent adds to the stepchild's stock of potential kin. If both biological parents are still involved in the stepchild's life, it's not clear what role the stepparent is supposed to play. Our society provides few guidelines, few norms. In the terms of my article, the role of the stepparent is incompletely institutionalized.

There is even greater variability in how more distant stepkin relate to the stepchildren. When Frank Furstenberg and I carried out a national study of grandparents, we asked them about relationships with stepgrandchildren. Once again, the younger the children had been when the grandparents had acquired them by virtue of an adult child's remarriage, the more the grandparents reported feeling that the children were like biological grandchildren. One stepgrandmother, who had not acquired her stepgrandchildren until they were teenagers, was asked what they called her:

> *Harriett. I insisted on that. They started by calling me Mrs. Scott. . . . But from the beginning, you realize, these children were in their teens, and it was hard to accept somebody from an entirely different family, and they didn't know me from Adam. . . . Now if they were smaller—you know, younger—it would have made a difference* (Cherlin & Furstenberg, 1992, p. 158).

It also made a big difference whether the stepgrandchildren were living with the grandparents' adult children (as when a son married a woman who had custody of children from a previous marriage) or were living most of the time in another household (as when a daughter married a man whose children lived with his former wife except for every other weekend and a month in the summer). Within these constraints, the closeness of the relationship depended on how much effort the stepgrandparents and their adult children put into creating the relationship. Being a steprelative depends on doing the work of kinship.

Building Stepfamilies

After a divorce, single parents and their children establish, often with some difficulty, agreed-upon rules and new daily schedules. They work out ways of relating to each other that may differ from those of earlier days. A daughter may become a special confidante to her mother; a son may assume new responsibilities, such as taking out the garbage, washing the car, and performing other tasks his father used to do. Put another way, single parents and children create a new family system. Then, into that system, with its shared history, intensive relationships, and agreed-upon roles, walks a stepparent. No wonder members of the stepfamily may have difficulty adjusting to his or her presence.

There is great variation in the types of stepfamilies that are formed today. Both partners may or may not have children from previous marriages. Those children, if they exist, may be young or adolescent, and their noncustodial parent may or may not see them regularly. Finally, the couple may have biological children after they remarry—or they may not. Even within each of these categories, there is great flexibility in how family members define their roles.

Nevertheless, research is beginning to suggest some general ways in which stepparents and stepchildren tend to interact during the life course of a typical

Table 14.1 Relations between stepparents and stepchildren		
	STEPPARENT	**STEPCHILDREN**
Transitional period (first 2 to 4 years)	Goes from "polite outsider" to "warm friend"	Young children: accepting of stepparent Early adolescents: may be distancing and resistant
Stabilization period (subsequent years)	Continued warmth Disengaged parenting Supportive of biological parent	Accepting of stepparent (but some long-term problems with late adolescents)

stepfamily. Table 14.1 summarizes these findings. I have labeled the first two to four years as the "transitional period," during which stepfamily members must adjust to the new family system (Bray, 1999). This is a time when parents are trying to build the stepfamily. I have labeled the subsequent years as the "stabilization period," when the new family system is firmly in place. These periods are approximate; a given stepfamily might have a shorter or longer transitional period, and some stepfamilies never stabilize.

THE TRANSITIONAL PERIOD

At the start, the stepparent is an outsider, almost an intruder into the system. At first, the stepparent may view himself or herself naively as a healer who will nurse the wounded family back to health (Papernow, 1988). But these initial efforts to help out may backfire. A stepdaughter may resent the intimacy and support a new stepfather provides to her mother; a son may not wish to relinquish certain responsibilities, such as washing the car, to a well-meaning stepfather who thinks fathers are supposed to do those chores. As Furstenberg and I wrote, "Stepparents quickly discover that they have been issued only a limited license to parent." The wiser ones among them accept the limits of their job description and bide their time (Furstenberg & Cherlin, 1991, p. 85).

The Stepparent as Polite Outsider   Given these difficulties, many stepparents take on the role of "polite outsider" during the early months of the stepfamily's existence (Hetherington & Stanley-Hagan, 2000). They don't attempt to discipline or control their stepchildren, nor do they actively back up the biological parent's efforts. Rather, they refrain from acting like a parent. They may even tone down displays of affection and support to the children. But as the family begins to adjust, the stepparent may display more warmth and support, and more actively back up the biological parent in efforts to supervise and discipline the children. Yet few stepparents actually discipline their stepchildren themselves. Instead, they try to support their partners while remaining relatively disengaged from active parenting themselves. They seek to be a warm and affectionate adult role model figure to the stepchildren—a "warm friend," so to speak (Hetherington & Jodl, 1994).

Until recently, there was no agreed-upon word by which a stepchild could call his or her stepparent. But in recent years, the use of the stepparent's first name has become increasingly common. If this usage becomes widespread, it will institutionalize the stepparent's role as neither parent nor stranger, but someone in between. That is, a child doesn't (usually) call a parent by his or her first name, nor use the first name of a stranger. Rather, the first-name usage suggests a role that is akin to that of a kindly uncle or aunt—a relative whom the child likes and can turn to for support, but not someone who has the authority to discipline the child.

Adjustment of the Stepchildren

As for the stepchildren, some show increased behavior problems in the early stage of a stepfamily (Bray, 1999). Some stepchildren also display resistance or hostility toward the stepparent, who may be surprised that his or her overtures are rejected. A key factor in how stepchildren respond is their age when the stepparent joins the household. Very young children are much more likely to consider a new stepparent a "real" parent (Marsiglio, 1992). While the evidence isn't precise enough to establish an age cutoff, I would speculate that if the stepparent arrives during the preschool years, a parentlike relationship is possible; but if the stepparent arrives in later years, that kind of relationship is much harder to establish. Still, if the stepparent arrives during the stepchild's elementary school years, the stepchild will probably accept the stepparent after an initial adjustment period. The outlook is especially favorable if the stepparent is a man (which is usually the case) and the stepchild a boy (Hetherington & Stanley-Hagan, 2000), because young boys seem to accept stepfathers more easily than young girls.

Research suggests that the most difficult time to start a stepfamily is when the children are in early adolescence (about ages 11 to 14). For both girls and boys, the transition to adolescene is a difficult time in which to adjust to a remarriage (Hetherington & Jodl, 1994). This is a time when children must come to terms with their own burgeoning sexuality. Having a parent's adult sexual partner move into the house—especially one for whom the traditional incest taboos do not hold—may be disconcerting.

Family therapists seem to agree that for a stepfamily to be successful, a remarried couple must build a boundary around themselves and work together to solve their problems. Their own marriage, rather than the custodial parent and child relationship, must become the dominant relationship within the family (Keshet, 1988; Papernow, 1988). To do so, they must reserve time for each other, even if that sometimes means deferring the demands of others. The task of the remarried couple is to create a shared conception of how their family is to go about its daily business. They cannot rely on generally accepted norms, as adults in first marriages do, because few norms exist. Instead, they must draw the blueprints themselves.

THE STABILIZATION PERIOD

Most stepfamilies come through the transition period successfully and form lasting bonds. As children emerge from early adolescene, relations with their stepparents generally improve. Even in stable stepfamilies, however, few stepparents take on a fully parentlike role. Instead, they perform a stepparent role that includes: (1) warmth toward, and support of, the stepchildren; (2) little disciplining of the stepchildren; and (3) support for the biological parent's childrearing style (Hetherington & Stanley-Hagan, 2000).

In sum, those stepparents who manage to integrate into the stepfamily successfully often play a valued role that is somewhere between that of parent and trusted friend—what one family therapist calls an **intimate outsider** role (Papernow, 1988). Teenage stepchildren, for example, may feel close enough to their stepparents to discuss with them issues that are too highly charged to discuss

intimate outsider a person, such as a stepparent, who plays a role in a family that is somewhere between that of a parent and that of a trusted friend

with their biological parents, such as sex, drugs, or their feelings about their parents' divorces. As one stepmother told Papernow:

> *Mary calls me her "motherly friend." Sometimes I think of myself as her mentor. I'm the one who helped her decide she could be an architect.*
>
> *She confides deeply in me, and it is such an honor and a pleasure to be so intimately involved in guiding her life, and yet to be seen as someone with enough distance that she can trust me not to take what she says personally. It is worth all the struggle to have this relationship with her* (Papernow, 1988, p. 81).

One leading researcher cautions, however, that a minority of stepchildren may be well-behaved until late adolescence or young adulthood, when they begin to show more stress and behavior problems (Bray, 1999). This phenomenon is similar to the "sleeper effect" Wallerstein (Wallerstein & Blakeslee, 1989) and others have noted. It occurs at a time when children begin to establish their own identity and independence, which may require some distancing from their parents. Bray (1999) speculates that older adolescents may once again be coming to terms with their parents' divorces. Unfortunately, stepparents may react with dismay and disengage even more from their stepchildren.

DIFFERENCES BETWEEN THE ROLE OF STEPMOTHER AND STEPFATHER

During this process, being a stepmother can be harder than being a stepfather. Prior to the twentieth century, most stepmothers moved into a household in which the children's mother had died—an event for which they were sometimes blamed. (See *Families in Other Cultures:* The Origins of the Wicked Stepmother, on pages 466–467). In the typical remarriage chain today, the children live with their biological mother and a stepfather; they visit their biological father and his new wife, their stepmother. Consequently, the typical stepmother does not live with her stepchildren; rather, she must establish a relationship during the visits. She is usually dealing with children whose primary tie is to their biological mother, with whom she must compete. In contrast, stepfathers compete with noncustodial fathers, many of whom, as has been discussed, see little of their children. Moreover, in the minority of cases in which the children live with the stepmother and the biological father, other difficulties can arise. In these atypical cases, the children may have been subject to a custody battle, or they may have been sent to live with the father because the mother couldn't control their behavior (Ihinger-Tallman & Pasley, 1987). And mothers who are noncustodial parents visit their children and telephone them more often than noncustodial fathers, creating competition with the stepmother (Furstenberg & Nord, 1985).

Stepfathers, in other words, can often fill a vacuum left by the departed biological father. Stepmothers must crowd into the space already occupied by the biological mother. Moreover, stepmothers may judge themselves according to the culturally dominant view that a mother should play the major role in rearing children; if so, they may fall short of these high standards. Stepfathers, in contrast, may hold themselves to the lower standard that a father is supposed to provide support to the mother but let her do most of the hands-on childrearing. If so, they may feel satisfied with their role performance, even if they are doing less than many dissatisfied stepmothers (Keshet, 1988).

The Origins of the Wicked Stepmother

"It is, perhaps, too much to expect that the second wife of a working man should have the same affection toward her husband's children by a former wife as towards her own," wrote Dr. Barnardo, a nineteenth-century English philanthropist and child welfare advocate. "But case after case has come before us in which the jealousy of a stepmother has led to the most cruel treatment of the little folks committed to her charge."[1] The good doctor was repeating a charge against stepmothers that is hundreds, if not thousands, of years old. For further confirmation, just ask Cinderella or Snow White. Where did this view of stepmothers come from, and how does it relate to stepmothers today?

The prefix "step" in Old English signified a family relationship caused by death. In fact, "stepchild" originally meant "orphan," and "stepmother" can be rendered as "one who becomes a mother to an orphan." The common meaning of stepmother, however, was a woman who married a man whose wife had died (Oxford English Dictionary, 1989). The term has long had the connotations of cruelty, neglect, and jealousy.

Pliny the Elder wrote in the first century A.D., "It is far from easy to determine whether she [Nature] has proved to man a kind parent or a merciless stepmother." Leonardo da Vinci, perhaps cribbing from Pliny, asked of Nature, "wherefore art thou thus partial, becoming to some of thy children a tender and benignant mother, to others a most cruel and ruthless stepmother?" Shakespeare had the Queen say in *Cymbeline* that "you shall not find me, daughter, after the slander of most stepmothers, evil-eyed unto you."[2] Numerous fairy tales contrast the wicked, jealous stepmother to the kindly but unfortunately deceased mother.

These connotations are rooted in the reality of stepfamilies in preindustrial societies. Because of the amount of labor it took to provide food, clothes, and shelter and to raise children, a family needed two parents in order to subsist. Yet it was common for a parent to die before her or his children reached adulthood. In particular, women faced a substantial risk of dying in childbirth. If a mother of small children died, her husband had no choice but to remarry quickly. Alone, he simply could not farm the land, perform

household tasks, and care for his children. If he attempted to do so, he might be risking his children's lives. Moreover, the strong patriarchal norms of preindustrial Western society discouraged him from even trying. Rather, economic necessity and social norms led him to remarry after a short period of mourning—often within several months (Mitterauer & Sieder, 1982).

Under these circumstances, the husband's remarriage choices were often limited. It was common for a second or third wife to be considerably younger than the husband; indeed, sometimes decades younger. These large age differences and the patriarchal norms sometimes led the husband to treat his second wife as if she were a child rather than a spouse (Mitterauer & Sieder, 1982). The young stepmother was relatively powerless before the older husband. In addition, she had little authority over the older children in the household, who could be roughly her age.

The stepmother's best strategy for gaining some power within the household was to bear and raise her own children. They would at least be bound to her by

RACIAL-ETHNIC DIFFERENCES

Low-income and racial-ethnic families sometimes face a different set of issues. David Mills describes the dynamic he has seen among stepfamilies that began when an unmarried teenager bore a child. The child was often raised partly by the mother and partly by the grandmother, who may herself have given birth to the mother as a teenager. Although the families Mills studied were white, this intergenerational family system has also been noted among poor African-American families (Burton, 1990). Mills found that there were frequent conflicts between the mother and the grandmother over how to raise the child. Sometime later, a stepfamily is formed when a man who is not the father of the child moves into the household as the mother's partner, or when the mother and child move in

The wicked stepmother is a staple of fairy tales such as Hansel and Gretel.

the typical emotional bonds between mother and child. As her biological children grew, she would be able to influence their actions; and in her old age, they would be more likely to provide for her.

One could therefore imagine a stepmother's desire to advance her biological children's interests within the household and her jealousy over the advancement of her stepchildren. One could also imagine that her stepchildren would be angry at her and resent her biological children.

And one could imagine the appeal of a story in which the stepmother wants her biological daughters, not her stepdaughter, to meet the prince at the ball. From household dynamics such as these, the malevolent image of the stepmother may have been formed.

Today, as noted earlier, the vast majority of remarriages are formed as a result of divorce rather than widowhood. If there are stepchildren, they probably live for most of the week with their biological mother, who, unlike the situation in the past, is still alive. The age difference between spouses in remarriages, although greater, on average, than in first marriages, is probably smaller than in the preindustrial past. Husbands and wives relate to each other as emotional equals more than in the past. The most direct route for wives to gain power in the household is not to raise loyal children but rather to work for pay outside the home. [➡ p. 296] In all these ways, stepmothers today face a situation so different from the past that perhaps we shouldn't even use the same term. In fact, the French have dropped the old, pejorative term for stepmother, *marâtre,* and replaced it with

belle-mère, literally "fine" or "beautiful" mother, a term which also means "mother-in-law." French scholars of the family lament the absence of a prefix, such as "step," with which to precisely label relationships brought about by remarriage. But the *belles-mères* of France may be fortunate that, unlike their Anglo-American counterparts, they no longer have to bear the stigma of an outmoded, archaic term.

Ask Yourself

1. Do you know anyone who fits the description of a wicked stepmother? Do you know anyone who might be described as a *belle-mère?*

2. If folktales like *Cinderella* and *Snow White* were based on real problems of the past, what kind of conflict would a modern-day children's tale describe?

[1]*Day and Night,* May 1885, p. 74. Cited in Cretney (1993).
[2]The quotations from Pliny the Elder and da Vinci are cited in Bartlett (1980). The quotation from Shakespeare is cited in Cretney (1993).

www.mhhe.com/cherlin

with him. In either case, this new stepfather soon faces situations in which he is urged to side with either the mother or the grandmother in their disputes about the child. If he criticizes the mother, he directly jeopardizes his relationship with her. But if he criticizes the grandmother too harshly, Mills observes, the mother may defend her and begin to reject him. Mills argues that this kind of tension makes it difficult for a stepfather to remain in an intergenerational family system for very long (Mills, 1988).

I don't want to leave the impression that stepfamily life is an interminable struggle. Most stepparents report that they are happy with their roles and their new families. After a period of adjustment, most stepchildren come to view their stepparents positively, although not quite as positively as children view their biological parents (Amato, 1999a). Moreover, there is a wide variation in the roles stepparents play. For example, in the National Survey of Families and Households, stepfathers were asked to agree or disagree with the statement "A stepparent is more like a friend than a parent to stepchildren." One-third agreed, half disagreed, and the rest were neutral (Marsiglio, 1992). Stepfamilies have worked out a variety of successful ways to develop a new family life.

The Effects of Remarriage on Children

Twenty years ago, I thought that remarriage would improve the overall well-being of children whose parents had divorced. For one thing, when a single mother remarries, her household income usually rises dramatically because men's wages are so much higher, on average, than women's wages. One national study found that 8 percent of children in mother–stepfather households were living below the poverty line, compared with 49 percent of children in single-mother households (Bachrach, 1983). Consequently, if a decline in the standard of living hurts the well-being of children in single-parent families, an increase after the mother remarries should improve it. In addition, the stepparent adds a second adult to the home. He or she can provide support to the custodial parent and back up the custodial parent's monitoring and control of the children's behavior. A stepparent can also provide an adult role model for a child of the same gender.

Despite these advantages, many studies now show that the well-being of children in stepfamilies is no better, on average, than the well-being of children in divorced, single-parent households. To be sure, most children in stepfamilies do not demonstrate serious problems (Amato, 1994; Hetherington & Jodl, 1994). Still, both groups of children show lower levels of well-being than children in two-biological-parent families. For example, psychologists Mavis Hetherington, Glenn Clingempeel, and several collaborators studied about 200 white households, divided into three groups: nondivorced, two-parent households; divorced, single-mother households in which the mothers had been divorced for about four years, on average; and stepfamilies that had just formed (four months' average duration) and in which the wife was the biological parent and the husband the stepparent. The sample was not selected randomly but rather recruited by such means as advertisements, examining marriage records, and sending notices to community organizations. All households had at least one child between 9 and 13 years of age; these early adolescents were the main focus of the study. Households were evaluated using multiple methods, including personal interviews with the parents and children, standardized tests given to the children, and videotaped family problem-solving sessions. Evaluations were conducted three times: at the start of the study, again about a year later, and yet again another nine months later (Hetherington & Clingempeel, 1992).

BEHAVIOR PROBLEMS

At all three evaluations, the children from both the single-mother and stepfamily households were not doing as well as the children in the nondivorced households. For example, all the mothers were asked which items on a list of behavior problems applied to their early-adolescent child. Scores above a certain level on this widely used behavior problems checklist are said to indicate serious difficulties that might warrant referral to mental health professionals. Even at the last assessment, about 25 to 30 percent of the children in the single-mother and stepfamily households were above this cutoff level, as opposed to 10 percent or less

A parent's remarriage means a new period of adjustment for a child such as this young ring bearer, whose siblings and would-be stepmother tried to convince him to march down the aisle.

of the children in nondivorced households; there was little difference between the former two groups (Maccoby, 1992).

In another research project, psychologists studied 100 stepfamilies and 100 first-marriage families, then followed most of them for three to four years (Bray, 1999). The project included extensive interviews, psychological assessments, and videotapes of family interactions. The authors reported that 20 percent of the children in stepfamilies had clinically significant behavior problems, compared to 10 percent of the children in first-marriage families—results similar to those of the Hetherington and Cligempeel study.

In addition, the sheer number of family transitions might impair the adjustment of children in stepfamilies. Having coped with a divorce, and possibly with the introduction of a live-in partner, these children must now cope with another major change in their family system. Some studies, as noted previously, have found a relationship between the number of family transitions a child has experienced, on the one hand, and behavior problems and subsequently having a baby before marrying.[4] [➡ p. 441] Finally, children and parents with certain unknown personal characteristics that impair family cohesion could be self-selecting into the population of divorced and remarried families.

AGE AT LEAVING HOME

Only one finding about the long-term effects on children of having lived in a stepfamily is well established. Children in stepfamilies—particularly girls—leave their households at an earlier age than children in single-parent households or two-parent households. They leave earlier either to marry or to establish independent

[4]See also Capaldi and Patterson (1991).

households prior to marrying. An analysis of a large, six-year national study of high school students showed this pattern for girls (Goldscheider & Goldscheider, 1993). In a British study, 23-year-olds who had left their parental homes were asked the main reason why they had left. Demographer Kathleen Kiernan reported that those who had lived in stepfamilies were substantially more likely to have said that they had left due to "friction at home" than those who had not lived in stepfamilies (Kiernan, 1992). Again, the differences were greater for girls. An analysis of the National Survey of Families and Households found that girls who had lived in a stepfamily were more likely to have left home by age 19 to marry or to live independently than girls who had lived with single parents or with two parents; the differences were much weaker for boys. If a girl had also lived with stepsiblings, her likelihood of leaving home by age 19 was even higher (Aquilino, 1991).

That tensions between stepchildren and their parents and stepparents lie behind the early home leaving is suggested by interviews in 1980 and 1983 with a national sample of currently married people. Those who had stepchildren in their households reported more family problems involving children. The authors hypothesize that one way these problems are resolved is by encouraging, or arranging for, the stepchildren to leave the household. During the three years between interviews, 51 percent of all the teenage stepchildren had left the households, compared with 35 percent of all the teenage biological children. Some may have chosen to move in with their other parent, some may have been forced to do so, and some may have left to go to school, establish their own residence, cohabit, or marry (White & Booth 1985). If this effect is indeed more pronounced for girls, it suggests that the "friction" in the household may be due to the disruption of the mother–daughter bond or to the presence of the mother's male sexual partner, whose relationship to the daughter is ambiguous.

Divorce and Remarriage: Some Lessons

What can be learned from these two chapters on divorce and remarriage? The evidence we have reviewed suggests three themes. First, the emphasis on personal fulfillment, the growth of women's economic independence, and the worsening economic prospects for young men since 1973 have made marriage more fragile. There is simply less glue holding couples together than there was a half century ago. Second, divorce, remarriage, nonmarital childbearing, and cohabitation are increasing the frequency with which people create their own kinship ties out of the many possibilities available to them—rather than accepting the set of relatives that automatically come with first marriages. These efforts, like the efforts of poor people in creating sharing networks and of gay men and lesbians in constructing friend-based ties, are changing the nature of kinship. Third, the increases in single-parent families and stepfamilies have altered many children's lives, causing short-term distress, increasing the risk of long-term harm, but leaving the majority relatively unscathed. Let us consider the implications of the developments.

THE PRIMACY OF THE PRIVATE FAMILY

The first theme, it seems to me, is this: The transformation of divorce from a highly restricted device used by wealthy men to protect against unwanted heirs, to a frowned-upon but tolerated option for disastrous marriages, and finally to an individual right for anyone whose marriage isn't personally fulfilling, represents a triumph of the private family. The changes in divorce law mirror changes in the way marriage has been viewed. Once it was an economic partnership in which sentiment was secondary and men were the masters of their homes. The public functions of marriage were dominant: reproducing the population (which wasn't an easy task given widespread disease and poverty), educating children, preparing them for their adult roles, and caring for the ill and the elderly. This is not to say that people didn't find their marriages satisfying, but satisfaction was likely to come primarily from keeping a family alive and fed, from passing one's craft on to one's children, or from marrying a daughter into a good family.

Those days are gone. With the rise of the private family in the twentieth century, marriage is now primarily an instrument of individual fulfillment, a means of personal growth, an expression of romantic love. As such, it is much more fragile, more vulnerable to crises, than ever before. When men and women each specialized in certain tasks and pooled their labor, their economic partnership tied them together. Now that the division of labor is less pronounced and men and women are more economically independent of each other, marriage is held together mainly by the bonds of sentiment.

It is easy to criticize the narcissistic excesses of the search for personal fulfillment in marriage. But as even some radical critics have understood, the expansion of private life has been a great social advance (Zaretsky 1986). It is an advance that the standard of living of most people in our society is high enough that they need not concern themselves daily with sustenance. It is an advance that they no longer need to labor 12 hours a day on the farm or in the factory. It is an advance that they have the time to pursue gratifying intimate relationships and that they have the luxury of marrying purely for love.

The changing nature of marriage has also been an advance for women. Once unable to sever a marriage unless they were subject to terrible cruelty, women (and men) now have the ability to divorce unilaterally. This option must provide them with greater leverage against the worst excesses of husband dominance. Nor do they need to marry as much as their ancestors did. Yet the gains for women have come at a price. A half century ago, when divorce was more difficult to obtain and stigmatizing to live with, wives who specialized in rearing children could be reasonably sure that their husbands would not abandon them. It was safe for them to withdraw from the labor market and let their earning power atrophy because their husbands, according to the bargain, would have to provide for them. Today they no longer have that protection. Choosing to be a homemaker is far riskier than it was in the 1950s. Just ask any of the older, divorced women who lived up to their part of the breadwinner-homemaker bargain only to see their husbands leave them.

A central contradiction of the current era of divorce, then, is that the law assumes that husbands and wives are economic equals, when in fact they still are not. To be sure, women's wages have increased enough that life as a single parent is much more feasible than it was a few decades ago. Still, if a woman chooses to end her marriage, she must often accept a steep drop in her standard of living, like a nun taking a vow of poverty before entering an order. And if a woman chooses to stay home and raise children, she cannot count on the lifetime support of her husband.

Men, however, are not the winners in every divorce. They, too, pay a cost under the new regime. The men who have gained the most are those who care the least about their children. Divorce law allows these men to walk away from their wives and children for a modest monthly fee; sadly, many do. The men who pay the highest price are those who care the most about being a daily part of their children's lives—for they no longer have the guarantee that if they fulfill their husbandly responsibilities, their wives will remain with them. On the contrary, if their wives initiate a divorce, they know they are likely to lose custody of their children, or at best to share it.

What, then, would we expect prudent women and men to do to protect themselves in the current system of unilateral divorce? A woman would be wise to develop good labor market skills in young adulthood and to maintain a connection to the labor market throughout her childrearing years. In fact, the trends in married women's employment are consistent with this strategy. A man who cares about living with his children would be wise to spend a substantial amount of time on childrearing throughout his marriage. That way his claims to his children will be far stronger in a custody dispute, should one arise. Although men seem to be doing somewhat more childrearing, this strategy isn't much in evidence. Perhaps men, on average, don't care as much about rearing their children as women do. Perhaps their resistance to household work is still too strong. Nevertheless, given the costs of the new system, we are likely to see continued investment by married women in developing job skills and careers and increased investment by men in caring for their children.

NEW KINSHIP TIES

Divorce, nonmarital childbearing, cohabitation, and remarriage are altering kinship in two fundamental ways that aren't yet fully appreciated. First, they are breaking the correspondence between family and household. Until recently, the unchallenged family unit in Western nations was the conjugal family of husband, wife, and children residing in the same household. At some points in the life cycle of the family they might welcome elderly parents, or young servants and apprentices, into their household. To be sure, the conjugal family members had many relatives living in other households. There was, however, a clear demarcation between the members of one's own household, who were the core of the family system, and those beyond the household's boundaries, who were the periphery. The correspondence between family and household is so deeply ingrained that we take it for granted. For example, our entire government apparatus for collecting statistics on "families" actually surveys households. The official Bureau of the Census definition of a family is two or more people living in the same household and related by blood, marriage, or adoption. This dinosaur of a definition is unlikely to survive for very long. But what will replace it is unclear. Statistically, we may have to give up the idea that we can count families simply by knocking on doors. We may have to accept that a family can be defined only in reference to a person, not a household.

Second, the rise in divorce, nonmarital childbearing, cohabitation, and remarriage is increasing the importance of what I have called created kinship, the ties that people have to actively construct, as opposed to assigned kinship, the ties that people automatically acquire at birth or through first marriage. [➡ p. 18] In this regard, kinship after divorce and remarriage is similar to the extended kin networks among low-income and racial-ethnic populations and to the efforts of gay men and lesbians to form alternative families. In all these situations, individuals find it in their interest to build their own family ties. Being a father or a mother was once a status assigned to a person automatically at the birth of his or her child. To be sure, people have children through their own efforts; nevertheless, one does not have to do anything else to be a parent, nor can one easily resign from the post. Being a grandparent was ascribed similarly. All that is still the case when children are born to, and raised by, two married parents.

Stepfamilies are increasing the importance of created kinship—ties that people such as these stepsiblings have to actively construct.

The creation of stepfamilies, though, adds a number of other potential kinship positions. Whether these positions are filled depends on the actions of the individuals involved. The most obvious positions are stepfather and stepmother. This chapter has described the wide variation in the roles stepparents play. Some are parentlike figures who are intensely involved with their stepchildren. Many others are more like friends or uncles and aunts. Others, particularly stepparents who don't live with their stepchildren every day, are more distant. In all cases, how much like a family member a stepparent becomes depends in large part on the effort he or she puts into developing a close relationship with stepchildren and also on the stepchild's actions. Intergenerational ties to stepgrandparents are even more dependent on individual action; they range from no contact to a kinlike role, depending in large part on the investment the stepgrandparents make.

Yet the challenge of created kinship is as follows: Kinship ties that can be created by people's actions can also be ended by lack of action. In contrast, it is much harder to end assigned kinship ties. Therefore, created kinship ties are more likely to change over the course of one's life than assigned kinship ties. Created ties may even change from year to year, as a stepparent moves into or out of the household or as contact diminishes with a stepgranddaughter who moves out of state. Just as containment within one household made families easy to spot, so, too, assignment at birth and first marriage made kinship easy to track. Now, family and kinship require new mental maps that can change from year to year. We are just beginning to draw them.

THE IMPACT ON CHILDREN

There is, finally, the important question of the effects of divorce and stepfamily life on children. I would argue that the effects are neither minor nor massive. On the one hand, the evidence suggests that most children who experience these events do not have serious, long-lasting problems because of them. Still, it must be said that we have not studied this topic long enough and intensively enough to reach a definitive conclusion. Evidence might come in over the next several years that changes this picture. Right now, however, the evidence suggests that divorce and stepfamily life do not inevitably scar children. On the other hand, it is clear that a minority of children do experience lasting problems that appear to be caused by divorce and remarriage. Some of these problems might have occurred even if the children's families had remained intact. Other problems, though, seem clearly linked to the disruption and its aftermath.

Let us suppose, for the sake of argument, that 10 percent of children from two-parent homes will grow up to have serious mental health problems as adults. Further, let us suppose that the prevalence of serious mental health problems is twice as high—20 percent—among children from maritally disrupted homes. A little algebra will show that if 4 in 10 children experience marital disruption (as current levels imply), the overall rate of serious mental health problems in the population would rise to 14 percent when this generation reaches adulthood.[5] An overall rise from an expected 10 percent (if there were no divorce in the population) to 14 percent may not seem like much. But it would require a 40 percent expansion of mental health facilities around the country and the training of 40 percent more mental health professionals. At current population levels, it would alter the lives of an additional three million people in each generation. It would mean that about 1 in 7, rather than 1 in 10, adults might need clinical help. In sum, it would mean a significant decline in mental health.

Consequently, even if only a minority of children will experience long-term problems, we should be troubled by this possibility. Some people might wish to work toward reducing the divorce rate. Although that is a worthy goal, it is unlikely to succeed (see Chapter 15). If the divorce rate can't be reduced much by government activity, we might wish to assist divorcing parents and children. We might promote conflict-resolution strategies for divorcing couples, urge that children be kept out of conflict, and provide guidelines on how to minimize the impact of divorce. We might wish to enforce child support obligations and guarantee custodial parents a minimum benefit. We might wish to encourage support groups and services in schools. In sum, we might take whatever steps we can to reduce the negative effects of divorce and remarriage on children.

[5]$(.40 \times .20) + (.60 \times .10) = .14$, or 14 percent.

Looking Back

1. What are the basic characteristics of remarriages and stepfamilies? Remarriages that involve children from a previous marriage create situations in which well-established rules about everyday family life don't apply. Today, most remarriages occur following a divorce rather than a death. Among divorced persons, the rate of remarriage has fallen since the 1960s, but the rate of cohabitation has risen. Remarriages are somewhat more likely to end in divorce than first marriages. Though stepfamilies have traditionally been defined in terms of remarriage following a divorce, the growth of nonmarital childbearing and cohabitation suggests an expanded definition that includes households in which two adults are married or cohabiting, and at least one child from a previous marriage or relationship is present.

2. How can we define "family" and "kinship" in the case of stepfamilies? One way to define a family in the case of stepfamilies is to focus on a household that contains a parent, that parent's current partner, and children from a previous union. A second way is to identify remarriage chains—relationships that link individuals across households, through the ties of a disrupted union and new unions. Remarriage chains can serve as support and exchange networks, although cooperation is less assured in these chains than in other kin networks. In first marriages, the bonds of kinship among parents and children are recognized almost automatically. Stepparents and other steprelatives, in contrast, must consciously create and maintain relationships in order to be recognized as kin. There is great variation in the degree to which they succeed at becoming like kin.

3. **How do stepparents, parents, and children go about building a stepfamily?** During the transitional period, which can last two to four years or even longer, stepparents and stepchildren adjust to each other's presence. Successful stepparents often play the role of "polite outsiders" who have limited involvement in the stepchildren's lives. With time they often become a "warm friend" to stepchildren, a trusted and liked figure who does not discipline them or wield authority. Stepchildren need time to adjust to a remarriage, and sometimes show increased behavior problems. Young children are more likely to accept a stepparent quickly; children in early adolescence, who are dealing with the changes of puberty, can be resistant to a new stepparent. In the long run, most stepchildren do adapt successfully to the addition of a stepparent to the family.

4. **How does the well-being of children in stepfamilies compare to the well-being of children in other kinds of families?** Many studies show that the well-being of children in stepfamilies is no better, on average, than the well-being of children in divorced, single-parent households. Both groups show lower levels of well-being than children in biological two-parent families. Several studies show that children in stepfamilies, especially girls, leave home earlier than children in other families.

5. **How have increases in divorce, remarriage, and related trends altered family life?** Divorce, nonmarital childbearing, cohabitation after divorce, and remarriage have altered family life in important ways. Because of the emphasis on personal fulfillment and the economic independence of women and men, marriages are now more fragile and vulnerable to crises. The nature of kinship has been altered, and the correspondence between household and family is breaking down. People are constructing new kinship ties to fit the new stepfamilies they have formed. While these new family forms cause short-term distress for many children and increase the risk of long-term harm to them, the majority of stepchildren grow up without serious long-term problems.

Thinking about Families

1. Are stepparents and stepchildren really related to each other?

2. What is the most complex remarriage chain you know of among your relatives and friends?

3. Should stepparents discipline their children as much as biological parents do?

4. **The Public Family** By and large, do stepfamilies do a good enough job of raising the next generation?

5. **The Private Family** What are the sources of the tension that sometimes exists between stepparents and stepchildren?

Key Terms

bilateral kinship   461
blood relatives   461
intimate outsider   464
remarriage chain   460
stepfamily   458

Families on the Internet   www.mhhe.com/cherlin

Note: While all the URLs listed were current as of the printing of this book, these sites often change. Please check our web site (http://www.mhhe.com/cherlin) for updates.

 A number of organizations provide online advice and information to stepparents. See, for instance, **www.stepfamilyinfo.org,** the web site for the Stepfamily Association of Illinois. At their home page, click on "site map," then on "stepfamily basics" to bring up a menu of topics. After browsing the site, determine the message this organization is trying to project to stepfamilies.

The About.com web site offers one of the most comprehensive collection of facts and research summaries. To access it, log onto **www.about.com,** then click on "parenting," and on the next page, "step-parenting." From the list of subjects, select "statistics." Do the research studies listed provide any new information about the relationships among stepfamily members?

Part Six

Family and Society

Where do all the great social changes of the twentieth century leave the institution of the family? That is the question to be addressed in the final part. • Chapter 15 begins by discussing the most fundamental changes in the family in the twentieth century, the lessened economic dependence of women and the weakening of marriage. The chapter then describes the emergence of a new form of kinship. It subsequently examines the implications of social change for the public family and the private family. • Any attempt to assess the overall state of the family necessarily involves the author's own interpretations. Consequently, my opinions are more prominent in this chapter than in previous ones. I have tried to clearly label my opinions as such. There is no single right answer to the difficult questions posed in this chapter; and readers are encouraged to consider what they have learned in this book and to draw their own conclusions.

Social Change and Families

Looking Forward

1. What are the two most fundamental changes in the American family over the past half century?

2. What is likely to happen to the relationship between the elderly and their families?

3. How have American children fared over the past several decades?

4. What should be done to improve children's family lives?

5. How has marriage evolved as a setting for personal life?

When Americans are asked about the state of the family, their responses are puzzling but instructive. In a 1999 national telephone survey by the *New York Times,* far more people mentioned family and children than any other response when asked, "What aspect of your life is most fulfilling and satisfying?"[1] Without doubt, then, people find deep meaning in their family lives. The survey also included a question about the great changes that have occurred in American family life over the past several decades: "In general, do you think that because of such things as divorce, more working mothers, or single parents, etc., family ties in the U.S. are breaking down—or don't you think so?" Seventy-seven percent responded that, yes, they thought family ties were breaking down—a very negative assessment. All the more surprising, then, were the answers to the next question: "What about in your own family? Are family ties breaking down, or not?" Eighty-two percent responded that their family ties were not breaking down. In other words, most people think that the family in general is in decline, but not their own families.

These seemingly contradictory responses reflect widespread ambivalence about the changes in American family life. People are concerned about the effects of day care on children, but they approve of decisions by women in their own families to work outside the home. They are worried about the consequences of divorce, but they don't expect their relatives to remain in unhappy marriages. They believe that ideally, children should be born to married couples, but they accept the occurrence of nonmarital births in their families.

In other words, many people share both the concern about family decline voiced by conservative commentators and the defense of newer family forms voiced by liberals. Although they may endorse traditional values, such as the superiority of the stable, two-parent family, they reserve the right to deviate from those values in their own lives. And they are loathe to tell others how to live their family lives. They may value the traditional family, but they accept family diversity as inevitable, and perhaps beneficial. When Alan Wolfe (1998, p. 110) conducted interviews to learn whether Americans could be divided into "traditionalists" and "modernists" in their beliefs about family life, he concluded: "The divisions over the family do not take place between camps of people; instead, they take place within most individuals." That is to say, many of us hold parts of both positions.

---

[1] All data that I cite from the survey come from unpublished tabulations. For an overview, see Cherlin (1999).

Many people, then, accept the fact that for better or worse, we live in an era with a variety of family forms, including cohabiting unions, dual-earner married couples, breadwinner-homemaker couples, single-parent families, and stepfamilies. One might ask whether these family forms are meeting society's need to ensure that the young are being raised well, and the old are well cared for. One might also ask whether individuals' needs for love, intimacy, companionship, and personal growth are being met. In other words, one might ask how well the family is fulfilling the functions of both the public and the private family at the beginning of the twenty-first century. That inquiry will be the subject of this chapter.

Two Fundamental Changes

First, however, it is worth reviewing the fundamental ways in which the family as a social institution has changed over the past half century. Two changes stand out: the lessened economic dependence of women on men and the weakening of marriage. Both have implications for American kinship.

THE LESSENED ECONOMIC DEPENDENCE OF WOMEN

The decline of the homemaker role and the movement of women into the paid labor force is probably the most significant shift in the family in the past half century. It has been discussed so often in this book that there's little need to say more. Here let me emphasize one point: To some extent, the movement toward greater economic independence is a movement back toward the situation of women a century or two ago. That is to say, married women probably had less economic independence in the 1950s than they had had 50 years earlier. In the nineteenth century, rural women were an important part of the family's farm labor. To be sure, as cities expanded, most urban white married women (and many urban black married women) rarely worked outside the home. Yet urban wives earned income by taking in boarders and lodgers or by doing other families' laundry or performing other services in their homes. By the 1950s, the greater affluence of the nation had nearly eliminated boarding and lodging, and rising wages placed the washing machine and dryer within the reach of many more families. As a result, opportunities to earn money while remaining at home declined. Still, the nineteenth-century economic activity of married women kept them at home, whereas the late-twentieth-century economic activity allows them (albeit with lower earnings than men) to live apart.

THE WEAKENING OF MARRIAGE

The greatest recent challenge to the institution of the family has been the weakening of marriage. In most societies at most times, marriage has been the central organizing principle for sexual activity and childbearing. Marriage, childbearing, and sexual activity overlapped in the 1950s to a great extent, possibly greater than in prior times. [➡ p. 214] Sexual intercourse, for the majority of women at least, was restricted to marriage (or to the men they were engaged to); consequently, few children were born outside marriage. Cohabitation was rare except among the poor. Marriage was more nearly universal than at any other time in the twentieth century. The probability that a marriage would end in divorce, although substantially higher than in the nineteenth century, was about half of what it is today. To be respectable, it was necessary to be married before living with a partner or having a child; to stay respectable, it was necessary to avoid divorce if at all possible.

Today, even though nearly 90 percent of whites and about two-thirds of African Americans eventually marry, the power of marriage to regulate people's personal lives is much weaker. Cohabitation both before and after marriage has become common and acceptable to most people. Although childbearing outside marriage is still frowned upon by many, it is tolerated by most. Divorce is considered to be unfortunate but acceptable if a partner wishes to end a marriage. Lifelong singlehood, although still uncommon, is also acceptable. In general, there is a greater acceptance of nonmarried adults.

The reasons for the weakening of marriage were discussed in previous chapters. Marriage is less economically necessary than it was when most people needed to pool their labor and earnings in order to subsist. Moreover, the aforementioned lessening of women's economic dependence on men has had an important effect. Even though women's wages remain, on average, lower than men's, it is less difficult now for a woman to support herself and her children. Also, the job prospects for young men without college educations have worsened since 1973, discouraging young adults from marrying. In the realm of values, marriage is increasingly viewed as a means of personal fulfillment, with the result that many married persons believe they are justified in obtaining a divorce if they feel unfulfilled. The quest for self-fulfillment may also prolong young adults' search for a spouse or lead them to try a cohabiting relationship first. Among those who do marry, relationships are more fragile and vulnerable to crises because there is less holding them together than when marriage was more of a necessity and the gendered division of labor was more strict.

Among African Americans, marriage has long been less central to family life, compared with ties to other kin, than it has been among whites; but over the past few decades, marriage has declined in importance even more. Among poor African Americans, the connection between marriage and childbearing is especially weak. Although marriage still remains an ideal, it is far from universal, and the great majority of children, especially first children, are born outside of marriage. Even when a woman does get married, it is not necessarily to the father of her first child. The decline of marriage among African Americans is linked both to the worsening labor market position of black men and to a cultural heritage of relying on extended kin in difficult times. [➡ p. 154] Hispanic groups vary greatly in the place of marriage in their family systems. Among the major groups, Puerto Ricans have the highest proportion of children living in single-parent families and Cubans the lowest. Mexican Americans display more three-generational households, suggesting the importance of extended family ties. Marriage is strongest among Asian Americans, many or them recent immigrants from societies in which marriage is nearly universal.

Still, marriage is not in danger of disappearing among Americans, and it remains the preferred form of union. (Recall that most cohabiting relationships either break up or end in marriage within a few years.) Most people choose to marry at some time in their lives, but the point is that they now have a choice. They don't have to be married in the sense that adults at midcentury did. Predictably, people spend less of their lives married and fewer children are raised by two married parents. What difference these changes mean for adults and children is a topic to be discussed below. (Social scientists have also been studying the changing nature of marriage in less developed nations; see *Families in Other Cultures:* World Revolution and Family Patterns, on pages 484–485.)

The Emergence of Created Kinship

In turn, the decline of lifelong marriage as the organizing principle of families has led to an important change in the nature of kinship, aspects of which have been discussed in several chapters. This change has received much less attention than the decline of marriage or the movement of married women into the paid workforce. Consider, for example, the following individuals: a poor woman receiving public assistance who is raising her children by sharing what little she has with her sister who lives in the same apartment building and her mother a block away. A gay man who celebrates Thanksgiving and Christmas with a network of friends who keep in touch and help one another out. A girl who spends part of every summer vacation at her stepfather's parents' beach house yet rarely sees her biological father's parents. All are creating new forms of family life by choosing their kin from the pool of eligibles around them. In the past, you acquired your relatives at birth; then, when you married, you acquired a spouse and in-laws. There was little choice in the matter; relatives came with birth and marriage like sweet scents and thorns come with roses.

CHOOSING ONE'S KIN

Today, people in a variety of settings are more likely to choose their own kin and create their own kinship networks. What all these settings have in common is that they are defined outside the boundaries of lifelong marriage. Marriage (both your parents' and your own) made kinship easy and automatic, but it also restricted the

As marriage has weakened as an institution, lifelong singlehood has become more acceptable.

$\mathcal{A}$ sociologist returned from a conference in Taiwan with a story told to him by a Taiwanese professor. The professor had begun the story by recounting an incident that had occurred when his father was a boy:

> My father and grandfather were riding in a carriage when my grandfather said, "See that little girl over there? That's the girl you are going to marry." My father never saw the girl again until his wedding day. When I was a boy, I thought my father very enlightened for allowing me to meet the woman I would marry before my wedding day. And recently, my daughter came home and asked me, "Dad, would you like to meet the man I'm going to marry?"

Taiwan is one of many societies in which the process of choosing a spouse—and indeed the very nature of marriage—changed dramatically during the twentieth century. In China, Japan, India, and elsewhere in Asia, parents used to select a son or daughter's spouse. Marriage often occurred at an early age—among girls, close to (or sometimes even before) puberty (Thornton & Fricke, 1989). Typically, the young wife would move into the home of her mother-in-law, who held considerable authority over her. In these ways, marriage was less an agreement between two individuals than a transaction between two families—the family of the groom and the family of the bride. What mattered most to the parents was making a match that would help the larger family by bringing in another healthy person to work the fields or to bear and care for children.

In these Asian families, the most important family bond was often between parents and children, rather than between husbands and wives. The succession of the family line from father to son and the obligation to care for parents in their old age were primary. Yet during the twentieth century, the ties between husbands and wives grew increasingly strong. One reason for this change was the growing availability of work for wages, which gave children a way to make a living that wasn't dependent on their parents' land. They could use their economic independence to make their own decisions about when and whom to marry. In addition, the spread of schooling gave children skills that were valuable in the labor market, introduced them to new ideas, and therefore undermined further their parents' ability to control their marriages (Caldwell, 1982).

In fact, William Goode argued in an influential 1963 book, *World Revolution and Family Patterns*, that family systems worldwide are converging toward a model in which the marital bond between husband and wife, rather than the bond between parent and child, will be the core of the family (Goode, 1963). Goode cataloged the great changes that had occurred during the previous half century in the family patterns of China, Japan, India, Arabic-speaking Islamic countries, and sub-Saharan Africa. He argued that the changes had been the result of the spread of industrialization—especially where it had brought young adults economic opportunities that their parents couldn't control. Among the related changes Goode noted were a decline in birthrates, an increase in women's holding jobs independently of male relatives, and greater sexual freedom among young adults.

What has happened since *World Revolution* was published? To a considerable extent, the trends Goode emphasized have continued in developing nations. Age at marriage has continued to rise, and more young adults have had a say in choosing whom they will marry. In Taiwan, where economic development has been rapid, 68 percent of women born in the early 1930s said that their parents had chosen their spouses, compared with just 11 percent of women born in the early 1960s (Thornton, Chang, & Lin, 1994). Moreover, the average Taiwanese woman today would give

possibilities for forging alliances. People who cannot rely, or choose not to rely, on marriage construe kinship differently. They cannot take it for granted. Rather, they must do the hard work of constructing a group of kin, a broader family, they can rely on. Recall the lesbian who told Kath Weston, "Gay people really have to work to make family." [➡ p. 266] In several chapters this new form of family making was labeled "created kinship," meaning kinship ties that people have to construct actively. The older form, based on blood relationships or first marriages, was called "acquired kinship."

Family patterns in Asia show a mixture of persistence and change. Arranged marriages, such as this one in India, are still common, but many young adults have a say in whom they will marry.

birth to 1.5 children at current rates, compared with 6.5 children at the rates prevalent in the 1950s (Freedman, Chang, Sun, & Weinstein, 1994; Population Reference Bureau, 2000).

Yet the prediction that all family systems would converge to a common, marriage-centered model has not proved accurate. Two developments suggest the limitations of this thesis. First, as previous chapters of this book have shown, the importance of marriage has declined in the United States and other Western nations, which Goode took as the model of the family patterns of the future. Cohabitation, childbearing outside marriage, divorce—all have increased dramatically since Goode's book was published. As he was writing about the growing

dominance of the married-couple family in developing nations, it was slipping away from him in Western nations.

Second, in newly developed countries in Asia, family ties to parents and other kin often remain strong and important, even though Goode's thesis about the increasing importance of the married-couple family has proved accurate. For example, in Japan, which has undergone perhaps the fastest economic development of any nation in history, many elderly people still live with one of their children. [➡ p. 378] In Taiwan and elsewhere, parents still play a collaborative role in choosing their children's spouses. Thus, the family patterns of the developing and newly developed nations of Asia show a mixture of persis-

tence and change, while family patterns in the Western nations have continued to move away from the married-couple model that dominated in the 1950s and early 1960s.

Ask Yourself

1. Do you know anyone whose marriage was arranged by family members? If so, what are the couple's culture and generation? Are they happily married?

2. Do you think that in Asia, marriage and the family will continue to evolve as they have in the United States? Why or why not?

www.mhhe.com/cherlin

Created kinship is based more on what people do for one another than on where they fit into a family tree. African Americans in Baltimore, you may remember, told Frank Furstenberg about the difference between *daddies,* who provide emotional and financial support to children, and the biological *fathers* of the children. [➡ p. 153] It was the daddies, not the fathers, who became part of the mother's and child's kinship network despite their lack of a biological link. Created kinship presents the opportunity to go outside the typical boundaries of kinship in order to find love and support. It is particularly valuable to people who can't find adequate support among blood-based or first-marriage–based kin. Lesbians and gay men, for example, are sometimes rejected by their parents. They cannot legally marry, and their partnerships have a high likelihood of eventually breaking up. In these circumstances, Weston tells us, they weave together a support network of long-term friends, partners, and biological kin to whom they can maintain ties. Poor African-American women who cannot find suitable spouses exchange help not only with their mothers and grandmothers but also with close friends and even daddies, creating kinshiplike relationships. A divorced mother whose ex-husband provides little child support can receive support from a live-in partner or second husband.

Yet created kinship also presents a challenge: It requires continual attention to maintain. In contrast, relations of blood and marriage are supported by strong social norms. Wives and husbands, for instance, take a public oath to support each other for better, for worse, in sickness and in health, until death (or, realistically, at least until divorce) do them part. Parents are supposed to support their young children, and adult children are supposed to assist their elderly parents. Society expects as much, and laws enforce these expectations. Moreover, evolutionary theory suggests that parents may also be predisposed to support their biological children and therefore ensure the survival of their genes into the next generation. Because of these strong supports, the relationships can be dormant for a period of time and then be reactivated. An adult daughter may be married and independent for years; then a divorce may leave her and her children in need of assistance. If she turns to her parents for support, they will usually provide it.

Lacking the strong support of social norms, legal obligations, and biological self-interest, created kinship ties must be kept active. If they are allowed to lapse, there is no guarantee that they can be revived. It is a risk, therefore, to withdraw from created kin, unless you are sure you won't be needing their help again. For example, it is risky for poor people to withdraw from the female-centered kinship networks that many of them rely upon for support. [➡ p. 127] Yet the sharing networks of the poor, although admirable in easing the hardships of poverty, may also make it difficult for the members of the networks to rise out of poverty.

THE FEMINIZATION OF KINSHIP

Because created kinship ties require continual maintenance, the system favors those who are willing to work at keeping kinship ties and penalizes those who aren't. A great deal of evidence, reviewed in earlier chapters, shows that women, on average, do much more kinship work than men. They are the ones, by and large, who run and maintain the sharing networks in poor African-American communities. They are the ones who retain the children after divorce and call upon relatives for help. Men, in contrast, seem to drift away from kinship except when they are married. Many divorced fathers, as was noted, have little to do with their children after a divorce. Many men in low-income communities have little to do with children they have fathered outside marriage. Divorced men receive comfort and support by remarrying, which they do more often than divorced women. It is unclear who provides comfort and support to the unmarried fathers in low-income communities. It seems likely that they find new partners and also rely on mothers, sisters, and grandmothers.

As marriage becomes less stable, and as kinship networks remain the work of women, more men will be left without adequate support from kin. The difference is most apparent in later life. For instance, stepfathers are less likely to receive assistance from their adult stepchildren than biological fathers are from their children. [➡ p. 376] Moreover, once a man's remarriage ends, his relationship with his stepchildren, as befits created kinship, often ends as well. What, then, will happen to a man who divorces his first wife, sees little of his children afterward, remarries, and then divorces again? Who will care for him in his old age? The evidence suggests that he is unlikely to receive assistance from anyone—unless he marries again.

Kinship, then, is becoming even more feminized than it previously was. Men's classic strategy for support is to marry and to let their wives keep up ties with relatives. This strategy worked well for men as long as most were married for life. Yet with the rises in divorce and childbearing outside marriage, men often become disconnected from kin. At first, many men gain economically because they don't share their higher incomes equitably with the mothers of their children. Yet men who become divorced may be the long-run losers in the decline of lifelong marriage and the rise of created kinship. They may be isolated unless they are remarried, distant from their adult children, and unable to forge links with other kin.

The changes in marriage and kinship reviewed so far are altering the ways in which families take care of children and the elderly. The question of how well families are managing these tasks leads to a perspective I have called the public family. From this perspective, we should ask how the great changes in families over the past few decades have affected their ability to care for the society's dependents.

Social Change and the Public Family: The Elderly

As for the elderly, the data in Chapter 11 suggest that their well-being has improved in several ways over the past few decades. First, they are living longer. Indeed, most elderly persons will live long enough to get to know their grandchildren. That was not true earlier in this century, when life expectancy was substantially lower. Second, their incomes are higher, allowing, for many, a comfortable retirement. The poverty rate among the elderly, as noted, is now lower than the poverty rate for the entire population. It is also true, however, that some elderly persons remain in need. African-American older people are less advantaged today due to the same forces that affect the black working-age population. Elderly women as a group have lower incomes than elderly men. Many of these women did little work outside the home while raising children, so they accrued substantially less in Social Security and private pension benefits than did elderly men. What is more, a disproportionate number of elderly people have incomes that are above the federal poverty line but not by much.

A SUCCESS STORY

Still, the well-being of the elderly represents a success story for American social policy and family caregiving. The standard of living of the elderly has improved because the growth of government programs such as Social Security and Medicare, and of private pension plans, has increased their health and standard of living. The Social Security taxes workers pay provide an indirect transfer of income from prime-age men and women to their parents' generation. This transfer system allows the elderly to feel financially independent of their children, when in fact they are receiving subsidies from the next generation as a whole. The elderly have used their better health and increased incomes to become more independent—to remain in, or move to, their own homes and apartments, for example. By and large, their relationships with their children remain warm, and contact is frequent. This pattern of autonomy and "intimacy at a distance" appears to be the preferred pattern for both the elderly and their adult children in the United States and other Western nations. (The major exception is the Hispanic elderly, who appear to have a stronger preference for living with their children. Although few data are available, I suspect that Asian-American elderly have similar preferences.)

The support family members provide is also crucial to the well-being of the elderly. When older persons become ill or infirm, their spouses and children provide most of the care they need. It is not true that Americans place most of their frail parents in nursing homes. Even among elderly persons with serious physical impairments, family members provide the majority of the care. Family care of the elderly saves billions of dollars a year that government health insurance programs would otherwise have to pay. Thus, the contribution of adult children to the well-being of their parents' generation is still crucial. Without it, government expenditures for Medicare and Medicaid would be substantially higher.

THE CALM BEFORE THE STORM

We can conclude that there is no worsening "problem" of the public family's care of the elderly. On the contrary, this is one of the few aspects of the public family in which the situation has improved. Nevertheless, one must wonder whether we are in the middle of the calm before the storm. The individuals who will be retiring during the 2000s will be the parents of the baby boom generation. These individuals, as noted, had more children than any other generation in the twentieth century. They will likely profit in old age from this investment in childrearing. The chances of an elderly person living near children and grandchildren will probably rise because the elderly will have more children. For the same reason, the chances that a frail elderly person can receive help from at least one child will probably also rise. In the nation as a whole, the number of working-age persons per retired person will rise, which will increase tax payments into the Social Security and Medicare funds.

This favorable demographic situation will change sharply after about 2010, when the baby boom children themselves begin to retire. The baby boomers are having fewer children than any previous generation—about two, on average, compared with the average of about three in their parents' generation. Whereas about 10 percent of people who will retire in the 1990s had no children, about 20 percent of the retirees after 2010 will have no children. Fewer children will mean fewer potential caregivers. It will also mean, on a national scale, fewer working-age persons per retiree and therefore a larger tax burden on workers. Even the steps already taken to shore up the Social Security system [➡ p. 362] may not be adequate to maintain the current level of retirement benefits. Health care costs could rise sharply unless further reforms are undertaken.

Moreover, there are other trends, already under way, that are worrisome in the long run. The increase in paid work among women—who have been the main caregivers—is reducing the number of people who can devote large

After 2010, when the baby boomers retire, the number of elderly persons per middle-aged daughter or son will increase greatly. Consequently, the elderly may not receive as much care from their families as today's elderly do.

amounts of time to caring for the elderly without the competing demands of employment. So far, it appears that caregivers are adding the demands of elder care to their other work and family responsibilities. Whether they will continue to do so is uncertain. One could argue that they shouldn't continue to do so; rather, men should increase their caregiving. In addition, as noted earlier, elderly men may be disadvantaged by the long-run consequences of divorcing and remarrying. The increase in divorce has left many men distant from their children; it seems unlikely that their children will provide as much support for them later in life as will children who have always remained close to their fathers.

In sum, our current achievements in supporting the elderly are substantial, but they could lead to a false sense of complacency. They could also lead us to overlook elderly persons who are not doing as well even today, such as unmarried women. Currently, an elderly wife receives either one-half of her husband's benefit or the benefit her own work history has entitled her to, whichever is larger. Her husband, of course, receives his own, typically higher benefit. If her husband dies, however, the widow must choose between receiving her husband's benefit or the benefit she received before his death—she cannot continue to receive both. The government could reduce the income gap between elderly women and men by providing more generous Social Security survivors' benefits to widows (Burkhauser & Smeeding, 1994). But, to pay for this change, Social Security taxes would have to be raised or benefits to married elderly couples would have to be reduced. Neither option is politically popular. Another way to reduce the burden of Social Security costs is to increase taxes on the benefits of the well-to-do elderly. Currently they pay taxes on half their Social

Security benefits. (See *Families and Public Policy:* Financing Social Security and Medicare, in Chapter 11.) Or the minimum age at which a person can retire and receive full benefits could be raised further. Yet the political power of the elderly will make reducing existing benefits difficult.

Some of today's remaining problems may ease without public action. The gap in the incomes of elderly women and elderly men, for instance, may narrow when the next generation of elderly women retires; they will have worked for pay much more and accrued higher retirement benefits. Still, a prudent policy-maker would anticipate the difficulties in supporting the elderly in the future and begin to confront them now. Efforts to contain the cost of Medicare will be necessary if its explosive growth is to be controlled. Some of the plans introduced in Congress during the unsuccessful attempt to reform health insurance in 1994 attempted to do so. One approach was to form large insurance-purchasing cooperatives that could bargain with hospitals and doctors for lower fees; another was to have the government itself regulate doctors' and hospitals' fees. In the end, proponents of competing plans could not agree, and no legislation was passed. Whether strong cost-containment measures will emerge from future congressional debates over health insurance remains to be seen.

Social Change and the Public Family: Children

An examination of the situation of the elderly suggests, then, that their well-being has improved, although it is not clear that the family should receive credit for it. As for children, the opposite judgment applies: Many indicators suggest that the well-being of children has declined, but it is not clear that the family should receive the blame for it. I concluded in Chapter 10 that the well-being of children in low-income families may have worsened since the 1950s and 1960s and that children in middle-income families have experienced a moderate decline. Yet the chapter also noted that if the comparison is extended back to 1940 or earlier, children's well-being is not worse than it used to be.

THE NONPOOR

Children in the shrinking middle—those who are neither poor nor privileged—are much better off, on average, than the poorest children, but their situation leaves little to cheer about. For one thing, they face a far higher likelihood that their parents will divorce than did children in 1960. Research on the long-term effects of divorce suggests two conclusions. [➡ p. 445] First, children whose parents divorce do face a higher risk of certain undesirable outcomes, such as not graduating from high school or having a child prior to marrying. Second, most children of divorce will still not experience these outcomes. I argued that the effects of divorce should be a source of concern to anyone interested in the well-being of children but that divorce does not cause the widespread devastation some observers suggest.

Divorce is likely to be followed by cohabitation and often by remarriage. One of the surprises in the recent research literature is the finding that children whose custodial parents remarry fare no better than children who remain in single-parent families. In retrospect, I think that I and other researchers focused too heavily on the beneficial effects of adding a second (usually male) income to the home and too little on the difficulties the addition of a stepparent poses to the postdivorce family system. Moreover, due to the increases in parental divorce, cohabitation, and remarriage, it has become much more common for children to live in a series of different family configurations. In fact, the effect of instability—of living in a succession of different arrangements—is perhaps the key question in gauging the consequences for middle-class children of the changes in family structure. Instability is central because it is an unavoidable by-product of high divorce, cohabitation, and remarriage rates. In contrast, if we concluded that the major problem for children after divorce stems from the lack of money and downward mobility of many single parents, we could provide more financial support to single parents, as many European countries do. Similarly, we could perhaps reduce the postdisruption conflict between parents by providing mediation and counseling services. But it's hard to see how to reduce instability and the resultant movement of people in and out of the child's household, except of course by lowering the rates of union formation and dissolution.

We don't know enough yet about the process of family breakup to distinguish the effects of instability per se from other effects such as income loss or parental conflict. As noted, there are some studies which suggest that instability itself does have negative effects, yet the evidence on the importance of instability, compared with, say, parental conflict, is still inconclusive. It seems obvious that it would be more difficult for children to adjust to different family situations two or three times than to adjust once (or not at all if one's parents remain together). Yet it is possible that, were society to mitigate the other effects of divorce, most children might adjust to the new situations without major difficulty.

Another great change for children in middle-income families has been the sharp increase in the number of mothers who work outside the home. (The increase has been smaller in low-income families because it has long been more common for both parents to work for pay.) Women's employment, it is true, does raise the likelihood that a couple will separate. But it would be an oversimplification to lump women's growing employment in with more problematic family trends, such as teenage sexual activity and childbearing. Much of the concern about the rise in mothers' employment has centered on the effects on children of being cared for outside the home while their parents work. Yet there is very little evidence that children are harmed by out-of-home care. The remaining uncertainty concerns the effects of full-time out-of-home care on children in the first year or two of life. Even for these children, a recent, large study found no harmful effects in most cases.

THE POOR

The weakening of marriage has produced what is surely the most dramatic change in the family lives of poor children, namely, the increase in the proportion who are living with just one parent. In 1995, 63 percent of poor children lived with one parent, up from 40 percent in 1969 (Hernandez, 1993; U.S. Bureau of the Census, 1996b). In sociology and social policy, the debates over changes in family structure have too often been dominated by those who see single-parent families as a sure sign of breakdown and inadequacy, on the one side, and those who defend them against all charges and even celebrate them. The classic example is the furor created by a 1965 report that Daniel Moynihan, then a Labor Department official and now a U.S. senator, wrote on black families. Alarmed by the rising numbers of single-parent families, Moynihan warned of disorganization and a "tangle of pathology." In response, a defensive and often uncritical literature arose which denied that single

There is widespread support for campaigns to discourage teenage childbearing and to encourage responsible fatherhood.

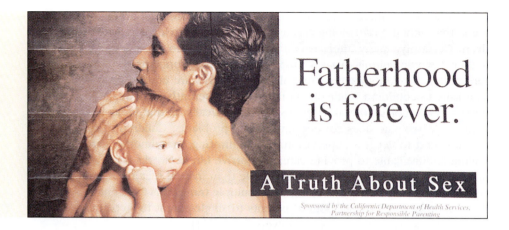

Fatherhood is forever.

A Truth About Sex

Sponsored by the California Department of Health Services, Partnership for Responsible Parenting

Louisiana have taken advantage of the option of covenant marriage. [➡ p. 416] And state legislators have resisted passing tough restrictions on divorce.

The objective of reducing nonmarital childbearing is less controversial. Teenage childbearing in particular, produces a consensus: Most people agree that it ought to be discouraged, although they don't agree on how. Some religious, community, and school groups are attempting to discourage adolescent sex by urging abstinence. Other groups accept the current level of sexual activity and urge teenagers to use contraceptives. In fact, adolescent sexuality did decline in the 1990s, especially among boys, while contraceptive usage went up—pleasing both the abstinence and contraception camps. [➡ p. 219] Moreover, teenage birth rates declined. This encouraging news was undercut somewhat by research suggesting that teenage childbearing may be more a reflection of a young woman's disadvantaged background than a cause of future problems. [➡ p. 223] If so, then discouraging teenage childbearing without addressing the underlying disadvantage might not make much difference to a young woman's life chances.

Assisting Single-Parent Families   The other approach to public policy on child welfare is to provide greater support for single-parent families. Many advocates of this approach believe that increases in the number of single-parent families result from broad economic and cultural trends that are not easily reversed by government programs. The pertinent economic trends are the movement of women into the workforce and the decline in the earning potential of noncollege-educated young men. Women's labor force participation increases their economic independence, reducing the necessity of their being married. Few people today would favor policies that restrict women's economic opportunities. The decline in poorly educated young men's job prospects has made them less attractive as marriage partners, and may thus have increased the likelihood that teenagers and young adults would bear children outside of marriage. The existence of welfare benefits may also encourage the formation of single-parent families, although evidence suggests that the effects are modest (Moffitt, 1992). (The effect of recent welfare reforms are not yet known.) Finally, recent evidence suggests that not all unmarried mothers are "single": See *Families and Public Policy: Fragile Families* on page 496.

The cultural trend behind the increase in single-parent families is increasing individualism, which has been rising in the United States at least since de Tocqueville noticed it in the 1830s but which appeared to take another quantum leap in the 1960s and 1970s. During this turbulent time of political and social protest, the divorce rate doubled, cohabitation emerged among the middle class, and sexual activity outside marriage became more acceptable. Advocates of strengthening marriage argue that cultural change can be reversed and that a concerted effort to reverse the recent rise in individualism should be mounted. Others respond that the cultural changes of the 1960s and early 1970s were consistent with the economic changes that were occurring, whereas the proposed cultural reversal would be inconsistent. That is to say, the increase in women's economic independence in the 1960s and early 1970s helped to create conditions under which divorce and nonmarital childbearing became more of an option. What was happening in the labor market reinforced, perhaps even propelled, what was happening culturally. The proposed cultural reversal, it is argued, would swim against the tide of women's economic independence and is therefore less likely to be successful.

This analysis of social trends leads to a pragmatic argument for assisting low-income single-parent families. Like it or not, they are here to stay in large numbers, and withholding aid from them would hurt their children (McLanahan & Sandefur, 1994). Some writers offer a more positive view: They maintain that two-parent families are not necessarily better for children, and that the diversity of family forms may be beneficial (Stacey, 1990). Either position translates into advocacy for increased support to single parents.

In the 1990s, little that was new in the way of direct assistance was provided. The 1996 welfare reform bill, which limited the amount of time a family could stay on the welfare rolls and strengthened work requirements, was the major new policy. Supporters claimed that it would help unmarried mothers by spurring them to take jobs. By 2000, the percentage of low-income single mothers in the workforce had increased substantially, and child poverty rates had declined, due partly to welfare reform and partly to the strong economy of the late 1990s (Blank & Card, 2000). Single parents who were working also benefited from increases in the Earned Income Tax Credit [➡ p. 199], the minimum wage, and childcare subsidies. Still, a majority of single-parent families who left the welfare rolls remained poor (Moffitt & Roff, 2000).

Assisting All Families

Almost all Western nations provide more financial assistance to parents than the United States, and this difference is an important reason why the United States has one of the highest percentages of children who are poor. [➡ p. 346] Many European countries provide universal child allowances—a fixed annual payment per child that the government pays to all parents, regardless of their incomes. The closest the United States comes to a universal child benefit is a $500 tax credit for each child under 17. But this tax credit is not universal because only families with income tax liabilities receive the credit; if parents don't earn enough money to pay income taxes (which is the case for many low-income families), they don't get the credit.

The argument for assisting poor families through universal benefits rather than means-tested (i.e., available only to parents with incomes below a certain level) benefits is that universal benefits acquire broad political support among families of all incomes. Some students of public policy have argued that only universal social programs, such as Social Security, gather enough political strength to retain adequate funding over the long run (Skocpol, 1991). The Achilles heel of universal programs, however, is that because of their universal

discussed, was increasing regulation of parents' relationships with their children. The second was decreasing regulation of adults' intimate relationships with one another.

THE DEREGULATION OF INTIMATE UNIONS

Let us consider the latter development. Prior to the twentieth century, when most families farmed land, marriage was the main way of controlling the flow of wealth across generations. For this reason, landowning parents sought to influence their children's choice of spouses. [➡ p. 49] Governments passed laws that reinforced parental control, such as by prohibiting interracial marriages or requiring parental permission. In the twentieth century, as the inheritance of land became less important, legal regulations on marriage weakened considerably. Laws concerning who is allowed to marry, who may marry whom, and who must give permission were overturned by courts or withdrawn by legislatures. For instance, in 1967, the Supreme Court unanimously struck down a Virginia law that prohibited interracial marriage. The judges found the law to be a violation of the equal protection clause of the Fourteenth Amendment to the Constitution. Moreover, the Court wrote,

> *The freedom to marry has long been recognized as one of the vital personal rights essential to the orderly pursuit of happiness by free men.*
>
> *Marriage is one of the "basic civil rights of man," fundamental to our very existence and survival. . . . Under our Constitution, the freedom to marry, or not marry, a person of another race resides in the individual and cannot be infringed by the State (Loving v. Virginia, 1967).*

The sweeping language of this decision suggested that the Court would not look favorably on other state restrictions on marriage. Marriage had become an individual decision, a basic personal right, rather than a socially approved way of transferring property, passing on wealth to descendants, or pooling labor. It had become essentially a private matter—a way of achieving a personally satisfying life. Other court decisions in the latter half of the twentieth century have endorsed a constitutional right to privacy in marriage that would never have been endorsed earlier in the nation's history. For example, the Supreme Court ruled in 1965 that a state law prohibiting the use of contraceptives by married couples violated marital privacy. [➡ p. 217] By the end of the 1980s, divorce had become an individual decision, as virtually every state enacted some form of "no-fault" divorce law allowing one spouse to obtain a divorce without demonstrating any particular fault or failing on the part of the other spouse, even if the other spouse objected. The law now emphasizes "private ordering," the idea that divorcing parents ought to have broad latitude to negotiate their own financial and custodial agreements (Maccoby & Mnookin, 1992).

An additional facet of the deregulation of marriage is the blurring of the legal and social boundaries between being in a married state and being in an unmarried state. U.S. courts have extended some, though not all, of the rights and protections of married couples to unmarried, cohabiting couples and their children, while maintaining in principle the difference between them. In 1972, the Supreme Court extended to unmarried individuals the right of privacy it had found for married persons in 1965 by overturning laws that prevented the sale of contraceptives to unmarried individuals. [➡ p. 217] A series of Supreme Court decisions starting in 1968 have invalidated nearly all laws that discriminate against children born outside marriage. Other Western nations have also ended most forms of discrimination against children born outside marriage and have held parents financially responsible for them. Generally, though, the surge in cohabitation is so new that the law is still in flux.

EXCESSIVE INDIVIDUALISM?

The increasingly private, self-fulfillment emphasis in marriage and cohabitation has been criticized and lamented by some. The issue is whether people's attention to their own personal satisfaction, to the growth and development of their psychological selves, has reached such extreme proportions that their capacity to make commitments to others has atrophied.[4] These "others" include not only family members but also neighborhoods, church groups, and communities—the groupings that give meaning and cohesion to society. In the twentieth-century United States, individualism is what economists call a "normal" good, meaning that the more income people have, the more of it they purchase. The elderly constitute the clearest example: They have used their higher incomes to purchase, or to remain in, separate homes and apartments. Similarly, young adults have used higher living standards to move out of their parents' homes (at least until the recent decline in their labor market prospects). Husbands and wives in unhappy marriages have used their greater economic independence to divorce.

Yet what seems excessive to the observer may seem justified and liberating to the actor. We are fortunate to live in a time and place where the standard of living is sufficiently high that a majority of the population can focus on their personal well-being. This luxury was not nearly as widespread 100, or even 50, years ago. As easy as it is to criticize excesses in others, few of us volunteer to rein in our own pursuit of happiness. Moreover, women's greater independence, some authors argue, has given them more control over their own sexual expression than previous generations had (Ehrenreich, Hess, & Jacobs, 1986). There is a case to be made, in other words, that the emphasis on individualism is an important advance that has improved societal levels of happiness. And although the case is rarely stated in words, many of us make it with actions in our own lives.

Individualism, it seems to me, can be judged a problem only if it interferes with important social functions. Yet that indeed is the charge, and in the realm of the family the specific charge is that adults have been too preoccupied with their own individual satisfaction to meet their obligations to children. In other words, it is alleged that the rise of the private family, focused on individual emotional satisfaction, has undercut the ability of the public family to carry out its responsibilities to children. There is some truth to this charge. For example, the pursuit of individual fulfillment is one factor in the greater instability of marriages and partnerships, and this instability in living arrangements, in turn, appears to be detrimental to children's well-being. It is a mistake, however, to hold individualism responsible for all of the increase in divorce, single-parent families, and the problems of children: Individualism did not cause the movement of manufacturing jobs from the United States to the Third World and the resulting deterioration

---

[4]See, for example, Bellah, Madsen, Sullivan, Swidler, & Tipton (1985).

in young people's labor market prospects. It did not cause the growth of the service sector of the economy during the twentieth century and the resulting expansion of opportunities in occupations that had been stereotyped as women's work. Culture and commitment have played a role in the case of children, but so has economic change. On the relative importance of each, reasonable people can, and do, disagree.

SHARING THE COST OF STABILITY

Moreover, the greater stability and security of marriage in previous generations were obtained at the cost of restricting women's lives more than men's. The breadwinner-homemaker norm restricted the ability of wives to pursue paid work. In a society in which money is the main medium of exchange, this restriction left wives dependent on their husbands. It also limited the fulfillment they could receive from achievements outside the home. There are still social conservatives who endorse this arrangement and would favor a return to the dominance of the breadwinner-homemaker family, but they are in the minority.

All others who are concerned about family need to confront the issue of how to enhance the stability and security of intimate unions without making women pay a disproportionate price. Is it possible to develop a new bargain between women and men that can provide both of them with a greater sense of security about their relationship and that can also provide more stability in their children's lives? Valerie Oppenheimer argues that, given their economic difficulties, young men should value having a second earner as a partner more highly than having a stay-at-home wife (Oppenheimer, 1994). But even if they do, one might ask how young women view these unions. In what Arlie Hochschild called a "stalled revolution," women have increased their financial contributions to marriages but men have not increased their household contributions commensurately (Hochschild, 1989). As a result, many wives are faced with a double burden of paid work and home work. Is it any wonder that women, given the option of living independently, find marriage less attractive and that many wives, as Hochschild writes, "cannot afford the luxury of unambivalent love for their husbands"?

If men wish to have the insurance of a second earner, they may need to do more around the house and with the children. There is evidence that men increased their share of housework moderately between 1965 and 1995. [➡ p. 298] Studies also show that boys in single-parent households do much more household work than boys in two-parent households; it's possible that as the 1970s and 1980s high-divorce-rate cohorts of children reach adulthood and marry, husbands will do a greater share of the domestic work (Goldscheider & Waite, 1991). In addition, it appears that the bargain between cohabiting couples stresses equity in wage earning and housework more than marriage does. If so, some cohabiting couples may carry this more equitable ethic into their marriages (Brines & Joyner, 1993).

Married men are more likely to share the domestic work if they value marital stability, and they are more likely to value marital stability if they also value living with their children every day. In an era of high divorce rates, men are at risk of losing the privilege of living with their children every day because they are rarely awarded (or even ask for) sole custody of children after a divorce. Sadly, from the evidence on divorced men's contact with their children, one might conclude that many men don't care if they see their children every day or even every week. The question is whether their preferences are changing or whether they will begin to change in the years ahead. Articles, books, and movies about the "new" fathers who actively rear their children indicate that our culture is giving men permission to care about raising their children much more than in the 1950s. The spread of joint legal custody also carries the message that fathers should be involved. So far, however, behavioral change appears to have lagged. Perhaps we will have to wait until the men who were divorced in the 1970s and 1980s reach old age and discover how little contact with, and support from, their kin they can muster. Perhaps then younger men will see the long-term costs of underinvesting in their children.

Even if men do change their behavior, divorce rates will probably not fall substantially. When women and men both work for pay, there are simply more alternatives to staying married. The typical ages at marriage are also unlikely to decline very much, especially if the job prospects of less-well-educated young men remain troubled. Cohabitation is likely to remain common and possibly increase. Marriage, particularly lifelong marriage, is unlikely to regain the predominant, indispensable place in family relations that it had in the past.

A Summing Up

Through hundreds of articles and books, the debates about the state of the family have bounced between those who argue that it is in deep decline and those who counter that it is in fine shape. Neither assertion is true. The social institution of the family is experiencing a period of great change, handling some of it well and limping through the rest. It is possible that some of the current changes will stretch its adaptability so thin that it will crack, but that judgment is premature. History has shown the family to be a resilient institution, able to alter its form to fit changing circumstances. Yet it is not infinitely adaptable. In examining the state of the family, one must be able to confront its problems without losing sight of its strengths.

One problem is that the family is an institution that was designed for scarcity and is now being asked to perform in an era of greater (although not uniform) prosperity. Throughout most of human history, people have been too preoccupied with subsisting from day to day and season to season to be concerned about personal fulfillment. Marriage and family provided an efficient way to pool the labor of women and men that was necessary to grow food (or earn enough money to buy it), to make or buy clothes and other goods, and to raise future sources of labor, namely children. Today, most people take these basic tasks for granted. Families are now being asked to carry the heavy responsibility of providing not merely sustenance but also emotional satisfaction. It is a relatively new demand, and the institution has not fully adjusted to it.

Another problem is that the family, in most places at most times, has been dominated by men; now it must adapt to a society in which women have substantial (although not yet full) independence. Male dominance was probably enforced first by greater physical strength, but then male dominance became so entrenched in Western law and social norms that the use of physical force usually wasn't necessary. For example, traditional English law held that wives had few legal rights because, upon marriage, the husband and wife became one legal person—effectively, the husband. A contemporary challenge is to modify the institution so that women and men share the benefits and burdens equitably.

The strengths of the family include the desires of most people for lasting intimacy and raising children.

The institution was also designed to raise many children in order that some would survive to adulthood; it now is being asked to raise one or two who will almost certainly survive to adulthood. Prior to the twentieth century, most couples did not experience sustained periods without children around because they began to have them soon after they were married and because one or both parents often died before all the children had grown up. Before the twentieth century, then, prolonged childless periods rarely existed by choice. Now an extended period without children in the household is common at the beginning of marriage and almost universal during the latter half. During these times, family relations necessarily focus on the relationship between the spouses. A consensus on what they should offer each other and expect from each other is still emerging.

The strengths of the family include the continuing desires of most adults to experience lasting bonds of intimacy and affection and to have children. Some sociologists think these desires are solely the result of the powerful socialization children receive. But there are theories that suggest they may also have a psychoanalytic component derived from early experiences with parents or an evolutionary component derived from the need to reproduce. Moreover, couples in first marriages can find strong support and guidance in the law and in social norms for the roles of spouse and parent.

In addition, the institution has demonstrated an ability to assume a great diversity of forms in different cultures and different eras. Countless anthropological studies show that non-Western societies have had family systems that are much less centered on the conjugal unit of husband, wife, and children. A final, and probably related, strength, which should humble those who predict its imminent demise, is its ability to outlast its critics. As with Mark Twain, its death has been greatly exaggerated. For instance, a concerned observer wrote in the *Boston Quarterly Review* of 1859: "The family, in its old sense, is disappearing from our land, and not only our free institutions are threatened but the very existence of our society is endangered" (Lantz, Schultz, & O'Hara, 1977, quoted at p. 413). Similar words can still be heard today—along with the words of those who celebrate its greater diversity. To be sure, the breadwinner-homemaker family is in decline. But although that type of family is the point of reference for many Americans, in historical perspective it is but a blip on the radar screen. The family is not disappearing, but exactly where it is heading we cannot yet be sure.

Looking Back

1. **What are the two most fundamental changes in the American family over the past half century?** One fundamental change in the American family is the lessened economic dependence of women on men. To some extent, this is a return to the situation of women a century or two ago. Another fundamental change is the weakening of marriage as the necessary institution for sexual activity and childbearing. Moreover, the decline of lifetime marriage has led to the emergence of created kinship. In a variety of family settings, people are now constructing kinship based more on what they do for one another than on their blood relationships.

2. **What is likely to happen to the relationship between the elderly and their families?** Changes in the lives of the elderly represent a success story for U.S. social policy, although minorities and women are not as well off economically as men. When the baby boom cohort retires starting around 2010, however, more elderly people will be depending on relatively fewer adult children to care for them and pay Social Security taxes. Because of high divorce rates, many elderly men will not have close ties with their children, who may be less willing than other children to provide assistance.

3. **How have American children fared over the past several decades?** Children in nonpoor families may have experienced a moderate decline in well-being since the mid-twentieth century. Parental divorce, which raises the risk of unwanted outcomes, is now more common. Although more middle-class mothers work outside the home today than in the past, no strong evidence links their employment to lowered well-being for their children. Among poor children, the decline in well-being has been greater. The percentage of poor children who live with single parents has increased sharply. Single-parent families are not as harmful to children as some critics suggest, but they do present some disadvantages.

4. **What should be done to improve children's family lives?** Experts disagree on how to strengthen families. Some believe that marriage is the superior family form, and that children would be helped most by efforts to promote marriage. In a similar vein, many people support efforts to discourage teenage childbearing, through either abstinence or contraception. Others urge that Americans accept the diversity of family forms as irreversible, and perhaps even beneficial. Such a position argues for direct assistance to both single- and two-parent low-income families.

5. **How has marriage evolved as a setting for personal life?** During the past century, the state has become less involved in regulating intimate adult relationships. Marriage has become fundamentally a private matter, a way of achieving a personally satisfying life. This private, self-fulfilling emphasis has been criticized as excessive, yet the emphasis on individual satisfaction may also be viewed as a social advance. Traditionally, marriage has been stabilized in part by restricting women's lives more than men's. The challenge is to enhance the stability and security of marriage and intimate relationships without forcing women to pay this price.

Thinking about Families

1. Do you hold both conservative (or traditional) beliefs and liberal (or modern) beliefs about families?

2. How can you tell whether a person is "kin" to another person?

3. Is marriage an outdated institution?

4. **The Public Family** How well are American families raising their children and caring for the elderly?

5. **The Private Family** How well are American families meeting the need for intimacy and emotional support?

Families on the Internet   www.mhhe.com/cherlin

*Note: While all the URLs listed were current as of the printing of this book, these sites often change. Please check our web site (**http://www.mhhe.com/cherlin**) for updates.*

The debates about the state of the family and its future can be monitored on the Internet. On the liberal side, the Council on Contemporary Families (**www.contemporaryfamilies.org**), defends the diversity of American families and argues that the institution is not in decline. On the center-right is the Institute for American Values (**www.americanvalues.org**), which promotes the idea that the decline of marriage and the increase in single-parent families have harmed children and weakened society. On the right is the Family Research Council (**www.frc.org**), which supports the "traditional family" in which women stay home to raise children, is strongly pro-life, and opposes gay rights. What evidence do these organizations cite in support of their positions on issues such as the growth of single-parent families?

Glossary

1965 Immigration Act   Act passed by the U.S. Congress which ended restrictions that had blocked most Asian immigration and substituted an annual quota.

acquired immune deficiency syndrome (AIDS)   A disease, caused by the **human immune deficiency virus (HIV),** that leaves the body unable to fight against disease.

activities of daily living (ADLs)   Personal care activities, including bathing, dressing, getting into and out of bed, walking indoors, and using the toilet.

ADLs   See **activities of daily living.**

AFDC   See **Aid to Families with Dependent Children.**

affective individualism   An outlook on personal relationships that emphasizes the emotional rewards to, and autonomy of, each individual more than that individual's obligations to care for and support others.

Aid to Families with Dependent Children (AFDC)   A federal program of financial assistance to low-income families, commonly known as "welfare" until it was replaced by Temporary Assistance to Needy Families (TANF) in 1996.

AIDS   See **acquired immune deficiency syndrome.**

alimony   Maintenance payments from an ex-husband to an ex-wife.

American Indian   The name used for a subset of all Native Americans, namely, those who were living in the territory that later became the 48 contiguous United States.

androgynous behavior   Behavior that has the characteristics of both genders.

annulment   A ruling that a marriage was never properly formed.

archival research   Research that uses printed or written documents stored in libraries or other data archives.

arranged marriage   A marriage in which the parents find a spouse for their child by negotiating with other parents.

Asian American   A person living in the United States who comes from or is descended from people who came from an Asian country.

assigned kinship   Kinship ties that people more or less automatically acquire when they are born or when they marry.

assimilation   The process by which immigrant groups merge their culture and behavior with that of the dominant group in the host country.

attachment   A bonding to another person that produces feelings of security, comfort, and ease when the other person is nearby.

authoritarian style (of parenting)   A parenting style in which parents combine low levels of emotional support with coercive attempts at control of their children.

authoritative style (of parenting)   A parenting style in which parents combine high levels of emotional support with inductive control of their children.

authority   The acknowledged right of someone to supervise and control others' behavior.

baby boom   The large number of people born during the late 1940s and 1950s.

barrio   A segregated Mexican-American neighborhood in a U.S. city.

berdache   In Native American societies, a man or woman who dressed like, performed the duties of, and behaved like a member of the opposite sex.

bilateral kinship   A system in which descent is reckoned through both the mother's and father's lines.

biosocial approach (to gender differences)   The theory that gender identification and behavior are based in part on people's innate biological differences.

birth cohort   All people born during a given year or period of years.

block grant   A fixed amount of money that the federal government gives each state to spend on a set of programs.

blood relatives   People who share common ancestors: parents and children, uncles and aunts, nephews and nieces, grandparents and grandchildren.

brideservice   A custom in which a prospective bridegroom agrees to work for a time for the bride's family.

bridewealth   A custom in which a prospective bridegroom's family makes a gift of money or livestock to the bride's family.

capitalism   An economic system in which goods and services are privately produced and sold on a market for profit.

centralizing women   Women who specialize in maintaining the links of kinship.

child abuse Serious physical harm (trauma, sexual abuse with injury, or willful malnutrition) of a child by an adult, with intent to injure.

cohabitation The sharing of a household by unmarried persons who have a sexual relationship.

cohort replacement model A model of changing public opinion in which each successive birth cohort experiences a different social environment and retains distinctive opinions throughout their adult life.

compadrazgo In Mexico, a godparent relationship in which a wealthy or influential person outside the kinship group is asked to become the *compadre,* or godparent, of a newborn child, particularly at its baptism.

companionate love The affection and partnership felt in a love relationship of long duration.

companionship marriage A marriage in which the emphasis is on affection, friendship, and sexual gratification.

comparable worth A system in which an expert body classifies jobs according to their "worth," as defined by attributes such as skill, effort, responsibility, and working conditions; wages or wage guidelines are then set according to the ranking of jobs.

comparable-worth discrimination A situation in which women and men do different jobs of equivalent value in the same company but the women are paid less.

comparison level for alternatives The level of satisfaction that a person thinks she or he would find in other relationships.

conflict theory A sociological theory that focuses on inequality, power, and social change.

conjugal family A kinship group comprising husband, wife, and children.

consensual union A cohabiting relationship in which a couple consider themselves to be married but have never had a religious or civil marriage ceremony.

contingent workers Workers who are hired temporarily or on a part-time basis and who typically do not receive fringe benefits such as health insurance, retirement pensions, and paid vacations.

coparenting An arrangement whereby divorced parents coordinate their activities and cooperate with each other in raising their children.

courtship A publicly visible process with rules and restrictions through which young men and women find a partner to marry.

courtship stage theories Descriptions of the stages of courtship that young adults must follow if their relationship is to result in marriage.

created kinship Kinship ties that people have to construct actively.

crisis period A period during the first year or two after parents separate when both the custodial parent and the children experience difficulties in dealing with the situation.

distribution of family income The proportion of the total income of all families in the nation that each family receives.

domestic violence Violent acts between family members or between women and men in intimate or dating relationships.

donor insemination A procedure in which semen is inserted into the uterus of an ovulating woman.

Earned Income Tax Credit (EITC) A refundable tax credit to low-income families with a child or children in which at least one parent is employed.

EITC See **Earned Income Tax Credit.**

elder abuse Physical abuse of an elderly person by a nonelderly person.

elderly population The group of people aged 65 years and over.

entitlement A program in which the government is obligated to provide benefits to anyone who qualifies, regardless of the total cost of the program.

era of divorce tolerance The time of a tolerant approach toward divorce, from the middle of the nineteenth century until, in the United States, 1970; the grounds for divorce were widened, and divorce was made more accessible to women.

era of restricted divorce The time of a restrictive approach toward divorce, until about the middle of the nineteenth century; divorces were usually granted only on the grounds of adultery or desertion, and generally only to men.

era of unrestricted divorce The time of a virtually unrestricted access to divorce, from, in the United States, 1970 to the present; divorces are usually granted without restriction to any married person who wants one.

evolutionary psychology The view that human behavior can be explained in terms of evolutionary pressure to behave in ways that maximize the chances of reproduction.

exchange theory A sociological theory that views people as rational beings who decide whether to exchange goods or services by considering the benefits they will receive, the costs they will incur, and the benefits t hey might receive if they were to choose an alternative course of action.

extended family A kinship group comprising the conjugal family plus any other relatives present in the household, such as a grandparent or uncle.

externalities   Benefits or costs that accrue to others when an individual or business produces something.

extramarital sex   Sexual activity by a married person with someone other than his or her spouse.

familial mode of production   A means of production in which the family produces nearly all its own food, makes most of its own clothes, and with the help of others builds its own dwelling.

family wage system   A division of labor in which the husband earns enough money to support his family and the wife remains home to do housework and childcare.

female-centered kinship   A kinship structure in which the strongest bonds of support and caregiving occur among a network of women, most of them relatives, who may live in more than one household.

feminist theory   A sociological theory that focuses on the domination of women by men.

fertility   The number of births in a population.

flextime   A policy that allows employees to choose, within limits, when they will begin and end their working hours.

formal sector   The part of a nation's economy that consists of jobs that meet legal standards for minimum wages, are relatively long-lasting and secure, include fringe benefits such as contributions to Social Security or health insurance, often have possibilities for advancement, and are sometimes unionized.

foster care   The removal of children from their parental home and their placement in another home.

free-rider problem   The tendency for people to obtain public goods by letting others do the work of producing them—metaphorically, the temptation to ride free on the backs of others.

frustration-aggression perspective   The theory that aggressive behavior occurs when a person is blocked from achieving a goal.

functionalist theory   A sociological theory that attempts to determine the functions, or uses, of the main ways in which a society is organized.

gender   The social and cultural characteristics that distinguish women and men in a society.

gender role   The different sets of behaviors that are commonly exhibited by women and men.

generativity   A feeling of concern about, or interest in, guiding and shaping the next generation.

gerontologist   A social/biological scientist who specializes in the study of aging.

gestation   Nine-month development of the fetus inside the mother's uterus.

Hispanic   A person living in the United States who traces his or her ancestry to Latin America.

HIV   See **human immune deficiency virus.**

human immune deficiency virus (HIV)   The virus that causes AIDS.

hunter-gatherers   People who wander through forests or over plains in small bands, hunting animals and gathering edible plants.

hypothesis   A speculative statement about the relationship between two or more factors.

ideal type   A hypothetical model that consists of the most significant characteristics, in extreme form, of a social phenomenon.

immigrant enclave   A large, dense, single-ethnic-group, almost self-sufficient community.

in vitro fertilization   A procedure in which eggs are removed from a woman, fertilized in a laboratory dish with sperm from a man, and then inserted into the uterus of either the genetic mother or a surrogate mother.

incest   Sexual relations with one's child, brother, or sister.

independent marriage   A marriage in which the emphasis is on self-development, flexible roles, and communication about problems.

informal sector   The part of a nation's economy that consists of temporary or casual jobs that sometimes offer illegal subminimum wages and that have little security, little possibility for advancement, and no fringe benefits.

initiator (of a divorce)   The person in a marriage who first becomes dissatisfied and begins the process of ending the marriage.

institutional marriage   A marriage in which the emphasis is on male authority, duty, and conformity to social norms.

interactionist approach (to gender differences)   The theory that gender identification and behavior are based on the day-to-day behavior that reinforces gender distinctions.

intergenerational solidarity   The characteristics of family relationships that knit the generations together.

internal economy   The way in which income is allocated to meet the needs of each member of a household, and whose preferences shape how income is spent.

intersexual   A person who is born with ambiguous sexual organs.

intimate outsider   A person, such as a stepparent, who plays a role in a family that is somewhere between that of a parent and that of a trusted friend.

joint legal custody (of children after a divorce)   The retaining by both parents of an equal right to make important decisions concerning their children.

joint physical custody (of children after a divorce)   An arrangement whereby the children of divorced parents spend substantial time in the household of each parent.

Kinsey Report   A 1948 book by zoology professor Alfred Kinsey detailing the results of thousands of interviews with men about their sexual behavior.

labor force   All people who are either working outside the home or looking for work.

labor market mode of production   A means of production in which people work for pay and thus produce less for their own use at home and buy and sell more on the market.

latent function   An unacknowledged, unstated reason behind social actions.

legal custody (of children after a divorce)   The right to make important decisions about the children and the obligation to have legal responsibility for them.

life-course perspective   The study of changes in individuals' lives over time, and how those changes are related to historical events.

lineage   A form of kinship group in which descent is traced through either the father's or the mother's line.

longitudinal survey   A survey in which interviews are conducted several times at regular intervals.

lower-class families   Families whose connection to the economy is so tenuous that they cannot reliably provide for a decent life.

manifest function   A publicly stated, acknowledged reason behind social actions.

marriage market   An analogy to the labor market in which single individuals (or their parents) search for others who will marry them (or their children).

masculinity   The set of personal characteristics that society defines as being typical of men.

matrilineage   A kinship group in which descent is through the mother's line.

mediating structures   Midlevel social institutions and groupings, such as the church, the neighborhood, the civic organization, and the family.

Medicaid   The government program of health insurance for people with incomes below the poverty line.

Medicare   The government program of health insurance for all elderly people.

mestizo   A person whose ancestors include both Spanish settlers and Native Americans.

middle-class families   Families whose connection to the economy provides them with a secure, comfortable income and allows them to live well above a subsistence level.

monogamy   A marriage system in which people are allowed only one spouse.

mortality   The number of deaths in a population.

nation   A people with shared economic and cultural interests.

nation-state   A term that combines the governmental and cultural connotations of the two words it comprises.

negative externalities   The costs imposed on other individuals or businesses when an individual or business produces something of value to itself.

new second generation   Children who are either immigrants themselves or who were born to immigrants after their families arrived in the United States.

no-fault divorce   The granting of a divorce simply on the basis of marriage breakdown due to "irreconcilable differences."

nonstandard employment   Jobs that do not provide full-time, indefinite work directly for the firm that is paying for it.

nonmarital birth ratio   The proportion of all births that occur to unmarried women.

non-Hispanic whites   People who identify their race as white but do not think of themselves as Hispanic.

norm   A widely accepted rule about how people should behave.

objectivity   The ability to draw conclusions about a social situation that are unaffected by one's own beliefs.

observational study (also known as field research)   A study in which the researcher spends time directly observing each participant.

oldest-old   The group of elderly people 85 years of age and over.

old-old   The group of elderly people 75 to 84 years of age.

parallel parenting   An arrangement whereby divorced parents gravitate toward a more detached style, going about their parenting business separately.

parental leave   Time off from work to care for a child.

passionate love   The sexually charged attraction that occurs at the start of many love relationships.

patriarchy   A social order based on the domination of women by men, especially in agricultural societies.

patrilineage   A kinship group in which descent is through the father's line.

patrilocal   A marriage residence rule in which the wife goes to live in her husband's parents' home.

pay equity   See **comparable worth.**

peer group   A group of people who have roughly the same age and status as one another.

permissive style (of parenting)   A parenting style in which parents provide emotional support but exercise little control over their children.

Personal Responsibility and Work Opportunity Reconciliation Act of 1996 (PRWORA)   The federal welfare legislation that requires most recipients to work within two years and that limits the amount of time a family can receive welfare.

physical custody (of children after a divorce) The right of a divorced spouse to have one's children live with one.

polyandry A form of polygamy in which a woman is allowed to have more than one husband.

polygamy A marriage system in which men or women (or both) are allowed to have more than one spouse.

polygyny A form of polygamy in which a man is allowed to have more than one wife.

positive externalities Benefits received by others when an individual or business produces something, but for which the producer is not fully compensated.

poverty line A federally defined income limit defined as the cost of an "economy" diet for a family of four, multiplied by three.

power The ability to force a person to do something even against his or her will.

prestige Honor and status in a society.

primary analysis Analysis of survey data by the people who collected the information.

principle of least interest In a dating relationship, the fact that the partner who is less interested in the relationship has more power because he or she could more easily leave it.

private family Two or more individuals who maintain an intimate relationship that they expect will last indefinitely—or in the case of a parent and child, until the child reaches adulthood—and who live in the same household and pool their income and household labor.

privilege A special advantage or benefit enjoyed by some individuals.

procreation The process of having and raising children.

production for exchange value Work for wages outside the home.

production for use value Work that produces goods and services used within the home.

pronatalism The belief that public policies should encourage people to have children.

psychoanalytic approach (to gender differences) The theory that gender identification and behavior are based on children's unconscious internalization of the qualities of their same-sex parent.

public family One adult, or two adults who are related by marriage, partnership, or shared parenthood, who is/are taking care of dependents, and the dependents themselves.

public goods Things that may be enjoyed by people who do not themselves produce them.

racial-ethnic group People who share a common identity and whose members think of themselves as distinct from others by virtue of ancestry, culture, and sometimes physical characteristics.

reflexivity A researcher's examination of the nature of the research process that she or he is undertaking.

relationship by blood The sharing of a common ancestor, including cross-generation ties (such as parent and child) and same-generation ties (such as brother and sister).

relationship-specific investment Time spent on activities such as childrearing that are valuable only in a person's current relationship.

remarriage chain A path that links individuals across households through the ties of disrupted unions and new unions.

remittances Cash payments sent by immigrants to family members in their country of origin.

responsive workplace A work setting in which job conditions are designed to allow employees to meet their family responsibilities more easily.

role overload The state of having too many roles with conflicting demands.

scientific method A systematic, organized series of steps that ensures maximum objectivity and consistency in researching a problem.

secondary analysis Analysis of survey data by people other than those who collected it.

selection effect The principle that whenever individuals sort, or "select," themselves into groups nonrandomly, some of the differences among the groups reflect preexisting differences among the individuals.

selection hypothesis The assertion that two groups differ because certain kinds of people select (or are selected into) one group more than the other.

service sector Workers who provide personal services such as education, health care, communication, restaurant meals, legal representation, entertainment, and so forth.

sex The biological characteristics that distinguish men and women.

sex-gender system The transformation of the biological differences between women and men into a social order that supports male domination.

sexual identity A set of sexual practices and attitudes that lead to the formation in a person's mind of an identity as heterosexual, homosexual, or bisexual.

sexual monogamy The state of having just one sex partner.

sexually based primary relationship An erotic, close relationship that is one of strong, frequent, and diverse interdependence that lasts over a considerable period of time.

social capital The resources that a person can access through his or her relationships with other people.

social class An ordering of all persons in a society according to their degrees of power, prestige, and privilege.

social exchange perspective   The theory that people calculate whether to engage in a particular behavior by considering the rewards and costs of that behavior and the rewards of alternatives to it.

social institution   A set of roles and rules that define a social unit of importance to society.

social learning perspective   The theory that individuals learn behavior they will later exhibit by observing what others do and seeing the consequences of these actions.

social network   A group of people who are linked through interaction with one another.

social role   A pattern of behaviors associated with a position in society.

Social Security Act of 1935   The federal act that created, among other provisions, Social Security, unemployment compensation, and aid to mothers with dependent children (later renamed Aid to Families with Dependent Children).

socialism   An economic system in which the number and types of goods produced, and who they are distributed to, are decided by the government rather than by the actions of a market.

socialization   The way in which one learns the ways of a given society or social group so that one can function within it.

socialization approach (to gender differences)   The theory that gender identification and behavior are based on children's learning that they will be rewarded for the set of behaviors considered appropriate to their sex but not for those appropriate to the other sex.

specialization model   A model of the marriage market in which women specialize in housework and child care and men specialize in paid work outside the home.

spillover   The fact that stressful events in one part of a person's daily life often spill over into other parts of her or his life.

state   A government that claims the right to rule a given territory and its population and to have a monopoly on force in that territory.

stem family   A kinship group comprising parents plus one child who remains at home.

stepfamily   A household in which two adults are married or cohabiting and at least one of the adults has a child present from a previous marriage or relationship.

Stonewall riot   The 1969 riot to which many writers date the emergence of the gay political movement.

surrogacy   A procedure in which a woman agrees to be artificially inseminated with a man's sperm, carry the fetus to term, and then turn the baby over to the man (and typically to his wife) when it is born.

survey   A study in which individuals from a geographic area are selected, usually at random, and asked a fixed set of questions.

symbolic interaction theory   A sociological theory that focuses on people's interpretations of symbolic behavior.

Temporary Assistance to Needy Families (TANF)   A federal program of financial assistance to low-income families that began in 1996, following passage of new welfare legislation. (See **Aid to Families with Dependent Children.**)

total fertility rate (TFR)   The average number of children a woman will bear over her lifetime if current birthrates remain the same.

transaction costs   The costs of organizing and carrying out exchanges.

transnational familes   Families that maintain continual contact between members in the sending and receiving countries.

'tweeners   The group of elderly people who have incomes that place them between the poor, who can qualify for public assistance over and above Social Security, and the middle class, who can supplement their Social Security checks with savings and pensions.

union   A stable, intimate relationship between two people who live in the same household but may or may not be married.

union formation   The process of beginning to live with a partner either through cohabitation or marriage.

upper-class families   Families that have amassed wealth and privilege and that often have substantial prestige as well.

value   A goal or principle that is held in high esteem by a society.

welfare state   A capitalist government that has enacted numerous measures, such as social security, unemployment compensation, and a minimum wage, to protect workers and their families from the harshness of the capitalist system.

Western nations   The countries of Western Europe and the overseas English-speaking countries of the United States, Canada, Australia, and New Zealand.

women-centered kinship   A kinship structure in which the strongest bonds of support and caregiving occur among a network of women, most of them relatives, who may live in more than one household.

working-class families   Families whose income can reliably provide only for the minimum needs of what other people see as a decent life.

young-old   The group of elderly people 65 to 74 years of age.

References

Acton, W. (1865). The function and disorders of the reproductive organs in youth, in adult age, and in advanced life: Considered in their physiological, social, and psychological relations. Philadelphia.

Adetunji, J. (1997). Assessing the mortality impact of HIV/AIDS relative to other causes of adult deaths in sub-Saharan Africa. In International Union for the Scientific Study of Population Committee on AIDS (Ed.), *The socio-demographic impact of AIDS in Africa.* Liège, Belgium: International Union for the Scientific Study of Population.

Akerlof, G. A., Yellen, J. L., & Katz, M. L. (1996). An analysis of out-of-wedlock childbearing in the United States. *Quarterly Journal of Economics, 111,* 277–317.

Alan Guttmacher Institute. (1999, April). Teenage pregnancy: Overall trends and state-by-state information. Available: www.agi-usa.org/pubs/tenn_preg_stats.html (Accessed 2 September, 2000).

Altman, L. K. (1997, July 15). AIDS deaths drop 19 percent in U.S., continuing a heartening trend. *New York Times,* pp. A1, A4.

Alwin, D. F. (1988). From obedience to autonomy: Changes in traits desired in children, 1924–1978. *Public Opinion Quarterly, 52,* 33–52.

Alwin, D. F. (1990). Historical changes in parental orientations to children. In N. Mandell (Ed.), *Sociological studies of child development* (pp. 65–86). Greenwich, CT: JAI Press.

Alwin, D. F. (1996). Coresidence beliefs in American society—1973 to 1991. *Journal of Marriage and the Family, 58,* 393–403.

Amato, P., & Booth, A. (1997). *A generation at risk: Growing up in an era of family upheaval.* Cambridge, MA: Harvard University Press.

Amato, P. R. (1993). Children's adjustment to divorce: Theories, hypotheses, and empirical support. *Journal of Marriage and the Family, 55,* 23–32.

Amato, P. R. (1994). The implications of research findings on children in stepfamilies. In A. Booth & J. Dunn (Eds.), *Stepfamilies: Who benefits? Who does not?* (pp. 81–87). Hillsdale, NJ: Lawrence Erlbaum.

Amato, P. R. (1996). Explaining the intergenerational transmission of divorce. *Journal of Marriage and the Family, 58,* 628–640.

Amato, P. R. (1998). More than money? Men's contribution to their children's lives. In A. Booth & A. C. Crouter (Eds.), *Men in families: When do they get involved? What difference does it make?* (pp. 241–278). Mahwah, NJ: Lawrence Erlbaum Associates.

Amato, P. R. (1999a). Children of divorced parents as young adults. In E. M. Hetherington (Ed.), *Coping with divorce, single-parenting, and remarriage* (pp. 147–163). Mahwah, NJ: Lawrence Erlbaum Associates.

Amato, P. R. (1999b). The postdivorce society. In R. A. Thompson & P. R. Amato (Eds.), *The postdivorce family: Children, parenting, and society* (pp. 161–190). Thousand Oaks, CA: Sage Publications.

Amato, P. R., & Gilbreth, J. G. (1999). Nonresident fathers and children's well-being. *Journal of Marriage and the Family, 61,* 557–573.

Amato, P. R., & Rezac, S. L. (1994). Contact with nonresident parents, interparental conflict, and children's behavior. *Journal of Family Issues, 15,* 191–207.

American Heritage Dictionary (3rd ed). (1997). New York: Houghton Mifflin.

Ammerman, N. T., & Roof, W. C. (1995). Old patterns, new trends, fragile experiments. In N. T. Ammerman & W. C. Roof (Eds.), *Work, family, and religion in contemporary society* (pp. 1–20). New York: Routledge.

Anderson, E. (1989). Sex codes and family life among poor inner-city youths. *Annals of the American Academy of Political and Social Science, 501,* 59–78.

Anderson, E. (1991). Neighborhood effects on teenage pregnancy. In C. Jencks & P. E. Peterson (Eds.), *The urban underclass* (p. 383). Washington, DC: The Brookings Institution.

Anderson, M. (1971). *Family structure in nineteenth century Lancashire.* Cambridge, England: Cambridge University Press.

Angell, R. (1936). *The family encounters the depression.* New York: Charles Scribner's Sons.

Angier, N. (1993, July 18). Study of sex orientation doesn't neatly fit mold. *New York Times,* p. 24.

Aquilino, W. S. (1991). Family structure and home-leaving: A further specification of the relationship. *Journal of Marriage and the Family, 53,* 999–1010.

Aquilino, W. S. (1994). Impact of childhood family disruption on young adults' relationships with parents. *Journal of Marriage and the Family, 56,* 295-313.

Arendell, T. (1986). *Mothers and divorce: Legal, economic, and social dilemmas.* Berkeley: University of California Press.

Ariès, P. (1960). *L'Enfant et la vie familiale sous l'ancien regime.* Paris: Librairie Plon.

Ariès, P. (1962). *Centuries of childhood: A social history of family life.* New York: Vintage Books.

Ariès, P. (1985a). Love in married life. In P. Ariès & A. Bejin (Eds.), *Western sexuality* (pp. 130-139). Oxford: Basil Blackwell.

Ariès, P. (1985b). Thoughts on the history of homosexuality. In P. Ariès & A. Bejin (Eds.), *Western sexuality* (pp. 62-75). Oxford: Basil Blackwell.

Astone, N., & McLanahan, S. (1991). Family structure, parental practices, and high school completion. *American Sociological Review, 56,* 309-320.

The average American woman spends 17 years raising children and 18 years helping aging parents. (1990, July 16). *Newsweek,* cover.

Baca Zinn, M., & Wells, B. (2000). Diversity within Latino families: New lessons for family social science. In D. H. Demo, K. R. Allen & M. A. Fine (Eds.), *Handbook of family diversity* (pp. 252-273). New York: Oxford University Press.

Bachrach, C. (1983). Children in families: Characteristics of biological step and adopted children. *Journal of Marriage and the Family, 45,* 171-179.

Baehr v. *Lewin.* (1993). 74 Haw. 530, 74 Haw. 645, 852 P.2d 44.

Bailey, B. L. (1988). *From front porch to back seat: Courtship in twentieth-century America.* Baltimore: Johns Hopkins University Press.

Bailey, J. M., & Dawood, K. (1998). Behavioral genetic, sexual orientation, and the family. In C. J. Patterson & A. R. D'Augelli (Eds.), *Lesbian, gay, and bisexual identities in families: Psychological perspectives* (pp. 3-18). New York: Oxford University Press.

Bailey, M., & Pillard, R. C. (1991). A genetic study of male sexual orientation. *Archives of General Psychiatry, 48,* 1089-1096.

Bailey, M., Pillard, R. C., Neale, M. C., & Agyei, Y. (1993). Heritable factors influence sexual orientation in women. *Archives of General Psychiatry, 50,* 217-223.

Bandura, A. (1973). *Aggression: A social learning analysis.* Englewood Cliffs, NJ: Prentice-Hall.

Bane, M. J. (1986). Household composition and poverty. In S. H. Danziger & D. H. Weinberg (Eds.), *Fighting poverty: What works and what doesn't* (pp. 209-231). Cambridge, MA: Harvard University Press.

Barcus, F. E. (1983). *Images of life on children's television: Sex roles, minorities, and families.* New York: Praeger.

Barringer, H. R., Gardner, R. W., & Levin, M. J. (1993). *Asian and Pacific Islanders in the United States.* New York: Russell Sage Foundation.

Bartlett, J. (1980). *Familiar quotations* (Ed. E. M. Beck). Boston: Little, Brown.

Bartlett, K. T. (1999). Improving the law relating to postdivorce arrangements for children. In E. M. Hetherington (Ed.), *Coping with divorce, single-parenting, and remarriage* (pp. 71-102). Mahwah, NJ: Lawrence Erlbaum Associates.

Baumgarth, W. (1986). The family and the state in modern political theory. In J. Peden & F. Glahe (Eds.), *The American family and the state* (pp. 19-47). San Francisco: Pacific Research Institute for Public Policy.

Baumrind, D. (1971). Current patterns of parental authority. *Developmental Psychology Monographs, 4* (1, Pt. 2).

Baxter, J. (1994). Is husband's class enough? Class location and class identity. *American Sociological Review, 59,* 220-235.

Bean, F., & Tienda, M. (1987). *The Hispanic population of the United States.* New York: Russell Sage Foundation.

Becker, G. S. (1991). *A treatise on the family* (Enlarged ed.). Cambridge, MA: Harvard University Press.

Bellah, R. N., Madsen, R., Sullivan, W. M., Swidler, A., & Tipton, S. M. (1985). *Habits of the heart: Individualism and commitment in American life.* Berkeley: University of California Press.

Belluck, P. (1998, March 20). Black youths' rate of suicide rising sharply. *New York Times,* p. A1.

Belsky, J., Spanier, G. B., & Rovine, M. (1983). Stability and change in marriage across the transition to adulthood. *Journal of Marriage and the Family, 45,* 567-577.

Belsky, J., Weinraub, M., Owen, M., & Kelly, J.F. (2001, April). *Quantity of Child Care and Problem Behavior.* Paper presented at the biennial meeting of the Society for Research on Child Development, Minneapolis, MN.

Bem, S. L. (1981). Gender schema theory: A cognitive account of sex-typing. *Psychological Review, 88,* 354-364.

Bem, S. L. (1993). *The lenses of gender: Transforming the debate on sexual inequality.* New Haven, CT: Yale University Press.

Bendix, R. (1960). *Max Weber: An intellectual portrait.* New York: Doubleday.

Benería, L., & Roldan, M. (1987). *The crossroads of class and gender: Industrial homework, subcontracting, and household dynamics in Mexico City.* Chicago: University of Chicago Press.

Bengtson, V., Rosenthal, C., & Burton, L. (1990). Families and aging: Diversity and heterogeneity. In R. H. Binstock & L. K. George (Eds.), *Handbook on aging and the social sciences* (3rd ed.) (pp. 263–287). New York: Academic Press.

Berger, B. (1986). On the limits of the welfare state: The case of foster care. In J. R. Peden & F. R. Glahe (Eds.), *The American family and the state* (pp. 365–379). San Francisco: Pacific Research Institute for Public Policy.

Berger, B., & Berger, P. (1983). *The war over the family: Capturing the middle ground.* Garden City, NY: Anchor Books.

Bergmann, B. R. (1986). *The economic emergence of women.* New York: Basic Books.

Berk, R. A., Campbell, A., Klap, R., & Western, B. (1992, October). The deterrent effect of arrest in incidents of domestic violence: A bayesian analysis of four field experiments. *American Sociological Review, 57,* 698–708.

Berk, S. F. (1985). *The gender factory: The apportionment of work in American households.* New York: Plenum Press.

Berkner, L. K. (1972). The stem family and the developmental cycle of the peasant household: An eighteenth-century Austrian example. *American Historical Review, 77,* 398–418.

Bernard, J. (1972). *The future of marriage.* New York: Bantam.

Bernhardt, A., Morris, M., & Handcock, M. S. (1995). Women's gains or men's losses? A closer look at the shrinking gender gap in earnings. *American Journal of Sociology, 101,* 302–328.

Bernstein, A. C. (1988). Unraveling the tangles: Children's understanding of stepfamily kinship. In W. R. Beer (Ed.), *Relative strangers: Studies of stepfamily processes* (pp. 83–111). Totowa, NJ: Rowan and Littlefield.

Berry, M., & Blassingame, J. (1982). *Long memory: The black experience in America.* New York: Oxford University Press.

Besharov, D. J., & Dembosky, J. W. (1996, October 3). Child abuse? Threat or menace? How common is it really? *Slate* [Online]. Available: www.slate.com (Accessed February 7, 1998).

Besharov, D. J., & Laumann, L. A. (2001). Don't call it child abuse if it's really poverty. In A. J. Cherlin (Ed.), *Public and private families: A reader, second edition.* (pp. 274–289). New York: McGraw-Hill.

Bianchi, S. M. (1995). The changing economic roles of women and men. In R. Farley (Ed.), *State of the Union: America in the 1990s.* Vol. 1 (pp. 107–154).

Bianchi, S. M., Milkie, M. A., Sayer, L. C., & Robinson, J. P. (2000). Is anyone doing the housework? Trends in the gender division of household labor. *Social Forces, 79,* 191–228.

Bianchi, S. M., & Spain, D. (1986). *American women in transition.* New York: Russell Sage Foundation.

Bianchi, S. M., & Spain, D. (1996). Women, work, and family in America. *Population Bulletin 51,* (3). Washington, DC: Population Reference Bureau.

Billingsley, A. (1992). *Climbing Jacob's ladder: The enduring legacy of African-American families.* New York: Simon and Schuster.

Black, A. (1924, August). Is the young person coming back? *Harper's,* p. 340.

Black, D., Gates, G., Sanders, S., & Taylor, L. (2000). Demographics of the gay and lesbian population in the United States: Evidence from available systematic data. *Demography, 37,* 139–154.

Blackwood, E. (1984). Sexuality and gender in certain Native American tribes: The case of cross-gender females. *Signs, 10,* 27–42.

Blake, J. (1989). *Family size and achievement.* Berkeley: University of California Press.

Blank, R. M. (1997). *It takes a nation: A new agenda for fighting poverty.* Princeton: Princeton University Press/Russell Sage Foundation.

Blank, R. M., & Card, D. (2000). The labor market and welfare reform. In R. M. Blank & D. Card (Eds.), *Finding jobs: Work and welfare reform* (pp. 1–19). New York: Russell Sage Foundation.

Bledsoe, C. (1990). Transformations in Sub-Saharan African marriage and fertility. *Annals of the American Academy of Political and Social Science, 501 (July),* 115–125.

Bledsoe, C. H. (1980). *Women and marriage in Kpelle society.* Palo Alto, CA: Stanford University Press.

Bledsoe, C. H., & Cohen, B. (Eds.) (1993). *Social dynamics of adolescent fertility in sub-Saharan Africa.* Washington, DC: National Academy Press.

Block, J. H. (1984). *Sex role identity and ego development.* San Francisco: Jossey-Bass.

Blood, R. O., & Wolfe, D. M. (1960). *Husbands and wives: The dynamics of married living.* New York: The Free Press.

Bloom, A. (1994, July 18). The body lies. *The New Yorker,* pp. 38–49.

Blumberg, P., & Paul, P. (1975). Continuities and discontinuities in upper-class marriages. *Journal of Marriage and the Family, 37,* 63–77.

Blumberg, R. L. (1991). Income under female versus male control: Hypotheses from a theory of gender stratification and data from the Third World. In R. L. Blumberg (Ed.), *Gender, family, and economy: The triple overlap* (pp. 97–127). Newbury Park, CA: Sage Publications.

Blumer, H. (1962). Society as symbolic interaction. In A. M. Rose (Ed.), *Human behavior and social processes* (pp. 179–192). Boston: Houghton Mifflin.

Blumstein, P., & Schwartz, P. (1983). *American couples: Money, work, sex.* New York: William Morrow Company.

Blumstein, P., & Schwartz, P. (1991). Money and ideology: Their impact on power and the division of household labor. In R. L. Blumberg (Ed.), *Gender, family, and economy: The triple overlap* (pp. 261–288). Newbury Park, CA: Sage Publications.

Bly, R. (1990). *Iron John: A book about men.* Reading, MA: Addison-Wesley.

Bohannan, P. (1971a). Divorce chains, households of remarriage, and multiple divorcers. In P. Bohannan (Ed.), *Divorce and after* (pp. 128–139). New York: Anchor Books.

Bohannan, P. (1971b). The six stations of divorce. In P. Bohannan (Ed.), *Divorce and after* (pp. 33–62). New York: Anchor Books.

Boocock, S. S. (1991). Childhood and child care in Japan: a comparative analysis. In S. E. Cahill (Ed.), *Sociological studies of child development: Vol. 4* (pp. 51–88). Greenwich, CT: JAI Press.

Booth, A., & Dabbs, James M., Jr. (1993). Testosterone and men's marriages. *Social Forces, 72,* 463–477.

Booth, A., & Edwards, J. N. (1992). Starting over: Why remarriages are unstable. *Journal of Family Issues, 13,* 179–194.

Booth, A., Johnson, D. R., Branaman, A., & Sica, A. (1995). Belief and behavior: Does religion matter in today's marriage? *Journal of Marriage and the Family, 57,* 661–671.

Boserup, E. (1970). *Woman's role in economic development.* London: George Allen and Unwin.

Boswell, J. (1982). Revolutions, universals, and sexual categories. *Salmagundi, 58–59,* 89–113.

Bott, E. (1957). *Family and social network.* London: Tavistock.

Bourdieu, P. (1980). Le capital social: Notes provisaire. *Actes de la recherche en sciences sociales, 3,* 2–3.

Bowler, M. (1999). Womens earnings: An overview. *Monthly Labor Review Online* [Online] 122 (December). Available: www.bls.gov/opub/mlr/mlrhome.htm (Accessed 15 July, 2000).

Bowles, S., & Gintis, H. (1976). *Schooling in capitalist America: Educational reform and the contradictions of economic life.* New York: Basic Books.

Bradbury, B., & Jantti, M. (1999). *Child poverty across industrialized nations.* Innocenti occasional papers, economic and social policy series, no. 71. Florence: UNICEF international child development centre.

Brand, E., Clingempeel, W. G., & Bowen-Woodward, K. (1988). Family relationships and children's psychological adjustment. In Hetherington & Arasteh (Eds.), *Impact of divorce* (pp. 299–324). Hillsdale, NJ: Lawrence Erlbaum Associates.

Bray, J. H. (1988). Children's development during early remarriage. In Hetherington & Arasteh (Eds.), *Impact of divorce* (pp. 279–298). Hillsdale, NJ: Lawrence Erlbaum Associates.

Bray, J. H. (1999). From marriage to remarriage and beyond. In E. M. Hetherington (Ed.), *Coping with divorce, single-parenting and remarriage* (pp. 253–271). Mahwah, NJ: Lawrence Erlbaum Associates.

Brien, M. J., Lillard, L. A., & Waite, L. J. (1999). Interrelated family building behaviors: Cohabitation, marriage, and nonmarital conception. *Demography, 36,* 535–551.

Brines, J., & Joyner, K. (1993). *Ties that bind: Principles of stability in the modern union.* Paper presented at the Annual Meeting of the Population Association of America, Cincinnati.

Brines, J., & Joyner, K. (1999). The ties that bind: Commitment and stability in the modern union. *American Sociological Review, 64,* 333–356.

Brod, H., & Kaufman, M. (Eds.). (1994). *Theorizing masculinities.* Thousand Oaks, CA: Sage Publications.

Brody, E., Kleban, M., Johnson, P., Hoffman, C., & Schoonover, C. (1987). Work status and parent care: A comparison of four groups of women. *The Gerontologist, 27,* 201–208.

Brody, E. M. (1981). Women in the middle and family help to older people. *The Gerontologist, 21,* 471–480.

Brooks-Gunn, J., Duncan, G. J., Klebanov, P. K., & Sealand, N. (1993). Do neighborhoods influence child and adolescent development? *American Journal of Sociology, 99,* 353–395.

Browning, C. R., & Laumann, E. O. (1997). Sexual contact between children and adults: A life course perspective. *American Sociological Review, 62,* 540–560.

Buchanan, C. M. et al. (1991). Caught between parents: Adolescents' experiences in divorced homes. *Child Development, 62,* 1008–1029.

Bulcroft, R., & Bulcroft, K. (1993). Race differences in attitudinal and motivational factors in the decision to marry. *Journal of Marriage and the Family, 55,* 338–355.

Bumpass, L. L. (1984). Children and marital disruption: A replication and update. *Demography, 21,* 71–82.

Bumpass, L. L., & Lu, H.-h. (2000). Trends in cohabitation and implications for children's family contexts in the United States. *Population Studies, 54,* 19–41.

Bumpass, L. L., Raley, R. K., & Sweet, J. A. (1995). The changing character of stepfamilies: Implications of cohabitation and nonmarital childbearing. *Demography, 32,* 1–12, 425–436.

Bumpass, L. L., & Sweet, J. A. (1989). National estimates of cohabitation. *Demography, 26,* 615–625.

Bumpass, L. L., Sweet, J. A., & Cherlin, A. (1991). The role of cohabitation in declining rates of marriage. *Journal of Marriage and the Family, 53,* 913–927.

Bumpass, L. L., Sweet, J., & Martin, T. C. (1990). Changing patterns of remarriage. *Journal of Marriage and the Family, 52,* 747-756.

Burgess, E. W., & Locke, H. J. (1945). *The family: From institution to companionship.* New York: American Book Company.

Burkhauser, R. V., & Smeeding, T. M. (1994). *Social security reform: A budget neutral approach to reducing older women's disproportionate risk of poverty,* Policy Brief, No. 2. Syracuse, NY: Center for Policy Research, Syracuse University.

Burstein, P., & Bricher, M. (1997). Problem definition and public policy: Congressional committees confront work, family, and gender, 1945-1990. *Social Forces, 75,* 135-169.

Burstein, P., & Wierzbicki, S. (2000). Public opinion and Congressional action on work, family, and gender, 1945-1990. In T. L. Parcel (Ed.), *Work and family: Research informing policy* (pp. 31-66). Thousand Oaks, CA: Sage Publications.

Burstein, P., Bricher, M., & Einwohner, R. L. (1995). Policy alternatives and political change: Work, family, and gender on the Congressional agenda, 1945-1990. *American Sociological Review, 60,* 67-83.

Burt, M. A. & Aron. L. (2000, February). America's homeless 11: Populations and services. Available: www.urban.org/housing/homeless/numbers/index.htm (Accessed July 2000).

Burtless, G., & Karoly, L. (1995). Demographic change, rising earnings inequality, and the distribution of personal well-being, 1959-1989. *Demography, 32,* 379-405.

Burton, L. (1990). Teenage childbearing as an alternative life-course strategy in multigenerational black families. *Human Nature, 1,* 123-143.

Buss, D. (1994). *The evolution of desire: Strategies of human mating.* New York: Basic Books.

Butterfield, F. (1997, February 3). '95 data show sharp drop in reported rapes. *New York Times,* p. A1.

Butz, W. P., & Ward, M. P. (1979). The emergence of countercyclical U.S. fertility. *American Economic Review, 69,* 318-328.

Byne, W. (1994, May). The biological evidence challenged. *Scientific American, 270,* 50-55.

Cain, M. (1983). Fertility as an adjustment to risk. *Population and Development Review, 9,* 688-702.

Caldwell, J. C. (1982). *Theory of fertility decline.* New York: Academic Press.

Caldwell, J. C., & Caldwell, P. (1993). The nature and limits of the sub-Saharan African AIDS epidemic: Evidence from geographic and other patterns. *Population and Development Review, 19,* 817-848.

Caldwell, J. C., Caldwell, P., & Orubuloye, I. (1992). The family and sexual networking in sub-Saharan Africa: Historical regional differences and present-day implications. *Population Studies, 46,* 385-410.

Calhoun, A. W. (1919). *A social history of the American family: Vol. 3. From 1865 to 1919.* New York: Barnes and Noble.

Callendar, C., & Kochems, L. (1983). The North American berdache, *Current Anthropology, 24,* 443-470.

Camarillo, A. (1979). *Chicanos in a changing society: From Mexican pueblos to American barrios in Santa Barbara and Southern California, 1848-1940.* Cambridge, MA: Harvard University Press.

Campbell, A. A. (1968). The role of family planning in the reduction of poverty. *Journal of Marriage and the Family, 30,* 236-245, quoted at 238.

Cancian, F. M. (1987). *Love in America: Gender and self-development.* Cambridge, England: Cambridge University Press.

Capaldi, D., & Patterson, G. (1991). Relation of parental transitions to boys' adjustment problems: 1. A linear hypothesis; 2. Mothers at risk for transitions and unskilled parenting. *Developmental Psychology, 27,* 489-504.

Caplow, T., Bahr, H. M., Chadwick, B. A., Hill, R., & Williamson, M. H. (1982). *Middletown families: Fifty years of change and continuity.* Minneapolis: University of Minnesota Press.

Carlson, A. (1986). What happened to the "family wage"? *The Public Interest, 83,* 3-17.

Carp, W. (1991). Family history, family violence: A review essay. *Journal of Policy History, 3,* 203-223.

Carter, H., & Glick, P. C. (1976). *Marriage and divorce: A social and economic study* (Rev. ed.). Cambridge, MA: Harvard University Press.

Castro, Janice. (1993, 29 March). Disposable workers. *Time,* pp. 42-46.

Cate, R. M., & Lloyd, S. A. (1992). *Courtship.* Newbury Park, CA: Sage Publications.

Cavan, R., & Ranck, K. (1938). *The family and the Depression: A study of 100 Chicago families.* Chicago: University of Chicago Press.

Center for Research on Child Well-Being. Fragile families research brief, number 1. Available: www.opr.princeton.edu/crcw/ff (Accessed 1 August 2000).

Chafe, W. H. (1972). *The American woman: Her changing social, economic, and political roles, 1920-1970.* New York: Oxford University Press.

Chambers, D. L. (1990). Stepparents, biological parents, and the law's perceptions of family after divorce. In S. D. Sugarman & H. H. Kay (Eds.), *Divorce reform at the crossroads* (pp. 102-129). New Haven, CT: Yale University Press.

Chan, R. W., Raboy, B., & Patterson, C. J. (1998). Psychosocial adjustment among children conceived via donor insemination by lesbian and heterosexual mothers. *Child development, 69,* 443–457.

Chao, R. (1994). Beyond parental control and authoritarian parenting style: Understanding Chinese parenting through the cultural norm of training. *Child Development, 65,* 1111–1119.

Chase-Lansdale, L., Brooks-Gunn, J., & Zamsky, E. (1994). Young multi-generational families in poverty: Quality of mothering and grandmothering. *Child Development, 65,* 373–393.

Chase-Lansdale, L., & Hetherington, E. M. (1990). The impact of divorce on life-span development: short and long term effects. In P. B. Baltes et al. (Ed.), *Life-span development and behavior: Vol. 10* (pp. 105–150). Hillsdale, NJ: Lawrence Erlbaum Associates.

Chase-Lansdale, P. L., Cherlin, A. J., & Kiernan, K. E. (1995). The long-term effects of parental divorce on the mental health of young adults: A developmental perspective. *Child Development, 66,* 1614–1634.

Chase-Lansdale, P. L., & Vanovskis, M. A. (1993). Adolescent pregnancy and child support. In R. Wolons (Ed.), *Children at risk in America* (pp. 202–229). Albany, NY: State University of New York Press.

Cherlin, A. (1977). The effects of children on marital dissolution. *Demography, 14,* 265–272.

Cherlin, A. J. (1978). Remarriage as an incomplete institution. *American Journal of Sociology, 84,* 634–650.

Cherlin, A. J. (1988). *The changing American family and public policy.* Washington, DC: Urban Institute Press.

Cherlin, A. J. (1988, October 27). Child support: Now everyone will be compelled to pay. *The Washington Post,* p. 23.

Cherlin, A. J. (1992). *Marriage, divorce, remarriage* (Rev. and enlarged ed.). Cambridge, MA: Harvard University Press.

Cherlin, A. J. (1993, December 30). Making deadbeats pay at work. *New York Times,* p. A19.

Cherlin, A. J. (1995). Child care for poor children. In P. L. Chase-Lansdale & J. Brooks-Gunn (Eds.), *Escape from poverty: What makes a difference for poor children?* Cambridge, England: Cambridge University Press.

Cherlin, A. J. (1999, 17 October). I'm O.K., you're selfish. *The New York Times Magazine,* pp. 44–46.

Cherlin, A. J. (2000, 11 December). Generation Ex-. *The Nation,* pp. 62–68.

Cherlin, A. J. (Ed.). (2001). *Public and private families: A reader* 2nd ed.. New York: McGraw-Hill.

Cherlin, A. J., Chase-Lansdale, P. L., & McRae, C. (1998). Effects of parental divorce on mental health throughout the life course. *American Sociological review, 63,* 239–249.

Cherlin, A., & Furstenberg, F. F., Jr. (1988). The changing European family: Lessons for the American reader. *Journal of Family Issues, 9,* 291–297.

Cherlin, A., & Furstenberg, F. F., Jr. (1992). *The new American grandparent: A place in the family, a life apart.* Cambridge, MA: Harvard University Press.

Cherlin, A. J., Furstenberg, F. F., Jr., Chase-Lansdale, P. L., Kiernan, K. E., Robins, P. K., Morrison, D. L., & Teitler, J. O. (1991). Longitudinal studies of the effects of divorce on children in Great Britain and the United States. *Science, 252,* 1386–1389.

Cherlin, A. J., Kiernan, K. E., & Chase-Lansdale, P. L. (1995). Parental divorce in childhood and demographic outcomes in young adulthood. *Demography, 32,* 299–318.

Chodorow, N. (1978). *The reproduction of mothering: Psychoanalysis and the sociology of gender.* Berkeley: University of California Press.

Christensen, K. E., & Staines, G. L. (1990). Flextime: A viable solution to work/family conflict? *Journal of Family Issues, 11,* 455–476.

Clark, R. L. (1990). Income maintenance policies in the United States. In R. H. Binstock & L. K. George (Eds.), *Handbook on aging and the social sciences* (pp. 382–397). New York: Academic Press.

Clarkberg, M. (1997). *The price of partnering: The role of economic well-being in young adults' first union experience.* Bronfenbrenner life course center working papers: Vol. 97-11. Ithaca, NY: Cornell University (33 pp.).

Clarkberg, M., Stolzenberg, R. M., & Waite, L. J. (1993). Attitudes, values, and the entrance into cohabitational unions [Discussion Paper 93–4]. Chicago: Population Research Center, National Opinion Research Center, and the University of Chicago.

Clymer, A. (1992, September 11). Family leave bill sent to president. *New York Times,* p. A26.

Coale, A. J., & Zelnik, M. (1963). *New estimates of fertility and population in the United States.* Princeton: Princeton University Press.

Cohen, R. (1971). Brittle marriage as a stable system: The Kanuri case. In P. Bohannan (Ed.), *Divorce and after* (pp. 205–239). Garden City, NY: Anchor Books.

Cohen, P. N., & Bianchi, S. M. (1999, December). Marriage, children, and women's employment: What do we know? *Monthly Labor Review,* 22–31.

Cohen, S., & Katzenstein, M. (1988). The war over the family is not over the family. In S. Dombusch & M Strober (Eds.), *Feminism, children, and the new families.* New York: The Guilford Press.

Colapinto, J. (2000). *As nature made him: The boy who was raised as a girl.* New York: HarperCollins.

Coleman, J. (1988). Social capital in the creation of human capital. *American Journal of Sociology, 94* (Suppl.), S95-S120.

Collier, J., Rosaldo, M., & Yanagisako, S. (1982). Is there a family? New anthropological views. In B. Thorne & M. Yalom (Eds.), *Rethinking the family: Some feminist questions* (pp. 25-39). New York: Longman.

Collins, R. (1971). A conflict theory of sexual stratification. *Social Problems, 19,* 3-21.

Coltrane, S. (1994). Theorizing masculinities in contemporary social science. In H. Brod & M. Kaufman (Eds.), *Theorizing masculinities* (pp. 39-60). Thousand Oaks, CA: Sage Publications.

Conger, R. D., Elder, J., Glen, H., Lorenz, F. O., Conger, K. J., Simons, R. L., Whitbeck, L. B., Huck, S., & Melby, J. N. (1990). Linking economic hardship to marital quality and instability. *Journal of Marriage and the Family, 52,* 643-656.

Connell, R. W. (1995). *Masculinities.* Cambridge, UK: Polity Press.

Cook, K., O'Brien, J., & Kollock, P. (1990). Exchange theory: A blueprint for structure and process. In G. Ritzer (Ed.), *Frontiers of social theory: The new syntheses* (pp. 151-181). New York: Columbia University Press.

Cooney, T. M., & Uhlenberg, P. (1990). The role of divorce in men's relations with their adult children after mid-life. *Journal of Marriage and the Family, 52,* 677-688.

Cooper, S. M. (1999). Historical analysis of the family. In M. B. Sussman, S. K. Steinmetz, & G. W. Peterson (Eds.), *Handbook of marriage and the family, second edition.* New York: Plenum.

Cott, N. (1977). *The bonds of womanhood: Woman's sphere in New England, 1780-1835.* New Haven, CT: Yale University Press.

Cowan, C. P., & Cowan, P. A. (1987). Men's involvement in parenthood: Identifying the antecedents and understanding the barriers. In P. W. Berman & F. A. Pederson (Eds.), *Men's transition to parenthood* (pp. 145-173). Hillsdale, NJ: Lawrence Erlbaum Associates.

Cowan, P. A., & Cowan, C. P. (in press). Becoming a family: Research and intervention. In I. Sigel & E. Brody (Eds.), *Family research, vol. 2.* Hillsdale, NJ: Lawrence Erlbaum Associates.

Cowley, G. (1997, May 19). Gender limbo. *Newsweek,* pp. 64-66.

Crenshaw, A. (1994, July 18-24). Paying the price for being married. *Washington Post National Weekly Edition, 21.*

Cretney, S. (1993, December). Step-parentage in English law. Paper presented at the International Colloquium on Stepfamilies Today, Paris.

Crimmons, E. M., Saito, Y., & Ingegneri, D. (1989). Changes in life expectancy and disability-free life expectancy in the United States. *Population and Development Review, 15,* 235-267.

The crisis in foster care: New directions for the 1990s. (1990, January). Washington, DC: Family Impact Seminar.

D'Antonio, W. V. (1985). The American Catholic family: Signs of cohesion and polarization. *Journal of Marriage and the Family, 47,* 395-405.

Danziger, S., & Weinberg, D. (1986). *Fighting poverty: What works and what doesn't.* Cambridge, MA: Harvard University Press.

Darling, C. A., Kallen, D. J., & VanDusen, J. E. (1984). Sex in transition, 1900-1980. *Journal of Youth and Adolescence, 13,* 385-399.

Darwin, C. (1871). *The descent of man and selection in relation to sex.* New York: Appleton.

Das Gupta, M., & Bhat, P. N. M. (1997). Fertility decline and increased manifestation of sex bias in India. *Population Studies, 51,* 307-315.

Davis, J. A., & Smith, T. (1997). General social surveys [Online]. Available: www.norc.uchicago.edu/gss.htm (Accessed November 7, 1997).

Davis, J. A., & Smith, T. W. (1996). *General social surveys, 1972-1996 cumulative code book.* Chicago: National Opinion Research Center.

Davis, J. A., Smith, T. W., & Marsden, P. (1999). *General social surveys, 1972-1998 cumulative code book.* Chicago: National Opinion Research Center, University of Chicago.

Davis, K. (1937). Reproductive institutions and the pressure for population. *Sociological Review, 29,* 289-306.

Davis, K. (1985). The meaning and significance of marriage in contemporary society. In K. Davis & A. Grossbard-Schechtman (Eds.), *Contemporary marriage: Comparative perspectives on a changing institution* (pp. 1-22). New York: Russell Sage Foundation.

Davis, N., & Robinson, R. (1988). Class identification of men and women in the 1970s and 1980s. *American Sociological Review, 53,* 103-112.

Deater-Deckard, K., Dodge, K. A., & Bates, J. E., Pettit. (1996). Externalizing behavior problems and discipline revisited: Non-linear effects and variation by culture, context, and gender. *Developmental Psychology, 32,* 1065-1072.

de Singly, F. (1993). *Sociologie de la famille contemporaine.* Paris: Editions Nathan.

Degler, C. N. (1980). *At odds: Women and the family in America from the revolution to the present.* New York: Oxford University Press.

Degler, C. N. (1990). Darwinians confront gender; or, there is more to it than history. In D. L. Rhode (Ed.), *Theoretical perspectives on sexual difference* (pp. 33–48). New Haven, CT: Yale University Press.

D'Emilio, J., & Freedman, E. B. (1988). *Intimate matters: A history of sexuality in America.* New York: Harper and Row.

Demos, J. (1970). *A little commonwealth: Family life in Plymouth Colony.* Oxford: Oxford University Press.

Department of the Interior. (1999). Indian statistics—population. Available: www.doi.gov/nrl/StatAbst/StatHome.html#BIA (Accessed August 2000).

Diekmann, A., & Englelhardt, H. (1999). The social inheritance of divorce: Effects of parent's family type in postwar Germany. *American Sociological Review, 64,* 783–793.

di Leonardo, M. (1987). The female world of cards and holidays: Women, families, and the work of kinship. *Signs, 12,* 440–453.

Diamond, M., & Sigmundson, H. K. (1997). Sex reassignment at birth: Long-term review and clinical implications. *Archives of Pediatric and Adolescent Medicine, 151,* 298–304.

Donnelly, A. C. (1994, June). National Committee to Prevent Child Abuse.

Dornbusch, S. M., Carlsmith, J. M., Bushwall, S. J., Ritter, P. L., Leiderman, H., Hastorf, A. H., & Gross, R. T. (1985). Single parents, extended households, and the control of adolescents. *Child Development, 56,* 326–341.

Dornbusch, S. M., & Strober, M. H. (1988). Our perspective. In S. M. Dornbusch & M. H. Strober (Eds.), *Feminism, children, and the new families* (pp. 3–24). New York: The Guilford Press.

Dumon, W. (1992). *National family policies in EC-countries in 1991.* Brussels: Commission of the European Communities, Directorate General for Employment, Industrial Relations and Social Affairs.

Duncan, G. J. (1984). *Years of poverty, years of plenty.* Ann Arbor: Institute for Social Research, University of Michigan.

Duncan, G. J. (1991). The economic environment of childhood. In A. C. Huston (Ed.), *Children in poverty* (pp. 23–50). New York: Cambridge University Press.

Duncan, G. J., & Brooks-Gunn, J. (1997). Income effects across the life span: Integration and interpretation. In G. J. Duncan & J. Brooks-Gunn (Eds.), *The consequences of growing up poor* (pp. 596–610). New York: Russell Sage Foundation.

Duncan, G. J., & Hoffman, S. D. (1985). Economic consequences of marital instability. In M. David & T. Smeeding (Eds.), *Horizontal equity, uncertainty, and economic well-being* (pp. 427–467). Chicago: University of Chicago Press.

Duncan, G. J., & Hoffman, S. D. (1991). Teenage underclass behavior and subsequent poverty: Have the rules changed? In C. Jencks & P. Peterson (Eds.), *The urban underclass* (pp. 155–174). Washington, DC: The Brookings Institution.

Duncan, G. J., & Rodgers, W. (1991). Has children's poverty become more permanent? *American Sociological Review, 56,* 538–550.

Dworkin, A. (1985). Against the male flood: Censorship, pornography, and equality. *Harvard Women's Law Journal, 8,* 1–30.

Easterlin, R. A. (1980). *Birth and fortune.* New York: Basic Books.

Eggebeen, D. J., & Hogan, D. P. (1990). Giving between generations in American families. *Human Nature, 1,* 211–232.

Eggebeen, D. J., Snyder, A. R., & Manning, W. D. (1996). Children in single-father families in demographic perspective. *Journal of Family Issues, 17,* 441–465.

Ehrenreich, B., Hess, E., & Jacobs, G. (1986). *Remaking love: The feminization of sex.* Garden City, NY: Anchor Books/Doubleday.

Ehrhardt, A. E. (1985). The psychobiology of gender. In A. S. Rossi (Ed.), *Gender and the life course.* New York: Aldine.

Eisenstadt v. *Baird.* (1972). (Vol. 438, p. 405). U.S.

Elder, G. H., Jr. (1974). *Children of the Great Depression: Social change in life experience.* Chicago: University of Chicago Press.

Elder, J., Glen, H. (1975). Age differentiation and the life course. *Annual Review of Sociology, 1,* 165–190.

Elder, J., Glen, H., Conger, R. D., Foster, E. M., & Ardelt, M. (1992). Families under economic pressure. *Journal of Family Issues, 13,* 5–37.

Elkin, F., & Handel, G. (1989). *The child and society: The process of socialization* (5th ed.). New York: Random House.

Ellwood, D. (1988). *Poor support: Poverty and the American family.* New York: Basic Books.

Emerson, R. M. (1972). Exchange theory, Part II: Exchange relations and network structures. In J. Berger, J. Zelditch, M. & B. Anderson (Eds.), *Sociological theories in progress: Vol. 2.* New York: Houghton Mifflin.

Emery, R. E. (1989). Family violence. *American Psychologist, 44,* 321–328.

Engels, F. (1972). *The origin of family, private property, and the state.* New York: International Publishers.

England, P. (1994). [Review of the Book *Gender play: Girls and boys in school*]. *Contemporary Sociology, 23,* 282–283.

England, P. (2000). Marriage, the costs of children, and gender inequality. In L. J. Waite, C. Bachrach, M. Hindin, E. Thomson, & A. Thornton (Eds.), *Ties that bind: Perspectives on marriage and cohabitation* (pp. 320-342). New York: Aldine de Gruyter.

England, P., & Farkas, G. (1986). *Households, employment, and gender: A social, economic, and demographic view.* New York: Aldine.

England, P., & Folbre, N. (1999). Who should pay for the kids? *Annals of the American Academy of Political and Social Science, 563,* 194-207.

Entwisle, D. R. (1985). Becoming a parent. In L. L'Abata (Ed.), *Handbook of family psychology and therapy: Vol. 1* (pp. 557-585). Homewood, IL: Dorsey Press.

Entwisle, D. R., & Doering, S. G. (1981). *The first birth: A family turning point.* Baltimore: Johns Hopkins University Press.

Epstein, C. F. (1988). Toward a family policy: Changes in mothers' lives. In A. J. Cherlin (Ed.), *The changing American family and public policy* (pp. 157-192). Washington, DC: Urban Institute Press.

Erikson, E. H. (1950). *Childhood and society.* New York: W. W. Norton.

Eschbach, K. (1993). Changing identification among American Indians and Alaska natives. *Demography, 30,* 635-652.

Evans, M. D. R. (1986). American fertility patterns: A comparison of white and nonwhite cohorts born 1903-1956. *Population and Development Review, 12,* 267-293.

Fagot, B. I. (1974). Sex differences in toddlers' behavior and parental reaction. *Developmental Psychology, 10,* 554-558.

Fagot, B. I., Leinbach, M. D., & Hagan, R. (1986). Gender labeling and the adoption of sex-typed behaviors. *Developmental Psychology, 22,* 440-443.

Families and Work Institute. (1998). The 1997 national study of the changing workforce, executive summary. Available: www.familiesandworkinst.org/summary/nscw.pdf (Accessed 30 September, 2000).

Farley, R., & Allen, W. (1987). *The color line and the quality of life in America.* New York: Russell Sage Foundation.

Federal Interagency Forum on Child and Family Statistics. (1997). *America's children: Key national indicators of well-being.* Washington, DC: U.S. Government Printing Office.

Ferree, M. M. (1990). Beyond separate spheres: Feminism and family research. *Journal of Marriage and the Family, 52,* 866-884.

Fine, G. A. (1987). *With the boys: Little league baseball and preadolescent culture.* Chicago: University of Chicago Press.

Fischer, D. H. (1978). *Growing old in America.* New York: Oxford University Press.

Fitch, C. A., & Ruggles, S. (2000). Historical trends in marriage formation. In L. J. Waite, C. Bachrach, M. Hindin, E. Thomson, & A. Thornton (Eds.), *The ties that bind: Perspectives on marriage and cohabitation* (pp. 59-88). New York: Aldine de Gruyter.

Flandrin, J. L. (1985). Sex in married life in the early Middle Ages: The church's teaching and behavioral reality. In P. Aries & A. Bejin (Eds.), *Western sexuality: Practice and precept in past and present times* (pp. 114-129). Oxford: Basil Blackwell.

Fonow, M. M., & Cook, J. (1991). Back to the future: A look at the second wave of feminist epistemology and methodology. In M. M. Fonow & J. Cook (Eds.), *Beyond methodology: Feminist scholarship as lived research* (pp. 1-15). Bloomington: Indiana University Press.

Forrest, J. D., & Singh, S. (1990). The sexual and reproductive behavior of American women. *Family planning perspectives, 22,* 206-214. *Fortune* (1991, May 20).

Foucault, M. (1980). *The history of sexuality: Vol. 1. An introduction.* New York: Vintage Books.

Fox, R. (1967). *Kinship and marriage.* Harmondsworth, England: Penguin Books.

Frazier, E. F. (1939). *The Negro family in the United States* (Rev. and abridged ed.). Chicago: University of Chicago Press.

Freedman, E. B. (1990). Theoretical perspectives on sexual difference: An overview. In D. L. Rhode (Ed.), *Theoretical perspectives on sexual differences* (pp. 257-261). New Haven, CT: Yale University Press.

Freedman, R., Chang, M., Sun, T., & Weinstein, M. (1994). The fertility transition in Taiwan. In Thornton & Lin (Eds.), *Social change and the family in Taiwan* (pp. 264-304). Chicago: University of Chicago Press.

Freeman, R. B., & Waldfogel, J. (2000). Dunning delinquent dads: Child support enforcement policy and never-married women. *Focus, 21* (number 1), 27-30.

Friedan, B. (1963). *The feminine mystique.* New York: Dell.

Friedman, D. E., & Galinsky, E. (1991). Work and family trends. In S. Zedeck (Ed.), *Work and family* (pp. 1-18). San Francisco: Jossey-Bass.

Frieze, I. H., & Brown, A. (1989). Violence in marriage. In L. Ohlin & M. Tonry (Eds.), *Family violence* (pp. 163-218). Chicago: University of Chicago Press.

Furstenberg, F. F., Jr. (1976). *Unplanned parenthood: The social consequences of teenage childbearing.* New York: The Free Press.

Furstenberg, F. F., Jr (1987). The new extended family: The experience of parents and children after remarriage. In K. Pasley & M. Ihinger-Tallman (Eds.), *Remarriage and stepparenting: Current research and theory* (pp. 42-61). New York: The Guilford Press.

Furstenberg, F. F., Jr., Brooks-Gunn, J., & Morgan, S. P. (1987). *Adolescent mothers in later life.* Cambridge, England: Cambridge University Press.

Furstenberg, F. F., Jr., & Cherlin, A. J. (1991). *Divided families: What happens to children when parents part.* Cambridge, MA: Harvard University Press.

Furstenberg, F. F., Jr., & Condran, G. A. (1988). Family change and adolescent well-being: A re-examination of U.S. trends. In A. J. Cherlin (Ed.), *The changing American family and public policy* (pp. 117-155).

Furstenberg, F. F., Jr., & Nord, C. W. (1985). Parenting apart: Patterns of childrearing after divorce. *Journal of Marriage and the Family, 47,* 893-904.

Furstenberg, F. F., Jr., Sherwood, K. E., & Sullivan, M. L. (1992). *Daddies and fathers: Men who do for their children and men who don't.* Parents' Fair Share Demonstration. New York: Manpower Demonstration Research Corporation.

Furstenberg, F. F., Jr., & Spanier, G. B. (1984). *Recycling the family: Remarriage after divorce.* Newbury Park, CA: Sage Publications.

Gagnon, J. H., & Simon, W. (1973). *Sexual conduct: The social sources of human sexuality.* Chicago: Aldine.

Galinsky, E. (1992). *Work and family: 1992 status report and outlook.* New York: Families and Work Institute.

Galinsky, E., Bond, J. T., & Friedman, D. E. (1993). *The changing workforce: Highlights of the national study.* New York: Families and Work Institute.

Galston, W. (1990/1991). A liberal-democratic case for the two-parent family. *The Responsive Community,* 14-26.

Gans, H. (1982). *The urban villagers: Group and class in the lives of Italian-Americans.* New York: The Free Press.

Garfinkel I., & McLanahan, S. (2000). Fragile families and child well-being: A survey of new parents. *Focus, 21* (number 1), 9-11.

Gates, G. J., & Sonenstein, F. L. (2000). Heterosexual genital activity among adolescent males: 1988 and 1995. *Family Planning Perspectives, 32,* 295-297, 304.

Gatz, M., Bengtson, V. L., & Blum, M. J. (1990). Caregiving families. In J. Birren & W. Schaie (Eds.), *Handbook of the psychology of aging* (3rd ed.) (pp. 404-426). Orlando, FL: Academic Press.

Gelles, R., & Cornell, C. P. (1990). *Intimate violence in families* (2nd ed.). Newbury Park, CA: Sage Publications.

Gelles, R. J. (1987). *Family violence.* Newbury Park, CA: Sage Publications.

Gelles, R. J., & Straus, M. A. (1979). Determinants of violence in the family: Toward a theoretical integration. In W. R. Burr, R. Hill, F. I. Nye, & I. L. Reiss (Eds.), *Contemporary theories about the family: Vol. 1* (pp. 549-581). New York: The Free Press.

Gelman, D. (1992, February 24). Is this child gay? Born or bred: The origins of homosexuality. *Newsweek,* pp. 46-53.

Geronimus, A. T. (1991). Teenage childbearing and social and reproductive disadvantage: The evolution of complex questions and the demise of simple answers. *Family Relations, 40,* 463-471.

Geronimus, A. T., & Korenman, S. (1992). The socioeconomic consequences of teen childbearing reconsidered. *Quarterly Journal of Economics, 107,* 1187-1214.

Gerth, H., & Mills, C. W. (1946). *From Max Weber: Essays in sociology.* New York: Oxford University Press.

Gilkes, C. (1995). The storm and the light: Church, family, work, and social crisis in the African-American experience. In N. Ammerman & C. Roof (Eds.), *Work, family and religion in contemporary society* (pp. 177-198). New York: Routledge.

Gill, R. (1991). Day care or parental care? *The Public Interest, 105,* 3-16.

Gillis, J. R. (1985). *For better or worse: British marriages, 1600 to the present.* Oxford: Oxford University Press.

Glass, J. L., & Estes, S. B. (1997). The family responsive workplace. *Annual Review of Sociology, 23,* 289-313.

Glendon, M. (1987). *Abortion and divorce in Western law.* Cambridge, MA: Harvard University Press.

Glendon, M. (1989). *The transformation of family law: State, law, and family in the United States and Western Europe.* Chicago: University of Chicago Press.

Glick, P. C. (1984). Marriage, divorce, and living arrangements: Prospective changes. *Journal of Family Issues, 5,* 7-26.

Gold, S. (1993). Migration and family adjustment: Continuity and change among Vietnamese in the United States. In H. McAdoo (Ed.), *Family ethnicity* (pp. 300-314).

Goldberg, C. (1998, January 16). Public still backs abortion, but wants limits, poll says. *New York Times,* p. A1.

Goldberg, C. (2000, 17 March). Vermont's house backs wide rights for gay couples. *The New York Times,* p. IA.

Goldin, C. (1977). Female labor force participation: The origin of black and white differences, 1870 and 1880. *Journal of Economic History, 37,* 87-108.

Goldscheider, C., & Uhlenberg, P. (1969). Minority group status and fertility. *American Journal of Sociology, 74,* 361-372.

Goldscheider, F. K. (1990). The aging of the gender revolution: What do we know and what do we need to know? *Research on aging, 12,* 531-545, quoted at 533.

Goldscheider, F. K. (1997). Recent changes in the U.S. young adult living arrangements in comparative perspective. *Journal of Family Issues, 18,* 708-724.

Goldscheider, F. K., & Goldscheider, C. (1993). *Leaving home before marriage: Ethnicity, familism, and generational relationships.* Madison: University of Wisconsin Press.

Goldscheider, F., & Goldscheider, C. (1994). Leaving and returning home in 20th century America. *Population Bulletin, 48* (4).

Goldscheider, F. K., & Waite, L. J. (1991). *New families, no families? The transformation of the American home.* Berkeley: University of California Press.

Goldstein, A. (2000, 6 March). When wives bring home more bacon. *The Washington Post,* p. 18.

Goldstein, J. R. (1999). The leveling of divorce in the United States. *Demography, 36,* 409-414.

Goldstein, J. R., & Kenney, C. T. (2000, 23 March). Marriage delayed or marriage forgone? New cohort forecasts of first marriage for U.S. women. Annual meeting of the Population Association of America. Los Angeles.

Golombok, S., Spencer, A., & Rutter, M. (1983). Children in lesbian and single-parent households: Psychosexual and psychiatric appraisal. *Journal of Child Psychology and psychiatry, 24,* 551-572.

Goode, W. J. (1963). *World revolution and family patterns.* New York: The Free Press.

Goode, W. J. (1971). Force and violence in the family. *Journal of Marriage and the Family, 33,* 624-636.

Goode, W. J. (1982). *The family* (2nd ed.). Englewood Cliffs, NJ: Prentice-Hall.

Goodstein, L. (2001a, January 30). Nudging church-state line, Bush invites religous groups to seek federal aid. *The New York Times,* p. 1ff.

Goodstein, L. (2001b, March 3). Bush's charity plan is raising concerns for the religious right. *The New York Times,* p. 1ff.

Gordon, L. (1988). *Heroes of their own lives: The politics and history of family violence.* New York: Viking.

Gordon, M. (1964). *Assimilation in American life.* New York: Oxford University Press.

Gottman, J. M. (1979). *Marital interaction: Experimental investigations.* New York: Academic Press.

Gove, W. R., Style, C. B., & Hughes, M. (1990). The effect of marriage on the well-being of adults. *Journal of Family Issues, 11,* 4-35.

Gray, F. (1990). Soviet women. *The New Yorker,* p. 55.

Greeley, A. M., Michael, R. T., & Smith, T. W. (1990, July/August). Americans and their sexual partners. *Society, 27,* 36-42.

Greenhouse, L. (2000, 29 June). The Supreme Court: The Nebraska case; Court rules that governments can't outlaw type of abortion. *The New York Times,* p. 1 ff.

Greeno, C. G. (1989). *Gender differences in children's proximity to adults.* Doctoral dissertation, Stanford University, Palo Alto, California.

Greenstein, T. N. (1990). Marital disruption and the employment of married women. *Journal of Marriage and the Family, 52,* 657-676.

Gregory, R. G., Anstie, R., Daly, A., & Ho, V. (1989). Women's pay in Australia, Great Britain, and the United States. In R. T. Michael, H. I. Hartmann & B. O'Farrell (Eds.), *Pay equity: Empirical inquiries* (pp. 222-242). Washington, DC: National Academy Press.

Greven, P. J. (1970). *Four generations: Population, land, and family in colonial Massachusetts.* Ithaca, NY: Cornell University Press.

Griswold del Castillo, R. (1979). *The Los Angeles barrio, 1850-1890: A social history.* Los Angeles, University of California Press.

Griswold v. *Connecticut.* (1965). 381 U.S. 479.

Groopman, J. (1997, August 11). To be poor and infected with H.I.V. *New York Times,* p. A29.

Gross, J. (1994, April 25). After a ruling, Hawaii weighs gay marriages. *New York Times,* p. A1.

Grossman, F. K., Eichler, L. S., & Winikoff, S. A. (1980). *Pregnancy, birth, and parenthood.* San Francisco: Jossey-Bass.

Grubb, W., & Lazerson, M. (1988). *Broken promises: How Americans fail their children.* Chicago: University of Chicago Press.

Gutman, H. G. (1976). *The black family in slavery and freedom, 1750-1925.* New York: Pantheon Books.

Guyer, J. (1988). Dynamic approaches to domestic budgeting: Cases and methods from Africa. In D. Dwyer & J. Bruce (Eds.), *A home divided: Women and income in the Third World* (pp. 155-172). Palo Alto, CA: Stanford University Press.

Gwartney-Gibbs, P., & Stockard, J. (1989). Courtship aggression in mixed-sex peer groups. In M. A. Pirog-Good & J. E. Stets (Eds.), *Violence in dating relationships* (pp. 185-204). New York: Praeger.

Haas, L. (1992). *Equal parenthood and social policy: A study of parental leave in Sweden.* Albany: State University of New York Press.

Haines, M. R. (1996). Long-term marriage patterns in the United States from colonial times to the present. *The History of the Family, 1,* 15-39.

Hajnal, J. (1982). Two kinds of preindustrial household formation systems. *Population and Development review, 8,* 449-494.

Haldeman, D. C. (1991). Sexual orientation conversion therapy for gay men and lesbians: Scientific examination. In Gonsiorek & Weinrich (Eds.), *Homosexuality: Research implications for public policy* (pp. 149-160). Newbury Park, CA: Sage Publications.

Hall, C. (1990). Strains in the firm of wife, children, and friends? Middle-class women and employment in early nineteenth-century England. In P. Hudson & W. Lee (Eds.), *Women's work and the economy in historical perspective* (pp. 106–131). Manchester, England: Manchester University Press.

Hall, S. (1904). *Adolescence: Its psychology and its relations to anthropology, sociology, sex, crime, religion and education.* 2 vols. New York: Appleton.

Halpern, R. (1993). Poverty and infant development. In C. H. J. Zeanah (Ed.), *Handbook of infant mental health* (pp. 73–86). New York, NY: Guilford Press.

Hamer, D. H., Hu, S., Magnuson, V. L., Hu, N., & Pattatucci, A. M. L. (1993). A linkage between DNA markers on the X chromosome and male sexual orientation. *Science, 261,* 321–327.

Hampton, R. L., & Newberger, E. (1985). Child abuse incidence and reporting by hospitals: Significance of severity, class, and race. *American Journal of Public Health, 75,* 56–60.

Handler, J. (1995). *The poverty of welfare reform.* New Haven, CT: Yale University Press.

Hansen, K. V. (1989). Helped put in a quilt: Men's work and male intimacy in nineteenth-century New England. *Gender & Society, 3,* 334–354, quoted at 338.

Hareven, T. K. (1982). *Family time and industrial time.* Cambridge, England: Cambridge University Press.

Harjo, S. (1993). The American Indian experience. In H. McAdoo (Ed.), *Family Ethnicity* (pp. 199–207).

Harrell-Bond, B. E. (1975). *Modern marriage in Sierra Leone.* The Hague: Mouton.

Hartmann, H. I. (1976). Capitalism, patriarchy, and job segregation by sex. *Signs, 1,* 137–169.

Harvey, D. (1993). *Potter Addition: Poverty, family, and kinship in a heartland community.* New York: Aldine de Gruyter.

Haveman, R. (1996). Does the growth in male earnings inequality reflect changing opportunities or changing choices? In AEI Conference Summary [Online]. Available: American Enterprise Institute for Public Policy Research.

Hawes, J., & Nybakkan, E. (1991). *American families: A research guide and historical handbook.* New York: Greenwood Press.

Hawes, J. M., & Hiner, N. R. (Eds.). (1991). *Children in historical and comparative perspective: An international handbook and research guide.* (pp. 31–70). New York: Greenwood Press.

Hayes, C. D. (1987). *Risking the future: Adolescent sexuality, pregnancy, and childbearing.* Washington, DC: National Academy Press.

Hayes, C. D., Palmer, J. L., & Zaslow, M. L. (1990). *Who cares for America's children? Child care policy for the 1990s.* Washington, DC: National Academy Press.

Heclo, H. (1986). The political foundations of antipoverty policy. In S. Danziger & D. Weinberg (Eds.), *Fighting poverty: What works and what doesn't* (pp. 312–340). Cambridge, MA: Harvard University Press.

Heise, L., Ellsberg, M., & Gottemoeller, M. (1999). *Ending violence against women.* Population Reports, Series L, no. 11. Baltimore, MD: Johns Hopkins School of Public Health.

Hendrick, S. S., & Hendrick, C. (Eds.). (1992). *Romantic love.* Newbury Park, CA: Sage Publications.

Henrikson v. *Gable.* 412 N.W. 2nd 702. (Mich. app. 1987).

Henry III, W. A. (1993, September 20). Gay parents: Under fire and on the rise. *Time.*

Hernandez, D. J. (1993). *America's children: Resources from family, government, and economy.* New York: Russell Sage Foundation.

Hernandez, D. J., & Charney, E. (1998). *From generation to generation: The health and well-being of children in immigrant families.* Washington, DC: National Academy Press.

Herskovits, M. J. (1990). *The myth of the Negro past* [Reissued with an introduction by Sindey W. Mintz]. Boston: Beacon Press.

Hertz, R. (1986). *More equal than others: Women and men in dual-career marriages.* Berkeley: University of California Press.

Herzog, E., & Sudia, C. E. (1973). Children in fatherless families. In B. Caldwell & N. Ricciuti (Eds.), *Review of child development research: Vol. 3* (pp. 141–232). Chicago: University of Chicago Press.

Hetherington, E. M. (1972). Effects of father absence on personality development in adolescent daughters. *Developmental Psychology, 7,* 313–326.

Hetherington, E. M. (1987). Family relations six years after divorce. In K. Pasley & M. Ihinger-Tallman (Eds.), *Remarriage and stepparenting* (pp. 185–205). New York: The Guilford Press.

Hetherington, E. M., & Clingempeel, W. G. (1992). Coping with marital transitions. *Monographs of the Society for Research in Child Development, 57* (Nos. 2–3).

Hetherington, E. M., Cox, R., & Cox, M. (1978). The aftermath of divorce. In J. Stevens & M. Mathews (Eds.), *Mother-child, father-child relations* (pp. 148–176). Washington, DC: National Association for the Education of Young Children.

Hetherington, E. M., & Jodl, K. M. (1994). Stepfamilies as settings for child development. In A. Booth & J. Dunn (Eds.), *Stepfamilies: Who benefits? Who does not?* (pp. 55–79). Hillsdale, NJ: Lawrence Erlbaum.

Hetherington, E. M., & Stanley-Hagan, M. (2000). Diversity among stepfamilies. In D. H. Demo, K. R. Allen & M. A. Fine (Eds.), *Handbook of family diversity* (pp. 173–196). New York: Oxford University Press.

Hirosima, K. (1997). Projection of living arrangements of the elderly in Japan: 1990–2010. *Genus, 53,* 79–111.

Hochschild, A. R. (1983). Attending to, codifying and managing feelings: Sex differences in love. In L. Richardson & V. Taylor (Eds.), *Feminist frontiers: Rethinking sex, gender, and society* (pp. 250–262). Reading, MA: Addison-Wesley.

Hochschild, A. R. (1989). *The second shift: Working parents and the revolution at home.* New York: Viking.

Hochschild, A. R. (1997). *The time bind: When work becomes home and home becomes work.* New York: Henry Holt and Company.

Hoeffer, B. (1981). Children's acquisition of sex-role behavior in lesbian-mother families. *American Journal of Orthopsychiatry, 51,* 536–544.

Hoem, B., & Hoem, J. M. (1988). The Swedish family: Aspects of contemporary developments. *Journal of Family Issues, 9,* 397–424.

Hofferth, S. (1984). Kin networks, race, and family structure. *Journal of Marriage and the Family, 46,* 791–806.

Hofferth, S. D. (1992). The demand for and supply of child care in the 1990s. In A. Booth (Ed.), *Child care in the 1990s: Trends and consequences* (pp. 3–25). Hillsdale, NJ: Lawrence Erlbaum.

Hoffman, K. L., Demo, D. H., & Edwards, J. N. (1994). Physical wife abuse in a non-Western society: An integrated theoretical approach. *Journal of Marriage and the Family, 56,* 131–146.

Hoffman, S. D., & Duncan, G. J. (1988). What are the economic costs of divorce? *Demography, 25,* 641–645.

Hoffman, S. D., Foster, M., & Furstenberg, F. F., Jr. (1993). Re-evaluating the costs of teenage childbearing. *Demography, 30,* 1–13.

Hogan, D., Hao, L., & Parish, W. P. (1990). Race, kin networks, and assistance to mother-headed families. *Social Forces, 68,* 797–812.

Holmes, S. (1990). Day care bill marks a turn toward help for the poor. *New York Times,* p. E4.

Hong, L. K. (1999). Chinese marriages and families: Diversity and change. In S. L. Browning & R. R. Miller (Eds.), *Till death do us part: A multicultural anthology on marriage* (pp. 23–44). Stamford, CT: JAI Press.

Hotz, V. J., McElroy, S. W., & Sanders, S. G. (1996). The costs and consequences of teenage childbearing for the mothers and the government. *Chicago Policy Review, 1,* 55–94.

House panel leader jeered by elderly in Chicago. *New York Times* (1989, August 19) p. 8.

Howell, N. (1979). *Demography of the Dobe Kung.* New York: Academic Press.

Hsia, H.-C., & Scanzoni, J. H. (1996). Rethinking the roles of Japanese women. *Journal of Comparative Family Studies, 27,* 309–329.

Huber, J. (1991). A theory of family, economy, and gender. In R. L. Blumberg (Ed.), *Gender, family, and economy* (pp. 35–51). Newbury Park, CA: Sage Publications.

Hurtado, A. (1995). Variation, combinations, and evolutions: Latino families in the United States. In R. Zambrana (Ed.), *Understanding Latino families* (pp. 40–61). Thousand Oaks, CA: Sage.

Ihinger-Tallman, M., & Pasley, K. (1987). *Remarriage.* Newbury Park, CA: Sage Publications.

Ingrassia, M., & McCormick, J. (1994, April 25). Why leave children with bad parents. *Newsweek,* pp. 52–58.

Institute for Social Research. (1998). The Monitoring the Future study [Online]. Available: www.isr.umich.edu/src/mtf/ (Accessed March 21, 1998).

Ishii-Kuntz, M. (2000). Diversity within Asian-American families. In D. H. Demo, K. R. Allen & M. A. Fine (Eds.), *The handbook of family diversity* (pp. 274–292). New York: Oxford University Press.

Jacklin, C. N. (1984). Sex-typing behavior and sex-typing pressure in child/parent interaction. *Archives of Sexual Behavior, 13,* 413–425.

Jacobs, J., & Gerson, K. (2000). The overworked American debate: New evidence comparing ideal and actual working hours. In T. Parcel & D. Cornfield (Eds.), *Work and Family: Research Informing Policy* (pp. 71–95). Thousand Oaks, CA: Sage Publications.

Jacobs, J., & Gerson, K. (2001). Overworked individuals or overworked families? Explaining trends in work, leisure, and family time. *Work and occupations, 28,* 40–63.

Jacobson, C. K., & Heaton, T. B. (1991). *Social Biology, 38,* 79–93.

Jacobson, P. (1959). *American marriage and divorce.* New York: Rinehart.

Jehl, D. (1994, June 15). President offers delayed proposal to redo welfare. *New York Times.* p. A1.

Jencks, C. (1994). *The homeless.* Cambridge, MA: Harvard University Press.

Jencks, C., & Peterson, P. (1991). *The urban underclass.* Washington, DC: The Brookings Institution.

Jeter, J. (1997, August 15). 'Covenant marriages' tie the knot tightly. *The Washington Post,* p. A1.

Joe, J. R., Sparks, S., & Tiger, L. (1999). Changing American Indian marriage patterns: Some examples from contemporary Western Apaches. In S. L. Browning & R. R. Miller (Eds.), *Till death do us part: A multicultural anthology on marriage* (pp. 5–21). Greenwich, CT: JAI Press.

Johnson, A. M., Wadsworth, J., Wellings, K., Bradshaw, S., & Field, J. (1992). Sexual lifestyles and HIV risk. *Nature, 360,* 410–412.

Johnson, W. R., & Skinner, J. (1986). Labor supply and marital separation. *American Economic Review, 76,* 455–469.

Johnston, L. D., O'Malley, P. M., & Bachman, J. G. (2001). *Monitoring the future: National results on adolescent drug use, Overview of Key Findings, 2000.* Institute for Social Research: University of Michigan.

Jones, J. (1985). *Labor of love, labor of sorrow: Black women and the family from slavery to the present.* New York, Basic Books.

Juhn, C., Murphy, K., & Pierce, B. (1993). Wage inequality and the rise in returns to skill. *Journal of Political Economy, 101,* 410-442.

Kalish, S. (1995). Multiracial births increase as U.S. ponders racial definitions. *Population Today, 23,* 1-2.

Kalleberg, A. L. (2000). Nonstandard employment relations: part-time, temporary, and contract work. *Annual Review of Sociology, 26,* 341-365.

Kalmuss, D. (1984). The intergenerational transmission of marital aggression. *Journal of Marriage and the Family, 46,* 11-19.

Kamerman, S. B., & Kahn, A. J. (1987). *The responsive workplace: Employers and a changing labor force.* New York: Columbia University Press.

Katz, J. (1976) *Gay American history.* New York: Harper and Row.

Katz, M. (1989). *The undeserving poor: From the war on poverty to the war on welfare.* New York: Pantheon Books.

Kaufman, J., & Zigler, E. (1987). Do abused children become abusive parents? *American Journal of Orthopsychiatry, 57,* 186-192.

Kaus, M. (1992). *The end of equality.* New York: Basic Books.

Kellam, S. G., Ensminger, M. E., & Turner, R. (1977). Family structure and the mental health of children. *Archives of General Psychiatry, 34,* 1012-1022.

Keller, S. (1991). The American upper class family: Precarious claims on the future. *Journal of Comparative Family Studies, 22,* 159-182.

Kelley, H., Berscheid, E., Christensen, A., Harvey, J., Huston, T., Levinger, G., McClintock, E., Peplau, L., & Peterson, D. (1983). *Close relationships.* New York: Freeman.

Kelley, H. H. (1979). *Personal relationships.* Hillsdale, NJ: Lawrence Erlbaum Associates.

Kempe, C. H., Silverman, F. N., Steele, B. F., Droegemuller, W., & Silver, H. K. (1962). The battered child syndrome. *Journal of the American Medical Association, 181,* 17-24.

Kertzer, D. I. (1991). Household history and sociological theory. *Annual Review of Sociology, 17,* 155-179.

Keshet, J. K. (1988). The remarried couple: Stresses and successes. In W. R. Beer (Ed.), *Relative strangers: Studies of stepfamily processes* (pp. 29-53). Totowa, NJ: Rowan and Littlefield.

Kessler, R., House, J., & Turner, J. (1987). Unemployment and health in a community sample. *Journal of Health and Social Behavior, 28,* 51-59.

Kiernan, K. E. (1992). The impact of family disruption in childhood on transitions made in young adult life. *Population Studies, 46,* 213-234.

Kimmel, D. C. (1992). The families of older gay men and lesbians. In L. Burton (Ed.), *Families and aging* (pp. 75-78). Amityville, NY: Baywood.

Kingston, P. W. (1990). Illusion and ignorance about the family-friendly workplace. *Journal of Family Issues, 11,* 438-454.

Kinsey, A. C., Pomeroy, W. B., & Martin, C. E. (1948). *Sexual behavior in the human male.* Philadelphia: W.B. Saunders.

Kirkpatrick, M., Smith, C., & Roy, R. (1981). Lesbian mothers and their children: A comparative study. *American Journal of Orthopsychiatry, 51,* 545-559.

Kitano, H. H. L. (1988). The Japanese American family. In C. H. Mindel & R. W. Habenstein (Eds), *Ethnic families in America: Patterns and variations* (pp. 258-275). New York: Elsevier Science Publishing.

Kitano, H. H. L., & Daniels, R. (1988). *Asian Americans: Emerging minorities.* Englewood Cliffs, NJ: Prentice Hall.

Klein, J. (1997, 16 June). In God they trust. *New Yorker,* pp. 40-48.

Kobrin, F. E. (1976). The fall of household size and the rise of the primary individual in the United States. *Demography, 13,* 127-138.

Koegl, P., Burnam, M., & Baumohl, J. (1996). The causes of homelessness. In J. Baumohl (Ed.), *Homelessness in America* (pp. 24-33). Phoenix, AZ: Oryx Press.

Kohn, M., & Slomczynski, K. (1990). *Social structure and self-direction: A comparative analysis of the United States and Poland.* Oxford: Basil Blackwell.

Kohn, M. L. (1969). *Class and conformity: A study in values.* Homewood, IL: Dorsey Press.

Kohn, M. L., & Schooler, C. (1978). The reciprocal effects of the substantive complexity of work and intellectual flexibility: A longitudinal assessment. *American Journal of Sociology, 84,* 24-52.

Komarovsky, M. (1971). *The unemployed man and his family.* New York: Octagon Books.

Komarovsky, M. (1992). The concept of social role revisited. *Gender & Society, 6,* 301-313.

Komter, A. (1989). Hidden power in marriage. *Gender & Society, 3,* 187-216.

Kornhaber, A., & Woodward, K. L. (1981). *Grandparents/grandchildren: The vital connection.* Garden City, NY: Anchor Press/Doubleday.

Koss, M. P. (1988). Hidden rape: Sexual aggression and victimization in a national sample of students in higher education. In A. W. Burgess (Ed.), *Rape and sexual assault II* (pp. 3-25). New York: Garland.

Kotlowitz, A. (1991). *There are no children here: The story of two boys growing up in the other America.* New York: Doubleday.

Kristof, N. D. (1996, 11 February). Who needs love! In Japan, many couples don't. *New York Times,* p. A1.

Landale, N., & Fennelly, K. (1992). Informal unions among mainland Puerto Ricans: Cohabitation or an alternative to legal marriage? *Journal of Marriage and the Family, 54,* 269-280.

Landale, N., & Forste, R. (1991). Patterns of entry into cohabitation and marriage among mainland Puerto Rican women. *Demography, 28,* 587-605.

Lantz, H., Schultz, M., & O'Hara, M. (1977). The changing American family from the preindustrial to the industrial period: A final report. *American Sociological Review, 42,* 406-421.

LaRossa, R., & LaRossa, M. (1981). *Transition to parenthood: How infants change families.* Newbury Park, CA: Sage Publications.

Larson, A. (1989). The social context of HIV transmission in Africa: A review of the historical and cultural bases of East and Central African sexual relations. In Australian National University (Ed.), *Health Transition Centre Working Papers,* no. 1.

Laslett, B. (1973). The family as a public and private institution: An historical perspective. *Journal of Marriage and the Family, 35,* 480-492.

Laslett, P., & Wall, R. (1972). *Household and family in past time.* Cambridge, England: Cambridge University Press.

Laumann, E. O., Gagnon, J. H., Michael, R. T., & Michaels, S. (1994). *The social organization of sexuality: Sexual practices in the United States.* Chicago: University of Chicago Press.

Lee, S. M. (1998). *Asian Americans: Diverse and growing* [Population Bulletin, vol. 53, no. 2]. Washington, DC: Population Reference Bureau.

Lehrer, E. L., & Chiswick, C. U. (1993). Religion as a determinant of marital stability. *Demography, 30,* 385-404.

Leridon, H., & Villeneuve-Gokalp, C. (1989). The new couples: Number, characteristics, and attitudes. *Population 44, English Selection,* no. 1, 203-235.

LeVay, S. (1991). A difference in hypothalmic structure between heterosexual and homosexual men. *Science, 253,* 1034-1037.

Lever, J. (1976). Sex differences in the games children play. *Social Problems, 23,* 478-487.

Levinson, D. (1988). Family violence in cross-cultural perspective. In V. B. Van Hasselt, R. L. Morrison, A. S. Bellack, & M. Hersen (Eds.), *Handbook of family violence* (pp. 435-455). New York: Plenum Press.

Levinson, D. (1989). *Family violence in cross-cultural perspective.* Newbury Park, CA: Sage Publications.

Levy, F. (1987). *Dollars and dreams: The changing American income distribution.* New York: Russell Sage Foundation.

Levy, F. (1998). *The new dollars and dreams: American incomes and economic change.* New York: Russell Sage Foundation.

Levy, F., & Michel, R. (1991). *The economic future of American families: Income and wealth trends.* Washington, DC: Urban Institute Press.

Levy, R. J. (1989). An introduction to divorce-property issues. *Family Law Quarterly, 23,* 147-160.

Lewis, O. (1965). *La vida: A Puerto Rican family in the culture of poverty—San Juan and New York.* New York: Random House.

Lewontin, R. (1995a, April 20). Sex, lies, and social science: *The New York Review of Books,* pp. 24-29.

Lewontin, R. (1995b, May 25). Sex, lies, and social science: An exchange. *New York Review of Books,* pp. 43-44.

Lichter, D. T., LeClere, F. B., & McLaughlin, D. K. (1991). Local marriage markets and the marital behavior of black and white women. *American Journal of Sociology, 96,* 843-867.

Lichter, D. T., McLaughlin, D. K., Kephart, G., & Landry, D. J. (1992). Race and the retreat from marriage: A shortage of marriageable men? *American Sociological Review, 57,* 781-799.

Liem, J. H., & Liem, G. R. (1990). Understanding the individual and family effects of unemployment. In J. Eckenrode & S. Gore (Eds.), *Stress between work and family* (pp. 175-204). New York: Plenum Press.

Light, I. (1972). *Ethnic enterprise in America: Business and welfare among Chinese, Japanese, and Blacks.* Berkeley: University of California Press.

Liker, J. K., & Elder, G. H., Jr. (1983). Economic hardship and marital relations in the 1930s. *American Sociological Review, 48,* 343-359.

Lin, C., & Liu, W. (1993). Intergenerational relationships among Chinese immigrants from Taiwan. In H. McAdoo (Ed.), *Family ethnicity* (pp. 271-286).

Lipman-Blumen, J. (1984). *Gender roles and power.* Englewood Cliffs, NJ: Prentice-Hall.

Liss, L. (1987). Family and the law. In M. B. Sussman & S. K. Steinmetz (Eds.), *Handbook of marriage and the family* (pp. 767-794). New York: Plenum Press.

Little, K. (1973). *African women in towns.* Cambridge, MA: Cambridge University Press.

Liu, K., Manton, K. G., & Liu, B. M. (1985). Home care expenses for the disabled elderly. *Health Care Financing Review, 7* (2), 51-59.

Lock, J. H. (1984). *Sex role identity and ego development.* San Francisco: Jossey-Bass.

Locke, H. J. (1951). *Predicting adjustment in marriage: A comparison of a divorced and a happily married group.* New York: Henry Holt.

Logan, J. R., & Spitze, G. D. (1996). *Family ties: Enduring relations between parents and their grown children.* Philadelphia: Temple University Press.

Lomnitz, L. (1977). *Networks and marginality: Life in a Mexican shantytown.* New York: Academic Press.

Lomnitz, L. (1987). *A Mexican elite family, 1820-1980: Kinship, class, and culture.* Princeton, NJ: Princeton University Press.

Lorber, J. et al. (1981). On the reproduction of mothering: A methodological debate. *Signs, 6,* 482-514.

Loving v. *Virginia.* (1967). 388 U.S. 1.

Luker, K. (1984). *Abortion and the politics of motherhood.* Berkeley: University of California Press.

Luker, K. (1996). *Dubious conceptions: The politics of teenage pregnancy.* Cambridge, MA: Harvard University Press.

Lundberg-Love, P., & Geffner, R. (1989). Date rape: Prevalence, risk factors, and a proposed model. In M. A. Pirog-Good & J. E. Stets (Eds.), *Violence in dating relationships: Emerging social issues* (pp. 169-184). New York: Praeger.

Luster, T., & Small, S. A. (1997). Sexual abuse history and number of sex partners among female adolescents. *Family Planning Perspectives, 29,* 204-211.

Lye, D. N., Klepinger, D. H., Hyle, P. D., & Nelson, A. (1992). *Childhood living arrangements and adult children's relations with their parents.* Annual meeting of the Population Association of America, Denver.

Lynd, R. S., & Lynd, H. M. (1929). *Middletown: A study in modern American culture.* New York: Harcourt, Brace, and World.

Maccoby, E. E. (1990). Gender and relationships: A developmental account. *American Psychologist, 45,* 513-520.

Maccoby, E. E. (1992). Family structure and children's adjustment: Is quality of parenting the major mediator? In M. Hetherington & W. G. Clingempeel (Eds.), Coping with marital transitions (pp. 230-238). *Monographs of the Society for Research in Child Development 57* (nos. 2-3).

Maccoby, E. E. (1998). *The two sexes: Growing up apart, coming together.* Cambridge MA: Harvard University Press.

Maccoby, E. E., & Jacklin, C. N. (1974). *The psychology of sex differences.* Palo Alto, CA: Stanford University Press.

Maccoby, E. E., & Mnookin, R. H. (1992). *Dividing the child: Social and legal dilemmas of custody.* Cambridge, MA: Harvard University Press.

MacDonald, K., & Parke, R. (1984). Bridging the gap: Parent-child play interaction and peer interactive competence. *Child Development, 55,* 1265-1277.

Macfarlane, A. (1970). *The family life of Ralph Josselin.* Cambridge, England: Cambridge University Press.

Macfarlane, A. (1978). *The origins of English individualism.* Oxford, England: Basil Blackwell.

Manegold, C. S. (1993, April 8). To Crystal, 12, school serves no purpose. *New York Times,* p. A1.

Manegold, C. S. (1994, August 25). Quiet winners in house fight on crime: Women. *New York Times,* p. A19.

Manning, W. D. (1993). Marriage and cohabitation following premarital conception. *Journal of Marriage and the Family, 55,* 839-850.

Manning, W. D., & Smock, P. (1995). Why marry? Race and the transition to marriage among cohabitors. *Demography, 32,* 509-520.

Marcus, S. (1964). *The other Victorians: A study of sexuality and pornography in mid-nineteenth-century England.* New York: Basic Books.

Mare, R., & Winship, C. (1991). Socioeconomic change and the decline in marriage for blacks and whites. In C. Jencks & P. Peterson (Eds.), *The urban underclass* (pp. 175-202). Washington, DC: The Brookings Institution.

Marsiglio, W. (1992). Stepfathers with minor children living at home: Parenting perceptions and relationship quality. *Journal of Family Issues, 13,* 195-214.

Marsiglio, W. (1993). Adolescent males' orientation toward paternity and contraception. *Family Planning Perspectives, 25,* 22-31.

Marsiglio, W., Amato, P., Day, R. D., & Lamb, M. E. (2000). Scholarship on fatherhood in the 1990s and beyond. *Journal of Marriage and the Family, 62,* 1173-1191.

Martel, J. L., & Kelter, L. A. (2000, February). The job market remains strong in 1999. *Monthly Labor Review* [Online] 123(2). Available: stats.bls.gov/opub/mlr/archive.htm (Accessed July 2000).

Martin, J., & Martin, E. (1978). *The helping tradition in the black family and community.* Chicago: University of Chicago Press.

Martin, L. G. (1989). The graying of Japan. *Population Bulletin, 44,* 1-43.

Martin, T. C., & Bumpass, L. L. (1989). Recent trends in marital disruption. *Demography, 26,* 37-51.

Marx, K. (1959). The eighteenth brumaire of Louis Bonaparte. In L. S. Feuer (Ed.), *Marx and Engels: Basic writings and philosophy* (pp. 318-348). Garden City, NY: Anchor Books.

Marx, K. (1977). *Capital:* Vol. 1. New York: Vintage Books.

Masheter, C. (1997). Healthy and unhealthy friendship and hostility between ex-spouses. *Journal of Marriage and the Family, 59,* 463-475.

Mathews, J. (1993, October 11-17). The quiet move toward benefits for gay couples. *The Washington Post National Weekly Edition.*

May, E. T. (1980). *Great expectations: Marriage and divorce in post-Victorian America.* Chicago: University of Chicago Press.

May, E. T. (1988). *Homeward bound: American families in the cold war era.* New York: Basic Books.

Mayer, S. E. (1997). *What money can't buy: Family income and children's life chances.* Cambridge, MA: Harvard University Press.

McAdoo, H. (1988). *Transgenerational patterns of upward mobility in African-American families.* Newbury Park, CA: Sage Publications.

McCurdy, K., & Daro, D. (1994). Current trends in child abuse reporting and fatalities: The results of the 1993 annual fifty state survey [Working Paper no. 808]. National Committee to Prevent Child Abuse. Chicago.

McGue, M., & Lykken, D. T. (1992). Genetic influence on risk of divorce. *Psychological Science, 3,* 368-373.

McLanahan, S., & Sandefur, G. (1994). *Growing up with a single parent: What hurts, what helps.* Cambridge, MA: Harvard University Press.

McLanahan, S. S. (1983). Family structure and stress: A longitudinal comparison of two-parent and female-headed families. *Journal of Marriage and the Family, 45,* 347-357.

McLanahan, S. S. (1994). The consequences of single motherhood. *The American Prospect, 18,* 48-58.

McLaughlin, D. K., & Lichter, D. T. (1997). Poverty and the marital behavior of young women. *Journal of Marriage and the Family, 59,* 582-594.

McLoyd, V. C. (1990). The impact of economic hardship on black families and children: Psychological distress, parenting and socioemotional development. *Child Development, 61,* 311-346.

McLoyd, V. C., Cauce, A. M., Takeuchi, D., & Wilson, L. (2000). Marital processes and parental socialization in families of color: A decade review of research. *Journal of Marriage and the Family, 62,* 1070-1093.

Mead, L. (1992). *The new politics of poverty: The nonworking poor in America.* New York: Basic Books.

Mellman, M., Lazarus, E., & Rivlin, A. (1990). Family ties, family values. In D. Blankenhorn, S. Bayme, & J. B. Elshtain (Eds.), *Rebuilding the nest* (pp. 73-92). Milwaukee: Family Service America.

Menaghan, E. G. (1989). Role changes and psychological well-being: Variations in effects by gender and role repertoire. *Social Forces, 67,* 693-714.

Merton, R. K. (1968). *Social theory and social structure* (Enlarged ed.) New York: The Free Press.

Meyer, D. R. (1999). Compliance with child support orders in paternity and divorce cases. In R. A. Thompson & P. R. Amato (Eds.), *The postdivorce family* (pp. 127-157). Thousand Oaks, CA: Sage Publications.

Meyer, D. R., & Garasky, S. (1993). Custodial fathers: Myths, realities, and child support policy. *Journal of Marriage and the Family, 55,* 73-89.

Meyering, A. (1990). La petite ouvrière surmenée: Family structure, family income, and women's work in nineteenth-century France. In P. Hudson & W. Lee (Eds.), *Women's work and the economy in historical perspective* (pp. 132-156). Manchester, England: Manchester University Press.

Michael, R. T., Hartmann, H. I., & O'Farrell, B. (1989). *Pay equity: Empirical inquiries.* Washington, DC: National Academy Press.

Michael, R. T., Laumann, E. O., & Gagnon, J. H. (1992). The number of sexual partners of adults in the United States. Harris School of Public Policy Studies, University of Chicago.

Mills, D. M. (1988). Stepfamilies in context. In W. R. Beer (Ed.), *Relative strangers: Studies of stepfamily processes* (pp. 1-28). Totowa, NJ: Rowan and Littlefield.

Min, P. (1993). Korean immigrants' marital patterns and marital adjustment. In H. McAdoo (Ed.), *Family ethnicity* (pp. 287-299).

Mintz, S., & Kellogg, S. (1988). *Domestic relations: A social history of American family life.* New York: The Free Press.

Mischel, W. (1966). A social-learning view of sex differences in behavior. In E. E. Maccoby (Ed.), *The development of sex differences* (pp. 56-81). Palo Alto, CA: Stanford University Press.

Mitterauer, M., & Sieder, R. (1982). *The European family.* Chicago: University of Chicago.

Modell, J. (1985). Historical reflections on American marriage. In K. Davis & A. Grossbard-Schectman (Eds.), *Contemporary marriage: Comparative perspectives on a changing institution* (pp. 181-196). New York: Russell Sage Foundation.

Modell, J. (1989). *Into one's own: From youth to adulthood in the United States.* Berkeley: University of California Press.

Modell, J., Furstenberg, F. F., Jr., & Strong, D. (1978). The timing of marriage in the transition to adulthood: Continuity and change 1860-1975. *American Journal of Sociology, 84* (Suppl.), S120-S150.

Modell, J., & Hareven, T. K. (1973). Urbanization and the malleable household: An examination of boarding and lodging in American families. *Journal of Marriage and the Family, 35,* 467-479.

Moffitt, R. (1990). The effect of the U.S. welfare system on marital status. *Journal of Public Economics, 41,* 101-124.

Moffitt, R. (1992). Incentive effects of the U.S. welfare system: A review. *Journal of Economic Literature, 30,* 1-61.

Moffitt, R., & Roff, J. (2000). The diversity of welfare leavers. In Welfare, children, and families: A three-city study [Online]. Available: www.jhu.edu/~welfare (Accessed 4 February, 2001).

Money, J., & Tucker, P. (1975). *Sexual signatures: On being a man or a woman.* Boston: Little, Brown and Company.

Moore, J. W., & Cuéllar, A. B. (1970). *Mexican Americans.* Englewood Cliffs, NJ: Prentice-Hall.

Morgan, S. P. (1988). Sons, daughters, and the risk of marital disruption. *American Journal of Sociology, 94,* 110–129.

Morgan, S. P., McDaniel, A., Miller, A. T., & Preston, S. H. (1993). Racial differences in household and family structure at the turn of the century. *American Journal of Sociology, 98,* 798–828.

Morgan, S. P., & Waite, L. J. (1987). Parenthood and the attitudes of young adults. *American Sociological Review, 52,* 541–547.

Morioka, K. (1996). Generational relations and their changes as they affect the status of older people in Japan. In T. K. Hareven (Ed.), *Aging and generational relations: Life-course and cross-cultural perspectives* (pp. 263–280). New York: Aldine de Gruyter.

Morley, R. (1994). Wife beating and modernization: The case of Papua New Guinea. *Journal of Comparative Family Studies, 25,* 25–52.

Morrison, D. R., & Cherlin, A. J. (1995). The divorce process and young children's well-being: A prospective analysis. *Journal of Marriage and the Family, 57,* 800–812.

Mortimer, J. T., & London, J. (1984). The varying linkages of work and family. In P. Voydanoff (Ed.), *Work and family: Changing roles of men and women* (pp. 20–35). Palo Alto, CA: Mayfield.

Mosley, J., & Thomson, E. (1995). *Fatherhood: Contemporary theory, research, and social policy* (W. Marsiglio, Ed.) (pp. 148–165). Thousand Oaks, CA: Sage.

Moss, P., & Deven, F. (1999) *Parental leave: Progress or pitfall?* London: Institute of Education, University of London.

Moynihan, D. (1973). *The politics of a guaranteed income: The Nixon administration and the family assistance plan.* New York: Random House.

Murray, C. (1984). *Losing ground: American social policy, 1950–1980.* New York: Basic Books.

Najman, J. M., Behrens, B. C., Andersen, M., Bor, W., O'Callaghan, M., & Williams, G. M. (1997). Impact of family type and family quality on child behavior problems: A longitudinal study. *Journal of the American Academy of Child and Adolescent Psychiatry, 36,* 1357–1365.

Nakonezny, P. A., Shull, R. D., & Rodgers, J. L. (1995). The effect of no-fault divorce law on the divorce rate across the 50 states and its relation to income, education, and religiosity. *Journal of Marriage and the Family, 57,* 477–488.

National Aging Information Center. (1996). *Limitations in activities of daily living among the elderly* [www.aoa.dhhs.gov/naic]. Washington, DC: U.S. Administration on Aging (17 March, 1998).

National Opinion Research Center. (1997). General Social Survey [Online]. Available: www.icpsr.umich.edu/GSS (Accessed August 29, 1997).

Neilson, J. M. (1990). Introduction in J. M. Neilson (Ed.), *Feminist research methods: Exemplary readings in the social sciences* (pp. 1–37). Boulder, CO: Westview Press.

Newman, K. (1988). *Falling from grace: The experience of downward mobility in the American middle class.* New York: The Free Press.

NICHD Early Child Care Research Network. (1997). The effects of infant child care on infant-mother attachment security: Results of the NICHD study of early child care. *Child Development, 68,* 860–879.

NICHD Early Child Care Research Network. (1998). Early child care and self-control, compliance, and problem behavior at twenty-four and thirty-six months. *Child Development, 69,* 1145–1170.

Nicholas, D. (1991). Childhood in medieval Europe. In J. M. Hawes & N. R. Hiner (Eds.), *Children in historical and comparative perspective* (pp. 31–52). New York: Greenwood Press.

Nock, S. L. (1998). *Marriage in men's lives.* New York: Oxford University Press.

Nock, S. L., Wright, J. D., & Sanchez, L. (1999). America's divorce problem. *Society, 36* (May–June), 43–52.

O'Brien, J. E. (1971). Violence in divorce prone families. *Journal of Marriage and the Family, 33,* 692–698.

O'Connell, M., & Bloom, D. E. (1987). Juggling jobs and babies: America's child care challenge. In *Population Trends and Public Policy Reports,* no. 12. Washington, DC: Population Reference Bureau.

O'Connell, M., & Moore, M. (1980). The legitimacy status of first births to U.S. women aged 15–24, 1939–1978. *Family Planning Perspectives, 12,* 16–25.

Oda, T. (1991). Tradition and innovation of the Japanese family in an aging society: Focusing on family support of the elderly. In *Proceedings of the Nihon University International Symposium on Family and the Contemporary Japanese Culture: An International Perspective* (pp. 361–406). Tokyo: University Research Center, Nihon University.

Ogawa, N., & Retherford, R. D. (1993). Care of the elderly in Japan: Changing norms and expectations. *Journal of Marriage and the Family, 55,* 585–597.

O'Hare, W. (1992). America's minorities—the demographics of diversity. *Population Bulletin, 47* (4).

Olasky, M. (1992). *The tragedy of American compassion.* Washington, DC: Regnery.

Olasky, M. (1997). Charitable aid should replace government welfare. In C. P. Cozie & P. A. Winters (Eds.), *Welfare: Opposing viewpoints* (pp. 56-64). San Diego, CA: Greenhaven Press.

Oliver, M., & Shapiro, T. M. (1995). *Black wealth/white wealth: A new perspective on racial inequality.* New York: Routledge.

Olson, J. S. (1979). *The ethnic dimension in American history.* New York: St. Martin's Press.

O'Neill, N., & O'Neill, G. (1972). *Open marriage: A new life style for couples.* New York: Evans.

O'Neill, W. L. (1967). *Divorce in the progressive era.* New Haven, CT: Yale University Press.

Oppenheimer, V. (1970). The female labor force in the United States. *Population Monograph Series, 5.* Berkeley: Institute of International Studies, University of California.

Oppenheimer, V. K. (1988). A theory of marriage timing. *American Journal of Sociology, 94,* 563-591.

Oppenheimer, V. K. (1994). Women's rising employment and the future of the family in industrial societies. *Population and Development Review, 20,* 293-342.

Oppenheimer, V. K., Blossfeld, H.-P., & Wackerow, A. (1995). United States of America. In H.-P. Blossfeld (Ed.), *The new role of women: Family formation in modern societies* (pp. 150-173). Boulder, CO: Westview Press.

Oppenheimer, V. K., Kalmijn, M., & Lim, N. (1997). Men's career development and marriage timing during a period of rising inequality. *Demography, 34,* 311-330.

Oppenheimer, V. K., & Lew, V. (1995). American marriage formation in the 1980s: How important was women's economic independence? In K. O. Mason & A.-M. Jensen (Eds.), *Gender and family change in industrialized countries* (pp. 105-138). Oxford: Clarendon Press.

Orbuch, T. L., Veroff, J., & Hunter, A. G. (1999). Black couples, white couples: The early years of marriage. In E. M. Hetherington (Ed.), *Coping with divorce, single parenting, and remarriage* (pp. 23-43). Mahwah, NJ: Lawrence Erlbaum Associates.

Orfali, K. (1991). The rise and fall of the Swedish model. In Prost, A., & Vincent, G. (Eds.), *A history of private life: Vol. 5, Riddles of identity in modern times* (pp. 417-449). Cambridge, MA: The Belknap Press of Harvard University Press.

Orloff, A. (1993). Gender and the social rights of citizenship: The comparative analysis of gender relations and welfare states. *American Sociological Review, 58,* 303-328.

Ortiz, V. (1995). The diversity of Latin families. In R. Zambrana (Ed.), *Understanding Latino families* (pp. 18-39). Thousand Oaks, CA: Sage.

Oxford English Dictionary (2nd ed.). (1989). Oxford: Clarendon Press.

Ozment, S. (1983). *When fathers ruled: Family life in reformation Europe.* Cambridge, MA: Harvard University Press.

Pagelow, M. D. (1988). Marital rape. In V. B. Van Hasselt, R. Morrison, A. S. Bellack & M. Hersen (Eds.), *Handbook of family violence* (pp. 207-232). New York: Plenum Press.

Pagnini, D. L., & Morgan, S. P. (1996). Racial differences in marriage and childbearing: Oral history evidence from the South in the early twentieth century. *American Journal of Sociology, 101,* 1694-1718.

Pagnini, D. L., & Rindfuss, R. R. (1993). The divorce of marriage and childbearing: Changing attitudes and behavior in the United States. *Population and Development Review, 19,* 331-347.

Pahl, J. (1989). *Money and marriage.* Hampshire, England: Macmillan.

Palmer, J. L. (1988). Financing health care and retirement for the aged. In I. V. Sawhill (Ed.), *Challenge to leadership: Economic and social Issues for the next decade* (pp. 173-214). Washington, DC: Urban Institute Press.

Palmer, J. L., & Gould, S. G. (1986). The economic consequences of an aging society. *Daedalus, 115* (1), 295-323.

Papanek, H. (1973). Men, women, and work: Reflections on the two-person career. *American Journal of Sociology, 78,* 852-872.

Papernow, P. (1988). Stepparent role development: From outsider to intimate. In W. R. Beer (Ed.), *Relative strangers: Studies of stepfamily processes* (pp. 54-82). Totowa, NJ: Rowan and Littlefield.

Parish, W. L., Hao, L., & Hogan, D. P. (1991). Family networks, welfare, and the work of young mothers. *Journal of Marriage and the Family, 53,* 203-215.

Parke, R. D. (1996). *Fatherhood.* Cambridge, MA: Harvard University Press.

Parsons, T. (1942). Age and sex in the social structure of the United States. *American Sociological Review, 7,* 604-616.

Parsons, T., & Bales, R. F. (1955). *Family, socialization, and the interaction process.* New York: The Free Press.

Pate, A. M., & Hamilton, E. E. (1992). Formal and informal deterrents to domestic violence: The Dade County spouse assault experiment. *American Sociological Review, 57,* 691-697.

Patillo-McCoy, M. (1999). *Black picket fences. Privilege and peril among the black middle class.* Chicago: University of Chicago Press.

Pattatucci, A. M. L. (1998). Biopsychosocial interactions and the development of sexual orientation. In C. J. Patterson & A. R. D'Augelli (Eds.), *Lesbian, gay, and bisexual identities in families: Psychological perspectives* (pp. 19-39). New York: Oxford University Press.

Patterson, C. J. (1992). Children of lesbian and gay parents. *Child Development, 63,* 1025-1042.

Patterson, C. J. (2000). Family relationships of lesbians and gay men. *Journal of Marriage and the Family, 62,* 1052-1069.

Patterson, C. J., & D'Augelli, A. R. (Eds.). (1998). *Lesbian, gay, and bisexual identities in families: Psychological perspectives.* New York: Oxford University Press.

Pearlin, L. I., & McCall, M. E. (1990). Occupational stress and marital support. In J. Eckenrode & S. Gore (Eds.), *Stress between work and family* (pp. 39-60). New York: Plenum Press.

Pearsall, P. (1987). Super marital sex: Loving for life. New York: Doubleday.

Peng, X., & Huang, J. (1999, October). Chinese traditional medicine and abnormal sex ratio at birth in China. *Journal of Biosocial Science, 31(4),* 487-503.

Peplau, L. A. (1991). Lesbian and gay relationships. In J. C. Gonsiorek & J. D. Weinrich (Eds.), *Homosexuality: Research implications for public policy.* Newbury Park, CA: Sage Publications.

Perry-Jenkins, M., Repetti, R. L., & Crouter, A. C. (2000). Work and family in the 1980s. *Journal of Marriage and the Family, 62,* 981-998.

Peters, E. H. (1986). Marriage and divorce: Informational constraints and private contracting. *American Economic Review, 76,* 437-454.

Peterson, G. W., & Rollins, B. C. (1987). Parent-child socialization. In S. K. Steinmetz (Ed.), *Handbook of marriage and the family* (pp. 471-507). New York: Plenum Press.

Peterson, J. L., & Zill, N. (1986). Marital disruption, parent-child relationships, and behavior problems in children. *Journal of Marriage and the Family, 48,* 295-307.

Phillips, R. (1991). *Untying the knot: A short history of divorce.* Cambridge, England: Cambridge University Press.

Pillemer, K., & Finkelhor, D. (1988). The prevalence of elder abuse: A random sample survey. *The Gerontologist, 28,* 51-57.

Pinker, S. (1997). *How the mind works.* New York: W. W. Norton.

Pleck, E. (1987). *Domestic tyranny: The making of American social policy against family violence from colonial times to the present.* New York: Oxford University Press.

Pleck, J. H. (1977). The work-family role system. *Social Problems, 24,* 417-427.

Pleck, J. H. (1985). *Working wives/working husbands.* Beverly Hills, CA: Sage Publications.

Pleck, J. H., & Ku, L. C. (1990). Sexual activity, condom use, and AIDS awareness among adolescent males. *Family Planning Perspectives, 22,* 206-214.

Pogrebin, L. (1983). *Family politics: Love and power on the intimate frontier.* New York: McGraw-Hill.

Polachek, S. (1979). Occupational segregation among women: Theory, evidence, and a prognosis. In C. Lloyd (Ed.), *Women in the labor market* (pp. 137-157). New York: Columbia University Press.

Polikoff, N. (1990). This child does have two mothers: Redefining parenthood to meet the needs of children in lesbian-mother and other nontraditional households. *Georgetown Law Journal, 78,* 459-515.

Pollack, W. S. (1998). *Real boys: Rescuing our sons from the myths of boyhood.* New York: Henry Holt.

Pollock, L. A. (1983). *Forgotten children: Parent-child relations from 1500 to 1900.* Cambridge, England: Cambridge University Press.

Popenoe, D. (1988). *Disturbing the nest: Family change and decline in modern societies.* New York: Aldine de Gruyter.

Popenoe, D. (1991). Family decline in the Swedish welfare state. *The Public Interest, 102,* 65-77.

Popenoe, D. (1994). The evolution of marriage and the problem of stepfamilies: A biosocial perspective. In A. Booth & J. Dunn (Eds.), *Stepfamilies: Who benefits? Who does not?* (pp. 3-27). Hillsdale, NJ: Lawrence Erlbaum.

Popenoe, D. (1996). *Life without father.* New York: Free Press.

Population Reference Bureau. (2000). 2000 World population report. Available: www.prb.org (Accessed 28 January, 2001).

Portes, A. (1996). *The new second generation.* New York: Russell Sage Foundation.

Portes, A., & Jensen, L. (1989). The enclave and the entrants: Patterns of ethnic enterprise in Miami before and after Mariel. *American Sociological Review, 54,* 929-949.

Portes, A., & Sensenbrenner, J. (1993). Embeddedness and immigration: Notes on the social determinants of economic action. *American Journal of Sociology, 98,* 1320-1350.

Portes, A., Stepick, A., & Truelove, C. (1986). Three years later: The adaptation process of Cuban and Haitian refugees in South Florida. *Population research and Policy Review, 5,* 83-94.

Presser, H. B. (1989). Can we make time for children? The economy, work schedules, and child care. *Demography, 26,* 523-543.

Presser, H. B. (1994). Employment schedules among dual-earner spouses and the division of household labor by gender. *American Sociological Review, 59,* 348-364.

Presser, H. B. (1999, 11 June). Toward a 24-hour economy. *Science, 284,* 177-179.

Presser, H. B. (2000). Nonstandard work schedules and marital instability. *Journal of Marriage and the Family, 62,* 93-110.

Preston, S. H., & Kono, S. (1988). Trends in the well-being of children and the elderly in Japan. In J. L. Palmer, T. Smeeding, & B. B. Torrey (Eds.), *The vulnerable* (pp. 277-307). Washington, DC: Urban Institute Press.

Preston, S. H., Lim S., & Morgan, S. P. (1992). African American marriage in 1910: Beneath the surface of census data. *Demography, 29,* 1-15.

Preston, S. H., & McDonald, J. (1979). The incidence of divorce within cohorts of American marriages contracted since the civil war. *Demography, 16,* 1-25.

Purcell, P., & Stewart, L. (1990). Dick and Jane in 1989. *Sex Roles, 22,* 177-185.

Qian, Z. (1997). Breaking the racial barriers: Variations in interracial marriage between 1980 and 1990. *Demography, 34,* 263-276.

Qian, Z., & Preston, S. H. (1993). Changes in American marriage, 1972 to 1987: Availability and forces of attraction by age and education. *American Sociological Review, 58,* 482-493.

Quadagno, J. S. (1994). *The color of welfare: How racism undermined the war on poverty.* New York: Oxford University Press.

Quadagno, J. S. (1999). *Aging and the life course.* New York: McGraw-Hill.

Queen, S. S., Habenstein, R. W., & Quadagno, J. S. (1985). *The family in various cultures* (5th Ed.). New York: Harper and Row.

Rainwater, L., & Smeeding, T. M. (1995). Doing poorly: The real income of American children in a comparative perspective. *Luxembourg Income Study, Working Paper 127* [Online]. Available: www.lissy.ceps.lu/index.htm (Accessed April 17, 1998).

Rainwater, L., & Yancey, W. L. (1967). *The Moynihan report and the politics of controversy.* Cambridge, MA: MIT Press.

Raley, R. (1995). Black-white differences in kin contact and exchange among never married adults. *Journal of Family Issues, 16,* 77-103.

Raley, R. (1996). A shortage of marriageable men? A note on the role of cohabitation in black-white differences in marriage rates. *American Sociological Review, 61,* 973-983.

Rank, M. R., & Cheng, L. (1995, August). Welfare use across generations: How important are the ties that bind? *Journal of Marriage and the Family, 57,* 673-684.

Reiner, W. (1997). To be male or female—that is the question. *Archives of Pediatric and Adolescent Medicine, 151,* 224-225.

Reinharz, S. (1992). *Feminist methods in social research.* New York: Oxford University Press.

Remez, L. (2000). Oral sex among adolescents: Is it sex or is it abstinence? *Family Planning Perspectives, 32,* 298-303.

Report cites heavy toll of rape among the young. (1994, June 23). *New York Times,* p. A12.

Reskin, B., & Padavic, I. (1994). *Women and men at work.* Thousand Oaks, CA: Pine Forge Press.

Richardson, L. W. (1977). *The dynamics of sex and gender: A sociological perspective.* Boston: Houghton Mifflin.

Riley, N. (1996). China's missing girls: Prospects and policy. *Population Today, 24,* 4-5.

Riley, N. (1997). Gender, power, and population change. *Population Bulletin, 52* (1).

Riley, N., & Gardner, R. W. (1997). *China's population: A review of the literature.* Liège, Belgium: International Union for the Scientific Study of Population.

Rindfuss, R. R., Morgan, S. P., & Swicegood, G. (1988). *First births in America: Changes in the timing of parenthood.* Berkeley, CA: University of California Press.

Rindfuss, R. R., & VandenHeuvel, A. (1990). Cohabitation: A precursor to marriage or an alternative to being single? *Population and Development Review, 16,* 703-726.

Risman, B. J. (1998). *Gender vertigo.* New Haven, CT: Yale University Press.

Roberts, R. E. L., Richards, L. N., & Bengtson, V. L. (1991). Intergenerational solidarity in families: Untangling the ties that bind. *Marriage and Family Review, 16,* 11-46.

Robins, P. K. et al. (1980). *A guaranteed annual income: Evidence from a social experiment.* New York: Academic Press.

Robinson, J. P. (1988, December). Who's doing the housework? *American Demographics,* p. 24 ff.

Robinson, R. V. (1993). Economic necessity and the life cycle in the family economy of nineteenth-century Indianapolis. *American Journal of Sociology, 99,* 49-74.

Rodgers, J. L., Nakonezny, P. A., & Shull, R. D. (1997). The effect of no-fault divorce legislation on divorce rates: A response to a reconsideration. *Journal of Marriage and the Family, 59,* 1026-1030.

Rodgers, W., & Thornton, A. (1985). Changing patterns of first marriage in the United States. *Demography, 22,* 265-279.

Roe v. *Wade.* (1973). 410 U.S. 113.

Roschelle, A. (1997). *No more kin: Exploring race, class, and gender in family networks.* Thousand Oaks, CA: Sage.

Rosen, E. I. (1987). *Bitter choices: Blue-collar women in and out of work.* Chicago: University of Chicago Press.

Rosenmayr, L., & Kockeis, E. (1965). *Umwelt und familie alter menschen.* Berlin: Luchterland-Verlag.

Rosenthal, E. (1998, 1 November). For one-child policy, China rethinks iron hand. *New York Times,* p. 1.

Rossi, A. S. (1977). A biosocial perspective on parenting. *Daedalus, 106,* 1-31.

Rossi, A. S. (1984). Gender and parenthood. *American Sociological Review, 49,* 1–19.

Rossi, A., & Rossi, P. (1990). *Of human bonding: Parent-child relations across the life course.* New York: Aldine de Gruyter.

Rossi, P. (1994). Troubling families: Family homelessness in America. *American Behavioral Scientist, 37,* 342–395.

Rothman, E. K. (1984). *Hands and hearts: A history of courtship in America.* Cambridge, MA: Harvard University Press.

Roussel, D. (1988). *La famille incertaine.* Paris: Éditions Odile Jacob.

Rubin G. (1975). The traffic in women. In R. R. Reiter (Ed.), *Toward an anthropology of women* (pp. 157–211). New York: Monthly Review Press.

Rubin, J. Z., Provenzano, F. J., & Luria, Z. (1974). The eye of the beholder: Parents' views on sex of newborns. *American Journal of Orthopsychiatry, 44,* 512–519.

Rubin, L. B. (1976). *Worlds of pain: Life in the working-class community.* New York: Basic Books.

Rubin, L. B. (1983). *Intimate strangers: Men and women together.* New York: Harper and Row.

Rubin, L. B. (1992). *Worlds of pain: Life in the working-class family* (Rev. ed.). New York: Basic Books.

Rubin, L. B. (1994). *Families on the fault line.* New York: HarperCollins.

Ruggles, S. (1987). *Prolonged connections: The rise of the extended family in nineteenth century England and America.* Madison, WI: University of Wisconsin Press.

Ruggles, S. (1994). The transformation of American family structure. *American Historical Review, 99,* 103–128.

Ruggles, S. (1997a). The effects of AFDC on American family structure. *Journal of Family History, 22,* 307–325.

Ruggles, S. (1997b). Reply to Oppenheimer and Preston. *Demography, 34,* 475–479.

Ruggles, S. (1997c). The rise of divorce and separation in the United States, 1880–1990. *Demography, 34,* 455–466.

Ryan, M. P. (1981). *Cradle of the middle class: The family in Oneida County, New York, 1790–1865.* Cambridge: Cambridge University Press.

Ryder, N. B. (1980). Components of temporal variations in American fertility. In R. W. Hiorns (Ed.), *Demographic patterns in developed societies* (pp. 15–54). London: Taylor and Francis.

Sandefur, G., & Tienda, M. (1988). *Divided opportunities: Poverty, minorities, and social policy.* New York: Plenum Press.

Sandefur, G. D., & Liebler, C. A. (1997). The demography of American Indian families. *Population Research and Policy Review, 16,* 95–114.

Santelli, J. S., Lindberg, L. D., Abma, J., McNeely, C. S., & Resnick, M. (2000). Adolescent sexual behavior: Estimates and trends from four nationally representative surveys. *Family Planning Perspectives, 32,* 156–165 and 194.

Sapiro, V. (1990). The gender basis of American social policy. In L. Gordon (Ed.), *Women, the state and welfare* (pp. 36–54). Madison: University of Wisconsin Press.

Savin-Williams, R. C., & Esterberg, K. G. (2000). Lesbian, gay, and bisexual families. In Demo, K. R. Allen & M. A. Fine (Eds.), *Handbook of family diversity* (pp. 197–215). New York: Oxford University Press.

Sawhill, I., & Chadwick, L. (1999, December). *Children in cities: Uncertain futures.* Survey series. Washington, DC: Brookings Institution.

Scanzoni, J. (1972). *Sexual bargaining: Power politics in American marriage.* Englewood Cliffs, NJ: Prentice-Hall.

Schaefer, R. T. (2001). *Sociology* (7th ed.). New York: McGraw-Hill.

Schaefer, R. T., & Lamm, R. P. (1998). *Sociology* (4th ed.). New York: McGraw-Hill.

Schlafly, P. (1978). *The power of the positive woman.* New York: Jove Publications.

Schneider, D. (1980). *American kinship: A cultural account* (2nd ed.). Chicago: University of Chicago Press.

Schneider, D., & Smith, R. (1973). *Class differences and sex roles in American kinship and family structure.* Englewood Cliffs, NJ: Prentice-Hall.

Schoen, R., Greenblatt, H. N., & Mielke, R. B. (1975). California's experience with non-adversary divorce. *Demography, 12,* 223–244.

Schoen, R., Urton, W., Woodrow, K., & Baj, J. (1985). Marriage and divorce in twentieth century American cohorts. *Demography, 22,* 101–114.

Schor, J. B. (1992). *The overworked American: The unexpected decline of leisure.* New York: Basic Books.

Schwartz, P. (1994). *Peer marriage.* New York: Free Press.

Schwartz, P., & Rutter, V. (1998). *The gender of sexuality.* Thousand Oaks, CA: Pine Forge Press.

Scott, J. (1986). Gender: A useful category for historical analysis. *American Historical Review, 91,* 1053–1075.

Seccombe, K. (2000). Families in poverty in the 1990s: Trends, causes, consequences, and lessons learned. *Journal of Marriage and the Family, 62,* 1094–1113.

Sedlak, A. J. (1991). *National incidence and prevalence of child abuse and neglect: 1988. Revised report.* Rockville, MD: Westat, Inc.

Sedlak, A. J., & Broadhurst, D. D. (1996). *Executive summary of the third national incidence study of child abuse and neglect.* Washington, DC: National Center on Child Abuse and Neglect, Administration for Children and Families, U.S. Department of Health and Human Services.

Seidman, S. (1991). *Romantic longings: Love in America*. New York: Routledge.

Seltzer, J. A. (1991). Relationships between fathers and children who live apart: The father's role after separation. *Journal of Marriage and the Family, 53,* 79-101.

Seltzer, J. (2000). Families formed outside of marriage. *Journal of Marriage and the Family, 62,* in press.

Serbin, L. A. (1984). The early development of sex differentiated patterns of social influence. *Canadian Journal of Social Science, 14,* 350-363.

Serbin, L. A., Sprafkin, C., Elman, M., & Doyle, A. (1984). The early development of sex-differentiated patterns of social influence. *Canadian Journal of Social Science, 14,* 350-363.

Sexton, J. (1996, May 12). As reports of child abuse rise, officials split up more families. *New York Times,* p. A1.

Shanas, E. (1980). Older people and their families: The new pioneers. *Journal of Marriage and the Family, 42,* 9-15.

Sharp, R. (1993, September 14). In latest recession, only Blacks suffered net employment loss. *Wall Street Journal,* p. 1.

Sheehan, S. (1995, December 11). Ain't no middle class. *New Yorker,* pp. 82-93.

Shelton, B. A., & Agger, B. (1993). Shotgun wedding, unhappy marriage, no-fault divorce? Rethinking the feminism-Marxism relationship. In P. England (Ed.), *Theory on gender/feminism on theory* (pp. 25-41). New York: Aldine de Gruyter.

Sherman, L., & Berk, R. (1984). *The Minneapolis domestic violence experiment.* Washington DC: The Police Foundation.

Sherman, L. W., & Smith, D. A. (1992, October). Crime, punishment, and stake in conformity: Legal and informal control of domestic violence. *American Sociological Review, 57,* 680-690.

Shilts, R. (1987). *And the band played on: Politics, people, and the AIDS epidemic.* New York: Penguin Books.

Shoemaker, N. (1991). Native American families. In J. Hawes & E. Nybakkan (Eds.), *American families: A research guide and historical handbook* (pp. 291-317). New York: Greenwood Press.

Silverstein, C. (1991). Psychological and medical treatments of homosexuality. In Gonsiorek & Weinrich (Eds.), *Homosexuality* (pp. 101-114).

Silverstein, M., & Bengtson, V. L. (1997). Intergenerational solidarity and the structure of adult child-parent relationships in American families. *American Journal of Sociology, 103,* 429-460.

Silverstein, M., & Waite, L. (1993). Are blacks more likely than whites to receive and provide social support in middle and old age? Yes, no, and maybe so. *Journals of Gerontology, 18,* S212-S222.

Skocpol, T. (1991). Targeting within universalism: Politically viable strategies to combat poverty in the United States. In C. Jencks & P. E. Peterson (Eds.), *The urban underclass* (pp. 411-436). Washington, DC: The Brookings Institution.

Skocpol, T. (1992). *Protecting mothers and soldiers: The political origins of social policy in the United States.* Cambridge, MA: The Belknap Press of Harvard University Press.

Smeeding, T. M. (1990). Economic status of the elderly. In R. L. Binstock & L. K. George (Eds.), *Handbook on aging and the social services* (pp. 362-381). New York: Academic Press.

Smeeding, T., Torrey, B. B., & Rein, M. (1988). Patterns of income and poverty: The economic status of children and the elderly in eight countries. In J. L. Palmer, T. Smeeding, & B. B. Torrey (Eds.), *The vulnerable* (pp. 89-119). Washington, DC: Urban Institute Press.

Smith, A. (1776). *The wealth of nations.*

Smith, D. S. (1973). Parental power and marriage patterns: An analysis of historical trends in Hingham, Massachusetts. *Journal of Marriage and Family, 35,* 419-428.

Smith, D. S. (1979). Life course, norms, and the family system of older Americans in 1900. *Journal of Family History, 4,* 285-298.

Smith, D. S., & Hindus, M. (1975). Premarital pregnancy in America, 1640-1971: An overview and interpretation. *Journal of Interdisciplinary History, 5,* 537-570.

Smith, J. P. (1994). Marriage, assets, and savings [Working paper]. RAND Corporation, Santa Monica, CA.

Smith, J. P., & Ward, M. P. (1985). Time-series growth in the female labor force. *Journal of Labor Economics, 3* (Suppl.), S59-S90.

Smith, P. K., & Daglish, L. (1977). Sex differences in parent and infant behavior in the home. *Child Development, 48,* 1250-1254.

Smith, T. W. (1999). The emerging 21st century American Family. GSS Social Change Report no. 42. Chicago: National Opinion Research Center.

Smith-Rosenberg, C. (1975). The female world of love and ritual: Relations between women in nineteenth-century America. *Signs, 1,* 1-29.

Smock, P. J. (2000). Cohabitation in the United States: An appraisal of research themes, findings, and implications. *Annual Review of Sociology, 26,* 1-20.

Smolensky, E., Danziger, S., & Gottschalk, P. (1988). The declining significance of age in the United States: Trends in the well-being of children and the elderly since 1939. In J. L. Palmer, T. Smeeding & B. B. Torrey (Eds.), *The Vulnerable* (pp. 29-54). Washington, DC: The Urban Institute Press.

Snarey, J. (1993). *How fathers care for the next generation.* Cambridge, MA: Harvard University Press.

Snipp, C. M. (1989). *American Indians: The first of this land.* New York: Russell Sage Foundation.

Soldo, B. J., & Agree, E. M. (1988). America's elderly. *Population Bulletin, 43* (3).

Soldo, B. J., & Hill, M. S. (1993). Intergenerational transfers: Economic, demographic, and social perspectives. *Annual Review of Gerontology and Geriatrics, 13,* 187-216.

Sommers-Flanagan, R., Sommers-Flanagan, J., & Davis, B. (1993). What's happening on music television: A gender-role content analysis. *Sex Roles, 28,* 745-753.

Sonenstein, F. L., Pleck, J. H., & Ku, L. C. (1991). Levels of sexual activity among adolescent males in the United States. *Family Planning Perspectives, 23,* 162-167.

South, S., & Lloyd, K. (1992). Marriage opportunities and family formation: Further implications of imbalanced sex ratios. *Journal of Marriage and the Family, 54,* 440-451.

South, S. J. (1991). Sociodemographic differentials in mate selection processes. *Journal of Marriage and the Family, 53,* 928-940.

Spain, D., & Bianchi, S. M. (1996). *Balancing act: Motherhood, marriage, and employment among American women.* New York: Russell Sage Foundation.

Spanier, G. B., & Furstenberg, F. F., Jr. (1987). Remarriage and reconstituted families. In M.B. Sussman & S. K. Steinmetz (Eds.), *Handbook of marriage and the family* (pp. 419-434). New York: Plenum Press.

Spira, A., et al. (1992, December 3). AIDS and sexual behavior in France. *Nature, 360,* 407-409.

Spitze, G., & Logan, J. (1990a). More evidence on women (and men) in the middle. *Research on Aging, 12,* 182-198.

Spitze, G., & Logan, J. (1990b). Sons, daughters, and intergenerational social support. *Journal of Marriage and the Family, 52,* 420-430.

Stacey, J. (1983). *Patriarchy and socialist revolution in China.* Berkeley: University of California.

Stacey, J. (1990). *Brave new families.* New York: Basic Books.

Stack, C. (1974). *All our kin: Strategies for survival in a black community.* New York: Harper and Row.

Stanley, S. M., Markman, H. J., St. Peters, M., & Leber, B. D. (1995). Strengthening marriages and preventing divorce: New directions in prevention research. *Family Relations, 44,* 392-401.

Stark, E., & Flitcraft, A. (1988). Violence among intimates. In V. B. Van Hasselt, R. Morrison, A. S. Bellack & M. Hersen (Eds.), *Handbook of family violence* (pp. 457-481). New York: Plenum Press.

Starr, J., & Raymond, H. (1988). Physical abuse of children. In V. B. Van Hasselt, R. Morrison, A. S. Bellack & M. Hersen (Eds.), *Handbook of family violence* (pp. 119-155). New York: Plenum Press.

Starving a child to death. [Editorial]. (1996, September 5). *New York Times,* p. A22.

Steiner, G. (1981). *The futility of family policy.* Washington, DC: The Brookings Institution.

Steinhauer, J. (1994, August 20). Increasingly, employers offer benefits to all partners. *New York Times,* p. A1.

Steinmetz, S. K. (1987). Family violence: Past, present, and future. In M. B. Sussman & S. K. Steinmetz (Eds.), *Handbook of marriage and the family* (pp. 725-765). New York: Plenum Press.

Stern, M. (1987). *Society and family strategy: Erie County, New York* (pp. 1850-1920). Albany: State University of New York Press.

Stets, J. E. (1992). Interactive processes in dating aggression: A national study. *Journal of Marriage and the Family, 54,* 165-177.

Stets, J. E., & Straus, M. A. (1989). The marriage license as a hitting license: A comparison of assault in dating, cohabiting, and married couples. In M. A. Pirog-Good & J. E. Stets (Eds.), *Violence in dating relationships* (pp. 33-52). New York: Praeger.

Stiglitz, J. E. (1988). *Economics of the public sector* (2nd ed.). New York: W.W. Norton.

Stoller, E. P., & Pugliesi, K. L. (1989). Other roles of caregivers: Competing responsibilities or supporting resources? *Journal of Gerontology, 44* (Suppl.), S231-S238.

Stone, L. (1977). *The family, sex, and marriage in England 1500-1800.* New York: Harper and Row.

Straus, M. A., & Gelles, R. J. (1986). Societal change and change in family violence from 1975 to 1985 as revealed by two national surveys, *Journal of Marriage and the Family, 48,* 465-479.

Suarez, Z. (1993). Cuban exiles: From golden exiles to social undesirables. In H. McAdoo (Ed.), *Family ethnicity: Strength in diversity* (pp. 164-176). Newbury Park, CA: Sage Publications.

Sudarkasa, N. (1980). African and Afro-American family structure: A comparison. *The Black Scholar,* (November–December) 37-60.

Sudarkasa, N. (1981). Interpreting the African heritage in Afro-American family organization. In Harriette Pipes McAdoo (Ed.), *Black families* (pp. 37-53). Beverly Hills, CA: Sage.

Swartz, M. J. (1958). Sexuality and aggression on Romonum Truk. *American Anthropologist, 60,* 467-486.

Sweeney, M. M. (1997, March). *Women, men, and changing families: The shifting economic foundations of marriage.* Paper presented at the annual meetings of the Population Association of America, Washington, DC.

Sweet, J. A., & Bumpass, L. L. (1987). *American families and households.* New York: Russell Sage Foundation.

Swidler, A. (1980). Love and adulthood in American culture. In N. J. Smelser & E. H. Erikson (Eds.), *Themes of work and love in adulthood* (pp. 120-147). Cambridge, MA: Harvard University Press.

Symons, D. (1979). *The evolution of human sexuality.* New York: Oxford University Press.

Tanner, M., Moore, S., & Hartman, D. (1995, September 19). The work versus welfare trade-off: An analysis of the total level of welfare benefits by state. *Policy Analysis* [Online] No. 240. Available: www.cato.org/pubs/pas/pa-240.html (Accessed February 7, 1998).

Tanner, N., & Zihlman, A. (1976, Part 1). Women in evolution. *Signs, 1* (3), 585-608.

Tasker, F., & Golombok, S. (1995). Adults raised as children in lesbian families. *American Journal of Orthopsychiatry, 65,* 203-215.

Tatara, T. (1993). U.S. child substitute care flow data for fiscal year 1992 and current trends in the state child substitute care populations [Voluntary Cooperative Information System Research Notes, no. 9]. Washington, DC: American Public Welfare Association.

Thibaut, J., & Kelley, H. H. (1959). *The social psychology of groups.* New York: John Wiley.

Thoits, P. A. (1986). Multiple identities: Examining gender and marital status differences in distress. *American Sociological Review, 51,* 259-272.

Thoits, P. A. (1992). Identity structures and psychological well-being: Gender and marital status comparisons. *Social Psychology Quarterly, 55,* 236-256.

Thomas, D. (1990). Intra-household resource allocation: An inferential approach. *Journal of Human Resources, 25,* 635-664.

Thompson, K. (Ed.). (1991). *To be a man: In search of the deeply masculine.* Los Angeles: Jeremy P. Tarcher, Inc.

Thorne, B. (1982). Feminist rethinking of the family: An overview. In B. Thorne & M. Yalom (Eds.), *Rethinking the family: Some feminist questions* (pp. 1-24). New York: Longman.

Thorne, B. (1992). Feminism and the family: Two decades of thought. In B. Thorne & M. Yalom (Eds.), *Rethinking the family: Some feminist questions* (Rev. ed.) (pp. 3-30). Boston: Northeastern University Press.

Thorne, B. (1993). *Gender play: Girls and boys in school.* New Brunswick, NJ: Rutgers University Press.

Thornton, A. (1985). Reciprocal influences of family and religion in a changing world. *Journal of Marriage and the Family, 47,* 381-394.

Thornton, A., Axinn, W. G., & Hill, D. H. (1992). Reciprocal effects of religiosity, cohabitation, and marriage. *American Journal of Sociology, 98,* 628-651.

Thornton, A., Axinn, W. G., & Teachman, J. D. (1994, May). *The influence of educational experiences on cohabitation and marriage in early adulthood.* Paper presented at the annual meeting of the Population Association of America, Miami.

Thornton, A., Chang, J., & Lin, H.-S. (1994). From arranged marriage toward love match. In A. Thornton & H.-S. Lin (Eds.), *Social change and the family in Taiwan* (pp. 148-177). Chicago: University of Chicago Press.

Thornton, A., & Fricke, T. E. (1989). Social change and the family: Comparative perspectives from the West, China, and South Asia. In J. M. Stycos (Ed.), *Demography as an Interdiscipline* (pp. 128-161). New Brunswick, NJ: Transaction Publishers.

Tienda, M. (1989). Puerto Ricans and the underclass debate. *Annals of the American Academy of Political and Social Science, 501,* 105-119.

Tilly, L. A., & Scott, J. W. (1978). *Women, work, and the family.* New York: Holt, Rinehart, and Winston.

Toshio, T. (1993). *U.S. child substitute care flow data for FY 92 and current trends in the state child substitute care populations.* VCIS research notes, vol. 9. Washington, DC: American Public Welfare Association.

Trafford, A. (1982). *Crazy time: Surviving divorce.* New York: Harper and Row.

Treas, J., & Bengtson, V. L. (1987). The family in later years. In M. B. Sussman & S. K. Steinmetz (Eds.), *Handbook of marriage and the family* (pp. 625-648). New York: Plenum Press.

Tribe, L. (1990). *Abortion: The clash of absolutes.* New York: W.W. Norton.

Troxel v. Granville. (2000). 137 Wash. 2d 1, 969 P.2d 21, *aff'd.*

Trussell, J. (1988). Teenage pregnancy in the United States. *Family Planning Perspectives, 20,* 262-272.

Tsuye, N. O. (1992, August). *Work and family life in Japan: Changes and continuities.* Annual meetings of the Population Association of America. Pittsburgh.

Turner, J. (1986). *The structure of sociological theory* (4th ed.) Chicago: Dorsey Press.

Tzeng, J. M., & Mare, R. D. (1995). Labor market and socioeconomic effects of marital stability. *Social Science Research, 24,* 329-351.

U.S. Administration for Children and Families. (1996, September). Fact sheet: Personal Responsibility and Work Opportunity Reconciliation Act of 1996. [Online.] Available: www.acf.dhhs.gov/programs/opa/facts/ prwora96.htm (Accessed March 6, 1998).

U.S. Administration for Children and Families. (2000). Changes in TANF caseloads since the enactment of the new welfare law. Available: www.acf.dhhs.gov/news/tables.htm (Accessed 9 August).

U.S. Bureau of Justice Statistics. (2000a). *Criminal victimization 1999* [NCJ 182734]. Washington, DC: U.S. Government Printing Office.

U.S. Bureau of Justice Statistics. (2000b). *Intimate partner violence* [NCJ 178247]. Washington, DC: U.S. Government Printing Office.

U.S. Bureau of Labor Statistics. (1988). *Labor force statistics derived from the Current Population Survey, 1948–1987*. Washington, DC:U.S. Government Printing Office.

U.S. Bureau of Labor Statistics. (1991). *Employment and earnings, 38,* (1). Washington, DC: U.S. Government Printing Office.

U.S. Bureau of Labor Statistics. (1999a). *Highlights of women's earnings in 1998* [Report 928]. Current population survey. Washington, DC: U.S. Government Printing Office.

U.S. Bureau of Labor Statistics. (1999b, February). Contingent and Alternative Employment Arrangements. In Current Population Survey [Online]. Available: http://stats.bls.gov/news.release/conemp.toc.htm (Accessed July 2000).

U.S. Bureau of Labor Statistics. (1999c, October). Report on the American workforce 1999. Available: stats.bls.gov/opub/rtaw/rtawhome.htm (Accessed July 2000).

U.S. Bureau of Labor Statistics. (2000a). *Highlights of women's earnings in 1999* [Report 943]. Washington, DC: U.S. Goyernment Printing Office.

U.S. Bureau of Labor Statistics. (2000b, January). Annual average tables. *Employment and earnings* [Online]. Available: stats.bls.gov/news.release/famee.toc.htm (Accessed August 2000).

U.S. Bureau of Labor Statistics. (2000c, June). Employment characteristics of families. Available: stats.bls.gov/news.release/famee.toc.htm (Accessed July 2000).

U.S. Bureau of the Census. (1975). *Historical statistics of the United States, Colonial Times to 1970.* Washington, DC: U.S. Government Printing Office.

U.S. Bureau of the Census. (1983). *America in transition: An aging society.* Current Population Reports, series P23-128. Washington, DC: U.S. Government Printing Office.

U.S. Bureau of the Census. (1991a). *Family disruption and economic hardship: The short-run picture for children.* Current Population Reports, Series P60-23. Washington, DC: U.S. Government Printing Office.

U.S. Bureau of the Census. (1991b). *Fertility of American women: June 1990.* Current population Reports, Series P20-454. Washington, DC: U.S. government Printing Office.

U.S. Bureau of the Census. (1991c). *Household and family characteristics. March 1990 and March 1989.* Current Population Reports, Series P20-447. Washington, DC: U.S. Government Printing office.

U.S. Bureau of the Census. (1991d). *Marital Status and Living Arrangements: March 1990.* Current Population Reports, Series P20-450. Washington, DC: U.S. Government Printing office.

U.S. Bureau of the Census. (1991e). *Statistical abstract of the United States, 1991.* Washington, DC: U.S. Government Printing Office.

U.S. Bureau of the Census. (1992a). *Marital status and living arrangements: March 1992.* Washington, DC: U.S. Government Printing Office.

U.S. Bureau of the Census. (1992b). *Marriage, divorce, and remarriage in the 1990s.* Washington, DC: Government Printing Office.

U.S. Bureau of the Census. (1992c). *Statistical abstract of the United States, 1992.* Washington, DC: U.S. Government Printing office.

U.S. Bureau of the Census. (1993a). *The Hispanic population of the United States: March 1992.* Washington, DC: U.S. Government Printing Office.

U.S. Bureau of the Census. (1993b). *Household and family characteristics: March 1992.* Current Population Reports, Series P20-467. Washington, DC: U.S. Government Printing Office.

U.S. Bureau of the Census. (1993c). *Marital status and living arrangements: March 1993.* Current Population Reports, Series P20-468. Washington, DC: Government Printing Office.

U.S. Bureau of the Census. (1993d). *Population projections of the United States, by age, race, sex, and Hispanic origin: 1993 to 2050.* Current population Reports, Series P25-1104. Washington, DC: U.S. Government Printing Office.

U.S. Bureau of the Census. (1993e). *Poverty in the United States: 1992.* Current Population Reports, Series P60-185. Washington, DC: U.S. Government Printing Office.

U.S. Bureau of the Census. (1993f). *Statistical abstract of the United States, 1993.* Washington, DC: U.S. Government Printing Office.

U.S. Bureau of the Census. (1993g). *We the Americans: Asians.* Washington, DC: U.S. Government Printing Office.

U.S. Bureau of the Census. (1993h). *We the Americans: Education.* Washington, DC: U.S. Government Printing Office.

U.S. Bureau of the Census. (1993i). *We the Americans: Our homes.* Washington, DC: U.S. Government Printing Office.

U.S. Bureau of the Census. (1994). *Marital Status and living arrangements, March 1993.* Current Population Reports, Series P20-478. Washington, DC: U.S. Government Printing Office.

U.S. Bureau of the Census. (1995, December). Minority- & women- owned business enterprises—1992. In Press Release, CB95-219 [Online]. Available: www.census.gov/csd/mwb/1992/view/b_press.txt (Accessed August 2000).

U.S. Bureau of the Census. (1996a). *1992 Economic Census.* Survey of Minority-Owned Business Enterprises—Hispanic, vol. MB92-2. Washington, DC: U.S. Government Printing Office.

U.S. Bureau of the Census. (1996b). *Marital status and living arrangements, March 1994.* Current Population Reports, Series P20-484. Washington, DC: U.S. Government Printing Office.

U.S. Bureau of the Census. (1996c). *Poverty in the United States: 1995.* Current Population Reports, Series P60-194. Washington, DC: U.S. Government Printing Office.

U.S. Bureau of the Census. (1996d, August). Minority- & women-owned business enterprises—1992. In Press Release, CB96-127 [Online]. Available: www.census.gov/Press-Release/cb96-127.html (Accessed August 2000).

U.S. Bureau of the Census. (1997a). *Family characteristics: March 1996* (update). Current Population Reports Series P20-495. Washington, DC: U.S. Government Printing Office.

U.S. Bureau of the Census. (1997b). *Health insurance coverage: 1996.* Consumer Income, Series P60-199. Washington, DC: U.S. Government Printing Office.

U.S. Bureau of the Census. (1997c). *Hispanic population from the March 1994 current population survey.* Washington, DC: U.S. Government Printing Office.

U.S. Bureau of the Census. (1997d). *Money income in the United States, 1996* [Series P20-197]. Current Population Reports. Washington, DC: U.S. Government Printing Office.

U.S. Bureau of the Census. (1997e). *Poverty in the United States: 1996.* Current Population Reports, Series P60-198. Washington, DC: U.S. Government Printing Office.

U.S. Bureau of the Census. (1997f). *Statistical abstract of the United States, 1997.* Washington, DC: U.S. Government Printing Office.

U.S. Bureau of the Census. (1998a). *Household and family characteristics, March 1998 (update).* Current Population Reports, Series P20-515. Washington, DC: U.S. Government Printing Office.

U.S. Bureau of the Census. (1998b). *Marital status and living arrangements: March 1998 (Update).* Current Population Reports, Series P20-514. Washington, DC: U.S. Government Printing Office.

U.S. Bureau of the Census. (1998c, December). Marital status and living arrangements: Detailed tables. In Current population reports [Online]. Available: www.census.gov/population/www/socdemo/ms-la.html (Accessed August 2000).

U.S. Bureau of the Census. (1999a). Interracial married couples: 1960 to present. Available: www.census.gov/population/socdemo/ms-la/tabms-3.txt (Accessed 5 August, 2000).

U.S. Bureau of the Census. (1999b). *Money income in the United States: 1998.* Current Population Reports, Series P60-206. Washington, DC: U.S. Government Printing Office.

U.S. Bureau of the Census. (1999c). *Poverty in the United States: 1998.* Current Population Reports, Series P60-207. Washington DC: U.S. Government Printing Office.

U.S. Bureau of the Census. (1999d). *Statistical abstract of the United States: 1999.* Washington, DC: U.S. Government Printing Office.

U.S. Bureau of the Census. (1999e). *Trends in premarital childbearing: 1930–1994.* Current population reports, Series P23-97. Washington DC: U.S. Government Printing Office.

U.S. Bureau of the Census. (1999f, January). *Marital status and living arrangements: Historical tables.* In Current Population Reports, Series P20-514 [Online]. Available: www.census.gov/population/www/socdemo/ms-la.html (Accessed August 2000).

U.S. Bureau of the Census. (1999g, February). *Poverty thresholds.* Available: www.census.gov/hhes/www/poverty.html (Accessed 30 Jung 2000).

U.S. Bureau of the Census. (1999h, March). *Detailed poverty tables.* In Current population survey [Online]. Available: www.bls.census.gov/cps/ads/sdata.htm (Accessed July 2000).

U.S. Bureau of the Census. (1999i, September). *Historical poverty tables.* In Current population survey [Online]. Available: www.census.gov/hhes/www/poverty.html (Accessed August 2000).

U.S. Bureau of the Census. (1999j, October). *Detailed income tabulations.* In Current population survey [Online]. Available: www.census.gov/hhes/www/income.html (Accessed July 2000).

U.S. Bureau of the Census. (1999k, October). *Historical income tables.* Available: www.census.gov/hhes/www/income.html (Accessed 30 June 2000).

U.S. Bureau of the Census. (2000a). *Child support for custodial mothers and fathers.* Current population reports, Series P20-212. Washington, DC: U.S. Government Printing Office.

U.S. Bureau of the Census. (2000b). *Educational attainment in the United States, March 1999.* Current Population Reports, Series P20-528. Washington, DC: U.S. Government Printing Office.

U.S. Bureau of the Census. (2000c). *The Hispanic population in the United States: Population characteristics, March 1999.* Current Population Reports, Series P20-527. Washington, DC: U.S. Government Printing Office.

U.S. Bureau of the Census. (2000d). *Money income in the United States.* Current Population Reports, Series P60-209. Washington, DC: U.S. Government Printing Office.

U.S. Bureau of the Census. (2000e). *Poverty in the United States, 1999.* Current Population Reports, Series P60-210. Washington, DC: U.S. Government Printing Office.

U.S. Bureau of the Census. (2000f). Table MS-2. *Estimated median age at first marriage, by sex: 1890 to the present.* Available: www.census.gov/population/socdemo/ms-la/tabms-2.txt (Accessed 27 June, 2000).

U.S. Bureau of the Census. (2000g). *Who's minding the kids? Child care arrangements.* Current Population Reports, Series P70-70. Washington, DC: U.S. Government Printing Office.

U.S. Bureau of the Census. (2000h, March). *Hispanic population of the United States.* In Current population survey [Online]. Available: www.census.gov/population/www/socdemo/hispanic/ho99-01.html (Accessed August 2000).

U.S. Bureau of the Census. (2000i, April). *Historical income tables.* In Current population survey [Online]. Available: www.census.gov/hhes/www/income.html (Accessed August 2000).

U.S. Bureau of the Census. (2000j, July). *Housing vacancies and homeownership historical tables.* In Current population survey/Housing Vacancy Survey, Series H-111 [Online]. Available: www.census.gov/hhes/www/hvs.html (Accessed July 2000).

U.S. Bureau of the Census, Population Estimates Program. (2000k, July). *National population estimates.* Available: www.census.gov/population/www/estimates/uspop (Accessed August 2000).

U.S. Bureau of the Census, Population Studies Branch. (2000l, July). *Puerto Rico Municipio population estimates.* Available: www.census.gov/population/www/estimates/puerto-rico.html (Accessed August 2000).

U.S. Bureau of the Census, Racial Statistics Branch. (1998, June). Interracial tables. Available: www.census.gov/population/www/socdemo/interrac.html (Accessed August 2000).

U.S. Bureau of the Census. (2001). Overview of race and Hispanic origin. Census 2000 brief. Washington, DC: U.S. Government Printing Office.

U.S. Bureau of the Census, & U.S. Department of Commerce. (1996). *Statistical brief,* vol. 96(4). Washington, DC: U.S. Government Printing Office.

U.S. Bureau of Justice Statistics, (2000a). *Criminal victimization 1999* [NCJ 182734].

U.S. Bureau of Justice Statistics. (2000b) *Intimate partner violence* [NCJ 178247].

U.S. Centers for Disease Control. (1988). *Understanding AIDS: A message from the Surgeon General.* Washington, DC: U.S. Government Printing Office.

U.S. Centers for Disease Control and Prevention. (1994). *HIV/AIDS surveillance report.* Washington, DC: U.S. Government Printing Office.

U.S. Centers for Disease Control and Prevention. (1996, September 27). Youth risk behavior surveillance—United States, 1995. *Morbidity and Mortality Weekly Report, 45*(SS-4), 1–83.

U.S. Centers for Disease Control and Prevention. (1997). *HIV/AIDS surveillance report.* Washington, DC: U.S. Government Printing Office.

U.S. Centers for Disease Control and Prevention. (1998, August 14). Youth risk behavior surveillance—United States, 1997. *Morbidity and Mortality Weekly Report, 47*(SS-3), 1–89.

U.S. Centers for Disease Control and Prevention. (2000a). *Births: Preliminary data for 1999.* National vital statistics report, vol. 48, no. 14. Washington, DC: U.S. Government Printing Office.

U.S. Centers for Disease Control and Prevention. (2000b, May). U.S. HIV and AIDS cases reported through December 1999 year-end edition. *HI V/AIDS Surveillance Report, 11*(2).

U.S. Centers for Disease Control and Prevention. (2000c, June 9). Youth risk behavior surveillance—United States, 1999. *Morbidity and Mortality Weekly Report, 49*(SSO5), 1–96.

U.S. Centers for Disease Control and Prevention. (2000d, July). Fact sheet: Youth risk behavior trends. In Youth Risk Behavior Surveillance System [Online]. Available: www.cdc.gov/nccdphp/dash/yrbs/index.htm (Accessed August 2000).

U.S. Department of Health and Human Services. (1997). *Trends in the well-being of America's children and youth: 1997* [Office of the Assistant Secretary for Planning and Evaluation]. Washington, DC: U.S. Government Printing Office.

U.S. Department of Health and Human Services. (2000). *Child maltreatment 1998: Reports from the states to the National Child Abuse and Neglect Data System.* Washington, DC: U.S. Government Printing Office.

U.S. House of Representatives. (1993). *1993 green book: Overview of entitlement programs.* Washington, DC: U.S. Government Printing Office.

U.S. House of Representatives, Committee on Post Office and Civil Service. (1992). Hearings, "America's Changing Profile." Serial no. 102–64. Washington, DC: U.S. Government Printing Office.

U.S. House of Representatives, Committee on Post Office and Civil Service. (1994). Hearings, "Review of Federal measurements of race and ethnicity." Serial no. 103–7. Washington, DC: U.S. Government Printing Office.

U.S. House of Representatives. (1996). *1996 green book.* Washington, DC: U.S. Government Printing Office.

U.S. House of Representatives. (2000). *2000 green book.* Washington, DC: U.S. Government Printing Office.

U.S. Internal Revenue Service. (2000). *Individual income tax returns, preliminary data, 1998.* Statistics of Income Bulletin, vol. Spring 2000. Washington, DC: U.S. Government Printing Office.

U.S. National Center for Health Statistics. (1979). *The national nursing home survey: 1977 summary for the United States.* Vital and Health Statistics, Series 13, no. 43. Washington, DC: U.S. Government Printing Office.

U.S. National Center for Health Statistics. (1986). *Aging in the eighties: Age 65 years and over and living alone, contacts with family friends, and neighbors.* Advance Data from Vital and Health Statistics, no. 116. Washington, DC: U.S. Government Printing Office.

U.S. National Center for Health Statistics. (1987). *Aging in the eighties: Functional limitations of individuals 65 and over.* Advance Data from Vital and Health Statistics, vol. 133. Washington, DC: U.S. Government Printing Office.

U.S. National Center for Health Statistics. (1991a). Advance report of final natality statistics, 1989. *Monthly Vital Statistics Report, 40* (8, Supplement). Washington, DC: U.S. Government Printing Office.

U.S. National Center for Health Statistics. (1991b). Advance report of final natality statistics, 1991. *Monthly vital Statistics Report, 42* (3, Supplement). Washington, DC: U.S. Government Printing Office.

U.S. National Center for Health Statistics. (1991c). Advance report of final marriage statistics, 1988. Monthly Vital Statistics Report 40 (4, Supplement). Washington, DC: U.S. Government Printing Office.

U.S. National Center for Health Statistics. (1993a). Advance report of final natality statistics. *Monthly Vital Statistics Report, 41* (9 Supplement). Washington, DC: U.S. Government Printing Office.

U.S. National Center for Health Statistics. (1993b). Annual summary of births, marriages, divorces and deaths: United States, 1992. *Monthly Vital Statistics Report, 41,* (13). Washington, DC: U.S. Government Printing Office.

U.S. National Center for Health Statistics. (1993c). Births, marriages, divorces, and deaths for 1992. *Monthly Vital Statistics Report, 41,* (12). Washington, DC: U.S. Government Printing Office.

U.S. National Center for Health Statistics. (1993d). Firearm mortality among children, youth, and young adults 1–34 years of age, trends and current status: United States, 1985–90. *Advance Data from Vital and Health Statistics, no. 231.* Washington, DC: U.S. Government Printing Office.

U.S. National Center for Health Statistics. (1993e). *Morbidity and Mortality Weekly Report, 42* (20). Washington, DC: U.S. Government Printing Office.

U.S. National Center for Health Statistics. (1994). Advance report of final natality statistics, 1992. *Monthly Vital Statistics Report, 43* (5, Supplement). Washington, DC: U.S. Government Printing Office.

U.S. National Center for Health Statistics. (1995). Annual summary of births, marriages, divorces, and deaths: United States, 1994. *Monthly Vital Statistics Report, 43,* (13). Washington, DC: U.S. Government Printing Office.

U.S. National Center for Health Statistics. (1996). Advance report of final natality statistics, 1994. *Monthly Vital Statistics Report 44* (11). Washington, DC: U.S. Government Printing Office.

U.S. National Center for Health Statistics. (1997a). Advance report of final natality statistics, 1995. *Monthly Vital Statistics Report, 45,* (11, supplement). [Online]. Available: www.cdc.gov/nchswww/ nchshome.htm (Accessed December 24, 1997).

U.S. National Center for Health Statistics. (1997b). Annual summary of births, marriages, divorces, and deaths: United States, 1996 [July 17]. *Monthly Vital Statistics Report, 45,* (12). Washington, DC: U.S. Government Printing Office.

U.S. National Center for Health Statistics. (1997c). Characteristics of elderly nursing home residents: Data from the 1995 national nursing home survey. *Advance Data from Vital and Health Statistics, 289.* Washington, DC: U.S. Government Printing Office.

U.S. National Center for Health Statistics. (1997d). Fertility, family planning, and women's health: New data from the 1995 National Survey of Family Growth. *Vital and Health Statistics,* Series 23, no. 19. Washington, DC: U.S. Government Printing Office.

U.S. National Center for Health Statistics. (1997e). Report of final natality statistics, 1995. *Monthly Vital Statistics Report, 45,* (11, supplement). Washington, DC: U.S. Government Printing Office.

U.S. National Center for Health Statistics. (2000a). *Births. Preliminary data for 1999.* National vital statistics reports, vol. 48, number 14. Washington, DC: U.S. Government Printing Office.

U.S. National Center for Health Statistics. (2000b). *Births: Final data for 1998.* National vital statistics report, vol. 48(3). Washington, DC: U.S. Government Printing Office.

U.S. National Center for Health Statistics. (2000c). *Deaths: Final data for 1998.* National vital statistics reports, vol. 48, no. 11. Washington, DC: U.S. Government Printing Office.

U.S. National Center for Health Statistics. (2000d, April 24). Variations in teen birth rates, 1991–1998: National and state trends. *National vital statistics report, 48*(6).

U.S. National Institute of Justice. (1998, November). *Prevalence, incidence, and consequences of violence against women: Findings from the National Violence against Women Survey.* Washington, DC: U.S. Government Printing Office.

U.S. National Institute of Justice. (2000a). Extent, nature, and consequences of intimate partner violence. Washington, DC: U.S. Government Printing Office.

U.S. National Institute of Justice. (2000b). The sexual victimization of college women. Washington, DC: U.S. Government Printing Office.

U.S. National Research Council Panel on Adolescent Pregnancy and Childbearing. (1987). *Risking the Future: Adolescent Sexuality, Pregnancy, and Childbearing.* Washington, DC: National Academy Press.

U.S. Office of Management and Budget. (1978). Race and ethnic standards for federal agencies and administrative reporting. *Federal Register 43, Statistical Policy Directive 15,* 19269-19270.

U.S. Senate, Special Committee on Aging. (1988). *Aging in America: Trends and projections.* Washington, DC: U.S. Government Printing Office.

Udry, J. R. (1994). The nature of gender. *Demography, 31,* 561-573.

Udry, J. R. (2000). Biological limits of gender construction. *American Sociological Review, 65,* 443-457.

Udry, J. R., Morris, N. M., & Kovenock, J. (1995). Androgen effects on women's gendered behavior. *Journal of Biosocial Science, 27,* 359-368.

Uhlenberg, P. (1979). Demographic change and the problems of the aged. In M. W. Riley (Ed.), *Aging from birth to death* (pp. 153-166). Boulder, CO: Westview Press.

Uhlenberg, P. (1980). Death and the family. *Journal of Family History, 5,* 313-320.

Uhlenberg, P. (1993). Demographic change and kin relationships in later life. *Annual Review of Gerontology and Geriatrics, 13,* 219-238.

Umberson, D. (1987). Family status and health behaviors: Social control as a dimension of social integration. *Journal of Health and Social Behavior, 28,* 306-319.

Umberson, D., & Chen, M. D. (1994). Effects of a parent's death on adult children: Relationship salience and reaction to loss. *American Sociological Review, 59,* 152-168.

Umberson, D., Wortman, C. B., & Kessler, R. C. (1992). Widowhood and depression: Explaining long-term gender differences in vulnerability. *Journal of Health and Social Behavior, 33,* 10-24.

UNAIDS. (2000, June). HIV/AIDS in Africa. Available: www.unaids.org/fact_sheets/index.html (Accessed 15 August 2000).

United Nations. (1995). *World population prospect: The 1994 revision.* NY: United Nations.

van Poppel, F., & de Beer, J. (1993). Measuring the effect of changing legislation on the frequency of divorce: The Netherlands. *Demography, 30,* 425-441.

Vaughan, D. (1990). *Uncoupling: Turning points in intimate relationships.* New York: Vintage Books.

Verhovek, S. H. (1994, May 9). Texas capital ends benefits for partners. *New York Times,* p. A1.

Veroff, J., Douvan, E., & Kulka, R. A. (1981). *The inner American: A self-portrait from 1957 to 1976.* New York: Basic Books.

Waite, L. J. (1995). Does marriage matter? *Demography, 32,* 483-507.

Waite, L. J., & Gallagher, M. (2000). *The case for marriage: Why married people are happier, healthier, and better off financially.* New York: Doubleday.

Waite, L. J., & Lillard, L. (1995). Til death do us part: Marital disruption and mortality. *American Journal of Sociology, 100,* 1131-1156.

Waller, W. (1938). *The family: A dynamic interpretation.* New York: Dryden.

Wallerstein, J. S., & Blakeslee, S. (1989). *Second chances: Men, women, and children a decade after divorce.* New York: Ticknor and Fields.

Wallerstein, J. S., & Kelly, J. B. (1980). *Surviving the breakup: How children and parents cope with divorce.* New York: Basic Books.

Wallerstein, J. S., Lewis, J. M., & Blakeslee, S. (2000). *The unexpected legacy of divorce.* New York: Hyperion.

Walsh, S. (2000, 17 July). Living large. *Washington Post National Weekly Edition,* pp. 18-19.

Watkins, S. S., Menken, J. A., & Bongaarts, J. (1987). Demographic foundations of family change. *American Sociological Review, 52,* 346-358.

Weber, M. (1949). *The methodology of the social sciences.* New York: Free Press.

Webster v. *Reproductive Health Services.* (1989). 109 S. Ct. 3040.

Webster, P. S. Orbuch, T. L., & House, J. S. (1995). Effects of childhood family background on adult marital quality and perceived stability. *American Journal of Sociology, 101,* 404-432.

Webster's Third New International Dictionary of the English language, unabridged (P. B. Gove, Ed.). (1976). Springfield, MA: Merriam.

Weinraub, M., Clemens, L. P., Sockloff, A., Ethridge, T., Gracely, E., & Myers, B. (1984). The development of sex role stereotypes in the third year. *Child Development, 55,* 1493-1503.

Weinrich, J. D., & Williams, W. L. (1991). Strange customs, familiar lives: Homosexualities in other cultures. In J. C. Gonsiorek & J. D. Weinrich (Eds.), *Homosexuality: Research implications for public policy* (pp. 44-59). Newbury Park, CA: Sage Publications.

Weisner, T. S. (1987). Socialization for parenthood in sibling caretaking societies. In J. B. Lancaster (Ed.), *Parenting across the life span: Biosocial dimensions* (pp. 237-270). New York: Aldine de Gruyter.

Weiss, R. S. (1975). *Marital separation.* New York: Basic Books.

Weiss, R. S. (1990). Bringing work stress home. In J. Eckenrode & S. Gore (Eds.), *Stress between work and family* (pp. 17-37). New York: Plenum Press.

Weitzman, L. J. (1979). *Sex role socialization.* Palo Alto, CA: Mayfield.

Weitzman, L. J. (1985). *The divorce revolution: The unexpected social and economic consequences for women and their children in America.* New York: The Free Press.

Welter, B. (1966, Summer). The cult of true womanhood. *American Quarterly,* pp. 151-174.

West, C., & Zimmerman, D. H. (1987). Doing gender. *Gender and Society, 2,* 125-151.

Westat Incorporated. (1981). *The national study of the incidence and severity of child abuse and neglect.* Washington, DC: National Center on Child Abuse and Neglect.

Weston, K. (1991). *Families we choose: Lesbians, gays, kinship.* New York: Columbia University Press.

White, L. (1994). Stepfamilies over the life course: Social support. In A. Booth & J. Dunn (Eds.), *Stepfamilies: Who benefits? Who does not?* (pp. 109-137). Hillsdale, NJ: Erlbaum Associates.

White, L. K. (1990). Determinants of divorce: A review of research in the eighties. *Journal of Marriage and the Family, 52,* 904-912.

White, L. K., & Booth, A. (1985). The quality and stability of remarriages: The role of stepchildren. *American Sociological Review, 50,* 689-698.

Whitehead, Barbara Dafoe. (1997). *The divorce culture.* New York: Knopf.

Whyte, M. K. (1990). *Dating, mating, and marriage.* New York: Aldine de Gruyter.

Williams, W. L. (1986). *The spirit and the flesh: Sexual diversity in American Indian culture.* Boston, MA: Beacon Press.

Wilson, K., & Portes, A. (1980). Immigrant enclaves: An analysis of the labor market experiences of Cubans in Miami. *American Journal of Sociology, 86,* 295-319.

Wilson, W. J. (1987). *The truly disadvantaged: The inner city, the underclass, and public policy.* Chicago: University of Chicago Press.

Wilson, W. J. (1996). *When work disappears.* New York: Knopf.

Wines, M. (1992, September 24). Vote is set today on veto by Bush. *New York Times,* p. A20.

Winship, C., & Mare, R. D. (1992). Models for sample selection bias. *Annual Review of Sociology 18,* 327-350.

Wolfe, A. (1998). *One nation, after all.* New York: Viking.

Wolfinger, N. H. (1999). Trends in intergenerational transmission of divorce. *Demography, 36,* 415-420.

Wong, M. G. (1988). The Chinese American family. In C. H. Mindel, R. W. Habenstein, & J. Wright (Eds.), *Ethnic families in America: Patterns and variations* (pp. 230-257). New York: Elsevier Science Publishing.

Wright, E. (1976). Class boundaries in advanced capitalist societies. *New Left Review, 98* (3), 41.

Wright, E. O., Shire, K., Hwang, S.-L., Dolan, M., & Baxter, J. (1992). The non-effects of class on the gender division of labor in the home: A comparative study of Sweden and the United States. *Gender & Society, 6,* 252-282.

Wright, G. C., & Stetson, D. M. (1978). The impact of no-fault divorce law reform on divorce in the American states. *Journal of Marriage and the Family, 40,* 575-580.

Wright, Lawrence. (1994, July 25). One drop of blood. *The New Yorker,* pp. 46-55.

Wu, L. L., & Martinson, B. C. (1993). Family structure and the risk of a premarital birth. *American Sociological Review, 59,* 210-232.

Wulczyn, F. H., & Goerge, R. M. (1992). Foster care in New York and Illinois: The challenge of rapid change. *Social Service Review, 66,* 278-294.

Yamamoto, C., & Kojima, K. (1996). Nuptiality and divorce in Japan: 1994 [In Japanese]. *Journal of Population Problems, 52,* 36-51.

Yanagisako, S. (1985). *Transforming the past: Tradition and kinship among Japanese Americans.* Stanford, CA: Stanford University Press.

Yanagisako, S. J., & Collier, J. F. (1987). Toward a unified analysis of gender and kinship. In J. F. Collier & S. J. Yanagisako (Eds.), *Gender and kinship: Essays toward a unified analysis* (pp. 14-50). Palo Alto, CA: Stanford University Press.

Yasuba, Y. (1962). *Birth rates of the white population in the U.S., 1800-1860.* Baltimore: Johns Hopkins University Press.

Young, I. M. (1994). Making single motherhood normal. *Dissent,* Winter, 89-93.

Young, M., & Willmott, P. (1986). *Family and kinship in east London.* London: Routledge and Kegan Paul.

Zaretsky, E. (1986). *Capitalism, the family, and personal life* (Rev. and expanded ed.). New York: Harper and Row.

Zelizer, V. (1985). *Pricing the priceless child: The changing social value of children.* New York: Basic Books.

Zeng, Y., Ping, T., Baochang, G., Yi, X., Onhua, L., & Yongping, L. (1993). Causes and implications of the recent increase in the reported sex ratio at birth in China. *Population and Development Review, 19,* 283-302.

Zhou, M., & Bankston, C. L., III. (1998). *Growing up American: How Vietnamese children adapt to life in the United States*. New York: Russell Sage Foundation.

Zill, N. (1988). Behavior, achievement, and health problems among children in stepfamilies: Findings from a National Survey of Child Health. In E. M. Hetherington & J. D. Arasteh (Eds.), *Impact of divorce, single parenting, and stepparenting on children* (pp. 325–368). Hillsdale, NJ: Lawrence Erlbaum Associates.

Acknowledgments

Chapter 1

P. 21, quotation from S. M. Dornbusch and M. H. Strober. 1988. "Our Perspective," in S. M. Dornbusch and M. H. Strober, eds., *Feminism, Children, and the New Families,* pp. 3–24. Reprinted by permission. Page 21, quotation from Kingsley Davis. 1985. "The Meaning and Significance of Marriage in Contemporary Society," in Kingsley Davis and A. Grossbard-Schechtman, eds., *Contemporary Marriage: Comparative Perspectives on a Changing Institution,* pp. 1–22. Permission granted by Russell Sage Foundation. P. 33, quotation from Alice S. Rossi. 1984. "Gender and Parenthood," *American Sociological Review,* 49 (1984), p. 15. Reprinted by permission of the American Sociological Association and the author.

Chapter 2

P. 71, Fig. 2.2 from Donald J. Hernandez. 1993. "Percentage of Children Aged 0–17 Living in Each of Four Types of Families, 1790–1989," *America's Children: Resources from Family, Government, and the Economy.* Reprinted by permission of Russell Sage Foundation.

Chapter 3

P. 94, quotation from *The American Heritage College Dictionary,* Third Edition. Copyright © 2000 by Houghton Mifflin Company. Adapted and reproduced by permission from *The American Heritage College Dictionary,* Third Edition. Pages 98–99, quotation in box from Barrie Thorne. 1993. *Gender Play: Girls and Boys in School.* Copyright © 1993 by Barrie Thorne. Reprinted by permission of Rutgers University Press. P. 100, quotation in box from R. T. Michael, H. I. Hartmann, and B. O'Farrell. 1989. *Pay Equity: Empirical Inquiries,* p. vii. Reprinted by permission of The National Academy Press. P. 103, quotation from Alice S. Rossi. 1984. "Gender and Parenthood," *American Sociological Review,* 49 (1984), p. 15. Reprinted by permission of the American Sociological Association and the author.

Chapter 4

P. 112, quotation from Susan Sheehan. 1995. From "Ain't No Middle Class" by Susan Sheehan. Originally appeared in *The New Yorker.* Copyright © 1995 by Susan Sheehan. This usage granted by permission of Lescher & Lescher, Ltd. P. 118, quotation in box from Peter H. Rossi. 1994. "Troubling Families: Family Homelessness in America." *American Behavioral Scientist,* 37: 342–395. Reprinted by permission of Sage Publications and the author. P. 129, Fig. 4.4 and quotation from James A. Davis and Tom W. Smith. 1996. *General Social Surveys, 1972–1996:* Cumulative Codebook. Reprinted by permission of National Opinion Research Center. P. 130, 131 quotations and Fig. 4.5 from Alice S. Rossi and Peter H. Rossi. 1990. *Of Human Bonding: Parent-Child Relations Across the Life Course.* (New York: Aldine de Gruyter) Copyright © 1990 by Walter de Gruyter, Inc., New York. Reprinted with permission from Alice S. Rossi and Peter H. Rossi, authors.

Chapter 5

P. 145, Fig. 5.1 from William P. O'Hare. 1992. "America's Minorities—The Demographics of Diversity," *Population Bulletin* 47, 4: Table 5. Reprinted by permission of Population Reference Bureau, Inc. P. 152, quotation from Andrew J. Cherlin and Frank F. Furstenberg Jr. 1992. *The New American Grandparent: A Place in the Family, A Life Apart,* p. 15. Published by Harvard University Press. Reprinted by permission of the authors. P. 155, quotation from Andrew J. Cherlin. 1992b. *Marriage, Divorce, Remarriage,* revised and enlarged edition. Copyright © 1992 by the President and Fellows of Harvard College. Reprinted by permission of Harvard University Press. Pp. 162–163, quotation from Nancy S. Landale and Katherine Fennelly. 1992. "Informal Unions Among Mainland Puerto Ricans: Cohabitation or an Alternative to Legal Marriage?" *Journal of Marriage and the Family,* 54: 2, p. 272. Copyright © 1992 by the National Council on Family Relations, 3989 Central Ave., N.E., Suite 550, Minneapolis, MN 55421. Reprinted by permission. P. 165, quotation from C. Lin & W. Liu. 1993. "Intergenerational Relationships among Chinese Immigrants from Taiwan," in H. McAdoo, ed., *Family Ethnicity,* pp. 271–286. Reprinted by permission of Sage Publications. P. 166, quotation from S. Gold. 1993. "Migration and Family Adjustment: Continuity and Change among Vietnamese in the United States," in H. McAdoo, ed., *Family Ethnicity,* pp. 300–314. Reprinted by permission of Sage Publications. P. 168, quotation from Alejandro Portes and Julia Sensenbrenner. 1993. "Embeddedness and Immigration: Notes on the Social Determinants of Economic Action," *American Journal of Sociology,* 98 (1993): 1320–50. Reprinted by permission of University of Chicago Press.

Chapter 6

P. 180, Table in box from Tom W. Smith. 1999. "The Emerging 21st Century American Family." *General Social Surveys: Social Change Report* No. 43, November 24, 1999. Reprinted by permission of National Opinion Research Center. Pp. 190-191, quotation and Fig. 6.1 from National Opinion Research Center. 1997. *General Social Survey.* Reprinted by permission of National Opinion Research Center. P. 196, quotation in box from Joe Klein. 1997. "In God They Trust." Copyright © June 19, 1997 by Joe Klein. This article originally appeared in *The New Yorker.* Reprinted by permission of the author.

Chapter 7

P. 215, Fig. 7.1 from Robert T. Michael, Edward O. Laumann, and John H. Gagnon. 1992. "The Number of Sexual Partners of Adults in the United States," unpublished paper, Harris School of Public Policy Studies, University of Chicago, 1992. Reprinted by permission of Robert T. Michael. P. 227, quotation and Fig. 7.4 from Edward O. Laumann, John H. Gagnon, Robert T. Michael, and Stuart Michaels. 1994. Tables 8.1 and 8.2. *The Social Organization of Sexuality.* Copyright © 1994 Edward O. Laumann, Robert T. Michael, CSG Enterprises, Inc., and Stuart Michaels. Reprinted with permission of The University of Chicago Press. Pp. 228-229, quotation in box from Richard Lewontin. 1995a. "Sex, Lies, and Social Science." *The New York Review of Books* (1995: 20/4, 25/5) pp. 29, 44. Copyright © NYREV Inc. Reprinted by permission of The New York Review of Books. P. 228, quotation in box from Edward O. Laumann, John H. Gagnon, Robert T. Michael, and Stuart Michaels. 1994. *The Social Organization of Sexuality,* p. 43. Copyright © 1994 Edward O. Laumann, Robert T. Michael, CSG Enterprises, Inc., and Stuart Michaels. Reprinted with permission of University of Chicago Press.

Chapter 8

P. 256, Fig. 8.1 from Scott J. South. 1991. "Sociodemographic Differentials in Mate Selection Preferences," *Journal of Marriage and the Family,* 53: 4, pp. 928-940. Copyright © 1991 by the National Council on Family Relations, 3989 Central Ave., NE, Suite 550, Minneapolis, MN 55421. Reprinted by permission. P. 264, quotation and Fig. 8.2 from Larry L. Bumpass, James A. Sweet, and Andrew Cherlin. 1991. "The Role of Cohabitation in Declining Rates of Marriage." *Journal of Marriage and the Family,* 53: 4, pp. 913-927. Copyright © 1991 by The National Council on Family Relations, 3989 Central Avenue, N.E., Suite 550, Minneapolis, MN 55421. Reprinted by permission. P. 272, Fig. 8.3 from Francesca M. Cancian. 1987. *Love in America: Gender and Self-Development.* Reprinted by permission of Cambridge University Press and the author. Pp. 274-275,

quotation in box from Francesca M. Cancian. 1987. *Love in America: Gender and Self-Development,* pp. 173-174. Reprinted by permission of Cambridge University Press and the author. P. 275, quotation in box from Deanna L. Pagnini and S. P. Morgan. 1996. "Racial differences in marriage and childbearing: Oral history evidence from the South in the early twentieth century." *American Journal of Sociology,* 101: 1702. Reprinted by permission of University of Chicago Press.

Chapter 9

P. 298, Fig. 9.3 from S. M. Bianchi, M. A. Milkie, L. C. Sayer, and J. P. Robinson. 2000. "Is Anyone Doing the Housework? Trends in the Gender Division of Household Labor." *Social Forces,* 79: 191-228. Reprinted by permission of University of North Carolina Press. P. 302, quotation from Leonard I. Pearlin and Mary E. McCall. 1990. "Occupational Stress and Marital Support," in John Eckenrode and Susan Gore, eds., *Stress Between Work and Family,* pp. 39-60. Copyright © 1990 Plenum Press. Reprinted by permission of Kluwer Academic/Plenum Press and Leonard I. Pearlin. P. 302, quotation from Robert S. Weiss. 1990. "Bringing Work Stress Home," in John Eckenrode and Susan Gore, eds., *Stress between Work and Family,* pp. 17-37. Copyright © 1990 Plenum Press. Reprinted with permission of Kluwer Academic/Plenum Press and Robert S. Weiss.

Chapter 10

P. 316, quotation from Catherine S. Manegold. 1993. "To Crystal, 12, School Serves No Purpose," *The New York Times* (April 8). Copyright © by The New York Times Company. Reprinted with permission. P. 323, Fig. 10.1 from Duane F. Alwin. 1990. "Percentage selecting characteristics as one of the three most important emphases in childrearing, by class," in Nancy Madell, ed., *Sociological Studies of Children and Youth,* vol. 3, pp. 65-68. Copyright © 1990 by JAI Press, a subsidiary of Elsevier Science. Reprinted by permission. P. 341, Fig. 10.4 from Donald J. Hernandez. 1993. *America's Children: Resources from Family, Government, and the Economy.* Reprinted by permission of Russell Sage Foundation. P. 343, Fig. 10.5 from Greg J. Duncan. 1991. "The Economic Environment of Childhood," in Aletha C. Huston, ed., *Children in Poverty.* Reprinted by permission of Cambridge University Press. P. 347, Fig. in box from B. Bradbury & M. Jantti. 1999. "Child Poverty across Industrialized Nations. *Innocenti Occasional Papers, Economic and Social Policy Series,* No. 71, Table 3.3: "Child Poverty Rates." Reprinted by permission of UNICEF International Child Development Centre, Florence, Italy.

Chapter 11

P. 354, quotation from Andrew J. Cherlin and Frank F. Furstenberg Jr. 1992. *The New American Grandparent:*

A Place in the Family, A Life Apart. Published by Harvard University Press. Reprinted by permission of the authors. P. 359, quotation from Alice S. Rossi and Peter H. Rossi. 1990. *Of Human Bonding: Parent-Child Relations Across the Life Course.* (New York: Aldine de Gruyter) Copyright © 1990 by Walter de Gruyter, Inc., New York. Reprinted with permission from Alice S. Rossi and Peter H. Rossi, authors. P. 364, Fig. 11.2 adapted in part from James A. Sweet and Larry L. Bumpass. 1987. *American Families and Households.* Reprinted by permission of Russell Sage Foundation. P. 367, quotation from Andrew J. Cherlin and Frank F. Furstenberg Jr. 1992. *The New American Grandparent: A Place in the Family, A Life Apart.* Published by Harvard University Press. Reprinted by permission of the authors. P. 366, quotation from *Webster's Third New International Dictionary.* Copyright © 1993 by Merriam Webster, Incorporated. Reprinted by permission. Pp. 368–369, quotation from Andrew J. Cherlin and Frank F. Furstenberg, Jr. 1992. *The New American Grandparent: A Place in the Family, A Life Apart.* Published by Harvard University Press. Reprinted by permission of the authors. Pp. 378–379, figure and quotation in box from Naohiro Ogawa and Robert D. Retherford. 1993. "Care of the Elderly in Japan: Changing Norms and Expectations," *Journal of Marriage and the Family,* 55: 3, pp. 585–597. Copyright © 1993 by The National Council on Family Relations, 3989 Central Ave., N.E., Suite 550, Minneapolis, MN 55421. Reprinted by permission.

Chapter 12
P. 398, quotation from Edward O. Laumann, John H. Gagnon, Robert T. Michael, and Stuart Michaels. 1994. *The Social Organization of Sexuality.* Copyright © 1994 Edward O. Laumann, Robert T. Michael, CSG Enterprises, Inc., and Stuart Michaels. Reprinted with permission of The University of Chicago Press. P. 401, quotation from Edward O. Laumann, John H. Gagnon, Robert T. Michael, and Stuart Michaels. 1994. *The Social Organization of Sexuality.* Copyright © 1994 Edward O. Laumann, Robert T. Michael, CSG Enterprises, Inc.,

and Stuart Michaels. Reprinted with permission of The University of Chicago Press. P. 405, quotation from Jan E. Stets. 1992. "Interactive Processes in Dating Aggression: A National Study." *Journal of Marriage and the Family,* 54: 1, pp. 165–177. Copyright © 1992 by The National Council on Family Relations, 3989 Central Avenue, N.E., Suite 550, Minneapolis, MN 55421. Reprinted by permission.

Chapter 13
P. 428, Fig. 13.2 from James A. Sweet and Larry L. Bumpass. 1987. Figure from *American Families and Households.* Reprinted by permission of Russell Sage Foundation. P. 435, Fig. 13.3 from Judith A. Seltzer. 1991. "Relationships between Fathers and Children Who Live Apart: The Father's Role after Separation," *Journal of Marriage and the Family,* 53: 1, p. 86. Copyright © 1991 by The National Council on Family Relations, 3989 Central Ave., N.E., Suite 550, Minneapolis, MN 55421. Reprinted by permission.

Chapter 14
P. 457, Fig. 14.1 from Larry L. Bumpass, James A. Sweet, and Andrew Cherlin. 1991. "The Role of Cohabitation in Declining Rates of Marriage." *Journal of Marriage and the Family,* 53: 4, pp. 913–927. Copyright © 1991 by The National Council on Family Relations, 3989 Central Ave., N.E., Suite 50, Minneapolis, MN 55421. Reprinted by permission. P. 461, quotation from Jamie K. Keshet. 1988. "The Remarried Couple: Stresses and Successes," in William R. Beer, ed. *Relative Strangers: Studies of Stepfamily Processes,* pp. 83–111. Reprinted by permission of Rowman & Littlefield Publishers, Inc. P. 462, quotation from Andrew J. Cherlin and Frank F. Furstenberg Jr. 1992. *The New American Grandparent: A Place in the Family, A Life Apart,* p. 158. Published by Harvard University Press. Reprinted by permission of the authors. P. 465, quotation from Patricia Papernow. 1988. "Stepparent Role Development: From Outsider to Intimate," in William R. Beer, ed., *Relative Strangers: Studies of Stepfamily Processes,* p. 81. Reprinted by permission of Rowman & Littlefield Publishers, Inc.

Photo Credits

Chapter 1

1.1 George Shelley/The Stock Market; 1.2 Steven E. Frischling/Corbis Sygma; 1.3a Lara Jo Regan/Gamma Liaison; 1.3b Michelle D. Bridwell/PhotoEdit; 1.3c Michael Newman/PhotoEdit; 1.4 Mark Peterson/Saba; 1.5 Frank Siteman/Stock, Boston; 1.6 Dion Ogust/The Image Works

Chapter 2

2.1 The Granger Collection; 2.2 National Gallery, London; 2.3 The Granger Collection; 2.4 North Wind Picture Archives; 2.5 Library of Congress, LC-USZC4—1733; 2.6 Library of Congress, LC-USZ6–1826; 2.7 Corbis-UPI/Bettmann

Chapter 3

3.1 Julie Houck/Stock, Boston; 3.2 Smithsonian American Art Museum, Washington, DC/Art Resource; 3.3 Sylvie Villeger/Explorer/Photo Researchers; 3.4 Tony Freeman/PhotoEdit; 3.5 V. Hazaticonos/Explorer/Photo Researchers; 3.6 Souza/Gamma Liaison; 3.7 Marc Bernheim/Woodfin Camp & Associates

Chapter 4

4.1 Alan S. Weiner/Gamma Liaison; 4.2 Bachmann/The Image Works; 4.3 R.Rotolo/Gamma Liaison; 4.4 Steve Rubin/The Image Works; 4.5 Lawrence Migdale/Photo Researchers; 4.6 Mark Peterson/Saba; 4.7 Ronnie Kaufman/The Stock Market

Chapter 5

5.1 Richard Hutchings/Photo Researchers; 5.2 Mark Richards/PhotoEdit; 5.3 Rudi Von Briel/PhotoEdit; 5.4 Owen Franken/Stock, Boston; 5.5 Bob Daemmrich/Stock, Boston; 5.6 Jack Kurtz/Impact Visuals; 5.7 David Butow/Saba; 5.8 Terry E. Eiler/Stock, Boston

Chapter 6

6.1 Gilles Mingasson/Gamma Liaison; 6.2 Paul Conklin/PhotoEdit; 6.3 S.Villeger/Explorer/Photo Researchers; 6.4 New York Times Pictures; 6.5 Joel Gordon; 6.6 Aaron Haupt/Stock, Boston; 6.7 AP/Wide World Photos

Chapter 7

7.1 Esbin Anderson/The Image Works; 7.2 Corbis-Bettmann; 7.3 Gilles Peress/Magnum; 7.4 Ellen B. Senisi/Photo Researchers; 7.5 Jose Pelaez/The Stock Market; 7.6 S. Noorani/Woodfin Camp & Associates; 7.7 David Young-Wolff/PhotoEdit

Chapter 8

8.1 Shia Photo/Impact Visuals; 8.2 David Young-Wolf/PhotoEdit; 8.3 Mike Yamashita/Woodfin Camp & Associates; 8.4 SuperStock; 8.5 Peter Southwick/Stock, Boston; 8.6 Jose Luis Pelaez/Stock, Boston; 8.7 Myrleen Ferguson/PhotoEdit; 8.8 Tom McCarthy/PhotoEdit

Chapter 9

9.1 Blair Seitz/Photo Researchers; 9.2 Jonathan Blair/Woodfin Camp & Associates; 9.3 Mark Richards/PhotoEdit; 9.4 Gary Wagner/Stock, Boston; 9.5 Kenneth Gabrielsen/Gamma Liaison; 9.6 David Young Wolff/PhotoEdit; 9.7 B. Busco/The Image Bank

Chapter 10

10.1 Joel Gordon; 10.2 Suzanne DeChillo/New York Times Pictures; 10.3 AFP/Corbis; 10.4 Nicol/Katz/Woodfin Camp & Associates; 10.5 Franz Pflugl/Stone; 10.6 William Campbell/Corbis-Sygma; 10.7 Hazel Hankin/Impact Visuals; 10.8 Chris Maynard/Gamma Liaison; 10.9 Dave Bartruff/Stock, Boston

Chapter 11

11.1 Hunter Freeman/Gamma Liaison; 11.2 Bob Daemmrich/Stock, Boston; 11.3 Steven Rubin/The Image Works; 11.4 Rhoda Sidney/Stock, Boston; 11.5 Dennis O'Clair/Stone; 11.6 David Wells/The Image Works

Chapter 12

12.1 Viviane Moos/Saba; 12.2 The Granger Collection; 12.3 Joel Gordon; 12.4 Rachel Epstein/PhotoEdit; 12.5 Gabe Palmer/The Stock Market; 12.6 B. Mahoney/The Image Works; 12.7 R. Lord/The Image Works

Chapter 13

13.1 Joel Gordon; 13.2 Corbis; 13.3 Michael Newman/PhotoEdit; 13.4 Michael Newman/PhotoEdit; 13.5 B. Daemmrich/The Image Works; 13.6 Jeff Greenberg/PhotoEdit; 13.7 A.Pizzi/The Stock Market

Chapter 14

14.1 Mark Richards/PhotoEdit; 14.2 Michael Newman/PhotoEdit; 14.3 Kim Kulish/Saba; 14.4 David Young-Wolff/PhotoEdit; 14.5 Illustration by Eloise Wilkin, Golden Press, Western Publishing Co., Inc.; 14.6 April Saul; 14.7 Mary Kate Denny/PhotoEdit

Chapter 15

15.1 Ken Cavanagh/Photo Researchers; 15.2 David Young-Wolff/PhotoEdit; 15.3 Jerry Cooke/Photo Researchers; 15.4 David Young-Wolff/PhotoEdit; 15.5 Steve Rubin/The Image Works; 15.6 [no 15.7] Bill Aron/PhotoEdit; 15.8 [no 15.7] Will & Deni Mcintyre/Photo Researchers

Name Index

548

Subject Index

Cherlin Online Learning Center Resources

Visit the Online Learning Center, a companion website for *Public and Private Families*, 3/e that offers students and professors a variety of resources and activities (www.mhhe.com/cherlin). Here are several samples of the study and research tools you can find on the Online Learning Center.

Test Your Comprehension

Multiple-Choice Quizzes

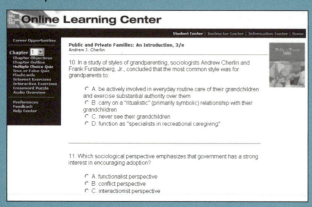

True-False Quizzes

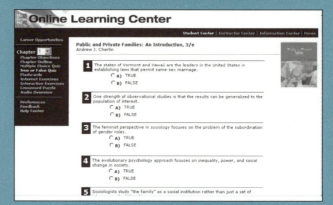

Glossary Flashcards

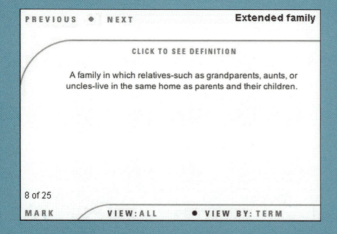

Glossary Crossword Puzzles

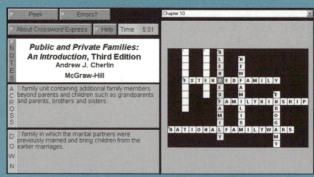